SPECIAL EDITION

USING

Microsoft®

Office Excel 2003

Patrick Blattner

800 East 96th Street,
Indianapolis, Indiana 46240

CONTENTS AT A GLANCE

1 Introduction 1

I Getting Started with Excel 2003
1 Getting Around Excel 9
2 Spreadsheet Basics 49
3 Editing Spreadsheets 63

II Formatting and Printing Excel Worksheets
4 Applying Number and Date Formats 91
5 Formatting and Printing 107

III Using Formulas and Functions
6 Function Fundamentals 159
7 Database Functions 189
8 Date and Time Functions .201
9 Engineering Functions 215
10 Financial Functions 233
11 Information Functions 265
12 Logical Functions 277
13 Lookup and Reference Functions 285
14 Math and Trigonometry Functions 303
15 Text Functions 325
16 Statistical Functions 343

IV Using Excel's Analysis Tools
17 Setting Up a List or Database in Excel 385
18 Using Excel's Data-Management Features 407
19 Outlining, Subtotaling, and Auditing
      Worksheet Data 439

V Creating and Modifying Charts
20 Building Charts with Excel 465
21 Modifying Excel Charts 505
22 Formatting Charts 533
23 Professional Charting Techniques 563

VI Using Excel in Business
24 Using PivotTables and PivotCharts 607
25 Using Analysis Tools: Goal Seek, Solver, and
      Data Tables 645
26 Using Excel in Business 675
27 Customizing Excel to Fit Your Working Style 703

VII Integrating Excel with Other Applications
28 Building Presentations with Excel 733
29 Using Excel with Access and Other Databases 755
30 Retrieving Data from OLAP Servers 789
31 Recording and Editing a Macro 809
32 Creating Interactive Excel Applications with VBA . .837

VIII Appendix
A What's on the CD 879

Index 887

SPECIAL EDITION USING MICROSOFT OFFICE EXCEL 2003

Copyright © 2004 by Que

International Standard Book Number: 0-7897-2953-9

Library of Congress Catalog Card Number: 2003103672

Printed in the United States of America

First Printing: September 2003

06   05   04   03   4   3

Que Publishing offers excellent discounts on this book when ordered in quantity for bulk purchases or special sales. For more information, please contact

U.S. Corporate and Government Sales
1-800-382-3419
corpsales@pearsontechgroup.com

For sales outside of the U.S., please contact

International Sales
1-317-581-3793
international@pearsontechgroup.com

Trademarks

Warning and Disclaimer

Associate Publisher
Greg Wiegand

Executive Editor
Rick Kughen

Development Editor
Todd Brakke

Managing Editor
Charlotte Clapp

Project Editor
Matthew Purcell

Indexer
Ginny Bess

Proofreader
Paula Lowell

Technical Editor
Helen Bradley

Team Coordinator
Sharry Lee Gregory

Multimedia Developer
Dan Scherf

Interior Designer
Anne Jones

Cover Designer
Anne Jones

TABLE OF CONTENTS

Introduction 1

New Features and Enhancements in Excel 2003 1

How This Book Is Organized 2
Part I: Getting Started with Excel 2003 3
Part II: Formatting and Printing Excel Worksheets 3
Part III: Using Formulas and Functions 3
Part IV: Using Excel's Analysis Tools 3
Part V: Creating and Modifying Charts 3
Part VI: Using Excel in Business 4
Part VII: Integrating Excel with Other Applications 4
Web Content 4

Conventions Used in This Book 4
Text Conventions 5
Special Elements 5

I Getting Started with Excel 2003

1 Getting Around Excel 9

Starting and Exiting the Excel Program 10

Identifying Workbook Elements 11
Using ScreenTips and What's This? Help 11
The New Workbook Task Pane NEW 12
Help, Search, and Clip-Art Task Panes NEW 13
Viewing Toolbars 15
Working with Excel Menus 19
Working with Shortcut Menus 20

Working with Workbooks 22
Coloring Workbook Tabs 23
Inserting Sheets 23
Naming Worksheets 24
Rearranging Worksheets 25
Grouping and Ungrouping Sheets 25
Using Worksheet Keyboard Shortcuts 27
Accessing Cells with Go To 28

Understanding Cell Basics 28

Entering Text 29
Labeling Columns and Rows 30
Adjusting Column Width and Row Height 31

Saving Excel Data 34

Performing a First-Time Save 34

Saving Your Workbook with a Password and File Encryption .NEW 35

Document Recovery NEW 37

Saving Excel Files in Alternative Formats 37

Saving an Excel Workbook as a Reusable Template 39

Controlling Your Worksheet View 40

Switching Between Open Workbooks 41

Freezing Columns and Rows 42

Splitting the Screen 43

Hiding and Unhiding Rows and Columns 45

Troubleshooting 46

Excel in Practice 47

2 Spreadsheet Basics **49**

Selecting Cells 50

Selecting Columns and Rows 53

Selecting Noncontiguous Ranges 54

Selecting Ranges on Grouped Worksheets 55

Naming Ranges for Fast Access 57

Troubleshooting 60

Excel in Practice 61

3 Editing Spreadsheets **63**

The Clipboard Viewer .NEW 64

Editing with the Keyboard 64

Editing a Group of Cells 65

Editing Using the Formula Bar 66

Moving Cell Content with Drag and Drop 68

Copying Cell Content with Drag and Drop 69

Creating a Data Series 70

Creating a Custom Fill Series 71

Creating a Custom Fill to Define Linear or Growth Trends 72

Creating a Custom List or Series 73

Replacing Data 75

Tracking Changes Made by Multiple Users NEW 75

Enabling and Disabling Revision Tracking 76

Accepting and Rejecting Changes 77

Using Comments to Explain Cell Content 79

Linking Excel Data .NEW. 82

    Establishing Links Between Worksheets or Workbooks 82

    Updating Links to a Workbook 83

    Locking Linked External Data 85

    Redirecting Links 85

    Breaking Links Between Files 85

Troubleshooting 86

Excel in Practice 86

II Formatting and Printing Excel Worksheets

4   Applying Number and Date Formats 91

Applying Common Numeric Formats from
    the Toolbar 92

Applying Built-In Formats 93

    Formatting the Date and Time 94

    Fractions 96

    Special 96

Creating Custom Formats 97

    Working with Date and Time Formatting Codes 98

    Working with Number and Text Formatting Codes 99

Applying Custom Currency 101

Working with Large Numbers 102

Pasting In Custom Characters 102

Creating Custom Conditions Codes 103

Repeating Characters 104

Excel in Practice 105

5   Formatting and Printing 107

Why Change the Formatting? 108

    Using the Formatting Toolbar 109

    Using the Format Cells Dialog Box 111

Changing the Font, Point Size, and Font Styles 112

    Changing the Font 112

    Setting the Point Size 113

    Adding Font Styles 114

    Formatting Individual Characters 115

    Resetting Excel's Default Font 115

Working with Styles 116

    Editing the Default Styles 116

    Creating and Applying Custom Styles 117

Merging Styles from One Workbook to Another 118

Formatting Titles with Merge and Center 119

Adjusting Alignment Within Cells, Columns, and Rows 119

Applying and Drawing Borders and Shading 122

Using Borders Effectively 122

Using Colors, Patterns, and Textured Fills 125

Using AutoFormat to Enhance Your Worksheets 126

Using the Drawing Toolbar 127

Ordering, Grouping, Moving, and Resizing Drawn Objects 131

Changing the Order of Overlapping Drawn Objects 131

Grouping Drawn Shapes and Lines 132

Combining Drawing Tools with Charts and Worksheets 133

Laying a Chart on a Bevel 133

Printing a Worksheet 135

Selecting a Printer 137

Choosing the Print Range 137

Previewing the Print Job 138

Using Page Break Preview 140

Working with Page Setup Options 141

Working with Orientation 142

Scaling the Printout 142

Choosing a Paper Size 143

Adjusting Print Quality 144

Setting Worksheet Margins 144

Creating Headers and Footers 147

Working with Sheet Settings 150

Troubleshooting 151

Excel in Practice 153

Media Matrix 153

Media Plan 153

Slider Charts 153

Inclusion Matrix with Webdings 154

Other Formatting Tips 156

III Using Formulas and Functions

6   Function Fundamentals 159

The Basic Parts of a Formula 160

Functions Versus Formulas 160

Arguments 160

Operators 160
Operator Order 161
Using Arithmetic Operators for Simple Math 162
Custom Functions 164
Applying a Name to a Range 164
Pasting a Named Range in a Formula 165

Using the AutoSum Feature 166

Editing Formulas 170
Dragging a Range Border to Change a Reference 172
Typing References Directly into a Formula 172

Writing Multiple Copies of a Formula 173
Copying Formulas with AutoFill 173
Entering Multiple Formulas All at Once 174

Using AutoCalculate for Quick Totals 175
Interpreting Formula Error Messages 177

Relative Versus Absolute Referencing 178

Using the Watch Window 180

Referencing Values in Other Worksheets and Workbooks 181
Referencing Other Worksheets 181
Applying Cubed Formulas 183
Referencing Other Workbooks 183
Updating Values in Referenced Workbooks 185

Troubleshooting 186

Excel in Practice 186

7 Database Functions 189

Database Functions Overview and Syntax 190

DAVERAGE 192

DCOUNT 193

DGET 194

DMAX 195

DMIN 196

DPRODUCT 197

DSUM 197

GETPIVOTDATA 198

Troubleshooting 199

Excel in Practice 200

8 **Date and Time Functions** 201

Date and Time Functions Overview 202

DATE 204

DAYS360 205

EDATE 206

MONTH 207

NETWORKDAYS 208

TODAY 209

WEEKDAY 210

YEAR 211

Troubleshooting 213

Excel in Practice 213

9 **Engineering Functions** 215

Engineering Functions Overview 216

BESSELI 218

BIN2DEC 219

COMPLEX 219

CONVERT 220

DEC2BIN 223

DELTA 223

GESTEP 224

HEX2BIN 225

IMCONJUGATE 225

IMPOWER 226

IMPRODUCT 227

IMSUB 228

IMSUM 229

OCT2BIN 230

Troubleshooting 230

Excel in Practice 231

10 **Financial Functions** 233

Financial Functions Overview 234

ACCRINT 238

ACCRINTM 239

COUPDAYBS 240

COUPDAYS 241

COUPNCD 242

COUPNUM 243

CUMIPMT 244

DISC 245

DURATION 246

FV 247

IPMT 248

MDURATION 249

NPER 250

NPV 251

ODDFPRICE 252

PMT 254

PRICE 255

PV 256

RATE 257

RECEIVED 258

TBILLPRICE 259

TBILLYIELD 260

YIELD 261

YIELDMAT 262

Troubleshooting 263

Excel in Practice 263

11 Information Functions 265

Information Functions Overview 266

CELL 267

COUNTBLANK 269

ERROR.TYPE 270

INFO 271

IS Functions 272

ISBLANK 273

ISNUMBER 274

Troubleshooting 275

Excel in Practice 276

12 Logical Functions 277

Logical Functions Overview 278

AND 278

IF 280

NOT 281

OR 282

Troubleshooting 283

Excel in Practice 283

13 Lookup and Reference Functions 285

Lookup and Reference Functions Overview 286

CHOOSE 287

HLOOKUP 288

INDEX (Array Form) 290

INDEX (Reference Form) 290

Using the Lookup Wizard 293

LOOKUP (Array Form) 294

LOOKUP (Vector Form) 295

OFFSET 296

Auto Update Charts Using the OFFSET Function 298

TRANSPOSE 299

VLOOKUP 300

Troubleshooting 301

Excel in Practice 301

14 Math and Trigonometry Functions 303

Math and Trigonometry Functions Overview 304

ABS 307

ACOS 308

ASIN 309

COMBIN 310

COUNTIF 311

DEGREES 313

LN 313

MODE 314

PERMUT 315

PI 316

RAND 316

ROMAN 317

SQRT 318

SUBTOTAL 319

SUM 320

SUMIF 321

TAN 322

Troubleshooting 323

Excel in Practice 323

15 Text Functions **325**

Text Functions Overview 326

CONCATENATE 328

EXACT 329

FIND 330

FIXED 331

LEN 332

LOWER 333

MID 334

PROPER 335

RIGHT 336

Add st, nd, rd, and th to the End of Numbers 337

SUBSTITUTE 338

TRIM 339

UPPER 340

Troubleshooting 341

Excel in Practice 341

16 Statistical Functions **343**

Statistical Functions Overview 344

AVERAGE 349

BINOMDIST 350

CHIDIST 351

CONFIDENCE 352

CORREL 353

COUNT 354

COUNTA 354

Returning the Last Record Entered 355

COUNTBLANK 356

COUNTIF 356

COVAR 358

EXPONDIST 358

FDIST 359

FORECAST 360

FREQUENCY 361

GEOMEAN 362

GROWTH 363

INTERCEPT 364

LARGE 365

LINEST 366

LOGEST 368

MAX 368

MEDIAN 369

MIN 370

MINA 371

MODE 371

NORMDIST 371

NORMINV 372

PERCENTILE 373

PERCENTRANK 373

POISSON 374

RANK 375

SLOPE 376

SMALL 377

STDEV 378

STDEVA 378

TREND 379

VAR 380

VARA 380

Troubleshooting 381

Excel in Practice 381

IV Using Excel's Analysis Tools

17 Setting Up a List or Database in Excel 385

Using Excel as a Database Program 386

Building an Effective List 386

Transposing List Data with the Paste Special Command 391

Transposing Tables with Formulas (Without Absolute Referencing) 391

Setting Up Date-Driven Lists 393

Creating Structured Lists from Data Contained in One Cell 394

Working with the Data Form 396

Viewing and Printing the List 399
    Keeping the Field Names from Scrolling 399
    Arranging Multiple Windows 400
    Inserting Data Ranges into a List 402
    Establishing Custom Views 403

Troubleshooting 405

Excel in Practice 405

18 Using Excel's Data-Management Features **407**

Data Management in Excel 408

Using Conditional Formatting with Lists 408

Using Formulas with Conditional Formatting 410

Using Formulas with Conditional Formatting to Create Timelines 411

Managing Data Using Text To Speech 413

Sorting a List 413

Filtering a List 416
    Managing the List with AutoFilters 417
    Using the Advanced Filter 421

Adding Form Controls to Your Worksheets 424
    Using Controls with Calculation Tables 429
    Using Controls with Charts 433
    Control Characteristics 435

Troubleshooting 436

Excel in Practice 437

19 Outlining, Subtotaling, and Auditing Worksheet Data **439**

Organizing and Auditing Your Data 440

Grouping or Outlining Data 440
    Grouping Data 441
    Changing the Outline Settings 447

Consolidating Data 447

Creating Automatic Subtotals 450

Validating and Auditing Data Entry .NEW. 453
    Data Validation 454
    Circling Invalid Data 457
    Auditing Precedents, Dependents, and Errors 458

Troubleshooting 460

Excel in Practice 460

20 Building Charts with Excel 465

An Overview of Excel Charts 466
   Chart Basics 466
   Chart Terms 467

Creating Charts with the Chart Wizard 469
   Selecting the Chart Type 470
   Specifying the Chart Source Data 471
   Choosing the Chart Options 475
   Choosing a Chart Location 484

Excel Chart Types 486
   Column Charts 487
   Bar Charts 488
   Line Charts 490
   Pie Charts 490
   Doughnut Charts 492
   Scatter Charts 493
   Area Charts 494
   Radar Charts 495
   Surface Charts 495
   Bubble Charts 496
   Stock Charts 497
   Cylinder, Cone, and Pyramid Charts 497
   Custom Charts 498

Printing Charts 500

Troubleshooting 501

Excel in Practice 502

V Creating and Modifying Charts

21 Modifying Excel Charts 505

Options for Improving Your Charts 506
   Moving and Resizing Embedded Charts 506
   Selecting Parts of a Chart for Editing 507

Changing the Chart Type 508

Changing a Data Series 510
   Selecting a Data Series or Data Point in a Chart 510
   Removing a Series from a Chart 510
   Adding or Adjusting Source Data 511

Adding a Secondary Axis to the Chart 514

Value Axis Scaling 516
   Changing the Maximum, Minimum, and Tick Mark Values 516
   Resizing the Plot Area 519
   Changing the Origin 520

Category Axis Scaling 521
   Repositioning the Axes 521
   Changing Tick Marks and Labels 523

Changing the Series Order 523
   Reversing the Categories 523
   Reversing the Values 525

Adding a Trendline to a Data Series 525
   Formatting the Trendline 527
   Trendline Options 528

Troubleshooting 530

Excel in Practice 531

22 Formatting Charts **533**

An Overview of Formatting Charts 534

Formatting Lines: Axes, Tick Marks, High/Low Lines, and Error Bars 534
   Formatting the Y-Axis, Secondary Y-Axis, and Z-Axis 534
   Formatting Axis Labels 537
   Adding High/Low Lines 538
   Adding Error Bars 538

Formatting Text: Data Labels, Titles, Legends, and Text Boxes 540
   Adding and Formatting Data Labels 540
   Adding and Formatting Chart Titles 543
   Formatting the Legend 544
   Inserting and Formatting Text on a Chart 545

Enhancing Charts with Shapes 546

Formatting Data Series 548
   Changing the Series Order 548
   Plotting Data on the Secondary Axis 549
   Exploding Pie Slices 549
   Changing the Data Series Angle in Pie or Doughnut Charts 549
   Formatting a Data Point 550

Changing the Border, Color, or Fill of a Chart Item 551
   Fill Effects 552
   Using Pictures as Backgrounds 554

Formatting 3D Charts 555
   Formatting the Walls of a 3D Chart 556
   Formatting the Floor of a 3D Chart 556
   Formatting the Data Series of a 3D Chart 557
   Formatting the 3D View 558

Troubleshooting 560

Excel in Practice 561

23 Professional Charting Techniques **563**

Formatting Charts for a Professional Look 564
  Key Elements in Professional Formatting 564
  Adding Pictures and Shapes to Charts 566

Creating Column Depth 573
  Working with the Secondary Axis, Overlap, and Gap Width 575
  Single Stacked Thermometers 578

Pie Chart Techniques 579
  Spinning the Pie Chart 579
  Organizing Pie Charts to Tell a Story 580
  Advanced Parsing of Pie Charts 580

Using Fill Effects to Show Variance in 3D Charts 582

Using Form Controls with Charts 584
  Creating Chart Models with Form Control Combo Boxes 587
  Creating Advanced Chart Models with Combo Boxes 588
  Creating Chart Models with Filters and Subtotals 588

Stacking Multiple Charts 590

Creating Cost and Production Curves with Charts for Variance 591

Linking Chart Text to Worksheet Cells 592

Charting Hidden Data 592

Creating Effective Multiple-Combination Charts 594
  Visual Display in Excel 595
  Combining Charts, Worksheets, Text, and Time 595
  Creating a Custom L-Bar Axis 595
  Building Single-Stack Charts 596
  Stacked Charts with Series Lines 597
  Detailed Time Analysis with Annotation 598
  Advanced Bar Chart Formats 600
  Advanced Analytical Chart Formats 600
  Creating Lifetime Profitability/Breakeven Charts 601

Troubleshooting 602

Excel in Practice 603

VI Using Excel in Business

24 Using PivotTables and PivotCharts **607**

Understanding PivotTables 608

Using the PivotTable and PivotChart Wizard 611
  Laying Out the PivotTable 613
  Setting PivotTable Options 618

Creating PivotCharts 623

Modifying PivotTables and PivotCharts 624
   Dragging Fields in a PivotChart 625
   Hiding Field Data 626
   Showing and Hiding Detail 626
   Performing Calculations on a PivotTable 628
   Hiding Columns or Rows 629
   Drilling Down in a Field 629
   Dragging a Field for a Page View 631
   Audit Your Totals 632
Working with Dates in PivotTables 633
Creating a PivotTable from Multiple Ranges 635
Saving and Editing PivotTables in HTML Format 636
Troubleshooting 638
Excel in Practice 638
   Grouping Data in Pivot Tables 638
   Managing Employee Hours and Costs with PivotTables 639

25 Using Analysis Tools: Goal Seek, Solver, and Data Tables **645**
Analyzing Your Data with Excel 646
Using Goal Seek 646
Using Solver 650
   Using Solver with Gantt Charts 657
   A Multiple-Project Solver Scenario 660
Creating Amortization Tables to Calculate Mortgage Payments 662
   Creating Active Tables with Spinners 665
   Multiple-Variable Tables 667
   Adding Scrollbars to the Mortgage Table 667
Using the Analysis ToolPak Add-In 669
Excel in Practice 672

26 Using Excel in Business **675**
Important Tools for Any Business 676
   Sell In Versus Sell Through 676
   Channel Velocity 677
   Cascading Schedules 677
   Reverse Schedules 678
   Summing the Total Velocity 679
   Automating Projected Cash Flows 679
   Transposing Tables with Formulas (Without Absolute Referencing) .. 680
   Averaging Positive Numbers Only in a Range 682
   Auto Lookup the Last Number in a Column 683
   P&L–Direct Contribution 684
   Financial Ratios 685

Resource Pools 687
Building Custom Functions 689
Producing a Line-Item Milestone Management Chart 692
Conditional Formats to Show Progress Against Baseline 693
Ramping Up Production on a Single Line Item 694

Value Chains 695
Creating a Market Opportunity Value Chain 695
Creating a Strategic Risk Factor Value Chain 697

Value Matrices 698
Creating a 2D Matrix 698
Creating a 3D Matrix 699

Excel in Practice 700

27 Customizing Excel to Fit Your Working Style 703

Why Customize Excel? 704

Changing the Default Excel Settings 704

Web Options Button 706

Changing Workbook Settings 706
Changing the Color Palette 706
Hiding Parts of the Workbook 709

Changing the Excel Window Settings 710
Adding and Removing Scrollbars 710
Customizing the Status Bar for Quick Analysis 711

Recent Option Tabs 712

Modifying Toolbars 714
Deleting Buttons from Toolbars 715
Displaying Text on Buttons 715
Changing the Button Images 716
Assigning Hyperlinks 718
Assigning Macros 718
Building Custom Toolbars 720
Deleting and Resetting Toolbars and Buttons 723

Customizing the Excel Menus 723
Creating a Custom Menu 725
Turning Personalized Menus On and Off 727

Troubleshooting 728

Excel in Practice 728

VII Integrating Excel with Other Applications

28 Building Presentations with Excel 733

Using Excel with Other Microsoft
  Office Programs 734

Copying Excel Data to a Word Document 734
  Pasting Excel Data as a Word Table 735
  Formatting Excel Data in a Word Document 736

Copying Excel Data to a PowerPoint Presentation 736
  Using Excel Ranges in a PowerPoint Slide 737
  Pasting a PivotTable into PowerPoint 738
  Pasting a Chart Over Images in PowerPoint 741
  Pasting Excel Images and Objects in PowerPoint 742
  Pasting Excel Data in a PowerPoint Datasheet 742

Copying Word and PowerPoint Data to an Excel Worksheet 744
  Adding Word Text to an Excel Worksheet 745

Combining Word, Excel, and PowerPoint Files with Hyperlinks 746
  Creating a Hyperlink 747
  Using Hyperlinks to Access a Range of Cells 749
  Updating Hyperlinks 749
  Deleting Hyperlinks 750

Troubleshooting 751

Excel in Practice 752

29 Using Excel with Access and Other Databases 755

Using Excel with Database Software 756

Using Access to Complement Excel 757
  When to Use Access Instead of Excel 757
  Sending Excel Data to Access for Further Analysis 759

Exporting Excel Data into Other Databases 766

Retrieving Data from Access and Other Relational Databases 767
  Where Corporate Data Is Found: Relational Databases and ODBC 767
  Querying the Database with the Query Wizard 769
  Using Microsoft Query 774
  Managing Database Data in Excel 781

Importing Data from Text Files 783
  Using the Convert Text to Columns Wizard 785

Troubleshooting 786

Excel in Practice 786

30 Retrieving Data from OLAP Servers 789

What Is OLAP? 790

Server Versus Client OLAP 791

Creating an OLAP Data Source Definition 792

Creating an OLAP PivotTable 794

Using OLAP PivotTables 795

Using OLAP PivotCharts 798

Saving Offline Cubes from Server Cubes 799

Performing OLAP Analysis on Database Data [NEW] 801
    Starting the OLAP Cube Wizard 801
    Selecting Cube Measures 802
    Organizing Data into Hierarchies 803
    Saving the Cube 804
    Using the Cube 805

Excel in Practice 805

31 Recording and Editing a Macro 809

Create Your Own Commands with Macros 810
    What Is a Macro? 810
    Why Create Your Own Commands? 811

Creating a Macro with the Macro Recorder 811
    What You Should Consider Before Recording 812
    Recording a Macro 813
    Where Are Macros Saved? 816
    Opening Workbooks That Contain Macros 816

Macro Playback 817
    Using the Macro Dialog Box 819
    Assigning a Keyboard Shortcut 820
    Assigning a Macro to a Toolbar or Menu 821
    Creating a New Toolbar or Menu for Macros 824
    Assigning a Macro to a Graphic Object 826

Editing a Macro 828
    Example: Editing a Sheet-Naming Macro 830

Deleting Macros, Custom Buttons, and Custom Menu Items .. 831

Macros to Help You Work Faster 832

Troubleshooting 833

Excel in Practice 834
    Applying Custom Headers 834
    Creating an AutoFit Column Macro 835

32 Creating Interactive Excel Applications with VBA 837
  Why Write Macros Rather Than Record Them? 838
  Introduction to Object-Oriented Programming 839
    Objects 839
    Collections 839
    Methods 840
    Properties 840
    Functions 841
    Putting It All Together 841
  Variables and Constants 842
    What Is a Variable? 842
    What Is a Constant? 844
  Understanding the Visual Basic Editor 845
  Getting Help with Visual Basic 847
  VBA Procedures 848
    Creating a Nonrecorded Procedure 849
    Creating a Function Procedure 852
  Control Structures 856
    Decision-Making Structures 856
    Loops 858
  Code-Writing Tips 861
    Using the Auto List Members and Auto Quick Info 861
    Writing Easy-to-Read Code 862
    Commenting Code 864
  Debugging 865
    Compiling a Project 865
    Stepping Through Code Using the Step Command and Breakpoints .. 866
    The Immediate Window 868
    Watching Variables and Expressions 869
  Automatic Execution of VBA Code 871
  Excel in Practice 873

A What's on the CD? 879
  WOPR COMMANDER 879
  ENVELOPER 880
  WorkBar 880
  FileNew Popup 880
  FloppyCopy 880
  Lookup Zip+4 881
  Insert Picture 881

Task Pane Customizer 881

Image Extractor/Editor 882

Document Notes 882

Date and Time Tools 882

Popup Contacts List 882

QuickMarks 882

Show/Hide All 882

Formatting Toolbar 882

Module Tools 883

City2Airport Smart Tags 883

WOPR Updater! 883

LITTLE WOPRs LIBRARY 884

Installing WOPR 2003 885

Security Considerations 885

Tech Support 886

TROUBLESHOOTING TABLE OF CONTENTS

Part 1: Getting Started with Excel 2003 7

Chapter 1: Getting Around Excel 9
Viewing More Sheet Tabs 46
Distinguishing One Version of a File from Another 46
Creating a Template from an Existing Workbook 46
Why Save to the Templates Folder? 46

Chapter 2: Spreadsheet Basics 49
Range Naming Errors 60
Deselecting Grouped Sheets 60
I've inherited a workbook that has all these named ranges associated with it.
  Every time I try to move or copy a sheet to a new workbook Excel prompts
  and asks whether I want to copy the ranges to the new workbook. How can I
  get rid of this? 60

Chapter 4: Editing Spreadsheets 63
Unaccepting Accepted Changes 86

Part 2: Formatting and Printing Excel Worksheets 89

Chapter 4: Applying Number and Date Formats 91

Chapter 5: Formatting and Printing 107
Changing the Default Font for the Active Workbook 152
Creating Permanent Styles 153
Where Did the Worksheet Title Go? 153

Chapter 6: Function Fundamentals 159
Common Formula Errors 186
Transposing Ranges with Formulas 186
AutoSum Won't Summarize the Entire List of Numbers 186

Chapter 7: Database Functions 189
Inserting PivotTables 199

Chapter 8: Date and Time Functions 201
#VALUE Using SUM(MONTH 213
#VALUE from NETWORKDAYS 213

Chapter 9: Engineering Functions 215
I need to convert one number to another form of measurement. 230
I get errors for most of the functions covered in this chapter. 230

Chapter 10: Financial Functions 233
When I follow the instructions for creating a formula using many of these
  functions I get a #NAME? Error. 263

Chapter 11: Information Functions 265
Activating Cells 275
Activating an Array 275
ISERROR 275

Chapter 12: Logical Functions 277
    Relative Timeline References 283

Chapter 13: Lookup and Reference Functions 285
    VLOOKUP Matching 301

Chapter 14: Math and Trigonometry Functions 303
    Quick Sum 323
    Creating Quick Relative Versus Absolute 323

Chapter 15: Text Functions 325
    Text in Formulas 341

Chapter 16: Statistical Functions 343
    Do you have a large list where you need to find the most common occurrence
      of a number? 381
    How do I find the largest value in a range? 381

Part 4: Using Excel's Analysis Tools 383

Chapter 17: Setting Up a List or Database
    in Excel 385
    Freeze Panes 405
    Unique Records 405

Chapter 18: Using Excel's Data-Management Features 407
    Intersecting Points in Lists or Tables 436
    Complex Formulas 436
    Formulas Are Slowing Down the Workbook 436
    Parsing a List of Names 437

Chapter 19: Outlining, Subtotaling, and Auditing Worksheet Data 439
    Displaying Tracer Arrows 460
    Auto Outline Doesn't Work 460

Part 5: Creating and Modifying Charts 463

Chapter 20: Building Charts with Excel 465
    Selecting a Chart Element 501
    Changing a Chart Sheet to an Embedded Chart 501
    Eliminating the Legend Border 501
    Saving a Formatted Chart As a Custom Chart 502
    Adding a Trendline 502
    Adding Data Labels 502

Chapter 21: Modifying Excel Charts 505
    Changing the Maximum Value for the Value Axis 530
    Changing the Chart Type of a Data Series 530
    Adding Data to a Chart 530
    Charting Dramatically Different Values on the Same Chart 530
    Customizing Tick Marks 531

Chapter 22: Formatting Charts 533
    Eliminating the Axis While Keeping Axis Labels 560

Eliminating Borders and Backgrounds 560
Formatting a Single Data Point 560
Offsetting the Categories 560
Eliminating Data Label Backgrounds 560
Reducing the Number of Units in a Picture 560

Chapter 29: Professional Charting Techniques 563
Moving Category Labels 602
Invisible Data Series 602
Moving a Chart with Objects 602
Aligning Chart Labels with Gridlines 603

Part 7: Using Excel in Business 731

Chapter 27: Customizing Excel to Fit Your Working Style 703
Retrieving Deleted Menus 728

Chapter 28: Building Presentations with Excel 733
Updating Links Between Files 751
Editing an Existing Hyperlink 751
Fixing Invalid Hyperlinks 752

Chapter 29: Using Excel with Access and Other Databases 755
Copying Visible Cells Only 786
When Access Can't Create an Index 786

Chapter 31: Recording and Editing a Macro 809
Increasing Macro Playback Speed 833
Runtime Errors 833

ABOUT THE AUTHOR

Patrick Blattner has authored *Special Edition Using Microsoft Excel 2000*, *Microsoft Excel 2000 Functions in Practice*, and *Special Edition Using Microsoft Excel 2002*. He has written about Excel in PC Computing Magazine and has spoken about it on Tech TV's live call-in television show "Call for Help."

A member of The Academy of Interactive Arts and Sciences, he spent several years in interactive media development with Disney Interactive in Southern California.

For the last several years he's been working with America Online as part of the AOL products group and resides in Northern Virginia.

DEDICATION

To Jim Kvistad, who's been serving his country during the last six months and has had to endure countless hours away from his family.

WE WANT TO HEAR FROM YOU!

As the reader of this book, *you* are our most important critic and commentator. We value your opinion and want to know what we're doing right, what we could do better, what areas you'd like to see us publish in, and any other words of wisdom you're willing to pass our way.

As an associate publisher for Que, I welcome your comments. You can email or write me directly to let me know what you did or didn't like about this book—as well as what we can do to make our books better.

Please note that I cannot help you with technical problems related to the *topic* of this book. We do have a User Services group, however, where I will forward specific technical questions related to the book.

When you write, please be sure to include this book's title and author as well as your name, email address, and phone number. I will carefully review your comments and share them with the author and editors who worked on the book.

Email: feedback@quepublishing

Mail: Greg Wiegand
QUE Publishing
201 West 103rd Street
Indianapolis, IN 46290 USA

For more information about this book or another QUE title, visit our Web site at www.quepublishing.com. Type the ISBN (excluding hyphens) or the title of a book in the Search field to find the page you're looking for.

INTRODUCTION

NEW FEATURES AND ENHANCEMENTS IN EXCEL 2003

Under the hood there have been a lot of improvements to Office Excel 2003 that will allow corporations and users to further customize Excel to fit their personal working environment.

Enhancements and new features you'll find in Excel 2003:

- Richer development tools

  Power users and IT departments can now further customize Excel using XML and InfoPath. This customization allows users and developers to build structured templates based on XML thus providing a more in-depth application development environment. Ultimately, this will make it easier for companies to collect and share data.

- Enhanced document management

  Rights management has become a common occurrence in daily business; with Excel 2003 you can control the policies for reading, printing, and copying documents to further put the creator of the document in control.

- In-depth cube analysis tools

  Access to Enterprise data enables you to create OLAP PivotTables, and use Excel's OLE DB, ActiveX Data Objects (ADO), DAO Data Access Objects, and data access technologies in an SQL Server environment.

- New Research task pane

  The new Research task pane allows you to research information on the Web or through a series of encyclopedias.

- Shared workspaces

  Available only with Windows Server 2003 running, users can save workbooks to shared workspaces to better collaborate in a team environment.

- Windows Sharepoint integration

  Use Sharepoint to manage an edit lists of information in Excel or transfer over to a Windows Sharepoint Service site.

- Permissions

  Available if you're running Windows Server 2003. Control your work and the distribution of your work with enhanced permissions that control whether a workbook can be saved, copied, or emailed with Windows Rights Management Services.

- Enhanced file recovery

  When a file becomes corrupt or crashes, the files are analyzed for errors and all recoverable documentation is saved with Excel's new Document Recovery feature.

- Improved encryption

  The encryption feature allows you to select a CryptoAPI-based encryption type with which you can create passwords up to 255 characters in length. This provides an ultra-secure workbook.

- Improved Help

  Through the improved Help task pane you can access client-side help or access Microsoft's online assistance from the Microsoft Web site.

- Enhanced collinearity detection

  Enhanced numerical detection allows Excel to identify calculations of the sum of squared deviations, normal distributions, and continuous probability distribution functions.

- Enhanced smart tags

  You can now associate smart tag actions with specific sections within a workbook. The smart tag will only appear when you hover over the smart tag with your mouse in that desired workbook section.

- Enhanced Clipboard viewer

  The enhanced Clipboard viewer is similar to the Excel 2002 Clipboard, except that the viewer is in the form of the task pane with multiple options for media and management. The new viewer allows you to manage clip art, photographs, movies, and sounds.

- Programmable task panes

  Using XML support in Excel 2003, you can program task panes to relate specifically to your business and or project.

HOW THIS BOOK IS ORGANIZED

Special Edition Using Microsoft Office Excel 2003 is divided into logically ordered and carefully divided sections. This makes it easier for you to find the topics you need, and ensures that the book flows from basic to advanced topics in a manner that enables you to read the book from start to finish, effectively building your Excel skills.

PART I: GETTING STARTED WITH EXCEL 2003

Chapter 1, "Getting Around Excel," Chapter 2, "Spreadsheet Basics," and Chapter 3, "Editing Spreadsheets," take you around some of Excel's new features and give you basic fundamentals to get around and manipulate the program on its basic levels. From adding and formatting worksheets to a workbook to using the new worksheet task pane, these chapters give you the basics. You'll also learn how to use the new smart tags that appear on your spreadsheet based on certain commands performed.

PART II: FORMATTING AND PRINTING EXCEL WORKSHEETS

In Chapter 4, "Applying Number and Date Formats," you'll learn all the basics from applying number and date formats to creating your own custom number and date formats. Chapter 5, "Formatting and Printing," takes you into the use of spreadsheets with drawing tools. From standard layouts to formatting cells, fonts, and styles, this is where you'll find it. After you learn these basics, you'll also learn the ins and outs of printing all elements in a spreadsheet.

PART III: USING FORMULAS AND FUNCTIONS

Chapters 6 through 16 take you through just about all the functions Excel offers. You start off with Chapter 6, "Function Fundamentals," and move into all the function categories by chapter including Chapter 7, "Database Functions," Chapter 8, "Date and Time Functions," Chapter 9, "Engineering Functions," Chapter 10, "Financial Functions," Chapter 11, "Information Functions," Chapter 12, "Logical Functions," Chapter 13, "Lookup and Reference Functions," Chapter 14, "Math and Trigonometry Functions," Chapter 15, "Text Functions," and Chapter 16, "Statistical Functions." With tons of examples, you should find just about every solution you'll need to solve problems in any business.

PART IV: USING EXCEL'S ANALYSIS TOOLS

Chapter 17, "Setting Up a List or Database in Excel," Chapter 18, "Using Excel's Data-Management Features," and Chapter 19, "Outlining, Subtotaling, and Auditing Worksheet Data," focus on Excel's data analysis and data-management features. Learn how to build a database or list; edit, sort, and filter the list; and use advanced filters to manipulate just about any list or database. Use form controls in conjunction with functions learned in previous chapters to automate and create custom form bid sheet models.

PART V: CREATING AND MODIFYING CHARTS

Chapters 20 through 23 take you on a comprehensive tour of Excel's considerable charting tools. From building a simple bar or pie chart to stacking multiple charts, you'll learn which chart type best depicts your data (Chapter 20, "Building Charts with Excel") and how to manipulate its appearance and content to express your numeric data effectively (Chapter 21, "Modifying Excel Charts" and Chapter 22, "Formatting Charts"). Learn professional techniques for making your charts stand out visually as well as in terms of their content, communicating complex data in a dynamic visual format. Also learn how to tie form controls such as drop-downs and radio buttons into your charts for automatic data manipulation (Chapter 23, "Professional Charting Techniques").

PART VI: USING EXCEL IN BUSINESS

In Chapters 24 through 27, you learn how to build and manage a database with PivotTables. Take advantage of Excel's new PivotTable task pane and improved PivotChart tools for data analysis to support your business decisions (Chapter 24, "Using PivotTables and PivotCharts"). Use Goal Seek, Solver, and Analysis ToolPak tools to solve simple or complex business and resource-loading problems (Chapter 25, "Using Analysis Tools: Goal Seek, Solver, and Data Tables"). Create cascading schedules and time-management tools found only in this book (Chapter 26, "Using Excel in Business"). Learn how to create custom functions that have relevance only to your business (Chapter 27, "Customizing Excel to Fit Your Working Style").

PART VII: INTEGRATING EXCEL WITH OTHER APPLICATIONS

Chapters 28 through 32 show you how to end your isolation and branch out—using Excel data in your PowerPoint presentations and Access tables. Chapter 28, "Building Presentations with Excel," provides the fundamentals for porting data over into other office applications for presentations or linked information. Chapter 29, "Using Excel with Access and Other Databases," focuses extensively on Excel's database access capabilities and on retrieving data from the Web. Learn how to build database queries and retrieve information from Access and from other databases. Chapter 30, "Retrieving Data from OLAP Servers," introduces you to OLAP PivotTables and data stores, how to create them, and how to use them. Use Excel's Cube Wizard to build and use cubes for quick data access and analysis offline. Chapter 31, "Recording and Editing a Macro," introduces you to recording and editing macros, while Chapter 32, "Creating Interactive Excel Applications with VBA," offers a crash course on using Visual Basic in Excel. Finally, Chapter 33, "Using Excel on the Web," shows you how to take advantage of new Web query options that allow you to manage your stock portfolios in Excel with simple refresh commands.

WEB CONTENT

Most readers of this book will be content to use Excel exactly as it comes out of the box. Therefore, many chapters deal only with customization that can be done simply by making choices in dialog boxes. But for those using Excel as a development environment, we have a special introduction chapter for going beyond the basic macro recordings using VBA. You can find this and other valuable information at http://www.quepublishing.com.

CONVENTIONS USED IN THIS BOOK

The special conventions used throughout this book are designed to help you get the most from the book as well as Excel 2002.

TEXT CONVENTIONS

Different typefaces are used to convey various things throughout the book. They include the following:

Typeface	Description
Monospace	Screen messages and Internet addresses appear in this special typeface.
Italic	New terminology and emphasized text will appear in italic.
Bold monospace	References to text you should type will appear in bold, monospace font.
Initial Caps	Menu names, dialog box names, and dialog box elements.

In this book, key combinations are represented with a plus sign. If the action you need to take is to press the Ctrl key and the S key simultaneously, the text tells you to press Ctrl+S.

SPECIAL ELEMENTS

Throughout this book, you'll find Tips, Notes, Cautions, Cross-References, and Troubleshooting Tips. These elements provide a variety of information, ranging from warnings you shouldn't miss to ancillary information that will enrich your Office experience but isn't required reading.

"SIGNATURE" TIPS

TIP FROM

Tips point out special features, quirks, or software tricks that will help you increase your productivity with Excel 2003.

NOTES

NOTE

Notes contain extra information or alternative techniques for performing tasks that we feel will enhance your use or understanding of the current topic.

CAUTIONS

CAUTION

If there is a potential problem with a feature or something you should be aware of to avoid errors or unwanted results, you'll find both a description of the situation and how to resolve or avoid it in the Caution format.

TROUBLESHOOTING

At the end of most chapters, you'll encounter a "Troubleshooting" section. This is where you learn how to solve or avoid common problems you might typically face with Excel 2003.

EXCEL IN PRACTICE

At the end of many chapters, you'll find an example of how to use that chapter's features to improve the overall functioning, legibility, and effectiveness of your worksheets. Often appearing in the form of before-and-after figures with explanatory callouts, these samples offer advice and practical examples for your own implementation.

CROSS-REFERENCES

Cross-references direct you to other locations in this book that provide supplemental or supporting information. They look like this:

→ For details on how to create custom number formats,, **see** "Creating Custom Formats," **p. 97**

Getting Started with Excel 2003

1 Getting Around Excel   3

2 Spreadsheet Basics   49

3 Editing Spreadsheets   63

CHAPTER 1

GETTING AROUND EXCEL

In this chapter

Starting and Exiting the Excel Program   10

Identifying Workbook Elements   11

Working with Workbooks 22

Understanding Cell Basics   28

Entering Text   29

Saving Excel Data   34

Controlling Your Worksheet View   40

STARTING AND EXITING THE EXCEL PROGRAM

If you're new to Excel, it won't be long before you're accustomed to performing various spreadsheet tasks simply and quickly. You'll want to start the program with as much speed and simplicity as possible. Choose one of the following methods to start Excel:

- From the Start menu, choose All Programs, and then select Microsoft Excel from the list. This method isn't the fastest, but you don't need to do anything special to use it—the menus are set up for you through your installation of Microsoft Office.

- Choose New Office Document from the Start menu, and choose the Blank Workbook icon from the General tab. Click OK to open Excel. Again, this isn't the fastest method, but the tools are already set up for you.

- Open an existing Excel workbook from within Windows Explorer, My Computer, or by using a desktop shortcut to that particular file.

→ To learn how to open an existing workbook file, **see** "Saving Excel Data," **p.34**.

- Create and use a shortcut icon on the desktop that takes you right into Excel. This requires you to create the icon in the first place, but you have to do that only once. From then on, you have the fastest method of starting Excel right on your desktop. To create a shortcut, follow these steps:

    1. Right-click any empty spot on your Windows desktop.
    2. Choose New, then Shortcut from the shortcut menu.
    3. In the Command Line text box, enter the path and filename for Excel, which should be in a Microsoft Office folder on your local drive. The default path is C:\Program Files\Microsoft Office\Office11\.

> **NOTE**
> If you're not sure of the exact location, click Browse. When you've found the program file (Excel.exe), double-click it or click Open to return to the Create Shortcut dialog box.

    4. Click Next.
    5. Type a name for your shortcut, or accept the default name as it appears in the Select a Name for the Shortcut text box.
    6. Click Finish. Your shortcut appears on the desktop. (You can tell a shortcut from a program icon by the small arrow in the lower-left corner of the icon image. Only shortcuts have this arrow.)

> **NOTE**
> You could also place the shortcut on the Windows task pane if you do not want to place on the desktop.

When you start Excel, you are immediately presented with a blank Excel workbook, ready for you to begin entering and editing your data.

You can exit Excel in any of the following ways:

- Choose File, Exit. Any open and unsaved workbooks will result in a prompt, asking you whether you want to save your work. After you respond to these prompts, the program will close.

- Click the Close button in the upper-right corner of the Excel application window. Using this button also results in prompts asking you to save any unsaved work, after which the application will be shut down. If you see two Close buttons, be sure to click the one on the Excel title bar; otherwise, you'll just close the workbook window.

- Right-click the taskbar icon for each of your Excel workbooks (a separate button appears on the taskbar for each open workbook) and choose Close from the shortcut menu for each open workbook. When all workbooks are closed, right-click the remaining Excel application button on the taskbar, and choose Close. The application will now be closed.

- Press Alt+F4 to exit the program.

If you need to close only the workbook you're working on and want to keep Excel open to work on other workbook files, choose File, Close from the menu, or press Ctrl+F4. If you haven't saved your work, you'll be prompted to do so before the workbook is closed. Find out more about saving your workbooks in Chapter 2, "Spreadsheet Basics."

IDENTIFYING WORKBOOK ELEMENTS

Before you start entering any text or numbers into your blank Excel workbook, it's a good idea to become familiar with the entire Excel window. Your Excel window contains the elements shown in Figure 1.1, all of which are part of a typical blank Excel workbook.

When a workbook is open and maximized, the Excel window contains two sets of Minimize, Maximize, and Close buttons. The uppermost set is associated with the Excel *application* (program), and the lower set controls the workbook window.

TIP FROM

If you're using a wheeled mouse, such as the Microsoft IntelliMouse, you can hold down the wheel button and drag up, down, left, or right within the window to scroll through your worksheet. You can also roll the wheel to scroll.

USING SCREENTIPS AND WHAT'S THIS? HELP

You can point to almost any element in your Excel window and, after a brief pause, a *ScreenTip* will appear to tell you the name of that particular element (see Figure 1.2).

1

Figure 1.1
This is the view upon
opening the Excel
2003 default window
and toolbars.

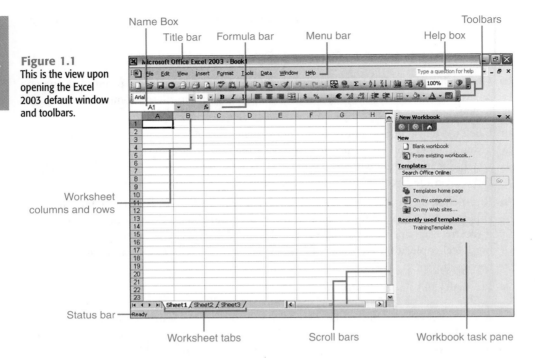

Figure 1.2
Use ScreenTips to
help familiarize your-
self with the names of
your Excel window
elements.

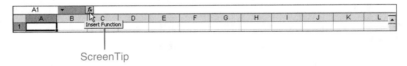

To gain access to Excel's full set of help files, choose Help, Microsoft Excel Help or press
F1. When the Office Assistant is enabled, it shows as an icon on the operating system tray.
If the Office Assistant has been disabled or you're using the standalone version of Excel, this
command displays the Help task pane.

In the task pane, you can search by topic using the search field, or if you're online you can
access Microsoft's communities, assistance center, or training site. I would suggest using the
search field to get started.

THE NEW WORKBOOK TASK PANE

The New Workbook task pane enables you to do several things from one pane, from
retrieving last-used workbooks to creating and storing Web templates. If you do not see the
task pane you can access it by choosing View and then Task Pane or by selecting Ctrl+F1.
You can also use the small drop-down menu at the top of the task pane next to the "X" to
access these panes—Getting Started, Help, Search Results, Clip Art, Research, Clipboard,

New Workbook, Template Help, Document Actions, Shared Workspace, Document Updates, and XML Source.

The task pane was created to help users have one centralized place for a host of tasks. The viewers available and their descriptions follow.

After you close the task pane, you access it again by selecting Task Pane from the View menu. In addition, the task pane is considered a toolbar and can be turned on and off using the Customize dialog box (Tools, Customize, Toolbars) or by selecting View, Toolbars, Task Pane (or the easiest way, View, Task Pane). You also can access the task pane's search mode by choosing File, File Search.

HELP, SEARCH, AND CLIP-ART TASK PANES

NEW You can use the help files in Excel for fast answers to questions. Microsoft has revised the help files so that you can access them faster and actually consume the information in the files. They've used a better format with more detailed information accompanied in many cases by screen shots. Notice the example in Figure 1.3. After you access the help files, you can close the task pane by simply clicking the X at the top-right corner of the pane. When you scroll over the icons, the links are highlighted to show selection.

Figure 1.3
Use the new redesigned help files to get quick answers to questions.

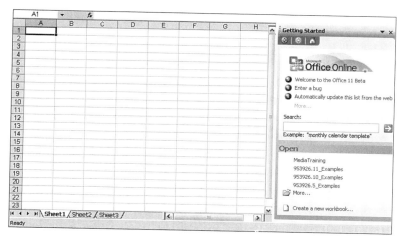

The task pane allows you to change the functionality of the pane by simply selecting the drop-down arrow to the left of the X at the top-right corner. Figure 1.4 shows the File Search task pane, which you get to by choosing File, File Search. The search option is for searching documents on your computer or network based on criteria, including file type, filename, date, and by text in the document. It also has a link at the bottom to Excel's Find & Replace command. This is via the Find command in this document link.

The Clipboard task pane allows you to see the objects copied. It stores the objects within the Clipboard and allows you to view the objects in the pane. If you're copying Excel objects or other Microsoft application data, you can view the copied elements all in one centralized place. To delete the individual elements, simply select the drop-down arrow that appears when you scroll over the individual object. Notice the Clipboard viewer in Figure 1.5.

Figure 1.4
By selecting the Search option from the drop-down menu on the top of the pane, you can search by file type, filename, date, and by text in the document.

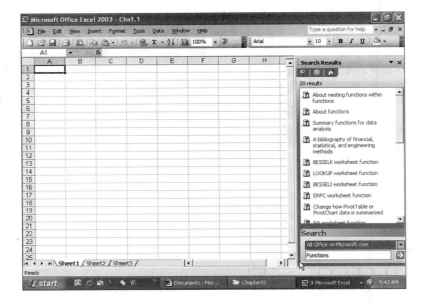

Items in Clipboard viewer

Figure 1.5
The Clipboard viewer is available within the pane by selecting the drop-down menu at the top of the pane.

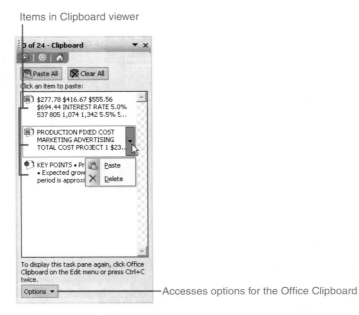

Accesses options for the Office Clipboard

Another option in the task pane drop-down menu is the Clip Art option. When you select it, a dialog box helps import clip art based on media files located on your local or network drives. After the clip art is imported, you can select from the thousands of individual clips in different categories to import into your documents. You can also access more clips from the Clips Online option. Notice the clips imported in the viewer in Figure 1.6.

Inserted clip art   Clip art available for insertion

Figure 1.6
The Clip Art task pane is available from the task pane drop-down menu. Simply click the image to insert it.

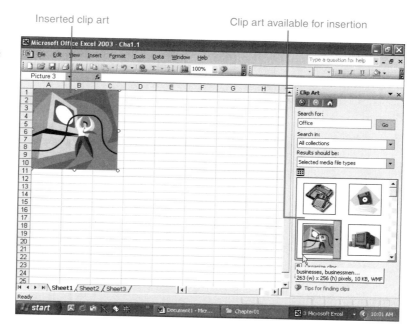

VIEWING TOOLBARS

The Excel window opens with a single row of icons displayed, which comprise two separate toolbars—the Standard and Formatting toolbars (see Figure 1.7). These two toolbars of icons contain buttons that represent some of the most frequently used Excel commands, as well as a number of buttons that you'll recognize from other Microsoft Office programs, assuming that you installed Excel with Microsoft Office instead of installing Excel as a standalone program.

Figure 1.7
Some of the most commonly used buttons from the Standard and Formatting toolbars are displayed on one strip.

Having these two toolbars share the same row was new to Excel 2000, and although it's the default, you might prefer to see all of both toolbars at once. To reset your toolbars and turn off the default, choose Tools, Customize, and click the Options tab. Check the Show Standard and Formatting Toolbars on two Rows option.

NOTE

> In this book, most figures show the Standard toolbar appearing below the menu bar, followed by the Formatting toolbar on a separate row.

If you prefer to keep them on the same row, keep in mind that the "one strip" look cannot display all the buttons from both toolbars. To view the obscured buttons, click the More Buttons button at the far-right end of a toolbar (see Figure 1.8).

Figure 1.8
Tools for formatting appear in a tool palette when More Buttons is clicked.

Tables 1.1 and 1.2 list each of the toolbar buttons on the Standard and Formatting toolbars and briefly explain their functions.

TABLE 1.1   BUTTONS ON THE STANDARD TOOLBAR

Button	Name	Description
	New	Creates a blank workbook.
	Open	Displays the Open dialog box, from which you can browse to find existing workbooks.
	Save	For a first-time save, this tool opens the Save As dialog box, enabling you to give the file a name and choose a location to save it. After you save the file, this button updates the saved file to include your latest changes.
	Permission	Permissions allow you to set restricted access to keep people from forwarding documents and even emailing them. You must first download Windows Rights Management software from Microsoft to access this functionality. Windows prompts you through the process if you do not already have rights software installed.

Button	Name	Description
	Email	Sends either the entire open workbook or the current worksheet as an email attachment.
	Print	Sends the currently selected sheet(s) directly to the printer.
	Print Preview	Displays a preview of the worksheet.
	Spelling	Runs a spell check of the text in the workbook.
	Research	Research opens the task pane in research mode where you can research information on the Web or through a host of dictionaries and research sites.
	Cut	Removes the selected content and places it on the Clipboard. Normally followed procedurally by pasting.
	Copy	Places a duplicate of the selected content on the Clipboard.
	Paste	Places the cut or copied content from the Clipboard to a new location. Contains a drop-down arrow allowing you to paste the data in different ways.
	Format Painter	Copies formatting from one range of cells to another.
	Undo	Cancels the last action. You can undo multiple operations by clicking the down arrow and selecting from the list.
	Redo	Reverses previous Undo operation(s).
	Hyperlink	Opens a dialog box from which you can choose to create a link to a document on your local or network drive, or to a Web page on the Internet.
	AutoSum	Automatically sums a column or row of numbers. Click once to choose the numbers to be summed, and then click again or press Enter to perform the calculation and insert the result. Contains a new drop-down arrow allowing you to select from a list of additional functions to automatically calculate.
	Sort Ascending	Performs an A to Z or 1 to 10 sort for a series of rows.
	Sort Descending	Performs a Z to A or 10 to 1 sort for a series of rows.
	Chart Wizard	Opens a wizard you can use to build a chart from selected cells in your worksheet.
	Drawing	Displays the Drawing toolbar, a series of tools for creating and formatting hand-drawn shapes and lines.

continues

TABLE 1.1   CONTINUED

Button	Name	Description
100% ▾	Zoom	Enlarges or reduces the display of your currently viewed worksheet area.
⊙	Microsoft Excel Help	Activates the Office Assistant if enabled—an animated character you can use to get help on a variety of Excel topics (Microsoft Office installations only). If the Office Assistant is not enabled, this button opens the normal Help task pane.

TABLE 1.2   BUTTONS ON THE FORMATTING TOOLBAR

Button	Name	Description
Arial ▾	Font	Shows the font currently in use; click the down-arrow button to see a list of fonts that you can apply along with their appearance.
10 ▾	Font Size	Indicates the current point size; click the down-arrow button to see a list of available point sizes. Choose one from the list or type your own number.
B	Bold	Makes the selection bold.
I	Italic	Makes the selection italic.
U	Underline	Underlines the selection.
≣	Align Left	Text is left-aligned by default. Use this button to realign previously centered or right-aligned text or to left-align numeric content.
≣	Center	Moves text or numeric content to the center of the cell.
≣	Align Right	Aligns the content of selected cells along the right side of the cell.
⊞	Merge and Center	Used primarily for titles, this button takes cell content in one cell and centers it across or down several contiguous (adjacent) cells, merging the cells into one cell. You can also unmerge the cells by depressing the button.
$	Currency Style	Turns standard numbers into currency by adding decimals, commas, and a dollar sign.
%	Percent Style	Turns standard numbers into a percent, with a percent sign.
,	Comma Style	Adds commas to numbers in excess of 999.99.

Button	Name	Description
	Increase Decimal	Extends the display of numbers to the right of the decimal point. The number 5.6, for example, can become 5.58 or 5.579. Each click of the button extends the number one digit.
	Decrease Decimal	Reduces the number of digits to the right of the decimal point. Each click removes one decimal place.
	Decrease Indent	Moves the cell content in selected cells closer to the left side of the cell, if any indent had been applied in the cell.
	Increase Indent	Moves cell content to the right.
	Borders	Opens a palette of border options for placing borders on any side of a cell or block of cells, including thick and double-bottom borders. This button also allows access to the Draw Borders feature.
	Fill Color	Applies or removes solid-color fills in cell backgrounds.
	Font Color	Changes the color of text or numbers in selected cells.

Many of Excel's tools require that you select a cell or cells before using the tool, so that Excel knows where you want to apply the format or perform the action that the button represents. If you don't consciously select a cell or cells, the toolbar will act upon the active cell.

Although you might not feel the need to do so until you're more familiar with Excel, you can always add and delete toolbars from your Excel window. To see a list of the different toolbars available in Excel, right-click any of the displayed toolbars, or choose View, Toolbars. Click the name of the toolbar you want to add to the screen.

To remove a currently displayed toolbar, display the list of toolbars and select the name of the toolbar you want to remove. The toolbar list is a toggle list—select them once, they're on; select them again, they're off. Many of the toolbars in Excel appear automatically, depending on what you're doing. For example, when working with a picture, the Picture toolbar will appear whenever the picture is selected. The same is true for the Chart toolbar, the WordArt, External Data, and so on.

→ For more information on customizing Excel's toolbars, **see** "Modifying Toolbars," **p. 714**.

WORKING WITH EXCEL MENUS

The Excel menus contain all the same tools that are represented on the toolbars, and more. To access Excel menus, click the name of the menu, or press Alt plus the underlined letter in the menu name. To close a menu you opened accidentally, press Esc or click the menu name again.

Microsoft Office menus contain the following three main features:

- **Commands**—The words you click to make things happen. If the words are followed by an ellipsis (…), a dialog box will open. If the command is followed by a right-pointing triangle, a submenu will appear.
- **Toolbar reference icons**—To familiarize you with the toolbar buttons that match your menu commands, they're reiterated in the menus.
- **Keyboard shortcuts**—If a keyboard shortcut is assigned to a given command, that shortcut will appear to the right of the command text.

If you prefer using the keyboard whenever possible, you can also issue menu commands by pressing the underlined letter in the command while the menu is displayed.

TIP FROM

> If Excel beeps repeatedly or refuses to insert entries as you type, you might have accidentally pressed the Alt key, which activates the menu bar without actually opening any particular menu. If one of the menu names looks different from the other menu names—boxed, or like a button—press Alt or Esc to deactivate the menu bar and return to the worksheet area.

Adaptive menus, which were introduced in Office 2000, are designed to be sensitive to the user. Each program begins by displaying a default set of commands when you open the menu; if you keep the menu open for a few seconds, additional (less commonly used) commands also appear. As you use these less-common commands, they join the others in the default set; the menus thus adapt to match your use of the program. If you prefer to have your menu commands remain static rather than adaptive, you can turn off this feature. Choose Tools, Customize, and on the Options tab, turn on the Always Show Full Menus check box. Click Close to put this change into effect and close the dialog box.

Figure 1.9 shows a typical Excel menu.

TIP FROM

> When adaptive menus are in use, you can display the entire menu immediately by double-clicking, rather than single-clicking, the top menu item (File, Edit, and so on). You also can click the last item on the open menu—a pair of downward-pointing arrows. If you don't do either of these actions, after a short delay in the menu, Excel will automatically display the full list of commands.

WORKING WITH SHORTCUT MENUS

Shortcut menus (also called *context menus*) are another type of menu that you'll find throughout Excel and all the other Office 2003 applications. By right-clicking various items in your workbook window, you can open menus that offer context-sensitive commands. Figure 1.10

shows a typical shortcut menu that appears when you right-click any cell (or selected range of cells) in your worksheet.

Figure 1.9
Although some commands are available only from the menus, most have toolbar and keyboard equivalents. Dimmed commands on menus are not available at that time.

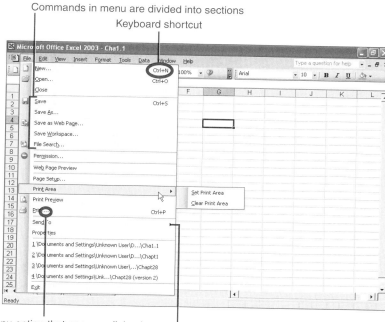

Commands in menu are divided into sections
Keyboard shortcut
... indicates menu option that opens a dialog box
Triangle indicates presence of a submenu

Figure 1.10
Commands appropriate for selected cells or cell content are displayed in the shortcut menu when you right-click any cell.

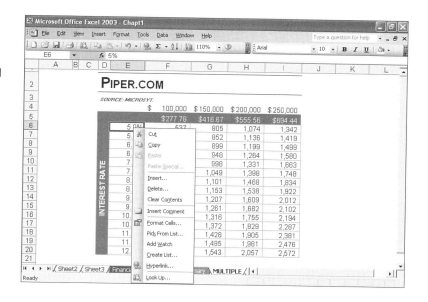

WORKING WITH WORKBOOKS

It's important to understand one concept from the outset—Excel files are *workbooks*, each of which contains three *worksheets* by default. You can access these worksheets by clicking their *sheet tabs*, or by using the *tab scrolling buttons* to the left of the tabs, as shown in Figure 1.11.

Figure 1.11
Click a worksheet's tab to select it. If you can't see the sheet you want, click the tab scrolling buttons to bring it into view.

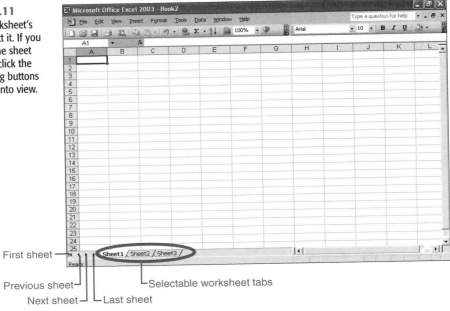

First sheet
Previous sheet
Next sheet — Last sheet
Selectable worksheet tabs

TIP FROM

If you want to quickly select a sheet that's out of view, right-click any of the tab scrolling buttons to see a shortcut menu listing all the sheets in the workbook. Select the sheet you want by choosing its name from the list.

The effect of each workbook containing a number of worksheets is that Excel files are three-dimensional. Each worksheet has a vertical height and a horizontal width and the entire workbook has depth, provided by the multiple worksheets it contains. You can use just one worksheet in a file or you may use many of them, depending on your application. Each can contain a different layout or they may be the same. These are some things you can do with worksheets in a workbook:

- You can add sheets to the default three with which each workbook starts. The number of sheets per workbook is limited only by the amount of memory on your computer.
- You can change sheet names. Sheet1, Sheet2, and so on are default sheet names. Worksheet names can be up to 31 characters long, including spaces.
- You can rearrange worksheet order and delete sheets.

- If you need to create a new worksheet that resembles an existing worksheet, you can copy the existing worksheet, paste the copy into the workbook, and edit the copy to meet your needs.

- You can group your worksheets and create several identical worksheets all at once, or you can create one worksheet and make a copy of it.

→ For more information on grouping sheets, **see** "Grouping and Ungrouping Sheets," **p. 25**

TIP FROM

Each new workbook opens with a number of sheets, which you can change by choosing Tools, Options and clicking the General tab. Change the setting for Sheets in New Workbook, and click OK. For more information about customizing Excel to meet your needs, see Chapter 27, "Customizing Excel to Fit Your Working Style."

COLORING WORKBOOK TABS

You can color the workbook tabs. If you have large workbooks in which several sheets might be dedicated to production numbers and other sheets dedicated to financial numbers, it's helpful to put these sheets together in a logical group and color them. To color the worksheet tab, simply right-click the tab and choose Color. Notice the example in Figure 1.12.

Figure 1.12
Right-click the sheet tab to access the Tab Color option.

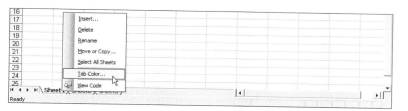

After you choose Color, a palette appears. The color palette enables you to change the color of the worksheet tab (see Figure 1.13). Select a color and then click OK. When the worksheet is active, a colored line appears at the bottom of the tab. When inactive, the whole tab is colored, as in the example in Figure 1.14. To change the colors in the palette, see Chapter 27.

INSERTING SHEETS

If the three sheets that came with your blank workbook aren't enough for you, add new ones. To insert a new worksheet, choose Insert, Worksheet. A new sheet appears to the left of the currently active sheet.

New sheets are added chronologically. For example, if you add Sheet 4 and then delete it, the next new sheet will be called Sheet 5, even though Sheet 4 is no longer in the workbook. When you right-click the sheet tab and click Insert you get a dialog called Insert from which you must select the Worksheet icon and click OK. Last, you can move a copy a worksheet to another location within the workbook or to another workbook by selecting the Edit menu and selecting Move or Copy Sheet.

Figure 1.13
The Format Tab Color dialog box enables you to choose a color for the tab from the color palette.

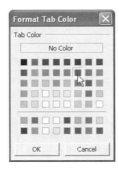

Figure 1.14
The inactive worksheet tabs appear completely colored when not selected.

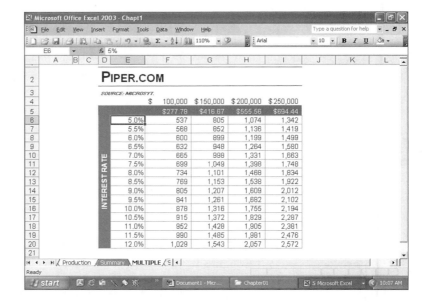

NAMING WORKSHEETS

Numeric worksheet names (Sheet1, Sheet2) don't tell you about the content of your sheets. Unless you happen to remember what data you've entered on your individual sheets, you're likely to spend a lot of time clicking through the worksheets.

To name a worksheet, you can use any of the following methods:

- Choose Format, Sheet, Rename.
- Double-click the sheet tab.
- Right-click the tab for the worksheet you want to rename and choose Rename from the shortcut menu.

All three techniques have the same result—the current sheet name is highlighted, and you can type the replacement text. To confirm your entry, click in any cell on the current sheet, click another sheet tab, or press Enter. To keep the previous name, press Esc before confirming the new name.

REARRANGING WORKSHEETS

When you insert a new sheet, it's added to the left of the sheet that was active at the time. In many cases, the new sheet isn't in the position where you want it, relative to the existing sheets.

To move a sheet, click and drag the sheet tab to a new position, watching the small down-pointing triangle that appears and follows the tab as you move it left and right. Your mouse pointer also is accompanied by a small page icon. When the triangle is pointing to the spot where you want to place your tab, release the mouse. Figure 1.15 shows a sheet tab being moved.

Figure 1.15
Rearrange your sheet tabs by dragging left and/or right until you find the correct location.

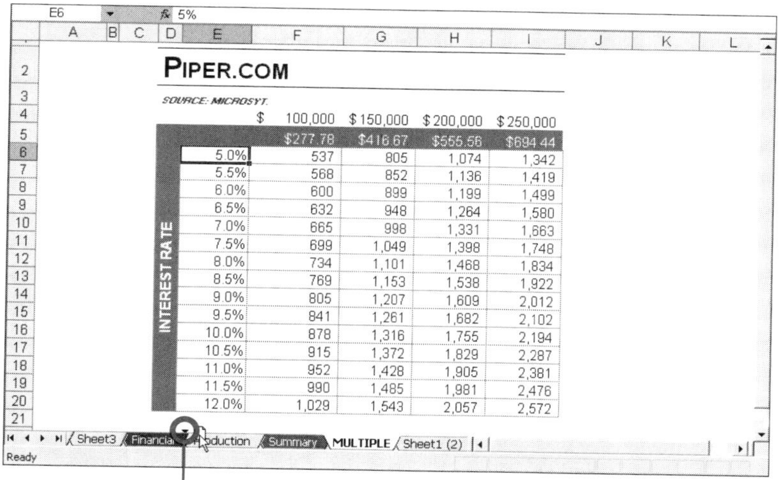

$	100,000	$ 150,000	$ 200,000	$ 250,000
	$277.78	$416.67	$555.56	$694.44
5.0%	537	805	1,074	1,342
5.5%	568	852	1,136	1,419
6.0%	600	899	1,199	1,499
6.5%	632	948	1,264	1,580
7.0%	665	998	1,331	1,663
7.5%	699	1,049	1,398	1,748
8.0%	734	1,101	1,468	1,834
8.5%	769	1,153	1,538	1,922
9.0%	805	1,207	1,609	2,012
9.5%	841	1,261	1,682	2,102
10.0%	878	1,316	1,755	2,194
10.5%	915	1,372	1,829	2,287
11.0%	952	1,428	1,905	2,381
11.5%	990	1,485	1,981	2,476
12.0%	1,029	1,543	2,057	2,572

Triangle indicates new position for worksheet

GROUPING AND UNGROUPING SHEETS

Sheets can be *grouped* (connected) to facilitate creating or formatting two or more identical sheets. For example, you can create one sheet and copy it to two other sheets, or you can group three blank sheets and enter and format the content once—no subsequent copying required. Because the sheets are connected before any content is entered, all the content is automatically placed on all the grouped sheets in the same exact locations on each sheet. It's important to note that, when sheets are grouped, almost anything you do happens to all the sheets. The following items point out things that happen on all sheets when sheets are grouped:

- Typing (including adding and deleting text)
- Almost any type of formatting (including text, column, row, and cell), including the removal of formatting
- Cut, copy, and paste (all methods, including right-drag and drag and drop)
- Changes to the File, Page Setup command
- Moving, copying, deleting, and coloring the tabs of sheets
- Several of the Window options on the View tab of the Tool, Options command, including page breaks, formulas, gridlines, row and column headers, and zeros values.

To group sheets, click one of the tabs that you want in the group and press the Ctrl key. With the Ctrl key held down, click the remaining tabs in the intended group of sheets. All the grouped sheets' tabs will turn white, and the indicator [Group] will appear in the title bar after the workbook name, as shown in Figure 1.16.

Group indicator

Figure 1.16
Select as many sheets as you need for your group with the Ctrl key.

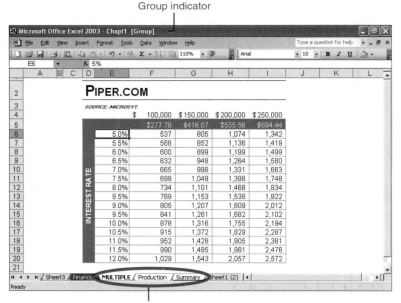

These three sheets are grouped

TIP

> To group a consecutive series of sheets, click the tab of the first sheet you want grouped, and then hold down the Shift key as you click the last tab of the sheet you want in the series. All the sheets between the first and last tab will be included in the group.

You can group *all* the sheets in a workbook by right-clicking any sheet tab and choosing Select All Sheets from the shortcut menu.

To *ungroup* your grouped sheets, click a sheet tab outside of the group, or right-click any of the grouped tabs and choose Ungroup Sheets from the shortcut menu.

CAUTION

> When entering group content, be sure to enter only the content that you want to be common to all the sheets in the group. If the group of sheets is intended to be quarterly sales reports for two or more companies, for example, stop entering group content and ungroup the sheets before entering any content specific to any individual company.

USING WORKSHEET KEYBOARD SHORTCUTS

With more than 16 million cells in a single worksheet, it's important to get where you're going as quickly as possible. Table 1.3 lists the keyboard shortcuts you can use to move from cell to cell in a worksheet.

TABLE 1.3   KEYBOARD WORKSHEET NAVIGATION

Keyboard Shortcut	Result
Tab	Moves one cell to the right.
Shift+Tab	Moves one cell to the left.
Enter	Moves one cell down.
Ctrl+Home	Moves back to cell A1 (called *Home*) from anywhere in the worksheet.
Ctrl+End	Moves to the last cell in the worksheet.
Home	Moves to the beginning of the current row.
Page Down	Moves down one screen.
Page Up	Moves up one screen.
Alt+Page Down	Moves one screen to the right.
Alt+Page Up	Moves one screen to the left.
Ctrl+Page Down	Moves to the next worksheet in the workbook.
Ctrl+Page Up	Moves to the previous sheet in the workbook.
Ctrl+Down Arrow	Navigates to the bottom of the data. End+down arrow will do the same.
Ctrl+Up Arrow	Navigates to the top of the spreadsheet data region. End+up arrow will do the same.
Ctrl+Right Arrow	Navigates to the right of the spreadsheet data region. End+right arrow will do the same.
Ctrl+Left Arrow	Navigates to the left of the spreadsheet data region. End+left arrow will do the same.

ACCESSING CELLS WITH GO TO

Although most keyboard shortcuts take you to a cell in relation to the cell you're in, the Go To shortcut—which you access by pressing the F5 key or Ctrl+G—opens a dialog box into which you can type any cell address. Press Enter after typing the address, and you are automatically placed in that cell. You can also type an address in the Name box located on the left side of the Formula bar and press Enter to jump to that address. The Go To dialog box offers an advantage over the Name box; the dialog box displays the address where the cell pointer was located before you jumped, so it's easy to jump back to the cell from which you came. You can also access the Go To dialog box by choosing Edit, Go To. The Special button opens the Go To Special dialog box, which lets you access formulas, conditional formatting, precedents, dependents, and more in an Excel workbook. Go To Special is also a good tool to use when auditing a workbook created by others. Go To also has the great capability to select all constants or formulas in a sheet or within a highlighted range.

For example, if you inherited a sheet with a lot of REF errors in various parts of a sheet, you can use the Go To, Special dialog box to select them all at once (for deletion or correction) by choosing the Formulas check box and deselecting all the types except Errors. If you have a sheet that's reused each month to enter that month's sales figures in various parts of a sheet, the Go To, Special dialog box lets you select only those cells that contain values. Choose Constants and deselect all the types except Numbers.

After the cells for either of the preceding examples are highlighted, you can delete them all or simply type in the new data/formulas throughout the selected cells.

UNDERSTANDING CELL BASICS

Cells are the bricks that build your worksheets and workbooks, each playing an integral part in the storage and manipulation of your text and numeric data. You can think of each cell as an individual container capable of storing text, numbers, and so on. The following is a list of basic information about cells—things that you should know to improve your use and understanding of Excel:

- A cell can hold up to 32,767 characters, which can consist of text, numbers, formulas, dates, graphics, or any combination of these. The amount of text you can view in a cell depends on the width of the column the cell is in and the formatting applied to the cell and its contents.

- Text, numbers, and formulas you type in a cell are immediately displayed in the Formula bar.

- Whenever a worksheet is active, at least one cell is also active (called the *active cell*). The active cell is designated by a heavy border around the cell called the *cell pointer*. If the Excel window is the active application, and the workbook window is active within it, that one cell's content—or lack thereof in the case of an empty cell—will appear in the Formula bar. The address of the cell (or name, if you've named it) will appear in the Name box.

- After you type data into a cell, press Enter to accept the entry and move down one cell, press the Tab key to accept the entry and move one cell to the right, or press an arrow key to accept the entry and move one cell in the direction of the arrow (pressing the up-arrow key, for instance, moves one cell up). You can also finish an entry by clicking the green check mark button located on the Formula bar. During the time a cell's entry is unfinished (designated by a cursor blinking inside the cell or on the Formula bar), many of Excel's commands cannot be executed.

- If you change your mind about an entry prior to finishing it, press Esc or click the Cancel button (the red X on the formula bar) to nullify the entry and start over.

- If you've already pressed Enter after completing an entry, you can reselect the cell and press Delete to quickly remove the entry, or simply type a new entry.

TIP FROM

> Almost everyone at one time or another forgets to finish entering data in a cell before attempting to access a command or some other object in the workbook. In many cases, Excel will finish entering the data for you. In some cases, though, Excel will beep.
>
> If you can't access something that you think you should be able to access, check two things:
>
> - Do you see the Cancel (red X) and Enter (green check mark) buttons on the Formula bar?
> - Does the word Enter appear on the status bar at the bottom left of the Excel window?
>
> If the answer is yes, you forgot to finish entering data into a cell. Do so by pressing Enter, Tab, by using one of the arrow keys, or by clicking the red X or green check mark on the Formula bar.

The remaining sections of this chapter discuss the intricacies of entering text and numbers into worksheet cells.

ENTERING TEXT

Text content in a spreadsheet seems like unnecessary fluff to some hard-core financial users. A necessary evil, text tells us which numbers are in which columns and rows, and which cells contain the results of formulas. For some users, that's more than enough text. Other users, however, take full advantage of Excel's text capabilities. Excel is a rich program capable of storing text in databases (names, addresses, comments), and can even be used for minor word processing.

No matter how detailed or concise your text entries are, Excel applies the following defaults to text:

- Text is automatically left-aligned. This includes numbers that Excel perceives as text due to the inclusion of nonnumeric content, such as Social Security numbers that include hyphens.

- Text doesn't wrap unless you tell it to. If you type text that exceeds the width of the cell, text will appear to flow into the next cell. If there is already data in the adjacent cell, the overflow will be *truncated*, meaning that the excess won't display unless you widen the column (this technique is covered later in this chapter). Even if the column isn't widened, the truncated content is merely hidden—it isn't deleted, proof of which can be found by examining the cell's content in the Formula bar, which displays the active cell's entire content, including the hidden overflow.

- Text is 10-point Arial by default. You can customize this default as needed.

- If you start to type an entry that resembles one you typed elsewhere in the same column, Excel might AutoComplete the entry for you.

- You can select from a list of entries you've already typed in the current column. Right-click the cell and select Pick from List from the context menu, or press Alt+down arrow. Then, select the entry you want to repeat.

- If you misspell a common word, you might notice that Microsoft Excel corrects it for you as you type. Excel includes an extensive set of *AutoCorrect* entries, shared with the other Office programs, that correct common misspellings, capitalization mishaps such as two initial capital letters at the beginning of a name, and so on. This feature can be a great help, but you might find some of the settings annoying.

TIP FROM

After you have completed your data entry, you can also check the spelling of all text entries—including sheet names, list headings, and so on—by choosing Tools, Spelling or clicking the Spelling button on the Standard toolbar. This only checks the selected or grouped sheets.

LABELING COLUMNS AND ROWS

Aside from the worksheet's title (which normally goes into cell A1), the first cells you normally fill in are column and row labels. These are the cells that tell you (and any other users of the worksheet) what to expect in the remaining cells in the worksheet. Figure 1.17 shows a worksheet in its first stages of development. By reading the labels that the user has typed into strategic locations, you can tell exactly what type of information will be stored, and how it will be manipulated. You even have an idea of what types of formulas will be used.

TIP FROM

If the current worksheet's information will be repeated on other sheets in the workbook, group the sheets before you type the labels and common content to save time and effort.

Row labels   Column labels

Figure 1.17
Other than the use of
in-house jargon, make
the worksheet labels
as clear and concise
as possible, designing
the sheet as if some-
one unfamiliar with
the data will be
using it.

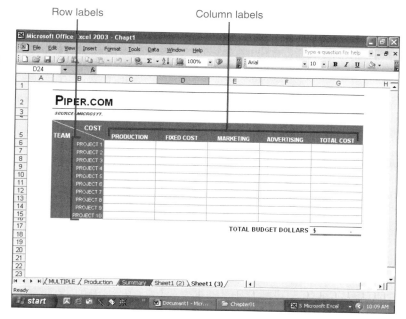

ADJUSTING COLUMN WIDTH AND ROW HEIGHT

As you type the worksheet titles, column headings, and row labels (as well as the data in the worksheet), you might need to make columns wider or narrower, or to adjust the height of the rows. Select the column line and drag it to the proper width, or double-click it and it will AutoFit. You can also select the row dividers and drag up and down to size the row height.

Truncated (chopped-off) text, error messages, and a cramped appearance to the worksheet content are all reasons to adjust the column width and row height. If you see #### symbols, try expanding the column width or double-clicking on the column line to get Excel to auto-expand and widen the column for you.

Excel will generally widen a column automatically to accommodate numeric entries (see the following Note), but text entries require manual adjustment. Row height will automatically increase if font size increases, but again, manual adjustments might become necessary from an aesthetic standpoint.

NOTE

When entering numbers, regardless of what's displayed in the cell, Excel stores the entire number with a precision of 15 significant digits. Digits after 15 are also stored, but rounded to zero.

continues

continued

By default, cells in a new worksheet use General format, and Excel automatically adjusts column width to display numbers you type into cells in some circumstances. Except for date formats and certain custom formats, if you apply a particular number format to a cell, such as Currency with two decimal places, Excel widens the cell to accommodate the specified format, but may round the decimal places.

In General format, this is what will happen to the column width and/or the number when you enter it into a cell:

- Numbers containing decimals are rounded visually to fit the default column width. (Excel retains the entire number value, of course, as you can see in the Formula bar when the cell is selected.)

- Numbers containing more than 11 total characters appear in scientific notation, which also may widen the column to show the notation properly.

- Columns are widened to accommodate numbers entered with commas, dollar signs, or percent signs, regardless of the number of digits, although decimals may be rounded.

- When numbers with fractions are entered, the column is adjusted to display the entire number, regardless of the number of digits (example: 111111111111111 ½). Digits beyond 15 are rounded to zero as usual. Fractional entries greater than 16 characters are rounded and no longer show the fractional format.

- Numbers consisting entirely of decimals are rounded to fit in the cell. Numbers without decimals that are fewer than 12 characters will automatically (if necessary) widen the column width. None of these scenarios will be true if you manually widen the column. Automatic column widths don't occur when the data is copied or moved.

Excel provides several methods for adjusting the size of rows and columns, as shown in the following list:

- The *AutoFit* feature adjusts selected columns or rows to accommodate the longest or tallest entry, respectively. Using the row and column lines as guides, double-click the bottom boundary on the selected row(s) or the right boundary on the selected column(s), as shown in Figure 1.18. The row/column will adjust to the size that fits the largest/widest entry. You also can invoke AutoFit by selecting the column(s) or row(s) and choosing Format, Column, AutoFit Selection or Format, Row, AutoFit.

- Choose Format, Column, Width or Format, Row, Height. In the resulting dialog box using the default font style and type, enter an exact measurement from 0 to 255 for the selected column(s) or row(s).

- Drag the right boundary of a column or the bottom boundary of a row. When dragging, the direction you drag determines the column's or row's new dimensions—drag to the right to widen a column, drag down to make a row taller. If you select more than one column or row, dragging the boundary of any column or row in the selection adjusts all the columns or rows in the selection. A ToolTip appears when you widen (drag) rows and columns. The width indicator represents the approximate width in characters based on the widest 10-pt. Arial character. The approximate height is in points, the same measurement technique used for font size.

Double-click here to adjust the entire set

Figure 1.18
Select a single column or row, or drag through a series of columns or rows, and adjust the width or height with one double-click.

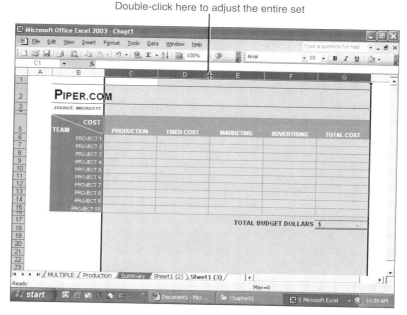

N O T E

If you're wrapping text and your row height keeps autoadjusting to fit the text in the cell, you can lock the row height by simply selecting Height under the Row option from the Format menu. Type a row height and click OK; this will lock the row and stop it from expanding.

C A U T I O N

If you adjust row height manually once and then make the content larger at a later time (requiring a taller row), the row will no longer adjust automatically. After you've tinkered with row height, you can continue to adjust row height manually each time you increase or decrease the font size, or you can double-click the bottom boundary of the row(s) to reset them to using automatic adjustment.

- To AutoFit an entire worksheet with one double-click, select the entire worksheet by clicking the Select All button in the upper-left corner of the worksheet window. Then, double-click any boundary between column control buttons to AutoFit all the columns, or any boundary between row control buttons to AutoFit all the rows. Click any individual cell to deselect the worksheet after making the desired adjustments.

1

CAUTION

> If cells display numbers in scientific notation, such as 78123E+12, AutoFit won't adjust the column to the width required to display the entire number. You might have to change the format of the cell for the number to display properly. See Chapter 7, "Database Functions," for more information on formatting numeric entries.

SAVING EXCEL DATA

The first rule you should learn with regard to any computer application is to save your work early and often. Excel is no exception to this rule, and is perhaps one of the applications where the rule is most important.

When is "early"? As soon as you've entered the worksheet title and column/row labels. Don't wait until you've entered all the numbers and built the formulas. Why save so early? Because programs crash, power failures happen unexpectedly, and we all make mistakes, such as closing a file without saving.

How often is often? Whenever you've entered more data or performed more calculations or formatting than you would want to repeat. Every five or ten minutes, depending on how fast you're working, isn't too often.

Excel, like all the Microsoft Office applications, makes it easy to save your work, providing toolbar buttons, menu commands, and keyboard shortcuts to accommodate anyone's work style. In addition, you're prompted before exiting a file without saving, as shown in Figure 1.19. (If you have the Office Assistant turned on, it asks this question in a dialog balloon.)

Figure 1.19
If you never have saved the file or you have made changes since the last time you saved, this prompt appears when you attempt to close a file.

PERFORMING A FIRST-TIME SAVE

The first time you save an Excel workbook (hopefully early in the worksheet development process), you'll need to name the file, choose a location for it, and in some cases choose a file format in which to save it.

You can execute a first-time save by any of the following methods:

- Choose File, Save.
- Choose File, Save As.
- Press Ctrl+S.

- Press Alt+F2, Alt+Shift+F2, or Shift+F12.
- Click the Save button on the Standard toolbar.

Whichever method you choose, the Save As dialog box opens the first time you save a file. Because Excel correctly assesses that the file hasn't been saved before, it opens this dialog box and gives you the opportunity to name the file and choose a folder in which to save it (see Figure 1.20).

Figure 1.20
Microsoft Office files will save to the My Documents folder by default.

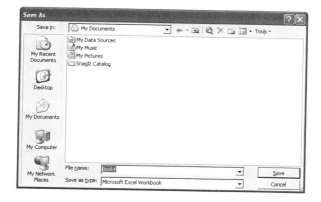

TIP FROM

It's a good idea to create subfolders (normally within a folder called My Documents) to categorize your files. By creating these folders, you make it easier to find the files, and simpler to copy or move them as a group to a backup disk or a network drive. You can create them in the Save As dialog box or through My Computer or Windows Explorer.

SAVING YOUR WORKBOOK WITH A PASSWORD AND FILE ENCRYPTION

If the content of your workbook is confidential, you can apply a password that will keep others from opening and/or editing the workbook. This security measure would be in addition to any security afforded by your network, operating system, or by the Excel Protection feature. To access the save options Advanced button, select the Data menu, select Options, and then choose the Security tab. You can encrypt the file by clicking the Advanced button in the Save Options dialog box. By selecting an RC4-based encryption type, you can create passwords up to 255 characters in length. This provides an ultrasecure workbook. When you encrypt a password using one of the RC4 algorithms, as shown in Figure 1.21, users of Excel 2000 and older will not be able to open the file. They will be prompted by their older versions to enter the password, but will never be able to enter one successfully, even if they are told what the password is. In other words, it will always return the Password Not Valid error. You used to be able to retrieve a lost password by purchasing (sometimes expensive) software that allows you to drag Word and Excel documents into their software window to instantly determine the password; however, the RC4 password encryption algorithms make this type of "password breaker" software obsolete.

Figure 1.21
Choose an encryption type to create an ultrasecure workbook.

1

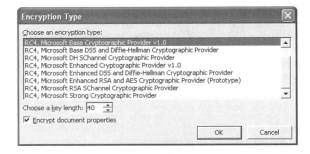

There is also an alternative to adding a password or encryption using the Save As command. Users can now attach passwords/encryption as well as provide digital signatures and remove personal data when they save by selecting Tools, General Options from the Save As dialog box, and then clicking the Security tab. Users of previous versions of Excel will find that the Save As technique is more familiar, and it does force the user to save the workbook after assigning the passwords.

You can set up a password on the first save, or by using File, Save As any time after that. Follow these steps to apply a password to the workbook:

1. In the Save As dialog box, open the Tools drop-down list and select General Options. The Save Options dialog box opens (see Figure 1.22).

Figure 1.22
Keep people from viewing or editing your workbooks by setting up a password that must be supplied each time someone attempts to open the file.

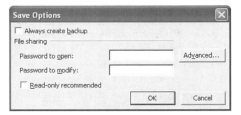

2. To set a password that will be required each time the file is opened, type the password in the Password to Open box. The password will appear as asterisks to prevent passers-by from seeing what you're typing.

3. For further security, add a password for modification in the Password to Modify box. This option requires the user to enter an additional password to be able to edit the workbook.

4. Click OK.

5. Reenter the password(s) in the Confirm Password dialog box, and click OK.

6. Click Advanced to encrypt the file. Select an encryption type and then click OK.

CAUTION

Don't forget your passwords! If you do, you won't be able to open or modify the file (depending on which functions you chose to secure with a password). There's no way to retrieve a forgotten password or reset it to a new password without the existing password. If you don't set an encryption type then it defaults to Office 97/2000 compatible and the password can be retrieved using password-breaking software.

TIP

Choose a password you won't forget, but that others can't guess. Passwords of five to eight characters are long enough to be harder to decipher, but not so long you forget them. If you password-protect a lot of spreadsheets, you could keep a list of your passwords in a secure place, just in case you forget. Or you could always set your passwords to be the first five characters of the filename, but rotated forward some number of characters. For example, the password for Project Status.xls could be tvsni. T is four letters after p, v is four letters after r, and so on. With this method, all you must remember is your rule. Finally, you could simply use the same password for all your workbooks.

None of these methods provides unbreakable security—someone could find your password list, figure out your single password, or figure out your password system. But all these methods deliver acceptable security for routine situations.

DOCUMENT RECOVERY

 Excel introduced a feature in its 2002 version, that is also included in Excel 2003, called document recovery. When a file becomes corrupt or when Excel crashes, the files are analyzed for errors and all recoverable documentation is saved. For example, if you have been working on a file and haven't saved in the last 30 minutes and the file crashes, chances are most of your data will be automatically saved. This is a huge timesaver. Excel will then prompt you with dialog boxes and or a document recovery task pane on the left side of the screen and asks which files you want to save. The status indicator tells you which file was corrupt by showing the status as [recovered] to the left of the document. If there is no corruption, the status is shown as [original].

SAVING EXCEL FILES IN ALTERNATIVE FORMATS

Most of the time, you'll want to let Excel save your files in the default XLS format for the currently installed version of Excel. This ensures that you'll be able to open the file in the current version of the software, and that all the formatting will be preserved with the file.

Sometimes, however, you'll need to save files to another file format. Following are some reasons for this change:

- You're going to share the file with a user who has an older version of Excel. Each new release of Excel has features the previous release didn't. Saving to an older version strips out those features so that the recipient using an older version of Excel can open and use the file.

- You'll be sending the file via email, and you don't know what software the recipient has. Saving the file in tab-delimited text (TXT) format will allow the user to open the file in any word-processing program, where the spreadsheet will appear as a block of tabbed text. When you save to this format, tabs are inserted between each cell so that the overall layout is preserved.

- You're sharing the file with someone who uses Lotus 1-2-3, Quattro Pro, Excel for the Macintosh, or dBASE. Choose the appropriate format for the software the recipient uses.

TIP FROM

> When saving a file in another spreadsheet or database software format (WK1, WKS, WQ1, DBF), if you're not sure of the version number, choose an older version (lower version number) so that you don't give the recipient a file that his or her version can't open or display properly.

- The current version of Excel is presenting problems and software errors, and it's been suggested that you save to a format that doesn't save the particular element that's causing problems. Normally, if this occurs, a Microsoft technical support person will tell you to save to the previous version format of Excel or a tab-delimited text (TXT) format so that you don't lose your work, and then reopen the file in the current version of Excel, and then try again.

- You're working on your company's intranet or Web server, or working internationally with other users and creating or saving files elsewhere via the Web. For these arrangements, you'll probably want to save the Excel files in HTML format (the language of the Web) rather than XLS format.

To save a file to a new format, follow these steps:

1. Choose File, Save As.
2. If necessary, choose a location and type a name for the file.
3. Open the Save As Type list box and scroll through the formats.
4. Select a format by clicking it in the list.
5. Press Enter or click Save.

TIP FROM

> If you're creating a new version of the file in an alternative format (for sharing with another user or as backup), give the file a different name (perhaps including the format's extension in the filename). You could add a 2 or an A to the existing filename so that even if you aren't displaying file extensions in the dialog boxes, you'll be able to tell the files apart.

SAVING AN EXCEL WORKBOOK AS A REUSABLE TEMPLATE

If the workbook you've created is one that you can envision creating again in the future, it's a labor-saving idea to save it as a *template* in addition to saving it as a normal Excel file.

Why a template? Because templates are like cookie cutters for new workbooks. When a file is saved as a template, it becomes a potential foundation for future workbooks, containing all the text, numbers, formulas, and formats that the file has in it. By using the template to start a new file, you save yourself all the entry and formatting that went into the creation of the original file.

The main advantage of using a template instead of Save As is that the user does not have to eliminate or update the old data from the old workbook. An actual template leaves all the cells containing the raw data blank—data that changes from one use to another. Each time they use the template, all they need do (in most cases) is punch in the raw data. Also, it prevents the user from accidentally saving the new data in an old file, which could happen if the user opened an old workbook, typed in data, and accidentally used the Save command before doing a Save As.

CREATING TEMPLATE CONTENT

It's important that your template not contain data that isn't applicable to each use of the template. For example, if you're saving a sales report workbook as a template, make sure that when you save it, none of the specific sales numbers are in the cells. You want the column and row labels, generic titles and page setups, and the formulas to be part of the file, but not any esoteric information that will have to be changed or deleted each time you use the template.

To save the current workbook as a template, follow these steps:

1. Choose File, Save As to open the Save As dialog box.
2. As needed, change the name of the file. Do not change the location because Excel will dictate this as soon as you choose the Template format for the file.
3. Open the Save As Type list box and choose Template (*.xlt)from the list. The Save In box automatically switches to the folder C:\Documents and Settings\Username\Application Data\Microsoft\Templates. On Windows 2000, the folder is C:\Documents and Settings\Username\Application Data\Microsoft\Templates, where \Username\ is the name they logged in under.
4. Click Save.

TIP FROM

You can create subfolder(s) within the Templates folder to house new templates. Templates stored in the Templates folder appear on the General tab in the New dialog box; templates stored in a subfolder of Templates are listed on a separate tab named for the subfolder.

STARTING A NEW WORKBOOK FROM A TEMPLATE

Whether you're starting a new workbook from a template you created or one of the installed Excel templates, follow these steps:

1. Choose File, New, and then select blank workbook from the task pane, as shown in Figure 1.23.

Figure 1.23
Excel looks for XLT files in the Templates folder and all of its subfolders. It displays a tab for any folder found to contain an XLT-formatted file.

2. Click the tab that corresponds to the name of the subfolder in which the template file is stored.

3. Double-click the template on which you want to base the new workbook, or click it once and press Enter.

The new workbook opens, filled with whatever content and formatting was part of the template file.

NOTE

> You aren't opening the template itself when you start a new workbook based on a template. You're using the template as a foundation, creating a completely separate file that contains the information, content, and settings you established in the template. Notice that the file is named Book#, and the original template filename doesn't appear on the title bar.

CONTROLLING YOUR WORKSHEET VIEW

You can switch between open workbook windows to tile or cascade the open windows; you can freeze a row of column headings onscreen for simplified data entry, or even hide a column or row of confidential information (so that it's not visible onscreen nor when printed). Figure 1.24 shows a table with frozen column headings and hidden columns. The following sections describe the techniques for freezing and hiding columns and rows, as well as how to split the window into multiple panes to focus in on multiple sections of the worksheet simultaneously.

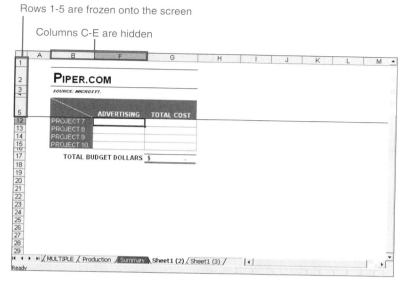

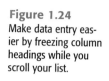

Figure 1.24
Make data entry easier by freezing column headings while you scroll your list.

SWITCHING BETWEEN OPEN WORKBOOKS

Windows gives you the power to have more than one program running at the same time, and within each program, more than one file open at a time. This capability would have little or no benefit if you couldn't also *switch* between those files and programs quickly and efficiently.

To switch between open Excel workbook windows, use one of the following methods:

■ Open Excel's Window menu and choose the desired numbered workbook file from the list.

CAUTION

> Watch out for slow responses, video pauses, or problems with screen colors when you have several workbooks open at the same time. The amount of memory in your computer will dictate how many workbooks you can have open without performance suffering. If you try to do too many things at once, Excel might crash or become unresponsive.

■ Click the Taskbar button for the workbook to which you would like to switch. Office 2003 displays each open file with its own button on the Taskbar, not just a button for the application itself. With this feature, you also can use Alt+Tab to switch between workbooks (keep in mind that this shortcut cycles between all open programs, not just Excel 2003).

- Press Ctrl+Tab or Ctrl+F6 to move to the next workbook. This workbook now becomes the active file.

- Press Ctrl+Shift+Tab or Ctrl+Shift+F6 to move to the previous workbook, making it the active file.

You also can view different workbooks at the same time, each in its own document window within the application window. The best way to do this is to choose Window, Arrange, and then choose Tiled or Horizontal from the Arrange Windows dialog box.

Choose horizontal or vertical tiling based on the layout of the workbooks.

TIP FROM

Obviously, if you have too many workbooks open at the same time, tiling them will create too many small windows. It's virtually impossible to view an entire spreadsheet through a small window. To make the tiled view more effective, keep the number of workbooks open to three or less, so that each window gives you enough room to scroll around and see a reasonable amount of content within each window.

FREEZING COLUMNS AND ROWS

Freezing part of a worksheet holds that part onscreen as you scroll the remainder of the worksheet. The most commonly frozen part of a worksheet is the row of column headings at the top of or to the left of a long series of rows containing data, such as in a name and address list. By freezing this row of headings, you can still see what data goes in which cell as you scroll down the rows, as shown in Figure 1.25.

Lines indicate frozen headings   Scrollable area

Figure 1.25
Freezing keeps the column headings onscreen no matter how many rows of data you must enter or edit.

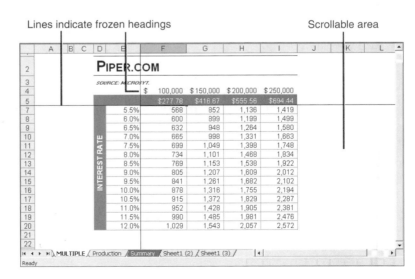

To freeze a row in the worksheet, follow these steps:

1. Click the row number *below* the row you want to freeze.

2. Choose Window, Freeze Panes. Everything above the selected row is now frozen in place.

If you scroll through the rows, you'll see that the frozen rows remain onscreen, regardless of how far down you scroll.

Freezing a column (normally column A) keeps vertical headings onscreen so that you can enter data that exceeds screen width from left to right. To freeze a column, select the column to the right of the one you want to freeze, and choose Window, Freeze Panes. When you scroll to the right, the frozen column remains onscreen. The freeze effect can also be saved with the file, but this can significantly increase the file size.

TIP FROM

You can freeze columns and rows at the same time by selecting a single cell and choosing Window, Freeze Panes. The rows above and columns to the left of the selected cell will be frozen. Use this technique to freeze row labels and column headings at the same time, as shown previously in Figure 1.25.

To unfreeze a frozen window, choose Window, Unfreeze Panes.

SPLITTING THE SCREEN

Splitting the Excel screen allows you to see two or four distinct parts of the same worksheet at the same time. This differs from freezing rows and/or columns in that each of the sections in the split can be scrolled separately. The upper and/or left portions of a frozen worksheet remain static. You'll find this feature particularly useful when comparing content within a worksheet, or if you need to cut or copy content from one area to another area that normally wouldn't appear on the same screen. Imagine that you have a worksheet containing data for all four quarters of the year—by splitting the screen into four parts, each one displaying a different quarter, you can do a quick visual analysis of the entire year.

By splitting the screen, you create the effect of two or four "cameras" on the worksheet content, each aimed at a different section of the sheet. Each camera can scroll and pan around the section at which it's aimed, and of course, you can remove the split(s) when the need has passed. Figure 1.26 shows a worksheet window split into four parts. A double-click on a split bar will eliminate the split. In a four-pane split, a double-click on the intersection of the split bars will remove all four panes.

To split the worksheet window into two parts, follow these steps:

1. To split into two panes, select the row or column that will mark the split by clicking its number or letter, respectively. Or, to split into four panes, click in one cell.

2. Choose Window, Split.

Draggable vertical split screen

Figure 1.26
If you need to compare or copy content from one area to another, split the worksheet window into two or four parts.

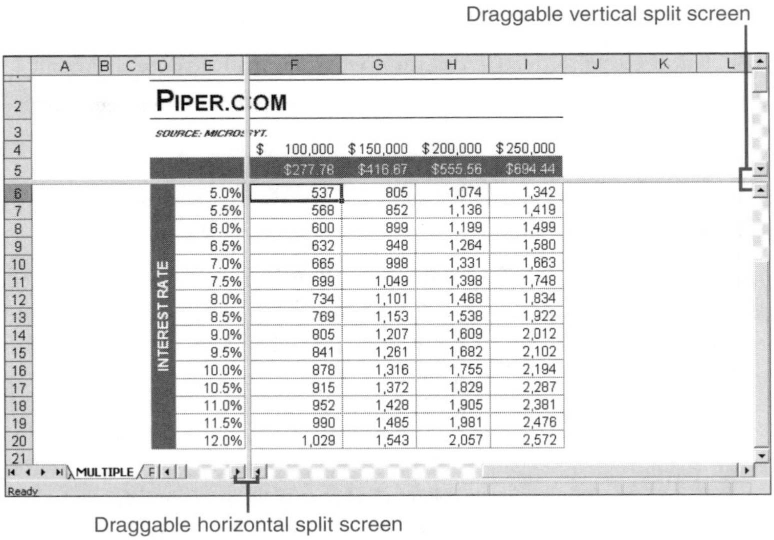

Draggable horizontal split screen

The worksheet now has either two or four sets of scrollbars for each side of the split, enabling you to scroll up, down, left, or right, within each section of the screen. Conceivably, you can be looking at the same cells in both sides of the split.

After creating the split, you can scroll to any location in the worksheet from within any and all of the sections.

NOTE

With a four-pane window split, the panes scroll in pairs. When scrolling up and down, the two upper panes scroll together. When scrolling left and right, the two left panes scroll together, and the two right panes scroll together.

Moving the *split bars* enables you to increase or decrease the size of any of the sections. To move a split bar, point to the bar. The mouse pointer turns into a two-headed arrow. Horizontal bars can be moved up or down, vertical bars left or right.

TIP FROM

To move all four sides of the split, point to the intersection of the vertical and horizontal bars. When the mouse pointer turns into a four-headed arrow, click and drag to move the intersection.

To remove the split, choose one of the following methods:

- Choose Window, Remove Split. All split bars will be removed.
- Double-click a split bar to remove it. To remove a four-way split, double-click the intersection of the two splits.
- Drag one of the split bars off the worksheet.

TIP FROM

> Use the *split boxes*, small buttons at the top of the vertical scrollbar and to the right of the horizontal scrollbar, to insert and move split bars. If you can't see the split boxes, unfreeze the window—you can't split a frozen window.

HIDING AND UNHIDING ROWS AND COLUMNS

Hiding rows and/or columns allows you to keep something from being printed if the content is of no interest to the person who'll be reading the printout (that might even be you), or to simplify the view of the worksheet, removing distracting or visually cluttering content while you work.

TIP FROM

> Hiding content also can be used to make confidential content invisible, but there are better ways to do that, such as password-protecting a workbook or placing the file in a network drive to which only you have access.

To hide a column or row, you can choose from the following two methods:

- Resize the column or row until it is so narrow that it literally disappears.
- Select the row(s) or column(s) and choose Format, Column (or Row), Hide, or right-click the selection and choose Hide from the context menu.

When a column or row is hidden, a thick border appears between the headings of the visible rows or columns where the hidden number or letter would normally appear.

To reveal hidden columns or rows, choose one of the following methods:

- Point to the thick boundary between column letters or row numbers. When the mouse pointer turns to a split two-headed arrow, double-click.
- Select the columns or rows that appear on either side of the hidden content, and choose Format, Column (or Row), Unhide.

CAUTION

> Observe the two-headed arrow carefully—a solid two-headed arrow is used for resizing visible columns and rows, whereas a split two-headed arrow is used for unhiding a column or row.

TROUBLESHOOTING

VIEWING MORE SHEET TABS

How can I see more of my sheet tabs?

After you've added and named sheets, you might find that not all of them are visible at the same time. You can do two things to avoid/rectify this situation. First, try to keep your sheet names short, using abbreviations such as Qtr1 Sales&Exp instead of First Quarter Sales and Expenses. Second, expand the sheet tab display area by clicking the *tab split box*—the little vertical bar at the left end of the horizontal scrollbar—and dragging it to the right. This reduces the width of the scrollbar and allows more room for your tabs.

DISTINGUISHING ONE VERSION OF A FILE FROM ANOTHER

How do I determine which file is which?

Aside from doing a visual check for differences in content, you can distinguish two different versions of an Excel file by checking the date and time modified for each file. You can see this information in the Open dialog box, Windows Explorer, or My Computer (in Details view), or by choosing File, Properties when the workbook is active. The Statistics tab in the Properties dialog box shows the date and time the file was last modified.

CREATING A TEMPLATE FROM AN EXISTING WORKBOOK

What if I've already added data to the file that I want to use as a template?

Before you save the file as a template, save it one last time in its current format. Then, delete any specific data, leaving only the labels, formulas, and any other text that you want to be on every worksheet created with the template. When you save the workbook as a template, the original file, prior to the deletions, will be left intact.

WHY SAVE TO THE TEMPLATES FOLDER?

I've placed my templates in a folder other than the Templates folder, and now I can't see them in the New dialog box. What do I do?

Only templates that are in the Templates folder or one of its direct subfolders (such as Spreadsheet Solutions) will appear in the New dialog box when you choose to create a new workbook based on a template. If you created or placed templates in some other folder, copy or move the templates—or the folder with its templates—to place them in C:\Documents and Settings\Username\Application Data\Microsoft\Templates.If you prefer to keep the templates where they are, use the Open dialog box to open a template, and then immediately save it with its new workbook name before making any changes (to avoid changing the template).

EXCEL IN PRACTICE

You can get rid of the gridlines to create a white canvas for a more professional spreadsheet appearance. To do this, simply select the entire sheet and choose the white fill color from the color palette (see Figure 1.27). Another way to clear the canvas is to remove the gridlines using Tools, Options, View Tab, and clicking the Clear the Gridlines check box.

Figure 1.27
Create a white canvas instead of showing all the lines on your spreadsheet by filling the entire sheet white.

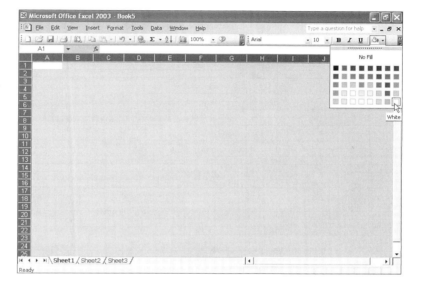

Create elbows for table displays. To create an elbow, type the column heading and row heading in the corner cell, place your cursor between the two words, and hold down the Alt key and press Enter. Then, adjust the column heading to the right as shown in Figure 1.28. Then, place a diagonal line between the two using the borders option to create a result similar to that in Figure 1.29.

Figure 1.28
Use the Alt key to stack the words in one cell, and then adjust the column label to the right.

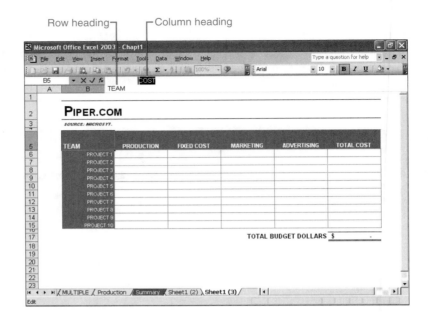

Figure 1.29
The final result of the elbow is two heading labels in one cell.

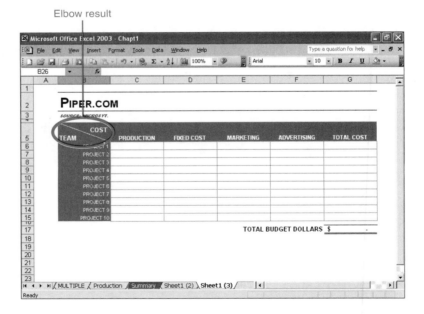

CHAPTER 2

SPREADSHEET BASICS

In this chapter

Selecting Cells   50

Selecting Columns and Rows   53

Selecting Noncontiguous Ranges   54

Selecting Ranges on Grouped Worksheets   55

Naming Ranges for Fast Access   57

SELECTING CELLS

After data entry, selecting worksheet content is probably the task most frequently performed in Excel. Selecting cells and ranges tells Excel where you are and what parts of a sheet you intend to change, and is an integral step in most formatting, calculation, and editing procedures. To select an individual cell, click it or use any of the keyboard shortcuts shown in Table 2.1 for worksheet navigation to move to the desired cell.

TABLE 2.1   KEYBOARD SHORTCUTS FOR SELECTING INDIVIDUAL CELLS

Keyboard Shortcut	Selects
Enter	The cell below the current cell.
Tab	The cell to the right of the current cell.
Shift+Tab	The cell to the left of the current cell.
Ctrl+Home	Cell A1.
Home	The first cell in the current row.
Ctrl+Arrow	Goes to the last formatted cell in a row or column. If no formatting, goes to the last row or column of the spreadsheet.
Shift+Arrow	Selects the entire range between the starting cell and the new destination cell.
Ctrl+Shift+Arrow	Selects the entire range between the starting cell and the last formatted cell. If no additional cell formatting or content is entered, it selects the end of the spreadsheet row or column.
Ctrl+*	Collapses the column of the current selection.

When a cell is *active* (the *current cell*), it appears with a thick border around it, as shown in Figure 2.1. This border, called the *cell pointer*, indicates the active cell. The Name box in the Formula bar displays the address of the active cell and the row number and column letter appear on a lighter background.

To select a range of cells, click and drag across them, dragging up, down, left, right, or a combination of these directions to select the desired range of cells. Release the mouse when the desired block of cells (two or more) is highlighted. Figure 2.2 shows a selected range of cells. The range in this example would have the address C7:H16—the colon representing the word *through*. The active cell is cell C7, which indicates that the range was selected from upper left to lower right; the cell pointer remains in the first cell selected and is part of the range. Notice that Excel highlights the row and column headings in a lighter background.

As you select a *contiguous* range—a range in which all the cells are adjacent to each other—Excel displays information in the Name box to match the selection. In this case, the designation 10R×6C indicates that the selection is 10 rows long and 6 columns wide. As soon as you complete the selection, the Name box goes back to displaying the address of the active cell.

Figure 2.1

Select a cell in preparation for entering or editing content, or to format the existing content of the cell.

Name box

Row number and column letter for selected cells

Formula bar

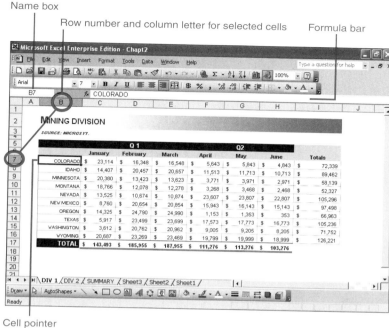

Cell pointer

Indicates selection is ten rows deep and six columns wide

Figure 2.2

The active cell color remains the same as the background. Other cells in the selected range show a transparent color (you can see the selected cells through the color).

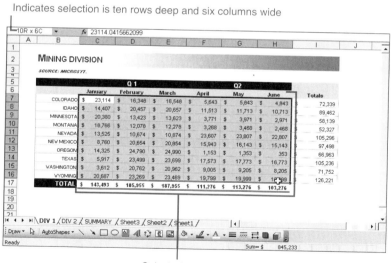

Selected range

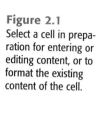

NOTE

Although this chapter's title lists them as two different things, both single cells and ranges of cells are considered ranges by Excel. You'll find this interchangeable terminology and concept in many areas, such as named ranges, covered later in this chapter.

CAUTION

Selected cells are vulnerable. If you accidentally press the spacebar or type a character while a cell or range of cells is selected, the content of the active cell (the one white cell of the range) will be deleted, replaced with a space or the character you typed. If this occurs, press Esc to cancel the entry if the cell is still selected. If you already accepted the entry, use the Undo feature to restore the original entry.

To Undo a change type Ctrl+Z, open the Edit menu and choose Undo, or click the Undo toolbar icon.

When a range of blank cells is selected, enter content by typing in the first cell and then pressing Enter or Tab. You automatically are moved to the next cell in the range—Enter moves you down a cell and Tab moves you to the right one cell. Continue typing content in each cell, pressing Enter or Tab after each one. This procedure changes the normal effect of pressing the Enter or Tab keys—normally the keys take you to the cell below or to the right of the current cell—and allow you to confine your edits to one area. If you select a block or range of cells for entry, using this method will also enable you to type entries across rows and columns without having to use any mouse or keyboard techniques to move the active cell into the next row or column. This is especially useful if you're referring to a printed document or written notes as a source for the entries.

TIP FROM

If you have selected a range that includes multiple rows, each press of the Enter key moves the cell pointer down until you reach the last row within the selection. Pressing Enter again moves the active cell to the top cell in the next column to the right of your selected range. Use Shift+Enter to move backward in a selection.

Alternatively, you can move left to right in a selection by pressing the Tab key. Use Shift+Tab to move right to left.

You also can select a range of cells by using the keyboard. To select a block of cells, follow these steps:

1. Use the most appropriate keyboard shortcut or click in the first cell in the desired range.

2. Press and hold down the Shift key.

3. Use the arrow keys to select cells to the right of, left of, above, or below the starting cell. To select larger blocks of text, use PgUp/PgDn or Alt+PgUp/Alt+PgDn.

4. When the desired block of cells is selected, release the Shift key.

2

TIP

It might be easier to use the Shift key and arrow keys to select a range when you're in the middle of a long data-entry session—it saves you the time of using the mouse and dragging through cells when your hands are already on the keyboard.

SELECTING COLUMNS AND ROWS

Selecting a range requires highlighting a block of cells. You can drag to select all the entries in a column or row, but in most cases, it's more efficient to select the entire row (all 256 cells) or column (all 65,536 cells), whether you're using the entire range of cells or not. To drag through an entire row or column could take several minutes just to scroll to the ends of the worksheet. It's much easier to click the column letter or row number to select the entire column or row, as shown in Figure 2.3.

Selected column

Figure 2.3
Click the column letter to select all 65,536 cells in the column.

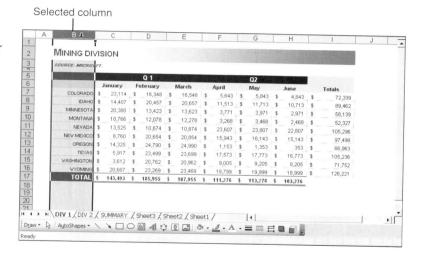

Notice that the color of the column or row heading is shaded when the entire column is selected. (This behavior might affect or be affected by background fills or patterns in the cells, however.)

If your worksheet includes background fills or patterns, the selection color might look unusual. See "Color Selection Looks Odd" in the "Troubleshooting" section at the end of this chapter.

You can select multiple columns or rows by dragging through the column letters or row numbers, as shown in Figure 2.4.

Table 2.2 lists keyboard shortcuts you can use to select rows or columns in a worksheet. The Result column in the table assumes that the active cell is in the row or column you want to select *before* you use these shortcuts.

Figure 2.4
Select a series of columns or rows to copy, move, format, or enter content for the entire selection.

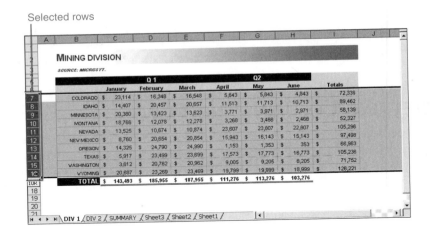

Selected rows

	January	February	March	April	May	June	Totals
COLORADO	$ 23,114	$ 16,348	$ 16,548	$ 5,643	$ 5,843	$ 4,843	$ 72,339
IDAHO	$ 14,407	$ 20,457	$ 20,657	$ 11,513	$ 11,713	$ 10,713	$ 89,462
MINNESOTA	$ 20,380	$ 13,423	$ 13,623	$ 3,771	$ 3,971	$ 2,971	$ 58,139
MONTANA	$ 18,766	$ 12,078	$ 12,278	$ 3,268	$ 3,468	$ 2,468	$ 52,327
NEVADA	$ 13,525	$ 10,674	$ 10,874	$ 23,607	$ 23,807	$ 22,807	$ 105,296
NEV MEXICO	$ 8,760	$ 20,654	$ 20,854	$ 15,943	$ 16,143	$ 15,143	$ 97,498
OREGON	$ 14,325	$ 24,790	$ 24,990	$ 1,153	$ 1,353	$ 353	$ 66,963
TEXAS	$ 5,917	$ 23,499	$ 23,699	$ 17,573	$ 17,773	$ 16,773	$ 105,236
WASHINGTON	$ 3,612	$ 20,762	$ 20,962	$ 9,005	$ 9,205	$ 8,205	$ 71,752
WYOMING	$ 20,687	$ 23,269	$ 23,469	$ 19,799	$ 19,999	$ 18,999	$ 126,221
TOTAL	$ 143,493	$ 185,955	$ 187,955	$ 111,276	$ 113,276	$ 103,276	

MINING DIVISION
SOURCE: MICROSYT.

TABLE 2.2   ROW AND COLUMN SELECTION WITH THE KEYBOARD

Keyboard Shortcut	Result
Ctrl+Spacebar	Selects the entire column
Shift+Spacebar	Selects the entire row
Ctrl+Shift+Spacebar or Ctrl+A	Selects the entire worksheet

TIP FROM

You can select the entire worksheet by clicking the Select All button (the blank gray button at the intersection of the column letters and row numbers) just below the Name box.

SELECTING NONCONTIGUOUS RANGES

When edits, formatting changes, or deletions you want to make are in multiple separate areas of a worksheet, you can select these *noncontiguous ranges* by adding the Ctrl key to the selection procedure.

To select multiple ranges that don't share adjacent cells, follow these steps:

1. Select the first cell or range of cells.
2. Release the mouse, and press and hold down the Ctrl key.
3. Using the mouse again, select the next cell or range of cells.
4. Repeat steps 2 and 3 until you've selected all the ranges you need. Figure 2.5 shows a worksheet with three noncontiguous ranges selected: B6:B17, C6:H6, and C17:H17.

After making these noncontiguous selections, you can delete or format all the selected areas at once.

Figure 2.5
Select the column and row labels, as well as the row of totals, so that you can apply formatting to all the selected cells at once.

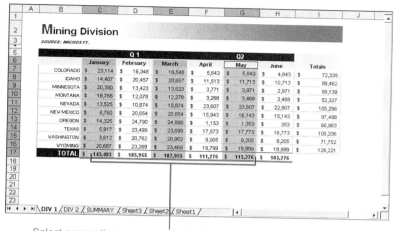

Select noncontiguous ranges by holding down the Ctrl key

TIP FROM

You can copy noncontiguous selections to the Clipboard only if all the selections are the same size and shape. For example, in Figure 2.5, you can select B7:H7, B11:H11, and B14:H14, and then copy that entire noncontiguous selection.

You'll notice that when you select the second range of cells, the active cell (starting cell) switches from the starting cell in the first range to the starting cell in the second range. The current cell will continue to move to each subsequent range you add to the group of selected ranges, ending up in the first cell of the last selected range.

TIP FROM

The Shift+F8 technique is a little-known technique but is great for selecting multiple ranges without having to hold the Ctrl key.

To use it on noncontiguous ranges, select the first range using whatever technique you want, press Shift+F8—the word Add appears on the status bar—and then select additional ranges using the mouse (no Ctrl key). When finished, press Shift+F8 again, or press the Esc key.

SELECTING RANGES ON GROUPED WORKSHEETS

In addition to being able to select contiguous or noncontiguous ranges on a single worksheet, you might occasionally want to select the same ranges on multiple worksheets within a workbook. Why might you want to select cells/ranges from several sheets at once? The following list offers some suggestions:

- **To speed up and simplify formatting changes**—Want to make all titles on all sheets look the same? Select them all at once and then apply the formatting.

- **To expedite editing a series of cells**—You know that a selected range of cells can be edited, cell by cell, with the Enter or Tab keys. What if you want to make changes to cell content on several sheets? Go through the workbook and select all the ranges, so as you edit and press Enter or Tab, you're taken automatically to the next cell in the series to be edited. Keep in mind, however, that grouped worksheets have the same selections on every sheet; you can't select one set of ranges on one worksheet and a different set on another worksheet.

- **To make a quick deletion**—Assume that your worksheets include multiple references to a sales rep you no longer employ or a product you no longer sell. Select the cells and ranges that refer to this person or product, and then press Delete. All cell content in those cells—in all worksheets included in the group—will be removed.

The process of selecting worksheets is called *grouping*. It's important to note that you should group worksheets for formatting, data entry, or deletions only if all the worksheets are structured identically. For example, if you group Sheet1 and Sheet2, select the range B2:B7 on Sheet1, and then switch to Sheet2, you'll find that the same cell coordinates are selected on Sheet2. If you add a range to the selection while on Sheet2, the added selection will be echoed on Sheet1. For this reason, if the sheets *aren't* structured identically (everything in exactly the same place on all sheets), restrict the use of this feature to editing content or changing page setup options—you can always press Enter to skip extra cells in the selection.

When working with grouped worksheets, you can select the ranges first and then group the worksheets, or group the worksheets and then make your selections. After all the ranges are selected and the worksheets grouped, you can make content changes, apply formatting, change page setup and application options, and so on.

To group worksheets, start by activating the first worksheet you want in the group. Then, hold down the Ctrl key while clicking the sheet tab for each additional worksheet you want to include in the group (see Figure 2.6). If you want to include a set of contiguous sheets, you can click the first sheet, hold down the Shift key, and click the last sheet tab. The sheet tabs for grouped worksheets turn white, and a [Group] indicator appears in the title bar of the workbook window. Grouped worksheets remain grouped until you click the sheet tab for an ungrouped sheet or right-click the sheet tab for one of the grouped sheets and select Ungroup Sheets from the resulting context menu.

After sheets are grouped, you can switch freely between the grouped sheets by clicking the sheet tab for the sheet you want to see. Notice that if you select a new range on the active sheet, it's simultaneously selected on all other sheets in the group (see Figure 2.7).

NOTE

If you group a sheet you didn't want, Ctrl+click the sheet tab to remove it from the group.

Figure 2.6
Grouped sheets remain grouped until you ungroup them. Any changes are applied to all the grouped sheets. So, formats or inputs on Div 2 sheet will also appear on Div 1 worksheet.

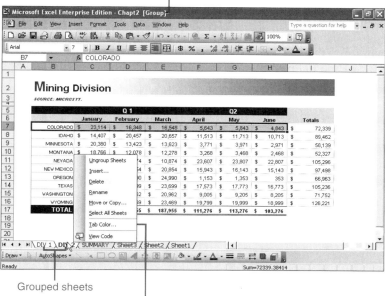

Group indicator

Grouped sheets

Right-click a tab to access the tab options

Figure 2.7
Selecting cells and ranges on grouped sheets makes it easy to edit and format cells within identical sheets.

Selected cells on the Div2 sheet

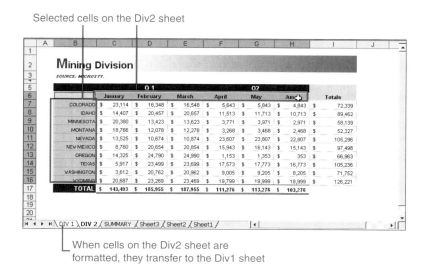

When cells on the Div2 sheet are formatted, they transfer to the Div1 sheet

NAMING RANGES FOR FAST ACCESS

After you enter some or all of a worksheet's content, you might find it easier to refer to cells and blocks of selected cells by name rather than a range of cell addresses. Just as it's easier to

2

find an employee by asking the receptionist for him by name than to comb the building on foot, looking in each cube or office, so finding cells and ranges by name is faster and easier than trying to find and remember cell addresses. Excel enables you to name individual cells or cell ranges so that you can find data by a logical name and refer to the cell ranges in formulas. You also can use named ranges in formulas, printing, and as a navigational tool for charting and filtering.

To name a cell or range of cells, follow these steps:

1. Select the cell(s), and choose Insert, Name, Define. This opens the Define Name dialog box, as shown in Figure 2.8.

2. In the Names in Workbook text box, type a name for the selected cell(s).

TIP FROM

> You can select or type a range of cells or a single cell address while in the Refers To box. This technique enables you to create several range names, clicking Add after naming each one, without having to repeatedly close and then reopen the dialog box after selecting cells or ranges with the mouse.

3. If you want to insert several ranges in one session click Add, enter a new range, and repeat step 2. If you want to add only one range name or have finished entering all range names, click OK.

Type the range name

Figure 2.8
Type the range name and click Add to insert several ranges in one session, or OK if you want to add only one range name. If you want to name several different ranges you will also have to select a different range, too.

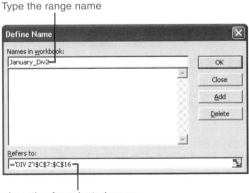

Location for selected range

NOTE

> A quick method for creating named ranges is to select the cell/range, and, using the Name box on the Formula bar, highlight the displayed cell address and replace it by typing a name for the cell/range. Press Enter to create the name.

Range names cannot begin with a number, resemble a cell address (such as FQ1999), or contain spaces or punctuation. You can use underscores in lieu of spaces, such as First_Quarter_1999. Although Excel allows range names to contain hundreds of characters, sticking to short names makes them easier to remember and use in formulas.

It's also good practice to stick to a consistent naming convention. For example, if you need to create several range names for various sales figures, begin each one of their range names with the word "Sales" (for example, SalesDallas, SalesNY, SalesLA, and so on). This will make it easier for users to locate the sales names because they'll be grouped together on the name list. It also makes it easier to remember the name when typing it into a formula or dialog box.

 Getting an error message when you type a range name? See "Range Naming Errors" in the "Troubleshooting" section at the end of this chapter.

When selecting cells to be named, they needn't be a contiguous range—use the Ctrl key to select several individual noncontiguous cells or ranges or a single rage as shown in Figure 2.9, and then give the group of selected cells a single name. This could be used to find and sum various sales totals throughout the worksheet, for example, giving them one name, such as Q1 Totals.

Name for selected range entered into Name box

Figure 2.9
Select single cells or ranges throughout the worksheet and then apply one name to the entire selection.

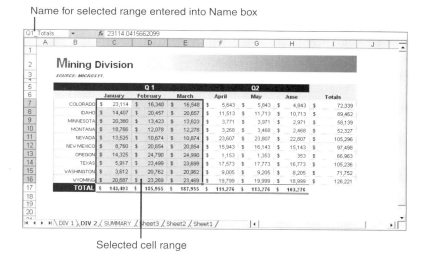

Selected cell range

After you've added a named range, you can access it by opening the Name box on the Formula bar. Figure 2.10 shows a series of named ranges.

To remove a named range, choose Insert, Name, Define, and select the named range from the list. Click the Delete button, and then click OK.

When a range name is selected from the
Name box, that range is selected in the worksheet

Figure 2.10
Select a range name
from the list, and the
cell or range it repre-
sents is immediately
selected.

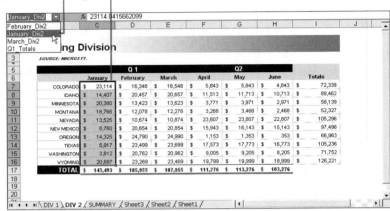

TROUBLESHOOTING

RANGE NAMING ERRORS

When I type the range name I want to create in the Name box, Excel displays the message `"That name is not valid"`.

You're probably attempting to use a space in the range name, or begin the range name with a number. Unfortunately, names such as `1999 Disbursements` are not allowed unless started by an underscore. For this type of name, put the year at the end, and replace the space with an underscore: `Disbursements_1999`.

DESELECTING GROUPED SHEETS

How can I deselect grouped sheets?

Simply select another sheet outside of the grouped sheets. If all sheets in the workbook are grouped together, Excel will automatically ungroup the sheets when you select another tab. You can also right-click on the tabs and then select Ungroup Sheets.

I'VE INHERITED A WORKBOOK THAT HAS ALL THESE NAMED RANGES ASSOCIATED WITH IT. EVERY TIME I TRY TO MOVE OR COPY A SHEET TO A NEW WORKBOOK EXCEL PROMPTS AND ASKS WHETHER I WANT TO COPY THE RANGES TO THE NEW WORKBOOK. HOW CAN I GET RID OF THIS?

From the Insert menu, select Name, then Define. Select the ranges that appear in the window and click Delete.

EXCEL IN PRACTICE

Excel's tools for selecting and naming ranges can be used to significantly reduce your setup time. Figure 2.11 shows a set of identical worksheets, created by grouping the sheets and selecting sections of their content. Simple formats were applied once, and that one action formatted all the sheets. This type of uniformity decreases the learning curve for users who have to work with the worksheets, and makes it easier for you to build worksheets quickly and consistently.

2

Row labels are all formatted on all selected sheets

Column headings

Figure 2.11
These sheets were grouped, and selections in all three sheets were simultaneously formatted to achieve a consistent look throughout the workbook.

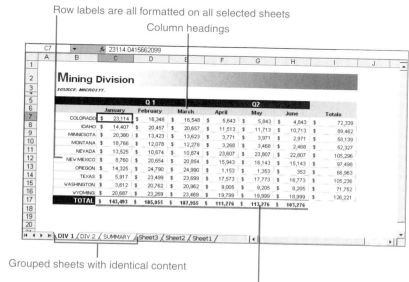

Grouped sheets with identical content

Totals are all formatted on selected sheets

CHAPTER 3

EDITING SPREADSHEETS

In this chapter

The Clipboard Viewer   64

Editing with the Keyboard   64

Creating a Data Series   70

Creating a Custom Fill Series   71

Creating a Custom Fill to Define Linear or Growth Trends   72

Creating a Custom List or Series   73

Replacing Data   75

Tracking Changes Made by Multiple Users   75

Using Comments to Explain Cell Content   79

Linking Excel Data 82

THE CLIPBOARD VIEWER

The Clipboard viewer maintains the items within its window so you can view, select, copy, and paste items at will. You can copy several items and paste them all at once with the Paste All command or even clear all copied items. To access the Clipboard viewer select the drop-down at the top of the worksheet task pane. If your task pane is not visible you access the task pane from the View menu and select Task Pane or press Ctrl+F1. The Clipboard viewer feature can be a hindrance to some users, but you can turn it off. To turn off the Clipboard viewer, select the Options button at the bottom of the Clipboard and select Collect Without Showing Office Clipboard, as shown in Figure 3.1.

Figure 3.1
To turn off the Clipboard viewer, click the Options button at the bottom of the Clipboard and choose the appropriate option.

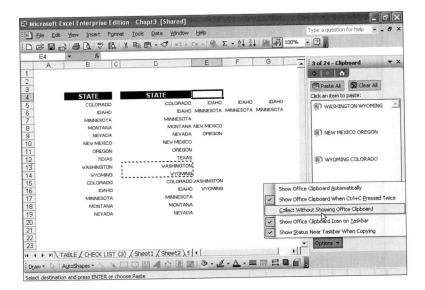

EDITING WITH THE KEYBOARD

When you click a cell that already contains data, pressing virtually any key on your keyboard temporarily replaces your content with the character or code associated with the key pressed. In your use of Excel, you'll find that you can use this feature to your own benefit (for intentional replacements) or in error (by pressing a key accidentally). To familiarize yourself with the keys that will edit your cell content, review the following:

- Alphanumeric keys (all the letters of the alphabet, the numbers 0 through 9, and all symbols and punctuation) will, when pressed, replace your selected cell content.
- The numeric keypad (active if Num Lock is on) will replace your content with numbers and mathematical symbols (/ * - + .).
- The spacebar will replace selected cell content with a space.

CAUTION

Pressing the spacebar in a cell doesn't empty the cell—it replaces the cell's contents with a space. To delete a cell's contents, select the cell and press the Delete key.

TIP FROM

If a cell containing data is accidentally edited by your pressing a key on the keyboard, press the Esc key immediately to return to the cell's original content. If you have already pressed Enter, click the Undo button, choose Edit, Undo, or press Ctrl+Z to undo the changes.

EDITING A GROUP OF CELLS

You also can edit a group of selected cells, whether in a single block or a group of two or more noncontiguous selections. This enables you to edit several cells quickly, saving you the time of selecting and editing each cell individually.

To edit a group of selected cells, follow these steps:

1. Select the group of cells you want to edit. If the cells are noncontiguous, hold down the Ctrl key as you drag over them to add them to the selection.

2. Starting with the cell that remains white (the first cell or active cell in your most recent selection), type your corrected data and/or make your corrections using the Formula bar.

3. Press the Enter key to move to the next cell in the block (see Figure 3.2). Hold down the Enter key to scroll through the information more quickly. If you prefer to move left to right through your selection, use the Tab key rather than Enter. Shift+Enter moves backward vertically; Shift+Tab moves backward horizontally.

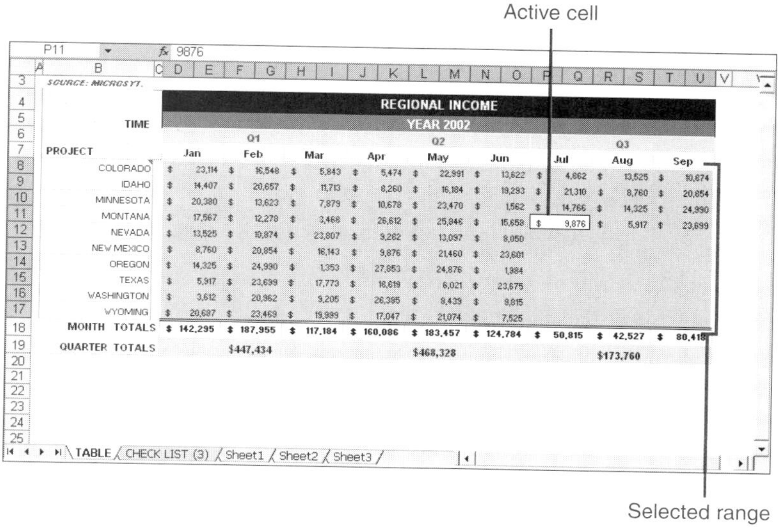

Figure 3.2
Excel moves down the selected block's columns and then starts at the top of the next column as you press the Enter key to complete each cell's edits.

Active cell

Selected range

4. Continue editing the cells in your selection, pressing Enter or Tab after each cell's edits are complete.

5. When you finish editing the cells, click any cell or use one of the arrow keys to deselect your block(s) of cells.

NOTE

If you want to place the same entry in multiple cells, select the cells (contiguous or non-contiguous), type the entry in one of the cells or in the Formula bar, and press Ctrl+Enter.

CAUTION

If you don't click outside the selected cells or use an arrow key at the end of your editing session, you will cycle through the selected cells again. This risks re-editing the first cells you edited in the current session.

EDITING USING THE FORMULA BAR

The Formula bar obviously displays more than formulas. If an active cell contains text or a number that isn't the result of a formula, this content also appears in the Formula bar. Figure 3.3 shows the Formula bar content for a selected cell.

Editing in the Formula bar

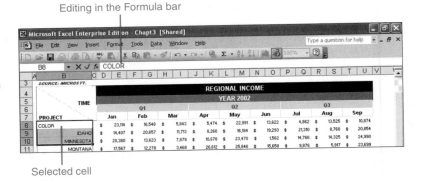

Figure 3.3
When a cell or range is selected the Formula bar shows the cell or active cell's contents.

Selected cell

To use the Formula bar to edit cell content, follow these steps:

1. Click the cell you want to edit. The cell's content appears in the Formula bar. You could also press F2 to edit directly in the cell.

2. In the Formula bar, use your mouse to select some or all of the cell's content (see Figure 3.4). You can select individual characters, words, or any portion of the cell content.

Press the Shift+arrow keys to select cell content

Figure 3.4
Press the Shift+arrow keys to select cell content.

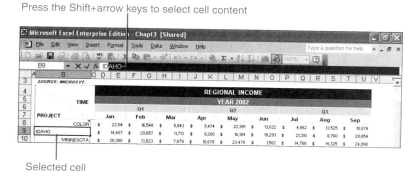

Selected cell

TIP FROM

Use your Backspace or Delete keys to remove a cell's content, one character at a time, on the Formula bar.

3

3. Type the replacement content—this will simultaneously remove and replace the Formula bar's selected content.

4. Press Enter to place your edited content in the cell.

If your selected cell contains a formula, the result of the formula appears in the cell, but the formula itself appears in the Formula bar with the formula syntax tip showing, as shown in Figure 3.5. To edit the formula, click in the Formula bar and delete/replace the numbers, operators, and cell addresses you need, and then press Enter. The formula is recalculated, and the new result appears in the cell.

Formula

Figure 3.5
To see whether a cell's content is a number typed directly into the cell or the result of a formula check the entry in the Formula bar.

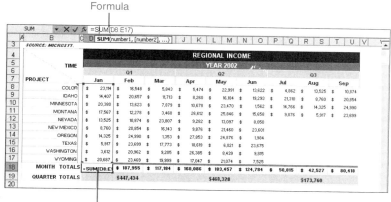

Formula cell

MOVING CELL CONTENT WITH DRAG AND DROP

You can drag any selection from one place to another by following these steps:

1. Select the cell or cells you want to move.
2. Point your cursor to the edge of the cell or block of cells, and look for your mouse to turn into a left-pointing arrow with four small black arrows attached.

> **NOTE**
>
> You cannot move (or copy) noncontiguous selections with drag and drop.

3. Click and drag the cell(s) to the desired location on the worksheet.
4. Release the mouse button to drop the selection in its new location.

If you attempt to drop the moved cell(s) where data already exists, you'll be prompted to confirm your desire to replace the contents of the destination cells.

> **TIP FROM**
>
> If drag and drop doesn't seem to work, choose Tools, Options, click the Edit tab, and check Allow Cell Drag and Drop.
>
> If you don't get the confirmation prompt after you drag and drop cells, the prompt is turned off. To turn it back on, choose Tools, Options, click the Edit tab, and check Alert Before Overwriting Cells.

> **CAUTION**
>
> Although you can drag the selected cell(s) to a spot outside the currently visible portion of the worksheet, you might find it difficult to control scrolling so that you arrive at your exact desired location. You might find that the sheet scrolls too fast.
>
> There's an informal name for this unintended fast scrolling: the Roadrunner Effect. To counteract it, rein in how far off the grid you move your mouse. When dragging and dropping downward, for example, if your mouse pointer is in the sheet tab area, scrolling is relatively slow. But if you move the mouse pointer into the status bar, scrolling speeds up significantly. So, don't just slam your mouse downward—keep it just off the edge of the grid.

If you need to move or copy cells between worksheets or workbooks, you can choose Window, Arrange, Tile or Cascade to position windows so that you can use drag and drop between them. If you prefer, you can use the Clipboard to move (cut) and copy.

NOTE

You can drag and drop onto other worksheets in your workbook by holding down the Alt key and dragging the selected cells to the other worksheet's tab, which causes that worksheet to open. Drag the selected cells where you want them.

COPYING CELL CONTENT WITH DRAG AND DROP

Moving cell content implies that it isn't in the right place or that it's no longer needed in its current location. Copying, on the other hand, allows you to leave the original cell and its content right where it is, and place a duplicate elsewhere on the worksheet. Just like moving, you can use drag and drop to copy a cell or cells from one place to another on your worksheet—again, it's a task best performed within a small area.

To copy a cell or group of contiguous cells to another location on the active worksheet, follow these steps:

1. Select the cell or cells you want to copy.

2. Point your cursor to the edge of the selected cell(s). Your mouse pointer turns into a left-pointing arrow with four small black arrows attached.

3. Press and hold the Ctrl key.

4. Drag your selected cells to another location, keeping the Ctrl key depressed as you drag. Figure 3.6 shows a block of cells being copied to another location.

Location to which selected cells will be copied

Figure 3.6
Select a range and hold Ctrl to copy cells to a new location.

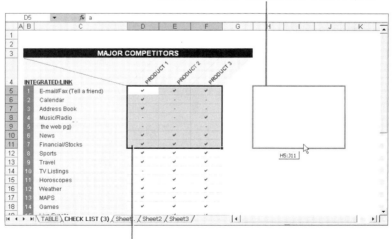

Selection of cells to be copied

5. When your desired location is reached, release the mouse button.

6. Release the Ctrl key.

CAUTION

> If you release the Ctrl key prior to releasing the mouse button, your copy procedure turns into a move, and the selected cells will be taken from their original location and moved to the spot where you released the mouse button. Be sure to release the Ctrl key after the cells' duplicates have been deposited in their new location.
>
> You should always release the mouse button first, then the keyboard. It's a Windows standard rule.
>
> When you attempt to move a cell's content to a cell that already contains data, you're prompted to confirm that this is your intention. Be aware that no such prompt appears when you drag and drop to copy a cell or cells, thus making it easy to accidentally overwrite data while copying.

CREATING A DATA SERIES

Excel allows you to create series out of numbers, dates, and custom lists. This feature can save a lot of time if you know how to apply it. Look at the example in Figure 3.7. By starting a series of months, you can have Excel finish the series for you by activating the cell, pointing to the fill handle in the lower-right corner of the cell (which changes your mouse symbol into a black cross), and then dragging in any of the four directions. The ScreenTip tells you what month you're currently at.

ScreenTip tells the last data element (month in this case) in the selected fill range

Fill handle

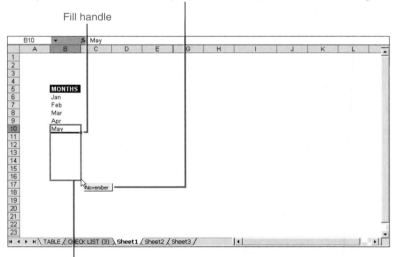

Figure 3.7
Use the ScreenTip to view the current date or month you're creating.

Drag the fill handle down to
extend the series of dates

When you let go of the handle, the fill series is copied in the range of cells with Excel's AutoFill Option button (see Figure 3.8). This icon appears when you let go of a copied cell. You can then apply another type of copy after the fact.

Figure 3.8
After you let go of the
series, the Auto Fill
options appear. Place
your cursor over the
indicator and click to
access the drop-down
menu items.

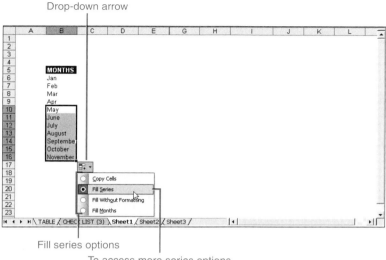

Drop-down arrow

Fill series options

To access more series options

By placing your cursor over the AutoFill Options indicator, a drop-down arrow appears. Select the drop-down list to access the menu and then select an additional option to change or modify the fill type.

CREATING A CUSTOM FILL SERIES

You can create a custom fill series by starting a series of dates or numbers and again using the fill handle, but this time hold the right mouse button down while dragging the fill handle. When you let go, the Fill Series menu appears, as shown in Figure 3.9. While right-dragging, Excel changes the mouse symbol back to an arrow. In other words, while right dragging, you will not see the familiar black cross symbol.

Figure 3.9
Select the fill handle,
and right-drag to
access the Fill Series
menu.

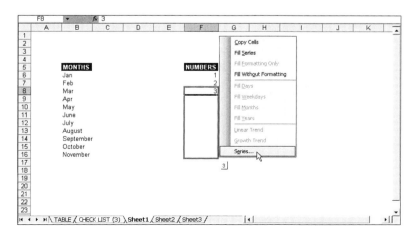

When you select the series from the Fill menu, the Series dialog box appears. The Step Value creates the amount of spacing or increments between numbers. For example, place 3 as the Step Value as shown in Figure 3.10 and the result is a series reflected in Figure 3.11 of 3,6,9,12, and so on.

Figure 3.10
Apply a step value to create increments between numbers.

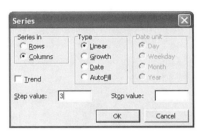

Figure 3.11
Notice the Step Value applied to the series with increments of 3.

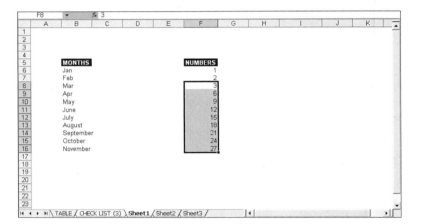

CREATING A CUSTOM FILL TO DEFINE LINEAR OR GROWTH TRENDS

You can use the custom fill to create linear or growth trends. For example, let's say you had to determine the growth of sales over the next few months based on the trends over the past four months. Here's a quick way to solve this problem. Similarly to the previous examples, you must use the right-drag with the fill handle. However, notice the example in Figure 3.12. First, you must select the entire series of numbers, and then select the fill handle, right-click and drag to the right, then let go and select Growth Trend. The result is shown in Figure 3.13 of the growth trend based on the historical information.

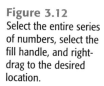

Figure 3.12
Select the entire series of numbers, select the fill handle, and right-drag to the desired location.

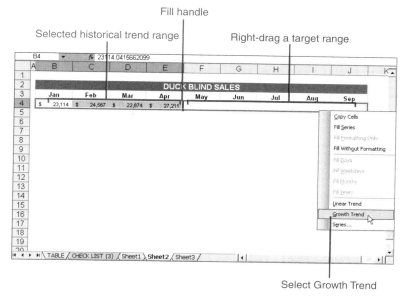

Fill handle

Selected historical trend range

Right-drag a target range

Select Growth Trend

Figure 3.13
After you select Growth Trend, the final result is the growth based on historical information.

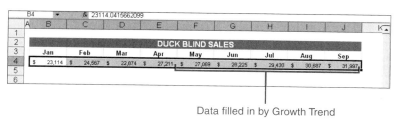

Data filled in by Growth Trend

CREATING A CUSTOM LIST OR SERIES

Companies often have custom data that pertains only to their organization, such as lists of employees, fiscal year, or selected states in which that the company does business. When you type a list once, that's the last time you should ever have to type it. Yes, you could copy and paste the list but that's not necessarily the most efficient way. The best way to handle this information is by creating a custom list so when you type in one of the states, you can then drag the fill handle to fill the rest of the states in automatically, in the order you pre-define (see Figure 3.14). Take Figure 3.15, for example. The list of states is the states a company normally has to type in. To automate this list or create a custom list, follow these steps:

1. Select the cell or cells you want in your custom list.

Figure 3.14
Start a state in the list and drag the fill handle.

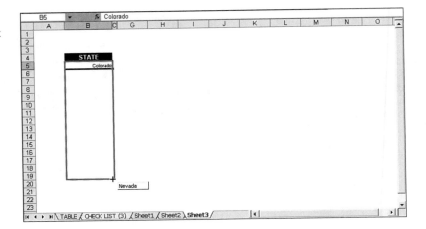

2. Choose Tools, Options.

3. From the Options dialog box, select the Custom Lists tab as shown in Figure 3.16. Click Import.

Figure 3.15
Create and select the list you must often type or that is specific to your organization.

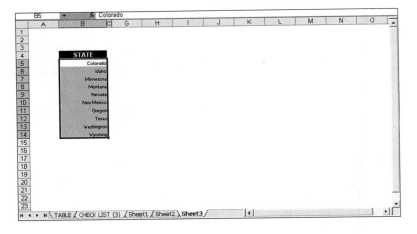

4. Click OK.

Selected custom list   Data in selected list

Figure 3.16
Create and select the
list you have to often
type or is specific to
your organization.

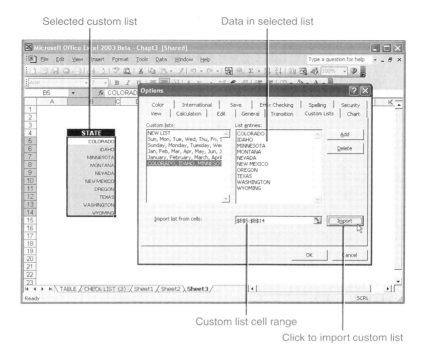

Custom list cell range

Click to import custom list

REPLACING DATA

You can find and replace names or information within cells similar to other Office applications. For replacing information in specific ranges or cells do this, select the range you want
to search. Choose Edit, Replace. In the Find What box, type the name or information
you're looking for and type the new information to replace it with in the Replace With box.
Click Replace All.

TRACKING CHANGES MADE BY MULTIPLE USERS

If you work with a team to build, edit, and maintain a workbook or if your workbook passes
through several hands on its way to completion, it can be useful to know who made which
changes to the workbook content. By using Excel's Track Changes feature, you can see
which person added which content, on which date, and at what time. You can also review
changes others made, and keep only the changes you want.

TIP FROM

> If you're a one-person editing team, you can track your own changes. Track Changes
> allows you to track not just who, but when a change was made, and that enables you to
> track your edits since your last save or after a certain date.

ENABLING AND DISABLING REVISION TRACKING

Track Changes must be turned on before you can begin tracking the evolution of your worksheet. If it isn't invoked, the changes someone else makes to your sheet will blend in with your content, and only your personal recollections will determine what's been added or changed.

To turn on and use Track Changes, follow these steps:

1. In the worksheet you want to track multiple users' changes in, choose Tools, Track Changes, Highlight Changes.

2. The Highlight Changes dialog box opens (as shown in Figure 3.17). Click the Track Changes While Editing check box.

Figure 3.17
Any edits or new entries made prior to turning on this feature will not be highlighted, nor will any data about their origin be saved or displayed.

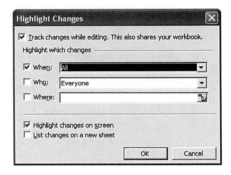

3. Select the amount and type of tracking you want to perform by clicking in the check boxes next to When, Who, and/or Where.

4. Leave on the Highlight Changes on Screen option so that cells containing new or edited content will be marked as such onscreen.

5. Click OK to close the dialog box and begin tracking changes.

TIP FROM

Use the Where option in the Highlight Changes dialog box to specify a range of cells in which to track changes. If a range is specified, Excel tracks changes only within that range.

Figure 3.18 shows a worksheet that has been edited by more than one user. The highlighted cells contain new/edited content, and the ScreenTip indicates who made the changes.

Figure 3.18
Cells containing changes contain a thin blue outline border with a small triangular change indicator in the upper-left corner.

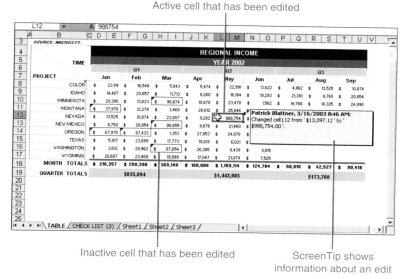

Active cell that has been edited

Inactive cell that has been edited

ScreenTip shows information about an edit

3

The List Changes on a New Sheet option in the Highlight Changes dialog box enables you to store a record of what's been added or changed in your workbook on a separate sheet, so that all changes can be seen in one place. Otherwise, you must scroll through the entire book to find all the changes your team has made.

This list contains only changes made through the date and time you enabled this feature. To update the list of changes, save the workbook and reenable this feature.

You can turn off the Track Changes feature by opening the Highlight Changes dialog box and removing the check mark in the Track Changes While Editing option box. A prompt appears to inform you that your workbook will no longer be in shared mode, which you must confirm by clicking Yes to turn off Track Changes.

ACCEPTING AND REJECTING CHANGES

After others have made their changes to your workbook, you can review the changes, keeping those you want and discarding those you don't:

1. Choose Tools, Track Changes, Accept or Reject Changes. The Select Changes to Accept or Reject dialog box appears. See Figure 3.19. (Excel might ask you to save your workbook first. If so, click OK.)

Figure 3.19
Choose whose changes to review, the time interval for which to review changes, and the range of cells for which to review changes.

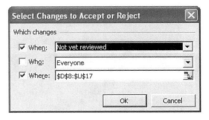

2. Decide what to review:
   - In the When area, choose to review either changes you haven't reviewed yet, or changes made after a certain date and time. When choosing a specific date, Excel places the current date in the box. To change the date, type a new one, separating month, day, and year with either a dash or a forward slash. To add a specific time, type one after the date, separating the two with a space.
   - In the Who area, choose to review changes made by all reviewers, all reviewers but you, or any specific reviewer.
   - In the Where area, choose the range of cells to review. If you leave this blank, you'll review the entire worksheet.

3. Click OK to begin reviewing changes. When Excel finds the first change, it highlights the cell on the spreadsheet with a marquee, and then describes it in the Accept or Reject Changes dialog box (Figure 3.20).

Figure 3.20
Excel describes the change and lets you choose to accept or reject it.

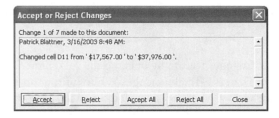

4. If more than one change was made to the cell, Excel lists them all. Click the one you want to keep.

5. Click Accept to keep the change or Reject to keep the cell's original value.

6. Excel finds the next change. You can continue to accept or reject each change in turn. You can also click Accept All to accept all the remaining changes in the workbook, or Reject All to keep each remaining changed cell's original value. You can also click Close at any time to stop the review process.

USING COMMENTS TO EXPLAIN CELL CONTENT

Many times, the content you add to or edit in a cell requires more explanation or supporting information than you can easily add to the worksheet. Explaining, for example, that the price contained in a particular cell includes a 5% discount is easy enough to do by typing this text in an adjacent cell. If, however, the 5% discount is offered only to certain customers or will be going up to 8% within the next few days, this extra information might be too cumbersome to add as actual worksheet content, especially if you print the data often but don't want these comments in the printout. This explanation or parenthetical information can be added in the form of a comment, a box containing text that appears whenever the mouse is positioned over the cell that needs explanation (see Figure 3.21).

Default text in comment box   Sizing handles

Figure 3.21
Drag the comment box handles to increase the size of the box.

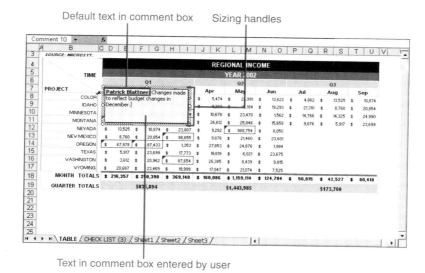

Text in comment box entered by user

TIP FROM

Reviewers can also use comments to ask questions of the workbook's owner or other editors.

To add a comment to your worksheet, follow these steps:

1. Click in the cell for which a comment is needed.

2. Choose Insert, Comment, or right-click the cell and choose Insert Comment from the shortcut menu.

3. A yellow comment box appears, containing your username (as you provided it during the installation of Office and as it appears on the User Name line in the General Tab of the Options dialog box). Click in the box to activate a cursor and begin typing your comment text.

4. Click in any other cell to close the comment box and store the entered comment text.

TIP

> You can format your comments so they look different from those others write. For example, if your comments have a light green background or use a different font, the person reviewing your comments will recognize yours just by the way they look. Use the Highlight tool on the Formatting toolbar to set a comment's background color. Use the font tools on the Formatting toolbar to change font attributes.

Cells that have an attached comment contain a small red triangle in the upper-right corner of the cell (see Figure 3.22). To view the comment, position your mouse pointer over the cell. The comment appears as long as your mouse remains over the cell.

TIP FROM

> You can set any comment so that it always displays. Right-click the cell and choose Show/hide Comments. You can also set your worksheet so that all comments display. Choose Tools, Options, click the Options dialog box's View tab, and then click Comment & Indicator. (You can also click None to never show comments or comment indicators, or click Comment Indicator to show indicators only.)

TIP FROM

> When you set any or all comments to always display, you can also print them with your workbook. Choose File, Page Setup, and then click the Sheet tab. Click the arrow at the end of the Comments box and choose either to print comments where they appear on the sheet, or to print comments at the end of the sheet. Click OK and then print the worksheet.

To delete a comment, right-click the cell and choose Delete Comment from the shortcut menu.

To edit a comment, right-click the cell and choose Edit Comment from the shortcut menu. The comment box becomes active, and you can click to position your cursor within it and begin editing.

The Reviewing toolbar helps you work with comments, especially when you're adding a lot of them or when you're reviewing several comments others have made in your workbook. To turn it on, choose View, Comments. Table 3.1 shows the buttons on this toolbar.

Figure 3.22
The comment displays as long as your mouse hovers over the interior of the cell to which a comment has been attached.

Red triangle in cell's upper-right corner indicates presence of a comment

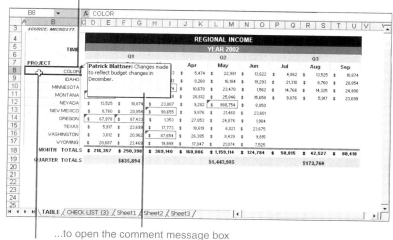

...to open the comment message box
Place the mouse cursor over the comment cell...

TABLE 3.1   REVIEWING TOOLBAR FUNCTIONS

Icon	Name	Function
	New Comment	Add a comment.
	Previous Comment	Find and show the previous comment.
	Next Comment	Find and show the next comment.
	Show Comment (or Show/Hide Comment)	Cause the currently selected comment to always display, or hide the currently selected comment.
	Show All Comments (or Hide All Comments)	Display or hide all comments.
	Delete Comment	Remove the currently selected comment.
	Create Microsoft Outlook Task	Make a task in Outlook out of the currently selected comment.
	Update File	Save new and changed comments in your workbook.
	Mail Recipient (as Attachment)	E-mail the workbook, with all its comments, to someone.

LINKING EXCEL DATA

So far, all the discussion of moving and copying has referred to content that exists in one or more locations, with no connection between the locations. Copying a section of a worksheet or an entire worksheet to another workbook saves you time and effort, but after the section or sheet is copied, the relationship between the source material and the target location might end (unless formulas are included that create links, as described shortly). If you go back to the source worksheet and change any of the data, the changes are not reflected in the place(s) to which the material was copied.

What if you want to establish a permanent relationship between the source material and the target? What if you need to copy a section of a worksheet to another workbook, and you want changes in the original (source) material to update the target (copied) material as well? To establish such a relationship, you must set up a *link* between the source and the target. Such a link uses *OLE* (*object linking and embedding*), a powerful Windows feature.

CAUTION

> If the target workbook will be transferred to or used on another computer or network, be sure to send along the source workbook also, or the link between the files will be broken. Be sure to place the files in folders at the new location that match the folder names at the old location, so that the path between the files remains the same (unless both files are in the same folder, in which case you don't have a problem). You might find that copying both files to the new location and then re-creating the link simplifies this process. See the later section "Breaking Links Between Files" for details.

ESTABLISHING LINKS BETWEEN WORKSHEETS OR WORKBOOKS

The simple Edit, Paste command places copied content in a new location. Choosing Edit, Paste Special enables you to create a link between the source and target worksheets or workbooks.

NOTE

> You can establish one or more links within a single worksheet, enabling you to enter repeated information once and have it update to one or more additional cells automatically.

To copy and link content between worksheets or workbooks in Excel, follow these steps:

1. When copying between workbooks, be sure both workbooks are open and have been saved.
2. Select and copy the source content in the source worksheet. This content will become the linked object.
3. Move to the target worksheet, select the cell where you want the linked data to begin, and choose Edit, Paste Special to open the Paste Special dialog box (see Figure 3.23).

Figure 3.23
In most cases, use the All option that's selected by default when creating a paste link.

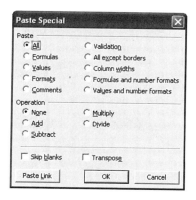

4. Make any selections pertaining to the content and formatting you want to include in the pasted material. In most cases, the default All selection is exactly what you need.

5. Click the Paste Link button. Note that this button doesn't open another dialog box, as you might expect. Instead, it immediately executes the link.

After linking a source and target, test the link by switching to the source cells and making a change to their content. Check the target, and see that the change is reflected. When viewing the target, notice that the Formula bar shows the link, listing the source location, as shown in Figure 3.24. The workbook name appears in brackets ([ ]), followed by the worksheet name with an exclamation point (!) and the range name or cell reference. In this example, the link is as follows:

`=[Chapt3.xls]Table!D8`

- The source workbook's name is Chapt3.xls (.xls is the file's extension).
- The source worksheet is named TABLE.
- The source cell is D8.

If the source workbook is closed, the link formula also includes the full path to the source file.

NOTE

> If you paste link blank cells, Excel displays 0 for the blank cell in the target location. To suppress the display of zeros, choose Tools, Options, click the View tab, and deselect the Zero Values option.

UPDATING LINKS TO A WORKBOOK

When you open a workbook that contains one or more links to other workbooks, you'll be prompted to update the links—that is, update the target to reflect any changes made in the source, as shown in Figure 3.25. You are prompted to update links only when one or more of the source workbooks are closed. If they're all open at the time you open the file containing links, Excel automatically updates the links. If you prefer, you can choose to keep the file's existing content intact and update the links later, as needed.

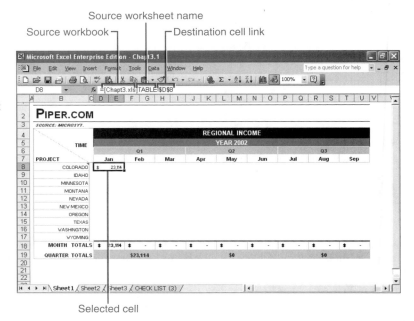

Figure 3.24
When a target cell is selected, the Formula bar displays the source filename, sheet name, and cell address.

Figure 3.25
If you aren't the primary editor of the source document, it might be safer to choose Don't Update, and then check the source document before updating the linked data.

To update a link between two workbooks after the target has been opened, follow these steps:

1. In the document containing the linked material (the target), choose Edit, Links to display the Links dialog box.

   Links can be edited only from within the target document. The Links command is disabled in the Edit menu if you attempt to access it from the source document or any unlinked workbook.

2. In the Links dialog box, click the link you want to update in the Source File list (see Figure 3.26).

Figure 3.26
It's a good idea to save the workbook before updating any links. If you regret having updated them, you can close the file without saving.

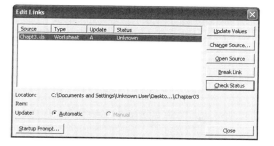

3. Click the Update Values button.

4. Click Close.

> To quickly update all links with one fast keystroke, press F9 in the workbook that contains linked data. Note, however, that this technique is useful only when the following conditions are in place:
> - The workbook containing the links has calculation set to Manual (choose Tools, Options, click the Calculation tab, and select Manual).
> - The source workbook is open. Keep in mind that if you've set your calculations to Manual none of the calculations will work unless you press F9.

LOCKING LINKED EXTERNAL DATA

Worksheets can occasionally include links to OLE-compatible applications other than Excel. To prevent accidental updates of these links, you can lock the links. Choose Tools, Options to open the Options dialog box, and click the Calculation tab. Remove the check mark in the Update Remote References box. To resume updates in the future, turn the option back on.

REDIRECTING LINKS

If you rename a workbook to which other workbooks are linked, the links break. You can repair the broken links by redirecting them to the renamed file. To do so, move to the target document (the workbook that contains the links) and choose Edit, Links. Click the Change Source button, and choose the appropriate file from the Change Links dialog box. By default, the cell addresses that were copied will be retained.

BREAKING LINKS BETWEEN FILES

You can break links by choosing Edit, Links, Break Link. Most broken links occur accidentally—the user changes the name of either the source or target file or moves one or both files to a new folder. Any change in name or location of either the source or target file will result in a broken link.

NOTE

To establish a new link to another document, you must re-create a link from scratch, starting with copying the source data and using the Edit, Paste Special command to link the source data to the target cells.

TIP FROM

You can also replace linked cells or break the link with the values that the cells contain. Copy the linked cell(s), choose Edit, Paste Special, select Values in the Paste Special dialog box, and then choose OK.

TROUBLESHOOTING

UNACCEPTING ACCEPTED CHANGES

What if I accept a change but later decide I want the original value back?

Excel has no "undo change" function (as Word does). However, Excel still remembers the last change made to a cell, even after you accept a change in it. Hover your mouse over the cell to see a ScreenTip that lists the last change. You can use this information to retype the value you want into the cell. It's unfortunate that this process isn't more automatic, but at least there is a way to restore original values.

TIP FROM

After you close a worksheet in which changes were tracked, the next time you open the worksheet, the change indicators don't appear. This is because Excel assumes you want to see changes only since the last time you saved. To see all your changes, choose Tools, Track Changes, Highlight Changes. Then, click the arrow at the end of the When box and choose All. Click OK. Change indicators appear for all changes made to the worksheet.

EXCEL IN PRACTICE

You can use Excel's font styles to create check marks. In Figure 3.27, a matrix has been created with check marks using the font style WebDings and the letter "a." Certain font styles can enhance worksheets and create characters other than letters. You could also use Excel's Symbol command from the Insert menu, as shown in Figure 3.28.

Figure 3.27
Create check marks with characters using the Webdings font style and the letter "a."

Create a matrix with check mark characters

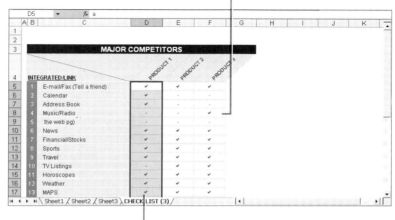

Use the font style WebDings and the letter "a" to create check marks

Figure 3.28
Excel's Symbol command allows you to access many symbols including characters in different languages.

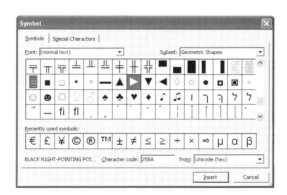

PART II

FORMATTING AND PRINTING EXCEL WORKSHEETS

4   Applying Number and Date Formats   91

5   Formatting and Printing   107

CHAPTER 4

APPLYING NUMBER AND DATE FORMATS

In this chapter

Applying Common Numeric Formats from the Toolbar   92

Applying Built-In Formats   93

Creating Custom Formats   97

Applying Custom Currency   101

Working with Large Numbers   102

Pasting In Custom Characters   102

Creating Custom Conditions Codes   103

Repeating Characters   104

APPLYING COMMON NUMERIC FORMATS FROM THE TOOLBAR

Numeric formatting changes the appearance of your numbers, displaying them as currency, percentages, dates, phone numbers, and so on. Although this formatting might seem purely cosmetic, it also serves an important purpose in defining the nature of your numbers (do the sales figures represent dollar volume or number of units sold?). It also helps ensure that your numbers appear in a digestible format (reducing the number of decimals displayed in a percentage, for example) so that they don't crowd or complicate your worksheet unnecessarily.

The most commonly applied number formats are applied directly from the Formatting toolbar, and each is described in Table 4.1.

TABLE 4.1 NUMBER FORMATTING TOOLS

Button	Name	Formatting
$	Currency Style	Displays numbers in an accounting style, where dollar signs appear left justified next to the number, and two decimal places appear to the right. Commas are used as a thousands delimiter by default.
%	Percent Style	Used to display decimals in the form of a percentage, such as .05 to 50% (percent).
,	Comma Style	Use this tool to add commas to your numbers in excess of 999. Two decimal places are added to the right of the number.
+.0 .00	Increase Decimal	Even if your decimals are currently zeros, this tool adds more of them. You can view a number to an unlimited number of decimal places with this tool, clicking once per desired decimal displayed. Note that Excel accurately displays only up to 14 decimals. Any decimal places after 14 appear as zeros.
.00 +.0	Decrease Decimal	If you've used the Increase Decimal tool and merely want to reverse your action or just want to see fewer numbers to the right of the decimal point, click this button. As you remove decimal places, numbers to the left of the removed numbers round up as required. For example, 5.682 becomes 5.68, then 5.7, and then 6 if the Decrease Decimal button is clicked three times.

These buttons apply the default settings for each of these number formats. It is important to note that no matter what you do to the appearance of the format of your numeric content, the original number you typed is being stored and used by Excel. In other words, your formats merely adjust the way the number looks in the worksheet and not the number itself. You can customize the way each format is applied by using the Format Cells dialog box (see the following section).

NOTE

Scientific notation is a way of compacting very large numbers into a short notation. 2.3987900109299 when formatted in scientific notation displays 2.4E+00; 00 equals no exponential power because it's a very small number; not the type typically used with the scientific format. However, if you remove the period in the number, making it a very large number (23987900109299), the scientific format would be useful in showing the large number in a compact format (2.4E+13 or 2.4 raised to the 13th power). You Z get 2.4E+13 when you choose to round the number to one decimal place. The actual number remains unaltered.

APPLYING BUILT-IN FORMATS

For many worksheets, Currency and Percentage formats will suffice. However, by using the Comma Style and Increase/Decrease Decimal buttons, a sufficient degree of customization for number formatting is available through the toolbar should the defaults be inappropriate for a particular worksheet.

Should you need to use any additional number formats or want to adjust your defaults automatically, follow these steps:

1. Select the cells you want to format.
2. Choose Format, Cells or right-click the selection and choose Format Cells from the shortcut menu, or press Ctrl+1 on the keyboard. The Format Cells dialog box opens.
3. Click the Number tab.
4. Select a category by clicking the name in the Category list.
5. For each category, a different set of options appears, except General and Text, which have no options associated with them. Figure 4.1 shows the settings for the Number category.

Figure 4.1
Apply the Number format when your numeric data will require decimal places (or zeros after the decimal point) or commas.

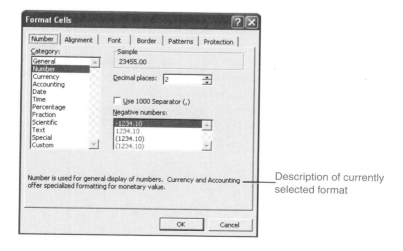

Description of currently selected format

6. Select the appropriate settings for any options you want to customize, and click OK.

NOTE

Your settings for the selected category apply only to the selected cells. To quickly apply numeric formats to all the numbers in the entire worksheet, you can select the entire worksheet before using the Format Cells dialog box. Be careful to apply only formats that will affect purely numeric content (no date formats), so that your text and date entries are not visually changed. If any unwanted results occur in a few cells throughout the worksheet, you can always reformat those cells later.

The example in Figure 4.2 has Excel's built-in category default formats applied to the numbers.

Figure 4.2
A listing of Excel's built-in default category default formats.

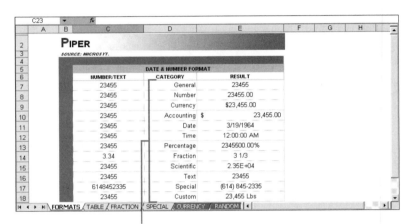

Built-in formats

FORMATTING THE DATE AND TIME

Dates and times are included in worksheets for information, for calculation, or both. By default, Excel converts typed dates depending on how they were entered as shown in Table 4.2. It's important to note that the following examples only work if you have Windows set to US date format. In countries that use dd-mm-yy as the default date format you will need to enter your numbers in that format instead. In addition, if you have set the short and long date formats for your system to be something other than the default, these may not be the default results used.

TABLE 4.2   DEFAULT DATE FORMATS

Typed Content	Stored As	Default Result
3/16/64	23452	3/16/64
3/16	37696	16-Mar
March 16, 1964	23452	16-Mar-64

If you want to have your typed dates formatted differently, follow these steps:

1. Select the cells that contain or will contain dates to be formatted.

TIP FROM

> If the cells that you want to format are scattered throughout your worksheet, use the Ctrl key to select them as a group before applying the format.

2. Choose Format, Cells.
3. Click the Number tab, and select the Date Category.
4. Select one of 15 date formats in the Type list.
5. After viewing the Sample, click OK.

Your Time Category settings are very similar, and eight Type options are available. Table 4.3 shows the Excel defaults for times as you type them into your worksheet cells.

TABLE 4.3   DEFAULT TIME FORMATS

Typed Content	Stored As	Default Format
1:50:15	.0765625	1:50:15
1:50 am	.076388889	1:50 AM
1:50 a	.076388889	1:50 AM
1:50 p	.576388889	1:50 PM

The Type list contains formats in a 12- and 24-hour clock, with or without seconds, and with or without the date accompanying the time.

NOTE

> If you'll be using your time entries in formulas, it will be easier to use the time in your formula if you apply a 24-hour format.

TIP

> The 24-hour clock starts at 0:00:00 and ends at 23:59:59. To figure out the 24-hour equivalent of a 12-hour-based time, add 12 if the time is PM. For example, 1:00PM is 13:00 in a 24-hour format. AM times are the same in both 12- and 24-hour clocks.

FRACTIONS

You can display decimals as fractions within Excel. Excel allows 1-, 2-, and 3-digit display fractions. Notice how the example in Figure 4.3 displays the number as a fraction within the cell. The number is created as a decimal and Excel displays the decimal as a fraction. You can change the display from hundreds to quarters and vice versa with the Fraction formatting option under Category in the Format Cells dialog box.

Figure 4.3
Decimals displayed as fractions in Excel.

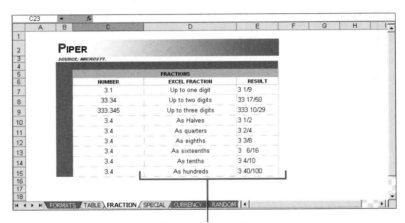

Default fractions in Excel

SPECIAL

The Special format is one of those formats few know about. If you have to enter any type of phone, Social Security, or ZIP Code numbers, this format can be invaluable as a timesaver. All you have to do is enter the exact number and Excel displays it in the special format you applied. It also takes into account country-specific items. For example, if you're in Canada, there is a Social Insurance Number format. All you have to do is select the country and Excel will display the country formats available. You then select the country format and your numbers will be automatically formatted. Notice the special formats in Figure 4.4.

Figure 4.4
Use special formats that allow you to type numerics and Excel will automatically format the special format for you.

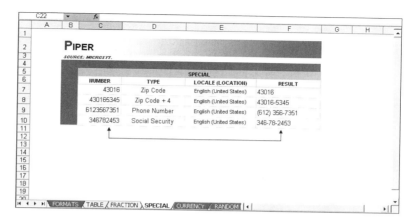

CREATING CUSTOM FORMATS

If Excel's built-in formats don't match what you're looking for, you can create a custom format. For example, you might want a date to show the weekday, month, date, and year, such as "Saturday, January 16, 1999." Or, you might want to make sure that if a number is less than 1, Excel omits the zero to the left of the decimal point. In both cases, you create a custom format.

To create a custom format, you must type a string of *formatting codes* (also simply called *codes*) that Excel can interpret. Here are the details:

1. Select the cell(s) to format.

2. Choose Format, Cells, click the Number tab, and choose the Custom Category.

3. In the Type field, type your custom format. In the list box below the Type field, you can choose a custom format upon which to base yours. For example, you can type dddd, mmmm d, yyyy to represent day-of-week, month, day, year, such as Tuesday, January 19, 1999. (The rest of this section explains how to develop custom formats.)

4. Click the OK button. Excel formats the cell(s) using your custom format, and adds your custom format to the list of available custom formats so you can use it again later.

The difficult part of this task is knowing what codes to type in step 3. The codes can be broken down into two groups: *date and time* codes and *number and text* codes.

TIP FROM

You can see the codes used by the built-in number formats by choosing the format as you normally would, and then (before exiting the Format Cells dialog box) click the Custom category. The number code used by the format you choose will appear on the Type line.

continues

continued

> For example, if you choose the Date category, choose the 3/14/01 format from the Type list, and then immediately switch to the Custom category, the "m/d/yy;@" number code for that date format will appear on the Type line.
>
> This technique is a great way to learn about the codes. It can also aid in building your custom code by using a built-in format's number code as a starting point.

WORKING WITH DATE AND TIME FORMATTING CODES

Table 4.4 lists the usable codes for date and time numbering formats. To use them, you need only type the combination of codes necessary to suit your needs. For example, "dddd, mmmm d, yyyy" changes 2/2/99 to Tuesday, February 2, 1999.

TABLE 4.4   DATE AND TIME FORMATTING CODES

Code	Meaning
d	Day, from 1 to 31.
dd	Day, from 01 to 31.
ddd	Three-letter day of week, such as Tue.
dddd	Day of week, such as Tuesday.
m	Month, from 1 to 12; or minute if the colon is used, from 1 to 60.
mm	Month, from 01 to 12; or minute if the colon is used, from 01 to 60.
mmm	Three-letter month, such as Aug.
mmmm	Month, such as August.
yy	Two-digit year, such as 99.
yyyy	Four-digit year, such as 2001.
h	Hour, from 0 to 23.
hh	Hour, from 00 to 23.
s	Second, from 0 to 59. Follow with .0 or .00 with additional digits to add tenths or hundredths of a second, respectively.
ss	Second, from 00 to 59. Follow with .0 or .00 with additional digits to add tenths or hundredths of a second, respectively.
AM/PM	AM or PM, as appropriate.
am/pm	am or pm, as appropriate.
A/P	A or P, as appropriate for am or pm.
a/p	a or p, as appropriate.

If you use one of the AM/PM, am/pm, A/P, or a/p codes, Excel formats time on a 12-hour clock. If you omit these codes, Excel formats time on a 24-hour clock.

Figure 4.5 shows a custom date format that shows a three-digit day code followed by a one-digit day code, followed by a three-digit year code.

Figure 4.5
Type your custom format in the Type box.

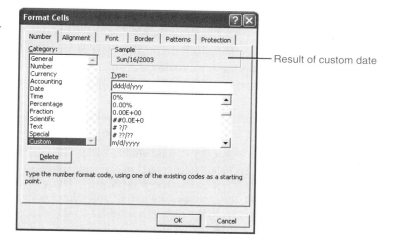

Result of custom date

TIP FROM

You can add a left and right bracket around any time or date code to make Excel show elapsed time. For example, if cell A1 contains 8/12/2001 10:15 and cell A2 contains 8/13/2001 9:42, and cell A3 contains =A2-A1, formatting cell A3 with [h]:mm:ss shows you how many hours, minutes, and seconds elapsed between the two dates.

WORKING WITH NUMBER AND TEXT FORMATTING CODES

Creating custom number formats can be more challenging than date/time formats, because Excel gives you a lot of flexibility. Table 4.5 shows the codes available for formatting numbers and text.

TABLE 4.5   NUMBER AND TEXT FORMATTING CODES

Code	Meaning
0	Digit placeholder. Use this code to ensure that the correct number of digits appears in a value. For example, if a cell contains .15 and you apply the format 0.000 to it, the cell will read 0.150. If the cell contained .15548, the 0.000 format would make it read 0.155.
?	Digit placeholder. This is similar to the 0 placeholder, but places spaces instead of zeros on the right of the decimal point. 0.??? applied to a cell containing .21 would yield 0.21.

continues

TABLE 4.5   CONTINUED

Code	Meaning
#	Digit placeholder. This is similar to the 0 placeholder, but does not pad a value with extra zeros. Use this placeholder mostly to show where to place commas. For example, #,### applied to a cell containing 123456789 yields 123,456,789.
.	Decimal point. Used in conjunction with other codes to signify decimal point placement. For example, 0.### applied to a cell that contains .1236 displays 0.124.
%	Percent symbol. This code multiplies the value by 100 and appends the percent symbol. Applying 0% to a cell containing 13 yields 1300%.
/	Fraction format. Use this code with the ? code to display numbers in fraction form. For example, applying ??/?? to a cell that contains 1.315 yields 1/4. Applying # ??/?? to the same cell yields 10/37. The more places you allow in the fraction, the more accurate it is. ?/? applied to a cell containing .270 yields 2/7, whereas applying ??/?? yields 11/40.
,	Thousands separator, as well as rounding and scaling agent. When you surround a comma with #s, 0s, or ?s, the comma separates hundreds from thousands, thousands from millions, and so on. #,### places a comma every third digit. When you place one comma at the end of a format, Excel rounds the number and displays it in thousands. When you place two commas at the end of a format, Excel rounds the number and displays it in millions. For example, #,###,###, displays 123456789 as 123,457. #,###,###,, displays 123456789 as 123.
E+ E- e+ e-	Scientific notation. Use these formats in conjunction with ?, #, and 0 to cause numbers to display in scientific notation. For example, #.##E-## (with no spaces and a capital E) applied to a cell that contains 545678132 displays 5.46 e 8. E- and e- display - before negative exponents but no sign before positive exponents. E+ and e+ display - before negative exponents and + before positive exponents.
( ) $ - + / space	Literals. Excel places these characters directly into the value unless they are preceded with an underscore.
\	Literal interpreter. Precede any character with the backslash, and Excel places that character directly into the value. For example, \t inserts the character t (but not the backslash) into the format. (To insert several characters in a row, use "text", described later in this list.)
_	Space inserter. This character leaves space equivalent to the width of the next character, to help you align elements. For example, _m leaves a space equal to the width of the m.
"text"	Literal string. For example, "Part No." inserts the text *Part No.* into the cell.
*	Repeater. Repeats the next character until the column is filled. Use only one asterisk per format.

Code	Meaning
@	Text placeholder. If a cell contains a text value, this character tells Excel where to show it. For example, if a cell contains the text "check," "Customer paid by "@"." displays *Customer paid by check.*
[color]	Color. Applies the specified color to the text. For example, [Red]#,###.## applied to a cell that contains 43567.4 displays 43,567.4 in red.

If a cell could contain a positive value, a negative value, zero, and/or text, you can apply a different format for each. Just write multiple formats, separating each with a semicolon. If you write two formats, the first applies to positive and zero values and the second applies to negative values. If you write three formats, the first applies to positive values, the second to negative values, and the third to zero. If you write four formats, they apply to positive, negative, zero, and text values, respectively. For example, you might write this format:

```
#,###; [red]#,###; "No balance"; "Note:"@
```

If the cell contains 2340, it displays 2,340. If the cell contains -4211, it displays 4,211 in red. If the cell contains zero, it displays *No balance.* If the cell contains the text "Non-negotiable," it displays *Note: Non-negotiable.* You might find it easier to use conditional formatting, described in the next section, to handle these kinds of situations.

APPLYING CUSTOM CURRENCY

You can apply custom currency symbols by turning on the Num Lock on your numeric keypad and entering the codes shown in Figure 4.6 while holding down the Alt key. For example, with the Num Lock turned on, hold down the Alt key and type 0165 to display the symbol for Yen. You could also wait and format the cells to show the symbols. Each symbol in the figure, except for the Yen, can be applied as part of a number format using the Symbol drop-down list for either the Currency or Accounting categories in the Format Cells (Number) dialog box.

Figure 4.6
You can easily apply custom currency symbols to your cells.

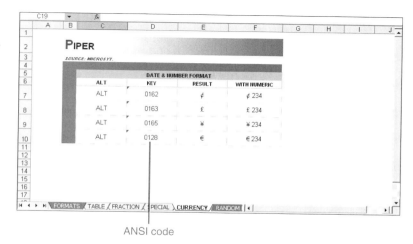

ANSI code

WORKING WITH LARGE NUMBERS

When you have a worksheet that contains numbers displayed in the millions or thousands, you might want to shrink these numbers down to make them more digestible, while retaining the value of millions. For example, ever notice charts or graphs with numbers displayed in two digits but called out as Numbers displayed as (000)? This can be done by applying the custom code formats shown in Figure 4.7. The original number is shown in millions and the results are created by applying the shown custom codes. Make sure you label the numbers appropriately or they could be misinterpreted.

Figure 4.7
You can display large numbers in simple reduced-digit formats.

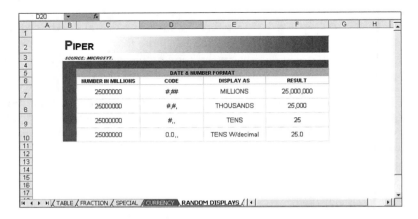

PASTING IN CUSTOM CHARACTERS

If you created a custom character or use a symbol or format often that takes special steps to create, you can paste the symbol in the custom formats. For example, the custom currency discussed and shown previously in Figure 4.7 shows the Yen symbol. The Yen symbol was created by turning on Num Lock, pressing the Alt key, and typing the ANSI code. Well, there's an easier way. Insert the ANSI code for the desired currency and then follow these steps to establish this character as a custom format:

1. Select the cell containing the character you want imported as a custom format.
2. Select the character in the formula bar, right-click the selected character, and choose Copy on the shortcut menu (or click the Copy button, or press Ctrl+C).
3. Then, press the Esc key or click the Cancel key (red X on the formula bar) to deselect the current selection. ·
4. Access the Number tab in the Format Cells dialog box and select Custom from the Category list.
5. In the Type text box, press Ctrl+V to paste the character into the custom format as shown in Figure 4.8.

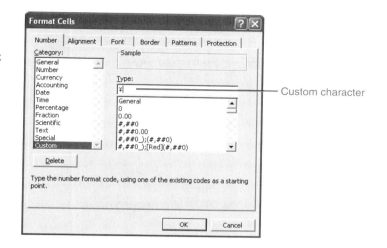

Figure 4.8
Paste custom characters into the custom formats Type text box to add them to your custom format options.

Custom character

CREATING CUSTOM CONDITIONS CODES

Excel allows you to create custom conditions. Another alternative might be to use the conditional formatting feature; however, you can also write your own custom condition codes. Codes or conditions must be enclosed in square brackets and the conditions are separated by a semicolon. For example, if you wanted to create a custom condition based on values below or equal to 50 and greater than 50, you could type the following condition codes into the Type format bar from the format cells dialog box under the Category Custom:

```
[Cyan][<=50];[Blue][>50]
```

→ For more information on setting formats using conditional formatting, **see** "Using Conditional Formatting with Lists," **p. 408**

A value in the cell would turn the color of Cyan if less than or equal to 50 and Blue if greater than 50 as shown in Figure 4.9. The following color codes are available in Excel:

```
[Black]
[Cyan]
[Magenta]
[White]
[Blue]
[Green]
[Red]
[Yellow]
```

You can also apply custom conditions with text. For example, to apply certain text based on positive or negative values, you apply the following condition code in the Type formula bar:

```
$0"Positive";$-0"Negative"
```

The Type format bar is located in the format cells dialog box under the Custom category. Figure 4.9 shows you the result of this formula. In the absence of special conditions, the first format is used for positive numbers and zero and the second for negative numbers.

Figure 4.9
Create custom conditions that apply colors and text based on values.

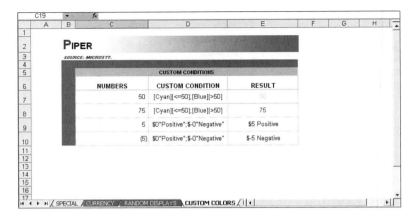

REPEATING CHARACTERS

You can fill cells with remaining characters or repeating characters. No matter what the column width, the repeating characters will always fill up the remaining space in a cell. If you have dollar values similar to how dollar values are filled out in checks and repeating characters take up the remaining space, this is a good way to establish the repeating characters. To create repeating characters, access the Type format bar (located in the Format Cells dialog box under the Custom category) and type the following into it:

`0*~`

The character that is repeated using this formula is the Tilde character. For your purposes, however, you can type any character after the asterisk that suits your needs. Notice the example in Figure 4.10.

TIP FROM

The asterisk is also used to help left align a character. It's how the accounting style is able to left align the $ in the cell. For example, `"¥" * #,##0.00` will left align the Yen symbol. The key to using the asterisk this way is to place a space between the asterisk and the rest of the number code to the right.

Code and characters to repeat   Repeating characters

Figure 4.10
Create repeating characters with custom code formats to fill the remaining spaces in cells.

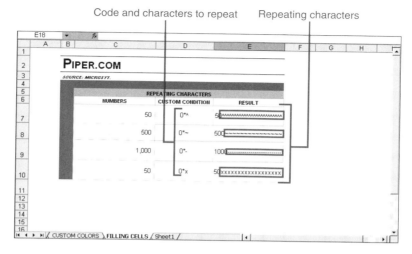

EXCEL IN PRACTICE

Excel's custom formats can make your spreadsheets not only look better but also make them simpler and more effective. Use Special formats, custom formats, and conditions to create results automatically as shown in Figure 4.11. All the results on the right are automated with custom formats.

Figure 4.11
Create custom formats that allow you to automate formatting procedures.

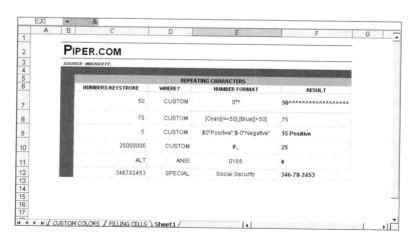

CHAPTER **5**

FORMATTING AND PRINTING

In this chapter

Why Change the Formatting?   108

Changing the Font, Point Size, and Font Styles   112

Working with Styles   116

Applying and Drawing Borders and Shading   122

Using AutoFormat to Enhance Your Worksheets   126

Using the Drawing Toolbar   127

Ordering, Grouping, Moving, and Resizing Drawn Objects   131

Combining Drawing Tools with Charts and Worksheets   133

Printing a Worksheet   135

Previewing the Print Job   138

Using Page Break Preview   140

Working with Page Setup Options   141

WHY CHANGE THE FORMATTING?

You could build an entire workbook with no special formatting at all. Excel's default styles, fonts, alignments, and other settings for text and numbers are sufficient for the legible and accurate display and printing of worksheet data. Why change formatting? Although Excel offers a logical grid format, your data often reads better with formatting. This includes creating bold headings to your lists as well as coloring text and worksheet cells. When you first open a workbook, it displays the default lines between columns and rows in Excel. If you don't want the row and column lines, you can select the entire worksheet and then fill the worksheet with the color white. This gives you a clean canvas with which to start. An alternative method is to select the Tools menu and choose Options, and then select the View tab. Under the Window Options on the View tab deselect Gridlines.

TIP FROM

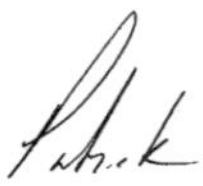

As a habit, before I ever start creating a worksheet or workbook, I fill the worksheets with white to create a canvas. In terms of creating a painting, it allows you to start with a clean, blank slate.

By formatting numbers, dates, columns, and headings, you can create a much easier-to-read spreadsheet. Notice the two examples in Figures 5.1 and 5.2. Figure 5.1 shows no special formatting and is a bit difficult to read.

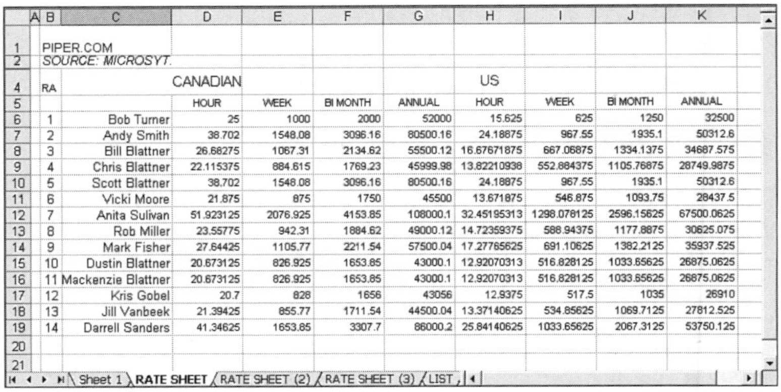

	A	B	C	D	E	F	G	H	I	J	K
1		PIPER.COM									
2		SOURCE: MICROSYT.									
4		RA		CANADIAN				US			
5				HOUR	WEEK	BI MONTH	ANNUAL	HOUR	WEEK	BI MONTH	ANNUAL
6		1	Bob Turner	25	1000	2000	52000	15.625	625	1250	32500
7		2	Andy Smith	38.702	1548.08	3096.16	80500.16	24.18875	967.55	1935.1	50312.6
8		3	Bill Blattner	26.68275	1067.31	2134.62	55500.12	16.67671875	667.06875	1334.1375	34687.575
9		4	Chris Blattner	22.115375	884.615	1769.23	45999.98	13.82210938	552.884375	1105.76875	28749.9875
10		5	Scott Blattner	38.702	1548.08	3096.16	80500.16	24.18875	967.55	1935.1	50312.6
11		6	Vicki Moore	21.875	875	1750	45500	13.671875	546.875	1093.75	28437.5
12		7	Anita Sulivan	51.923125	2076.925	4153.85	108000.1	32.45195313	1298.078125	2596.15625	67500.0625
13		8	Rob Miller	23.55775	942.31	1884.62	49000.12	14.72359375	588.94375	1177.8875	30625.075
14		9	Mark Fisher	27.64425	1105.77	2211.54	57500.04	17.27765625	691.10625	1382.2125	35937.525
15		10	Dustin Blattner	20.673125	826.925	1653.85	43000.1	12.92070313	516.828125	1033.65625	26875.0625
16		11	Mackenzie Blattner	20.673125	826.925	1653.85	43000.1	12.92070313	516.828125	1033.65625	26875.0625
17		12	Kris Gobel	20.7	828	1656	43056	12.9375	517.5	1035	26910
18		13	Jill Vanbeek	21.39425	855.77	1711.54	44500.04	13.37140625	534.85625	1069.7125	27812.525
19		14	Darrell Sanders	41.34625	1653.85	3307.7	86000.2	25.84140625	1033.65625	2067.3125	53750.125
20											
21											

Sheet 1 | RATE SHEET | RATE SHEET (2) | RATE SHEET (3) | LIST

Figure 5.1
Notice there is not special formatting to this figure, which can make it a bit difficult to read.

Figure 5.2 shows the same worksheet as shown in Figure 5.1, with formatting applied. Although formatting might take a few extra minutes, your worksheets will be able to tell a story without explanation.

Even a small amount of formatting can make a worksheet easier to interpret—the formatting is used to draw the reader's eye to important information. Worksheets that will be published for customers, reports, or an Internet or intranet site will be much better received if they have a more polished, visually appealing look.

Title font is larger than the rest

Elbow effect

Merged cells

Tiered title

Figure 5.2
The worksheet title is called out with a larger font size, and the column and row headings are tiered and aligned in an informative way. The worksheet also includes number formatting.

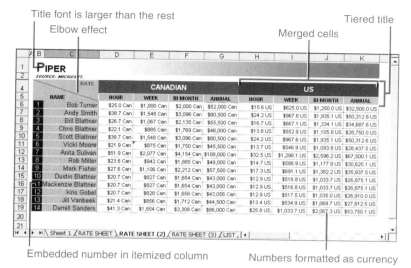

Embedded number in itemized column

Numbers formatted as currency

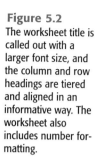

If you want readers to understand the overall content of the worksheet, see what information is being stored, and go right to the bottom line, make column headings and titles stand out through use of boldfacing or by applying a dynamic font, and draw attention to the bottom line—totals and the results of important formulas.

USING THE FORMATTING TOOLBAR

Excel's Formatting toolbar offers the most common tools used for changing the appearance of text. Table 5.1 shows the tools that change the appearance of text.

5

TABLE 5.1   TEXT FORMATTING TOOLS ON THE FORMATTING TOOLBAR

Button	Name	Method of Use/Formatting Effect
Arial	Font	Click the down arrow to see a list of fonts. Select a font from the list to apply to the selected cells, or text or numbers within a cell.
100%	Font Size	Click the down arrow to see a list of point sizes for the selected cell(s), or text or numbers within a cell. The larger the point size number in the Font Size box, the larger the text will be.
B	Bold	Click the Bold button once to boldface the selected cell content, or selected text or numbers within a cell. If the selection is already bold, clicking this button removes the bold format.

continues

TABLE 5.1 CONTINUED

Button	Name	Method of Use/Formatting Effect
I	Italic	Like the Bold button, the Italic button works by clicking it to apply the format. You also can click this button to remove italic formatting from a selection.
U	Underline	Click the Underline button to apply an underline to selected cell(s) or text or numbers within a cell. The underline spans spaces between words. Click the button again to remove the for mat. This is different from applying a bottom border to the entire cell, a technique discussed later in this chapter.
▤	Align Left	Text is left aligned by default. You can apply this alignment to numeric content as well by selecting a cell or cells and clicking the Align Left button.
▤	Center	Useful for titles and column headings, centering cell content creates equal space to the left and right of the content in each selected cell.
▤	Align Right	Numbers are right aligned by default. You also can apply right alignment to text. This format is especially effective for row headings.
▤	Merge and Center	Used primarily for worksheet titles, this button enables you to center text in a single cell that spans multiple columns. Merge and Center also enables you to merge and center text across multiple rows. Click to merge and center and click again to remove merge and center.
A	Font Color	Change the color of the cell content. Click the button to see a palette of 40 different colors, and click one of the colors to apply it to the selected cell(s) or text or numbers within a cell.

The remaining tools on the Formatting toolbar are for number formatting. The Borders and Fill Color tools are discussed later in this chapter.

TIP FROM

> When you're formatting a worksheet, it might be easier for you if you display the Formatting toolbar on its own row. Click the drop-down arrow on the end of the Formatting toolbar and choose Show Buttons on Two Rows.

When applying formats from the toolbar, several tools toggle—one click to apply the for-mat, a second click to remove it. For those that aren't toggles (alignment, color, Merge and Center), use the Undo button or press Ctrl+Z to remove the format.

→ To find out more about customizing toolbars (adding, moving, and deleting buttons), **see** "Modifying Toolbars," **p. 714**

USING THE FORMAT CELLS DIALOG BOX

For more control, more options, and a preview of the formatting tools' effects before you apply them, you can use the Format Cells dialog box, opened by choosing Format, Cells or right-clicking a cell or selection and choosing Format Cells from the context menu, or pressing Ctrl+1 on the keyboard. (Be sure to have the cells you want to format selected before opening the dialog box.)

The Format Cells dialog box contains six tabs, two of which apply to worksheet text:

- **Alignment**—Change not just the horizontal alignment (left, center, right) that you can adjust quickly from the toolbar, but the vertical alignment (top, center, bottom, and justified), and the orientation of the text (see Figure 5.3). You can rotate text up to 180°, an especially effective format for long column headings. You can also stack the text, useful for printing column headings vertically.

  The Text Control settings on this tab also enable you to make selected cells' text wrap within the cell, shrink to fit the current cell dimensions, or merge the selected cells into one cell.

Figure 5.3
Change the position of cell content with the Alignment tab's tools.

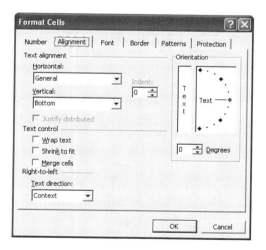

- **Font**—Choose a font, size, style, and color for the selected cells' text. You can see a preview before applying the formats to the worksheet, as shown in Figure 5.4.

After making changes to the formats with one or both of these tabs, click OK to apply the changes to the selected cell(s) in the worksheet. You can undo any formatting by choosing Edit, Undo, or pressing Ctrl+Z.

NOTE

If you can no longer Undo the formatting, select the cells that you want to "unformat" and choose Edit, Clear, Formats. The selected cell(s) revert to default formats.

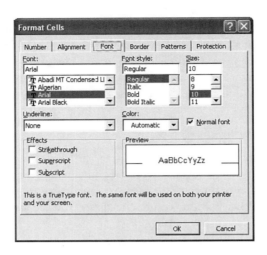

Figure 5.4
Preview font formats with the Font tab's Preview box.

CHANGING THE FONT, POINT SIZE, AND FONT STYLES

The default font in Excel—Arial, 10 points—is an effective generic font. It's available on virtually anyone's computer, and it's highly readable. Although you can format specific cells and cell ranges for visual impact, most users leave the majority of their cells, especially those containing numbers, in this default font. There's nothing wrong with that. But one of the simplest—and fastest—ways to dress up the worksheet and simultaneously draw attention to the more important text and numbers within the sheet is to make subtle changes to the font in certain areas of the worksheet. Fonts and font styles (bold, italic, and so on) can be applied with the Formatting toolbar or the Format Cells dialog box.

CHANGING THE FONT

The fastest way to change the font for a particular cell or range—including noncontiguous ranges—is to select the cell(s), click open the Font box on the Formatting toolbar, and click the font you want. Office 2003 shows each font's appearance (not just the name) in the drop-down list, as shown in Figure 5.5. TrueType fonts are indicated with a double T icon; printer fonts have a printer icon. (For more details on using fonts and printing with Windows, consult your Windows documentation.)

If scrolling the list is too cumbersome, you can type the font's name in the Font box, although this technique works only when you know the font's exact name—if you want the Zurich XBlk BT font, you have to type it just like that. If you don't remember the exact name, you can click the arrow at the end of the Font box and type the first letter of the font you want, to jump to that part of the list. When you select a font in the list, it replaces whatever appears in the Font box.

Font box   Font style

Figure 5.5
The Font list shows
the available fonts
installed on your
computer.

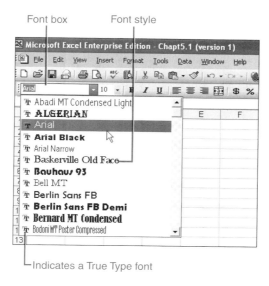

└ Indicates a True Type font

You can control whether to view font styles with their names. Choose Tools, Customize,
click the Options tab, and select or deselect List Font Names in Their Font. If you have a
slower PC, you might find that deselecting this setting will make the Font box work faster.
Because this is an Office setting, changing it in one program changes it for all Office
programs.

SETTING THE POINT SIZE

Measurements in typography are expressed in *picas* and *points*. There are six picas in an inch
and 12 points in a pica, which means that there are 72 points in an inch.

Although many typographical measurements are absolute, font measurement is slippery. The
size of type is measured in points—say, 11-point Times New Roman or 24-point Arial
Black. This is a measurement from the top of an *ascender* to the bottom of a *descender* in the
font. The letter d has an ascender—the *stem* that rises above the *bowl*, or round part, of
the d. The letter g has a descender—that is, the stem that extends below the bowl of the g.
If you superimpose a Times New Roman d over a Times New Roman g, the number of
points between the top of the ascender and the bottom of the descender is the font's point
size. Unfortunately, one 12-point font might not look to be the same size as another 12-
point font. Compare Arial to Times New Roman at the same point size. Arial appears to be
much larger than Times New Roman. That's because your eye determines the "size" by
looking at everything but the ascenders and descenders.

You can specify the desired point size for cells and ranges. The default point size is 10,
which provides decent readability in the default Arial font. However, many users prefer titles
to be larger, footnotes to be relatively tiny, and so on. The Size box, located next to the

5

Font box on the Formatting toolbar, is a drop-down list that you can use to select the point size, or you can just type the desired point size (see Figure 5.6). Typing the point size offers the advantage of being able to specify a point size that isn't included in the list of default point sizes for that font—even in-between point sizes such as 10.5. However, keep in mind that this option isn't useful if your printer can't size the font to that specification.

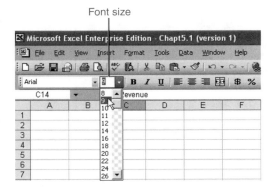

Figure 5.6
Select or type the desired point size.

If you apply a larger point size, Excel automatically adjusts the height of the row to accommodate the new setting. The opposite isn't true, however; applying a smaller point size doesn't automatically reduce the row height unless you apply the point size to the entire row.

ADDING FONT STYLES

Now that you have the right font and point size in place, you might want to apply a *font style* (also called *character styles*) to add emphasis to the text or numbers in the cell. Three choices are reflected on the Formatting toolbar: Bold (**B**), Italic (*I*), or Underline (U). Select the characters or cells to which you want to apply the font style, and click the appropriate buttons.

TIP FROM

Some fonts offer special bold and italic styles that are "true" italics and bolds. Clicking the Bold or Italic buttons causes Windows to create a bold or italic version of the font. True italics and bolds generally look better than their created counterparts. For example, the Franklin Gothic Demi font also came with Franklin Gothic Heavy and Franklin Gothic Book variants. Book is essentially the normal typeface, whereas Demi is bold and Heavy is very bold.

You also can use shortcut keys to apply the font styles. Press Ctrl+B for bold, Ctrl+I for italic, or Ctrl+U for underline. The same shortcut keys toggle to remove the designated font style.

FORMATTING INDIVIDUAL CHARACTERS

Although you most likely will change the font, point size, or character style for entire cells, you can format individual characters, words, numbers, sentences, and so on within a cell. Select the character(s) on the formula bar and apply the formatting as desired.

You also can reverse the formatting for individual characters within a cell. If you have formatted a particular cell as bold, for example, you can make one or more characters "not bold" by selecting those characters and clicking the Bold button to remove the boldfacing.

If you increase the point size for individual characters, Excel adjusts the row height to accommodate the new point size, just as if you had changed the entire cell.

RESETTING EXCEL'S DEFAULT FONT

If you don't like Arial as the default Excel font, or you prefer a larger font (you probably wouldn't want a smaller font for the default), you can change the default setting.

To reset Excel's default font and font size, follow these steps:

1. Choose Tools, Options. The Options dialog box opens.
2. Click the General tab.
3. Adjust the Standard Font setting and/or the Size setting as needed (see Figure 5.7).
4. Click OK to apply the changes.

Figure 5.7
Choose a legible font and an appropriate size as the new default for Excel worksheets.

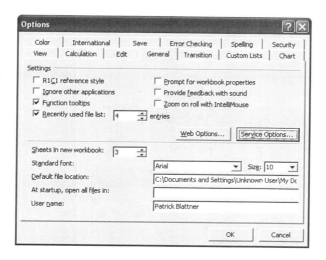

This change doesn't affect any open workbooks (it's not retroactive), and you must restart Excel before the changes can take effect.

You can change the default font for just the active workbook. See "Changing the Default Font for the Active Workbook" in the "Troubleshooting" section at the end of this chapter.

CAUTION

> Make sure you've selected a legible alternative for the default font—one that all users of your workbooks will have on their computers, and that can be read easily when printed, photocopied, and faxed. Also, choose a font that won't clash with any other fonts your organization uses in its letterhead or publications.

WORKING WITH STYLES

Styles are collections of formats, designed to make several formatting changes at once through the application of the style to a cell or range. For example, the Normal style—the default style that's applied to all new Excel content—consists of specific font, alignment, border, pattern, and other settings. To work with styles, choose Format, Style to open the Style dialog box.

EDITING THE DEFAULT STYLES

You can edit the default styles in the current workbook to apply the attributes you want. You might want cells formatted in Currency style to have a different background color, for example, so that they're more noticeable (or less). Changes to styles apply in the current workbook only.

 If you want to change the default styles permanently or create new styles that will apply to new workbooks, see "Creating Permanent Styles" in the "Troubleshooting" section at the end of this chapter.

To edit a style, follow these steps:

1. Choose Format, Style. The Style dialog box appears.
2. In the Style Name list, select the style you want to edit (see Figure 5.8).

Figure 5.8
Select the style to edit.

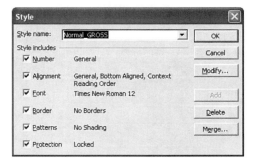

3. In the Style Includes section of the dialog box, turn any of the elements on or off by clicking the check boxes.
4. Click the Modify button to specify the settings for the selected options. This action opens the Format Cells dialog box (refer to Figure 5.4).

5. Using one or more of the six tabs in the Format Cells dialog box, select the new settings for the style.

6. Click OK to close the Format Cells dialog box and return to the Style dialog box.

7. Click OK. Excel immediately updates any cells with that style to reflect the formatting changes.

CREATING AND APPLYING CUSTOM STYLES

If you use Microsoft Word, you might already be comfortable with the process of creating custom styles to use for headings, bulleted lists, and so on. Excel's styles are comparable to those in Word, and offer just as many formatting possibilities. A common use for Excel styles is to create a certain "look" for worksheet titles used for a particular business. For worksheets disseminated outside your division or company, specific design standards might have been set up that require worksheets and charts to look alike. (In such circumstances, custom styles might already have been set up by someone else in your company. See the next section for details on how to combine those styles with yours.)

You create custom styles in either of the following ways:

- Design the style "from scratch" in the Style dialog box using the Format Cells dialog box.

- Select a cell that already contains the formats you want to store in a named style, and use it as an example to establish the settings for the new style.

The methods are almost identical, and are closely related to the technique for editing a default style. Follow these steps:

1. If you're creating a style by example, select a cell that's using the formats you want. If not, skip this step, or select any cells to which you want to apply the new style you're creating.

2. Choose Format, Style to open the Style dialog box.

3. Type a name for the new style in the Style Name box.

4. Select any settings you want in the Style Includes section of the dialog box.

5. Click the Modify button to open the Format Cells dialog box, and make any necessary changes. Then, click OK to return to the Style dialog box.

6. If you want to apply the style immediately to the selected cells, click OK. If you just want to add the style to the list of styles without applying it, click Add. You can then close the dialog box with the Close button, or continue adding styles before you click the Close button.

To apply a style, select the cell(s) you want to format with the style, choose Format, Style, select the style in the Style Name list, and click OK.

The Style toolbar button works like the Font list and the Size list, but you use it to select from a list of styles. You can add the Style list to any toolbar, as described in the section "Modifying Toolbars" in Chapter 27, "Customizing Excel to Fit Your Working Style."

MERGING STYLES FROM ONE WORKBOOK TO ANOTHER

The Merge button in the Style dialog box enables you to select another open workbook and merge any styles from that workbook with those in the active workbook. This feature saves time and effort by enabling you to create or edit styles in one workbook and then use them in other workbooks. For businesses with a standard set of styles, this feature also helps ensure consistency.

Merging the styles from one workbook to another overwrites existing styles with the same name (such as the default Normal style). Excel asks you to confirm this overwrite, but only once—you must either confirm or deny the overwrite for the entire set of styles.

To merge styles, follow these steps:

1. Open the source workbook, containing the styles you want to merge.
2. Open or create the target workbook.
3. In the target workbook, choose Format, Style.
4. Click the Merge button to open the Merge Styles dialog box (see Figure 5.9).

Figure 5.9
Choose another open workbook's styles to merge the styles from the selected workbook. This helps create consistency throughout workbooks and their worksheets.

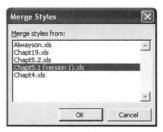

5. In the Merge Styles From list, select the source workbook whose styles you want to merge with the active workbook.
6. Click OK. Excel asks you to confirm (if the styles are different) that you want to merge styles that have the same name. This process will overwrite all existing styles with the same name.
7. Click Yes if you want to overwrite all existing styles with those in the source workbook. Click No if you don't.
8. Click OK or Close to exit the Style dialog box.

FORMATTING TITLES WITH MERGE AND CENTER

The worksheet title is normally the first thing someone notices when viewing a worksheet. The title normally tells the reader what sort of information will be found in the worksheet or what purpose the worksheet serves.

Making the title stand out is important for worksheets that will be published—on paper or on the Web. This chapter has discussed applying various formats to enhance worksheet text, and certainly those formats will be applied to the title. However, to place the title above and across the width of the worksheet is a popular effect, requiring use of Excel's Merge and Center tool. The Merge and Center effect is frequently enough to make titles stand out, even if no other special formatting is applied to the title text.

To center the title across the worksheet, follow these steps:

1. Assuming the title is in cell D3 or a cell to the left of and above the worksheet or a portion thereof, select the title and the blank cells to its right, as shown in Figure 5.10.

2. Click the Merge and Center button on the Formatting toolbar. The cells are merged into one cell, with the title centered across the cell (see Figure 5.11).

D3 is the cell in which the title was typed

Figure 5.10
Select the cells across which you want to center the title. They will be merged into one long cell, with the title centered across it.

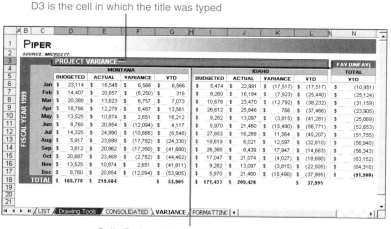

Cells D3:L3 will be merged into one cell

ADJUSTING ALIGNMENT WITHIN CELLS, COLUMNS, AND ROWS

By default, Excel aligns text to the left, and numbers and dates to the right. You can change the alignment of cell content by changing the number formats for numeric data, or by selecting a new alignment.

Why would you change cell alignment? The motivation is normally aesthetic, as changing alignment helps to change the worksheet's overall appearance, and can help to set certain cells apart, such as column headings.

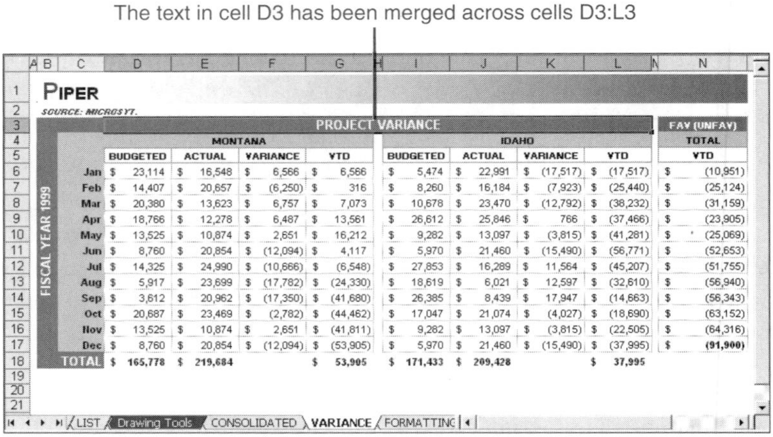

The text in cell D3 has been merged across cells D3:L3

Figure 5.11
Keep the title visually separate from the rest of the worksheet content through the use of Merge and Center.

	MONTANA				IDAHO				FAV (UNFAV) TOTAL
	BUDGETED	ACTUAL	VARIANCE	YTD	BUDGETED	ACTUAL	VARIANCE	YTD	YTD
Jan	$ 23,114	$ 16,548	$ 6,566	$ 6,566	$ 5,474	$ 22,991	$ (17,517)	$ (17,517)	$ (10,951)
Feb	$ 14,407	$ 20,657	$ (6,250)	$ 316	$ 8,260	$ 16,184	$ (7,923)	$ (25,440)	$ (25,124)
Mar	$ 20,380	$ 13,623	$ 6,757	$ 7,073	$ 10,678	$ 23,470	$ (12,792)	$ (38,232)	$ (31,159)
Apr	$ 18,766	$ 12,278	$ 6,487	$ 13,561	$ 26,612	$ 25,846	$ 766	$ (37,466)	$ (23,905)
May	$ 13,525	$ 10,874	$ 2,651	$ 16,212	$ 9,282	$ 13,097	$ (3,815)	$ (41,281)	$ (25,069)
Jun	$ 8,760	$ 20,854	$ (12,094)	$ 4,117	$ 5,970	$ 21,460	$ (15,490)	$ (56,771)	$ (52,653)
Jul	$ 14,325	$ 24,990	$ (10,666)	$ (6,548)	$ 27,853	$ 16,289	$ 11,564	$ (45,207)	$ (51,755)
Aug	$ 5,917	$ 23,699	$ (17,782)	$ (24,330)	$ 18,619	$ 6,021	$ 12,597	$ (32,610)	$ (56,940)
Sep	$ 3,612	$ 20,962	$ (17,350)	$ (41,680)	$ 26,385	$ 8,439	$ 17,947	$ (14,663)	$ (56,343)
Oct	$ 20,687	$ 23,469	$ (2,782)	$ (44,462)	$ 17,047	$ 21,074	$ (4,027)	$ (18,690)	$ (63,152)
Nov	$ 13,525	$ 10,874	$ 2,651	$ (41,811)	$ 9,262	$ 13,097	$ (3,815)	$ (22,505)	$ (64,316)
Dec	$ 8,760	$ 20,854	$ (12,094)	$ (53,905)	$ 5,970	$ 21,460	$ (15,490)	$ (37,995)	**$ (91,900)**
TOTAL	**$ 165,778**	**$ 219,684**		**$ 53,905**	**$ 171,433**	**$ 209,428**		**$ 37,995**	

PIPER — SOURCE: MICROSYT. — PROJECT VARIANCE — FISCAL YEAR 1999

LIST / Drawing Tools / CONSOLIDATED \ VARIANCE / FORMATTING

ALIGNING CELL CONTENT

To change the alignment of a single cell or any range of selected cells, you can use the Formatting toolbar or the Format Cells dialog box. First do one of the following: choose Format, Cells; right-click the cell or range and choose Format Cells; or press Ctrl+1. Then click the Alignment tab (refer to Figure 5.4). The dialog box gives you more options for changing the cells' alignment, as described in the following list:

- **Horizontal**—This option in the Format Cells dialog box gives you choices ranging from General (meaning that alignment will be dictated by the type of content—text will be left-aligned, numbers and dates right-aligned) to Center Across Selection.

TIP FROM

> Center Across Selection is nearly the equivalent of the Merge and Center button on the Formatting toolbar, but not quite. If you use Merge and Center to place a title across A1:A5, clicking A1 selects the entire merged "cell" A1:A5. If you use Center Across Selection, clicking A1 just selects A1. Center Across Selection doesn't merge the cells; it just visually moves the title across the selection. The text remains in the first cell.

- **Vertical**—This setting enables you to align cell content to the top, middle, or bottom of a cell. By default, cells are bottom-aligned.

You can use the Decrease Indent and Increase Indent buttons to change the horizontal position of cell content within the cell. Before or after entering content into the active cell, click the Increase Indent button to move the content to the right, in small increments. To move the content to the left, click the Decrease Indent button.

ROTATING AND WRAPPING TEXT

The Alignment tab in the Format Cells dialog box also gives you access to tools for rotating text to any angle you need, and for choosing whether or not text will wrap in a cell.

Used primarily for column headings, the Orientation feature enables you to drag the wand to any position on the semicircle or enter a specific number of degrees of rotation for the text. However, some fonts don't look very good when rotated, as Figure 5.12 shows. When you rotate text, be sure it's readable.

Figure 5.12
Formats and text apply to angled formats.

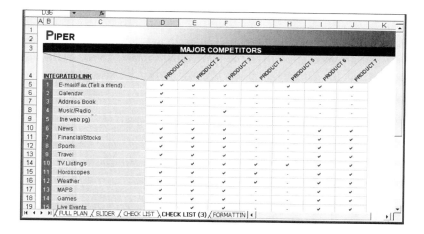

Wrapping text is frequently a better option than rotating it when you want it to fit a particular column width. Choosing Wrap Text enables you to type a phrase, sentence, paragraph, or more into a cell and have it wrap within the cell's current width. The cell grows taller to accommodate the wrapping text. You can also force Excel to wrap the text in the cell as you type—press Alt+Enter at the point where you would like the text to wrap onto the next line. This is handy when you want line breaks to occur at specific points. In addition, you can stack text by typing the first word or number and then pressing Alt+Return.

The Shrink to Fit and Merge Cells options are tools that give you more control over text placement. Shrink to Fit makes the text (or numbers) reduce in point size so that it fits in the cell's current dimensions. (Note that this can sometimes make cell entries tiny and unreadable.)

Use Merge Cells to make one large cell out of two or more contiguous cells. You can do this before or after the selected cells have content.

Wrapping text has particular advantages when it comes to column headings in lists. Many users place two or three line/word headings (for example, Total Sales) in separate cells. Doing so prevents Excel from correctly selecting a list when it comes to their list management features (such as sorting, filtering, subtotaling, and using PivotTables). Placing the headings on multiple lines within one cell allows those features to work correctly.

TIP FROM

Like fonts, alignment effects should be kept to a minimum. Using too many different alignments in a single sheet can be distracting for the reader.

APPLYING AND DRAWING BORDERS AND SHADING

You can apply borders from the Format Cells dialog box, which you find by choosing Cells from the Format menu and clicking the Borders tab. Another method is involves clicking the downward pointing arrow to the right of the Borders button on the Formatting toolbar and selecting a border to apply from those shown. You can also draw borders with the new Draw Borders command from the Formatting toolbar. To access the Draw Borders command, select the Borders drop-down arrow and click Draw Borders.

Notice Figure 5.13, when the worksheet is filled with white to create a canvas affect (or when gridlines are disabled), Excel plots the corners of each cell when the Draw Borders command is selected. When you select the Draw Borders command, the cursor turns into a pencil and allows you to apply borders one click at a time or by holding down the left mouse button, you can draw borders around several cells at once. Briefly, you turn off the borders by clicking the Draw Border button or by pressing the Esc key. Using borders and/or shading in worksheets is an effective method for enhancing and improving a worksheet's appearance and highlighting important information.

To erase the lines drawn, choose the Erase button and click and drag over the lines you want to erase.

Figure 5.14 shows a worksheet with borders and shading applied for both cosmetic and functional reasons.

Don't have a color printer? It's still worthwhile to add color to worksheets. Whether you're publishing the worksheet to the Web or sending it to another user to view onscreen, the use of color is never wasted. Even a black-and-white printout is enhanced by the use of color, as the colors are translated into subtly varying shades of gray. Also, if you want to use color but have your printer always print in black and white, you can turn the Black and White feature off on by selecting File, Page Setup and clicking the Sheet tab.

USING BORDERS EFFECTIVELY

By default, worksheet gridlines don't print. This means that borders added to cells in a worksheet are the only lines that appear on the hard copy. You print Excel's gridlines using the Gridlines option on the Sheet tab of the Page Setup dialog (File, Page Setup), but that will print all the gridlines for the entire print range. With proper use of borders, your printouts will be much cleaner and more effective.

What purpose do borders serve? Borders draw attention and create separations.

Figure 5.13
Use the Draw Borders tool from the Formatting toolbar to quickly draw borders on the worksheet.

Click down arrow to access Draw Borders tool

The Draw Borders command button

Cell plotting dots

Pencil cursor

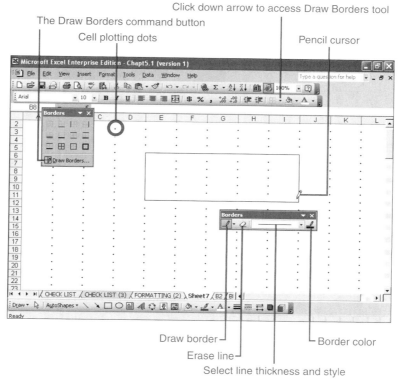

Draw border

Erase line

Select line thickness and style

Border color

Figure 5.14
Use borders and shading to draw attention to specific numbers or to create a barrier between sections in a worksheet.

White borders

Shaded cells

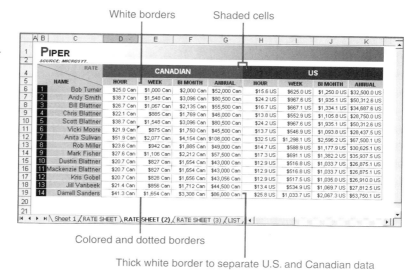

Colored and dotted borders

Thick white border to separate U.S. and Canadian data

5

To apply quick borders instead of drawing them, you can use the Borders button on the Formatting toolbar. Follow these steps:

1. Select the cell or cells to which you want to apply a border.
2. Click the down-arrow button to the right of the Borders button to display a drop-down palette of border styles.
3. Choose one of the 12 border options from the Borders palette.

   Notice that the button face changes to display the border style you selected. If you make another selection in the worksheet and click the button (instead of clicking the down arrow to display the list), Excel applies the border style shown on the button face to the new selection.

The Borders button applies thick, thin, or double lines to any cell or group of cells you select. If you want more variety, use the Borders tab in the Format Cells dialog box, as described in the following steps:

1. Select the cell or range of cells to be bordered.
2. Choose Format, Cells or right-click the range and choose Format Cells to display the Format Cells dialog box.
3. Click the Border tab (see Figure 5.15).

Click border buttons or inside the border box to add borders

Figure 5.15
The Border box serves as a tool for previewing borders as well as applying them.

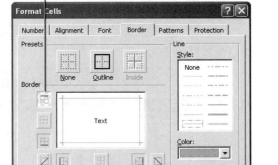

4. Choose a line style and, if you want, a color for the borders.
5. In the Border box, click the sides around the word *Text* to indicate on which side of the selected cell(s) you want borders applied, or click the buttons that surround the box to choose which sides to border. If you have multiple cells selected, as in Figure 5.17, the

word *Text* appears twice, and you can click the Inside button or click between the two words to insert borders between cells. You can also access additional Border styles and color using the Line Style and Line Color buttons on the Draw Borders toolbar.

6. Click OK to apply the border(s) to the selected cell(s).

TIP FROM

> To remove borders, select the cell(s), click the Borders button, and select the No Border option in the upper-left corner of the palette. Or use the Eraser from the Borders toolbar.

USING COLORS, PATTERNS, AND TEXTURED FILLS

Shading cells can mean more than simply applying a shade of gray behind the cell content. Excel gives you 56 different solid colors and 18 different pattern fills to add visual interest and excitement to your worksheets.

To apply colors and patterns to selected cells, follow these steps:

1. Select the cell(s) and choose Format, Cells.
2. Click the Patterns tab (see Figure 5.16).

Figure 5.16
Choose a color, a pattern, or both, and preview the selection in the Sample window.

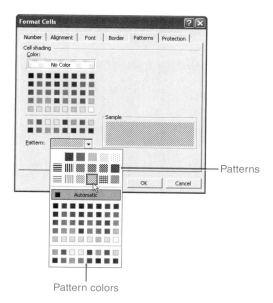

3. To add color, click a solid color from the Color palette.
4. If desired, open the Pattern list box and choose a pattern. You can combine color and pattern by choosing a color and then a pattern, or vice versa.

> If you choose both a color and a pattern, the pattern will appear in black on top of the
> selected color. You can make a number of nice combinations by experimenting. The pat-
> tern can be a color other than black. For example, to add a light blue fill with a light yel-
> low checkered pattern, you would simply choose a light blue color on the color palette.
> Then, on the Pattern drop-down, choose a light yellow color. Access the Pattern drop-
> down again and choose one of the checkered patterns (such as Thin Horizontal
> Crosshatch), and then click OK.

5. Click OK to apply the color and/or pattern to the selection.

To apply a fill color quickly, select the cell or cells to be colored, and click the Fill Color
button on the Formatting toolbar. Choose one of the 40 colors on the palette.

To remove both fill color and pattern, select the cell(s), open the Fill Color list, and choose
No Fill on the palette. To remove one or the other, open the Format Cells dialog box, click
the Patterns tab, and click No Color in the Color list or Solid in the Pattern list.

> If you're using Excel to create a fill-in form, using patterns in empty cells can tell the user
> not to use those cells, or create a visually interesting separation between parts of the
> form.

USING AUTOFORMAT TO ENHANCE YOUR WORKSHEETS

If you would rather not spend your time selecting fonts and choosing when and where to
apply shading and borders, let Excel make these choices for you. Excel's *AutoFormat* feature
offers a series of preformatted effects that you can apply to any range of cells within a
worksheet. The options button on the AutoFormat dialog box also offers formats that apply
to the following: Number, Border, Font, Patterns, Alignment, and Width/Height.

To use AutoFormat, follow these steps:

1. Select the range of cells you want to format, keeping the following rules in mind:
   - You must have two or more contiguous cells selected to use AutoFormat.
   - AutoFormat can't be applied to multiple ranges.

2. Choose Format, AutoFormat.

3. Select a format from the list of samples (see Figure 5.17).

4. Clicking the Options button displays a list of the formats that will be applied with the
   selected AutoFormat. You can deselect any of the options you don't want AutoFormat
   to apply.

5. Click OK.

To select an AutoFormat sample, click it

Figure 5.17
By default, the AutoFormat's fonts, sizing, shading, and borders will be applied as shown in the sample.

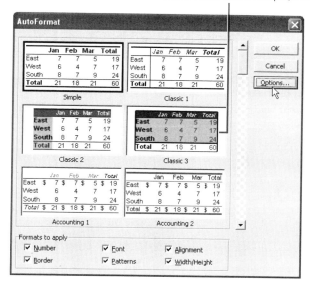

CAUTION

If you've already sized columns and rows before using AutoFormat, deselect the Width/Height option. AutoFormat sizes the columns and rows to fit the widest/tallest entry, which might result in a cramped or crowded look for the worksheet.

In some cases, the size and content of the selected range and the AutoFormat you chose don't match—for example, a border might be applied indicating a total where you don't have one. If this occurs, remove the offending formatting effect or use Undo to remove the AutoFormat. At this point, you can reapply the AutoFormat, and choose not to apply the borders (or whatever format didn't work well with the selected cells).

NOTE

If you find that you're turning off more than one or two of the formats to apply, this can be an indication that AutoFormat isn't appropriate for the currently selected range. Although AutoFormat is a timesaver, it might not be the best formatting solution in every situation.

USING THE DRAWING TOOLBAR

The Drawing toolbar enables you to add shapes, lines, text boxes, artistic text, business strategy diagrams, and clip art to your Office documents and manipulate them in terms of their size, placement, and colors. Table 5.2 explains the buttons.

TABLE 5.2 THE DRAWING TOOLBAR

Button	Name	Button Function
Draw ▾	Draw	Click this button to display a menu of commands that enable you to manipulate the placement of and relationship between your drawn objects.
	Select Objects	Use this arrow tool to click drawn objects. Using this tool tells Excel that you're dealing with your drawn objects and not the worksheet's cell content.
AutoShapes ▾	AutoShapes	Click this button to display a list of AutoShape categories, such as Basic Shapes and Flowchart. From these categories, choose shapes from a palette of drawing tools.
	Line	Use this tool to draw straight lines of any length. You can later format the lines to varying lengths and styles, as well as add arrowheads to make the line point to something.
	Arrow	If you know your line will be an arrow, draw one using this tool. You can later select arrowheads for one or both ends of the line.
	Rectangle	This tool enables you to draw simple rectangles and squares.
	Oval	Draw elliptical shapes and true circles with this tool.
	Text Box	When you need a text object that can be placed on top of your cells anywhere on the worksheet, use this tool to create the box and type the text.
	Insert WordArt	Create artistic text headlines and banners with this tool. The WordArt program, with its own toolbars and menus, opens to give you the ability to create text objects with a wide variety of color, shape, and fill options.
	Insert Diagram or Org chart	Creates org chart layouts and business strategy diagrams.
	Insert Clip Art	Click this button to view and insert objects from a categorized list of clip-art images that were installed with Office XP. The Office XP CD also contains extra clip-art images that you can add as needed—navigate to your CD-ROM drive to access them.
	Picture From File	Click this button to view and insert pictures from your personal picture files.
	Fill Color	Choose from a palette of solid colors to fill your drawn shape or a range of cells on a worksheet.

5

Button	Name	Button Function
	Line Color	Click the button to display a palette of colors that you can use to color your line, arrow, or the outline of a shape.
	Font Color	Apply a color to a shape's text or text within your worksheet cells.
	Line Style	Choose from various line weights and styles for double and triple lines.
	Dash Style	If you want your line to be dashed, dotted, or a combination thereof, click this button and select a style from the palette.
	Arrow Style	Turn a simple line into an arrow or change the arrowheads on your existing arrow line. Choose from 10 styles.
	Shadow Style	Choose from 20 shadow settings, each with a different light source and angle. Applying a shadow gives your object depth, and it can be applied to shapes or lines.
	3D Style	Apply up to 20 3D effects to your shapes. Unlike a shadow, which merely repeats the object in a flat 2D state behind the original, 3D settings add sides and depth to your object, and shade the sides for a true 3D effect.

You can display the Drawing toolbar by right-clicking any existing toolbar and choosing Drawing from the list, or by choosing View, Toolbars, Drawing.

TIP FROM

You can turn your Drawing toolbar (or any toolbar, for that matter) into a floating toolbar by dragging it from the edge of the window onto your worksheet area. Click the left edge of the toolbar and drag the entire toolbar out onto the worksheet. After you release your mouse, the toolbar appears with its own title bar, which you can use to move the floating toolbar anywhere you want onscreen.

5

When using the Drawing toolbar, keep the following concepts in mind:

- The Drawing toolbar's drawing tools (Line, Arrow, Rectangle, Oval, and all the AutoShapes) work by clicking them and then drawing the associated shape or line by dragging across the worksheet to create a custom size shape or line. For shapes other than lines, you can quickly create a shape without default size by clicking once on the worksheet.

- Each time you click and then use a drawing tool, the tool turns off as soon as the object is created. To draw another one, you must reclick the tool.

To avoid having to reclick a drawing tool to draw another shape, double-click the drawing tool (Line, Arrow, Rectangle, Oval), and you can draw an infinite number of objects with that tool. To turn off the tool, click it again or press the Esc key.

- Buttons with a down arrow (triangle) display a palette or menu when you click the down arrow.

- In the case of the Fill, Line, and Font Color tools, clicking the button itself will apply the color displayed on the button to the selected object. The button face changes to show any new color you select from the palette.

- The Line, Dash, and Arrow style tools display a palette although there is no triangle on/next to the button (see Figure 5.18).

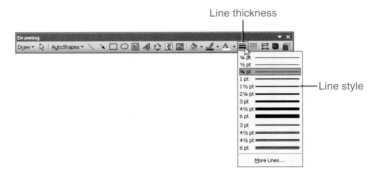

Figure 5.18
Choose the line thickness from the palette that appears when you click the button. The thickness will apply to the selected object.

- The Draw and AutoShapes buttons display a menu and submenus/palettes as opposed to performing a task or applying a format (see Figure 5.19).

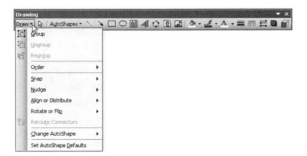

Figure 5.19
Choose a Draw command to affect the placement of your drawn objects or their relationship to other shapes and lines.

Drawn objects float over the worksheet content. Be careful to place them so they don't obscure something important—they're intended to enhance your worksheet, not compete with it.

ORDERING, GROUPING, MOVING, AND RESIZING DRAWN OBJECTS

After you draw lines and shapes on your worksheet, you'll probably want to move them around a bit so they line up just right, adjust their size, and even resolve unintended overlap of objects. Several techniques will help you.

CHANGING THE ORDER OF OVERLAPPING DRAWN OBJECTS

The objects you draw, if overlapping, will stack in the order in which they were drawn—first drawn on the bottom, last drawn on the top. Because you might not draw things in the order you need them to appear in overlapped groupings, you might want to change this order.

To restack your overlapping objects, follow these steps:

1. Click the object that you want to move up or down in the stack of drawn objects.

2. Choose Draw, Order; then select the command that matches your needs—moving the item to the very top or bottom, or moving it up or down one layer in the stack. Your choices are

   - **Bring to Front**—Takes the object from wherever it is in the stack and puts it above all other objects on the worksheet. This, of course, affects only items currently on top of the object you're adjusting.

   - **Send to Back**—Places the selected object on the bottom layer of all drawn objects, but it remains above the worksheet content layer.

   - **Bring Forward**—To move items one layer at a time (from fourth in the stack to third, for example), choose this command.

   - **Send Backward**—Move the selected object down toward the bottom, one layer at a time.

3. The object remains selected in its new stacking order, as Figure 5.20 shows. If moving one layer at a time (Bring Forward or Send Backward), you can repeat the command until the object is where it belongs.

Figure 5.20
Selecting the white square and choosing Draw, Order, Bring Forward places it on top of the rectangle.

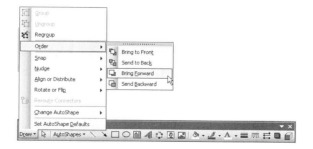

GROUPING DRAWN SHAPES AND LINES

After you've painstakingly aligned two or more objects in relation to one another, you don't want to accidentally move one of the objects out of place, changing its relative position. Or, perhaps you want to move the objects, but you want to move them as a group, so their relative positions remain unchanged. To accomplish this, the objects must be selected and grouped, so that Excel sees them as one unit.

To group two or more drawn shapes and/or lines on your worksheet, follow these steps:

1. Click the first item in your group (the order in which you click the items is immaterial).

2. Press and hold the Ctrl or Shift key.

3. One at a time (with the Shift key still pressed), click the other objects you want to include in the group. When the entire group of objects is selected (handles appear around each one of them, as shown in Figure 5.21), choose Draw, Group.

Select each object

Figure 5.21
As you build your group, handles appear on or around each selected item.

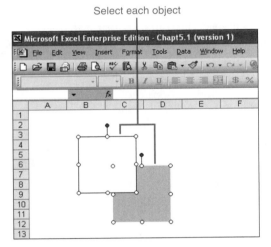

After it's grouped, the entire group of items has one set of handles, as shown in Figure 5.22.

NOTE

Grouping is not the same as temporarily selecting multiple items for quick recoloring, resizing, or moving. Grouped objects remain a unit, even after you deselect them. If you click again on any item in the group, the entire group is selected.

You can ungroup your items at any time by selecting the group (click any one item in the group) and choosing Draw, Ungroup. Use the Regroup command to put any one selected item back in a group with the items with which it was formerly grouped.

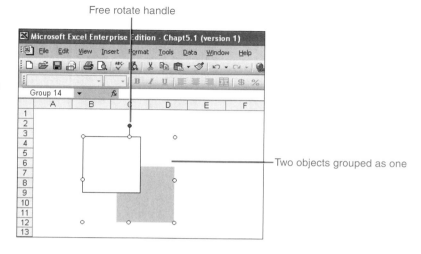

Figure 5.22
One set of eight handles surrounds the entire group, even if the items in the group are scattered around a large area of the worksheet.

COMBINING DRAWING TOOLS WITH CHARTS AND WORKSHEETS

Understanding how and when to use tools, as well as how to combine tools to create dramatic effects, can enhance your charts, worksheets, and tables. The difficulty is that no set rule exists to help you decide which tools to combine, or even how to combine them. This chapter attempts to show you some ideas on how to effectively combine tools to enhance your information. Start by picking up magazines, newspapers, and periodicals to get ideas for presentations, and then visualize which tools it would take to re-create the presentation shown in the literature.

For the most part, there are few presentations that you can't re-create with all the tools available in Excel. The drawing tools, in particular, offer a wide variety of opportunities for improving your charts and worksheets—making them more understandable and simultaneously more interesting. The following sections of this chapter take off from those basics, combining drawing objects in unique and sometimes unexpected ways to give your worksheets and charts a polished look.

LAYING A CHART ON A BEVEL

You can lay charts on bevels to give them a "raised-off-the-surface" look. The next time you look through one of the top financial publications, chances are you'll see this technique in use. It works especially well for onscreen presentations, but also can look great in print. Notice that in Figure 5.23 the chart is actually lying on the bevel and the chart area is filled with the same fill as the background of the sheet. The plot area is formatted white.

Figure 5.23
Lay the chart on a bevel object to give the chart a "raised-off-the-surface" appearance.

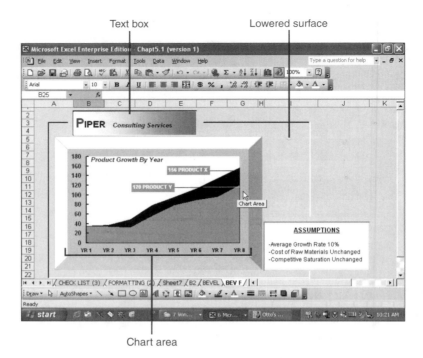

Text box   Lowered surface

Chart area

To lay a chart on a bevel, perform the following steps:

AutoShapes ▾

1. On the Drawing toolbar, click the AutoShapes button, select Basic Shapes, and click the Bevel tool (fourth row, second from the right), as shown in Figure 5.24.

2. Drag the bevel object to size it so that its raised portion approximately matches the height and width of the chart (see Figure 5.25).

Figure 5.24
The bevel is found on the AutoShapes button under Basic Shapes.

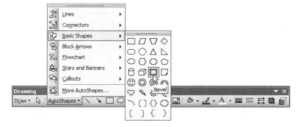

3. Adjust the degree of the beveling (the raised portion of the bevel object), if desired, by dragging the yellow sizing handle.

4. Drag the chart over the surface of the bevel. (If necessary, right-click the bevel and select Order, Send to Back to bring the chart to the front.)

5. Drag the chart to fit the size of the surface of the top of the bevel, as shown in Figure 5.26.

Size the raised area of the bevel with this handle

Figure 5.25
Size the bevel to an adequate size for the chart.

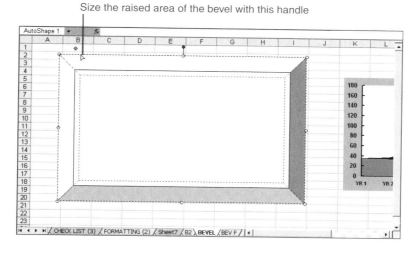

Size the chart to fit the bevel

Figure 5.26
Lay the chart on the bevel and drag the chart size to fit the top surface so that the lines and corners meet.

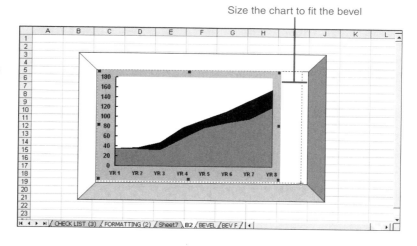

5

6. Format the chart area as gray.

7. Select and format the plot area as white.

8. Select the entire worksheet by clicking the Select All button in the upper-left corner of the worksheet frame.

9. Apply a light-gray fill.

PRINTING A WORKSHEET

Although many worksheets will be viewed onscreen, the need to create tangible evidence of your spreadsheet content is undeniable. It's important to document your work as a backup, as well as for people with whom you share your work who might be without the use of or access to a computer. Some users find it easier to edit a worksheet on paper than onscreen, making notes and drawing on the worksheet to indicate changes in content, placement, and formatting. Printed worksheets also are handy for carrying to meetings, especially if you need to hand out copies to several people.

Printing your worksheet can be as simple as a click of a button, or it can be more complex, depending on what you want to print and how much control you want to have over the content and appearance of your printout. Excel gives you the tools for either approach, most of which can be accessed from within the Print dialog box.

To print a single copy your active worksheet immediately, with standard Print options, click the Print button on the Standard toolbar.

To set Print options such as number of copies or which pages to print, choose File, Print. The Print dialog box opens, as shown in Figure 5.27.

Figure 5.27
Use the Print dialog box to choose the printer, which pages, and the number of copies you want in your printout.

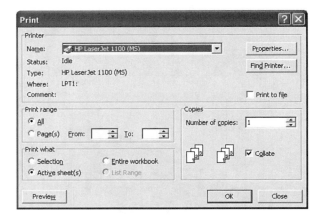

TIP

You can also invoke the print dialog box by pressing Ctrl+P.

The Print dialog box both gives and asks for information. It is divided into the following four main sections:

- **Printer**—Set the default or currently selected printer that will generate your print job. You can choose an alternate printer as needed.

    The selected printer's properties—its settings, options, and capabilities—are available through the Properties button found in the Printer section of the Print dialog box.

- **Print Range**—Choose to print all pages of your worksheet or a select few.

- **Print What**—A powerful section of the Print dialog box, this enables you to print the Active Sheet or Sheets (if you've grouped two or more sheets) or print the Entire

Workbook. You also can print just a Selection, a single cell or a range of cells from within the active sheet, or a selected chart.

- **Copies**—Choose the Number of Copies of the selected pages, sheets, or workbook you'll need. By default, Collate is turned on, if your printer supports this feature. In the case of printouts consisting of two or more sets of the selected pages, you'll want to leave it on. Collate prints a document in its entirety before it prints the next copy of a document; if you clear the Collate check box, Excel prints the selected Number of copies of each page, and you'll have to collate the separate pages into complete document sets by hand.

TIP FROM

> If you forgot to preview your worksheet before issuing the Print command, you can click the Preview button in the Print dialog box. To find out more about previewing before printing, see the section "Previewing the Print Job" in this chapter.

Detailed coverage of all the options found in the Print dialog box is provided throughout this chapter.

SELECTING A PRINTER

If you're on a network and have physical access through the network to more than one printer, you can choose an alternate printer before you begin your print job. If you're on a standalone computer but have more than one printer, you also can change printers before your printout is created.

To change printers, click the Name drop-down arrow in the Print dialog box to display a list of printers accessed by your computer and choose a different printer from the list.

You can click the Print to File check box in the Printer section of the Print dialog box to create a print job in the form of a computer file—the file then can be run through Windows Explorer, My Computer, or the Run command on the Start menu. By running the file, you will send the print job to the printer selected when the file was created. You needn't have Excel open to run the file.

TIP FROM

> Be sure you've previewed and set up your worksheet to print exactly the way you want it to before you print it to a file, because when you print the file later, you won't have the opportunity to preview it or change print settings.

CHOOSING THE PRINT RANGE

Don't confuse print range with print area, which will be covered later in this chapter. A *print range* refers to the pages within your worksheet that will be printed—the physical pages, determined by page breaks (both naturally occurring and forced by the user) within the worksheet content. The *print area* is a manually defined range of cells that you select and designate as a range to be divided into pages and printed. Setting a print area is done before you use the Print dialog box, and is discussed in greater detail later in this chapter.

TIP FROM

> To quickly print a specific range of cells, select the range in the worksheet, and then click File, Print. In the Print dialog box, under Print What, click the Selection option, and then click OK.

Your print range choices are All or Page(s), the latter requiring a range (From and To) of page numbers be entered. To print a single page, enter that page number in both the From and To boxes. If you leave the default choice All selected, all the pages in defined print areas in the active worksheet will be printed; if you haven't defined print areas, all data in the active worksheet will be printed, including any empty rows and columns between ranges of data.

After you've set a Print range and any other options you want, send the file to the printer by clicking OK.

PREVIEWING THE PRINT JOB

What if you don't know how your worksheet has been broken into pages? Although there are onscreen indications of page breaks, it can be hard to tell precisely where an integral section of information falls (see Figure 5.28). Excel's Print Preview feature lets you check your worksheet over before committing it to paper.

Figure 5.28
Look for dashed vertical and/or horizontal lines on your worksheet, indicating page breaks.

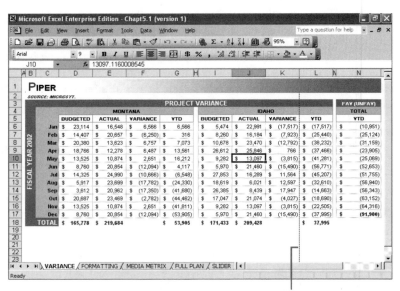

Page break line

Other good reasons for previewing before printing are to check page headers and footers (be sure they're up to date and correct, and not overlapping the data area), and to make sure all the data is visible. Occasionally, numbers that are visible on your screen will be slightly too wide for the column on a printed page, and will print as ###### (before you waste time and paper, you can widen the column until all the numbers are displayed in Print Preview).

To see what your printed page will look like, choose File, Print Preview, or click the Print Preview button on the Standard toolbar. The Print Preview window shows you a small view of your first page, and a set of text buttons, as shown in Figure 5.29.

Figure 5.29
A bird's-eye view of your worksheet through Print Preview makes it easier to see what changes you need to make before printing.

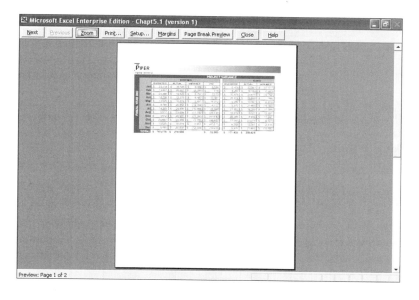

Use the Print Preview toolbar buttons to view subsequent and previous pages in your worksheet, and to alter the layout and appearance of your printout:

- **Next/Previous**—Use these buttons to move from page to page within your Preview.
- **Zoom**—If you need to be able to read your worksheet text, click the Zoom button to see a 100% view of your page. (Clicking the Zoom button is the same as clicking the page with your mouse, which looks like a small magnifying glass when hovering over the page.)
- **Print**—The Print button sends the document directly to the printer; if you access Print Preview from the File menu, clicking this option sends you to the Print dialog.
- **Setup**—This button opens the Page Setup dialog box (discussed later in this chapter).
- **Margins**—This button displays margin lines and column markers. You can use the mouse to quickly change margin and column widths by dragging the lines and markers.

> **NOTE**
>
> There are two sets of margins on your worksheet—the inner set are for the worksheet content, and the outer set (at the top and bottom) define the distance of your header and/or footer from the edge of the paper.

- **Page Break Preview**—To see and adjust how your page breaks were applied, click this button. This topic is covered in detail in the next section.
- **Close**—Click this button to return to your worksheet.
- **Help**—Click this button to access Print Preview–related help.

> **TIP FROM**
>
> Always look at a preview of your worksheet before printing—you'll save paper by not printing things you don't want, and you'll save time by spotting and fixing problems before committing them to paper.

USING PAGE BREAK PREVIEW

As the data in your worksheet accumulates, it can exceed the size of a single page. The space allocated to a single page is determined by the size of your paper and the margins set within that page. With the break preview, you can drag the line to set the page breaks.

Page Break Preview gives you a big overview of how your worksheet breaks into pages. To enter Page Break Preview, choose View, Page Break Preview. Notice the page break preview in Figure 5.30.

Figure 5.30
Page Break Preview shows that this worksheet is not ready to be printed, because the pages break the Idaho side of the table in half (the pages should break cleanly between the tables).

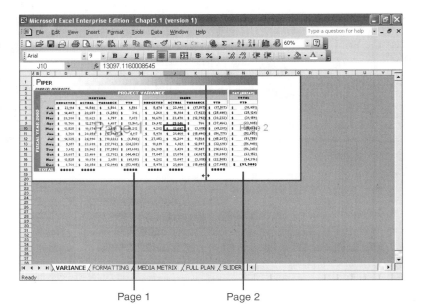

Page 1   Page 2

TIP FROM

You also can see a Page Break Preview by clicking the Page Break Preview button in the standard Print Preview window of your worksheet.

To use Page Break Preview to adjust your page breaks, follow these steps:

1. Choose View, Page Break Preview. Page breaks appear onscreen as blue lines, running horizontally and vertically in the worksheet.

2. Point to the page break that you want to adjust—you can adjust breaks side-to-side or up-and-down.

3. When your mouse pointer turns into a two-headed arrow, click and drag the page break borders to the desired location. Automatic page breaks (those that Excel sets using page margins) are broken blue lines; manual page breaks (those that you set) are solid blue lines.

4. Choose View, Normal to return to your worksheet.

CAUTION

If you drag any of the page breaks beyond the page margins while using Page Break Preview, Excel accommodates you by shrinking the printed text so that everything you want to print on a single page will be printed on a single page. This is a quick and convenient way to adjust page *scaling*, which is covered later in this chapter.

WORKING WITH PAGE SETUP OPTIONS

After you've created and formatted your worksheet, you'll need to set up the printed pages so they'll resemble what you created onscreen. To set ground rules for the layout, content, and output of your printed pages, click File, Page Setup to open the Page Setup dialog box.

TIP FROM

If you're looking at the pages in Print Preview and decide to change the page setup, click the Setup button on the Print Preview toolbar to open the Page Setup dialog box.

In the Page Setup dialog box, you'll find these four tabs:

- **Page**—Adjust the orientation, scaling, paper size, and print quality of your printed output (see Figure 5.31).
- **Margins**—Although you can adjust them manually in Print Preview, this tab enables you to enter specific measurements for your margins (if you want margins identical side-to-side, it's easier to set them by measurement than by eye). You also can adjust your header and footer margins, and center the entire worksheet on the page both horizontally and vertically.

Figure 5.31
Choose from four areas to control and adjust the appearance of your worksheet, both onscreen and on paper.

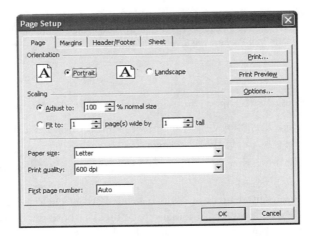

- **Header/Footer**—Click this tab to enter text or automatic entries into the header and/or footer of your worksheet printout.
- **Sheet**—This tab's settings enable you to choose a specific Print Area, set Print Titles for multiple-page worksheets, and choose the worksheet features (gridlines, column/row headings) that will be included in your printout.

WORKING WITH ORIENTATION

Your worksheet orientation determines how your worksheet content will be applied to the paper. By default, your worksheet orientation is 8.5×11 inches and Portrait. If your worksheet, or the portion of it you want to print, is wider than it is long, you can switch to Landscape orientation by clicking the Landscape option under Orientation.

TIP FROM

Sometimes, a switch to Landscape orientation doesn't create enough width for your worksheet. Consider using legal-size paper for 14 inches of printed width, scaling the worksheet down to fit on a single page, or reducing the left and right margins.

SCALING THE PRINTOUT

Another method of controlling the printed output of your worksheet is *scaling*. By scaling back, or shrinking, the size of your worksheet content—text, numbers, graphics—more of the worksheet fits on a page, thus reducing the number of pages in the entire printout. Reducing the number of pages, especially if it keeps as much of the worksheet as possible on one page, makes your printout easier to read. The downside to scaling down is that data on the page becomes smaller and might be more difficult to read.

To change the scale of your worksheet pages, follow these steps:

1. Choose File, Page Setup.

2. On the Page tab choose one of the following two scaling options:

    • **Adjust the percentage**—Use the spin box arrows or type a percentage in the Adjust to box to increase or decrease the percentage of original. For example, reducing the number to 75% will give you 25% more worksheet on the page.

    • **Fit to a specific number of pages**—Your worksheet's pagination is based on the width and height of the worksheet. Choose how many pages wide and tall your printout will be. This is usually the most practical option—decide how many pages you want, and let Excel figure out the scale. If you type one value and leave the other blank, Excel will work it out for you. For example, if you know you want to constrain the printout to 1 page wide but you don't know how many pages tall this would make the printout, just set the 1 page wide option and delete the entry in the tall box—then Excel will work out how many pages tall this will be.

3. If you're finished setting up the page, click OK to close the Page Setup dialog box, or click Print to open the Print dialog box.

TIP FROM

Before adjusting your page scaling, it's a good idea to preview your worksheet with Print Preview so that you can see the current pagination, especially when using the Fit To option. Fit To causes Excel to squeeze the worksheet into the specified number of pages, potentially resulting in print so tiny that you'll want to change the settings immediately.

CHOOSING A PAPER SIZE

The default paper size for your worksheets is letter size, 8.5×11 inches. Excel gives you additional choices, including envelope sizes, on the Page tab of the Page Setup dialog box. The paper size choices depend on the printer's driver. To display the sizes, open the Paper Size drop-down list.

As you probably won't print your worksheets on envelopes, your main paper size options are as follows:

- Letter (8.5×11 inches)
- Legal (8.5×14 inches)
- A4 (210mm×297mm)
- Executive (7.25×10.5 inches)
- JIS B5 (182mm×257mm)

NOTE

> A4 paper size is used primarily in Europe, and is slightly longer than Letter size. Be sure that the paper size you choose actually matches your paper so that none of your content is lost (prints off the page) or you fail to take advantage of the full paper size.

Bear in mind that you can adjust all the page setup options—changing orientation, scaling, and paper size—to meet the needs of your worksheet printout.

→ To find out more about changing orientation, **see** the section "Working with Orientation" **p. 142**
→ To find out more about scaling pages, **see** the section "Scaling the Printout" **p. 142**

ADJUSTING PRINT QUALITY

Print quality refers to the resolution of your printout and it's yet another option you can control on the Page tab. Click the Print Quality drop-down arrow to display a list of resolutions that reflect the capabilities of the printer or printers to which your computer can send output. If your printer is capable of 600dpi (dots per inch) output, 600dpi and 300dpi (and perhaps 100dpi and 72dpi, depending on your model printer) dpi output options will be offered in the list box. You cannot choose a dpi setting higher than your printer can handle.

NOTE

> If you feel that your printer is capable of a higher dpi setting than is offered among your print quality settings, click the Options button in the Page Setup dialog box to view your selected printer's properties. (You can also use the Windows Control Panel to open the Printers window and check the Properties of your printer.) You might have the wrong driver set up for your printer or perhaps the settings for your printer have been changed from the default settings. Consult your printer's documentation before making any changes to the Properties settings.

SETTING WORKSHEET MARGINS

The Margins tab in the Page Setup dialog box has options for setting specific numbers for your top, bottom, left, and right margins (see Figure 5.32). The default margins are 1 inch from the top and bottom, and .75 inch from the left and right.

To enter new margins for your worksheet, follow these steps:

1. Choose File, Page Setup.
2. Click the Margins tab.
3. In the Top margin box, type a new margin setting, or use the spin arrows to increase or decrease the number in .25" increments.
4. Set the Bottom, Left, and Right margins the same way.
5. Click OK to close the dialog box when you're finished, or Print to open the Print dialog box.

Figure 5.32
Although you can adjust your margins quickly from within Print Preview, this dialog box enables you to set more precise margins.

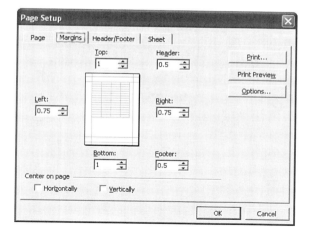

TIP FROM

> In addition to using the spin box arrows to increase or decrease the margin settings, you can use the up and down arrows on your keyboard to adjust the number in .25-inch increments.

SETTING HEADER AND FOOTER MARGINS

While in the Margins tab of the Page Setup dialog box, you'll notice that two additional spin boxes are offered. These settings let you control the placement of your header and footer content (if any) in relation to the edge of the paper. By default, these margins are set at .5 inch, just a half inch beyond the default top and bottom margins.

When setting new header and footer margins, keep your sheet margins in mind—if you've reduced your top and bottom margins to allow more worksheet content on the page, you'll have to reduce your header and footer margins, too. You need to reduce them enough so that they don't run into your sheet content, but not so much that they're off the page. Figure 5.33 shows reduced margins for the top, bottom, header, and footer on a worksheet. The header and footer margins are the topmost and bottommost margins on the page (if you point at a margin line and press the mouse button when you see the two-headed arrow, the status bar tells you at which margin you're pointing). The margins for the top and bottom of the data are the innermost margins.

To set header and footer margins, follow these steps:

1. Choose File, Page Setup, and click the Margins tab.
2. Type the Header setting you need, or use the spin box triangles to increment or decrement the measurement.
3. Set the Footer margin the same way.
4. Click OK.

Left margin   Header margin   Top margin   Right margin

Figure 5.33
Top and bottom margins of .5 inch should have .25-inch header and footer margins.

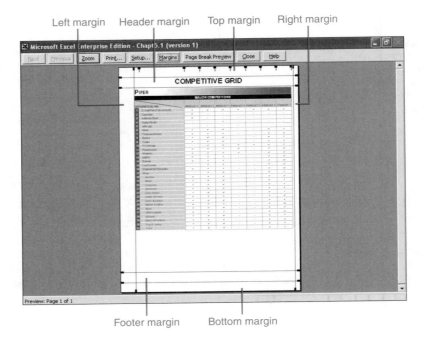

Footer margin   Bottom margin

NOTE

Many worksheets don't require header or footer text—their content is either completely self-explanatory, or their use is informal. In any case, Excel inserts no header or footer content by default. Earlier versions inserted the worksheet name, but user requests resulted in Microsoft's deletion of that automatic insertion. The creation of header and footer content is covered later in this chapter.

→ To learn how to set header and footer text, **see** the section "Creating Headers and Footers," **p. 147**

CENTERING THE WORKSHEET ON THE PAGE

Although technically unrelated to setting margins, the options for centering your worksheet on the page are found on the Margins tab. The Center on Page options are Horizontally or Vertically. You can select both options to place your worksheet in the actual center of the paper.

CAUTION

If your centering doesn't seem to work, check your margin settings. If your margins are not equal on opposite sides of the worksheet, your content will not appear centered on the page. You also might need to check your printer's settings; some printers have predefined margins on each side of the paper, and these settings might not be equal.

CREATING HEADERS AND FOOTERS

Although not required for a worksheet printout, header and/or footer content can be very useful. Your worksheet already has space allocated for header and footer content, and you can use this space for information that will help your readers interpret your worksheet content.

ENTERING HEADER AND FOOTER CONTENT

Headers are good places for information that identifies the document, such as a company name, department name, or report title. That kind of information can take up valuable screen space and interfere with data lists and tables if you place it on the worksheet. In a header, it appears where it's needed (on the top of all printed pages) and stays out of your way when you work with the data.

Footers are efficient places for automatic dates, times, and page numbers. Automatic dates and times always print the date and time when the report was printed, so you know whether it's current, and page numbers tell you whether you have the entire report. Like headers, footers place the information where it's needed (at the bottom of all the printed pages) and out of your worksheet space.

Header and footer content can be totally automated. By clicking preset buttons in the custom header and footer dialogs, you can place the filename, worksheet name, current date, current time, page number, and total number of pages in the header or footer. Automated information is always correct and current, no matter what changes you make in the worksheet, and you can format it to be as elegant or mundane as you want.

To create header and/or footer content, follow these steps:

1. Choose File, Page Setup.
2. Click the Header/Footer tab, as shown in Figure 5.34.

Figure 5.34
You can choose built-in headers and footers, or create your own.

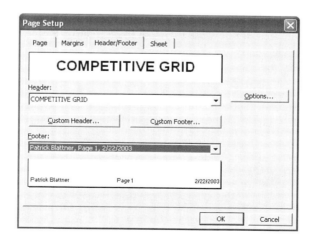

3. Choose from several built-in headers and footers in the Header and Footer drop-down lists, or follow steps 4–7 to create custom, formatted headers and footers.

4. Click the Custom Header button to open the Header dialog box, as shown in Figure 5.35.

Figure 5.35
Type your header text and/or click the field buttons to insert automatic content such as page numbers or the date.

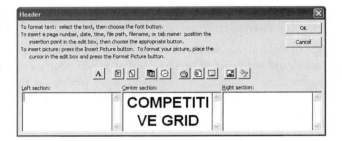

TIP FROM

The ampersand is a field code character, and won't appear in your header/footer text. To include an ampersand, type two ampersands.

5. Each of the three boxes represents a section of the header. Type your text and use the field buttons to create custom header content.

6. Click OK.

7. Back in the Page Setup dialog box, click the Custom Footer button, and repeat steps 5 and 6 if you want to create a custom footer.

8. Click OK to close the Page Setup dialog box.

Your header and/or footer will appear whenever you print that worksheet, but only for that worksheet. If your header or footer is tall, you'll need to reset page margins so it doesn't overlap the worksheet area. If you want to delete the header or footer completely, click (none) in the Header or Footer drop-down list.

INSERTING HEADER AND FOOTER FIELDS

Some of the automatic information that you might want to add to your header and footer is available through the Custom Header and Custom Footer buttons. Table 5.3 describes each button.

TABLE 5.3   HEADER AND FOOTER FIELD BUTTONS

Button	Name	Code	Function
A	Font		Opens a Font dialog box, from which you can format selected characters in the header or footer.

Button	Name	Code	Function
	Page Number	&[Page]	Inserts the correct page number on each page of your printout.
	Total Pages	&[Pages]	Inserts the total number of pages in your printout.
	Date	&[Date]	Inserts the current date at the time of printing.
	Time	&[Time]	Inserts the current time at printing. This is especially useful in worksheets that are undergoing changes and updates on a daily basis—the time will help you be sure you have the most current copy.
	Path and File	&[Path] &[File]	Inserts the path and filename of the workbook.
	File Name	&[File]	Inserts just the filename. If the file hasn't been saved, the default Book number will be inserted instead. If you subsequently save the file, the new filename will replace the default name.
	Sheet Name	&[Tab]	Inserts the sheet name. This is useful if you've named your worksheets.
	Insert Picture		Inserts a picture into the header of the document. The picture must be the same height as the header or footer area; otherwise, the picture will appear cropped. This is one of the main reasons Excel added the Format Picture button.
	Format Picture		Allows for the adjustment of size, rotate, scale, crop and adjustment of the image within the header.

NOTE

Use the Total Pages field button as an accompaniment to the Pages button. For example, type the word **Page**, and then click the Page Number button. Then, type a space, type **of**, type another space, and then click the Total pages button. Your result looks like Page 3 of 6. This helps readers keep the pages in order and know immediately whether they're missing a page.

CAUTION

If it's important that a particular date be displayed in your header or footer, type the date rather than using the Date button. The Date button inserts the current date, which changes each time you open and print the file on a new date; but a date you type will remain the same, regardless of the date on which you print the file.

If you are inserting the current date or time, you are relying on your computer's system date and/or time (so keep in mind that your system clock needs to be correct).

5

TIP FROM

You can type the automatic field codes yourself, if you want to, but the buttons are faster and foolproof.

WORKING WITH SHEET SETTINGS

The Sheet tab in the Page Setup dialog box, shown in Figure 5.36, gives you more control over what appears on your printout. The dialog box is divided into the following main areas:

- **Print Area**—Click the Collapse Dialog button to reduce the dialog box, enabling you to drag through a range of cells in your worksheet, selecting them as your print area. This is not the fastest way to set print areas, but if the Page Setup dialog box is already open, you can set and change print areas here.

Figure 5.36
You can set print areas in the Page Setup dialog box.

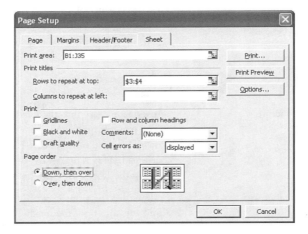

- **Print Titles**—If your data requires multiple printed pages, you can end up without labels to identify the columns and rows in your pages; setting print titles ensures that all the data in the printed pages is identified.
- **Print**—Choose which elements of your worksheet to print or not print (Gridlines, Row and Column Headings, Comments, and Errors), and how your printout will be processed in terms of color (Black and White, Draft Quality).
- **Page Order**—Choose the direction Excel will take in paginating your worksheet.

TIP FROM

You can move from tab to tab in any dialog box by pressing Ctrl+Tab or Ctrl+Shift+Tab.

SELECTING A PRINT AREA

If you don't want to print the entire worksheet, you need to set a print area. There are three ways to do this:

- Select a range of cells and choose File, Print Area, Set Print Area. The selected range becomes your permanent print area. To set multiple print areas, select the first range, then press Ctrl while you select the remaining ranges, and then choose File, Print Area, Set Print Area. Each of the print areas will be printed on a separate page, and they'll all print the worksheet's header and footer.

- To print a specific range quickly without setting a permanent print area, select the range to print, then click File, Print, and then choose Selection from the Print What section of the Print dialog box.

- Click File, Page Setup. In the Sheet tab, click in the Print Area box, and drag to select a range of cells (use the Collapse Dialog button if the box is in the way). To select multiple print ranges, you can type a comma between each print range (see Figure 5.37), or press Ctrl while selecting additional print ranges.

Figure 5.37
Select multiple print areas by typing a comma between each range.

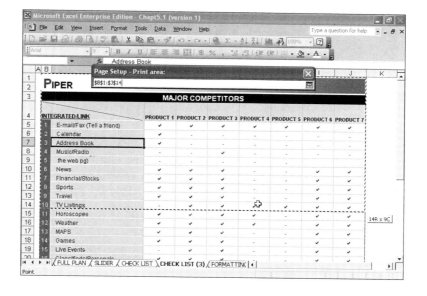

TROUBLESHOOTING

Printing problems are usually related to your printer rather than to the application through which you're printing (Excel, in this case). Some common printing problems and their potential solutions appear in Table 5.4.

TABLE 5.4   PRINTING PROBLEMS AND SOLUTIONS

Printing Problem	Possible Cause/Solution
One or two columns or rows flow onto a second or other unwanted subsequent page.	Too much data to fit on the page. Try reducing margins, or scaling the page to fit on a specific number of pages.
Printing takes too long.	A lot of graphic content—fonts, drawings, clip art. Increase the amount of memory in your printer or reduce the amount of graphic content in your worksheet, if possible. If you're on a network, try printing to a printer with more memory. If you have an ordinary laser printer, don't be surprised if it doesn't have enough memory to print even the smallest WordArt graphic.
Portions of your worksheet didn't print.	A print area has been defined that doesn't include the parts that are missing from your printout. Reselect the entire desired sections to print, and choose File, Print Area, Set Print Area to reset.
Excel is ignoring the page breaks you set up.	Your Page Setup options might be in conflict with one another. Choose File, Page Setup, and on the Page tab, check the Fit To option, and specify the number of pages that your worksheet should print to.

If you're experiencing a lot of printing problems and none of the software-driven solutions seem to help, try reinstalling your printer driver. From the Start menu, choose Settings, Printers. Within the Printers window, double-click the Add Printer icon, and look for your printer's manufacturer and model. If your printer model does not appear on the list, you'll need to use the driver disks or CD-ROM that came with your printer and choose the Have disk option in the wizard. Follow the Add Printer procedure to install a new driver, which will appear as a copy of your original driver in the Printers window.

After the new driver is installed, delete the original icon for your printer so that your printer will utilize the newly installed driver, represented by the Copy icon. Restart your computer before printing again.

It's also a good idea to check your printer manufacturer's Web site periodically. Updated drivers are often available for free download.

CHANGING THE DEFAULT FONT FOR THE ACTIVE WORKBOOK

How can I change the default font for the active workbook only?

Display the workbook whose default font you want to change. Choose Format, Style to open the Style dialog box, select the Normal style in the Style Name list, and click the Modify button to open the Format Cells dialog box. Click the Font tab, if necessary, and change the font as needed. Choose OK twice.

CREATING PERMANENT STYLES

I want to use styles I've created or modified in other workbooks. How do I do that?

Open the workbook whose styles you want to save permanently. Then, open a new workbook and merge the styles to the new workbook. In the new workbook, choose File, Save As. In the Save As Type list, choose Template (*.xlt). In the File Name box, assign the filename book. Store the file in the XLStart folder.

WHERE DID THE WORKSHEET TITLE GO?

I selected a row and clicked the Merge and Center button to merge the cells and center the title. Now I can't find the title, although it still appears in the Formula bar.

A common error when centering a title across the columns of a worksheet is selecting the entire row that contains the title. If you do this and then click the Merge and Center button, you'll merge all 256 cells of that selected row into one cell, and center the title across those 256 cells. Be sure to select only the cells that span the worksheet or a major portion of it.

EXCEL IN PRACTICE

The following examples offer some unique ways to use fonts, objects, and formats to achieve visual results using Excel. Because of Excel's tool sets and flexibility you can enhance spreadsheets to become powerful visual aides.

MEDIA MATRIX

If you have to define objectives for campaigns and then reveal strengths and weaknesses, you can create a media matrix on a spreadsheet with drawing tools. With the proper objects applied, you can decide what media to buy and how much to buy. For example, TV might offer strong image advertising and brand awareness but other campaigns might be more effective in their reach to the consumer. Look at the example in Figure 5.38. With the use of Wingdings2 font, octagon and oval objects, along with spreadsheet formats, you can create visual concepts for media spending and impact.

MEDIA PLAN

What if you had to plot out a media campaign over weeks in several markets? This would include a multidimensional matrix that would not only show the weeks and months of the campaign but also the regions in which you're going to market the campaign. By applying tiered timelines, colored cells with different colors per campaign and the regions along the left column, you can see the saturation of the campaigns as shown in Figure 5.39.

SLIDER CHARTS

Slider charts are often used in comparing two sets of data against high or low usage and or outcome. Notice the example in Figure 5.40 comparing Adult versus Young consumers as applied to the digital economy. The questions are in alignment with each slider from low to high, the adults are denoted by an oval with the letter A, and the young consumers are also denoted by an oval with the letter Y. The cumulative effect of each is called out to the right of the slider bar.

Wingding lowercase U   Octagon   Wingding V   Drawing objects

Figure 5.38
Apply drawing tools to spreadsheets to create visual media plans and spending.

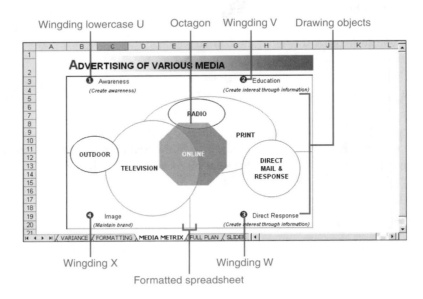

Wingding X   Formatted spreadsheet   Wingding W

Weekly campaigns   Schedule media campaigns to see saturation

Figure 5.39
Create multidimensional tables that show media saturation over time with proper cell alignment and formatting.

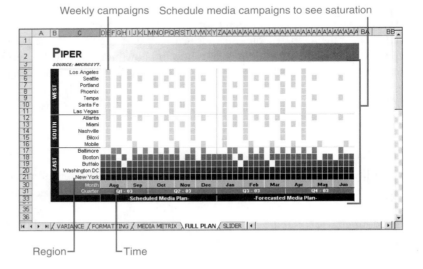

Region   Time

INCLUSION MATRIX WITH WEBDINGS

Another example of a matrix can be used when comparing multiple products that have different options or functionality. Take for example the comparison shown in Figure 5.41

where the products are viewed from left to right and the functionality within each product is down the left column. The unique thing to note in this example is the use of the Webdings font style. The Webdings font lowercase "a" produces a check mark. This provides a great visual for the checked-off functionality per product.

Figure 5.40
Use drawing objects to slide along a low-to-high usage bar for visual slider charts.

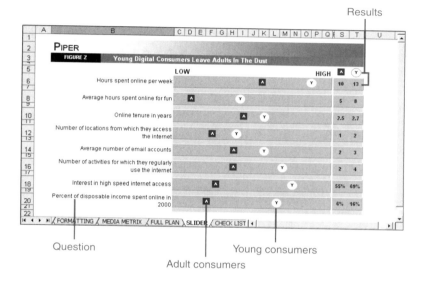

Results

Question

Adult consumers

Young consumers

Figure 5.41
Create compelling grids by using other fonts such as Webdings.

Functionality

Product

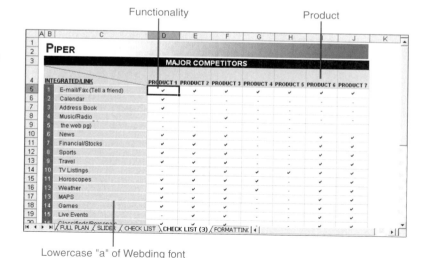

Lowercase "a" of Webding font

5

OTHER FORMATTING TIPS

The type of formatting you apply to a worksheet depends largely on its use and who will be seeing it. For worksheets that only you will see, formatting probably will be restricted to things that make the worksheet easier to read, such as increasing font size for onscreen viewing.

Worksheets that are shared with others often are formatted for clarity, visual impact, and a professional look. In some cases, you'll spend more time formatting than you did entering the data! To make the most of Excel's formatting tools without taking a lot of time, keep things simple (see Figure 5.42). Use shading to improve clarity and draw attention to important data, use borders and boldface to set column or row headings apart, and use fonts sparingly—you'll save time choosing them, and the worksheet won't look too "busy." It's a good idea to use the same formatting on many (if not all) of the worksheets—this strategy can help your work have a signature look that people will associate with you.

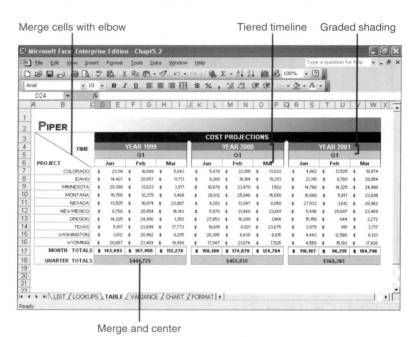

Figure 5.42
Use font sizes, merge, and center along with colors to create professional tables. Keep the font style the same for a consistent look and feel.

PART III

USING FORMULAS AND FUNCTIONS

6 Function Fundamentals 159

7 Database Functions 189

8 Date and Time Functions 201

9 Engineering Functions 215

10 Financial Functions 233

11 Information Functions 265

12 Logical Functions 277

13 Lookup and Reference Functions 285

14 Math and Trigonometry Functions 303

15 Text Functions 325

16 Statistical Functions 343

CHAPTER **6**

FUNCTION FUNDAMENTALS

In this chapter

The Basic Parts of a Formula   160

Using the AutoSum Feature   166

Editing Formulas   170

Writing Multiple Copies of a Formula   173

Using AutoCalculate for Quick Totals   175

Relative Versus Absolute Referencing   178

Using the Watch Window   180

Referencing Values in Other Worksheets and Workbooks   181

THE BASIC PARTS OF A FORMULA

A *function* in Excel is a built-in formula that performs a mathematical operation or returns information specified by the formula. For example, if you had a list of a thousand numbers and wanted to manually look for the highest value, it could take a while. That's where Excel can help. It has a MAX function that searches a specified range and returns the highest value. Using another example, if you wanted to calculate the average from a list of numbers, you could use the AVERAGE function to calculate the average instead of manually creating a formula that added the numbers and divided by the count of those numbers. In all, Excel has more than 450 built-in functions, so if you know which ones do what, you can save countless hours. In addition to the numerous functions already available, you'll also learn how to create your own custom functions. If you have specific calculations that are customized to you or your business, you can create your own set of custom functions. While we cover several functions throughout this book not all functions have been discussed. If you need additional information you can always type a question in the search field in the menu bar. In addition, you can also click on the Insert Function command in the formula bar.

FUNCTIONS VERSUS FORMULAS

The function is the built-in formula provided by Excel. The *formula* is the function with its arguments. As with every formula created in Excel, each function starts with an = sign. For example, if you place the formula Average(B3:B20), where Average is the function name and (B3:B20) is the argument, nothing happens; however, place an = sign in front of Average and it activates the function. Think of it in terms of using a key to start your car.

ARGUMENTS

An argument is the reference behind the function. The reference being a number, a text string, a logical value, a cell reference, or worksheet names can be used as an argument. For example, if you were to calculate the average of cells B3:B20 in a list, the argument is the cell-range reference shown as (B3:B20) behind the function. Table 6.1 shows examples of arguments used in Excel.

TABLE 6.1   ARGUMENT TYPES

Argument	Example
Numbers	1,2,3
Text	"January"
Logical Values	(True or False)
Cell References	B7 or B7:B20

OPERATORS

Operators are mathematical symbols that are broken into four categories: arithmetic operators, comparison operators, text operators, and reference operators. An operator tells Excel what kind of calculation you want to perform. For example, to divide 7 by 3, the operator is the front slash key (/) and tells Excel to divide. In essence, it's a language that tells Excel what operation you want it to do. You could use voice recognition to tell Excel to divide or you could learn the keystroke language as shown in Table 6.2.

TABLE 6.2   KEYSTROKE OPERATORS

Arithmetic	Explanation	Example
+	Addition	2+3
-	Subtraction	5-1
-	Negation	-7
*	Multiplication	7*3
/	Division	7/2
%	Percent	90%
^	Exponentiation	7^2

Comparison	Explanation	Example
=	Equal to	B1=D1
>	Greater than	B1>D1
<	Less than	B1<D1
>=	Greater than or equal to	B1>=D1
<=	Less than or equal to	B1<=D1
<>	Not equal to	B1<>D1

Text	Explanation	Example
&	Adjoins text or cell references or any combination thereof	"Scott " & "Blattner" produces "Scott Blattner"

Reference	Explanation	Example
:	Includes cells of a column or row between the designated limits	B3:B20
,	Separates arguments in a function	(B3,B20)

OPERATOR ORDER

When creating complicated formulas or formulas that include more than one operator, there is a specific order Excel uses to calculate the answer. The order is listed in Table 6.3. Meaning, if you were to create a formula that contained % and the operator +, the % would be calculated first. Also note, multiplication is performed before addition so 2+4*3 results in the sum of 14 rather than 18.

TABLE 6.3   EXCEL'S OPERATOR ORDER

Arithmetic	Operator Precedence	Description
1	%	Percent
2	^	Exponentiation
3	*	Multiplication
4	/	Division
5	+ –	Addition
6	-	Subtraction
7	&	Ampersand (adjoins text)
8	>, >=, <, <=, =, <>	Comparisons

USING ARITHMETIC OPERATORS FOR SIMPLE MATH

To perform direct mathematical operations in a formula (as opposed to using Excel's built-in functions), you use arithmetic operators. *Arithmetic operators* in a formula tell Excel which math operations you want to perform. Arithmetic operators were also discussed earlier in this chapter.

A simple formula might consist of adding, subtracting, multiplying, or dividing cells. Excel can also perform exponentiation, so you can enter a number and exponent (such as 5^4, or 5 to the fourth power), and Excel will use the ultimate value of the exponent in the formula calculation. You can use percentages in a formula the same way—instead of entering 25% as a fractional value (25/100) or a decimal value (0.25), you can enter 25% in a formula; Excel will calculate and use its decimal value in the math operation.

- **Parentheses**—All calculations within parentheses are completed first.
- **Negation**—Making a number negative (such as -5) precedes any other operations, so that the negative value is used in the remaining calculations.
- **Percent**—Percentages (for example, 12%) are calculated next, so that the actual value (in this case, .12) is used in the remaining calculations.
- **Exponentiation**—Exponents (for example, 10^3, which means 10 cubed) are calculated next, so that the actual value is used in the remaining calculations.
- **Multiplication**—Performed after parenthetical operations and before all other calculations.
- **Division**—Follows any multiplication and is on the same level of precedence as multiplication.
- **Addition**—Performed after all divisions.
- **Subtraction**—Follows any additions and is on the same level of precedence as addition.

6

CONTROLLING THE ORDER OF OPERATIONS

Although Excel follows a set order of operations when it calculates a formula, you can alter the order in a specific formula by using parentheses to break the formula into segments. Excel performs all operations within sets of parentheses first, and you can use this to get exactly the order of operations you want.

If multiple operations are encased in multiple sets of parentheses, the operations are performed from inside to outside, then follow the order of operations, and then left to right. Table 6.4 shows results of rearranging parentheses within the same formula. Each parenthetical calculation is performed first; then, the results of those first calculations are used for the second set of calculations, which follow the order of operations. All operations on the same level (in this case, all the additions) are then performed left to right.

TABLE 6.4   THE RESULTS OF REARRANGING PARENTHESES

Formula	Result
=(1+2)*3+4+5	18
=1+2*3+4+5	16
=1+2*(3+4)+5	20
=1+2*(3+4+5)	25
=(1+2)*(3+4)+5	26
=(1+2)*(3+4+5)	36

You must enter parentheses in pairs. If you forget a parenthesis, you'll see a message telling you there's an error. Sometimes Excel takes a guess at where you want the missing parenthesis and displays a prompt box. If the guess is right, click Yes; if it's wrong, click No and fix the formula yourself.

TIP FROM

If your formula is long and contains many sets of parentheses, it can be difficult to find the missing parenthesis by eye. Instead, open the formula for editing, and use the arrow keys to move the cursor (the insertion point) through the formula one character at a time. Whenever the cursor moves over a parenthesis, both parentheses in the pair are momentarily darkened. If the parenthesis is not temporarily darkened when the cursor passes over it, that's the one missing a matching parenthesis for the set. The Range Finder (color feature used to color code range references) also color codes multiple parentheses, allowing the user to identify individual pairs of parentheses of the same color.

NESTING CALCULATIONS WITHIN A FORMULA

Some calculations are more complex than can be handled with isolated sets of parentheses; they require parenthetical sets that are *nested*, or contained within larger parenthetical sets.

This isn't so common in simple mathematical formulas, but is very common when you use functions.

Nested calculations use parentheses to force Excel to follow the order of operations that you want, even as it follows the standard order of operations. Figure 6.1 shows a simple example of the changes you can make by nesting parentheses within other parentheses.

Figure 6.1
Nesting parentheses within other parentheses alters the calculation even more. Proper formula construction is critical to the outcome of a formula.

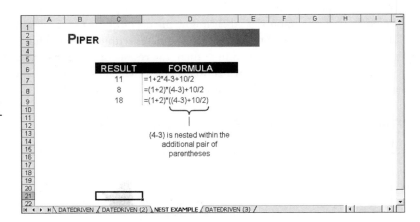

To simplify the principle: Excel calculates the innermost parentheses first, and then uses those quantities to calculate within the next outer level of parentheses, and so forth through all the nested levels. When all the parenthetical quantities have been calculated, Excel uses those quantities to calculate the formula by following the order of operations.

CUSTOM FUNCTIONS

You can create custom functions in Excel using Excel's Visual Basic for Applications macro language. However, be sure Excel has not already addressed a function that will work for your specific needs. Note the following custom function example.

If you were in the construction industry, and had a specific calculation that included a formula with rates that were specific to your company and equipment, and a profit rate that was also specific to your company, you could create a custom function called =TRUCKRATE(xxx). Now, every time you estimate an amount of material to be moved and it includes the use of a Cat 777 truck, it would calculate the amount of material based on the 777 truck base rate plus overhead.

→ **See** Chapter 27, "Customizing Excel to Fit Your Working Style," to learn more about creating custom functions.

APPLYING A NAME TO A RANGE

If you frequently write formulas that reference the same range, you can apply a name to that range and use the name in your formulas. So, instead of the range appearing in a formula as

B7:B16, it would appear as a name called Channel. The SUMIF formula in Figure 6.2 uses ranges in the formula as follows:

```
=SUMIF(B7:B16,B17,D7:D16)
```

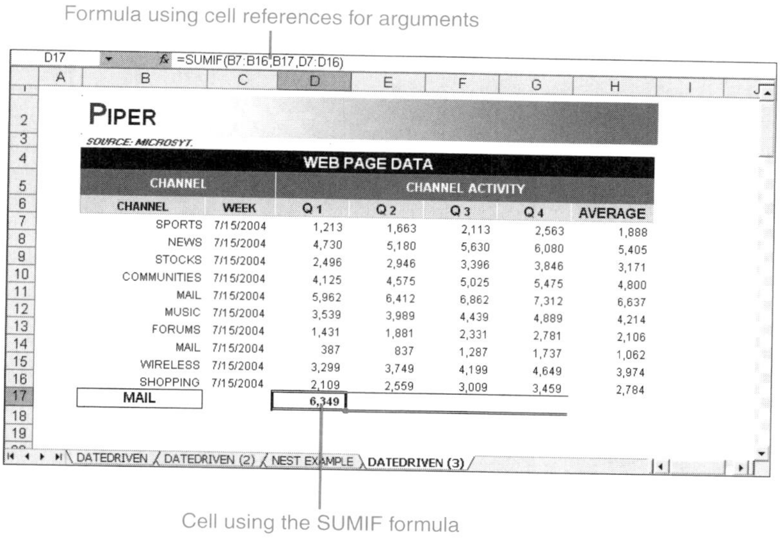

Formula using cell references for arguments

Figure 6.2
This formula uses ranges and criteria.

Cell using the SUMIF formula

The same SUMIF formula uses named ranges to accomplish the same result:

```
=SUMIF(Channels,Cell_Reference,Q_ONE)
```

To apply a name to a range, follow these steps:

1. Choose Insert, Name, Define.
2. Type the name of the range in the Names in Workbook text box.
3. Press the Tab key twice or click the Range Finder (red arrow) button to activate the Refers To text box.
4. Select the range the name will refer to.
5. Click Add (if you want to include more named ranges) or OK (if you're done).

PASTING A NAMED RANGE IN A FORMULA

After you've named ranges within a workbook, you can then paste them into a formula. To paste a named range into a formula, follow these steps:

1. Start a formula—in this case:
   ```
   =sumif(
   ```
2. Choose Insert, Name, Paste, or press F3 to open the Paste Name dialog box.

3. From the Paste Name dialog box, select the name of the range as shown in Figure 6.3, and then click OK. The Channels name refers to the channel names in range B7:B16, the Cell Reference name refers to cell B17, and the Q_One name refers to the Q1 figures in range D7:D16.

Figure 6.3
Paste the named ranges in the appropriate locations within the formula.

Range names available in workbook

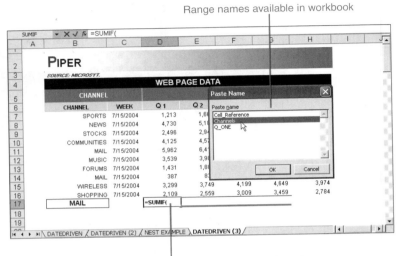

Start the formula and then paste the names in the formula

USING THE AUTOSUM FEATURE

A simple way to summarize numbers is by using a feature called Autosum. It allows you to perform various calculations like average, count, or sum and automatically calculates the numbers for you. The AutoSum feature has a drop-down menu that allows you to select the type of mathematical calculation you want instead of forcing the SUM function into a cell. You can apply the most common functions with one click. To access the most common functions, click the down arrow on the right side of the AutoSum button. When applying analytical functions against rows or columns, use the AutoSum feature for a quick summary. Because AutoSum looks for the first blank cell as a stopping point, be careful to ensure that any blank cells that appear intermittently are filled with zero values. The most common functions appear in the AutoSum drop-down menu as shown in Figure 6.4: Sum, Average, Count, Max, and Min. You can also choose More Functions to launch the Insert Function command.

To use AutoSum for summing data, follow these steps:

1. Click in the cell where you want to display the formula result.

2. Click the AutoSum button on the Standard toolbar.

Excel guesses which cells you want to include and surrounds them with an animated border (as shown in Figure 6.5).

AutoSum drop-down menu function choices

Figure 6.4
When you click the
down arrow next to
the AutoSum button,
the drop-down menu
appears.

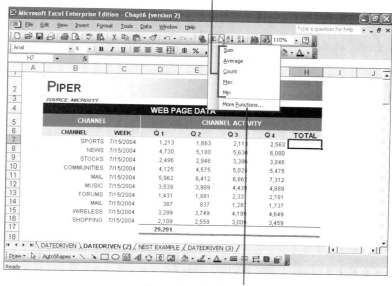

Launches the Insert Function dialog box

The SUM function in the formula bar

Enter button on
the Formula bar

AutoSum button ─┐ ┌─ AutoSum drop-down menu

Figure 6.5
When you click
AutoSum, an ani-
mated border sur-
rounds the cells
included in the for-
mula.

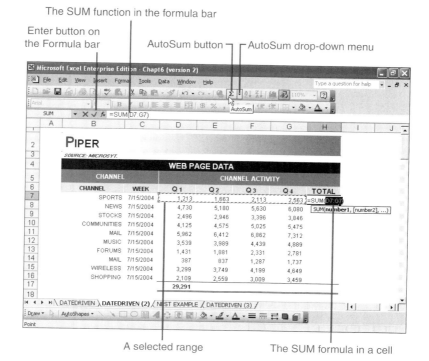

A selected range   The SUM formula in a cell

3. If the formula doesn't have an obvious row or column to sum, or if it guesses wrong, drag to select the cells you want to sum. The animated border surrounds all the cells you drag.

4. When the range is correct, press Enter (or click the Enter button, the green check mark left of the Formula bar) to complete the formula.

If you want to create SUM functions for several columns or rows in a table, follow these steps:

1. Drag to select all the cells that you want to display totals in, either across the bottom or down the right side of the table.

2. Click the AutoSum button.

   Each cell is automatically filled with a SUM formula that sums the contents of the column above it (see Figure 6.6).

Figure 6.6
Select a range and click AutoSum for quick summaries.

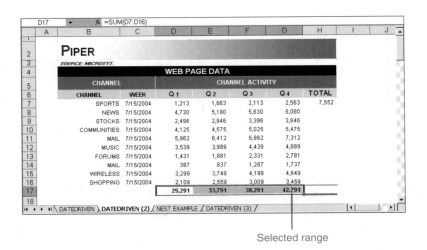

Selected range

When using the AutoSum feature, you can also choose any of the other functions included with Excel. For example, if you have a list of categories—in this case, channels from an Internet company—and you want to be able to sum all the occurrences of one channel, you could use the Insert Function command from the forumula bar to help write the formula. Notice the example in Figure 6.7. For every occurrence of the mail channel, the activity should be summed in Q1. This is one of the most commonly used functions in Excel. To use this feature, follow these steps:

1. Select More Functions from the AutoSum drop-down menu.

2. Select the SUMIF function from the Insert Function dialog box as shown in Figure 6.7, and click OK.

Selected function

Figure 6.7
Use the Insert
Function command
from the AutoSum
drop-down menu to
open the Insert
Function dialog box
shown here.

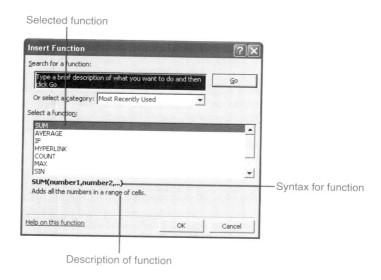

Syntax for function

Description of function

3. Either type or select the Range containing the category you're looking for on the range line in the edit box and use the Tab key to move down to the next line. In this example, B7:B16 is selected and the range is named. The range name is "Channels". You can learn more about named ranges in Chapter 2.

4. Either type or select the cell containing the text criteria in the Criteria edit box. In this case, it's cell B17 "Mail" shown as the named range "Cell_Reference" (see Figure 6.8).

Refers to a named range

Figure 6.8
Define the arguments
in the Function dialog
box for the SUMIF
formula.

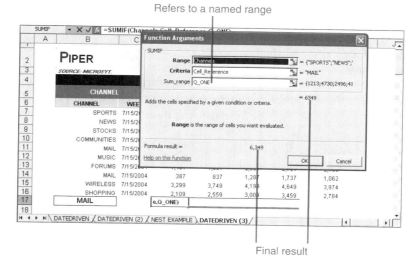

Final result

5. Either type or select the range you want to sum in the Sum_Range edit box. For Q1 in Figure 6.8, it's D7:D16 or the named range Q_1. By clicking in the edit field, Excel will now auto-name the range to help user easily identify the range by its title row.

6. Click OK.

The final result is the total values summed for every occurrence of mail as shown in Figure 6.9.

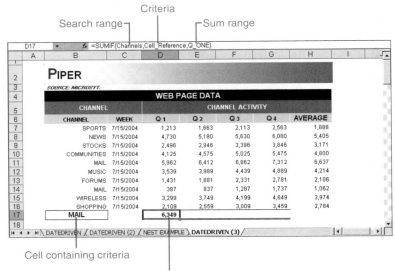

Figure 6.9
The total for all occurrences of mail in Q1 is applied to cell D17.

Use cell references whenever possible, (or named range tied to a cell reference), such as B17 instead of "MAIL" in the formula is because now you can type another reference (Criteria) in the cell where the word "Mail" is and the formula will respond to the new reference (Criteria). Using text directly in the formula is called hard coding. If you want to change the criteria when you hard code formulas, you must edit the text in the function each time you want it changed. One reason you should always use a cell reference, (or named range tied to a cell reference), such as B17 instead of "MAIL" in the formula is because now you can type another reference (Criteria) in the cell where the word "Mail" is (for example, "STOCKS")and the formula will respond to the new reference (Criteria) by displaying the total for that channel.

EDITING FORMULAS

When you need to change a formula, either the calculation or the referenced cells, you can edit the formula in the Formula bar or in the cell.

To edit in the Formula bar, click the cell that contains the formula, and then click anywhere in the Formula bar. Use regular text-editing techniques to edit the formula—click-and-drag to select characters you want to change; then delete or type over them. Press Enter to complete the formula.

To edit the formula in the cell, double-click the cell. The cell switches to edit mode and the entire formula is visible (as shown in Figure 6.7). You can select and edit the formula just as you would in the Formula bar.

NOTE

> You can also press F2 to switch to edit mode for the selected cell you want to edit.

NOTE

> If, you double-click the formula cell (or press F2), the cell references are selected but the cell doesn't change to edit mode, choose Tools, Options, and select the Edit tab. Click the Edit Directly in Cell check box to turn it on, and then click OK.

Whether you edit a formula in the Formula bar or in the cell, the references in the formula are highlighted in color, and the corresponding cell ranges on the worksheet are surrounded by borders that are color-matched to the range references in the formula, as shown in Figure 6.10. Although you can't see the actual colors in this figure, the callouts point them out, and they'll appear on your screen.

Figure 6.10
The colors in the formula match the colors outlining the references.

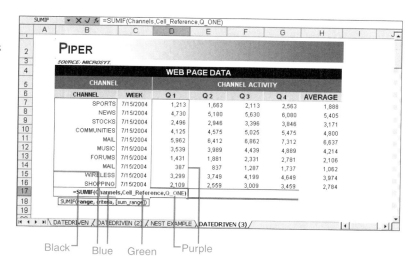

Black   Blue   Green   Purple

If you need to change the cell references so the formula calculates based on different cells, you can choose from several techniques. You can type new references; highlight the range you want to change and click and drag to select a new range on the worksheet; or use range names.

NOTE

To get out of a cell without making any changes, or to undo any changes you've made before entering them, press Esc or click the Cancel button (the red X left of the Formula bar).

DRAGGING A RANGE BORDER TO CHANGE A REFERENCE

If you need to expand or collapse existing references (for example, if you added new columns or rows to a table and need to adjust the formula to include them), you can move or resize the colored range border (indicated in Figure 6.10) to encompass the new cells. You can also move and resize the range border to reduce the range included in the formula.

To move a range border to surround different cells without changing its size, drag any side of the border while your mouse displays four small black arrows on top of its normal white arrow. To expand or reduce the size of a range border, drag any fill handle—located at each corner of the color box—to change the size of the range (see Figure 6.11). Your mouse will display two small black arrows while dragging.

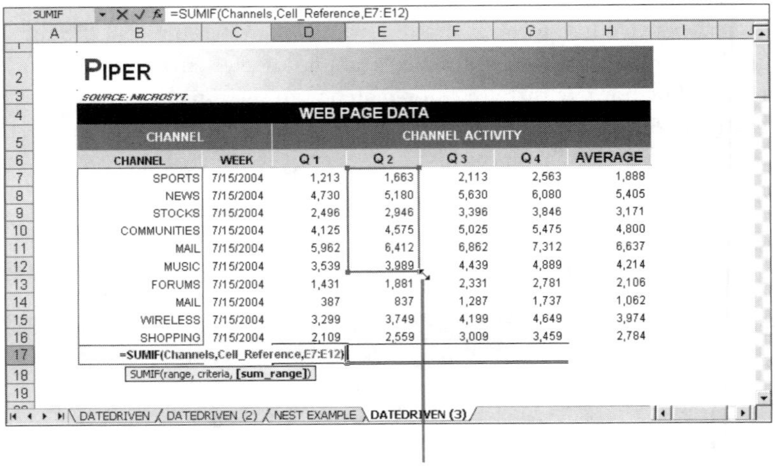

Figure 6.11
You can edit a range reference by moving or resizing its colored borders.

Drag the fill handle to adjust the sum range

TYPING REFERENCES DIRECTLY INTO A FORMULA

If you would rather use your keyboard, you can type range references directly into the formula. Use common text-editing techniques to delete and replace characters in your references; be sure to use a colon to separate the upper-left cell of a reference from the lower-right cell of a reference to a range, and remember to separate multiple range references with commas. If you need to reference ranges on other worksheets and other workbooks, the typing becomes a bit more complex; you'll learn about those later in this chapter, in "Referencing Other Workbooks and Worksheets."

WRITING MULTIPLE COPIES OF A FORMULA

Suppose you have a table similar to the one shown in Figure 6.11 (shown in the following section), and you need to add identical formulas at the end of each row. Instead of entering each formula individually, there are a couple of ways to create copies of your formula quickly. One method uses AutoFill to copy a formula to several more cells. Another method creates multiple copies when you enter the formula.

COPYING FORMULAS WITH AUTOFILL

When you copy a formula, each formula adjusts its references automatically so that the calculation is correct when pasted into a new location. For example, when you write a formula that averages the values in the four cells to the left (like the formula in Figure 6.11), each copy of the formula will sum the values in the four cells to its left. This works because the formula uses relative references.

To AutoFill a formula, follow these steps:

1. Enter your formula in the first cell (in this example, in the cell at the top of the column), as shown in Figure 6.11.

2. Select the cell containing the formula. The active cell (or range) has a small black box in the lower-right corner, called a *fill handle*.

3. Point the mouse at the fill handle; when the mouse pointer becomes a black cross, click and drag down to fill cells with copies of the formula (see Figure 6.12). You can use AutoFill to copy formulas in all four directions in your worksheet (up, down, left, and right).

Cell containing original formula

Figure 6.12
Using the fill handle, you can drag to AutoFill the formula to adjoining cells.

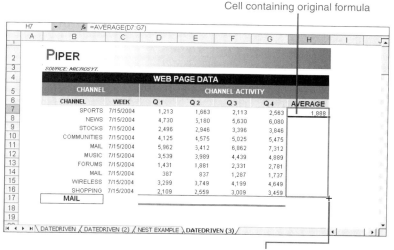

Drag the fill handle to select the range of cells to which you want to copy the original formula

4. At the end of the range, release the mouse button. The cells you dragged are filled with copies of the formula, as illustrated in Figure 6.13.

Figure 6.13
When you release the mouse pointer, the cells are filled.

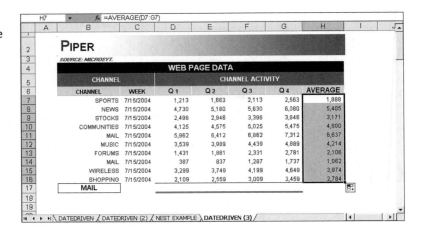

TIP FROM

You can use AutoFill to fill out a table (for example, a loan payments table) by copying an entire row or column of entries and formulas. Select the range of cells you want to copy, and drag the fill handle on the lower-right corner of the range.

Also, if your data is extremely long, you can AutoFill an adjacent column by double-clicking the fill handle instead of dragging it.

Entering Multiple Formulas All at Once

If you've already entered a formula and need to copy it across a row or down a column, use the autofill feature. But to enter multiple copies of a formula you can enter them all at the same time.

To enter the same formula in several cells at once, follow these steps:

1. Select all the cells in which you want to enter the formula (see Figure 6.14). They can be in a single row or column, any rectangular range, or in noncontiguous ranges (press Ctrl to select noncontiguous ranges).

2. Create your formula by whatever means you normally use, but don't press Enter when finished.

3. When the formula is complete, press Ctrl+Enter. The formula is entered in all the selected cells simultaneously (see Figure 6.15).

Figure 6.14
To enter multiple copies of a formula all at once, select all the cells first.

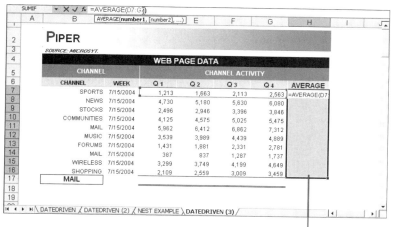

Selected range of cells to which the formula will be applied ⌐

Figure 6.15
Press Ctrl+Enter to enter the formula in all the selected cells.

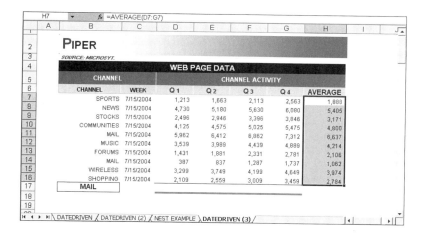

USING AUTOCALCULATE FOR QUICK TOTALS

6

Sometimes you need a quick and impermanent calculation—you need to know right now what your expense account entries add up to, or how many items there are in a list. You can use *AutoCalculate* to get quick answers.

To use AutoCalculate, select the cells you want to calculate. The answer appears in the AutoCalculate box on the status bar (see Figure 6.16).

When you install Excel, AutoCalculate is set to calculate sums by default; but you're not limited to quick sums. You can also, for example, obtain a quick count of the items in a long product list or a quick average of your list of monthly phone bills. You can switch the calculation to Average, Count, CountNums, Max, or Min (or None to turn the feature off). To switch the calculation, right-click anywhere on the status bar (see Figure 6.17) and click the calculation you want on the shortcut menu.

Selected range

Figure 6.16
Select two or more cells and see the automatic calculation of those entries displayed on the status bar.

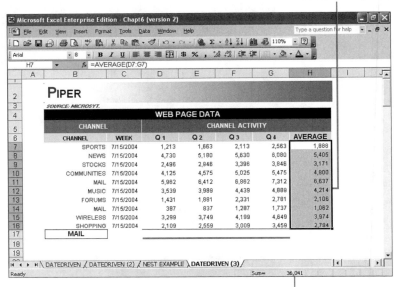

Result of AutoCalculate

Figure 6.17
Choose a different AutoCalculate function.

TIP FROM

AutoCalculate retains whatever function you set until you change the function again.

AutoCalculate appears in the status bar only when two or more calculable cells are selected. For example, if the AutoCalculate function is set to Sum and you select cells that contain only text entries, AutoCalculate won't appear (because there's nothing to sum).

AutoCalculate offers the following functions:

- **Average**—Averages numeric values in the selected cells; ignores blank cells and nonnumeric values.
- **Count**—Counts all entries, whether numeric, text, or logical; ignores blank cells.
- **CountNums**—Counts only numeric values; ignores blank cells and nonnumeric values.
- **Max**—Returns the single maximum numeric value in the selected cells.
- **Min**—Returns the single minimum numeric value in the selected cells.
- **Sum**—Sums numeric values in the selected cells; ignores blank cells and nonnumeric values.

INTERPRETING FORMULA ERROR MESSAGES

When something prevents a formula from calculating, you'll see an error message instead of a result. The "something" might be a reference that was deleted from the worksheet, an invalid arithmetic operation such as dividing by zero, or a formula attempting to calculate a named range that doesn't exist. It can also be something as simple as a misspelled function name.

Table 6.5 lists the error messages and their probable causes (some have several probable causes, and you must do some detective work to find the problem). Excel has tools that can help you track down the source of an error.

TABLE 6.5   ERROR VALUES

Error	Meaning	How to Fix
#####	Technically not an error, this means the column isn't wide enough to display the value.	Widen the column.
#VALUE!	Wrong type of argument or operand (for example, calculating a cell with the value #N/A).	Check operands and arguments; be sure references are valid.
#DIV/0!	Formula is attempting to divide by zero.	Change the value or cell reference so that the formula doesn't divide by zero.
#NAME?	Formula is referencing an invalid or nonexistent name.	Be sure the name still exists or correct the misspelling.
#N/A	Most often means no value is available or inappropriate arguments were used.	In a lookup formula, be sure the lookup table is sorted correctly.

continues

6

TABLE 6.5   CONTINUED

Error	Meaning	How to Fix
#REF!	Excel can't locate the referenced cells. (For example, referenced cells were deleted.)	Click Undo immediately to restore references and then change formula references or convert formulas to values.
#NUM!	Incorrect use of a number (such as SQRT(-1)), or formula result is a number too large or too small to be displayed.	Be sure that the arguments are correct, and that the result is between $-1*10^{307}$ and $1*10^{307}$.
#NULL!	Reference to intersection of two areas that do not intersect.	Check for typing and reference errors.
Circular	A formula refers to itself, either directly or indirectly.	Click OK and then look at the status bar to see which cell ontains the circular reference. Use the Trace Precedents and Trace Dependents buttons on either the Circular Reference or Auditing toolbars to find the culprit references.

NOTE

If you are working with extremely large or small numbers keep these limitations of Excel in mind:

- This is the largest value to be typed in a cell: 9.99999999999999^{307}
- This is the smallest negative value you can type in a cell: -9.99999999999999^{307}
- The smallest allowed positive number is 2.229E-308.
- The largest allowed negative number is -1^{-307}.

RELATIVE VERSUS ABSOLUTE REFERENCING

When you specify a cell or range of cells in a worksheet in a formula, it is called *cell or range referencing*. When you want the reference to adjust to its new location when you copy the formula, it is called *relative referencing*. When you anchor or lock the row or column reference to a cell or range in a formula so that it does not change when copied, that is called *absolute referencing*. For example, if you write a formula that you need to drag horizontally or vertically, you might need to anchor one or more of the reference cells or ranges for the

6

correct results. A cell becomes anchored by applying the dollar sign before the column and/or row.

Note the result of the following:

- **=B6**—Relative row and column reference.
- **=$B6**—Column is anchored or absolute; row is relative.
- **=B$6**—Row is anchored or absolute; column is relative.
- **=$B$6**—Both column and row are anchored or absolute.

In the example in Figure 6.18, the formula references the channel range B11:B18, the channel references cell B6, and the sum range is C11:C18. The reason to create a partial absolute reference in this example is because you'll want to drag (copy) the formula to the right to summarize all the corresponding quarters for the sports channel.

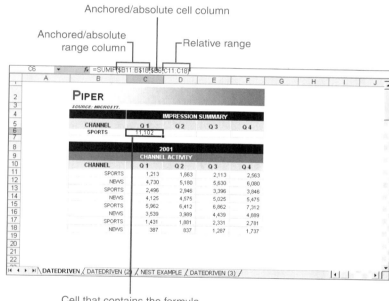

Figure 6.18
If you anchor or apply absolute referencing, you can drag formulas but maintain the proper referencing.

In the example in Figure 6.19, the absolute or anchored references in the formula after it has been copied to the right remain the same while the sum range (F11:F18) adjusts to its new column F.

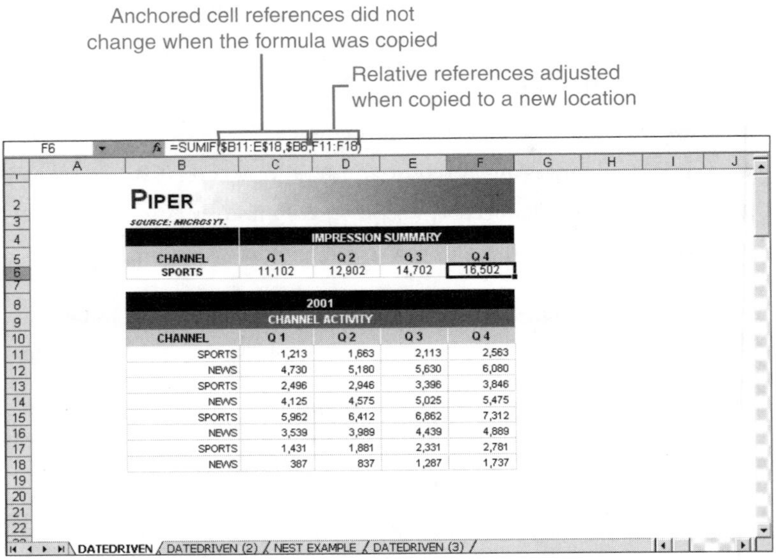

Anchored cell references did not
change when the formula was copied

Relative references adjusted
when copied to a new location

Figure 6.19
The anchored or
absolute referencing
maintains integrity
when the formula is
copied to the right
while the sum range
adjusts its column
reference to the right.

| F6 | ▼ | f_x =SUMIF($B11:E$18,$B6,F11:F18) |

	A	B	C	D	E	F	G	H	I	J
2		**PIPER**								
3		*SOURCE: MICROSYT.*								
4				IMPRESSION SUMMARY						
5		CHANNEL	Q 1	Q 2	Q 3	Q 4				
6		SPORTS	11,102	12,902	14,702	16,502				
7										
8				2001						
9				CHANNEL ACTIVITY						
10		CHANNEL	Q 1	Q 2	Q 3	Q 4				
11		SPORTS	1,213	1,663	2,113	2,563				
12		NEWS	4,730	5,180	5,630	6,080				
13		SPORTS	2,496	2,946	3,396	3,846				
14		NEWS	4,125	4,575	5,025	5,475				
15		SPORTS	5,962	6,412	6,862	7,312				
16		NEWS	3,539	3,989	4,439	4,889				
17		SPORTS	1,431	1,881	2,331	2,781				
18		NEWS	387	837	1,287	1,737				
19										
20										
21										
22										

DATEDRIVEN / DATEDRIVEN (2) / NEST EXAMPLE / DATEDRIVEN (3) /

USING THE WATCH WINDOW

The Watch Window helps evaluate formulas within workbooks or worksheets. It's a for-
mula-management tool that shows you the formula and where it is. If you share workbooks
with others, the Watch Window can help identify formulas and errors within formulas. To
access the Watch Window, right-click over the toolbar and select Watch Window from the
drop-down list. The Watch Window docks at the top of the workbook as shown in Figure 6.20. Also, the watch window creates a split screen effect when dragged to any side of
the Excel window. The Watch Window docks at the top of the workbook as shown in
Figure 6.20 when you double-click its title bar.

The Watch Window is really a throwback to Excel's old Info window. In versions prior to
Excel 97, the Info window (Tools, Options, View Tab, Info Window check box) was used to
analyze a cell's information, which included its value, formula, range names used, protection,
formatting, dependents and precedents, and the note (now called comments). The old Info
window was more robust; it showed more info about the cell, but it could analyze only one
cell at a time.

6

Watch Window's information for the currently selected cell

Figure 6.20
The Watch Window
allows you to track
formulas' addresses.

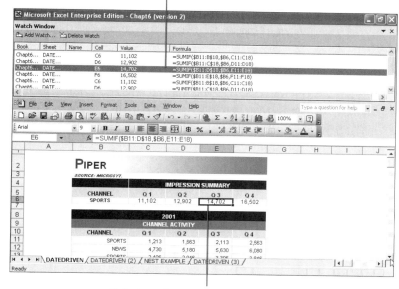

Select a cell and click Add Watch to view
the cell's information in the Watch Window

REFERENCING VALUES IN OTHER WORKSHEETS AND WORKBOOKS

You can write formulas that calculate values in other worksheets and other workbooks, which is a common way to compile and summarize data from several different sources. When you write formulas that reference other worksheets and workbooks, you create links to those other worksheets and workbooks.

REFERENCING OTHER WORKSHEETS

Suppose you have a workbook that contains separate worksheets for each division in your company. You can combine data from each division's worksheet in a Summary sheet in that same workbook to compile and analyze data for the entire company. Formulas on the Summary sheet will need to reference data on the individual division sheets (these are called *external references*). You can create external references by switching to the other worksheet and clicking and dragging the cells you want to reference, just as in a same-worksheet reference; the only difference is that the cells are located on a different worksheet.

To reference data from another worksheet in your formula, follow these steps:

1. Begin building the formula.

2. When you are ready to insert the reference from another worksheet, click the tab for that worksheet.

TIP FROM

Sometimes it's easier to work in two windows, side by side on your screen. To open a second window, click Window, New Window. Then, click Window, Arrange, and in the Arrange Windows dialog box, click an arrangement (Tiled always works well), and click OK. Then, select the second worksheet in one of the windows.

3. Locate the cell (or cells) that you want to reference, and select it. If you're referencing a range, drag across the range to select it. The sheet name and cell reference appear in the Formula bar, as shown in Figure 6.21.

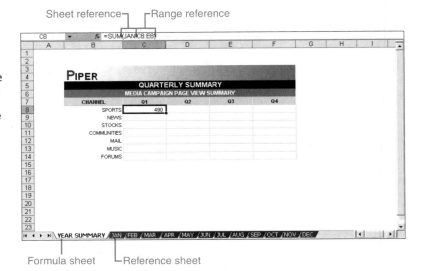

Figure 6.21
A three-dimensional worksheet (external references) equals the sheet name, followed by an exclamation point, followed by the cell reference (which can be relative or absolute).

4. Continue building your formula by typing the remaining operators. If your formula requires cells from other worksheets (or from the original worksheet), repeat steps 2 and 3 to add them.

5. When the formula is complete, press Enter.

You can also enter three-dimensional(external references) worksheet references by typing them. The syntax for an external worksheet reference is

```
SheetName!CellReference
```

If the sheet name contains spaces, enclose the sheet name in single quotation marks, like this:

```
'Year End Summary'!CellReference
```

If you change the sheet name after you've written formulas referencing it, no problem! Because they're in the same workbook, the formulas automatically update to show the current sheet name.

APPLYING CUBED FORMULAS

A cubed formula is formula that summarizes information across multiple sheets in a workbook. (see also Chapter 24 using PivotTables and PivotCharts. Although not recommended, there is a data-management style of workbooks that spread data across worksheets with a need to summarize the individual sheets onto a summary page. Instead, you could apply all the data on one sheet and use pivot tables to summarize the data on another sheet, but if you're stuck with the former data-management philosophy, do the following. First, make sure you set up your worksheets identical to each other by grouping or copying and pasting the like tables onto the separate worksheets. Notice in Figure 6.22, the formula =Sum(Jan:Dec!C8:E8) summarizes all sheets from January through December. To summarize only January and December, the formula would be =Sum(Jan!C8:E8,Dec!C8:E8).

Figure 6.22
Summarize multiple sheets of information with one simple formula.

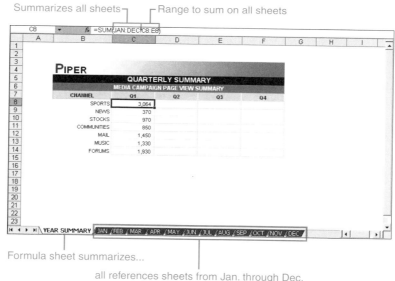

Summarizes all sheets ⌐ ⌐ Range to sum on all sheets

Formula sheet summarizes...

all references sheets from Jan. through Dec.

REFERENCING OTHER WORKBOOKS

If you need to reference data in another workbook (called a *source* workbook), you can write formulas with external workbook references, also referred to as *links*. For example, employees in another city send you their Excel files with operational data for their division. The following steps show how to reference two additional workbooks. To write a formula using external workbook references (links), follow these steps:

1. Open the workbooks you want to use, including the source workbook(s) and the destination workbook in which the formula will be written.

2. Select the cell in the destination workbook to start building your formula.

3. Begin the formula with an equal sign (=). In this example, you could also use the AutoSum button on the Standard toolbar to start the formula.

4. Click in one of the source workbooks, and then select the cell (or cells) you want to include in the formula.

   The cell reference is added to the formula, but because it's located in another workbook, the reference includes both the workbook and worksheet names (see Figure 6.23). The workbook name is in square brackets and is followed by the worksheet name; the worksheet name is separated from the cell reference by an exclamation point, like this:

   `[WorkbookName]WorksheetName!CellReference`

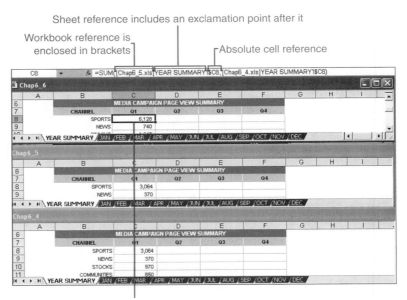

Figure 6.23
Using multiple windows is the easiest way to work in multiple workbooks.

5. Continue building your formula by typing operators and clicking in other workbooks to select additional cell references.

6. Complete the formula by pressing Enter.

The formula in the destination workbook shown in Figure 6.23 calculates the sum of the cells in the two source workbooks. All three workbooks are now linked by the formula.

You can also enter external workbook references by typing them. The syntax for an external workbook reference is

`[BookName.xls]SheetName!CellReference`

If the book name or the sheet name contains spaces, enclose the entire book-and-sheet reference in single quotation marks, like this:

```
'[North Division.xls]Year End Summary'!CellReference
```

UPDATING VALUES IN REFERENCED WORKBOOKS

The workbook that contains the formula is called the *dependent* or target workbook, and the workbook that contains the data being referenced is called the *source* workbook. If the values in the source workbooks change, the formula that references them can update its results automatically.

If the source workbook is open when you open the dependent workbook, the formula is automatically updated with no questions. If the source workbook is closed when you open the dependent workbook, you'll be asked whether you want to update all linked information. The dialog box will offer several options:

- If you click Update, all formulas containing external references are updated with current values from the source workbooks, even if those values have changed.

- If you click Don't Update, the formula won't be updated with current values but will retain its previous values, which saves you time spent waiting for a large workbook to recalculate.

- If you choose Update and one or more source workbooks cannot be found, a new additional prompt appears allowing you to click a Continue button (which opens the workbook without correcting the problem), or click an Edit Links button, which opens the Edit Links command and allows the user to either Break the link or change the Source.

   The Edit Links dialog box also contains a check status button and a Startup Prompt button, which allows the user to customize what happens when the workbook opens.

- To edit the links in a workbook, click Edit, Links. In the Edit Links dialog box, click Change Source. In the Change Links dialog box, locate and click the name of the moved or renamed source workbook, and click OK. Click OK to close the Links dialog box, and the link is permanently fixed (until you move, delete, or rename the source again).

TIP FROM

If you don't want the formula to recalculate, ever, or be bothered by the links that need updating every time you open the workbook, you can break the link and save the current formula result as a value. To break a link, choose Edit, Links, and then select Break Link from the Edit Links dialog box.

6

TROUBLESHOOTING

COMMON FORMULA ERRORS

After entering a formula, I am getting unusual results, and sometimes no result at all.

Formula errors are most often the result of a typo or the inclusion of a cell or range reference that doesn't contain appropriate values for the formula. Typos can include misspellings, missing or inappropriate operators, or missing parentheses.

Be sure that all nested functions, ranges, and arguments are held within a complete pair of parentheses, and that each left parenthesis has a matching right parenthesis.

TRANSPOSING RANGES WITH FORMULAS

You can transpose ranges with formulas by using the replace feature in the Edit menu to remove and replace the "=" sign in the formula with an "*". By doing this you deactivate the formula allowing relative references to remain intact. Once the cells are transposed use Excel's replace feature to replace the "*" with the "=" sign and the formula will reactivate.

AUTOSUM WON'T SUMMARIZE THE ENTIRE LIST OF NUMBERS

AutoSum looks for the first blank cell and stops there. Make sure you enter a zero value as opposed to leaving the cell blank so AutoSum will include the numbers above the zeroed cell.

EXCEL IN PRACTICE

When inheriting workbooks from others, you can run trace precedents to view cells that reference other workbooks and worksheet cells. Auditing tools help show relationships of precedents and dependents. Notice Figure 6.24 and 6.25. Figure 6.24 shows auditing precedents from other worksheets or workbooks denoted by the icon and Figure 6.25 shows the relationships of one formula with references to other cells on the worksheet. If you inherit workbooks, this will help you understand the layout and logic.

Figure 6.24
Trace precedents with icons denoting formulas reference other worksheets.

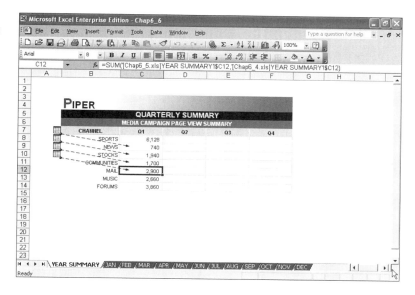

Figure 6.25
Trace precedents with lines denoting the relative and absolute referencing.

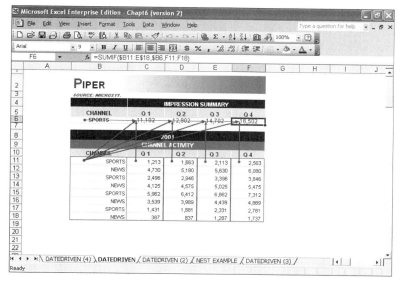

CHAPTER 7

DATABASE FUNCTIONS

In this chapter

Database Functions Overview and Syntax   190

DAVERAGE   192

DCOUNT   193

DGET   194

DMAX   195

DMIN   196

DPRODUCT   197

DSUM   197

GETPIVOTDATA   198

DATABASE FUNCTIONS OVERVIEW AND SYNTAX

Database functions operate over ranges that can span more than one row or column. One of the key benefits of database functions is the capability to set up criteria ranges for creating complex criteria. For example, if you have to look up maximum or minimum numbers through a period of time over a span of years, database functions work great for a quick reference lookup. As with all functions, you can reference the database with a range name or with the cell references; either way works.

Although database functions as well as many other functions work well for managing and looking up data, if at all possible you should use PivotTables to manage large lists, data stores, or databases of information. Not only is this method the fastest and most efficient way to manage data but you can also apply the dBASE functions to PivotTables. This chapter covers the database functions listed in Table 7.1 that appear in bold font.

→ For more information on implementing PivotTables, **see** Chapter 24, "Using PivotTables and PivotCharts."

TABLE 7.1   DATABASE FUNCTIONS

Function	Syntax	Description
DAVERAGE	=DFUNCTION(database,field,criteria)	Indicates the average of the values that meet the specified criteria.
DCOUNT	=DFUNCTION(database,field,criteria)	Counts the number of cells that contain numbers that meet the specified criteria.
DCOUNTA	=DFUNCTION(database,field,criteria)	Counts nonblank cells containing numbers or text that meet the specified criteria.
DGET	=DFUNCTION(database,field,criteria)	Returns a singlevalue that meets the specified criteria.
DMAX	=DFUNCTION(database,field,criteria)	Extracts the highest value that meets the specified criteria.
DMIN	=DFUNCTION(database,field,criteria)	Extracts the lowest value that meets the specified criteria.
DPRODUCT	=DFUNCTION(database,field,criteria)	Returns the product of the values that meet the specified criteria.
DSTDEV	=DFUNCTION(database,field,criteria)	Returns the calculation of the standard deviation of a sample population based on the values that meet the specified criteria.

7

Function	Syntax	Description
DSUM	`=DFUNCTION(database,field,criteria)`	Returns the total of the values that meet the specified criteria.
DVAR	`=DFUNCTION(database,field,criteria)`	Estimates the variance of a sample population, based on the values that meet the specified criteria.
DVARP	`=DFUNCTION(database,field,criteria)`	Estimates the variance of an entire population, based on the values that meet the specified criteria.
GETPIVOTDATA	`=DFUNCTION(Data_Field, pivot_table, field 1, item1, field 2, item 2…)`	Returns a value of data stored in a PivotTable.

If you have large data stores or databases, DFUNCTION can be quite useful. With all database functions, you can use cell references within the formula, text or hard code references, or column numbers to reference the column number from left to right in a list. The general syntax for DFUNCTION is as follows:

`=DFUNCTION(database,field,criteria)`

- The *database* argument refers to the range encompassing the entire list or database, including any field (column) headings.
- The *field* argument refers to a particular column in the list that contains the data that you want calculated. If you omit the data in the cells for the *field* argument, the function operates on the entire list. The field argument must be included.
- The *criteria* argument specifies the basis on which you want the function to select particular cells. Another way to describe it is that criteria is the specific requirements you set for the return. If you omit the data in the cells for the *criteria* argument, the function operates on the entire range specified in the *field* argument.

The database range can be a reference range of cells (Example 1a) or a named range (Example 2a) on all database functions. In this example, I've used the term SalesRange for a named range, which could refer to a range such as C3:F17.

1a. `=DFUNCTION(C3:F17,field,criteria)`
2a. `=DFUNCTION(SalesRange,field,criteria)`

The <u>field</u> can be the number of the column such as 3, meaning the third column in the list (Example 1b). It can be a cell reference such as C3 that contains the column heading that you want calculated (Example 2b). The <u>field</u> can also be the column heading's text.

7

However, the text must be enclosed in quotation marks, although it is not case sensitive (Example 3b).

1b. `=DFUNCTION(Database,3,Criteria)`

2b. `=DFUNCTION(Database,C3,Criteria)`

3b. `=DFUNCTION(Database,"Column Heading Name",Criteria)`

The *criteria* argument is the range containing restrictions on which data should be included in the calculation. This means that you can specifically call out parameters or criteria to isolate the results, such as the sum of all numbers greater than 30, with the DSUM function.

DAVERAGE

The DAVERAGE function averages the numbers that span over a range based on criteria you specify.

`=DAVERAGE(database,field,criteria)`

The *criteria* argument is the range containing restrictions on which data should be included in the calculation. This means that you can specifically call out parameters or criteria to isolate the results, such as the sum of all numbers greater than 30, with the DSUM function.

The DAVERAGE function counts the total number of entries and divides the total of the numbers by the number of entries. When sampling data or populations, or analyzing sales data over large ranges, the DAVERAGE function quickly summarizes and returns the average. Notice the example in Figure 7.1. The channel campaign media impressions for the Piper.com company spans four years and six channels. The first set of criteria looks up the average for the year 2000 for all impressions greater than 5,000 and less than 6,000 with a result of 5,600. The met criteria are pointed out in the figure with the bullets. The second example uses the column number to specify the criteria and the third example hard codes "1999". These are three unique examples of using the DAVERAGE syntax for results.

NOTE

> Because no criteria are specified in C19 the last two example functions operate on all the data.

7

Figure 7.1
The DAVERAGE function can be used to average numbers in lists based on data that meets the specified criteria.

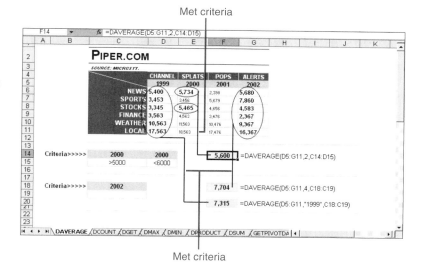

DCOUNT

The DCOUNT function counts the number of cells containing numbers.

```
=DCOUNT(database,field,criteria)
```

Cells that contain text, blank cells, and errors are ignored. To include those other types, use DCOUNTA. If you have a list or database, the database can be referenced as a cell reference or as a named range. The field is the number of the column in the database from left to right or the column heading in quotation marks (not case sensitive).

TIP FROM

> Although database functions serve a unique purpose in Excel, you should familiarize yourself with PivotTables to manage large data stores or databases.

The criteria argument is a range that contains the constraints from which the function operates. For example, let's say you had a large database that had several blank cells as well as cells containing numbers, only in some of which you were interested. The criteria could specify to count all numbers having a value of more than 4,000 and less than 7,000, as shown in Figure 7.2 in Example 1. Example 2 takes into account the criteria greater than 12,000 in column 4 of the database, and Example 3 hard codes the column, "1999". You can reference the CD for the workbook examples and work with the criteria to see the examples in action.

7

Figure 7.2
The DCOUNT function counts the number of cells that contain numbers and that meet specified criteria.

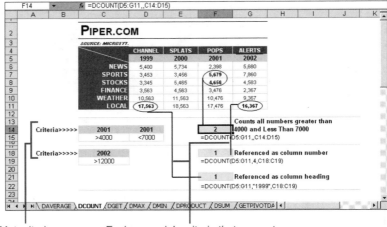

Met criteria　　　　Each example's criteria that are met

DGET

The DGET function extracts a number within a database at two intersecting points.

=DGET(database,field,criteria)

For example, if you have rate tables used in conjunction with a financial model, the DGET function can be used to retrieve rates based on criteria in the criteria range. The database argument is the range or named range of the database; and the field is referenced as either the column heading in quotation marks or the column number from left to right. The criteria argument is a range that is referenced and the function operates from the parameters set. Notice the example in Figure 7.3; the DGET formula looks in the list in B6:F10, locates the Rate 2 field (or heading), and applies the criteria in B13:F14 to look up Product C. If more than one value meets the specified criteria, DGET returns a #NUM! error. Example 2 shows another use of the function using text within the function for looking up the column header versus using the actual column number in B19.

Figure 7.3
The DGET function finds a number at two intersecting points.

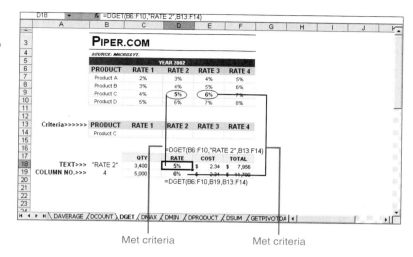

Met criteria   Met criteria

DMAX

The DMAX function looks up the highest value in a range or database.

`=DMAX(database,field,criteria)`

The database argument is the range or named range of the database; and the field is referenced as either the column heading in quotation marks or the column number from left to right. The criteria argument is a range that is referenced, and the function operates from the parameters set. The field can also be a cell reference. For example, notice the formula in Figure 7.4 that references the column heading Minnesota in cell F23. The criteria look up the highest temperature that is less than 20 degrees. If you type a new column heading, or state in this case, in the cell reference F23, the DMAX formula searches through that column heading in the database. The cell reference could be Minnesota or 1, meaning column 1 of the database. Either way works. You can use cell references for the field in all database functions. When you look at the figure, you'll notice that Minnesota in cell F23 is not case sensitive, and neither is the criteria range. The circle points out the result after the criteria are met. To change the result to another state, all you would need to do is type in the state in cell F23 and remove the "<20" in the criteria range and type "<20" under the state you're looking up.

Figure 7.4
The DMAX function finds the maximum value in a database range with criteria or parameters.

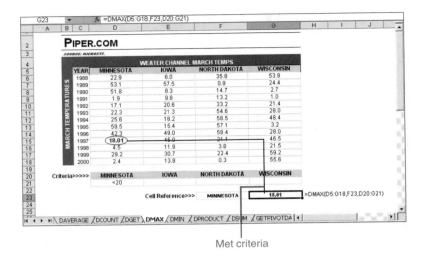

Met criteria

DMIN

The DMIN function is like the DMAX function but looks up the lowest value in a range or database.

```
=DMIN(database,field,criteria)
```

The database argument is the range or named range of the database; and the field is referenced as either the column heading in quotes or the column number from left to right. The criteria argument is a range that is referenced, and the function operates from the parameters set. The field can also be a cell reference. Notice the example in Figure 7.5; the criteria are set for all values greater than 0 and the cell reference is for Minnesota or column 1 of the list or database. The circle points out the exact result and cell in which the criteria were met within column 1 for Minnesota.

Figure 7.5
The DMIN function is like the DMAX function but looks up the minimum value within a list or database.

| G23 | ▼ | fx | =DMIN(D5:G18,F23,D20:G21) |

PIPER.COM

SOURCE: MICROSTT.

WEATER CHANNEL MARCH TEMPS

YEAR	MINNESOTA	IOWA	NORTH DAKOTA	WISCONSIN
1988	22.92	6.0	35.8	53.9
1989	53.08	57.5	0.9	24.4
1990	-18.50	8.3	14.7	2.7
1991	1.94	9.8	13.2	1.0
1992	-17.40	20.6	33.2	21.4
1993	-4.00	21.3	54.6	28.0
1994	25.57	18.2	58.5	48.4
1995	59.47	15.4	57.1	3.2
1996	42.30	49.0	58.4	28.0
1997	18.01	45.0	21.1	46.5
1998	4.46	11.9	3.8	21.5
1999	29.22	30.7	22.4	59.2
2000	2.44	13.8	0.3	55.6

Criteria>>>>>	MINNESOTA	IOWA	NORTH DAKOTA	WISCONSIN
	>0			

Cell Reference>>> MINNESOTA 1.94 =DMIN(D5:G18,F23,D20:G21)

DAVERAGE / DCOUNT / DGET / DMAX \ DMIN / DPRODUCT / DSUM / GETPIVOTDA |

Met criteria

DPRODUCT

The DPRODUCT function returns the product of multiplying the values that meet the specified criteria.

=DPRODUCT(database,field,criteria)

In the syntax for this function, the database argument is the range or named range of the database; the field is referenced as either the column heading in quotes or the column number from left to right. The criteria argument is a range that is referenced, and the function operates from the parameters set. The field can also be a cell reference. In Figure 7.6, the product is the multiplication of the cost and the markup. As well, the parameters are Unit 1 with a cost greater than $2 and a markup less than 30%. The product is 2.88. Of course, this is a simple example to illustrate parameters and the operation of the function.

NOTE

> The DPRODUCT will multiply all the total figures for all the totals that pass the criteria. For example, if the Unit 1 record in row 11 had a markup percentage of 29%, yielding a total of 5.55, the 5.55 (which now passes the criteria) would be multiplied by the 2.88 (cell G6), the other total that passed the criteria. The DPRODUCT result would be 15.97.

Figure 7.6
The DPRODUCT function multiplies the numbers based on parameters set in the criteria range of a given list or database.

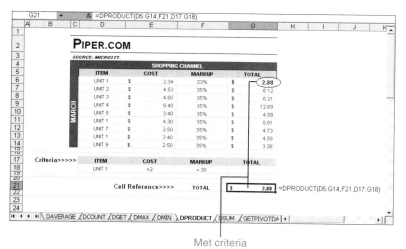

Met criteria

DSUM

DSUM returns the total of the values that meet the specified criteria within a list or database.

=DSUM(database,field,criteria)

The DSUM function operates much like the SUM function except that it operates on a database with criteria. The database argument is the range or named range of the database; the `field` is referenced as either the column heading in quotes or the column number from left to right. The `criteria` argument is a range that is referenced, and the function operates from the parameters set. The `field` can also be a cell reference. The criteria enable you to apply constraints, as shown in the example in Figure 7.7. Notice the criteria apply the sum of all sales for the cars produced later than 1995 and earlier than 2000. The sum of sales dollars from 1996 through 1999 equals $974,746. The cars column is hard coded in the example as text; you could also express the field argument as a cell reference or as a column number. You should use cell references to maintain the flexibility to scroll across columns.

Figure 7.7
The DSUM function sums up all numbers that fall within the specified criteria; in this case, it sums up all car sales later than 1995 and earlier than 2000.

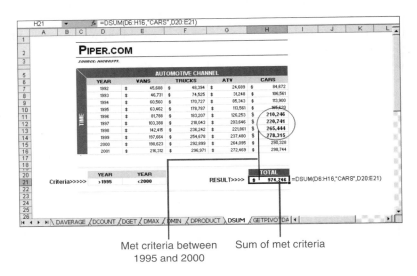

Met criteria between 1995 and 2000   Sum of met criteria

GETPIVOTDATA

GETPIVOTDATA returns a value of data stored in a PivotTable. Excel 2003 allows you to type = in a cell and then select the cell in a PivotTable to automatically create the formula within the cell.

`=GETPIVOTDATA(pivot_table,name)`

- The *pivot_table* argument refers to the PivotTable that contains the data you want to retrieve. This can be a reference to any cell within the PivotTable or a named range that refers to the PivotTable.

- The *name* is the text string enclosed in double quotation marks or referenced as your lookup criteria.

- The second argument can specify multiple column and row headings with a corresponding search item in each (all in quotation marks), which enables the user to pull out a specific value in a table with multiple row/column layers.

TIP

> If you want to reference a cell in a PivotTable but do not want Excel to write a PivotTable formula in that cell, do the following: If B4 references a cell in the PivotTable then type =B4. Don't click the PivotTable. This is important because when you are creating an extended list from a PivotTable, you can then drag the formula down with relative referencing.

The GETPIVOTDATA function can extract total sums from a PivotTable or pull multiple sets of data and find the information at their intersecting points. For example, notice the PivotTable in Figure 7.8. The months are shown down the left side and the years across the top. The formula to look up a grand total for the year 2000 is

```
=GETPIVOTDATA(E6,"Sum of 2000")
```

In this formula, E6 selects the entire PivotTable, and "Sum of 2000" in quotation marks is the column heading. Looking up information at intersecting points, such as the sum of August for the year 2000, is not case sensitive. The formula would read

```
=GETPIVOTDATA(E4,"Aug Sum of Sales")
```

Or

```
=GETPIVOTDATA("Sum of 2000",$E$6,"MONTH","AUG")
```

Figure 7.8
The GETPIVOT-
DATA function can
be used to extract
total sums or to find
the intersecting
points of sets of data.

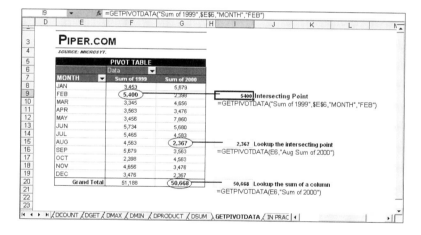

TROUBLESHOOTING

INSERTING PIVOTTABLES

When I click a PivotTable, it automatically inserts the PivotTable formula. How can I get around this?

If you want to reference a cell in a PivotTable but do not want Excel to write a PivotTable formula in that cell, do the following: Type =B4 if B4 references a cell in the PivotTable.

Don't click the PivotTable. This is important because when you are creating an extended list from a PivotTable, you can then drag the formula down with relative referencing.

EXCEL IN PRACTICE

When structuring your database and criteria, be sure to create a logically organized table to allow for dynamically changing the criteria, for example C14:D15 where cells C15 and D15 can be changed producing new results. Notice the example in Figure 7.9. By changing the criteria in cells C14:D15, the result of the DAVERAGE function in cell F14 changes. You should use dynamic cell referencing instead of hard coding as shown in cell F20.

Figure 7.9
As a rule, remember to use cell referencing in formulas instead of hard coding; this makes your formula dynamic based on the criteria.

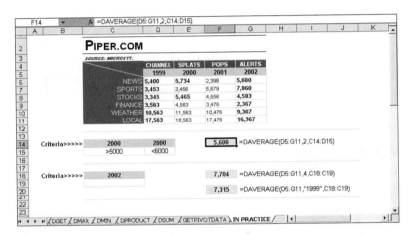

CHAPTER **8**

DATE AND TIME FUNCTIONS

In this chapter

Date and Time Functions Overview   202

DATE   204

DAYS360   205

EDATE   206

MONTH   207

NETWORKDAYS   208

TODAY   209

WEEKDAY   210

YEAR   211

DATE AND TIME FUNCTIONS OVERVIEW

Date and time functions are powerful functions that allow you to automate and manage information dealing with time elements. For example, if you have a daily report that goes out and you always want the report to include the day it was printed, you could manually enter the current date into a cell before printing or let Excel's TODAY() date function do it for you. The date and time formulas can do much more than provide a simple date in a cell; they can also help you manage time by calling out due dates, weekends, holidays, or dates that are past due. You can find maturity dates, and create calculators that manage your bills and combine formulas to see workdays in the future.

Unlike most other numeric data, when you enter a date or a formula that calculates a date, in most cases, Excel automatically displays the result in an easily readable date format. The date is actually a serial number representing the time elapsed since 12:00 AM, January 1, 1900. For example, Jan 1, 1900 = 1 where Jan 2, 1900 = 2 and so on. When you are comparing two dates, Excel is looking at the serial numbers. Therefore, one date minus another date is one serial number subtracted from another serial number, with the result converted back into a date format. This chapter covers the functions listed in Table 8.1 that are marked in bold.

Some functions require the Analysis ToolPak to be installed. To install the analysis select the Tools menu and choose Add-Ins. Then check Analysis toolpak and click OK.

TABLE 8.1   DATE AND TIME FUNCTIONS

Function	Syntax	Description
DATE	=DATE(*year*,*month*,*day*)	Returns the DATEVALUE as a serial number.
DATEVALUE	=DATEVALUE(*date_text*)	Converts a text date to a DATEVALUE as a serial number.
DAY	=DAY(*serial_number*)	Returns the corresponding day of the month as a serial number, from 1 to 31.
DAYS360	=DAYS360(*start_date*, *end_date*)	Returns the number of days between two set dates that you specify.
EDATE	=EDATE(*start_date*,*months*)	Returns the value or serial number of the date specified by you and which is the number of months. Use EDATE to calculate the maturity date or date due that falls on the same day of the month as the date of issue.
EOMONTH	=EOMonth(*start_date*,*months*)	Returns the calculated maturity dates or dates due that fall in the last day of the month.

Function	Syntax	Description
HOUR	=HOUR(*serial_number*)	Returns the hour as a serial number integer between 0 and 23.
MINUTE	=MINUTE(*serial_number*)	Returns the serial number that corresponds to the minute.
MONTH	=MONTH(*serial_number*)	Returns the corresponding serial number of the month between 1 and 12.
NETWORKDAYS	=NETWORKDAYS(*start_date*, *end_date*,*holidays*)	Returns the number of working days between two dates. Excludes weekends and specified holidays.
NOW	=NOW()	Returns the current date and time in the form of a serial number. There are no arguments for this function. This function updates the date and time each time the worksheet it appears on recalculates.
SECOND	=SECOND(*serial_number*)	Returns the corresponding serial number of seconds as an integer between 0 and 59.
TIME	=TIME(*hour*,*minute*,*second*)	Returns the corresponding serial number of time as fraction or decimal between 0 and 0.99999999.
TIMEVALUE	=TIMEVALUE(*time_text*)	Returns the serial number represented by text as time.
TODAY	=TODAY()	Returns the current date as a serial number. There are no arguments for this function. This function updates the date each time the worksheet it appears on recalculates.
WEEKDAY	=WEEKDAY(serial_number, return_type)	Returns the corresponding day of the week as a serial number.
WORKDAY	=WORKDAY(start_date,days, holidays)	Returns date and time functions. A number representing the date that is the number of days (specified by days) before or after start_date. You can exclude dates with the holidays argument.
YEAR	=YEAR(*serial_number*)	Returns the corresponding year as a serial number in the form of an integer.
YEARFRAC	=YEARFRAC(*start_date*, *end_date*,*basis*)	Returns the calculated fraction of the year represented by whole numbers between two dates.

DATE

The DATE function returns the date value, or serial number as shown in Figure 8.1 in cell C13, of a given year, month, and day.

```
=DATE(year,month,day)
```

Excel automatically formats this function in a date format; however, the date format is actually a serial number that starts from the time 12:00 AM on January 1, 1900, and is formatted as a date. Use the DATE function to convert a given month, day and year into a serial number (by itself or in conjunction with other formulas). The syntax descriptions are in the following order of year,month,day. You can use the DATE function in conjunction with other formulas, as in the example in Figure 8.1. If you need to find out the actual calendar day of the year a day falls on, use the formula =B7-Date(Year(B7),1,0), where cell B7 references a cell with a date in it. You can calculate the days to date and the remaining days in the year.

- **Year**—The serial number in Windows operating systems that falls between 1900 and the year 9999. For Macintosh, the number is 1904 to 9999.

- **Month**—The serial number representing the month of the year from 1 to 12. If greater than 12, it adds that number to the first month in the year specified.

- **Day**—The serial number representing the day of the month. If that number is greater than 31, it adds the number of days to the first day in the month.

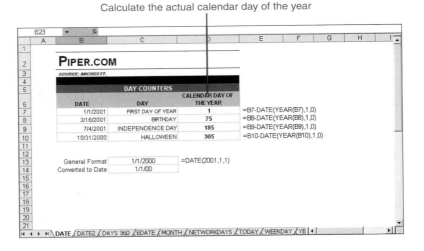

Figure 8.1
Use the DATE and YEAR function to calculate the day of the year a date falls on.

Notice the following example in Figure 8.2 using the DATE function in conjunction with the YEAR and MONTH function. If you wanted to find out how many days were in a given month of a specified year, you could use this function, where D8 is a day in a given month of a given year and the result cell returns the last day of that month. As you can see, the only change from 2000 to 2001 is in the month of February from 29 days to 28 days. Also, Excel considers the 0th day of a month to be the last day of the previous month.

Figure 8.2
The DATE function can also be used to plot the last day of each month in a year.

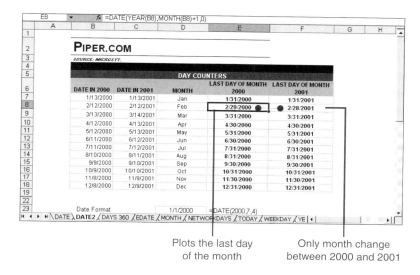

Plots the last day of the month

Only month change between 2000 and 2001

DAYS360

DAYS360 returns the number of days between two set dates based on a 360-day year.

```
=DAYS360(start_date,end_date)
```

The DAYS360 function is used primarily for accounting systems based on a 360-day year—if, for example, you calculate payments based on 12 30-day months. In Figure 8.3, you'll notice the DAYS360 function in cell D7 calculates the number of days between the start date of 3/16/2000 and 3/16/2005 to be 1800. This number divided by 30 gives you the number of payments. The second example builds the 30-day divisor into the formula as shown in D11 and is basically a combination of the two formulas in the first example. And last, you'll see that the DAYS360 function is used with text dates in cell D15, and that the dates are enclosed by quotation marks and are separated with a comma. Text dates are entered in the format, mm,dd,yyyy.

- **Start and End Date**—The start and end dates for which you want the number of days returned between. If the end date is less than the start date, the result is a negative number.

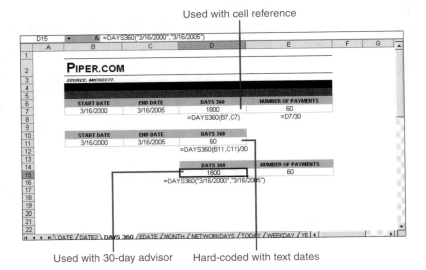

Figure 8.3
The DAYS360 formula operates on a 360-day year accounting system—12 30-day months.

Used with cell reference

Used with 30-day advisor   Hard-coded with text dates

EDATE

EDATE returns the value or serial number of the date specified by you and which is the number of months before or after the specified date. Use EDATE to calculate the maturity date or date due that falls on the same day of the month as the date of issue.

=EDATE(start_date,months)

The EDATE function is found in the Analysis ToolPak. If you don't see the EDATE function, you must first install the Analysis ToolPak and then enable the ToolPak by choosing Tools, Add-Ins. In Figure 8.4, the start date in cell B8 is 3/16/1999 and the number of months to maturity is in cell C8; therefore, the result would equal 4/16/1999. A –1 would result in the date 2/16/1999. The second example in cell D18 uses a text date entry and the months to maturity is 7, resulting in the date 10/16/1999. Note that because this function returns a serial number, you might have to apply a date format to the cell containing the formula.

- **Start Date**—The start date to maturity.

Figure 8.4
The EDATE function calculates the maturity date or date due that falls on the same day of the month as the date of issue.

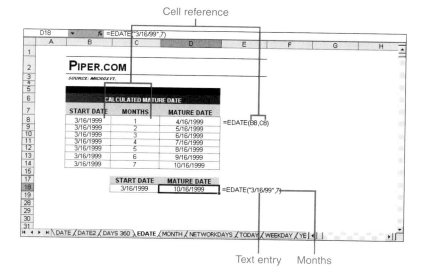

Cell reference

Text entry   Months

MONTH

MONTH returns the corresponding serial number of the month between 1 and 12 for a specified date.

`=MONTH(serial_number)`

The MONTH function operates off the serial number or day of the year. For example, 1 equals the first day of the year and falls in January. You can use the MONTH formula with the serial number in parentheses or as a cell reference. For example, embed the MONTH function with the SUM and IF function in the form of an array to sum the total values in a given month. The example in Figure 8.5 shows the month value of March in cell B14 as 3 and the function and formula is in cell C14. (Bullets denote the cells that were added.) After you enter the formula, make sure you hold down Ctrl+Shift and press Enter to activate the array. The MONTH function combined with the SUM and IF function can be a powerful tool when managing lists of information. (see the "YEAR" section later in this chapter).

- **Serial Number**—The serial number is a number between 1 and 12 that represents a month in a year. The serial number can be extracted from text in quotes or as a cell reference.

Figure 8.5
Use the MONTH function to sum up the values in a given month.

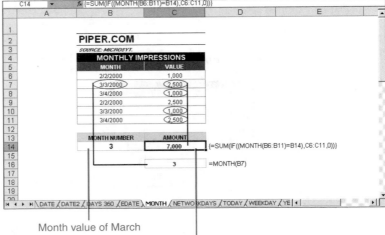

Month value of March

Sum of impressions in March

NETWORKDAYS

NETWORKDAYS returns the number of working days between two dates (excludes weekends and specified holidays):

=NETWORKDAYS(start_date,end_date,holidays)

The NETWORKDAYS function allows you to find out the total number of working days between two dates excluding the weekends and holidays. This is an extremely important function when calculating schedules that have to be completed within specific timeframes. In Figure 8.6, the first example in cell E6 is used to calculate actual working days between two dates and excluding holidays. The function refers to the following cells and what they represent:

- B6=Start Date
- C6=End Date
- D6:D9=Holidays

You can also use text referencing within the formula enclosed by quotation marks; however, I recommend against hard coding text within formulas. To keep functions dynamic, use cell referencing and the function remains dynamic, changing when you apply new dates or holidays. You could also add your vacation days to the holiday number to get a more accurate account. This function requires the Anaylsis ToolPak be installed.

- **Start Date**—The date that represents the start date.
- **End Date**—The date that represents the end date.
- **Holidays**—This is optional; however, you can use one or more holidays in the form of text in the formula or in a range of cells.

8

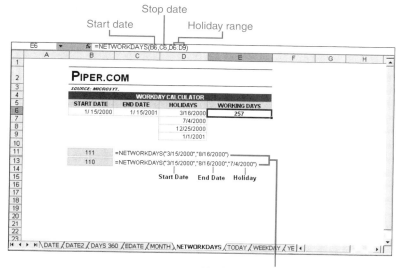

Figure 8.6
The NETWORK-
DAYS function
allows you to find the
number of working
days between two
dates, excluding
weekends and holi-
days.

Hard-coded dates and holidays

TODAY

TODAY returns the current date as a serial number. There are no arguments for this function.

=TODAY( )

The TODAY function is a powerful, dynamic function that allows you to see the current day every time the workbook is opened, calculated, or printed. You could place the TODAY function in a cell on a report so you always have the current day posted on the report, or you could use the TODAY function to calculate the total days you have left to complete a project or pay a bill. In conjunction with the NETWORKDAYS function, you can create a quick snapshot of a project (see Figure 8.7). The NETWORKDAYS function supplies the total workdays within a given timespan excluding weekends and holidays. The TODAY function in cell E6, denoted as Current Date, operates as a walking day, or dynamic day, that changes every time you open the workbook. The Remaining Days left in the project cell uses the results of both the Current Date cell and the Total Working Days cell within the project.

Figure 8.7
The TODAY function can operate as a time-management tool to calculate the remaining days within a project.

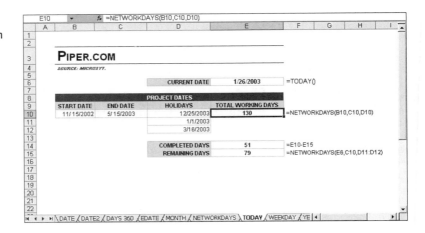

WEEKDAY

WEEKDAY returns the corresponding day of the week as a serial number.

=WEEKDAY(serial_number,return_type)

The WEEKDAY function is another function that can be a powerful tool when combined with other functions. It returns the number corresponding to the day of the week between 1 and 7, where the first day of the week is Sunday and the seventh day is Saturday. If your date format is 1/1/00 and you're planning your work schedule, you can type in the cell, =WEEKDAY("1/1/00"), or reference a cell containing a date. However, what if you are planning dates in the future for approvals and final production of a media campaign? You probably plot out dates in the future not realizing some of those dates actually fall on the weekend. In this case, you can create a weekday kicker formula that kicks a date that falls on Saturday to Friday and kicks a date that falls on Sunday to Monday. With this formula, you are assured that all dates within your plan will fall on a weekday as opposed to a weekend. In Figure 8.8, the Review and Revision dates actually fall on Sunday and Saturday; however, the weekday formula used in conjunction with an IF function converts the day to Monday and Friday. The weekday formula returns the day of the week, which the IF function then uses to add one day to the Date Due if it's a Sunday (1), the first day of the week, and subtracts one day if it's a Saturday (7), the seventh day of the week.

- **Serial Number**—The serial number is the date time code used by Microsoft Excel. You can specify the serial number as text and Excel will automatically convert the serial number text to the day value, or you can apply the day value.

- **Return Type**—This number determines the type of return value. 1 or omitted, returns 1 (Sun) through 7 (Sat), or 2 returns 1 (Mon) through 7 (Sun), or 3 returns 0 (Mon) through 6 (Sun).

8

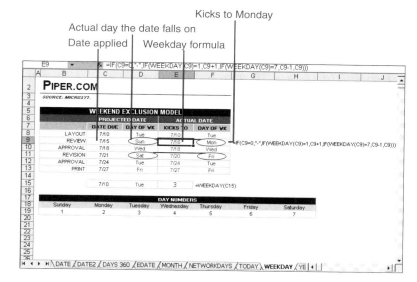

Figure 8.8
The WEEKDAY function can act as a date manager by kicking days that fall on weekends to weekdays.

YEAR

YEAR returns the corresponding year as a serial number in the form of an integer, a date time code between the numbers 1900 and 9999.

`=YEAR(serial_number)`

The serial number is the code that Excel uses for date and time calculations. The date and value of Windows date systems is any date from 1/1/1900 to 12/31/9999. The date value of Macintosh systems is any date from 1/1/1904 to 12/31/9999. In the Options dialog box (choose Tools, Options), you can change the date system of an Excel for Windows system to the 1904 date system found on the Calculation tab. The year value of `=YEAR("1/1/2000")` results in 2000. The serial number of `=YEAR(0.007)` results in 1900; if you're using the 1904 date system, the same year value of `=YEAR(0.007)` results in 1904.

- **Serial Number**—The serial number is the date time code used by Microsoft Excel. You can specify the serial number as text and Excel will automatically convert the serial number text to the year value, or you can apply the year value.

You can use the YEAR function to summarize all the values within a list that fall within a given year. The YEAR function combined with the SUM and IF function in the form of an array can be a powerful data-management tool. When your list contains a date range from B9:B15 and a number range from C9:C15, use the cell reference of B19 to input the year (see Figure 8.9). This way, you can input 2000 or 2001 and the formula will respond and summarize the totals for that year. Be sure to activate the array by holding down Ctrl+Shift and then pressing Enter. Note, in the example =YEAR(B19) is just the year value of the number 2000.

Figure 8.9
Embed or nest the YEAR function within the SUM and IF functions to total the values over any given year.

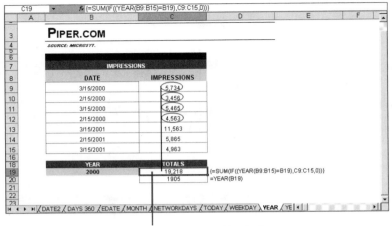

Sum of all values that meet the year 2000 criteria

To summarize all numbers in a list that fall within a given month and year, you can take the previous example one step further by adding a Month condition in the form of an array (be sure to activate the array by holding down the Ctrl+Shift key and then pressing Enter). In Figure 8.10, the Year condition in cell B20 is 2000 and the Month condition in cell C20 is 2. The formula looks through the date range, finds all conditions that meet B20 and C20, and then adds the adjacent values in the range C9:C15. The bullets denote the result cells.

TIP FROM

Another way to write this formula without using an embedded `if` statement is
`{=SUM((YEAR(B9:B15)=B20)*(MONTH(B9:B15)=C20)*(C9:C15))}`.

Figure 8.10
Embed or nest the YEAR and MONTH functions within the SUM and IF functions to total the values over any given months and years within a list.

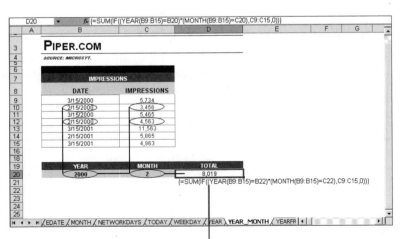

Use this function to summarize values within a month and year

TROUBLESHOOTING

#VALUE USING SUM(MONTH

When I use a SUM(MONTH formula, I get a #Value return.

Make sure you press Ctrl+Shift+Enter to activate the array, which is the multiple adjacent ranges the formula is referencing

`{=SUM((YEAR(B9:B15)=B20)*(MONTH(B9:B15)=C20)*(C9:C15))}`.

#VALUE FROM NETWORKDAYS

I can't get NETWORKDAYS to work. It returns #Value!

Make sure you have the Analysis ToolPak installed. This is commonly overlooked. Without the Analysis ToolPak installed, the formula won't work. Choose Tools, Add-Ins. In the Add-Ins dialog box, check the Analysis ToolPak.

EXCEL IN PRACTICE

Use data validation to automate your year and month lookups. Notice the pop-up scroll box that appears in the cell in Figure 8.11.

Figure 8.11
Create automated drop-down lists that allow for selecting numbers within a given list using data validation.

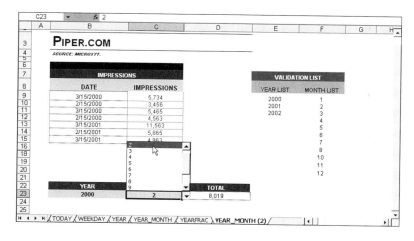

To create an automated drop-down in a cell when the cell is selected, select Data, Validation. Under Allow, choose List. Under Source, select the range of the Month List as shown in Figure 8.12. This way, when you select the cell, a drop-down list or pop-up menu appears and the formula reacts to the month selected.

Figure 8.12
The SUM (IF
formula reacts to
the selected month
and year because it
is set up with cell
referencing.

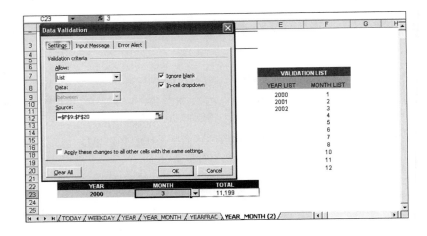

CHAPTER

9

ENGINEERING FUNCTIONS

In this chapter

Engineering Functions Overview   216

BESSELI   218

BIN2DEC   219

COMPLEX   220

CONVERT   223

DEC2BIN   223

DELTA   223

GESTEP   224

HEX2BIN   225

IMCONJUGATE   225

IMPOWER   226

IMPRODUCT   227

IMSUB   228

IMSUM   229

OCT2BIN   230

ENGINEERING FUNCTIONS OVERVIEW

Engineering functions are built-in formulas that allow you to apply engineering analysis against statistical and logical information. The bold font functions in Table 9.1 are covered in this chapter. (To use these functions the Analysis ToolPak must be installed. To install the Analysis ToolPak, select Tools, Add In and then check Analysis ToolPak.)

TABLE 9.1 ENGINEERING FUNCTIONS

Function	Syntax	Description
BESSELI	=BESSELI(*x*,*n*)	Returns the Bessel function of the first kind in modified form for imaginary arguments.
BESSELJ	=BESSELJ(*x*,*n*)	Returns the actual Bessel function of the first kind. X is the value at which to evaluate the function. N is the order of the Bessel function.
BESSELK	=BESSELK(*x*,*n*)	Returns the Bessel function of the second kind in modified form for imaginary arguments.
BESSELY	=BESSELY(*x*,*n*)	Returns the Bessel function of the second kind, also known as the Weber or Neumann function. X is the value at which to evaluate the function. N is the order of the function.
BIN2DEC	=BIN2DEC(*number*)	Converts a binary number to decimal form.
BIN2HEX	=BIN2HEX(*number*,*places*)	Converts a binary number to hexadecimal.
BIN2OCT	=BIN2OCT(*number*,*places*)	Converts a binary number to octal.
COMPLEX	=COMPLEX(*real_num*, *I_num*,*suffix*)	Converts real and imaginary coefficients into a complex number of the form x + yi or x + yj, where i and j are imaginary suffix components.
CONVERT	=CONVERT(*number*,*from_unit*, *to_unit*)	Converts from one measurement system to another.
DEC2BIN	=DEC2BIN(*number*,*places*)	Converts decimal numbers to binary.
DEC2HEX	=DEC2HEX(*number*,*places*)	Converts decimal numbers to hexadecimal.
DEC2OCT	=DEC2OCT(*number*,*places*)	Converts decimal numbers to octal.
DELTA	=DELTA(*number1*,*number2*)	Tests whether numbers or values are equal.
ERF	=ERF(*lower_limit*, *upper_limit*)	Returns the integrated error function between lower limit and upper limit.
ERFC	=ERFC(*x*)	Returns a complementary ERF function integrated between x and infinity. X is the lower bound for integrating ERF.

Function	Syntax	Description
GESTEP	=GESTEP(*number*,*step*)	Returns the value of 1 if the number is greater than or equal to the step, or threshold, otherwise 0.
HEX2BIN	=HEX2BIN(*number*,*places*)	Converts hexadecimal numbers to binary.
HEX2DEC	=HEX2DEC(*number*)	Converts hexadecimal numbers to decimal.
HEX2OCT	=HEX2OCT(*number*,*places*)	Converts hexadecimal numbers to octal.
IMABS	=IMABS(*inumber*)	Returns the absolute value (Modulus) of a complex number in x+yi or x+yj text format.
IMAGINARY	=IMAGINARY(*inumber*)	Returns the coefficient of a complex number in x+yi or x+yj text format.
IMARGUMENT	=IMARGUMENT(*inumber*)	Returns the Theta argument as an angle expressed in radians.
IMCONJUGATE	=IMCONJUGATE(*inumber*)	Returns the complex conjugate of a complex number in x+yi or x+yj text format.
IMCOS	=IMCOS(*inumber*)	Returns the cosine of a complex number in x+yi or x+yj text format.
IMDIV	=IMDIV(*inumber1*,*inumber2*)	Returns the quotient of complex numbers in x+yi or x+yj text format.
IMEXP	=IMEXP(*inumber*)	Returns the exponential of complex numbers in x+yi or x+yj text format.
IMLN	=IMLN(*inumber*)	Returns the natural logarithm of a complex number in x+yi or x+yj text format.
IMLOG10	=IMLOG10(*inumber*)	Returns the common logarithm (base 10) of a complex number in x+yi or x+yj text format.
IMLOG2	=IMLOG2(*inumber*)	Returns the base 2 logarithm of a complex number in x+yi or x+yj text format.
IMPOWER	=IMPOWER(*inumber*,*number*)	Returns a complex number in x+yi or x+yj text format raised to a power.
IMPRODUCT	=IMPRODUCT(*inumber1*, *inumber2*,...)	Returns the product from 2 to 29 complex numbers in x+yi or x+yj text format.
IMREAL	=IMREAL(*inumber*)	Returns real coefficient of complex numbers in x+yi or x+yj text format.
IMSIN	=IMSIN(*inumber*)	Returns the sine of a complex number in x+yi or x+yj text format.
IMSQRT	=IMSQRT(*inumber*)	Returns the square root of a complex number in x+yi or x+yj text format.

continues

TABLE 9.1	CONTINUED	
Function	**Syntax**	**Description**
IMSUB	=IMSUB(*inumber1,inumber2*)	Returns the difference of two complex numbers in x+yi or x+yj text format.
IMSUM	=IMSUM(*inumber1, inumber2,...*)	Returns the sum of two complex numbers in x+yi or x+yj text format.
OCT2BIN	=OCT2BIN(*number,places*)	Converts an octal number to binary.
OCT2DEC	=OCT2DEC(*number*)	Converts an octal number to decimal.
OCT2HEX	=OCT2HEX(*number,places*)	Converts an octal number to hexadecimal.

BESSELI

The BESSELI function returns the BESSEL function in modified form for imaginary arguments:

=BESSELI(x,n)

The BESSELI function is found only if the Analysis ToolPak is installed. In addition, it must be turned on by choosing Tools, Add-Ins. Both x and n must be numeric and greater than zero. Notice the example in Figure 9.1. Where the value is 2 and the integer is 1, the BESSELI function results in 1.5906.

- **x**—The value to evaluate the function.
- **N**—The order of the BESSEL function. Truncated if not an integer.

The *n*th order modified BESSEL function of the variable x is

$$I_n(x) = (i)^{-n} J_n(ix)$$

Figure 9.1
The BESSELI function returns the modified BESSEL function for imaginary arguments.

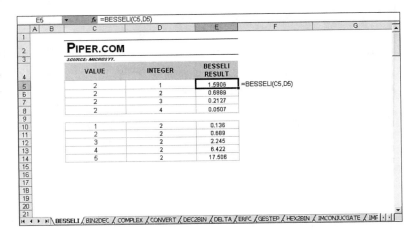

BIN2DEC

The BIN2DEC function converts a binary number to decimal form:

`=BIN2DEC(number)`

The BIN2DEC function is found only if the Analysis ToolPak is installed. In addition, it must be turned on by choosing Tools, Add-Ins. The number cannot be more than 10 characters. Notice the example in Figure 9.2, where the Binary Number is 10000010 and the conversion to a decimal results in 130.0000.

- **NUMBER**—The binary number to convert. The most significant number is the sign bit. The remaining 9 bits are magnitude bits. Cannot contain more than 10 characters (10 bits).

Binary numbers converted to a decimal

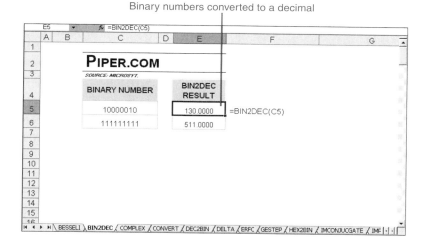

Figure 9.2
Use the BIN2DEC function to convert a binary number to a decimal. The binary number cannot be more than 10 characters.

COMPLEX

Use the COMPLEX function to convert real and imaginary coefficients into a complex number of the form x+yi or x+yj:

`=COMPLEX(real_num,I_num,suffix)`

The COMPLEX function is found only if the Analysis ToolPak is installed. It must be turned by choosing Tools, Add-Ins. Lowercase "i" and "j" must be used for the suffix argument for the function to work. The suffixes must match also. Notice the example in Figure 9.3. Where the Real Imaginary Coefficient is 3 and the Imaginary Coefficient is 4, the result is 3+4i.

- **Real_Num**—The real coefficient of the complex number.
- **I_Num**—The imaginary coefficient of the complex number.
- **SUFFIX**—Either the "i" or "j" suffix for the imaginary component. If omitted, it's assumed to be "i." Suffix must be in lowercase.

Figure 9.3
Converts real and imaginary coefficients into a complex number.

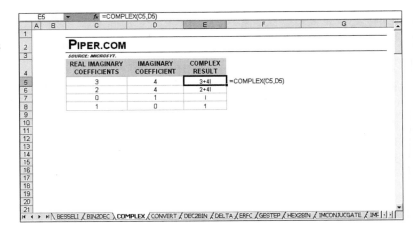

CONVERT

CONVERT interprets or converts data from one measurement system to another:

`=CONVERT(number,from_unit,to_unit)`

The CONVERT function is found only if the Analysis ToolPak is installed. Notice the conversion examples and how the formula is structured in Figure 9.4. The conversion tables in Tables 9.2 and 9.3 show the conversion text that must be used to convert units of measure.

Figure 9.4
Converts measurement units from one unit to another.

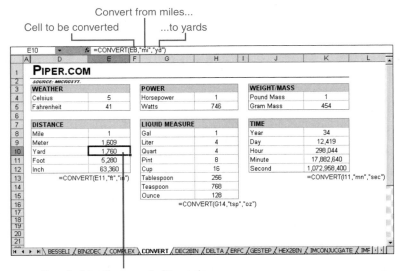

- **NUMBER**—The number to convert.
- **From_unit**—Measurement unit to convert from.
- **To_unit**—Measurement unit to convert to.

TABLE 9.2 CONVERSION TABLE

Unit Type	From Unit to Unit	Unit Type	From Unit to Unit
Weight and Mass		*Force*	
Gram	"g"	Newton	"N"
Slug	"sg"	Dyne	"dyn"
Pound mass	"lbm"	Pound force	"lbf"
Ton	"u"	*Energy*	
Distance		Joule	"J"
Meter	"m"	Erg	"e"
Statute mile	"mi"	Thermodynamic calorie	"c"
Nautical mile	"Nmi"	IT calorie	"cal"
Inch	"in"	Electron volt	"eV"
Foot	"ft"	Horsepower hour	"HPh"
Yard	"yd"	Watt-hour	"Wh"
Angstrom	"ang"	Foot-pound	"flb"
Pica(1/72 in.)	"Pica"	BTU	"BTU"
Time		*Power*	
Year	"yr"	Horsepower	"HP"
Day	"day"	Watt	"W"
Hour	"hr"	*Magnetism*	
Minute	"mn"	Telsa	"T"
Second	"sec"	Gauss	"ga"
Pressure		*Temperature*	
Pascal	"Pa"	Degree Celsius	"C"
Atmosphere	"atm"	Degree Fahrenheit	"F"
mm of Mercury	"mmHg"	Degree Kelvin	"K"

continues

TABLE 9.2   CONTINUED

Unit Type	From Unit to Unit	Unit Type	From Unit to Unit
Liquid Measure		*Liquid Measure*	
Teaspoon	"tsp"	U.K. Pint	"uk_pt"
Tablespoon	"tbs"	Quart	"qt"
Fluid ounce	"oz"	Gallon	"gal"
Cup	"cup"	Liter	"l"
U.S. Pint	"pt"		

The abbreviations for conversions in Table 9.3 are case sensitive.

TABLE 9.3   ADDITIONAL CONVERSIONS

Prefix	Multiplier	Abbreviation
exa	1E+18	"E"
peta	1E+15	"P"
tera	1E+12	"T"
giga	1E+09	"G"
mega	1E+06	"M"
kilo	1E+03	"k"
hecto	1E+02	"h"
deka	1E+01	"e"
deci	1E-01	"d"
centi	1E-02	"c"
milli	1E-03	"m"
micro	1E-06	"u"
nano	1E-09	"n"
pico	1E-12	"p"
femto	1E-15	"f"
atto	1E-18	"a"

DEC2BIN

The DEC2BIN function converts decimal numbers to binary:

`=DEC2BIN(number,places)`

DEC2BIN is found only if the Analysis ToolPak is installed. The number returns a 10 character binary. The sign bit being the most significant, the remaining 9 bits are magnitude bits. Negatives are represented using twos-complement notation. Notice the example in Figure 9.5. Where the Decimal Number is 2 and the Places is 3, the conversion to a binary results in 010.

- **NUMBER**—The number to convert. Cannot be less than –512 or greater than 511.
- **PLACES**—The number of characters to use. If PLACES is omitted, it uses the least characters necessary. If the value is not an integer, the value is truncated. Use when you want to pad the result with leading zeros to achieve uniformity.

Figure 9.5
Converts decimals to binary numbers.

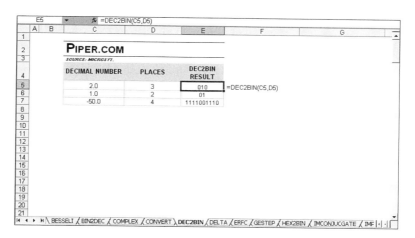

DELTA

DELTA tests whether numbers or values are equal and returns a number result of either 0 or 1—sometimes referred to as Kronecker: DELTA helps count the number of equal pairs by summing several DELTA functions.

`=DELTA(number1,number2)`

The DELTA function is found only if the Analysis ToolPak is installed. If the first number is 1 and the second number is 2, the result is 0 (False). However, if the first number is 1 and the second number is 1, the result is 1 (True), similar to a True or False logical test, except the return is a number instead of a text result. Notice the example in Figure 9.6.

- **Number 1**—The first number.
- **Number 2**—The second number. If omitted, assumes 0.

Figure 9.6
DELTA tests whether
two numbers are
equal with a numeric
result.

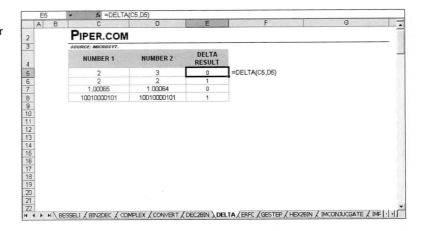

GESTEP

The GESTEP function returns the value of 1 if the number is greater than or equal to a specified step value, otherwise 0:

```
=GESTEP(number,step)
```

The GESTEP function is found only if the Analysis ToolPak is installed. The Analysis ToolPak must be turned on by choosing Tools, Add-Ins. Notice the example in Figure 9.7. Where the number is equal to or greater than the step, the result is 1. Otherwise, the result is 0. You can use this to sum up only those values that exceed the step value.

- **NUMBER**—The number to test against the step value.

- **STEP**—The step value is the threshold value the number is tested upon. If the value for step is omitted, it assumes 0.

Figure 9.7
Returns the value of 1
if the number is
greater than or
equal to the step,
otherwise 0.

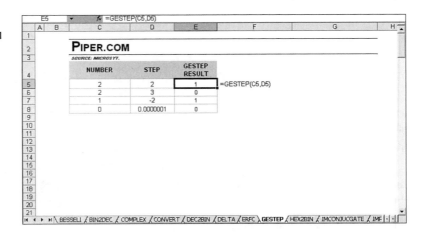

HEX2BIN

Convert hexadecimal numbers to binary with the HEX2BIN function:

=HEX2BIN(number,places)

HEX2BIN is found only if the Analysis ToolPak is installed. Notice in the example in Figure 9.8, the binary number is converted to a hexadecimal and then the HEX2BIN function converts the hexadecimal back to a binary number. The number variable cannot contain more than 10 characters. The most significant bit of the number variable is the sign bit (40th bit from the right). The remaining 9 bits are magnitude bits. Negative numbers are represented using twos-complement notation. If the number variable is negative, it cannot be less than FFFFFFFE00, and if it is positive, it cannot be greater than 1FF:

- **NUMBER**—The number to convert. Cannot be less than –512 or greater than 511.

- **PLACES**—The number of characters to use. If PLACES is omitted, it uses the least characters necessary. If the value is not an integer, the value is truncated. Use when you want to pad the result with leading zeros to achieve uniformity.

Figure 9.8
Converts hexadecimal numbers to binary numbers.

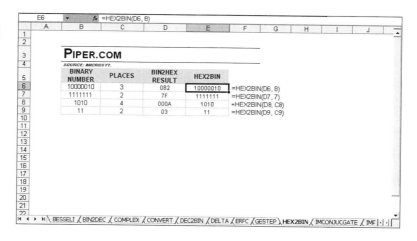

IMCONJUGATE

Imconjugate returns the complex conjugate of a complex number in x+yi or x+yj text format:

=IMCONJUGATE(inumber)

IMCONJUGATE is found only if the Analysis ToolPak is installed. Where the complex number in Figure 9.9 is 3+4i, the complex conjugate results in 3-4i.

- **Inumber**—The complex number you want converted to the complex conjugate.

Where the formula is

IMCONJUGATE("3+4i") equals 3 - 4i

Figure 9.9
Returns the complex conjugate of a complex number in x+yi or x+yj text format.

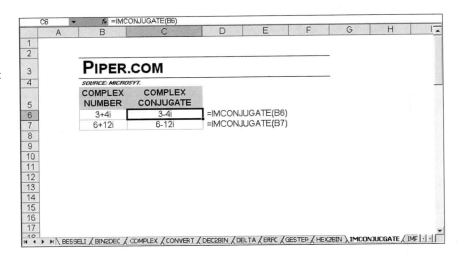

IMPOWER

Returns a complex number raised to a power in x+yi or x+yj text format:

=IMPOWER(inumber,number)

The IMPOWER function is found only if the Analysis ToolPak is installed and turned on by choosing Tools, Add-Ins. The example in Figure 9.10 shows the complex numbers with the powers to raise the numbers to and the result.

- **Inumber**—The complex number to raise to a power.
- **NUMBER**—The power to raise the complex number to.

The number being raised to the power is calculated as follows:

$$(x + yi)^n = r^n e^{n\theta} = r^n \cos n\theta + ir^n \sin n\theta$$

where

$$r = \sqrt{x^2 + y^2}$$

and

$$r = \sqrt{x^2 + y^2}$$

and:

$$\theta = \tan^{-1}\left(\frac{y}{x}\right)$$

→ To obtain the complex number of real and imaginary coefficients, **see** the "COMPLEX" section on **p. 219**

Figure 9.10
Returns a complex number raised to a power in x+yi or x+yj text format.

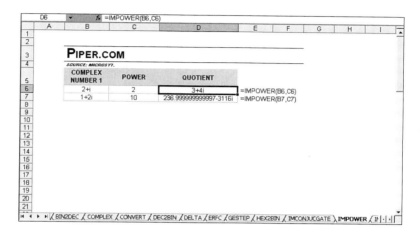

IMPRODUCT

IMPRODUCT returns the product from 2 to 29 complex numbers in x+yi or x+yj text format:

=IMPRODUCT(inumber1,inumber2,...)

The IMPRODUCT function is found only if the Analysis ToolPak is installed and turned on by choosing Tools, Add-Ins. The example in Figure 9.11 shows the complex numbers and their products. You can use from 1 to 29 complex numbers:

- **Inumber 1,2...**—1 to 29 complex numbers to multiply.

The product of two complex numbers:

$$(a + bi)(c + di) = (ac - bd) + (ad + bc)i$$

→ To obtain the complex number of real and imaginary coefficients, **see** the "COMPLEX" section on **p. 219**

Figure 9.11
Returns the product from 2 to 29 in complex numbers $x+yi$ or $x+yj$ text format.

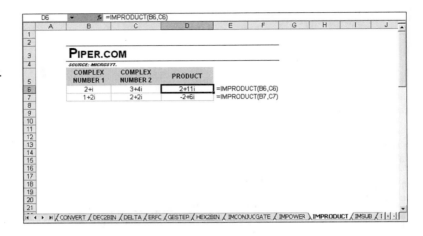

IMSUB

Returns the difference of two complex numbers in $x+yi$ or $x+yj$ text format:

`=IMSUB(inumber1,inumber2)`

The IMSUB function is found only if the Analysis ToolPak is installed and turned on by choosing Tools, Add-Ins. The example in Figure 9.12 shows the difference when two complex numbers are subtracted.

- **Inumber 1**—The complex number to subtract from Inumber 2.
- **Inumber 2**—The complex number to subtract from Inumber 1.

The difference between two complex numbers is

$$(a+bi)-(c+di)=(a-c)+(b-d)i$$

→ To obtain the complex number of real and imaginary coefficients, **see** the "COMPLEX" section on **p. 219**

Figure 9.12
Returns the difference of two complex numbers x+yi or x+yj in text format.

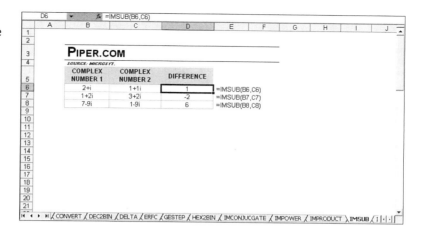

IMSUM

IMSUM returns the sum of two complex numbers x+yi or x+yj in text format:

=IMSUM(inumber1,inumber2,...)

The IMSUM function is found only if the Analysis ToolPak is installed and turned on by choosing Tools, Add-Ins. The example in Figure 9.13 shows the sum of 1–29 complex numbers when added together.

- **Inumber 1**— Inumber 1,2...—1 to 29 complex numbers to add.

The addition or sum of two complex numbers is

$$(a+bi)+(c+di)=(a+c)+(b+d)i$$

→ To obtain the complex number of real and imaginary coefficients, **see** the "COMPLEX" section on **p. 219**

Figure 9.13
Returns the sum of two complex numbers x+yi or x+yj in text format.

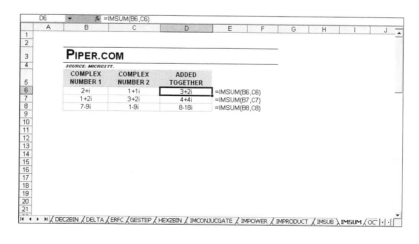

OCT2BIN

OCT2BIN converts an octal number to binary:

`=OCT2BIN(number,places)`

The OCT2BIN function is found only if the Analysis ToolPak is installed and turned on by choosing Tools, Add-Ins. The number cannot be more than 10 characters. The sign bit being the most significant, the remaining 29 bits are magnitude bits. Negatives are represented using twos-complement notation. Notice the example in Figure 9.14. Where the Binary Number is 10000010 and the Places is 3, the conversion to a Octal results in 202, and the conversion back to the binary results in 10000010.

- **NUMBER**—The number in which to convert. If the number is negative, it ignores the places and returns 10-character binary. The number cannot be greater than 777 and less than or equal to 7777777000.

- **PLACES**—The number of characters to use.

Figure 9.14
Converts an octal number to a binary number.

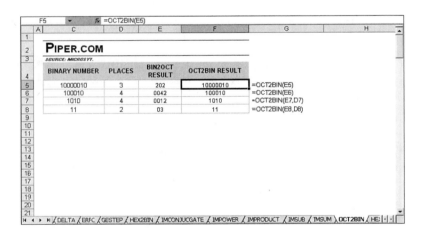

TROUBLESHOOTING

I NEED TO CONVERT ONE NUMBER TO ANOTHER FORM OF MEASUREMENT.

Use the CONVERT function. It interprets or converts data from one measurement system to another: `=CONVERT(number,from_unit,to_unit)`

I GET ERRORS FOR MOST OF THE FUNCTIONS COVERED IN THIS CHAPTER.

Make sure the Analysis ToolPak is installed. To install the Analysis ToolPak, select Tools, Add In and then check Analysis ToolPak.

EXCEL IN PRACTICE

To really take advantage of formulas or functions, the best practice is to create dynamic scenarios. This means using cell referencing. When you hard-code numbers in functions or formulas, you have to change the numbers directly in the formula for new results. If you use cell referencing, you can set up tables and change the numbers in the table and the formula will respond. It also makes it easier to understand the variables included in the formula. Notice the example in Figure 9.15. The binary numbers are set up in column B, the Places in column C, the BIND2DEC result in Column D, and the formula in Column E references the cells in D8 and C8 as shown.

Figure 9.15
Use cell referencing with formulas so you can create changes with dynamic results.

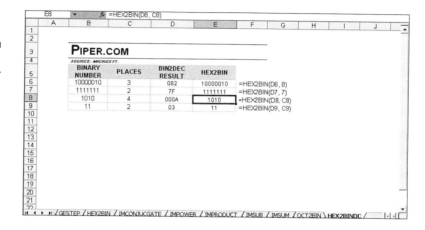

CHAPTER 10

FINANCIAL FUNCTIONS

In this chapter

Financial Functions Overview   234

ACCRINT   238

ACCRINTM   239

COUPDAYBS   240

COUPDAYS   241

COUPNCD   242

COUPNUM   243

CUMIPMT   244

DISC   245

DURATION   246

FV   247

IPMT   248

MDURATION   249

NPER   250

NPV   251

ODDFPRICE   252

PMT   254

PRICE   255

PV   256

RATE   257

RECEIVED   258

TBILLPRICE   259

TBILLYIELD   260

YIELD   261

YIELDMAT   262

FINANCIAL FUNCTIONS OVERVIEW

Financial functions can be used to calculate house mortgage payments, annuities, accrued interest, and just about any other financial calculation for future, present, or past values. Excel has more than 50 financial functions that can operate independently or can be combined with other functions for a more customized situation. The financial functions are also accompanied by descriptions of the syntax. This helps in understanding the function as a whole. You should take note that when creating functions to return date results, you might have to format the result in a date format. If the return is in digit format, change the cell format from the Format menu. Before moving on to the examples, many of these financial functions require dates for some of their arguments. Errors can occur when text dates are used. To avoid these errors, date arguments should be in the form of dates, not in the form of text. If you suspect the date is text, convert it using DATEVALUE or use the DATE function to explicitly define the date. Also, note that many of these functions require the Analysis ToolPak. To turn on the Analysis ToolPak, choose Tools, Add-Ins.

The functions in Table 10.1 presented in bold are included with examples in this chapter.

TABLE 10.1 FINANCIAL FUNCTIONS

Function	Syntax	Description
ACCRINT	=ACCRINT(*issue*, *first_interest*,*settlement*, *rate*,*par*,*frequency*,*basis*)	Returns the accrued interest for security that pays periodic interest
ACCRINTM	=ACCRINTM(*issue*,*maturity*, *rate*,*par*,*basis*)	Returns the accrued interest for security that pays interest at maturity
AMORDEGRC	=AMORDEGRC(*cost*,*date_ purchased*,*first_period*, *salvage*,*period*,*rate*,*basis*)	Returns depreciation for each accounting period
AMORLINC	=AMORLINC(*cost*,*date_ purchased*,*first_period*, *salvage*,*period*,*rate*,*basis*)	Returns depreciation for each accounting period
COUPDAYBS	=COUPDAYBS(*settlement*, *maturity*,*frequency*,*basis*)	Returns the number of days from the start date of thecoupon period to the settlement
COUPDAYS	=COUPDAYS(*settlement*, *maturity*,*frequency*,*basis*)	Returns the number of days in the coupon period that includes the settlement date
COUPDAYSNC	=COUPDAYSNC(*settlement*, *maturity*,*frequency*,*basis*)	Returns the number of days from the settlement date to the next coupon date
COUPNCD	=COUPNCD(*settlement*, *maturity*,*frequency*,*basis*)	Returns the number that is representative of next coupon date after the settlement date

Function	Syntax	Description
COUPNUM	=COUPNUM(*settlement*, *maturity*,*frequency*,*basis*)	Returns the total number of coupons payable between the settlement and maturity date, rounded up to the nearest whole coupon
COUPPCD	=COUPPCD(*settlement*, *maturity*,*frequency*,*basis*)	Returns the number of the previous coupon date before the settlement date
CUMIPMT	=CUMIPMT(*rate*,*nper*,*pv*, *start_period*,*end_period*, *type*)	Returns the cumulative interest on a loan between start and stop dates
CUMPRINC	=CUMPRINC(*rate*,*nper*,*pv*, *start_period*,*end_period*, *type*)	Returns the cumulative principal amount between start and stop dates
DB	=DB(*cost*,*salvage*,*life*, *period*,*month*)	Returns the asset depreciation for a period using the fixed-declining balance method
DDB	=DDB(*cost*,*salvage*,*life*, *period*,*factor*)	Returns the asset depreciation for a period using the double-declining balance method, or another method you specify
DISC	=DISC(*settlement*,*maturity*, *pr*,*redemption*,*basis*)	Returns the security discount rate
DOLLARDE	=DOLLARDE(*fractional_ dollar*,*fraction*)	Converts a fraction dollar price into a decimal dollar price
DOLLARFR	=DOLLARFR(*decimal_dollar*, *fraction*)	Converts a decimal dollar price into a fraction dollar price
DURATION	=DURATION(*settlement*, *maturity*,*coupon*,*yield*, *frequency*,*basis*)	Returns the duration for an assumed par value of $100 using the Macauley method
EFFECT	EFFECT(*nominal_rate*,*npery*)	Returns the effective interest rate annually, giving the nominal annual interest rate and the number of compounding periods per year
FV	=FV(*rate*,*nper*,*pmt*,*pv*,*type*)	Returns the future value of periodic payments and a constant interest rate
FVSCHEDULE	=FVSCHEDULE(*principal*, *schedule*)	Returns the future value of the initial principal after applying several compound interest rates

continues

TABLE 10.1 CONTINUED

Function	Syntax	Description
INTRATE	=INTRATE(*settlement*, *maturity*,*investment*, *redemption*,*basis*)	Returns the interest rate of a fully invested security
IPMT	=IPMT(*rate*,*per*,*nper*,*pv*, *fv*,*type*)	Returns the interest payment for a period of time based on an investment with periodic constant payments and a constant interest rate
IRR	=IRR(*values*,*guess*)	Returns the internal rate of return for a series of cash flows represented by numbers in the form of values
MDURATION	=MDURATION(*settlement*, *maturity*,*coupon*,*yield*, *frequency*,*basis*)	Returns a modified duration of a security with an assumed par value of $100
MIRR	=MIRR(*values*,*finance_rate*, *reinvest_rate*)	Returns a modified internal rate of return for several periodic cash flows
NOMINAL	=NOMINAL(*effective_rate*, *npery*)	Returns the nominal annual interest rate given an effective rate and a number of compounding periods per year
NPER	=NPER(*rate*,*pmt*,*pv*,*fv*,*type*)	Returns the number of periods for an investment based on periodic constant payments and a constant interest rate
NPV	=NPV(*rate*,*value1*,*value2*,...)	Calculates the net present value of an investment with the discount rate and several future payments and income
ODDFPRICE	=ODDFPRICE(*settlement*, *maturity*,*issue*,*first_ coupon*,*rate*,*yield*, *redemption*,*frequency*,*basis*)	Returns the value of a security based on a per $100 face value and an odd first period
ODDFYIELD	=ODDFYIELD(*settlement*, *maturity*,*issue*,*first_coupon*, *rate*,*pr*,*redemption*, *frequency*,*basis*)	Returns the security yield with an odd first period
ODDLPRICE	=ODDLPRICE(*settlement*, *maturity*,*last_interest*, *rate*,*yield*,*redemption*, *frequency*,*basis*)	Returns the per $100 face value of a security having an odd last coupon period

Function	Syntax	Description
ODDLYIELD	=ODDLYIELD(settlement, maturity,last_interest, rate,pr,redemption, frequency,basis)	Returns the security yield that has an odd last coupon period
PMT	=PMT(rate,nper,pv,fv,type)	Calculates the loan payment for a loan based on constant payments and constant interest rates
PPMT	=PPMT(rate,per,nper,pv, fv,type)	Returns the principal payment for a period of an investment based on periodic constant a constant interest rate
PRICE	=PRICE(settlement,maturity, rate,yield,redemption, frequency,basis)	Returns the value of a security based on price per $100 face value and periodic payments
PRICEDISC	=PRICEDISC(settlement, maturity,discount, redemption,basis)	Returns the value of a discounted security based on a price per $100 face value
PRICEMAT	=PRICEMAT(settlement, maturity,issue,rate, yield,basis)	Returns the value of a security that pays interest at maturity and price per $100 face value
PV	=PV(rate,nper,pmt,fv,type)	Returns the present value based on an investment
RATE	=RATE(nper,pmt,pv,fv, type,guess)	Returns per period the interest of an annuity
RECEIVED	=RECEIVED(settlement, maturity,investment, discount,basis)	Returns the amount received at maturity based on a fully invested security
SLN	=SLN(cost,salvage,life)	Returns the straight-line depreciation on an asset based on one period
SYD	=SYD(cost,salvage,life,per)	Returns the sum-of-years-digits depreciation of an asset based on a specified period
TBILLEQ	=TBILLEQ(settlement, maturity,discount)	Returns the bond equivalent yield for a treasury bill
TBILLPRICE	=TBILLPRICE(settlement, maturity,discount)	Returns the price per $100 face value for a treasury bill
TBILLYIELD	=TBILLYIELD(settlement, maturity,pr)	Returns the yield for a treasury bill

10

continues

TABLE 10.1 **CONTINUED**

Function	Syntax	Description
VDB	=VDB(cost,salvage,life, start_period,end_period, factor,no_switch)	Returns the depreciation of an asset for a period you specify
XIRR	=XIRR(values,dates,guess)	Returns the internal rate of return for a schedule of cash flows that are not necessarily periodic
XNPV	=XNPV(rate,values,dates)	Returns the present value for a schedule of cash flows that are not necessarily periodic
YIELD	=YIELD(settlement,maturity, rate,pr,redemption, frequency,basis)	Returns the yield of the security based on a yield that pays periodic interest
YIELDDISC	=YIELDDISC(settlement, maturity,pr,redemption, basis)	Returns the annual yield for a discounted security
YIELDMAT	=YIELDMAT(settlement, maturity,issue,rate,pr, basis)	Returns the annual yield based on a security that pays interest at maturity

Understanding Financial Terms and Definitions

The functions covered in this chapter must assume you have a basic familiarity with financial terms and processes. If you need more information, I suggest you reference from the Web site Investorwords.com. It can provide you with a basic crash-course on the terms and definitions used in this chapter.

ACCRINT

ACCRINT returns accrued interest for securities that pay periodic interest:

=ACCRINT(issue,first_interest,settlement,rate,par,frequency,basis)

The ACCRINT function is found only if the Analysis ToolPak is installed. It must be turned on using the Add-Ins command on the Tools menu. Notice the example in Figure 10.1. The example is set up with cell referencing so that you can make adjustments to dates, percentages, par values, and so on. By using cell referencing instead of applying the dates in the formula, your formula becomes more flexible.

- **Issue**—The date of the security issue.
- **First Interest**—The first interest date of the security.
- **Settlement**—The security settlement date is the date the security is traded to the buyer after the issue date.
- **Rate**—The security's annual coupon rate.

- **Par**—The security's par value. If you omit par, ACCRINT uses the default of $1,000.
- **Frequency**—The number of payments per year. Quarterly is 4, semiannually is 2, and annually is 1.
- **Basis**—The day count basis to use. If omitted, the function uses 0. Refer to Figure 10.1 for a list of choices.

The ACCRINT formula is calculated as

$$ACCRINT = par \times \frac{rate}{frequency} \times \sum_{i=1}^{NC} \frac{A_i}{NL_i}$$

Figure 10.1
The ACCRINT function returns the interest for a security that pays interest periodically.

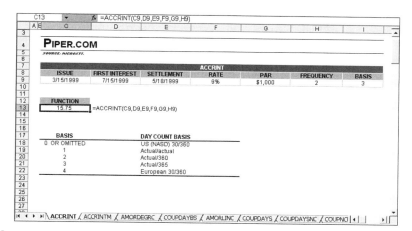

ACCRINTM

ACCRINTM returns accrued interest for securities that pay interest at the maturity date.

=ACCRINTM(issue,maturity,rate,par,basis)

The ACCRINTM function is found only if the Analysis ToolPak is installed. In addition, it must be turned on by choosing Tools, Add-Ins. Notice the example in Figure 10.2. The example is set up with cell referencing so that you can make adjustments to dates, percentages, par values, and so on. By using cell referencing instead of applying the dates in the formula, your formula becomes more flexible.

- **Issue**—The date of the security issue.
- **Maturity**—The date the security matures.
- **Rate**—The security's annual coupon rate.
- **Par**—The security's par value. If you omit par, ACCRINTM uses the default of $1,000.
- **Basis**—The day count basis to use. If omitted, the function uses 0. See Figure 10.2 for a list of choices.

The ACCRINTM formula can be calculated with

$$ACCRINTM = par \times rate \times \frac{A}{D}$$

Figure 10.2
The ACCRINTM function returns the accrued interest for the security that pays interest at maturity.

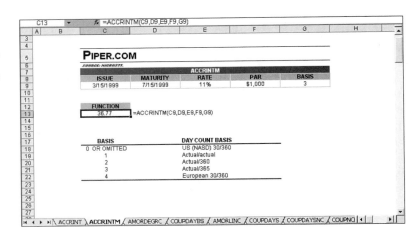

COUPDAYBS

COUPDAYBS returns the number of days from the beginning of the period to the coupon-period settlement date:

`=COUPDAYBS(settlement,maturity,frequency,basis)`

The COUPDAYBS function is found only if the Analysis ToolPak is installed and turned on by choosing Tools, Add-Ins. Notice in Figure 10.3, the bond settlement date (the date a buyer purchases a coupon, such as a bond) is 5/15/1999 and the maturity date (the date the bond expires) is 7/15/2000. The frequency is semiannual and the basis is Actual/actual. The number of days between the coupon day and the settlement is 120. By using cell referencing instead of applying the dates in the formula, your formula becomes more flexible.

- **Settlement**—The security's settlement date. This is the date after the issue date when the security is traded to the buyer.
- **Maturity**—The security's maturity date. The date when the security expires.
- **Frequency**—The number of payments per year—Annual = 1; Semiannual = 2; Quarterly = 4.
- **Basis**——The day count basis to use. If omitted, 0 is used. See additional choices in Figure 10.3.

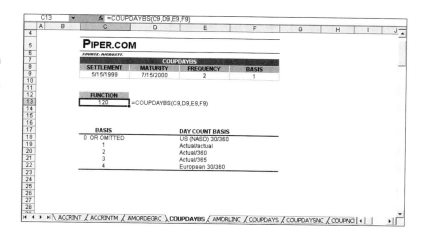

Figure 10.3
The COUPDAYBS function returns the number of days from the start date of the coupon period to the settlement.

COUPDAYS

COUPDAYS returns the number of days in the period that contains the coupon period settlement date.

=COUPDAYS(settlement,maturity,frequency,basis)

The COUPDAYS function is found only if the Analysis ToolPak is installed and turned on by choosing Tools, Add-Ins. In Figure 10.4, you'll see that the bond settlement date (the date a buyer purchases a coupon such as a bond) is 5/15/1999, and the maturity date (the date the bond expires) is 7/15/2000. The frequency is semianual and the basis is Actual/actual. The number of days between the coupon day and the settlement is 181. By using cell referencing instead of applying the dates in the formula, your formula becomes more flexible.

- **Settlement**—The security's settlement date. This is the date after the issue date when the security is traded to the buyer.
- **Maturity**—The security's maturity date. The date when the security expires.
- **Frequency**—The number of payments per year—Annual = 1; Semiannual = 2; Quarterly = 4.
- **Basis**—The day count basis to use. If omitted, 0 is used. See additional choices in Figure 10.4.

Figure 10.4
COUPDAYS returns the number of days in the period that contains the coupon period settlement date.

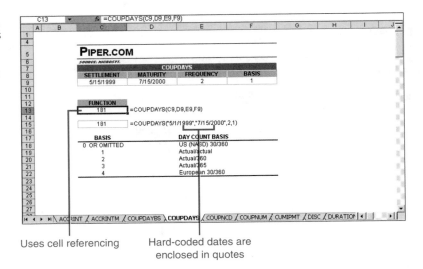

Uses cell referencing

Hard-coded dates are enclosed in quotes

COUPNCD

COUPNCD returns the number that represents the next coupon date after the settlement date.

=COUPNCD(settlement,maturity,frequency,basis)

The COUPNCD function is found only if the Analysis ToolPak is installed and turned on by choosing Tools, Add-Ins. The cell the function is in must also be in a date format. In Figure 10.5, the bond settlement date (the date a buyer purchases a coupon such as a bond) is 5/15/1999 and the maturity date (the date the bond expires) is 9/15/2000. The frequency is semiannual and the basis is Actual/actual. The next coupon date after the settlement date is 9/15/1999. By using cell referencing instead of applying the dates in the formula, your formula becomes more flexible because it will automatically update based on inputs in the proper cells. When you apply dates in the formula it's called "hard coding" and is more apt to include errors.

- **Settlement**—The security's settlement date. This is the date after the issue date when the security is traded to the buyer.
- **Maturity**—The security's maturity date. The date when the security expires.
- **Frequency**—The number of payments per year—Annual = 1; Semiannual = 2; Quarterly = 4.
- **Basis**—The day count basis to use. If omitted, 0 is used. See additional choices in Figure 10.5.

Figure 10.5
COUPNCD returns the number of the next coupon date after the settlement date.

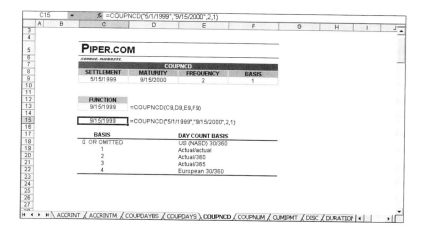

COUPNUM

COUPNUM returns the total number of coupons to be paid between the settlement and maturity dates, rounded up to the nearest whole coupon.

```
=COUPNUM(settlement,maturity,frequency,basis)
```

The COUPNUM function is found only if the Analysis ToolPak is installed and turned on by choosing Tools, Add-Ins. When you look at Figure 10.6, you'll see that the bond settlement date (the date a buyer purchases a coupon such as a bond) is 5/15/1999 and the maturity date (the date the bond expires) is 9/15/2000. The frequency is semiannual and the day count basis is Actual/actual. Where Actual/actual is an accounting term for the day count basis to use for certain annuities. The total number of coupons payable between the settlement and maturity date is 3. By using cell referencing instead of applying the dates in the formula, you give your formula greater flexibility.

- **Settlement**—The security's settlement date. This is the date after the issue date when the security is traded to the buyer.
- **Maturity**—The security's maturity date. The date when the security expires.
- **Frequency**—The number of payments per year—Annual = 1; Semiannual = 2; Quarterly = 4.
- **Basis**—The day count basis to use.

Figure 10.6
The COUPNUM function returns the total number of coupons payable between the settlement and maturity date, rounded up to the nearest whole coupon.

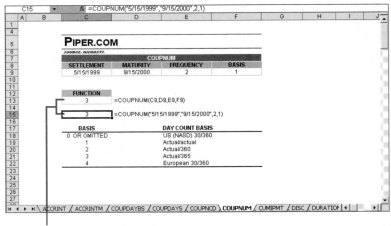

Payable coupons between settlement and security

CUMIPMT

CUMIPMT returns the cumulative interest on a loan between start and stop dates:

=CUMIPMT(rate,nper,pv,start_period,end_period,type)

The CUMIPMT function is found only in the Analysis ToolPak, which must be turned on by choosing Tools, Add-Ins. As you see in Figure 10.7, the rate is 7% on the loan, the number of payments on a 30-year mortgage is 360, and the present value of the loan is $250,000. The cumulative interest for the second year of the loan starts with 13 and ends with 24 (number in months). The type is 0 (payment at the end of the period). The cumulative interest on the loan for the second year of the mortgage is $20,759. The ABS function is used in conjunction with the formula to convert the value to an absolute value. Without the ABS function, the result would be -20,759. Note that you can also place a minus sign between the equal and the function name to convert it to a positive value.

■ **Rate**—The interest rate of the loan.

■ **Nper**—The number of payment periods.

■ **Pv**—The present value of the loan.

■ **Start_Period**—The first payment period. Payment periods start with one.

■ **End_Period**—The last period in the calculation.

■ **Type**—The payment timing.

Figure 10.7
Use CUMIPMT to
return the cumulative
interest on a loan
between start and
stop dates.

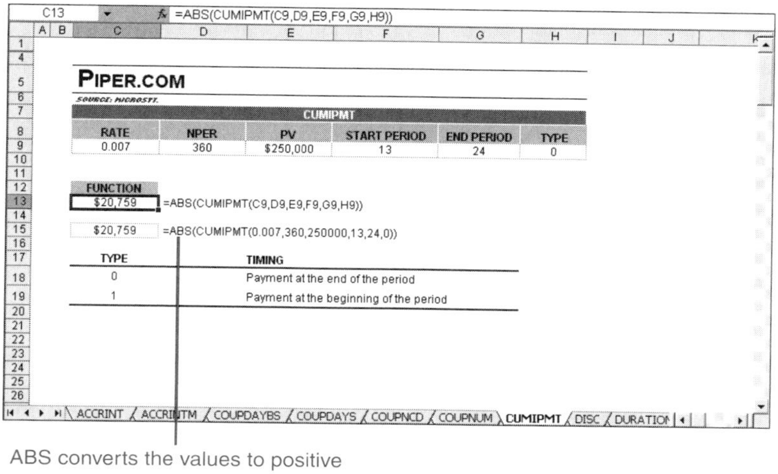

ABS converts the values to positive

10

DISC

DISC returns the security discount rate:

```
=DISC(settlement,maturity,pr,redemption,basis)
```

The DISC function is found only if the Analysis ToolPak is installed and turned on by choosing Tools, Add-Ins. In Figure 10.8, the bond settlement date (the date a buyer purchases a coupon such as a bond) is 5/15/1999 and the maturity date (the date the bond expires) is 11/15/1999. The security price per $100 face value is $95. The redemption value is $100. And the basis is Actual/360. The bond discount rate equals 9.92%. By using cell referencing instead of applying the dates in the formula, your formula becomes more flexible.

- **Settlement**—The security's settlement date. This is the date after the issue date when the security is traded to the buyer.
- **Maturity**—The security's maturity date—the date when the security expires.
- **Pr**—The security price per $100 face value.
- **Redemption**—The security redemption value per $100 face value.
- **Basis**—The day count basis to use.

Figure 10.8
The DISC function returns the security discount rate.

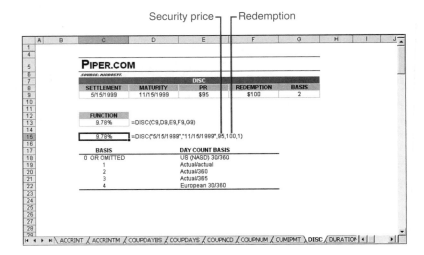

DURATION

DURATION returns the Macauley duration for an assumed par value of $100:

```
=DURATION(settlement,maturity,coupon,yield,frequency,basis)
```

The Duration function is found only if the Analysis ToolPak is installed and turned on by choosing Tools, Add-Ins. Notice that in Figure 10.9 the bond settlement date (the date a buyer purchases a coupon such as a bond) is 5/15/1999 and the maturity date (the date the bond expires) is 5/13/2007. The security's annual coupon rate is 8.7%. The security's annual yield is 9.2%. The frequency is semiannual and the basis is Actual/actual. The weighted average equals 5.89 years. By using cell referencing instead of applying the dates in the formula, your formula becomes more flexible.

- **Settlement**—The security's settlement date. This is the date after the issue date when the security is traded to the buyer.
- **Maturity**—The security's maturity date. The date when the security expires.
- **Coupon**—The security's annual coupon rate.
- **Yield**—The security's annual yield.
- **Frequency**—The number of payments per year—Annual = 1; Semiannual = 2; Quarterly = 4.
- **Basis**—The day count basis to use.

Figure 10.9
The DURATION method is the weighted average of the present value of the cash flows and is used as a measure of a bond's price response to changes in the yield.

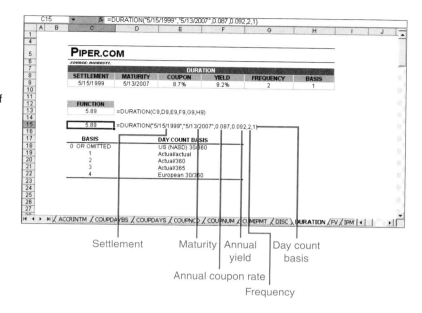

FV

FV returns the future value of an investment based on periodic constant payments and a constant interest rate:

```
=FV(rate,nper,pmt,pv,type)
```

The FV function is used primarily for finding the payments over a period of time to reach a specific goal or lump sum. As you should notice in Figure 10.10, the deposit amount or present value is $1,000, the interest earned is 7%, and you plan on depositing $200 per month over the period of the annuity of 12 months at the beginning of each period. The value or worth at the end of the annuity is $3,599. Use the ABS function to convert the formula to an absolute value as shown in cell C17.

- **Rate**—The interest rate per period.
- **Nper**—The number of payment periods in an annuity.
- **Pmt**—The payment made per period. Typically containing principal and interest and does not change over the life of the loan.
- **Pv**—The present value that a series of payments is worth right now. If omitted, Excel assumes zero.
- **Type**—The timing of the payment. When the payments are due.

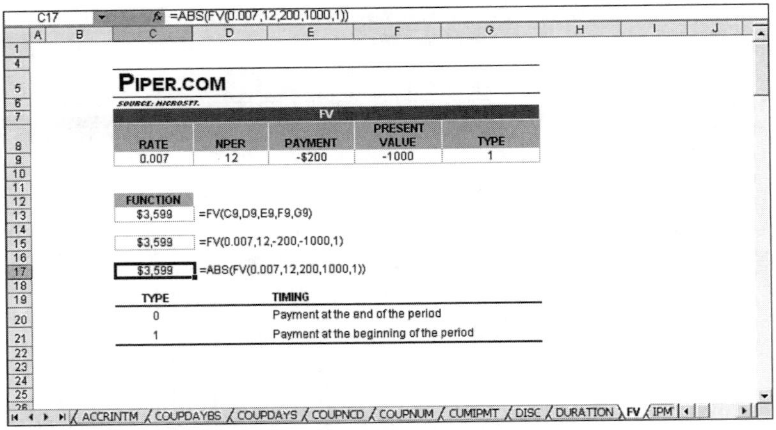

Figure 10.10
FV returns the future value of periodic payments and a constant interest rate.

IPMT

IPMT returns the interest payment for a given period of time based on an investment with periodic constant payments and a constant interest rate:

=IPMT(rate,per,nper,pv,fv,type)

The IPMT function returns an interest payment for a specific period of time. As shown in Figure 10.11, the interest rate per period is .7%. Period 1 is the period in which to find the payment when spread out over a total of 36 payments. The present value or lump sum amount that the future payments is worth right now is $10,000. As you see, the future value of the loan in this case is 0 and the payment is at the end of each period. So, the interest payment for the first period of the loan in the example equals $70. The first example shows the function using cell referencing, the second shows hard-coded numbers, and the third displays the ABS function to convert the value to a positive number. By default, the value will be negative.

- **Rate**—The interest rate per period.
- **Per**—The period for which you want to find the interest. This must be in the range of 1 to Nper.
- **Nper**—The number of payment periods in an annuity.
- **Pv**—The present value that a series of payments is worth right now. If omitted, Excel assumes zero.
- **Fv**—The future value or cash balance you want to attain upon the last payment.
- **Type**—The timing of the payment. When the payments are due.

Figure 10.11
Use IPMT to determine the interest payment for a period of time based on an investment with periodic constant payments and a constant interest rate.

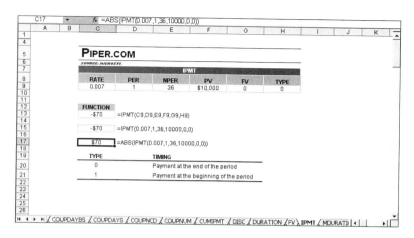

MDURATION

MDURATION returns the modified duration of a security with an assumed par value of $100:

=MDURATION(settlement,maturity,coupon,yield,frequency,basis)

The MDURATION function is found only if the Analysis ToolPak is installed and turned on by choosing Tools, Add-Ins. Figure 10.12 shows that the settlement date is 5/15/1999 and the maturity date is 9/15/2004. The coupon's rate is 7.8% and the yield of the coupon is 9.2%. You'll also see that the frequency is semiannual and the basis is Actual/actual. This means that the modified duration equals 4.18. The two examples show the same result: the first using cell referencing and the second with hard-coded dates and numbers within the formula.

- **Settlement**—The security's settlement date. This is the date after the issue date when the security is traded to the buyer.
- **Maturity**—The security's maturity date—when the security expires.
- **Coupon**—The security's annual coupon rate.
- **Yield**—The security's annual yield.
- **Frequency**—The number of payments per year—Annual = 1; Semiannual = 2; Quarterly = 4.
- **Basis**—The day count basis to use.

The modified duration is calculated as follows:

$$\text{MDURATION} = \frac{\text{DURATION}}{1 + \left(\dfrac{\text{Market yield}}{\text{Coupon payments per year}} \right)}$$

Figure 10.12
The MDURATION function returns the modified duration of a security with a par value assumed of $100.

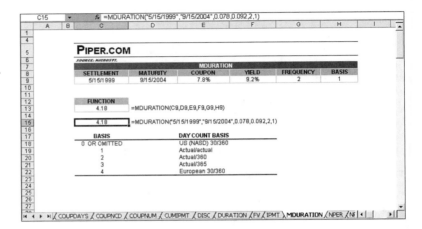

NPER

NPER returns the total number of periods for an investment. This is based on a periodic constant payment and a constant interest rate.

`=NPER(rate,pmt,pv,fv,type)`

Notice the example in Figure 10.13. The interest rate is 3%, the payment per period is $350. The current present value is $11,500. The future value of the loan, or the amount you want to attain after the last payment is zero (the loan is paid off). And the payment type is zero (at the end of the period). The number of periods (NPER) to pay off the loan would equal 23. Note that not specifying a value for FV will result in a negative number of periods.

- **Rate**—The interest rate per period.
- **Pmt**—The payment made per period, which cannot change over the life of the loan or annuity (typically is the principal and interest).
- **Pv**—The present value that a series of payments is worth right now. If omitted, Excel assumes zero.
- **Fv**—The future value or cash balance you want to attain upon the last payment.
- **Type**—The payment timing—when the payments are due. See Figure 10.13 for Type descriptions.

Figure 10.13
Use the NPER function to return the total number of periods for an investment. This is based on periodic constant payment and a constant interest rate.

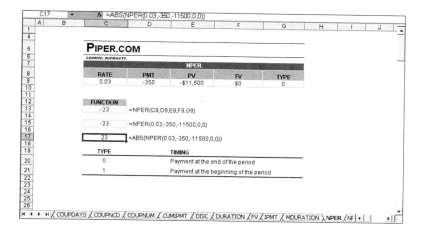

NPV

NPV calculates the net present value of an investment with the discount rate and several future payments and income:

=NPV(rate,value1,value2,...)

For example, let's say you invested $35,000 in a business and you expect to receive over the next four years a return of $7,000, $13,000, $15,000, and $18,000. With an annual discount rate of 9%, the net present value of the investment would be $6,145, as shown in Figure 10.14. This example can be simplified by using one range for the payments instead of individually identifying each one, as follows: =NPV(C9,D9:H9). Additionally, Negative values are investment amounts (payments) and positives are receipts (income). Also, payments/income must be made at equal time intervals.

- **Rate**—The discount rate over the entire period.
- **Value**—1–29 arguments representing the payments and income.

NPV can be calculated as

$$NPV = \sum_{i=1}^{n} \frac{values_i}{(1+rate)^i}$$

Figure 10.14
NPV calculates the net present value of an investment with the discount rate and several future payments and income.

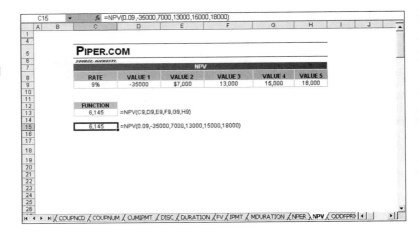

ODDFPRICE

ODDFPRICE returns the value of a security based on a per $100 face value and an odd (short or long) first period:

```
=ODDFPRICE(settlement,maturity,issue,first_coupon,rate,yield,
➥redemption,frequency,basis)
```

For example, take a look at Figure 10.15. You'll see that the settlement date is 11/11/1996 and the maturity date is 3/1/2011. The issue date is 10/15/1996 with the first coupon date being 3/1/1997. The security's interest rate is 9.3%. The yield is 7.8% and the redemption value is $100 with the frequency set semiannually. The basis is Actual/actual. You'll also see that the price per $100 face value of the security is $113. The ODDFPRICE function is found only if the Analysis ToolPak is installed and turned on by choosing Tools, Add-Ins.

- **Settlement**—The security's settlement date. This is the date after the issue date when the security is traded to the buyer.

- **Maturity**—The security's maturity date—the date when the security expires.

- **Issue**—The security's actual issue date.

- **First_Coupon**—The date of the security's first coupon.

- **Rate**—The interest rate of the security.

- **Yield**—The annual yield of the security.

- **Redemption**—The redemption value of the security per $100 face value.

- **Frequency**—The number of payments per year—Annual = 1; Semiannual = 2; Quarterly = 4.

- **Basis**—The day count basis to use.

The odd short first coupon is calculated as

$$ODDFPRICE = \left[\frac{redemption}{\left(1+\frac{yld}{frequency}\right)^{\left(N-1+\frac{DSC}{E}\right)}}\right] + \left[\frac{100 \times \frac{rate}{frequency} \times \frac{DFC}{E}}{\left(1+\frac{yld}{frequency}\right)^{\frac{DSC}{E}}}\right]$$

$$+ \left[\sum_{k=2}^{N}\frac{100 \times \frac{rate}{frequency}}{\left(1+\frac{yld}{frequency}\right)^{\left(k-1+\frac{DSC}{E}\right)}}\right]$$

$$- \left[100 \times \frac{rate}{frequency} \times \frac{A}{E}\right]$$

The odd long first coupon can be determined using

$$ODDFPRICE = \left[\frac{redemption}{\left(1+\frac{yld}{frequency}\right)^{\left(N+N_q+\frac{DSC}{E}\right)}}\right]$$

$$+ \left[\frac{100 \times \frac{rate}{frequency} \times \left[\sum_{i=1}^{NC}\frac{DC_i}{NL_i}\right]}{\left(1+\frac{yld}{frequency}\right)^{\left(N_q+\frac{DSC}{E}\right)}}\right]$$

$$+ \left[\sum_{k=2}^{N}\frac{100 \times \frac{rate}{frequency}}{\left(1+\frac{yld}{frequency}\right)^{\left(k-N_q+\frac{DSC}{E}\right)}}\right]$$

$$- \left[100 \times \frac{rate}{frequency} \times \sum_{i=1}^{NC}\frac{A_i}{NL_i}\right]$$

Figure 10.15
To return the value of a security based on a per $100 face value and an odd (short or long) first period, use the ODDFPRICE function.

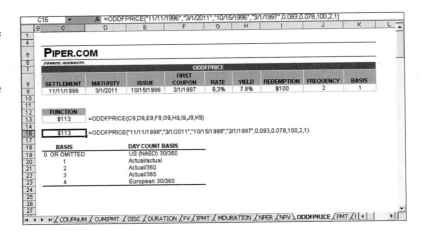

PMT

PMT calculates the loan payment for a loan based on constant payments and constant interest rates: A constant payment could be described as a monthly payment.

=PMT(rate,nper,pv,fv,type)

In Figure 10.16, the rate on the loan is 6% and the total number of payments is 24 (2 years). The present value of the loan or principal amount is 20,000 and the future value of the loan after it's paid off is 0. The monthly payment would be $886 dollars. Use the ABS function to convert the default negative value to a positive number.

- **Rate**—The interest rate of the loan.
- **Nper**—The number of total payments.
- **Pv**—The present value or the principal amount.
- **Fv**—The future value or cash balance you want to attain upon the last payment—for a loan it would be zero.
- **Type**—The payment timing—when the payments are due.

Figure 10.16
Calculate the loan payment for a loan based on constant payments and constant interest rates using the PMT function.

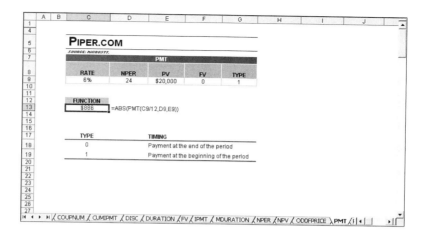

PRICE

PRICE returns the value of a security based on price per $100 face value and periodic interest payments:

```
=PRICE(settlement,maturity,rate,yield,redemption,frequency,basis)
```

Figure 10.17 shows the settlement date is 11/11/1999. The maturity date is 3/1/2011, and the annual coupon rate is 5.9%. The annual yield of the security is 6.8% and the redemption is $100. With seminannual frequency, the basis is Actual/actual resulting in the value of the security being $93. The PRICE function is found only if the Analysis ToolPak is installed and turned on by choosing Tools, Add-Ins.

- **Settlement**—The security's settlement date. This is the date after the issue date when the security is traded to the buyer.
- **Maturity**—The security's maturity date—the date when the security expires.
- **Rate**—The annual coupon rate of the security.
- **Yield**—The annual yield of the security.
- **Redemption**—The redemption value of the security per $100 face value.
- **Frequency**—The number of payments per year—Annual = 1; Semiannual = 2; Quarterly = 4.
- **Basis**—The day count basis to use.

PRICE is calculated as follows:

$$PRICE = \left[\frac{redemption}{\left(1 + \frac{yld}{frequency}\right)^{\left(N-1+\frac{DSC}{E}\right)}} \right] + \left[\sum_{k=1}^{N} \frac{100 \times \frac{rate}{frequency}}{\left(1 + \frac{yld}{frequency}\right)^{\left(k-1+\frac{DSC}{E}\right)}} \right]$$

$$- \left(100 \times \frac{rate}{frequency} \times \frac{A}{E} \right)$$

Figure 10.17
Return the value of a security based on price per $100 face value and periodic interest payments with the PRICE function.

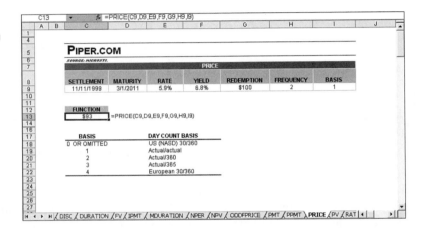

PV

Based on an investment, PV returns the present value:

`=PV(rate,nper,pmt,fv,type)`

For example, on a car loan, the present value is the amount of the loan to the lender. Figure 10.18 presents a PV example. If you can afford monthly payments of $500 a month, and can get a loan for 5.8%, what amount could you afford on a three-year loan? The formula `=PV(C9/12,D9*12,E9)` would result in a total loan amount over three years of $16,485.

- **Rate**—The interest rate of the loan. If the annual interest rate is 6% and you make monthly payments, the interest rate is 6%/12 =.50%.
- **Nper**—The number of total payments—12 months per year at 2 years would be 12*2 =24.
- **Pmt**—The payment made each period. It must remain constant. Typically, it includes principal and interest.
- **Fv**—The future value or cash balance you want to attain upon the last payment. For a loan it would be zero. For a future amount you want to attain with payments, it would be the total goal amount.
- **Type**—The payment timing—when the payments are due.

PV is calculated as follows:

$$pv * (1+rate)^{nper} + pmt(1+rate*type) *$$
$$\left(\frac{(1+rate)^{nper}-1}{rate}\right) + fv = 0$$

Figure 10.18
Based on an investment, PV returns the present value; for example, the total amount you could afford for a car loan.

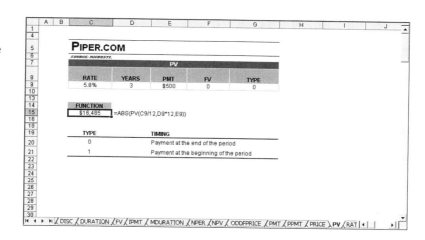

RATE

RATE returns the interest of an annuity per period:

=RATE(nper,pmt,pv,fv,type,guess)

The RATE function is calculated by iterations and can have many solutions. If results of RATE do not converge within .00000001 after a total of 20 iterations, the result returns #NUM. In Figure 10.19, the number of periods is 48 (a four-year loan), the payment is $200 a month, and the present value of the loan is $8,000. The monthly rate is .77%. Multiply the rate times 12 for the yearly rate as shown.

- **Nper**—The number of total periods on an annuity.
- **Pmt**—The payment made each period, which must remain constant. Typically, it includes principal and interest.
- **Fv**—The future value or cash balance you want to attain upon the last payment. For a loan it would be zero.
- **Type**—The payment timing. When the payments are due.
- **Guess**—What you assume the rate will be. If omitted, Excel assumes 10%.

Figure 10.19
RATE returns the
per-period interest of
an annuity.

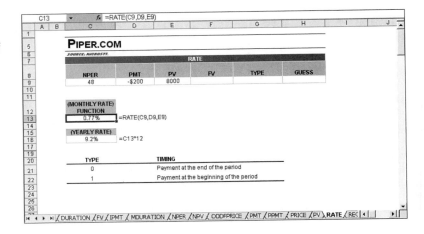

10 RECEIVED

Based on a fully invested security, RECEIVED returns the amount received at maturity:

`=RECEIVED(settlement,maturity,investment,discount,basis)`

The RECEIVED function is found only if the Analysis ToolPak is installed and turned on by choosing Tools, Add-Ins. Figure 10.20 shows the function with the dates in the formula and as a cell reference. The settlement date is 11/15/1999 and the maturity date is 2/15/2000. You also see that the total amount of the security investment is $500,000 and the discount rate is 5.75% with a day count basis of 2 or Actual/360. The amount received at maturity results in $507,457.

- **Settlement**—The security's settlement date. This is the date after the issue date when the security is traded to the buyer.
- **Maturity**—The security's maturity date—the date when the security expires.
- **Investment**—The total amount invested in the security.
- **Discount**—The discount rate of the security.
- **Basis**—The day count basis to use.

RECEIVED can be calculated as follows:

$$RECEIVED = \frac{investment}{1 - (discount \times \frac{DIM}{B})}$$

Figure 10.20
Based on a fully invested security, RECEIVED returns the amount received at maturity.

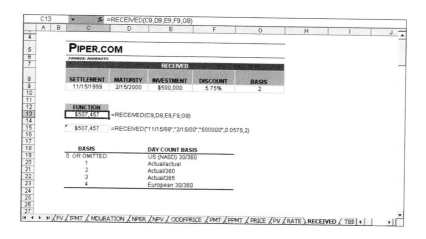

TBILLPRICE

The TBILLPRICE function returns the price per $100 face value of a treasury bill:

=TBILLPRICE(settlement,maturity,discount)

The TBILLPRICE function is found only if the Analysis ToolPak is installed and turned on by choosing Tools, Add-Ins. In Figure 10.21, for example, the treasury bill's settlement date is 11/15/1999 and the maturity date is 2/25/2000. The treasury bill's discount rate is 8.9% and the result is $97.48 price per $100 face value.

- **Settlement**—The treasury bill's settlement date. This is the date after the issue date when the security is traded to the buyer.
- **Maturity**—The treasury bill's maturity date—when the security expires.
- **Discount**—The discount rate of the treasury bill.

TBILLPRICE is calculated as follows:

$$TBILLPRICE = 100 \times (1 - \frac{discount \times DSM}{360})$$

Figure 10.21
For a treasury bill, TBILLPRICE returns the price per $100 face value.

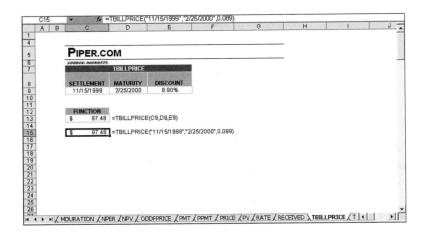

10 TBILLYIELD

The TBILLYIELD function returns the yield for the treasury bill:

=TBILLYIELD(settlement,maturity,pr)

The TBILLYIELD function is found only if the Analysis ToolPak is installed and turned on by choosing Tools, Add-Ins. As you see in Figure 10.22, the treasury bill's settlement date is 11/15/1999 and the maturity date is 2/25/2000. The treasury bill's discount rate is $97.64 and the yield result is 8.53%.

- **Settlement**—The treasury bill's settlement date. This is the date after the issue date when the security is traded to the buyer.
- **Maturity**—The treasury bill's maturity date—when the security expires.
- **PR**—The price per $100 for the treasury bill.

TBILLYIELD is calculated as

$$TBILLYIELD = \frac{100 - par}{par} \times \frac{360}{DSM}$$

Figure 10.22
For a treasury bill, `TBILLYIELD` returns the yield.

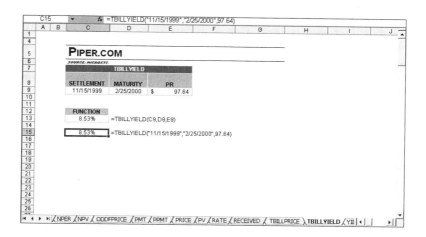

YIELD

The `YIELD` function returns the yield on a security that pays on period interest.

`=YIELD(settlement,maturity,rate,pr,redemption,frequency,basis)`

This is a function found only if the Analysis ToolPak is installed and turned on by choosing Tools, Add-Ins. In Figure 10.23, for example, the settlement date of the security is 11/15/1999 and the maturity date is 2/9/2009. The rate is 5.8% and the security's price per $100 face value is $98. The frequency is semiannually, and the basis is 30/360(4), resulting in a yield of 6.08%.

- **Settlement**—The security's settlement date. This is the date after the issue date when the security is traded to the buyer.
- **Maturity**—The security's maturity date—when the security expires.
- **Rate**—The annual coupon rate of the security.
- **PR**—The price of the security.
- **Redemption**—The redemption value of the security per $100 face value.
- **Frequency**—The number of the payments per year—Annual = 1; Semiannual = 2; Quarterly = 4.
- **Basis**—The day count basis to use.

`YIELD` can be calculated as

$$YIELD = \frac{(\frac{redemption}{100} + \frac{rate}{frequency}) - (\frac{par}{100} + (\frac{A}{E} \times \frac{rate}{frequency}))}{\frac{par}{100} + (\frac{A}{E} \times \frac{rate}{frequency})} \times \frac{frequency \times E}{DSR}$$

Figure 10.23
Based on a yield that pays periodic interest, this function returns the yield of the security.

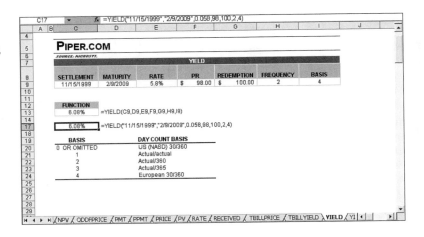

YIELDMAT

Based on a security that pays interest at maturity, YIELDMAT returns the annual yield:

```
=YIELDMAT(settlement,maturity,issue,rate,pr,basis)
```

It can be found only if the Analysis ToolPak is installed and turned on by choosing Tools, Add-Ins. The example in Figure 10.24 shows the settlement date of the security is 11/15/1999 and the maturity date is 6/9/2000. The issue date of the security is 6/18/1999. The rate is 5.8%, the security's price per $100 face value is $98, and the basis is 30/360(4). This means that the annual interest for the security is 9.30%.

- **Settlement**—The security's settlement date. This is the date after the issue date when the security is traded to the buyer.
- **Maturity**—The security's maturity date—when the security expires.
- **Issue**—The issue date of the security.
- **Rate**—The interest rate of the security.
- **PR**—The price of the security.
- **Basis**—The day count basis to use.

Figure 10.24
YIELDMAT returns
the annual yield
based on a security
that pays interest at
maturity.

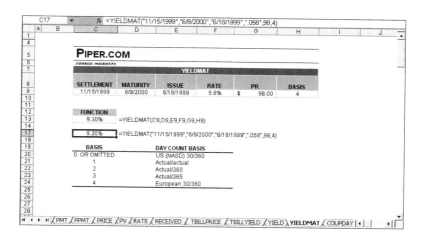

TROUBLESHOOTING

When I follow the instructions for creating a formula using many of these functions I get a #NAME? Error.

If you get the #NAME? Error you need to install the Analysis ToolPak. To install, go to Tools, Add-Ins, and then select the Analysis ToolPak and click OK.

EXCEL IN PRACTICE

Notice the two examples of the COUPDAYS function in Figure 10.25. The first example uses cell referencing and the second hard codes the numbers in the formula. Whenever possible, use cell referencing with formulas so that your models or formulas remain dynamic. If you hard code numbers within formulas, you run the risk of error every time you want to update the numbers within the formula. The COUPDAYS function is found only if the Analysis ToolPak is installed and turned on by choosing Tools, Add-Ins. In Figure 10.26, you'll see that the bond settlement date (the date a buyer purchases a coupon such as a bond) is 5/15/1999, and the maturity date (the date the bond expires) is 7/15/2000. The frequency is semianual and the basis is Actual/actual. The number of days between the coupon day and the settlement is 181. By using cell referencing instead of applying the dates in the formula, your formula becomes more flexible.

- **Settlement**—The security's settlement date. This is the date after the issue date when the security is traded to the buyer.

- **Maturity**—The security's maturity date. The date when the security expires.

- **Frequency**—The number of payments per year—Annual = 1; Semiannual = 2; Quarterly = 4.

- **Basis**—The day count basis to use. If omitted, 0 is used.

Figure 10.25
Use cell referencing whenever possible instead of hard coding numbers in formulas.

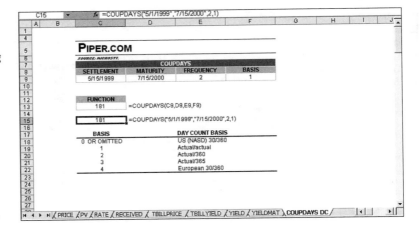

10

CHAPTER **11**

INFORMATION FUNCTIONS

In this chapter

Information Functions Overview   266

CELL   267

COUNTBLANK   269

ERROR.TYPE   270

INFO   271

IS Functions   272

INFORMATION FUNCTIONS OVERVIEW

Information functions generally return logical results and can be used in many business situations. Combined with other functions, the information functions can manage lists of data and provide feedback based on a logical result. For example, if you were tracking dates where certain items were received and then delivered, you could use the ISBLANK function combined with the IF function to return the result of numbers, widgets, or pages delivered. For a more in-depth explanation of this, see "ISBLANK," later in this chapter. This chapter covers the functions in Table 11.1 that are marked in bold.

TABLE 11.1   INFORMATION FUNCTIONS

Function	Syntax	Description
CELL	=CELL(*info_type*,*reference*)	Returns information about a cell's location, formatting, or contents in the upper-left cell in a reference.
COUNTBLANK	=COUNTBLANK(*range*)	Counts the number of empty cells in a specified range.
ERROR.TYPE	=ERROR.TYPE(*error_val*)	Returns the corresponding number value associated with an error type in Microsoft Excel.
INFO	=INFO(*type_text*)	Returns operating environment information.
ISBLANK	=ISBLANK(*value*)	Returns TRUE if the value or values contain empty cells.
ISERR	=ISERR(*value*)	Returns TRUE if the value results in an error value used in Microsoft Excel, except #NA.
ISERROR	=ISERROR(*value*)	Returns TRUE if the value results in any error value used in Microsoft Excel.
ISEVEN	=ISEVEN(*number*)	Returns TRUE or FALSE if the number is even or odd, TRUE being even and FALSE being odd.
ISLOGICAL	=ISLOGICAL(*value*)	Returns TRUE if the value is logical.
ISNA	=ISNA(*value*)	Returns TRUE if the value associated with the error type is #NA.
ISNONTEXT	=ISNONTEXT(*value*)	Returns TRUE if the value of any item is nontext, including blank cells.
ISNUMBER	=ISNUMBER(*value*)	Returns TRUE if the value is a number.
ISODD	=ISODD(*number*)	Returns FALSE if the number is even and TRUE if the number is odd.
ISREF	=ISREF(*value*)	Returns TRUE if the value is a reference, including range names.
ISTEXT	=ISTEXT(*value*)	Returns TRUE if *value* refers to text.

Function	Syntax	Description
N	=N(*value*)	Returns the value converted to a number.
NA	=NA()	Returns the error value associated with #NA.
TYPE	=TYPE(*value*)	Returns the type of value, for example, Number = 1, Text = 2, Logical Value = 4, Error Value = 16, and Array = 64. Use TYPE when the behavior of another function depends on the type of value in a particular cell.

CELL

The CELL function returns information about the cell such as the format, or whether it's general or some type of number format.

=CELL(*info_type*,*reference*)

The CELL function is primarily used to provide compatability with other spreadsheet programs. Table 11.2 lists the possible results from using this function based on the info type.

TABLE 11.2   INFO_TYPE EXAMPLES AND DESCRIPTIONS

Info Type	Return
Address	Reference of the first cell in reference as text.
Col	The column number of the cell referenced.
Color	Returns zero unless formatted in color for negative values; then it returns 1.
Contents	Contents of the upper-left cell in reference.
Filename	Full path and filename as text.
Format	The text value of the number format in a cell.
Parentheses	If the cell is formatted with parentheses, Excel returns 1; otherwise, it returns zero. Note that Excel can *format* numerical data in parentheses (similar to using a dollar sign for a monetary value). In these cases the parentheses are ignored.
Prefix	Text value of the label prefix.
	Returns (') for left-aligned text.
	Returns (") for right-aligned text.
	Returns (^) for centered text.
	Returns (\) for fill-aligned text and empty text.
	Returns (" ") for anything else.
Protect	Zero for unlocked cells and 1 for locked.

continues

TABLE 11.2   CONTINUED

Info Type	Return
Row	Row number of the cell referenced.
Type	The text value of the type of data in a cell.
	Returns (b) for blank cells.
	Returns (1) for text.
	Returns (v) for anything else.
Width	The column width of the cell referenced, rounded off to an integer.

Figure 11.1 shows an example of the results this function generates. If the INFO_TYPE is "Format," and the format of the cell in the reference argument changes, the cell function will not update the value until the worksheet is recalculated, meaning the cell must be activated before you press Return. Notice the examples shown in Figure 11.1, where E5 shows a negative ($265.00). The CELL function is applied with all the different info type information in column C about cell E5.

Figure 11.1
The CELL function returns formatting, location, and content information about the cell referenced or selected.

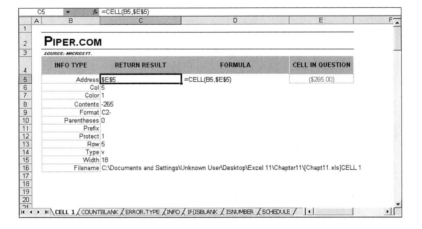

Here's an example, not shown in the figure, of the CELL function used to determine whether a cell is protected: C5:C16 contains cell functions that determine the protection of B5:B16.Ex: C5=CELL("protect",B5), C6=CELL("protect",B6), and so on.

To add up unprotected cells in a range in the form of an array, the example could be {=SUM((C5:C16=0)*B5:B16)}, where the array-entered formula adds up only the unprotected cells in the range B5:B100.

- **INFO_TYPE**—This is the text that tells Excel what kind of value you're looking for. See Table 11.2 for examples and descriptions.

■ **REFERENCE**—This is the cell you want information about. When omitted, information is returned for the last cell that was changed. See Table 11.3 for examples and descriptions.

Additional cell formatting return types are shown in Table 11.3.

TABLE 11.3   REFERENCE EXAMPLES AND DESCRIPTIONS

If Format Is...	Cell Returns...
General	G
0	F0
#,##0	,0
0.00	F2
#,##0.00	,2
$#,##0_);($#,##0)	C0
$#,##0_);[Red]($#,##0)	C0-
$#,##0.00_);($#,##0.00)	C2
$#,##0.00_);[Red]($#,##0.00)	C2-
0%	P0
0.00%	P2
0.00E+00	S2
#?/? or #??/??	G
m/d/yy or m/d/yy h:mm or mm/dd/yy	D4
d-mmm-yy or dd-mmm-yy	D1
d-mmm or dd-mmm	D2
mmm-yy	D3
mm/dd	D5
h:mm AM/PM	D7
h:mm:ss AM/PM	D6
h:mm	D9
h:mm:ss	D8

COUNTBLANK

COUNTBLANK counts the number of empty cells in a specified range:

```
=COUNTBLANK(range)
```

If you have a formula that returns a blank text result—a space for example, that cell is also counted. In Figure 11.2, the COUNTBLANK function can be used to track percent complete in tables where you have steps in process.

■ **RANGE**—This is the range in which you're looking for blank cells.

As shown in Figure 11.2, the formula =COUNTBLANK(D7:D12) returns 1 as the result because one of the six cells within the step 1 range are blank. When a date is entered into one of the blank cells within the specified range, the number of blank cells decreases.

Figure 11.2
The COUNTBLANK function returns the number of blank cells within the specified range.

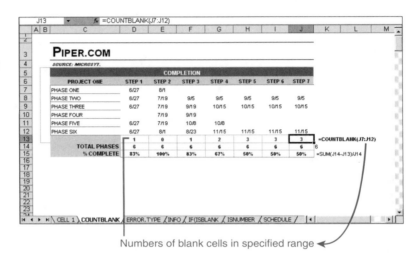

Numbers of blank cells in specified range ◄—

ERROR.TYPE

Returns the corresponding number value associated with an error type in Microsoft Excel. This could, for example, be used for the purposes of auditing a workbook (though it is rarely used):

=ERROR.TYPE(*error_val*).

The table example in Figure 11.3 shows the Excel number result and the error type. You can use the ERROR.TYPE function with the IF function to display custom text messages instead of errors as shown in cell F19 of Figure 11.3. In the example, the range F19:F25 uses an auditing illustration for data that's been incomplete or not properly filled out. The example states that if the error type equals a specific error number(type), then return the desired text within parentheses in the formula.

■ **ERROR_VAL**—This is the error value of the number you're looking for. This is usually used in the form of a reference to another cell containing a formula you want to test. So, for example, it would be a cell address.

Figure 11.3
The ERROR.TYPE function returns the Excel number result associated with the Excel error type.

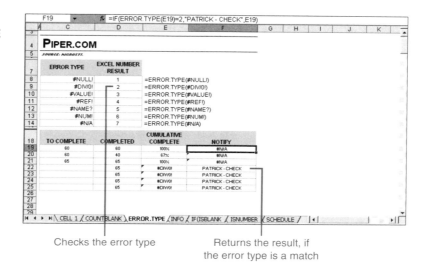

Checks the error type   Returns the result, if
                               the error type is a match

INFO

The INFO function can be used to retrieve vital information about your current operating system:

=INFO(*type_text*)

For example, if you are working within a workbook created by another person, and, for some reason the calculations weren't working, you could type the formula =INFO("recalc") and Excel would return either manual or automatic, meaning if you have the automatic calculation feature turned off in your options, the return would be manual; if turned on, it would be automatic. The INFO text types and descriptions are shown in Table 11.4 and the formulas in practice with the return results are shown in Figure 11.4. You can write the formula using cell referencing or you can type the "text type" in quotation marks within the formula, such as =INFO("Recalc").

■ **TYPE_TEXT**—The information you want returned.

For example, the text type within Table 11.4 can be applied in the following manner within the formula =INFO("Directory") to return the result or applied with cell referencing as shown in Figure 11.3.

TABLE 11.4   INFO TEXT TYPES AND DESCRIPTIONS

Text Type	Return
Directory	Path of the current directory or folder
Memavail	Amount of memory available in bytes

continues

TABLE 11.4 CONTINUED

Text Type	Return
Memused	Amount of memory being used for current data
Numfile	Number of active worksheets currently open
Origin	A1 reference style
Osversion	Current operating system version as text
Recalc	Current recalculation mode; "Automatic" or "Manual"
Release	Version of Microsoft Excel
System	Name of operating environment; "pcdos" for PC, "mac" for Mac
Totmem	Total memory available including in-use

Figure 11.4
The INFO function can provide quick information about a system or operating environment including certain Excel settings.

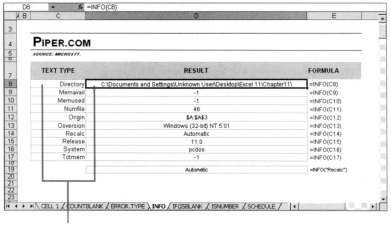

Looks up information based on Text Type column

IS FUNCTIONS

The IS functions return logical results after a test on a cell or a range of cells:

=ISFUNCTION(NUMBER)

These functions alone provide the logical test. However, when combined with other functions such as the IF function, they become a powerful decision-making tool for analyzing data and returning a logical test with a numeric result. The following IS functions in Table 11.5 are available in Excel.

TABLE 11.5   IS FUNCTION RETURNS

IS **Function**	**Syntax**	**Description**
ISBLANK	=ISBLANK(*value*)	Returns TRUE if the value or values contain empty cells
ISERR	=ISERR(*value*)	Returns TRUE if the value results in an error value used in Microsoft Excel, except #NA
ISERROR	=ISERROR(*value*)	Returns TRUE if the value results in any error value used in Microsoft Excel
ISEVEN	=ISEVEN(*number*)	Returns TRUE or FALSE if the number is even or odd, TRUE being even and FALSE being odd
ISLOGICAL	=ISLOGICAL(*value*)	Returns TRUE if the value is logical
ISNA	=ISNA(*value*)	Returns TRUE if the value associated with the error type is #NA
ISNONTEXT	=ISNONTEXT(*value*)	Returns TRUE if the value of any item is nontext, including blank cells
ISNUMBER	=ISNUMBER(*value*)	Returns TRUE if the value is a number
ISODD	=ISODD(*number*)	Returns FALSE if the number is even and TRUE if the number is odd
ISREF	=ISREF(*value*)	Returns TRUE if the value is a reference, including range names
ISTEXT	=ISTEXT(*value*)	Returns TRUE if *value* refers to text

Again, the IS functions alone provide only a TRUE/FALSE result. However, when used in conjunction with other functions, they can be powerful management tools. Note some of the following IS functions in use with others.

ISBLANK

The ISBLANK function can be used in accordance with the SUM and IF functions to track information based on the input of dates within a range of cells.

=ISBLANK(*value*)

Note the formula as shown in Figure 11.5 in cell I19:

- **VALUE**—This is the cell or range you want tested.

The following formula looks up the cells with dates in them within the range and returns the actual page (ACT) count from the column D range.

{=SUM(IF(ISBLANK(I8:I18),0,$D$8:$D$18))} Ctrl+Shft+Enter to activate the array.

NOTE

Use IS formulas, such as the ISBLANK formula shown in Figure 11.5, to manage completion by dates. You can also use PivotTables to produce the same results.

For example, let's say you are tracking steps in a process. In this case, the chapters in a book have to go through four steps before being complete. When you place a date completed in the intersecting cell for the chapter and step completed, the formula takes into account the actual page count from column D and adds up the column. The percent complete shows the total chapters complete through the steps.

Figure 11.5
Combine the ISBLANK function with SUM and IF to look up entered dates in a range and return a numeric result from another range.

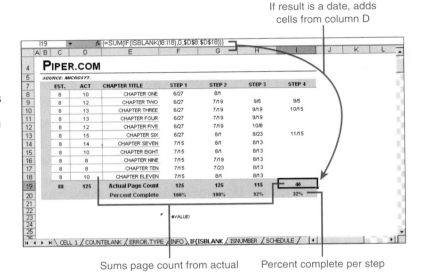

If result is a date, adds cells from column D

Sums page count from actual

Percent complete per step

ISNUMBER

ISNUMBER returns a logical result of true if the cell has a number and false if it does not.

=ISNUMBER(*value*)

This function can be combined with cell references to return a text result based on whether a number meets the criteria of the number specified in the formula. Notice the example in Figure 11.6. If there is a number in the "Mortgage Received" column, the result appears as "Paid" else "-". Tables are commonly composed of multiple functions, as shown in the figure, to display results.

- **VALUE**—This is the cell or range you want tested.

Figure 11.6
Combine the
`ISNUMBER` function
with the `IF` function
to return results
based on whether the
criteria are met.

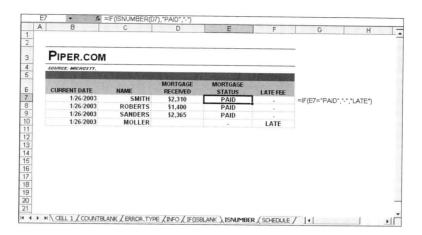

TROUBLESHOOTING

ACTIVATING CELLS

I'm using the cell function and it's not returning the proper results.

Make sure you recalculate the formula by selecting and activating the cell—meaning your cursor is showing up in the cell—and then press Return.

ACTIVATING AN ARRAY

When applying the SUM(IF(ISBLANK example earlier in the chapter, the corresponding number is incorrect.

Chances are you have not activated the array by pressing Ctrl+Shift+Enter. Make sure the array brackets appear, and make sure your reference ranges are equal or referencing the same number of adjacent cells.

ISERROR

ISNUMBER returns TRUE if the value results in an error.

`=ISERROR(value)`

You can use the `ISERROR` function combined with the IF and SUM function to filter out an errors in a data range. The IF function filters out the errors and the sum function then summarizes the filtered list. For example, if you have a range of values where some of the cells randomly have #DIV/0! A normal sum function will result in the form of #DIV/0!. To get around this use the following formula in the form of an array. After you've entered the formula remember to activate the array by pressing Ctrl+Shift+Enter

`{=SUM(IF(ISERROR(DATA),"",Data))}`

EXCEL IN PRACTICE

You can create floating timelines that appear on spreadsheets only when numbers are present. Notice the example in Figure 11.7. The formula =If(isnumber(U9),U$4,"") says, "If there is a number in cell U9 then return the value displayed in U4." U4 is the master timeline for the Gantt chart. This example shows the output of frames of animation over weeks. By applying the floating timeline, you can create referencing to dates without having to realign to a single timeline.

NOTE

A Gantt chart is used for displaying information over time. In general, it's popular for project programs but can often be useful when working on Excel data.

Figure 11.7
Use the ISNUMBER function to return results only if there is a number in a cell.

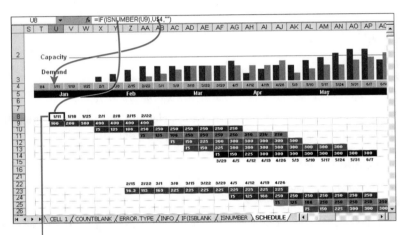

Floating timeline using the ISNUMBER function

CHAPTER 12

LOGICAL FUNCTIONS

In this chapter

Logical Functions Overview   278

AND   278

IF   280

NOT   281

OR   282

LOGICAL FUNCTIONS OVERVIEW

Logical functions test cells and ranges and return a logical result in the form of text (True or False) or numbers (1 or 0). A logical function operates under a logical test. For example, if you want to apply a simple addition based on whether a cell has a number in it, you could use an IF function to test the cell and then apply the simple addition if the logical result is true. This chapter covers the functions in Table 12.1 that appear in bold.

TABLE 12.1   LOGICAL FUNCTIONS

Function	Syntax	Description
AND	=AND(*logical1,logical2,...*)	Returns TRUE if all of the arguments are true in the formula, and FALSE if one or more are false.
FALSE	=FALSE()	Returns the value FALSE. No arguments are associated with this function.
IF	=IF(*logical_test, value_if_true,value_if_false*)	Returns a value or result if one condition is TRUE, and returns another value or result if the condition is FALSE.
NOT	=NOT(*logical*)	Returns the reverse value of its arguments. If FALSE returns TRUE, if TRUE returns FALSE.
OR	=OR(*logical1,logical2,...*)	Returns FALSE if all arguments are false, and TRUE if any argument is true.
TRUE	=TRUE()	Returns the value TRUE. No arguments are associated with this function.

AND

AND returns TRUE if all the arguments are true in the formula, and FALSE if any one argument is false.

=AND(logical1,logical2,...)

The AND function can operate on text, numbers, or cell references. The AND function alone serves as a simple logical test function. However, when it is combined with other formulas, the AND function enables you to combine several tests into one, and then apply the results depending on whether the test result is true or false. Notice the example in Figure 12.1. The AND function operates on the text applying False if FALSE appears within the selected range. Another way to look at it is if two values such as 1 appear in one cell and 2 appears in another, the test would result in FALSE, but if both cells had 1 in them the result would be

TRUE. In the range C6:D6, all tests are True, thus applying the True result. Notice the second and third examples in Figure 12.1. The AND function is combined with IF to perform a logical test on multiple combinations. The example in cell D10—
=IF(AND(C10>C9,C10<D9),"QUALIFY")—states, if the value in C10 is greater than 10 and the value in C10 is less than 30, apply the text QUALIFY. All conditions/tests/arguments in the AND function must be met for the person to QUALIFY. The next test applies the same logic, except the result is false because, although 32 is greater than 10 it *is not* less than 30 so both tests do not evaluate to True.

- **LOGICAL VALUE 1, 2** ...—The test results in a logical TRUE or FALSE return. Up to 30 conditions can be tested together.

When test is TRUE...

Figure 12.1
The AND logical function can stand alone as a logical test or be used in conjunction with other functions, such as IF, to test multiple conditions.

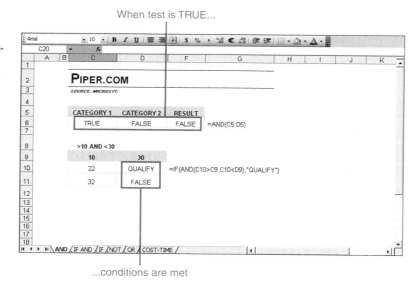

...conditions are met

Another example of using the AND function with the IF function is in conjunction with time-lines. If you want to plot names, numbers, symbols, text, or colors over time, you can create dynamic time lines using Gantt charts. Notice the example in Figure 12.2. The formula in cell G8—=IF(AND(G$7>=$D8,H$7<=$E8),$F8,"")—states: If the date in G7 is greater than or equal to the start date in cell D8, and the date in H7 is less than or equal to the stop date in cell E8, then plot the result of cell F8 ($50) in cell G8." Otherwise, leave G8 blank. Apply the color by using conditional formats.

→ For more information using conditional formats, **see** "Using Conditional Formatting with Lists," **p. 408**

Figure 12.2
Use the AND function in conjunction with the IF formula when building dynamic time lines to automatically move money, names, colors, and symbols.

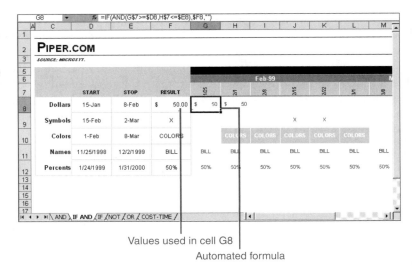

Values used in cell G8

Automated formula

IF

The IF function returns a value or result if one condition is true, and returns another value or result if the condition is false.

```
=IF(logical_test,value_if_true,value_if_false)
```

The IF function is one of the most commonly used logical functions in Excel. This function can be used in conjuction with other functions, embedded within itself to perform up to seven logical tests per cell. You've already seen the IF function in action with the AND function example earlier in this chapter. Notice the example in Figure 12.3. Three different logics are used in conjuction with IF. The first example applies the logic of whether a student has passed or failed. The result is applied to cell E4. The formula in E4— =IF(D4="PASS","GRADE 7","GRADE 6")—states: If the text result is in cell D4 = "PASS", apply the result GRADE 7 or return GRADE 6. The first value applied is the true value, and the second value applied is the false value based on whether the logical test is met.

- **LOGICAL_TEST**—This test is the criteria on which the inputs will be assessed. The possible outputs of the test are TRUE and FALSE.

- **VALUE IF TRUE**—This value is the output when your Logical test value returns TRUE. This can be a character, word, or formula. If you leave the field blank, "TRUE" will be the output.

- **VALUE IF FALSE**—This value is the output when your Logical test value returns FALSE. This can be a character, word, or formula. If you leave the field blank, "FALSE" will be the output.

Figure 12.3
The IF formula performs the logical test and applies the TRUE result value first after the logical test is met and the FALSE value if the test is not met.

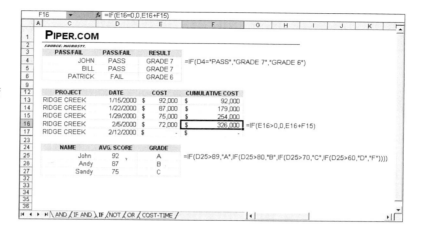

Notice the second example in Figure 12.3. The formula in cell F16 asks the logical question—if cell E16 equals zero then apply zero, else apply the formula E16 + F16. The last example in Figure 12.3 shows an automated grading formula with an embedded IF statement. The formula applies the text results of the grades A–F based on whether the logical test is met. The formula is structured so that the only false value is F and occurs only if all other true values are not met. The formula—

=IF(D25>89,"A",IF(D25>80,"B",IF(D25>70,"C",IF(D25>60,"D","F"))))—states the following conditions:

> If the value in cell D25 is greater than 89, apply the result of A else
>
> If the value in cell D25 is greater than 80, apply the result of B else
>
> If the value in cell D25 is greater than 70, apply the result of C else
>
> If the value in cell D25 is greater than 60, apply the result of D else
>
> F

The formula embeds an IF function with only the True values being met. The last value after all other logical tests are applied is F or the False value.

NOT

NOT returns the opposite of the logical value:

=NOT(logical)

If the logical value is False, NOT returns True. If two cells are equal, NOT returns False. NOT can be used when evaluating two cells in lists of information. For example, if two cells can never equal each other, NOT returns a False logical value if the cells match. Notice the first example in Figure 12.4. The first condition in cell D4 is the logical value False and the formula returns the opposite, True. The second example shows two cells not equaling each other in cells C8 and D8 and the logical value again returns True. If cell C9 is less than D9 in the third example, the logical value is False even when the condition appears True. The last example—=IF(NOT(COUNTA(C12:D12)<2),"HOLIDAY CONFLICT,"")—could be used if you were planning holidays for workers within a plant. If one employee always has to be on call, the function would call out a False logical value to notify that all employees were taking off the same week.

> **NOTE**
>
> COUNTA counts the number of cells that are not empty in the range.

- **LOGICAL**—This is the value that can be evaluated with a True or False condition. If True, NOT returns False, if False, NOT returns True.

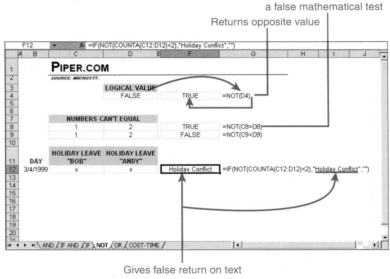

Figure 12.4
The NOT function can be used when calling out employees that are marking weeks off for holidays within the same week. The logical value returned would equal False.

Returns opposite result on a false mathematical test

Returns opposite value

Gives false return on text values that are equal

OR

OR returns FALSE if all arguments are false, and TRUE if one or more arguments are true:

=OR(logical1,logical2,...)

The OR function can be used as a standalone function when looking for one true statement or can be used in conjuction with other functions to return logical information. The first example in Figure 12.5 shows one true test being met in the range D7:F7. The second example displays no true values in the range D8:F8 and returns the logical value of False.

The last example displays the OR function used in conjunction with the EXACT function in the form of an array. EXACT compares two text strings and returns TRUE if they are the same. The array range is D12:D23. If you have a list of ISBN numbers, SKUs, and so on that span 1,000 rows and you want to know whether there is a match with a number, this formula tells you whether the number exists in the list with a True result. After the formula is entered, remember to press Ctrl+Shift+Enter to activate the array.

→ For more information on the EXACT function, **see** "Exact," **p. 329**

- **LOGICAL1, LOGICAL2** ...—These are the conditions to be met to test a logical true or false result. You can use up to 30 conditions within the formula.

Figure 12.5
The OR function returns the logical result of True if only one true result is met.

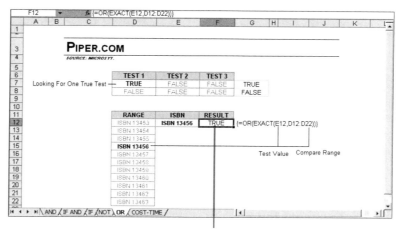

True, if result is within list

TROUBLESHOOTING

RELATIVE TIMELINE REFERENCES

When creating a timeline with the IF and AND functions, my values don't appear when I drag the formula to the right.

Make sure you apply proper relative referencing. For the dates on the timelines, you want to anchor the rows and for the dates in your table, you want to anchor the columns. See the example shown in Figure 12.6.

EXCEL IN PRACTICE

The IF function combined with the AND function can be used as powerful time-management tools. The automated cashflow formula in Figure 12.6 is driven off the timeline and the corresponding table to the left. The formula plots the weekly dollars across the timespan of the project. The function as shown in cell M6 is =IF(AND(M$5>=$G6,N$5<=$H6),$F6,"").

The function reads as follows: If M5 is greater than or equal to the date in G6 and the date in N5, which is the next week, is less than or equal to the date in H6, then plot the value in F6 or else plot nothing.

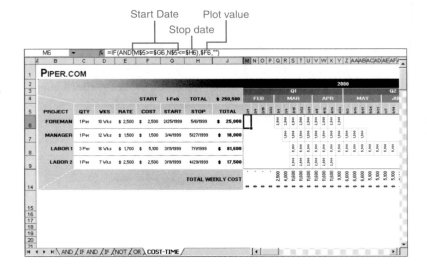

Figure 12.6
Use the IF function combined with the AND function to create automated cash flows over time.

CHAPTER **13**

LOOKUP AND REFERENCE FUNCTIONS

In this chapter

Lookup and Reference Functions Overview   286

CHOOSE   207

HLOOKUP   288

INDEX (Array Form)   290

INDEX (Reference Form)   290

Using the Lookup Wizard   293

LOOKUP (Array Form)   294

LOOKUP (Vector Form)   295

OFFSET   296

Auto Update Charts Using the OFFSET Function   298

TRANSPOSE   290

VLOOKUP   300

LOOKUP AND REFERENCE FUNCTIONS OVERVIEW

Lookup and reference functions are probably some of the most frequently asked, "How do I?" questions of all functions. Because so many people use Excel to manage data stored in lists in some form or fashion, at times you'll need to look up information associated with an item. For example, if you have several product names in a database and want to look up the associated inventory number for the product, you could do this several ways using Excel's lookup functions. You could, for example, use the VLOOKUP function or combine the INDEX and MATCH functions to pinpoint the inventory number. This chapter covers the functions in Table 13.1 that appear in bold font.

TABLE 13.1 LOOKUP AND REFERENCE FUNCTIONS

Function	Syntax	Description
ADDRESS	=ADDRESS(*row_num*,*column_num*, *abs_num*,*A1*,*sheet_text*)	Returns the cell address in relative or absolute form. Returns the actual location of the cell on the spreadsheet.
AREAS	=AREAS(*reference*)	Returns the number of areas in a reference. An *area* is a range of contiguous cells or a single cell.
CHOOSE	=CHOOSE(*index_num*,*value1*, *value2*,...)	Uses the index number to return a value from a list of up to 29 choice arguments.
COLUMN	=COLUMN(*reference*)	Returns the relative column number based on a given reference.
COLUMNS	=COLUMNS(*array*)	Returns the number of columns in an array or reference.
HLOOKUP	=HLOOKUP(*lookup_value*, *table_array*,*row_index_number*, *range_lookup*)	Searches for a pecified value in an array based on a table's top row.
HYPERLINK	=HYPERLINK(*link_location*, *cell_contents*)	Creates a shortcut to jump to a document stored within a workbook or storage device or hyperlink function to link to a URL, such as a stock page on the Web.
INDEX (Array Form)	=INDEX(*array*,*row_num*, *column_num*)	Returns the value of an element selected by the row number and column letter indexes within a table or array.
INDEX (Reference Form)	=INDEX(*reference*,*row_num*, *column_num*,*area_num*)	Returns the reference of the scell based on the intersection of a particular row and column within a table or array.

Function	Syntax	Description
INDIRECT	=INDIRECT(*ref_text*,*A1*)	Returns the reference based on a text string.
LOOKUP (**ArrayForm**)	=LOOKUP(*lookup_value*,*array*)	Looks in the first row or column of an array, and returns the specified value from the same position in the last row or column of the array.
LOOKUP (**Vector Form**)	=LOOKUP(*lookup_value*, *lookup_vector*,*result_vector*)	Returns the value from the same position in a second one-row or one-column range based on a lookup value located in the first one-row or one-column range.
MATCH	=MATCH(*lookup_value*, *lookup_array*,*match_type*)	Returns the position of an item in an array that matches a specified value in specified order.
OFFSET	=OFFSET(*reference*,*rows*, *columns*,*height*,*width*)	Returns a reference to a range that is a specific number of rows and columns from a cell or range of cells.
ROW	=ROW(*reference*)	Returns the row number based on a reference.
ROWS	=ROWS(*array*)	Returns the number of rows in an array or reference.
TRANSPOSE	=TRANSPOSE(*array*)	Returns a horizontal range of cells as vertical or vice versa.
VLOOKUP	=VLOOKUP(*lookup_value*, *table_array*,*column_index_num*, *range_lookup*)	Looks for a value in the leftmost column of a table and returns a value from the column number you specify.

CHOOSE

Based on a list of arguments, CHOOSE uses the index number to return an index number from a list of up to 29 arguments:

```
=CHOOSE(index_num,value1,value2,...)
```

The CHOOSE function can be used as a standalone function or in conjunction with other functions. See how CHOOSE indexes in cell D20 of Figure 13.1. If the value is 3, it indexes to the third value—in this case, "Robert." The CHOOSE premise is quite simple: The index number indexes the value or text within the formula from left to right. The result in the figure if cell A1 is 1 would be APPROVE, 2 would be DECLINE, and 3 would be SEND TO MANAGER; the value can be text, cells, and ranges. The index number can also be a cell reference. Notice the formula in cell D7 in Figure 13.1.

13

NOTE

> If the index number is larger than the number of values then the function will return an error.

- **Index_Num**—Specifies the position of the value. So, if the index number is 3, it would result in the third value over. Such as =CHOOSE(**3**,Value1,Value2,**Value3**,Value4).

- **Value 1, Value 2…**—The values are arguments from 1 to 29. These numbers can be cell references, formulas, functions, text, and defined names.

One way you can use the CHOOSE function is with form controls. For example, use the CHOOSE function with the Option button from the Form Control toolbar. Notice that in the example in Figure 13.1, the CHOOSE formula references the control's link cell A1, which prompts an automated response for the indexing result. In this example, Approve equals 1 and would produce the text result of APPROVE. The Decline option results in a 2 in the link cell, which would produce a text result of DECLINE in the CHOOSE function. Where the Send To Mgr. option equals 3, the text result would be the third choice in the CHOOSE function, SEND TO MGR. This simple example of using one formula response generated from another formula's result demonstrates how forms are created using form controls.

→ To learn more about formulas and form controls, **see** Adding Form Controls to Your Worksheets," **p. 424**

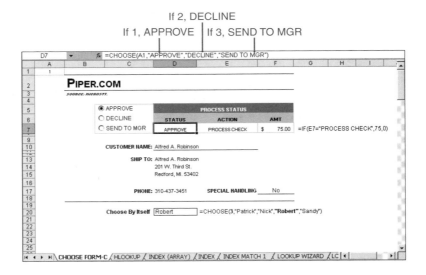

If 1, APPROVE   If 2, DECLINE   If 3, SEND TO MGR

Figure 13.1
The CHOOSE function with form controls creates an automated indexing result based on the cell link.

HLOOKUP

The HLOOKUP function searches for a column heading that is defined in the table array and then it returns a value associated with the row index.

=HLOOKUP(lookup_value,table_array,row_index_number,range_lookup)

You can use text reference for the lookup value as shown in the first example in Figure 13.2. Using text for the lookup value produces the following formula: =HLOOKUP("Q2",D11:G15,2), which results in $65,087. The quarter specifies the column heading, the table array includes the entire data table and the headings, and 2 is the number of rows indexed down. The range lookup argument is not necessary in this example.

The second example is a more efficient way to use the HLOOKUP function because the formula acts upon the values input in the cells to the left. With cell referencing, your formula becomes a live working model. Now you can apply different region numbers for index values as well as column headings, and the function will return the index and column heading result.

In the second example in Figure 13.2, you see that =HLOOKUP(C9, D11:G15,B9) results in $31,785. The quarter reference for the lookup value is Q3, which the formula is referencing in cell C9, the table array includes the column headings, and the index value is referenced to the number of rows down the left side, which the formula is getting from the value in cell B9.

- **Lookup_Value**—This is the value to be looked up in the first row of the table. This can be values, references, and text strings.

- **Table_Array**—The table or range in which you are looking up information. You can also use references to names or range names for the table array.

- **Row_Index_Number**—Specifies the lookup row within the table array in which the result will be returned.

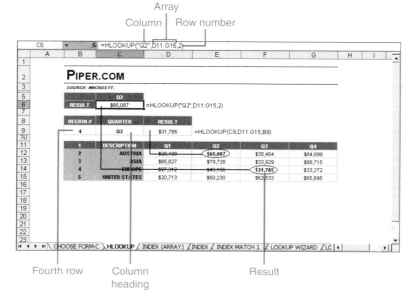

Figure 13.2
The HLOOKUP function looks up the column heading of a table array and indexes the number of rows that follow as specified.

INDEX (ARRAY FORM)

Based on a table or array, INDEX (Array Form) returns the value of an element selected by the row number and column letter indexes

`=INDEX(array,row_num,column_num)`

The INDEX function in the form of an array allows you to expand the flexibility of the array function by specifying a row number and column number over several rows and columns, as shown in the examples in Figure 13.3. The range is B10:D20, the row number of the range referenced is 2, and the column nubmer is 3, which results in $4,021.

- **Array**—This is the range of cells or the array constant in the formula.
- **Row_Num**—Specifies the row within the array from which to return the value.
- **Column_Num**—Specifies the lookup column number from left to right within the array.

The example—`=INDEX(B10:D20,2,3)`—results in $4,021 because it is the second row and the third column over in the table array.

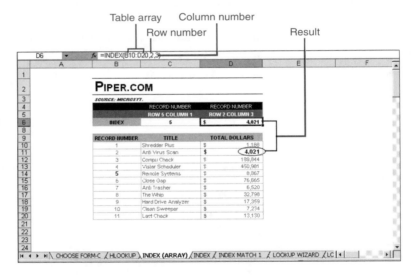

Figure 13.3
The INDEX function in the form of an array creates database function flexibility by allowing you to specify a range of columns and rows and look up an intersecting point.

INDEX (REFERENCE FORM)

Based on the intersection of a particular row and column, INDEX (Reference Form) returns the reference of the cell:

`=INDEX(reference,row_num,column_num,area_num)`

The INDEX function in the form of a reference is one of the more useful lookup functions because it can be used with other functions or form controls as a cell reference or as a text reference. To illustrate, Figure 13.4 shows three examples using the index function on a list.

The first example—=INDEX(B8:B11,2)—results in 2, because it is the second row down on the single-column range.

The second example is used with the MATCH function to match text from another column shown as

=INDEX(C7:D18,MATCH(B22,C7:C18,),MATCH("Product",C7:D7,))

The result is the product name, where C7 through D18 specifies the range of the ISBN number and the product names, and the first nested match function specifies the ISBN input number cell reference. The MATCH range includes the same range as the index, and the second nested MATCH function calls out the column title heading in quotation marks and specifies the column heading range. The last example takes a form control into account. The form control cell reference link in cell A1 indexes down to the fourth record and returns the index range of the fourth record in the range from E8:E18. When formatting the form control, use the D8:D18 product range. To learn more about form controls and functions, see Chapter 18. Note that part of the ISBN list is hidden to allow all three examples to fit on one screen. The result is that the product name for the given ISBN number is extracted from the list which is defined by the range C7:D18 in the function. The first nested match function MATCH(B22,C7:C18,) looks up the ISBN number from cell B22 in the range C7:C18 and returns its row number (2). The second MATCH function MATCH("Product",C7:D7,) looks up the word Product in the range C7:D7 and returns its location (2). The INDEX function thus evaluates to =INDEX(C7:D18,2,2) which extracts the value at the intersection of the second row and second column of the range C7:D18—that is, Anti Virus Scan.

- **Reference**—The reference to cell ranges. You can use one or more.
- **Row_Num**—The number of the row within the reference to return the reference for.
- **Column_Num**—The number of the column within the reference from which to return the reference.
- **Area_Num**—This is the range within the reference to return a result for from a specified range. For example, 1 might refer to the first range, 2 would refer to the second, and so on.

Because the INDEX and MATCH functions are so critical and useful, Figure 13.5 shows the importance of these functions. As you see in the figure, the INDEX function is combined with the nested MATCH function performed over another list. Based on a lookup value such as an ISBN number or any number that identifies a product in a list over a range, you can look up numbers or text. Notice how the ISBN identifier returns the text value of the product title highlighted in the list. This formula might look like this:

=Index(D10:E25,Match(D8,D10:D25,),Match(Title,D10:E10,))

Where D10:E25 is the table range.

Where D8,D10:D25 references the first match of 7111 in the ISBN range.

Where "Title",D10:E10 references the word title from the range of title range.

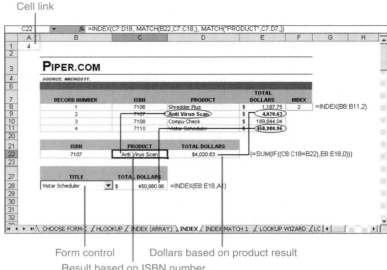

Figure 13.4
The INDEX function in the reference form returns the reference or value of two intersecting points.

The formula returns the text result of the title.

The function Match(D8,D10:D25,) returns the row in the range D10:D25, which contains the value in cell D8—that is, row 6.

And Match("Title",D10:E10,) returns the position in the range D10:E10, which contains the word Title—that is, position 2. And lastly, the formula now evaluates to =INDEX(D10:E25,6,2), which returns the value at the intersection of row 6 column 2 of the range D10:E25, that is, the value "Shredder".

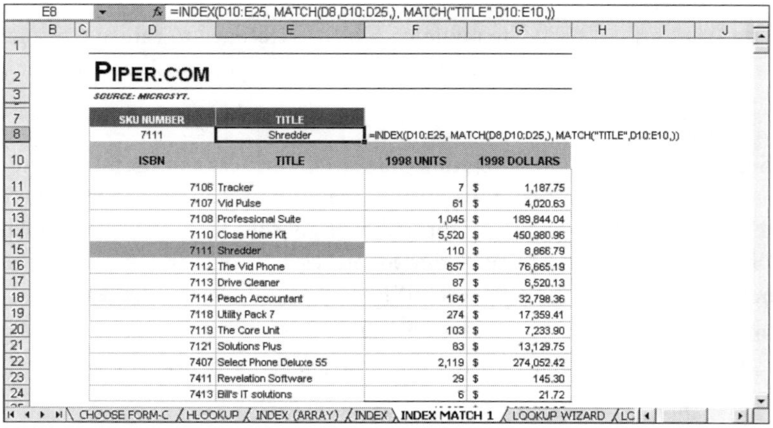

Figure 13.5
The INDEX function with the MATCH function can include the return of a value or of text.

USING THE LOOKUP WIZARD

You can use the Lookup Wizard to help create complex lookup formulas. To use the Lookup Wizard, you must first activate it. To activate the Lookup Wizard, follow these steps:

1. Choose Tools, Add-Ins.
2. Check Lookup Wizard in the Add-Ins dialog box.
3. Click OK.
4. The Lookup Wizard installs, or you are required to insert the Office 2003 CD to install the wizard. If you have downloaded the product via a company's intranet you may need to contact your system administrator.

To use the Lookup Wizard, follow these steps:

1. Choose Tools, Lookup.
2. Step 1 of 4 of the wizard starts. Select the range you want to search and click Next (see Figure 13.6). Make sure to include the row and column headings within your selection.
3. In step 2 of 4, select the column heading that contains the values to look up. Then, select the row that contains the values to find. Select the row label. If the proper label doesn't exist, choose No Row Label Matches Exactly and manually type in the row label.

NOTE

Excel automatically hard codes the row so your formula will actually look like the following:

```
=INDEX($E$9:$F$15, MATCH("BMW528I",$E$9:$E$15,), MATCH("2002
UNITS",$E$9:$F$9,))
```

In the example, I replaced the hard code "BMW528I" with the actual cell reference of E19 to make the lookup dynamic.

4. Step 3 of 4 allows you to copy the formula to a single cell or copy the formula and lookup parameters. The default is to a single cell.
5. Step 4 of 4 allows you to choose the formula cell destination. When complete, click Finish.

When the wizard completes its lookup it generates a result in the cell destination (see Figure 13.7).

13

Figure 13.6
Step 2 of the Lookup Wizard allows you to specify the columns and rows to search.

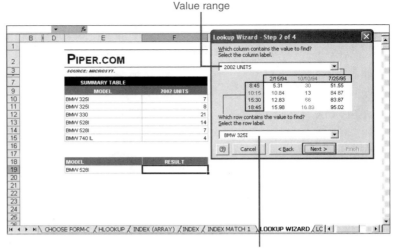

Figure 13.7
The Lookup Wizard returns a final result.

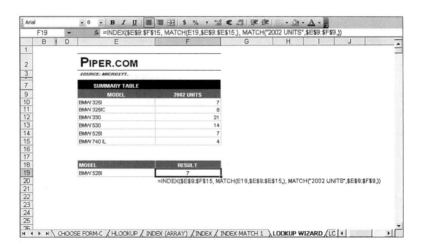

LOOKUP (ARRAY FORM)

LOOKUP (Array Form) looks in the first row or column of an array, and returns the specified value from the same position in the last row or column of the array.

`=LOOKUP(lookup_value,array)`

The LOOKUP function Array Form differs from the Vector Form in that the Vector Form looks up the value in one row or column range, and the Array Form allows you to specify the location of the lookup value.

- **Lookup_Value**—This is the value LOOKUP searches for in the first vector.
- **Array**—The range that contains only one row or column.

LOOKUP (Vector Form)

Based on a range of one row or one column, LOOKUP (Vector Form) returns the value from the same position in a second row or column from the first row.

=LOOKUP(lookup_value,lookup_vector,result_vector)

The LOOKUP function Vector Form looks for the value in the first vector or range and returns the result from the second vector or range. More simply put, this function looks up the value in the first range and applies the result of the same position in the second range (see Figure 13.8). Notice in the timeline example, the LOOKUP function searches for the greatest value in the range. For example, =LOOKUP(1,D9:M9,D8:M8) looks up the value of 1 in the range D9:M9. It finds the largest value (the one furthest to the right in the range), in the sixth position across. It then returns the corresponding value from the range D8:M8—the value in sixth position in this range is "Jun". Use this form when the value you want to look up is in the first row or column. The lookup array/range must be sorted in ascending order to obtain the correct answer.

- **Lookup_Value**—This is the value LOOKUP searches for in the first vector.
- **Lookup_Vector**—The range that contains only one row or column.
- **Result_Vector**—The range that contains only one row or column and must be the same size as the Lookup_Vector.

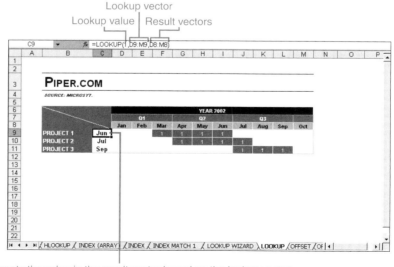

Figure 13.8
The LOOKUP function looks up values in one vector (range) and returns the result of another vector (range).

June represents the value in the result vector based on the lookup vector

OFFSET

The OFFSET function returns a reference to a range that is a specific number of rows and columns from a cell or range of cells:

```
=OFFSET(reference,rows,columns,height,width)
```

For example, if you were giving a presentation and wanted the presentation to be interactive, you could use the OFFSET function to return different locations for a chart reference as shown in Figure 13.9. The first example shows the OFFSET function being used to look up or offset the Year 1 unit sales for Asia to Year 2. The formula is =OFFSET(C6,0,2), where C6 is the current location, or ground zero. The number of rows down is 0, and 2 is the number of columns over. The height of the return is the first row and the first column from the new position. If the row reference had been 2, the return value would have been 10,750. However, the result returns the value in cell E6 of 8,696. Further, the formula is =OFFSET(C6,0,2), where C6 is the current location, or ground zero. The number of rows down is 0 *(leaving the row number unchanged)*, and 2 is the number of columns over *relative to column C; that is, column E*. The height of the return is the first row and the first column from the new position; that is, *Cell E6*.

It's important to note that the examples don't need the last two arguments (height and width). They are both assumed to be 1 if they are omitted. When used within another function, the last two arguments help create a new range height and width starting at the new offset position. Using height and width numbers other than 1 in a cell containing just an offset formula results in an error. If OFFSET is used inside another function that is expecting to see a reference then OFFSET returns the address and not the value.

- **Reference**—The range or cell of adjacent cells on which you want to base the offset.
- **Rows**—The number of rows up or down you want the base to refer or offset to.
- **Columns**—The number of columns left or right you want the base to refer or offset to. For example, using three would mean the individual offset column is three positions to the right of the reference.
- **Height**—(Optional) The height in the number of rows that you want the reference to return. This must be a positive number.
- **Width**—(Optional) The width in the number of columns that you want the reference to return. This must be a positive number.

As you can see in Figure 13.10, you can use the OFFSET function in conjunction with other functions.

In this particular example, the OFFSET function is used with the IF function to trigger a response based on a cell reference. The cell reference in C12 is used to determine which year's sales you want in your offset table. The IF function in cell E14 checks cell C12 for the year. If it's Year 2, the OFFSET function is used to obtain Year 2 sales. If cell C12 contains anything other than Year 2, it defaults to Year 1 sales as shown in Figure 13.10. The column chart to the right of the Tables is based on the Offset table. Changing C12 to Year 1 automatically updates the sales figures in the offset table, which in turn displays Year 1 sales figures in the chart, as shown in Figure 13.11.

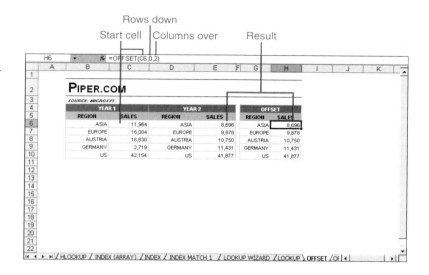

Figure 13.9
The OFFSET function returns a location offset from the current location on the worksheet.

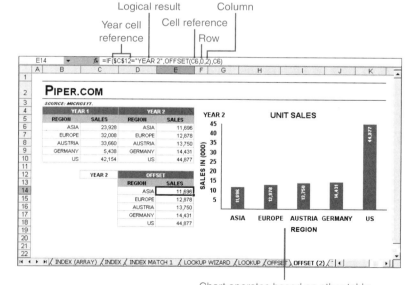

Figure 13.10
The OFFSET function in conjunction with the IF function can be used to create a table that corresponds with the logical result in cell E14. The chart is based on the offset table.

13

If value in Cell C2 doesn't equal "Year 2"...

Figure 13.11
With the OFFSET function, if the logical result is not met, the result defaults to Year 1.

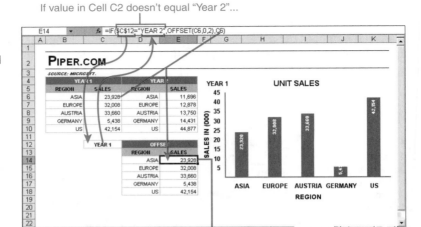

...place value of Cell C6 into cell

AUTO UPDATE CHARTS USING THE OFFSET FUNCTION

Do you ever have to update data on a regular basis and then change the chart information to match the new data? There's a couple of ways you can automatically update charts from updated data—one is with plot visible cells only, and the other is by using a more efficient solution with the OFFSET function and NAMED ranges (see Figure 13.12). In Figure 13.12 the Date range starts at A2 and the Traffic range starts at B2. To create an auto update chart follow these steps:

Figure 13.12
Use the OFFSET function with NAMED ranges to create an auto-updating chart.

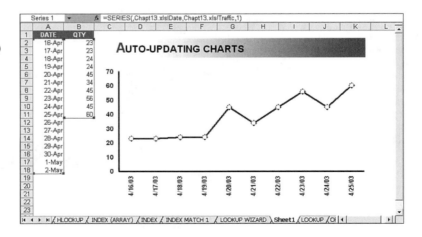

1. Establish your list range similar to that in Figure 13.11.

2. Start by setting up a named range for the date column. From the Insert menu choose Name then Define.

3. In the names in workbook field type **DATE.** In the Refers to field type this formula:

   `=OFFSET(Sheet1!$A$2,0,0,COUNTA(Sheet1!$A:$A)-1)`

4. Click Add and then click OK. The OFFSET function refers to the first cell in the range for the Date data and the COUNTA function refers to the column of data.

5. Now set up a named range for the traffic column. From the Insert menu choose Name then Define.

6. In the names in workbook field type **Traffic.** In the Refers to field type this formula:

   `=OFFSET(Sheet1!$B$2,0,0,COUNTA(Sheet1!$B:$B)-1)`

7. Click Add. The OFFSET function refers to the first cell in the range for the traffic data and the COUNTA function refers to the column of data.

8. Now, select the chart data series.

9. Replace the range references with the NAMED ranges in the formula bar. Refer to the formula bar in Figure 13.11. In the case of this example you can also refer to the workbook provided on the CD. The formula will now look as follows:

   `=SERIES(,Chapt13.xls!DATE,Chapt13.xls!TRAFFIC,1)`

10. After you have entered the NAMED ranges press Return or Enter. Now, when you add data new dates to the x axis will be applied automatically.

TRANSPOSE

TRANSPOSE returns a horizontal range of cells as vertical or vice versa.

`=TRANSPOSE(array)`

It operates similarly to TRANSPOSE in the Paste Special command. The trick to making this function work is selecting your destination range first before typing the TRANSPOSE function. Use Ctrl+Shift+Enter instead of Enter to fill the entire highlighted range with the new transposed data. Notice how Figure 13.13 shows building the TRANSPOSE function in progress and Figure 13.14 shows the final result. This function must be entered in the form of an array for the function to work. Press Ctrl+Shift+Enter to activate the array. Should your initial range not contain the same number of columns and rows, you will need to select the destination range in the opposite configuration. For example, if the initial range is B5:E7 (3 rows by 4 columns), you will need to select B9:D12 (4 rows by 3 columns) as a destination range.

■ **Array**—This is the range of cells you want to transpose on the worksheet. This starts with the first row of the range and then transposes starting with the first column of the new array.

Figure 13.13
Be sure to select the region of the destination of the transposed table.

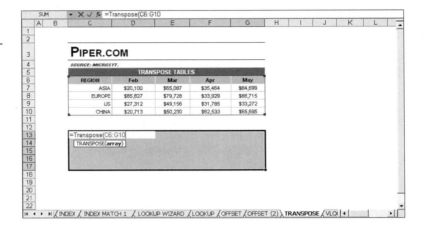

Figure 13.14
The result of the TRANSPOSE function operating on a table. Press Ctrl+Shift+Enter instead of Enter to enter the formula as an array and fill the entire highlighted range with the new transposed data.

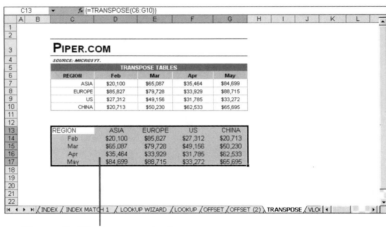

The result of the transposed cells

VLOOKUP

VLOOKUP looks for a value in the leftmost column of a table and returns a value from the column number that you specify:

=VLOOKUP(lookup_value,table_array,column_index_num,range_lookup)

VLOOKUP is one of those functions that has multiple purposes, and is useful in just about every walk of business life. If you have employee timesheets on a weekly or daily basis, this is a good formula to use when looking up the rate for the employee and matching it to the name of the employee in the list. In Figure 13.15, =VLOOKUP(F6,$C$6:$D$8,2,FALSE) produces the rate of the employee from the rate table. The lookup range must not include the column headings.

In this example, F6 is the lookup value—the employee's name—C6:D8 is the rate table referenced, and 2 is the column index number from the rate table in which you want a value return. The `range_lookup` argument determines what type of search to perform. TRUE (or omitted) means it searches for an approximate match, FALSE means finds an exact match. If an approximate match is needed, the first column in the lookup table must be in ascending order.

Figure 13.15
The VLOOKUP function can be used to combine employee rates with the names in a list.

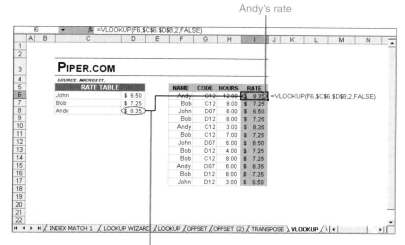

Andy's rate

Match names to rate tables

TROUBLESHOOTING

VLOOKUP MATCHING

VLOOKUP is returning the wrong value.

The `range_lookup` argument determines what type of search to perform. TRUE (or omitted) means it searches for an approximate match, FALSE means finds an exact match. If an approximate match is needed, the first column in the lookup table must be in ascending order.

EXCEL IN PRACTICE

The VLOOKUP function combined with a list of employees can look up the rates of the employees. Take this example one step further as shown in Figure 13.16 and create a PivotTable that summarizes the list of employees' hours and dollars from the list. You can make an extended range for the source data of the table so that when you add to the list, the PivotTable automatically includes the new list data in the summary PivotTable.

To create an automatic summary like the one in Figure 13.16, set up your Rate Table first. Then, create your list with the VLOOKUP function referencing the table. Then, select the range of the list, or select an extended range the list will never grow to, such as E7:H40,000. From that list, create a PivotTable summarizing the total values for each employee.

Figure 13.16
Use tables, lists, VLOOKUP, and PivotTables to automatically manage employee costs.

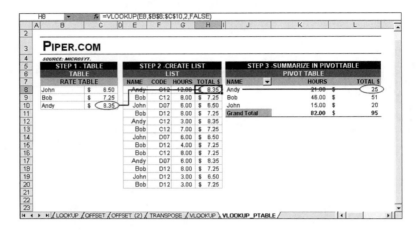

CHAPTER 14

MATH AND TRIGONOMETRY FUNCTIONS

In this chapter

Math and Trigonometry Functions Overview 304

ABS 307

ACOS 308

ASIN 309

COMBIN 310

COUNTIF 311

DEGREES 313

LN 313

MODE 314

PERMUT 315

PI 316

RAND 316

ROMAN 317

SQRT 318

SUBTOTAL 319

SUM 320

SUMIF 321

TAN 322

MATH AND TRIGONOMETRY FUNCTIONS OVERVIEW

Math and Trigonometry functions in Excel can be used to perform calculations as stand-alone functions or combined to create complex formulas. Trigonometry is simply the study of how sides and angles of a triangle relate to each other. So, this chapter when referring to trig functions is all about triangles. Yep, it's that simple. And, some quick comments about sine and cosine. Sine is the ratio of the height to the hypotenuse and cosine is the ratio of the base to the hypotenuse. Where the hypotenuse is the longest leg of a right triangle. Sine and cosine are referred to frequently within the chapter. Table 14.1 functions presented in bold are included with examples in this chapter.

TABLE 14.1   MATH AND TRIGONOMETRY FUNCTIONS

Function	Syntax	Description
ABS	=ABS(*number*)	Returns the absolute value of a number.
ACOS	=ACOS(*number*)	Returns the arccosine or inverse cosine of a number. The arccosine is the angle whose cosine is a number.
ACOSH	=ACOSH(*number*)	Returns the inverse hyperbolic cosine of a number.
ASIN	=ASIN(*number*)	Returns the arcsine, or inverse sine of a number.
ASINH	=ASINH(*number*)	Returns the inverse hyperbolic sine of a number.
ATAN	=ATAN(*number*)	Returns the arctangent, or inverse tangent of a number.
ATAN2	=ATAN2(*x_num*,*y_num*)	Returns the arctangent, or inverse tangent of the specified x and y coordinates.
ATANH	=ATANH(*number*)	Returns the inverse hyperbolic tangent of a number between –1 and 1.
CEILING	=CEILING(*number*, *significance*)	Returns number rounded up, away from zero, to the nearest multiple you specify.
COMBIN	=COMBIN(*number*, *number_chosen*)	Returns the total number of combinations for a given number of items.
COS	=COS(*number*)	Returns the cosine of a given angle.
COSH	=COSH(*number*)	Returns the hyperbolic cosine of a number.
COUNTIF	=COUNTIF(*range*,*criteria*)	Counts the number of cells in a specified range that meet criteria you specify.

14

Function	Syntax	Description
DEGREES	=DEGREES(*angle*)	Converts radians into degrees.
EVEN	=EVEN(*number*)	Returns a number rounded up to the nearest even integer.
EXP	=EXP(*number*)	Returns E (which equals the base logarithm constant of 2.71828182845904) raised to the power of a number you specify.
FACT	=FACT(*number*)	Returns the factorial of a number.
FACTDOUBLE	=FACTDOUBLE(*number*)	Returns the double factorial of a number.
FLOOR	=FLOOR(*number*, *significance*)	Rounds number down, toward zero, to the nearest multiple you specify.
GCD	=GCD(*number1*,*number2*,...)	Returns the greatest common divisor of two or more integers.
INT	=INT(*number*)	Rounds number down to the nearest integer (no decimals).
LCM	=LCM(*number1*,*number2*,...)	Returns the least common multiple of integers.
LN	=LN(*number*)	Returns the natural logarithm of a number.
LOG	=LOG(*number*,*base*)	Returns the logarithm of a number to the base you specify.
LOG10	=LOG10(*number*)	Returns the base 10 logarithm of a number.
MDETERM	=MDETERM(*array*)	Returns the matrix determinant of an array.
MINVERSE	=MINVERSE(*array*)	Returns the inverse matrix for the matrix stored in an array.
MMULT	=MMULT(*array1*,*array2*)	Returns the matrix product of two arrays.
MOD	=MOD(*number*,*divisor*)	Returns the remainder after number is divided by divisor.
MODE	=MODE(*Number1*,*Number2*,...)	Returns the value that appears the most times within a list or range of cell.
MROUND	=MROUND(*number*,*multiple*)	Returns number rounded to the desired multiple.
MULTINOMIAL	=MULTINOMIAL(*number1*, *number2*,...)	Returns the ratio of the factorial of a sum of values to the product of factorials.
ODD	=ODD(*number*)	Returns number rounded to the nearest odd integer.
PERMUT	=PERMUT(*number*, *number_chosen*)	Returns the number of permutations for a given number of objects that can be selected from number objects.

14

continues

TABLE 14.1 CONTINUED

Function	Syntax	Description
PI	=PI()	Returns the number 3.14159265358979, the mathematical constant pi, accurate to 15 digits. There are no arguments associated with this function.
POWER	=POWER(*number*,*power*)	Returns the result of a number raised to a power.
PRODUCT	=PRODUCT(*number1*, *number2*,...)	Multiplies all the numbers given as arguments and returns the product.
QUOTIENT	=QUOTIENT(*numerator*, *denominator*)	Returns the integer portion of a division, discarding the remainder.
RADIANS	=RADIANS(*angle*)	Converts degrees to radians.
RAND	=RAND()	Returns an evenly distributed number greater than or equal to 0 and less than 1. There are no arguments associated with this function.
RANDBETWEEN	=RANDBETWEEN(*bottom*,*top*)	Returns a random number between the qnumbers you specify.
ROMAN	=ROMAN(*number*,*form*)	Converts an Arabic numeral to Roman, as text.
ROUND	=ROUND(*number*,*num_digits*)	Rounds a number to a specified number of digits.
ROUNDDOWN	=ROUNDDOWN(*number*, *num_digits*)	Rounds a number down toward 0.
ROUNDUP	=ROUNDUP(*number*,*num_digits*)	Rounds a number up, away from 0.
SERIESSUM	=SERIESSUM(*x*,*n*,*m*, *coefficients*)	Returns the sum of a power series based on the mathematical **SERIES** formula, which can be found in Excel's **SERIESSUM** help topic.
SIGN	=SIGN(*number*)	Determines the sign of a number, returning a 1 for positive, a 0 for zero, and a −1 for negative.
SIN	=SIN(*number*)	Returns the sine of the given angle.
SINH	=SINH(*number*)	Returns the hyperbolic sine of a number.
SQRT	=SQRT(*number*)	Returns the positive square root of a number.
SQRTPI	=SQRTPI(*number*)	Returns the square root of (number*pi).
SUBTOTAL	=SUBTOTAL(*function_num*, *ref1*,*ref2*,...)	Calculates a subtotal from a range based on 11 different functions: AVERAGE, COUNT, COUNTA, MAX, MIN, PRODUCT STDEV, STDEVP, SUM, VAR, and VARP.

14

Function	Syntax	Description
SUM	=Sum(*number1*,*number2*,...)	Adds the numbers in a range or multiple ranges of cells.
SUMIF	=SUMIF(*range*,*criteria*, *sum_range*)	Adds the numbers in a range based on criteria you specify.
SUMPRODUCT	=SUMPRODUCT(*array1*, *array2*,*array3*,...)	Multiplies corresponding components in the given arrays, and returns the sum of those products.
SUMSQ	=SUMSQ(*number1*,*number2*,...)	Returns the sum of the squares of the arguments.
SUMX2MY2	=SUMX2MY2(*array_x*,*array_y*)	Returns the sum of the difference of squares of corresponding values in two arrays.
SUMX2PY2	=SUMX2PY2(*array_x*,*array_y*)	Returns the sum of the sum of squares in corresponding values in two arrays.
SUMXMY2	=SUMXMY2(*array_x*,*array_y*)	Returns the sum of the difference of squares of corresponding values in two arrays
TAN	=TAN(*number*)	Returns the tangent of the given angle.
TANH	=TANH(*number*)	Returns the hyperbolic tangent of a number.
TRUNC	=TRUNC(*number*,*num_digits*)	Truncates number to an integer, removing the fractional part of the number. Unlike the INT function, TRUNC does not round down.

ABS

The ABS function returns the absolute value of a number—the number without its sign:

=ABS(number)

In other words, the ABS function always returns a positive number. The NUMBER argument can be a value; a single-cell range, such as ABS(A1); or a multiple-cell range; which returns an array of values. Following is an example of using ABS in a multiple-cell range.

This is the function you would use for looking at the absolute differences of a set of data from a given value. As shown in Figure 14.1, ABS can be used to find the value from a data range that is closest to the average of that data. For example, notice in the figure that the average of the random set is in cell E8 and the formula in E12 finds the next closest value to that average. This formula creates an array of absolute differences, as calculated by the ABS function, between the data and the average of the data. This is matched to the minimum difference, and the INDEX function returns the desired value based on that match. The formula shown in the figure is an array formula. To enter an array formula, hold down

14

Ctrl+Shift+Enter. Notice a less complex use of the ABS function that returns the absolute value of a real number in cell G16. For example, –9 would result in 9.

■ **NUMBER**—The real number you want to convert to an absolute.

Figure 14.1
The ABS function can be used to create arrays of absolute differences to be used in complex formulas.

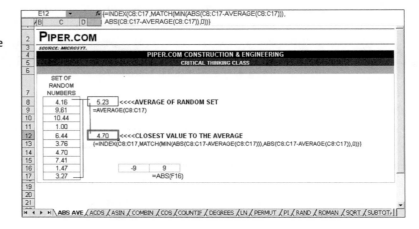

ACOS

The ACOS function returns the arccosine of a number in radians in the range 0 (zero) to pi:

`=ACOS(number)`

The arccosine is the angle of the number's cosine. As with all normal trigonometric functions in Excel, you can convert the result from radians to degrees by multiplying it by `180/PI()`.

Notice the example of the ACOS function shown in Figure 14.2. The equation is Cos B=b²-a²-c²/-2ac, where a = 18.2, b = 20.3, and c = 24. The numbers in the example were hard coded into the formula; you could also create the following example using cell referencing to make the formula dynamic based on inputs in cells C7:C9, assuming the three numbers in Figure 14.2 are in cells C7:C9. This function is an example of the Law of Cosines, which finds the measure of the angle opposite side b of a triangle, given the length of each of all three sides:

`=ACOS((C8^2-C7^2-C9^2)/(-2*C7*C9))*180/PI()`

You can use `180/PI()` to convert radians to degrees, or simply use the DEGREES function. For example, the following formula also works (which also demonstrates the use of the DEGREES function):

`=DEGREES(ACOS((20.3^2-18.2^2-24^2)/(-2*18.2*24)))`

■ **NUMBER**—This is the cosine of the angle you want. It must be from –1 to 1. To convert the result from radians to degrees multiply the number by `180/PI()`.

Figure 14.2
The ACOS function returns an angle of which cosine is the given number.

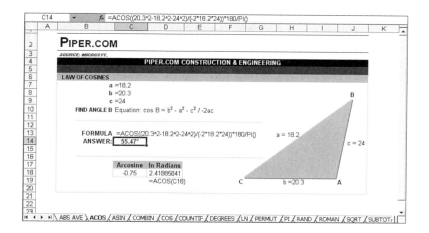

ASIN

The ASIN function returns the arcsine of a NUMBER:

```
=ASIN(number)
```

Where sine is the number, Arcsine returns the angle. The returned angle is given in radians in the range –pi/2 to pi/2.

As with all normal trigonometric functions in Excel, you can convert the result from radians to degrees by multiplying it by 180/PI() or use the DEGREES function to convert radians to degrees. While engineers, scientists and mathematicians are used to measurements of angles in radians, it's easier for most to understand angles in the form of degrees.

Notice the example of the ASIN function shown in Figure 14.3. The destination of the plane flying at 450 miles per hour is at 16 degrees south of west. If the wind velocity is 30 miles per hour from the east, what course should the pilot set?

- Cell E8: 450 miles per hour
- Cell E9: direction south of west
- Cell E10: wind velocity in miles per hour

The formula

```
=E9+ASIN(E10*SIN(RADIANS(E9))/E8)*180/PI()
```

results in the following course the pilot should set: 17.05 south of west.

- **NUMBER**—The sine of the desired angle. It must be from –1 to 1.

14

Figure 14.3
The ASIN function returns an angle in which sine is the given number.

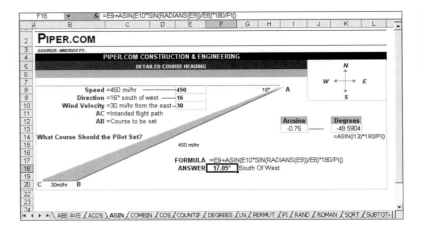

COMBIN

The COMBIN function returns the NUMBER of combinations for a given number of items:

```
=COMBIN(number,items)
```

Use COMBIN to determine the total possible number of groups for a given number of items. Combinations are similar to permutations in that groupings of objects are made from a larger set of objects. With permutations, the internal order is significant, but it isn't with combinations.

The ITEMS argument is the number of items in each combination and it must be between zero and the value of the number argument for the function to work correctly. Although non-integer values can be used in the COMBIN function, they have no mathematical significance, and they are automatically rounded to integers.

Notice in the example in Figure 14.4, there are 8 linemen, 6 receivers, 4 running backs, and 2 quarterbacks on a given football team. How many different ways can a team of 11 offensive players be chosen if 5 linemen, 3 receivers, 2 running backs, and 1 quarterback are used? The answer: 13,440. Notice in the example how the formula is set up. In essence, it reads Combin(firstset,Secondset) and multiply it by Combin(firstset,Secondset), then multiply by Combin(firstset,Secondset) and multiply by Combin(firstset,Secondset).

Another way to use the COMBIN function could be to calculate the odds of the California Lottery as shown in cell D19 of Figure 14.4, because COMBIN(52,6) will give you all the combinations of 6 numbers in the 52 total number format. That said, your odds stand at 1 in 20,358,520.

- **NUMBER**—The number of items.
- **ITEMS**—The number of items in each combination.

$$\binom{n}{k} = \frac{P_{k,n}}{k!} = \frac{n!}{k!(n-k)!}$$

Figure 14.4
Use the COMBIN function to return the number of combinations that can be used with different sets of data.

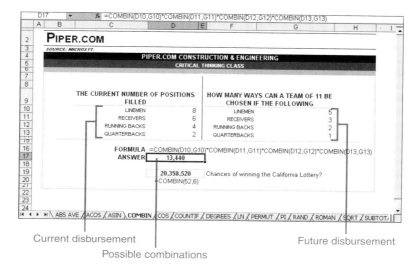

Current disbursement

Possible combinations

Future disbursement

CAUTION

> When you hard code formulas (place the number or text in the formula), you lose efficiency. The best way to handle functions and formulas is through cell referencing. Meaning, set your numbers up in corresponding cells and where the formula calls for that number or syntax, type the cell reference. If you set your formulas up this way, they become dynamic and you can change the result by creating new inputs in the cell references.

COUNTIF

The COUNTIF function counts the number of cells within a range that meet the given criteria:

`=COUNTIF(range,criteria)`

The RANGE argument is the range of cells from which you want to count cells. It is important to note that this argument cannot be a calculated array, unlike many functions that do not differentiate between a worksheet range and an array.

The CRITERIA argument is the criteria in the form of a number, expression, or text that defines which cells will be counted. Whatever you decide to use in this argument, Excel must be able to convert it into a Boolean (TRUE/FALSE) expression that defines the criteria.

The second argument of the COUNTIF function also can accept a range of data. An outstanding example of using this range argument is in the formula that returns the average of all

14

numbers greater than zero. Often, you'll have a range of numbers that you need to average and want to exclude all the zero values. Using the AVERAGE function will include all numbers in its calculation, including zero and negative numbers. COUNTIF can help screen out those undesirable values. See Table 14.2 for additional COUNTIF formula variations.

In Figure 14.5, range C7:C15 contains six values that are greater than 0. The average of those values is rounded to 24. The COUNTIF formula in cell F7 counts all values within the specified range greater than zero.

A slightly less complicated formula in cell D17 could be

`{=AVERAGE(IF(C7:C15>0,C7:C15))}`

- **RANGE**—The range of cells to count: C7:C15.
- **CRITERIA**—The criteria in the form of an expression is all values greater than zero: ">0".

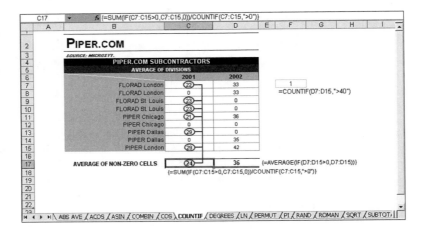

Figure 14.5
The COUNTIF function can be used in an array formula to calculate the average of all values in a range greater than zero.

TABLE 14.2 VARIATIONS IN USING THE COUNTIF FORMULA

Function Formula	Result
=Countif(Range,25)	Returns the number of cells containing the value of 25.
=Countif(Range,">0")	Returns the number of cells with values greater than 0.
=Sum(if(Range>0,Range,0)/countif (range,">0")) Ctrl+Shft+Enter	Averages all positive values greater than zero.
=Countif(Range,"*")	Returns the number of cells that contain text.
=countif(Range,"??")	Returns the number of text cells that contain two characters. Add an additional question mark for three, four, and so on.
=countif(Range,"2001")	Returns the number of cells that contain the text 2001.

Function Formula	Result
=countif(Range,"*2001*")	Returns the number of cells that have 2001 anywhere within the text or sentence. Cells containing 2001 in a numeric value are ignored.
=countif(Range,"North*")	Returns the number of cells starting with North, such as North East, North West, North, and so on.
=countif(Range,today())	Returns the number of cells that return today's date.

DEGREES

The DEGREES function converts radians into degrees:

=DEGREES(angle)

Using this function is equivalent to multiplying a value in radians by 180/PI(). The formula DEGREES(PI()) equals 180 because pi radians describes an arc of a hemisphere. While radians are frequently used by scientists, engineers, and mathematicians, measurements in degrees are more easily understood by the general public.

Notice the example of the DEGREES function shown in Figure 14.6.

- **ANGLE**—The angle in the form of radians you want to convert.

Figure 14.6
The DEGREES function converts radian measure to central angle measure.

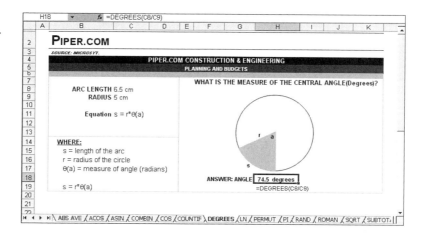

LN

The LN function returns the natural logarithm of a number. Natural logarithms are based on the constant (2.71828182845904). A logarithm is an exponent used in calculations to show perceived levels of variable quantities. In the following case, this refers to the perceived level of population growth.

=LN(number)

The LN function can be used in problems that calculate exponential growth, such as the population growth in Figure 14.7. In this example, the growth rate is 5%, the current population is 5,000,000, and you want to know how many years it will take to reach the population of 10,000,000. The formula is

`=(LN(I12)-LN(F12))/C8`

where cell I12 is the future population, cell F12 is the current population, cell C8 is the growth rate, and the result is 13.9 years.

- **NUMBER**—The NUMBER argument is the positive real number for which you want the natural logarithm.

LN is the inverse of the EXP function, so the formula LN(EXP(22.3)) equals 22.3. You also can use LOG if a more flexible approach is needed.

Figure 14.7
Use the LN function to estimate population growth over time.

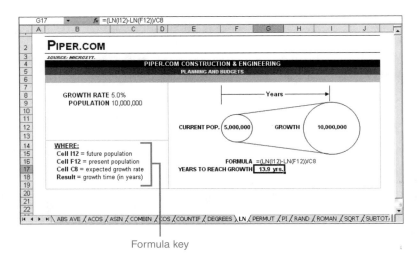

Formula key

MODE

MODE returns the value that appears the most times within a list or range of cells.

> **NOTE**
> MODE is actually a statistical function but is often mistaken for a math and trig function.

`=Mode(Number1,Number2,…)`

Use the MODE function to find out the most recurring information in a list. For example, if you have a list and want to find out what number appears the most times within the list simply use the following formula:

`=MODE(Data)`

Here are some caveats to using the MODE function:

- If the data contains no duplicating numbers or data points it will result in the #N/A error value.

- If the data contains text, logical values, or empty cells, those data points are ignored. Cells containing an actual value of zero are included

This will return the actual number that most frequently occurs. A common next step might be to ask how many times that number actually appears within the list. You can find this out by combining the COUNTIF function with the MODE function. Use the following formula to count the occurrence of that number within the list:

```
=COUNTIF(Data,MODE(Data))
```

PERMUT

The PERMUT function returns the number of permutations for a certain number of objects that can be selected from number objects:

```
=PERMUT(Number,Number_chosen)
```

The PERMUT function operates on the subset of the whole, where the order of the subset is of importance. Also find the PERMUT function in Chapter 16, "Statistical Functions." For example, in Figure 14.8, there are nine players on a baseball team. If the pitcher is excluded, what is the number of ways to arrange the first five positions in the batting order? The result is 6,720.

- **NUMBER**—The integer that describes the number of the total set.
- **NUMBER CHOSEN**—The number of objects in the permutation.

Figure 14.8
Use the PERMUT function to find the number in order of a subset of the whole.

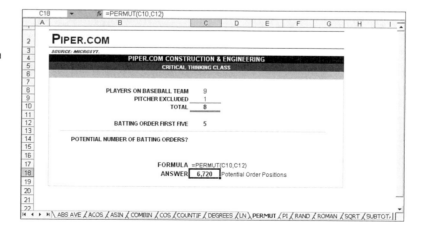

PI

The PI function returns the approximate number 3.14159265358979, the mathematical constant pi, accurate to 15 digits:

=PI()

Notice the example in Figure 14.9. Where the radius of the circle is 6.75, the calculation to find the area from the radius is =PI()*(D11^2) and the result is 143.14. The formula for the area of the circle is pi*r².

Figure 14.9
To find the area of a circle with the known radius, use the PI function.

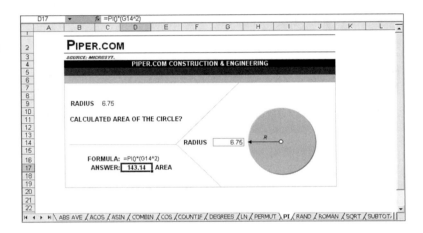

RAND

The RAND function returns an evenly distributed random number greater than or equal to 0 and less than 1. A new random number is returned every time the worksheet is calculated.

=RAND()

The RAND function is a volatile function. This means that the value returned by that function is changed each time the worksheet is recalculated. To prevent the result of the RAND function from changing the next time the worksheet calculates, the formula must be converted to its value. To do this, either choose the Copy and Paste Special commands from the Edit menu and then choose the Values option from the dialog box, or highlight the formula in the formula bar and press F9 and Enter.

For example, you can return a value between 0 and 2 with RAND()*2. In Figure 14.10, the RAND Function returns random numbers between point A and B: =RAND()*(b-a)+a.

14

Figure 14.10
The RAND function can be used to create random numbers between two points as shown.

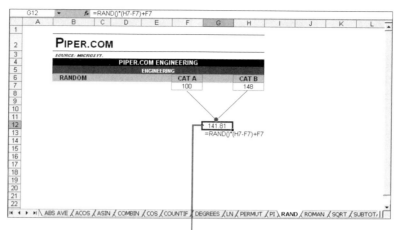

Random number between CAT A and CAT B

ROMAN

The ROMAN function converts an Arabic numeral to Roman, as text:

=ROMAN(number,form)

The NUMBER argument is the Arabic numeral you want converted, and the FORM argument is a number specifying the type of Roman numeral you want. If the number is negative or greater than 3,999, an error value is returned. The Roman numeral style ranges from Classic to Simplified (0 to 4), becoming more concise as the value of form increases, meaning:

- **NUMBER**—The number you want converted.
- **FORM**—Specifies the type of Roman numeral, where numbers 1 through 3 provide more precise levels of accuracy:

  Classic: =ROMAN(cell,0) or =ROMAN(cell) or =ROMAN(cell, TRUE)

  More precise: =ROMAN(cell,1)

  More precise: =ROMAN(cell,2)

  More precise: =ROMAN(cell,3)

  Simplified: =ROMAN(cell,4) or =ROMAN(cell, FALSE)

The example in Figure 14.11 converts B9:B18 and J9:J12 to Roman numerals.

14

Figure 14.11
Use the ROMAN function to convert Arabic numerals to Roman.

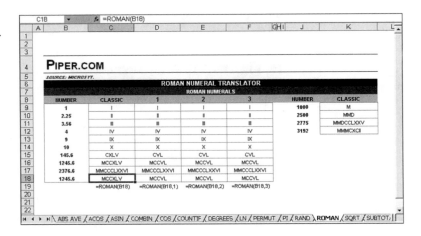

SQRT

The SQRT function can be used to return the positive square root of a number or in conjunction with the cosine and radians to return the length of an unknown where the square root of 64 is 8, as shown in Figure 14.12. Or in other words, The SQRT function can be used to return the positive square root of a number as shown in cell C19 of Figure 14.12 where the square root of 64 is shown to be 8. It can also be used in trigonometric calculations, for example, in conjunction with the cosine and radian functions, using the law of cosines, to return the length of the side of a triangle where the length of the other two sides and the size of the angle between them is known. In Figure 14.12 this formula is used to calculate the length of side b of the triangle (cell C14):

```
b = sqrt(a² + c² - 2ac cos B)
```

```
=SQRT(number)
```

The result for the length of b is 21.60.

- **NUMBER**—The NUMBER argument is the number for which you want the square root. If number is negative, SQRT returns an error value.

14

Figure 14.12
The SQRT function can be used to return the positive square root of a number or in conjunction with the cosine and radians to return the length of an unknown.

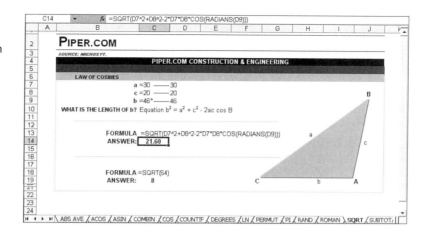

SUBTOTAL

The SUBTOTAL function returns a subtotal in a list or database:

`=SUBTOTAL(fnum,ref1,ref2,...)`

You can apply this function to a list or database data table automatically by using the Subtotals command on the Data menu. After the subtotal list is created, you can modify it by editing the SUBTOTAL function. The capability of the SUBTOTAL function to return information from a filtered list makes it one of the most powerful of Excel's functions. If there are other subtotals within ref1, ref2, (or nested subtotals), these nested subtotals are automatically ignored. The SUBTOTAL function also ignores any hidden rows that result from a list being filtered. This is important when you want to subtotal only the visible data that results from a list that you have filtered as shown in Figure 14.13. If any of the references are 3D references, SUBTOTAL returns an error value.

The SUBTOTAL function can be used either with the normal filter (available by selecting Data, Filter) or by using the advanced filter (Data, Filter, Advanced Filter). The example shown in Figure 14.13 uses the standard auto filter. In this case, the data table has been filtered to show only the February results. You can apply multiple analysis against any list with SUBTOTAL by applying the type of calculation number as shown here in the FNUM place.

- **FNUM**—The FNUM argument is a number from 1 to 11 that specifies which function to use in calculating subtotals within a list. There can be up to 29 arguments.
- **CELL REFERENCE or RANGE**—The cell or range in which to reference.

The 11 FNUM arguments are as follows:

AVERAGE	STDEV
COUNT	STDEVP
COUNTA	SUM

14

MAX   VAR

MIN   VARP

PRODUCT

Figure 14.13
Use the SUBTOTAL function with FNUM arguments to reference information quickly in lists or subtotal filtered information so it sums only the filtered visible cells.

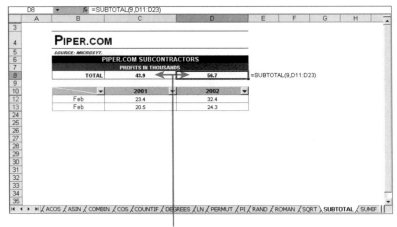

Subtotals the sums for visible cells only

SUM

The SUM function adds all the numbers in a range of cells:

```
=SUM(number1,number2, ...)
```

If an argument is an array or reference, only numbers in that array or reference are counted. Empty cells, logical values, and text in the array or reference are ignored. Any error values in any reference arguments result in the SUM function returning an error.

TIP FROM

> A quick way to create a SUM formula with multiple reference arguments is to type "=SUM(" and click the first cell or group of cells to be used in the formula. Then, press Shift+F8. Each range that you highlight from that point will be added to the formula with the necessary comma separator for that argument.

- **NUMBER**—The NUMBER arguments are 1 to 30 arguments for which you want the total value or sum.

The SUM function can accept only 30 arguments, but there is a simple workaround to this limitation. Each argument can contain up to 30 arguments of its own as long as they are enclosed by parentheses. The following example illustrates how this is done:

```
=SUM((A1,B2,C3),(A2,B3,C4))
```

The SUM function is one of the functions in Excel that can operate on a 3D range where a 3D range is a range used across multiple sheets within a workbook. The following formula is an example of the use of a 3D-range argument:

```
=SUM(Sheet1:Sheet4!A1)
```

In this case, the values in the sheets from Sheet1 to Sheet4 inclusive are summed. However, sheet names do not necessarily reflect sheet positions and only those sheets that are "between" Sheet1 and Sheet4 will be included in the result. So essentially, if Sheet 5 is physically located between Sheet 1 and Sheet 4 (on the list of tabs) in this example, it *would* be counted.

SUMIF

The SUMIF function adds the cells specified by a given criteria:

```
=SUMIF(range,criteria,sumrange)
```

It is important to note that the RANGE and SUMRANGE arguments do not have to reside on the same worksheet (example shown later in this section).

```
=SUMIF(Sheet1!A1:A10,">5",Sheet2!A1:A10)
```

In this case, the values in the range Sheet2!A1:A10 are summed if the corresponding values in the range Sheet1!A1:A10 are greater than 5.

An example of the utility of the SUMIF function is shown in Figure 14.14. The table represents profits from a variety of divisions. The formula shown in G7 summarizes this information according to region names that fit given criteria. The *, or wildcard character, matches any word in B7:B14 that starts with "PIPER" and sums the values in the range C7:C19. So, the result is 127.1. In this case, the wildcard character "*" is concatenated with the cell text to allow matches based on strings contained in text. You might also notice that the criteria and sumrange arguments in these formulas are partially relative references. This allows the formulas to be filled across for each Year column and then filled down for the "Piper" and "Florad" summary rows.

- **RANGE**—The range of cells you want evaluated.
- **CRITERIA**—The criteria in the form of a number, expression, or text that defines which cells will be added. The criteria can also be a cell reference that contains part or all of the criteria, as in the example.
- **SUMRANGE**—The actual cells to sum. The cells in SUMRANGE are summed only if their corresponding cells in the range match the criteria. If SUMRANGE is omitted, the cells in the RANGE argument are summed.

The RANGE argument cannot be a calculated array, unlike many functions that do not differentiate between a worksheet range and an array. Whatever you decide to use in this argument, Excel must be able to convert it into a Boolean expression that defines the criteria.

14

Figure 14.14
The SUMIF function can use wildcard characters to summarize the totals for divisions spread out through several states or countries as shown.

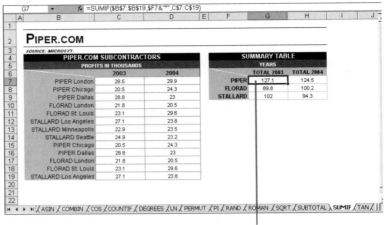

Sum of all divisions that start with PIPER

TAN

The TAN function returns the tangent of the given angle:

=TAN(number)

As with all normal trigonometric functions in Excel, you can convert the result from radians to degrees by multiplying it by 180/PI(). The number is the angle to be converted or changed to a tangent.

Notice the example of the TAN function shown at the bottom of Figure 14.15. The angle of "a" is 56 degrees and the measurement from the survey point is 145 feet. Where length of side A = length of adjacent side of the right angled triangle * tangent of angle a, what is the height of the tower? The result is 214.97 feet.

Figure 14.15
The TAN function can be used in survey measurements along with RADI- ANS to return results that are not directly measurable.

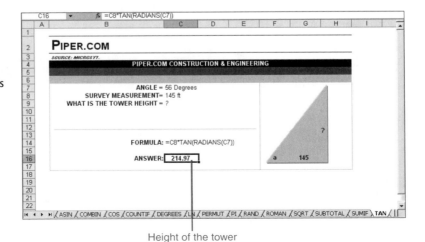

Height of the tower

TROUBLESHOOTING

QUICK SUM

I have multiple ranges to add to a SUM formula. What's the best way to do this?

There are two simple ways to do this: Start the SUM formula with =sum(, select your first cell or range, press the Ctrl key and select the next set, and so on. This method automatically separates your cells or ranges with a comma separator. The second way to create a SUM formula with multiple reference arguments is to type =SUM(and click the first cell or group of cells to be used in the formula. Then, press Shift+F8. Each range that you highlight from that point will be added to the formula with the necessary comma separator for that argument.

CREATING QUICK RELATIVE VERSUS ABSOLUTE

When creating absolute referencing in cells, is there a better way than typing the dollar sign in front of the rows and columns?

There is a quicker and safer way. Highlight or select the cell or range in the formula bar. Press F4 and both rows and columns will become absolute. Press F4 again and the rows remain absolute and the columns are relative. Press F4 again and the columns remain absolute and the rows are relative. Press F4 again and the formula is back to relative.

EXCEL IN PRACTICE

One of the most common yet misunderstood functions is the SUBTOTAL function. In Figure 14.16, the list beneath the summary table is filtered. You can apply the SUBTOTAL function to sum the visible cells of a filtered list. In this example it's imperative you use the SUBTOTAL function instead of SUM because the SUM function adds visible and nonvisible cells.

Figure 14.16
Use the SUBTOTAL function to summarize visible cells only in a list.

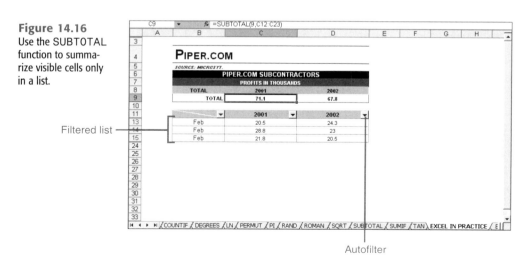

Filtered list

Autofilter

CHAPTER 15

TEXT FUNCTIONS

In this chapter

Text Functions Overview   326

CONCATENATE   328

EXACT   329

FIND   330

FIXED   331

LEN   332

LOWER   333

MID   334

PROPER   335

RIGHT   336

Add st, nd, rd, and th to the End of Numbers   337

SUBSTITUTE   338

TRIM   339

UPPER   340

TEXT FUNCTIONS OVERVIEW

Text functions can be used in several ways. They can return the number of characters in text strings, remove extra spaces and nonprintable characters from cells, return exact data within a string, change the case of text strings, and even combine text from other cells. If you inherit workbooks from other people, you will eventually have to clean up or manipulate the data. Text functions allow you to create consistency throughout the workbook. Because certain functions are case sensitive, it's good practice to create consistency throughout lists and tables. This chapter covers the functions in Table 15.1 that are marked in bold.

TABLE 15.1   TEXT FUNCTIONS

Function	Syntax	Description
CHAR	=CHAR(*number*)	Returns the character specified by a number.
CLEAN	=CLEAN(*text*)	Removes all nonprintable characters from text.
CODE	=CODE(*text*)	Returns a numeric code for the first character in a text string.
CONCATENATE	=CONCATENATE(*text1*,*text2*,...)	Joins several text strings into one text string.
DOLLAR	=DOLLAR(*number*,*decimals*)	Converts a number to text using currency format, with the decimals rounded to the specified place.
EXACT	=EXACT(*text1*,*text2*)	Compares two text strings and returns TRUE if they're exactly the same, and FALSE otherwise.
FIND	=FIND(*find_text*,*within_text*, *start_num*)	Finds one text string within another text string, andreturns the number of the starting position of find_text, from the leftmost character of within_text.
FIXED	=FIXED(*number*,*decimals*, *no_commas*)	Rounds a number to a specified number of decimals, formats the number in decimal format using a period and commas, and returns the result as text.
LEFT	=LEFT(*text*,*num_char*)	Returns the first character or characters in a text string based on the number of characters you specify.
LEN	=LEN(*text*)	Returns the number of characters in a text string.
LOWER	=LOWER(*text*)	Converts all uppercase letters in a text string to lowercase.

Function	Syntax	Description
MID	=MID(*text,start_num,num_char*)	Returns a specific number of characters from a text string, starting at the position you specify.
PROPER	=PROPER(*text*)	Capitalizes the first letter of each word in a text string and any other letters in text that follow any character other than a letter.
REPLACE	=REPLACE(*old_text,start_num, num_chars,new_text*)	Replaces a portion of a text string with a different text string based on the number of characters you specify.
REPLACEB	=REPLACEB(*old_text,start_num, num_bytes,new_text*)	Replaces part of a text string with a different text string based on the number of bytes you specify.
REPT	=REPT(*text,number_times*)	Repeats text a given number of times.
RIGHT	=RIGHT(*text,num_chars*)	Returns the last character or characters in a text string based on the number of characters you specify.
SEARCH	=SEARCH(*find_text, within_text, start_num*)	Returns the number of the character at which a specific character or text string is first found, reading from left to right. SEARCH is not case sensitive and can include wildcard characters.
SEARCHB	=SEARCHB(*find_text, within_text,start_num*)	Returns the number of the character at which a specific haracter or text string is first found, based on its byte position, reading from left to right.
SUBSTITUTE	=SUBSTITUTE(*text,old_text, new_text,instance_num*) =T(*value*)	Substitutes new_text for old_text in a T text string. Returns the text referred to by value.
TEXT	=TEXT(*value,format_text*)	Converts a value to text in a specific number format.
TRIM	=TRIM(*text*)	Removes all spaces from text except for single spaces between words.
UPPER	=UPPER(*text*)	Converts text to uppercase.
VALUE	=VALUE(*text*)	Converts a text string that represents a number to a number.

CONCATENATE

The CONCATENATE function is one of the more useful functions you'll find in Excel. CONCATE-NATE can be used to join text in several forms. One reason it's useful is when you inherit spreadsheets from other creators you'll often need to clean up the cells and text. Often, this includes the combination of information within one cell and this is where concatenate comes in.

```
=CONCATENATE(text1,text2,...)
```

Using this function by itself joins a city and state as shown in the first example in Figure 15.1; however, you also can place characters between the adjoined text by inserting them within a pair of open and close quotation marks.

NOTE

> If you adjoin numbers with the ampersand or the CONCATENATE function, the result is converted to text.

The characters or text can include spacing, dashes, commas, numbers, other functions, and so on. Notice some of the different ways the CONCATENATE function can join text in separate cells. You can also use the ampersand (&). If you want to adjoin three or more cells with the ampersand, it would appear as follows: =A1&B1&C1. If you want to separate the three cells with a space, it would be =A1&" "&B1&" "&C1. Notice how each adjoined cell or text is separated by the ampersand.

- **TEXT 1, TEXT 2...**—Text is the text to be joined. You can join from 1 to 30 items per cell.

TIP FROM

> Using & to connect strings does NOT have CONCATENATE's 30-item limit.

Patrick

Figure 15.1
The CONCATE-NATE function allows you to join text from separate cells into the same cell.

Ampersand joins text with next characters ⎯

Quotes allow for text insertion

EXACT

EXACT compares two text strings and returns TRUE if they're exactly the same, and FALSE otherwise. EXACT is case sensitive.

```
=EXACT(text1,text2)
```

The EXACT function compares two text strings to see whether they are the same. The EXACT function can operate from text within the function or via cell referencing. The EXACT function is case sensitive as shown in the following examples.

- **TEXT 1, TEXT 2...**—The text is the first text string and then the second text string.

For example:

```
=EXACT("BILL","bill") results in FALSE.
=EXACT("BILL","BILL") results in TRUE.
```

As you see in Figure 15.2, there are two examples comparing ranges of cells with the EXACT function. The first displays TRUE when an asset is complete using cell referencing. The second compares a single cell reference to a range in the form of an array. If you had a list of assets, and all assets had unique identities, you might want to determine whether the asset is in the list. For this, you would use the EXACT function with the OR function in the form of an array as shown here and in cell F16 of Figure 15.2. Be sure to activate the array by pressing Ctrl+Shift+Enter.

```
ARRAY {=Or(Exact(Cell Reference, Compare Range))}
```

Figure 15.2
The EXACT function tests two sets of information and displays a logical value of TRUE or FALSE depending on whether the information is equal.

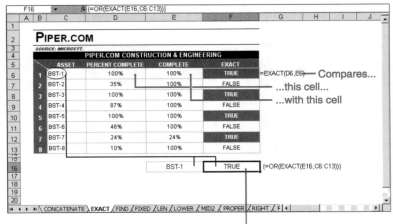

Looks up a cell against a range

FIND

FIND locates one text string with another text string and returns the number of the starting position of find_text, from the leftmost character of within_text. The FIND function is case sensitive.

=FIND(find_text,within_text,start_num)

- **FIND_TEXT**—The find_text is the text you want to locate or find.
- **WITHIN TEXT**—The within_text refers to the text string you're looking within.
- **START NUM**—The start_num refers to the number from left to right from which to start looking for the text. For example, Patrick where the "t" character would be third as the start_num.

For example:

=FIND("W","Wally Bill"), where W is the first character in the string, results in 1.

=FIND("a","Wally Bill"), where a is the second character in the string, results in 2.

NOTE

It's important to note that FIND looks only for the first instance of the text it's looking for. If, for example, we were looking for "a" in, "Wally Ball," the result would still be 2.

If you had a cell that contained the names of people and the cities and states they lived in, you could combine the FIND function with the MID function to extract a text string. The MID function is explained later in this chapter.

15

In Figure 15.3, the formula =Mid(C6,1,Find(" ",C6,1)-1) results in the extraction of the first word, which in this case is a name in the cell, regardless of the length of the first name. The MID function (covered later in this chapter) looks at cell C6 and starts with the first text string; the FIND function also starts with cell C6 and looks for the first space as noted in the quotation marks. The formula then takes the position of the space found and subtracts 1 to return the result.

To take this explanation a step further, the formula =Mid(C6,1,Find(" ",C6,1)-1) extracts the first word from a string regardless of the length of the string. The FIND function looks for a space in the text in cell C6 beginning at character 1. It finds this space at position 6. Then 1 is deducted from this resulting in a formula which now evaluates to this: =Mid(C6,1,5). The MID function (covered later in this chapter) now extracts a five-character string from cell C6 beginning at character position 1.

Figure 15.3
The FIND function combined with the MID function can extract text strings in cells regardless of the string length.

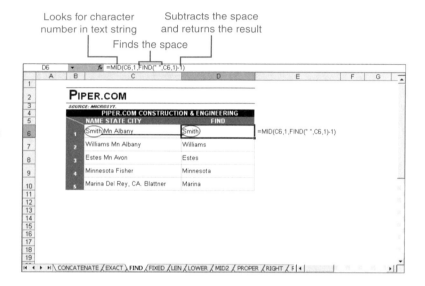

FIXED

The FIXED function rounds a number to a specified number of decimals, formats the number in decimal format using a period and commas, and returns the result as text:

=FIXED(number,decimals,no_commas)

The FIXED function can round numbers in a cell. You can use the FIXED function with text in the function or with cell referencing. Use the FIXED function to round numbers to decimals, hundreds, and thousands. The examples in Figure 15.4 round a number to decimals, tens, hundreds, and thousands using the FIXED function.

NOTE

> The difference between FIXED and ROUND is that FIXED returns its answer in the form of text. FIXED results can be used only in other numeric calculations if converted back to a number using the VALUE function.

- **NUMBER**—The number refers to the number you want to round or convert to text.
- **DECIMALS**—The decimals refer to the number of decimal places to the right. If no decimals are specified it assumes 2.
- **NO COMMAS**—The no commas is a logical result in that if TRUE, it prevents the function from including any commas in the text returned result. For example, the formula =Fixed(2345.24,1,TRUE) would result in 2345.2 without commas.

Figure 15.4
Use the FIXED function to round numbers in a cell.

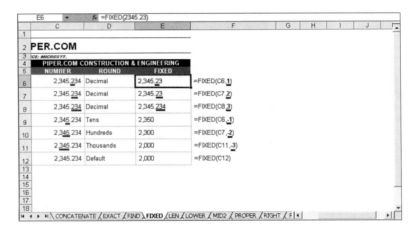

LEN

LEN returns the number of characters in a text string:

=LEN(text)

The LEN function on its own returns the number of characters in a text string. For example, if you had the name Bob in cell A1 and you typed in cell B1 =LEN(A1) the result would be 3. This is an extremely powerful tool when combined with other functions. See also, the "RIGHT" function.

- **TEXT**—The text refers to the text string, word, or multiple words that you want to find the total number of characters. For example, the formula =LEN(" Hello") would result in 5.

Because spaces also count as one character, =LEN("Mn Albany") would result in 9. While the usefulness of this function may not seem clear, in reality, when combined with other functions in Excel, the LEN function becomes a powerful tool for extracting text strings. If you work in an environment in which you have to clean workbooks that were set up improperly, or you've inherited lists of information and have to extract text strings within cells for your own particular purposes, use the LEN function in conjunction with other Excel functions. In the example in Figure 15.5, say you wanted to extract the equipment brand from the equipment type. The function =RIGHT(C17,LEN(C17)-FIND(" ",C17)) results in Caterpillar, because the function extracts the text to the right of the space. (See the "RIGHT" section later in this chapter.)

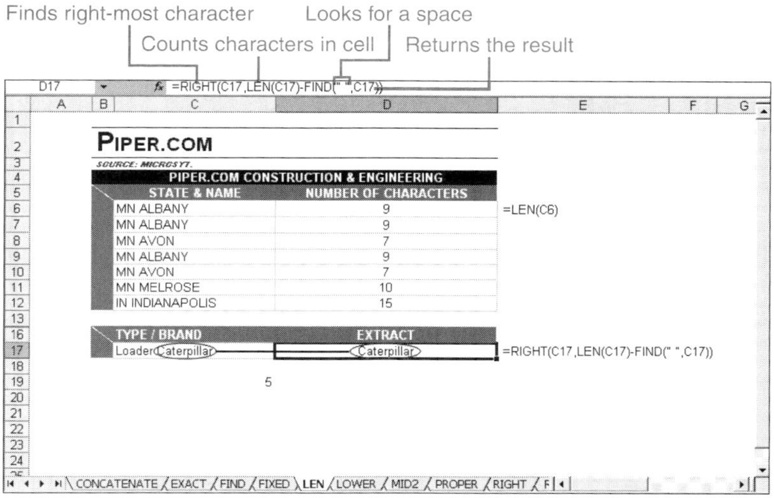

Figure 15.5
Use LEN with other functions in Excel for text extraction.

LOWER

LOWER converts all letters in a text string to lowercase:

=LOWER(text)

The LOWER function is primarily a cleaning function. If you have inconsistent data in lists and you want all characters to result in lowercase, use the LOWER function. In Figure 15.6, the LOWER function converts all the uppercase names to lowercase. Use Paste Special and paste as values back into the original location in the list after you've converted all characters to lowercase. This function can be used with text in a cell or with cell referencing as demonstrated in the figure.

For more information on Paste Special See also Chapter 17, "Setting Up a List or Database in Excel."

- **TEXT**—This is the text within the cell you want to convert to lowercase characters.

Figure 15.6
Use the LOWER function to clean lists of information that are inconsistent.

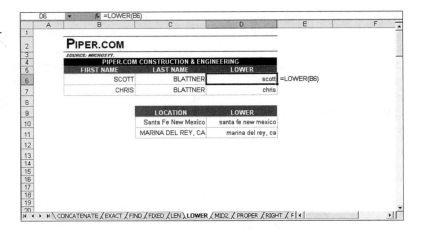

MID

Use the MID function to return a specific number of characters from a text string, starting at the position you specify:

```
=MID(text,start_num,num_char)
```

- **TEXT**—The text is the text string or word you want to extract from.
- **START_NUM**—The start_num is the number of the character within the text string or word you want to extract from.
- **NUM_CHAR**—The num_char is the number of characters to extract from the start_num point to the right.

You can use text within the formula or use cell referencing. For example, =MID("Chris",1,4) returns only the first four characters in the string—Chri. =MID("Hobbe",2,4) returns the text string starting with the second character in the string—obbe. Combined with the FIND function, you can create a powerful tool to dynamically extract any text within a string as shown in Figure 15.7 and described in this section. If you have a URL and you want to extract the actual name from a list of URLs and the name appears in different locations in each URL, you could use the following formulas to do so.

In cell C6, the formula used to extract any text name from a URL is

```
=MID(B6,FIND("Sports",B6),6)
```

If the name doesn't appear in the URL, it will return a #Value error. To eliminate this, use the function found in cell C10 in Figure 15.7 and shown here:

```
=IF(ISERROR(FIND("Sports",B11)),"",MID(B11,FIND("Sports",B11),6))
```

Figure 15.7
Use the MID function as a standalone function or in combination with other functions such as FIND.

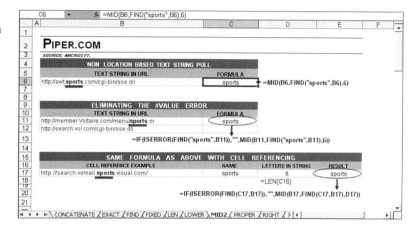

To set up the same formula as shown here with cell referencing, see the formula in Figure 15.7 located in cell E17 and shown here. This will allow you to dynamically pull any text string from a URL.

```
=IF(ISERROR(FIND(C17,B17)),"",MID(B17,FIND(C17,B17),D17))
```

PROPER

PROPER capitalizes the first letter of each word in a text string or sentence.

```
=PROPER(text)
```

The PROPER function is another cleaning tool function. It places initial caps on each word within the text string specified in the formula, or text within a cell if you are using cell referencing. The result of =PROPER("PATRICK") would be Patrick. Notice that the example in Figure 15.8, used with cell referencing on lists, can quickly clean up the list.

- **TEXT**—The text is the text in the text string, word, or sentence to convert to proper. Meaning, the first character is capitalized in each word.

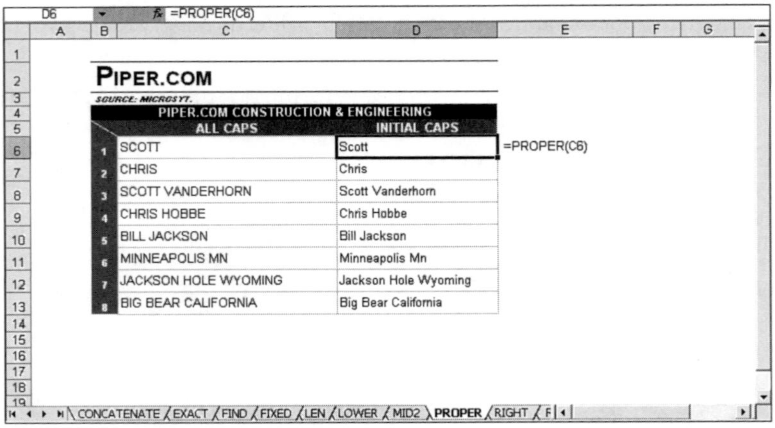

Figure 15.8
The PROPER function creates text with initial caps.

		D6	▼	fx =PROPER(C6)			

PIPER.COM

SOURCE: MICROSYT.

	PIPER.COM CONSTRUCTION & ENGINEERING	
	ALL CAPS	**INITIAL CAPS**
1	SCOTT	Scott	=PROPER(C6)
2	CHRIS	Chris
3	SCOTT VANDERHORN	Scott Vanderhorn
4	CHRIS HOBBE	Chris Hobbe
5	BILL JACKSON	Bill Jackson
6	MINNEAPOLIS MN	Minneapolis Mn
7	JACKSON HOLE WYOMING	Jackson Hole Wyoming
8	BIG BEAR CALIFORNIA	Big Bear California

CONCATENATE / EXACT / FIND / FIXED / LEN / LOWER / MID2 \ **PROPER** / RIGHT / F

RIGHT

RIGHT returns the last character or characters in a text string:

=RIGHT(text,num_chars)

The text can be in the form of text within the formula or as a cell reference. (Refer to the "LEFT" section earlier in this chapter.) The NUM_CHARS argument is the number of characters to return.

- **TEXT**—This is the text string, word, or sentence you want to extract characters from.

- **NUM_CHARS**—This indicates the number of characters you want to extract starting from the right moving left.

For example, =RIGHT("Patrick",4) would return rick, as shown in Figure 15.9. When including text within the formula, you need quotes. When you use cell referencing, you don't.

Finds the space

Figure 15.9
The RIGHT function in conjunction with the LEN and FIND functions can be used to extract the right-most words.

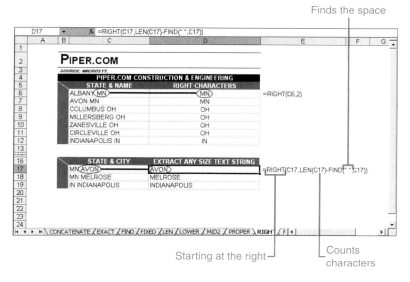

Starting at the right⏤

Counts characters

ADD st, nd, rd, AND th TO THE END OF NUMBERS

You can use the IF, OR, VALUE, RIGHT, and CHOOSE functions together to create automated ordinals, where an ordinal is an adjective used to describe the numerical position of an object. In Figure 15.10, B7 contains the number 1. If your list of numbers begin in cell B7, the formula would be

```
=B7&If(Or(Value(Right(B7,2))={11,12,13}),"th",If(Or(Value(Right(B7))
➥={1,2,3}),Choose(Right(B7),"st","nd","rd"),"th"))
```

This code adds the following results to the end of ordinary numbers:

1st

2nd

3rd

4th

15

Figure 15.10
You can add ordinals to the end of numbers automatically.

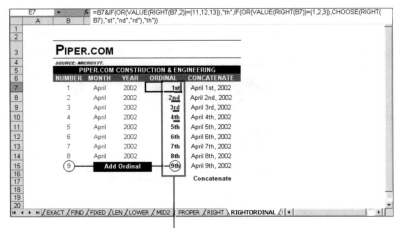

Adds ordinals to ordinary numbers

SUBSTITUTE

The SUBSTITUTE function replaces old text within a text string with new text.

=SUBSTITUTE(text,old_text,new_text,instance_num)

The text can be in the formula or used as a cell reference. The examples in Figure 15.11 show the SUBSTITUTE function in the first example using complete cell referencing from one cell to another. The second example gives a mix of cell referencing and text directly in the formula. For the formula =SUBSTITUTE("Melrose",C11,"Farming"), where C11 equals Melrose, the result is Farming.

- **TEXT**—This is the text in a cell you want to substitute.
- **OLD_TEXT**—This is the text you want to replace.
- **NEW_TEXT**—This is the new text to replace the old text with.
- **INSTANCE_NUM**—This is the number of instances you want to replace the old text with. For example, if you want to replace every occurrence of old text, use "][". If replacing just one occurrence, use 1.

Figure 15.11
The SUBSTITUTE function replaces one text string or cell for another.

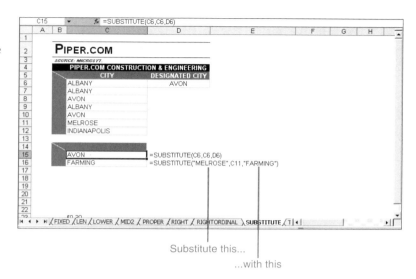

Substitute this...

...with this

TRIM

The TRIM function is another cleaning function that removes spacing between words:

```
=TRIM(text)
```

For example, if you inherit a list of information and there is random spacing between the text at different locations, you can trim away the spacing by referencing the cell. For example, in Figure 15.12 the left column shows a mixture of spacing. However, by applying the TRIM function to the right, you can eliminate the spacing. Use the Paste Special command to paste the cleaned text back into the original column as values. This function is specifically useful when data is imported from other applications, particularly mainframe and DOS applications, where spacing often is used as separators in lists and forms.

- **TEXT**—This is the text or cell reference containing the text from which you want to remove all the excess spaces.

Figure 15.12
The TRIM function can trim random spacing from cells.

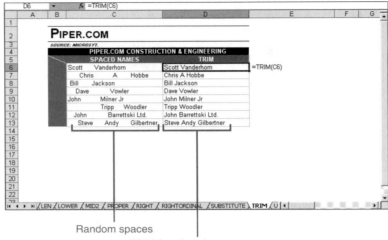

Random spaces

TRIM function cleans spaces

UPPER

Similar to the LOWER function, the UPPER function converts all text within a cell to uppercase:

=UPPER(text)

For example, =UPPER("upper") would result in UPPER. Cell referencing can also be used as shown in Figure 15.13.

- **TEXT**—This is the text or cell reference containing text that you want to change to uppercase.

Figure 15.13
The UPPER function converts all text to uppercase.

TROUBLESHOOTING

TEXT IN FORMULAS

When using functions such as LEFT *and* RIGHT, *I get the* #NAME? *error.*

If you're placing text in formulas, enclose the text in quotation marks, such as
=RIGHT("Bill",2). An easier way would be to place Bill in a cell such as A1, and then the
formula could be used with cell referencing such as =RIGHT(A1,2).

EXCEL IN PRACTICE

By knowing which text functions do what, you can simplify your life and become extremely
efficient when it comes to managing data. Notice in Figure 15.14 that the initial list has tons
of inconsistencies. By using the following functions, you can quickly clean up and modify
this list: Notice the functions used in cells C16:F16.

- **TRIM function**—Removes all the unnecessary spaces in a cell.
- **PROPER function**—Creates initial caps on all text.
- **CONCATENATE function**—Adjoins text from different cells.

Figure 15.14
Use text functions to
quickly manipulate
poorly organized lists
of information.

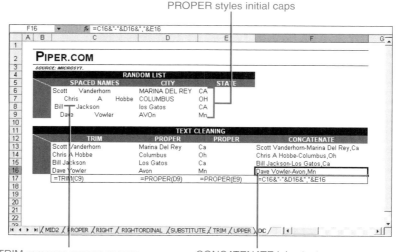

CHAPTER 16

STATISTICAL FUNCTIONS

In this chapter

Statistical Functions Overview   344

AVERAGE   349

BINOMDIST   350

CHIDIST   351

CONFIDENCE   352

CORREL   353

COUNT   354

COVAR   358

EXPONDIST   358

FDIST   359

FORECAST   360

FREQUENCY   361

GEOMEAN   362

GROWTH   363

INTERCEPT   364

LARGE   365

LINEST   366

LOGEST   368

MAX   368

MEDIAN   369

MIN   370

MINA   371

MODE   371

NORMDIST   371

NORMINV   372

PERCENTILE   373

PERCENTRANK   373

POISSON   374

RANK   375

SLOPE   376

SMALL   377

STDEV   378

STDEVA   378

TREND   379

VAR   380

VARA   380

STATISTICAL FUNCTIONS OVERVIEW

Statistical functions are among the most widely used functions in Excel. You can calculate the average of a group of numbers and determine probabilities, distributions, and trends. For example, the BETADIST function is used to measure variations in the percentage of a particular variable across samples. This chapter describes 38 of the 81 statistical functions in Excel and most are accompanied by an example to help illustrate the value of the function. The functions in bold in Table 16.1 are discussed in this chapter.

16

TABLE 16.1   STATISTICAL FUNCTIONS

Function	Syntax	Description
AVEDEV	=AVEDEV(*number1*,*number2*,...)	Returns the average of the absolute deviations of data points from their mean.
AVERAGE	=AVERAGE(*number1*,*number2*,...)	Returns the average of the arguments.
AVERAGEA	=AVERAGEA(*value1*,*value2*,...)	Calculates the average of the values in the list of arguments. Text and logical values are included in the calculation.
BETADIST	=BETADIST(*x*,*alpha*,*beta*,*A*,*B*)	Returns the cumulative beta probability density function.
BETAINV	=BETAINV(*probability*,*alpha*, *beta*,*A*,*B*)	Returns the inverse of the umulative cbeta probability density function.
BINOMDIST	=BINOMDIST(*number_s*, *trials*, *probability_s*,*cumulative*)	Returns the individual term binomial distribution probability.
CHIDIST	=CHIDIST(*x*,*degrees_freedom*)	Returns the one-tailed probability of the chi- squared distribution.
CHIINV	=CHINV(*probability*, *degrees_freedom*)	Returns the inverse of the one-tailed probability of the chi-squared distribution.
CHITEST	=CHITEST(*actual_range*, *expected_range*)	Returns the test for independence.
CONFIDENCE	=CONFIDENCE(*alpha*,*standard_dev*, *size*)	Returns the confidence interval for a population mean.
CORREL	=CORREL(*array1*,*array2*)	Returns the correlation coefficient of the array1 and array2 cell ranges.
COUNT	=COUNT(*value1*,*value2*,...)	Counts the number of cells that contain numbers within the list of range arguments.

Function	Syntax	Description
COUNTA	=COUNTA(*value1*,*value2*,...)	Counts the number of cells that are not empty within the list of range arguments.
COUNTBLANK	=COUNTBLANK(*range*)	Counts empty cells in a specified range of cells.
COUNTIF	=COUNTIF(*range*,*criteria*)	Counts the number of cells within a range that meet a given criteria.
COVAR	=COVAR(*array1*,*array2*)	Returns covariance, the average of the products of deviations for each data-point pair.
CRITBINOM	=CRITBINOM(*trials*,*probability_s*, *alpha*)	Returns the smallest value for which the cumulative binomial distribution is greater than or equal to a criterion value.
DEVSQ	=DEVSQ(*number1*,*number2*,...)	Returns the sum of squares of deviations of data points from their sample mean.
EXPONDIST	=EXPONDIST(*x*,*lambda*,*cumulative*)	Returns the exponential distribution.
FDIST	=FDIST(*x*,*degrees_freedom1*, *degrees_freedom2*)	Returns the F probability distribution.
FINV	=FINV(*probability*, *degrees_freedom1*, *degrees_freedom2*)	Returns the inverse of the F probability distribution.
FISHER	=FISHER(*x*)	Returns the Fisher transformation at X.
FISHERINV	=FISHERINV(*y*)	Returns the inverse of the Fisher transformation.
FORECAST	=FORECAST(*x*,*known_y's*, *known_x's*)	Calculates or predicts a future value by using existing values. Uses linear regression.
FREQUENCY	=FREQUENCY(*data_array*, *bins_array*)	Calculates how often values occur within a range of values, and then returns a vertical array of numbers.
FTEST	=FTEST(*array1*,*array2*)	Returns the result of an F-test.
GAMMADIST	=GAMMADIST(*x*,alpha,*beta*, *cumulative*)	Returns the gamma distribution.
GAMMAINV	=GAMMAINV(*probability*, *alpha*,*beta*)	Returns the inverse of the gamma cumulative distribution.

16

continues

TABLE 16.1   CONTINUED

Function	Syntax	Description
GAMMALN	=GAMMALN(*x*)	Returns the natural logarithm of the gamma function.
GEOMEAN	=GEOMEAN(*number1*, *number2*,...)	Returns the geometric mean of an array or range of positive data.
GROWTH	=GROWTH(*known_y's*,*known_x's*, *new_x's*,*const*)	Calculates predicted exponential growth by using existing data.
HARMEAN	=HARMEAN(*number1*, *number2*,...)	Returns the harmonic mean of a data set.
HYPGEOMDIST	=HYPGEOMDIST(*samples*, *number_sample*,*population_s*, *number_population*)	Returns the hypergeometric distribution.
INTERCEPT	=INTERCEPT(*known_y's*,*known_x's*)	Calculates the point at which a line will intersect the y-axis by using existing x-values and y-values.
KURT	=KURT(*number1*,*number2*,...)	Returns the Kurtosis of a data set.
LARGE	=LARGE(*array*,*k*)	Returns the *k*th largest value in a data set.
LINEST	=LINEST(*known_y's*,*known_x's*, *const*,*stats*)	Calculates the statisticsfor a line by using the "least squares" method to calculate a straight line that best fits your data, and returns an array that describes the line.
LOGEST	=LOGEST(*known_y's*,*known_x's*, *const*,*stats*)	Regression analysis. Calculates an exponential curve that fits your data and returns an array of values that describes the curve in regression analysis.
LOGINV	=LOGINV(*probability*,*mean*, *standard_dev*)	Returns the inverse of the lognormal cumulative distribution function of X, wherein (x) is normally distributed with parameters MEAN and STANDARD_DEV.
LOGNORMDIST	=LOGNORMDIST(*x*,*mean*, *standard_dev*)	Returns the cumulative LOGNORMAL distribution of X, wherein (x) is normally distributed with parameters MEAN and STANDARD_DEV.
MAX	=MAX(*number1*, *number2*,...)	Returns the largest value in a set of values.

Function	Syntax	Description
MAXA	=MAXA(*value1*,*value2*,...)	Returns the largest value in a list of arguments. Text and logical values are included in the calculation.
MEDIAN	=MEDIAN(*number1*, *number2*,...)	Returns the median, the number at the midpoint, of a given set of numbers.
MIN	=MIN(*number1*, *number2*,...)	Returns the smallest number in a set of values.
MINA	=MINA(*value1*,*value2*,...)	Returns the smallest value in a list of arguments. Text and logical values are included in the calculation.
MODE	=MODE(*number1*,*number2*,...)	Returns the most frequently occurring, or repetitive, value in an array or range of data.
NEGBINOMDIST	=NEGBINOMDIST(*number_f*, *number_s*,*probability_s*)	Returns the negative binomial distribution.
NORMDIST	=NORMDIST(*x*,*mean*,*standard_dev*, *cumulative*)	Returns the normal cumulative distribution for the specified mean and standard deviation.
NORMINV	=NORMINV(*probability*, *mean*,*standard_dev*)	Returns the inverse of the normal cumulative distribution for the specified mean and standard deviation.
NORMSDIST	=NORMSDIST(*z*)	Returns the standard normal umulative distribution function.
NORMSINV	=NORMSINV(*probability*)	Returns the inverse of the standard normal cumulative distribution.
PEARSON	=PEARSON(*array1*,*array2*)	Returns the Pearson product moment correlation coefficient, r, a dimensionless index that ranges from -1.0 to 1.0 inclusive and reflects the extent of a linear relationship between two data sets.
PERCENTILE	=PERCENTILE(*array*,*k*)	Returns the kth percentile of values in a range.
PERCENTRANK	=PERCENTRANK(*array*,*x*, *significance*)	Returns the rank of a value in a data set as a percentage of the data set.
PERMUT	=PERMUT(*number, number_chosen*)	Returns the number of permutations for a given number of objects that can be selected from a number of objects.

continues

16

TABLE 16.1   CONTINUED

Function	Syntax	Description
POISSON	=POISSON(*x*,*mean*,*cumulative*)	Returns the Poisson distribution and predicts events over time.
PROB	=PROB(*x_range*,*prob_range*, *lower_limit*,*upper_limit*)	Returns the probability that values in a range are between two specified limits.
QUARTILE	=QUARTILE(*array*,*quart*)	Returns the quartile of a data set.
RANK	=RANK(*number*,*ref*,*order*)	Returns the rank of a number in a list of numbers.
RSQ	=RSQ(*known_y's*,*known_x's*)	Returns the square of the Pearson roduct moment correlation coefficient through data points in known_y's and known_x's.
SKEW	=SKEW(*number1*,*number2*,...)	Returns the degree of asymmetry of a distribution around its mean.
SLOPE	=SLOPE(*known_y's*,*known_x's*)	Returns the slope or rate of change of the regression line through data points in known_y's and known_x's.
SMALL	=SMALL(*array*,*k*)	Returns the kth smallest value in a data set.
STANDARDIZE	=STANDARDIZE(*x*,*mean*, *standard_dev*) STANDARD_DEV.	Returns a normalized value from a distribution characterized by MEAN and
STDEV	=STDEV(*number1*,*number2*,...)	Estimates standard deviation based on a sample. Nonnumeric values are ignored.
STDEVA	=STDEVA(*value1*,*value2*,...)	Estimates standard deviation based on a sample. STDEVA acts upon values. Text and logical values are included in the calculation.
STDEVP	=STDEVP(*number1*,*number2*,...)	Calculates standard deviation based on the entire population given as arguments.
STDEVPA	=STDEVPA(*value1*,*value2*,...)	Calculates standard deviation based on the entire population given as arguments. Text and logical values are included in the calculation.
STEYX	=STEYX(*known_y's*,*known_x's*)	Returns the standard error of the predicted y-value for each x in the regression.

Function	Syntax	Description
TDIST	TDIST(*x*,*degrees_freedom*, *tails*)	Returns the probability for a student's t-distribution.
TINV	=TINV(*probability*, *degrees_freedom*)	Returns the inverse of the student's t-distribution for the specified degrees of freedom.
TREND	=TREND(*known_y's*,*known_x's*, *new_x's*,*const*)	Returns values along a linear trend using the method of least squares.
TRIMMEAN	=TRIMMEAN(*array*,*percent*)	Returns the mean of the interior of a data set.
TTEST	=TTEST(*array1*,*array2*, *tails*,*type*)	Returns the probability associated with the student's t-test.
VAR	=VAR(*number1*,*number2*,...)	Estimates the variance of a sample population.
VARA	=VARA(*value1*,*value2*,...)	Estimates the variance of a sample population. Text and logical values are included in the calculation.
VARP	=VARP(*number1*,*number2*,...)	Calculates variance based on the entire population.
VARPA	=VARPA(*value1*,*value2*,...)	Calculates variance based on the entire population. In addition to numbers, text and logical values, such as TRUE and FALSE, are included in the calculation.
WEIBULL	=WEIBULL(*x*,*alpha*,*beta*, *cumulative*)	Returns the Weibull distribution.
ZTEST	=ZTEST(*array*,*x*,*sigma*)	Returns the two-tailed P-value of a z-test.

AVERAGE

AVERAGE returns the average (also known as *arithmetic mean*) of its arguments:

=AVERAGE(number1,number2,...)

AVERAGE is one of the most widely used functions in Excel. It is calculated by taking the sum of the values in a data set and dividing by the number of values in the data set. See Figure 16.1 for examples of the AVERAGE function.

■ **number** *n*—You can specify up to 30 arguments for the AVERAGE function. The arguments can be cell references, arrays, or range names. Blank cells or cells containing text or logical values are ignored. Cells that contain a zero (0) are included in the Average calculation.

16

Figure 16.1
The AVERAGE function calculates the average of the values in a range.

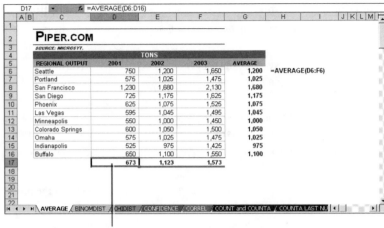

Average of cell values from D6 to D16

BINOMDIST

BINOMDIST returns the individual term binomial distribution probability.

=BINOMDIST(number_s,trials,probability_s,cumulative)

The BINOMDIST function is used to find the probability that an outcome will occur x times in n performances of an experiment or trial. The trials are known as *Bernoulli trials*. The BINOMDIST function is used when

- The number of trials (or tests) is fixed.
- Each repetition of the trial results in one of two possible outcomes—success or failure.
- The trials are independent and performed under identical conditions.
- Probability of success (denoted by p) is constant throughout the experiment.

The arguments passed to BINOMDIST are

- **number_s**—Represents the number of successes in trials in the form of an integer; must be a positive number but smaller than the number of trials.
- **trials**—The number of trials in the form of an integer.
- **probability_s**—The probability of success on each trial; must be a positive number less than 1.
- **cumulative**—A logical value that determines the form of the function. If TRUE, then BINDOMIST returns the cumulative distribution function (the probability that there are no more than number_s successes). If FALSE, then BINOMDIST returns the probability mass function (the probability that there are exactly the number_s successes).

As shown in Figure 16.2, the cumulative binomial distribution when the `cumulative` argument is TRUE is 99.9%, which means it's almost a certainty that no more than nine trials will be successful. The cumulative arguments appear in cells F5:F6.

Cumulative arguments

Figure 16.2
The BINOMDIST
function returns the
individual term bino-
mial distribution
probability.

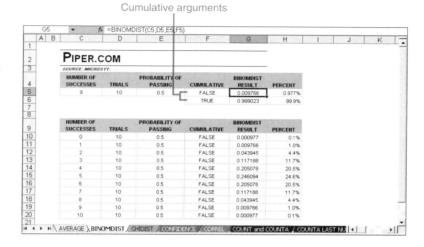

Figure 16.2
The BINOMDIST
function returns the
individual term bino-
mial distribution
probability.

CHIDIST

CHIDIST returns the one-tailed probability of the chi-squared (X^2) distribution; the area in the right tail under the chi-squared distribution curve.

=CHIDIST(x,degrees_freedom)

The CHIDIST function is used in conjunction with the CHITEST function to perform hypothesis tests, including experiments with more than two categories (goodness-of-fit tests or *multinomial experiments*); contingency tables (independence and homogeneity tests); and variance and standard deviation of a single population.

For example, an experiment might hypothesize that farmers who do not till the soil before planting a crop will yield a larger harvest. By comparing the observed results with the expected ones, you can decide whether the hypothesis is valid.

- **x**—The value at which you want to evaluate the distribution.
- **degrees freedom**—The degrees of freedom are typically the number of observations that can be chosen freely and is usually denoted by *df*.

Small degrees of freedom skew the distribution curve to the right. Large degrees of freedom skew the distribution curve to the left, making it more symmetrical like a normal distribution. Figure 16.3 shows the results of several CHIDIST calculations using different values of X and degrees of freedom.

Figure 16.3
If the CHITEST result is more than the CHIDIST result, the hypothesis is typically rejected.

16

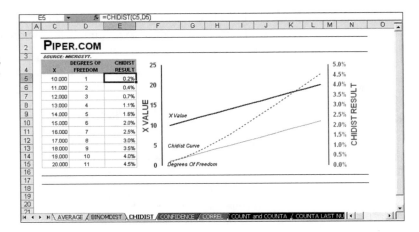

	E5	▼	*fx* =CHIDIST(C5,D5)			

X	DEGREES OF FREEDOM	CHIDIST RESULT
10.000	1	0.2%
11.000	2	0.4%
12.000	3	0.7%
13.000	4	1.1%
14.000	5	1.6%
15.000	6	2.0%
16.000	7	2.5%
17.000	8	3.0%
18.000	9	3.5%
19.000	10	4.0%
20.000	11	4.5%

PIPER.COM
SOURCE: MICROSYT.

CONFIDENCE

CONFIDENCE returns the confidence interval for a population mean:

=CONFIDENCE(alpha,standard_dev,size)

The confidence interval is a range on each side of a sample mean, indicating the lowest (or earliest) and highest (or latest) values. Figure 16.4 shows the prices for efficiency apartments in various cities. After you calculate CONFIDENCE, you subtract the result from the mean to get the low interval and add the result to the mean to get the high interval. As noted in Figure 16.4, the low for the rent is $574, the high is $782, and the mean is $678.

- **alpha**—The significance level used to determine the confidence level. The confidence level equals 1-alpha (shown as a percentage). If alpha (the significance level) is .1, then the confidence level is 90%. Typical confidence levels are 90%, 95%, and 99%.

- **standard_dev**—The standard deviation for the data set.

- **size**—The sample size.

Figure 16.4
Although not part of the CONFIDENCE function, you must calculate the mean using the AVERAGE function.

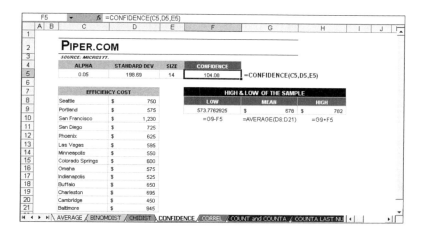

CORREL

CORREL returns the correlation coefficient between two data sets:

=CORREL(array1,array2)

Essentially, the CORREL function compares relationships between two data sets. For example, in Figure 16.5, the correlation between the monthly average temperature and the monthly average water usage (in gallons) is 0.954163749.

The value of the correlation coefficient always lies between –1 and +1. A correlation coefficient close to +1 indicates a positive correlation, as one variable increases, the other variable increases. A correlation coefficient close to –1 indicates a negative correlation, as one variable increases, the other variable decreases. A correlation coefficient close to zero (0) indicates there is little or no correlation between the variables.

- **array1**—The first set of values; can be a cell range, range name, or array.
- **array2**—The second set of values; can be a cell range, range name, or array.

NOTE

> The number of data points in each array must be the same. If array1 has 12 data points, array2 must also have 12 data points.

The equation for the correlation coefficient is

$$\rho_{x,y} = \frac{Cov(X,Y)}{\sigma_x \cdot \sigma_y}$$

where

$$-1 \le \rho_{xy} \le 1$$

and

$$Cov(X,Y) = \frac{1}{n}\sum_{i-1}^{n}(x_i - \mu_x)(y_i - \mu_y)$$

Figure 16.5
Cells that contain text, logical values, or are empty, are ignored. Cells containing zero (0) are included in the CORREL calculation.

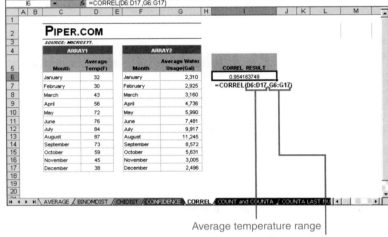

Average temperature range
Average water use range

COUNT

COUNT counts the number of cells that contain *numbers* within the list of arguments:

`=COUNT(value1,value2,...)`

The COUNT function is used only to count the number of numerical entries in a range. Figure 16.6 shows a comparison between the COUNT and the COUNTA functions. Where COUNT calculates the number of cells with a numerical value, COUNTA simply counts the number of cells that contain any value (that is, cells that are not blank).

- **value n**—You can specify up to 30 arguments for the COUNT function. The arguments can be cell references, arrays, or range names. Blank cells or cells containing text are ignored. Cells that contain a zero (0) or dates are included in the COUNT calculation.

COUNTA

COUNTA counts the number of cells that are not empty:

`=COUNTA(value1,value2,...)`

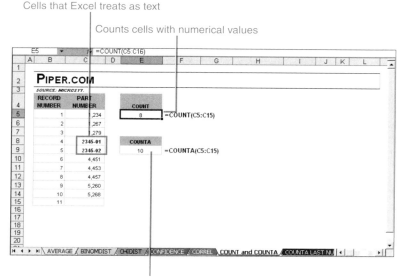

Cells that Excel treats as text

Counts cells with numerical values

Figure 16.6
Numbers with symbols are treated as text by Excel and are therefore not included in the COUNT function calculation.

Counts all non-empty cells

Use the COUNTA function to count the number of cells in a range that contain text, numbers, or a combination of text and numbers. Although you can use COUNTA to generate the number of clients or employees in a list, it counts each entry, not unique entries.

TIP FROM

> To count unique entries, combine the SUM and the COUNTIF functions. For example, if the range to be counted is C6:C46, the formula would be
> ```
> =SUM(1/COUNTIF(C6:C46,C6:C46))
> ```
> You must array enter the formula (using Ctrl+Shift+Enter) for this formula to count properly.

Refer to Figure 16.6 for a comparison between the COUNT and the COUNTA functions.

■ **value n**—You can specify up to 30 arguments for the COUNTA function. The arguments can be cell references, arrays, or range names. Blank cells are ignored. All other cells are counted.

RETURNING THE LAST RECORD ENTERED

If you maintain a list of information, you can return the last record entered two ways. The first is with PivotTables using extended ranges; the second is by using the OFFSET function with the COUNTA function. In Figure 16.7, the formula is

```
=Offset(C4,Counta(C:C)-1,0)
```

16

Where `Offset(C4` is the first cell in the range, `Counta(C:C)` includes the entire column, and `-1` subtracts the last blank cell. Also, this function relies on there being no data in column C beyond the list entries and one heading cell.

Although a bit more complex, you can retrieve the last entry in a column regardless of any blanks using the following array formula:

`{=INDIRECT(ADDRESS(MAX((C5:C65536<>"")*ROW(C5:C65536)),COLUMN(C5:C65536),4))}`

Note that you can't use the entire column (C:C) for the range. Also, whenever possible, try to limit the upper bound (65536). For example, if you know your list will never exceed 10,000 rows, use C5:C10000. This will increase the formula's calculation speed significantly.

The result will always match the farthest entry down the list as long as there are no blanks in the list.

Figure 16.7
Use the OFFSET and the COUNTA functions to dynamically display the last entry in a list.

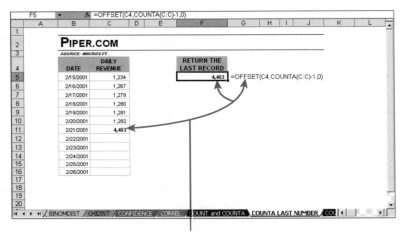

Always counts the last record

COUNTBLANK

COUNTBLANK counts the blank cells in a range (it functions the opposite of COUNTA):

`=COUNTBLANK(range)`

In the COUNTBLANK function shown in Figure 16.8, any cells that are blank or formulas that return "" (empty text) as the formula results are counted.

■ **range**—The range to be counted.

COUNTIF

COUNTIF counts the number of cells in a range that meet a given criterion:

`=COUNTIF(range,criteria)`

Blank cells

Figure 16.8
Use the COUNT-BLANK function to identify or count the blank cells within a list or range.

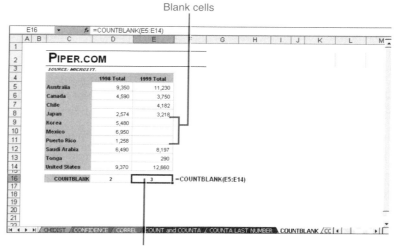

Number of blank cells counted

Use COUNTIF when you only want to count part of a range, as shown in Figure 16.9. The first example in this figure counts the number of times the name Patrick occurs in the name range, the second counts all quantities above 0, and the third counts all quantities greater than 10.

- **range**—The range to be counted.
- **criteria**—The criteria you want to evaluate; can be a number (14), a cell reference (G5), an expression (E5>10), or text ("Victorian Décor").

Number of occurences of "Patrick" in the specified range

Figure 16.9
use the COUNTIF function to count cells with conditions such as greater than zero or equal to Patrick.

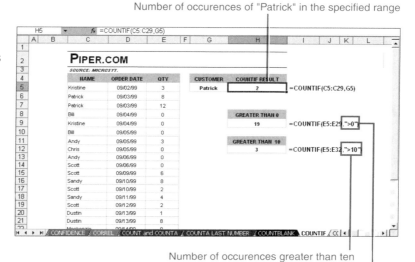

Number of occurences greater than ten

Number of occurences greater than zero

COVAR

COVAR returns covariance, the average of the products of deviations for each data point pair.

`=COVAR(array1,array2)`

The COVAR function is used to determine whether a relationship exists between two data sets. Note that the data sets must contain an identical number of items. The data values must also be integers. Figure 16.10 shows an example of the COVAR function.

- **array1**—The first set of values; can be a cell range, range name, or array.
- **array2**—The second set of values; can be a cell range, range name, or array.

The equation for the covariance is

$$Cov(X,Y) = \frac{1}{n}\sum_{i-1}^{n}(x_i - \mu_x)(y_i - \mu_y)$$

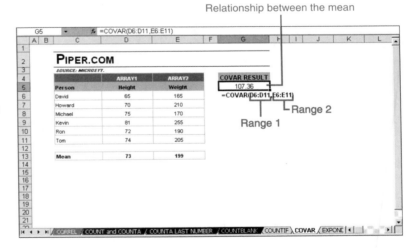

Figure 16.10
If the data set contains text, logical values, or blank cells, those cells are ignored. Cells that contain a zero (0) are included in the COVAR calculation.

EXPONDIST

EXPONDIST returns the exponential distribution.

`=EXPONDIST(x,lambda,cumulative)`

The exponential probability distribution deals with the lapse of time between two successive occurrences or events, when the average number of occurrences per unit of time is known. Note that both x and λ must be numeric, or a #VALUE! error will occur. Figure 16.11 shows an example of this function.

- **x**—The value of the function.

- **lambda ([λ])**—The parameter value.

- **cumulative**—A logical value that indicates which form of the exponential function to provide. If TRUE, then EXPONDIST returns the CUMULATIVE DISTRIBUTION function. If FALSE, then EXPONDIST returns the probability density function.

The formula for the probability density function is

$$f(x;\lambda) = \lambda e^{-\lambda x}$$

The formula for the cumulative distribution function is

$$F(x;\lambda) = 1 - e^{-\lambda x}$$

Figure 16.11
The cumulative argument dictates which formula is used to calculate EXPONDIST.

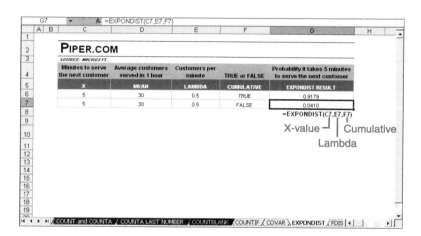

FDIST

FDIST returns the F probability distribution.

=FDIST(x,degrees_freedom1,degrees_freedom2)

The FDIST function is used for analysis of variance, which is to determine whether two data sets have different degrees of diversity (for example, male and female). This function returns the one-tailed probability of the FDIST distribution. Figure 16.12 shows an example in which the FDIST is approximately .025, the area in the right tail under the FDIST distribution curve. This is the *significance level*. The significance level represents the probability of rejecting the statement you assume is true (the null hypothesis). In this case, that probability is 2.5%.

- **x**—The value at which to evaluate the function; must be a positive number.
- **degrees freedom1**—The numerator of freedom.
- **degrees freedom2**—The denominator of freedom.

16

Figure 16.12
FDIST returns the probability of rejecting the statement you assume is true.

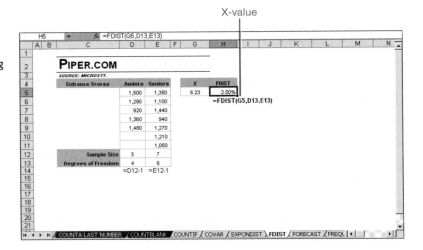

FORECAST

FORECAST calculates or predicts a future value by using existing values.

=FORECAST(x,known_y's,known_x's)

Use the FORECAST function when you want to predict a value based on the trend of the existing or known data. Figure 16.13 shows a forecast for the next year, based on sales from the past three years. Notice the formula in Figure 16.13 where cell H5 is the next year and E6:G6 are the values and the E5:G5 are the years.

- **x**—The data point of the value you want to predict.
- **known_y's**—The known values for the known data points; the dependent variable.
- **known_x's**—The known data points—typically increments of time (years, quarters, months); the independent variable.

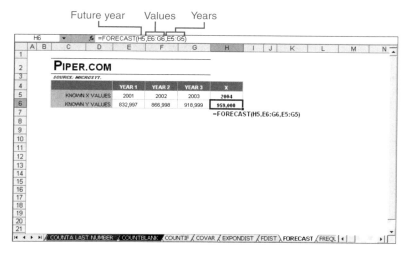

Figure 16.13
FORECAST can
only predict one
future value. See the
TREND function
later in this chapter to
predict more than
one value.

FREQUENCY

FREQUENCY calculates how often values occur within a range of values, and then returns a vertical array of numbers.

`=FREQUENCY(data_array,bins_array)`

Figure 16.14 shows the FREQUENCY function used to count how the number of test scores fall within ranges of scores. Because this function returns an array, the following must be true:

- The result range must be selected *before* you begin the function.
- The function must be an array entered by using Ctrl+Shift+Enter, instead of just pressing Enter.

The data_array is the list of student scores. The bins_array is the list of max scores (G5:G9). Because this function always returns one more element than the number of elements in the bins_array, the range selected for the frequencies is H5:H10.

- **data_array**—The array of values for which you want to count frequencies (the test scores in Figure 16.14).
- **bins_array**—The array of intervals into which you want to group the values in the data_array.

16

Array of score intervals ┐ ┌ Array of test scores

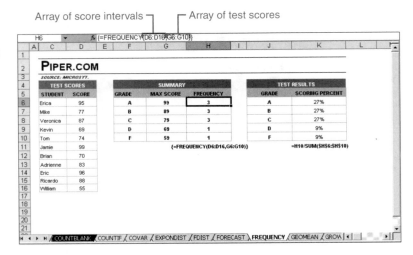

Figure 16.14
The data array is from D6:D16, and the bins array is in cells G6:G10.

GEOMEAN

GEOMEAN returns the geometric mean of an array or range of positive data.

=GEOMEAN(number1,number2,...)

Use the GEOMEAN when you want to calculate the average growth rate of compound interest, assuming variable interest rates. Figure 16.15 demonstrates the GEOMEAN function and its different result compared to the AVERAGE function.

■ **number n**—Up to 30 arguments can be specified, including cell references or an array.

The equation for the geometric mean is

$$GM_{\overline{y}} = \sqrt[n]{y_1 y_2 y_3 \cdots y_n}$$

Figure 16.15
GEOMEAN calculates average growth rate assuming compound interest with variable rates are known.

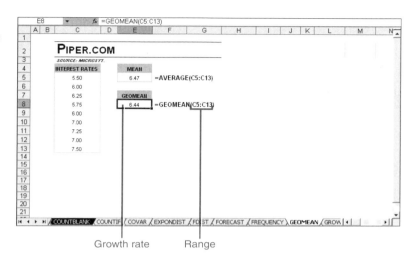

Growth rate   Range

GROWTH

GROWTH calculates predicted exponential growth by using existing data:

=GROWTH(known_y's,known_x's,new_x's,const)

Using an existing data set of values and increments, and supplying a new set of increments, the GROWTH function generates the predicted set of corresponding values (the new y values). In Figure 16.16, the exponential growth values (the predicted y-values) have been calculated. The known_y and known_x values are based on the formula $y=b*m^x$. A set of new y-values is predicted for the entire time increment, not just for the additional time increments you specify. Because these new y-values are based on the growth equation (and not on the known y values), the first three y-values predicted do not match the known y values for the same increment.

- **known_y's**—The known values for the known data points; the dependent variable. Each value must be a positive number.
- **known_x's**—The known data points—typically increments of time (years, quarters, months); the independent variable. An optional argument. If omitted, assumed to be the array {1,2,3…}, the same size as the known_y's.
- **new_x's**—The data points of those values you want to predict. An optional argument. If omitted, assumed to be the same as the known_x's.
- **const**—TRUE or FALSE indicating whether the slope (*b*) is = 1 (FALSE) or not (TRUE).

Because this function returns an array:

- The result range must be selected *before* you begin the function.
- The formula must be array entered by using Ctrl+Shift+Enter, instead of just Enter.

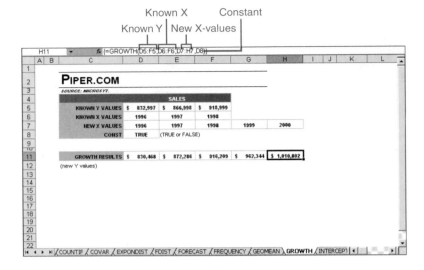

Figure 16.16
GROWTH calculates predicted growth over time.

16

INTERCEPT

INTERCEPT calculates the point at which a line will intersect the y-axis by using existing x-values and y-values:

```
=INTERCEPT(known_y's,known_x's)
```

The INTERCEPT function tells you the value of y when x is zero. Figure 16.17 shows an example.

- **known_y's**—The known values for the known data points; the dependent variable.
- **known_x's**—The known data points. If increments of time (years, quarters, months), convert or substitute consecutive integers. The independent variable.

$$a = \overline{Y} - b\overline{X}$$

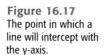

Figure 16.17
The point in which a line will intercept with the y-axis.

Intercept value of line and y-axis

x-values

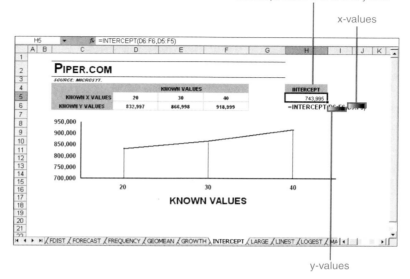

y-values

LARGE

LARGE returns the *k*th largest value in a data set:

=LARGE(array,k)

The LARGE function is used to retrieve a value based on its standing or rank in the data set. Figure 16.18 shows an example of the LARGE function returning the third largest number from the list.

- **array**—The range of data from which you want to return the *k*th largest value.
- **k**—The position (from the largest) of the data point you want to return.

Figure 16.18
LARGE returns a value from a data set based on a rank number you specify. To return the *k*th smallest value, use the SMALL function.

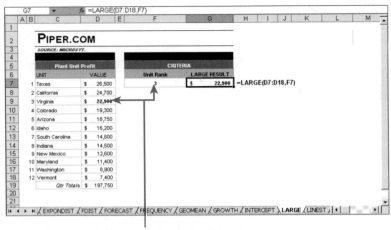

Returns third largest value in the data set

LINEST

LINEST calculates a straight line that best fits your data, using the "least squares" method (see Figure 16.19).

=LINEST(known_y's,known_x's,const,stats)

The LINEST function uses the equation

$y = mx + b$

If there are multiple ranges of x-values, the equation is

$y = m1x1 + m2x2 + ... + b$

Because the result is an array, the formula must be array entered by using Ctrl+Shift+Enter, instead of just pressing Enter.

- **known_y's**—The known values for the known data points; the dependent variable.
- **known_x's**—The known data points. The independent variable. An optional argument. If omitted, assumed to be the array {1,2,3...}, the same size as the known_y's.
- **const**—TRUE or FALSE indicating whether the y-intercept (b) is = 0 (FALSE) or not (TRUE).
- **stats**—If stats is TRUE, LINEST returns the additional regression statistics, so the returned array is {mn,mn-1,…,m1,b; sen,sen-1,…,se1,seb; r2,sey; F,df; ssreg,ssresid}. If stats is FALSE or omitted, LINEST returns only the m-coefficient and the constant b (see Table 16.2).

NOTE

> Before you start the function, if stats will be FALSE, select a range of cells one cell high and two cells wide (as in this example). If stats will be TRUE, select a range of cells five cells high and two cells wide.

Figure 16.19
LINEST results in both the slope (M) of the straight line and y-intercept (b) that fits the data.

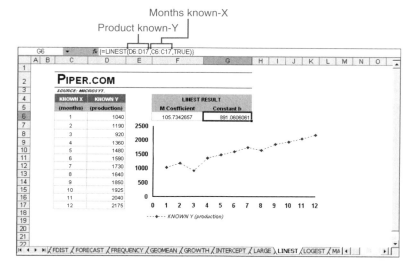

Months known-X
Product known-Y

TABLE 16.2   REGRESSION STATISTICS RETURNED WHEN THE stats ARGUMENT IS TRUE

Statistic	Description
$se_1, se_2, \ldots, se_n$	The standard error values for the coefficients $m_1, m_2, \ldots, m_n$.
se_b	The standard error value for the constant b (se_b = #N/A when const is FALSE).
r^2	The coefficient of determination. Compares estimated and actual y-values, and ranges in value from 0 to 1. The closer r^2 is to 1, the more correlation there is between the estimated y-value and the actual y-value. If r^2 is 0, the regression equation is not helpful in predicting a y-value.
se_y	The standard error for the y estimate.
F	The F statistic, or the F-observed value. Use the F statistic to determine whether the observed relationship between the dependent (y) and independent (x) variables occurs by chance.
df	The degrees of freedom. Use the degrees of freedom to help you find F-critical values in a statistical table. Compare the values you find in the table to the F statistic returned by LINEST to determine a confidence level for the model.
ss_{reg}	The regression sum of squares.
ss_{resid}	The residual sum of squares.

16

LOGEST

LOGEST, which is used in regression analysis, calculates an exponential curve that fits your data and returns an array of values that describes the curve:

```
=LOGEST(known_y's,known_x's,const,stats)
```

The LOGEST function is used in regression analysis. The equation for the curve is $y=b*m^x$. Because the result is an array, the formula must be array entered by using Ctrl+Shift+Enter, instead of just Enter. Figure 16.20 shows an example of LOGEST.

- **known_y's**—The known values for the known data points; the dependent variable.
- **known_x's**—The known data points. If omitted assumed to be the array {1,2,3...} the same size as the known_y's.
- **const**—TRUE or FALSE indicating whether to force b to be = 1 (FALSE) or not (TRUE). When TRUE or omitted, b is calculated normally.
- **stats**—If stats is TRUE, LOGEST returns the additional regression statistics. If stats is FALSE or omitted, LOGEST returns only the M coefficient and the Constant b.

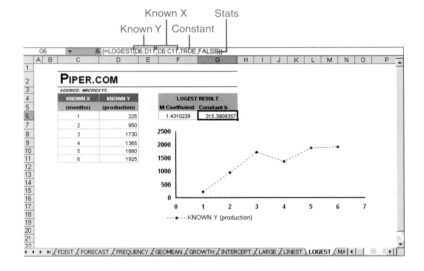

Figure 16.20
The LOGEST function returns values that describe the existing curve. Use the GROWTH function to predict future values on the curve.

MAX

MAX returns the largest value in a set of values:

```
=MAX(number1,number2,...)
```

Use the MAX function to display the largest value in a range. In Figure 16.21, the MAX function looks up the largest value in the range D7:D17. The MAX function is also used in conjunction with the IF, YEAR, and MONTH functions to look up the largest value in a specified year and month. Be sure to activate the array by pressing Ctrl+Shift+Enter for the array formula to work.

You could also achieve the same result by eliminating the IF function with the following array:

`{=MAX((YEAR(C7:C17)=E7)*(MONTH(C7:C17)=F7)*D7:D17)}`

- **number _n_**—The cell reference(s), range name, or array that makes up the data set. Up to 30 unique arguments (data sets) can be specified.

Looks up the largest value in a year and month

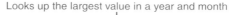

Figure 16.21
Use the MAX function to return the largest value in a range. Although the MAX function evaluates cells containing numerical data, you can use _MAXA_ when you need to evaluate data containing text or logical values.

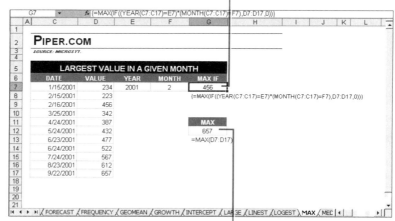

Maximum value in a range

MEDIAN

MEDIAN returns the median of the given numbers.

`=MEDIAN(number1,number2,...)`

The median is the number in the middle of a set of numbers, as opposed to the mean, which is the average of the set of numbers. When the data set contains an odd number of values, the value in the middle is returned (as shown in Figure 16.22). When the data set contains an even number of values, the middle two values are averaged to determine the median.

- **number _n_**—The cell reference(s), range name, or array that makes up the data set. Up to 30 arguments (unique data sets) can be specified.

16

The middle number is a set of numbers

Figure 16.22
The MEDIAN function does not average the entire set of numbers, but returns the middle number in the set or the average of the two middle numbers (if the data set contains an even number of values).

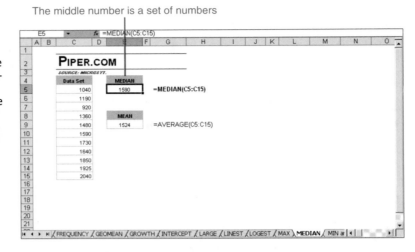

MIN

MIN returns the smallest number in a set of values:

=MIN(number1,number2,...)

Use the MIN function to display the smallest sales figure, loss due to shrink, employee absentee rate, and so on, in a group of values. In Figure 16.23, the MIN function returns the lowest value within a range.

■ **number n**—The cell reference(s), range name, or array that makes up the data set. Up to 30 arguments (unique data sets) can be specified.

The minimum absentee rate in a range

Figure 16.23
Although the MIN function evaluates cells containing numerical data, use MINA when you need to evaluate data containing text or logical values.

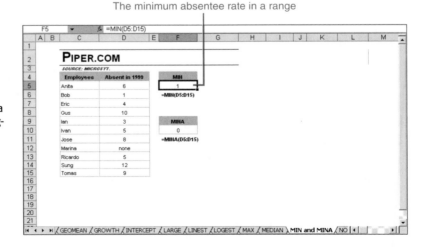

MINA

MINA returns the smallest value in a list of arguments:

`=MINA(value1,value2,...)`

The MINA function differs from the MIN function in that it will also evaluate logical values such as TRUE, FALSE, and text. TRUE evaluates to one (1); FALSE evaluates to zero (0). Arguments that contain text also evaluate to zero. Refer to Figure 16.23 for a comparison of MIN and MINA.

- **value n**—The cell reference(s), range name, text representations of numbers, array, or logical values that makes up the data set. Up to 30 arguments (unique data sets) can be specified. Text values in an array argument are ignored.

16

MODE

MODE returns the value that appears the most times within the list or range:

`=Mode(Number1,Number2,…)`

Use the MODE function to find out the most recurring information in a list. For example, if you have a list and want to find out what number appears the most often within the list simply use the following formula. Where the range is C5:C15 and the number that occurs the most times is 8.

`=MODE(C5:C15)`

- If the data contains no duplicating numbers or data points it will result in the #N/A error value.
- If the data contains text, logical values, or empty cells, those data points are ignored. Cells containing an actual value of zero are included.

A common next step might be to ask how many times that number actually appears within the list. You can find this out by combining the COUNTIF function with the MODE function. Use the following formula to count the occurrence of that number within the list:

`=COUNTIF(C5:C15,MODE(C5:C15))`

NORMDIST

NORMDIST returns the normal cumulative distribution for the specified mean and standard deviation:

`=NORMDIST(x,mean,standard_dev,cumulative)`

The NORMDIST function is frequently used in statistics and hypothesis testing. There is also the *standard* normal distribution function (NORMSDIST).

- **x**—The value for which you want the distribution.
- **mean**—The arithmetic mean of the distribution.
- **standard_dev**—The standard deviation of the distribution.
- **cumulative**—A logical value that determines the form of the function. If TRUE, the cumulative distribution is returned. If FALSE, the probability mass function is returned.

NORMINV

NORMINV returns the inverse of the normal cumulative distribution for the specified mean and standard deviation:

`=NORMINV(probability,mean,standard_dev)`

The NORMDIST function returns a probability, the NORMINV function returns *x*, the value that corresponds to the given probability, mean, and standard deviation. NORMINV uses an iterative technique for calculating the function. The default maximum number of iterations is 100. If a result is not reached within those iterations, the #N/A value is returned. You can change the number of iterations under Tools, Options, Calculation tab.

Figure 16.24 shows an example of the NORMINV function.

- **probability**—The probability corresponding to the normal distribution.
- **mean**—The arithmetic mean of the distribution.
- **standard_dev**—The standard deviation of the distribution.

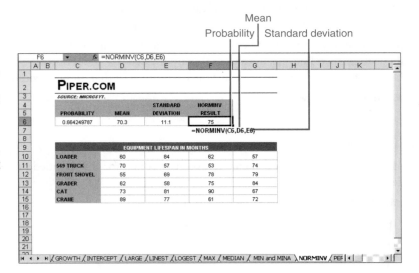

Figure 16.24
The NORMINV function returns the inverse of the normal cumulative distribution. You can see the inverse of the standard normal distribution function by using the NORMSINV function.

PERCENTILE

PERCENTILE returns the *k*th percentile of values in a range:

`=PERCENTILE(array,k)`

The PERCENTILE function is used to determine a threshold of acceptance. In Figure 16.25, for example, the price-earning ratios of 12 companies is given. To find the value of the seventieth percentile (the k value), the result is 28.3. In this example, 70% of the companies have a price to earnings ratio of less than 28.3 and those remaining 30% are greater than 28.3

- **array**—The data set that defines relative standing.
- **k**—The percentile value between 0 and 1.

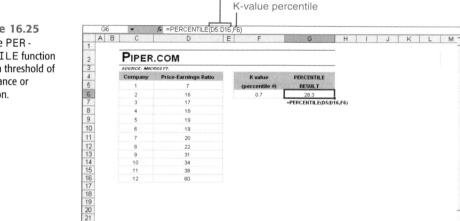

Figure 16.25
Use the PER-CENTILE function to set a threshold of acceptance or rejection.

PERCENTRANK

PERCENTRANK returns the rank of a value in a data set as a percentage of the data set:

`=PERCENTRANK(array,x,significance)`

This function returns the percentage of values in the data set that are smaller than *x*—the relative standing of an observation in a data set. In Figure 16.26, about 73% of the companies have a price-earnings ratio of less than 31. The remaining 27% of the companies have a price-earnings ratio of greater than 31.

- **array**—The data set with numeric values that defines relative standing.
- **x**—The value for which you want to know the rank.
- **significance**—An optional value that identifies the number of significant digits for the percentage value that is returned. If omitted, three (3) digits are returned.

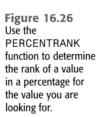

Figure 16.26
Use the PERCENTRANK function to determine the rank of a value in a percentage for the value you are looking for.

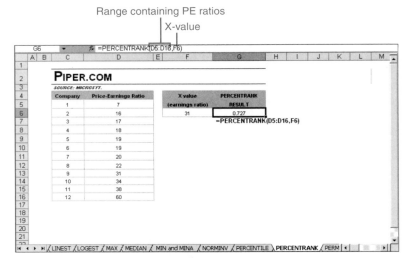

POISSON

POISSON returns the Poisson distribution. Basically, it predicts the number of events that occur over time.

```
=POISSON(x,mean,cumulative)
```

The Poisson probability distribution is applied to experiments or estimations with random and independent occurrences. The occurrences are always considered within an interval (time, space, or volume). Using a known average number of occurrences for the interval, the POISSON function computes the probability of a certain number of occurrences at the x interval. Figure 16.27 shows the Poisson probability distribution for the number of people arriving at a bank branch within a one-hour time period. Therefore, there is an 80% chance that 17 people (X) will come into the bank in an hour, when the average is 14 per hour.

- **x**—The number of occurrences within the interval.
- **mean**—The average and, therefore, expected number of occurrences.
- **cumulative**—A TRUE/FALSE value that determines the form in which the Poisson probability distribution will be returned. If TRUE, the cumulative probability is returned (the probability that the number of occurrences will be *between* zero and *x*). If FALSE, the probability mass function is returned (the probability that exactly *x* events will occur).

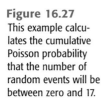

Figure 16.27
This example calculates the cumulative Poisson probability that the number of random events will be between zero and 17.

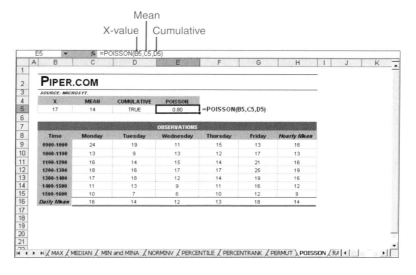

RANK

RANK returns the rank of a number in a list of numbers:

```
=RANK(number,ref,order)
```

In Figure 16.28, the RANK function is used to provide the relative position of the number you specify in relation to the other numbers in the data set. Be sure the data set is sorted in either ascending or descending order. Make the order number zero for descending and any other value for ascending.

- **number**—The number of the rank you want to determine.
- **ref**—The data set of values being assessed.
- **order**—An indicator of how the numbers should be ranked. If zero (0) or omitted, the list is ranked as if it were in descending order. If any nonzero value, the list is ranked as if it were in ascending order.

Although duplicate numbers are treated as having the same rank, the numbering is affected when duplicates are present. In Figure 16.28, there are several duplicates; number 84 appears twice. 84 is ranked third, and 81 is ranked fifth; no number is ranked fourth. The result of the number 78 is the 7th ranked result in the descending data list.

Figure 16.28
Be sure the data set is sorted by the values, either ascending or descending. RANK calls out the rank of a given number in a data set.

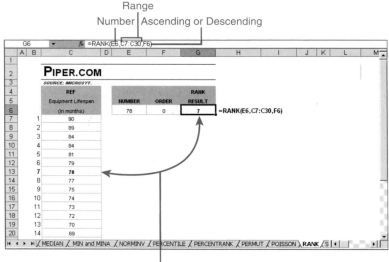

The number 78 has a rank of 7 in the specified range

SLOPE

SLOPE returns the slope of the regression line through data points in known_y's and known_x's: For example, you may use SLOPE when defining slopes on roadways for engineering and construction.

=SLOPE(known_y's,known_x's)

The slope of a line is the vertical distance divided by the horizontal distance between any two points on the line. Figure 16.29 shows the result of calculating the slope for a set of sales data.

- **known_y's**—The set of data points or values; the dependent variable.
- **known_x's**—The set of independent data points.

The equation for the slope of the regression line is

$$b = \frac{n\sum xy - \left(\sum x\right)\left(\sum y\right)}{n\sum x^2 - \left(\sum x\right)^2}$$

Figure 16.29
The slope of a line is the amount of change in y due to a change of one unit in x.

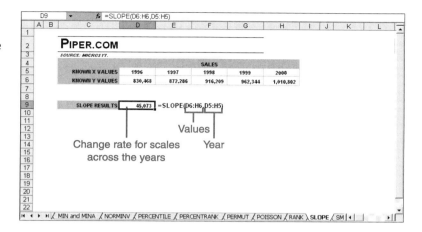

SMALL

SMALL returns the *k*th smallest value in a data set:

=SMALL(array,k)

The SMALL function is used to retrieve a value based on its standing or rank in the data set. Figure 16.30 shows an example of the SMALL function returning the third smallest number from the list.

- **array**—The range of data from which you want to return the *k*th smallest value.
- **k**—The position (from the smallest) of the data point you want to return.

Figure 16.30
SMALL returns the position of the specified smallest value in the data set. To return the largest value, use the LARGE function.

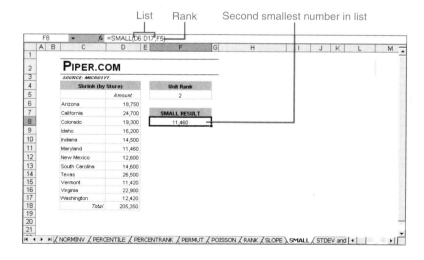

STDEV

STDEV estimates standard deviation based on a sample:

`=STDEV(number1,number2,...)`

The standard deviation is a measure of how widely dispersed values are from the arithmetic mean (the average) value. Figure 16.31 shows the STDEV calculated for a *random* sample of college entrance scores from a local high school. If your data set is the entire population, use the STDEVP function.

- **number n**—Arguments can be cell references, arrays, or range names. Blank cells or cells that contain text, or logical values are ignored. Cells containing a zero (0) are included in the calculation. You can specify up to 30 arguments for the STDEV function.

The equation for STDEV is

$$\sqrt{\frac{n\sum x^2 - \left(\sum x\right)^2}{n(n-1)}}$$

Figure 16.31
The STDEV function is used with a sample data set. Use the STDEVP function if the data set represents the entire population and not a sample.

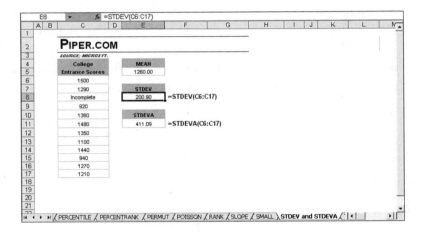

STDEVA

STDEVA estimates standard deviation based on a sample that might be comprised of numbers, text, or logical values:

`=STDEVA(value1,value2,...)`

Similar to STDEV, the STDEVA function calculates the average of its arguments. The difference is that STDEVA does not ignore text or logical values (TRUE and FALSE). Text and FALSE are evaluated as zero (0) and TRUE is evaluated as one (1). Refer to Figure 16.31 for a comparison of the STDEV and STDEVA functions.

- **value** *n*—Cells that contain a zero (0), text, or logical values are included in the STDEVA calculation. Arguments can be cell references, arrays, or range names. Blank cells are ignored. You can specify up to 30 arguments for the STDEVA function.

TREND

TREND returns the y-values along a linear trendline that best fits the values in a data set: Use TREND to forecast future values over time based on historical performance or data.

=TREND(known_y's,known_x's,new_x's,const)

Using the least squares method, the TREND function determines the values that plot a straight line based on a data set. In Figure 16.32, the trend values have been calculated. The known_y and known_x values are based on the formula $y=m*x+b$. Because the new y values (the values that the function returns) are along the linear trendline that best fits your data (based on the trend equation), the new y values do not match the known y values.

Because this function returns an array, the result range must be selected *before* you begin the function, and the formula must be array entered by using Ctrl+Shift+Enter, instead of just Enter.

- **known_y's**—The known values for the known data points; the dependent variable.
- **known_x's**—The known data points. If omitted, assumed to be the array {1,2,3...}, the same size as the known_y's.
- **new_x's**—The new x-values for which you want TREND to return corresponding y-values. If omitted, assumed to be the same as the known_x's.
- **const**—TRUE or FALSE indicating whether the y-intercept (*b*) is = 0 (FALSE) or not (TRUE).

Figure 16.32
Use TREND to forecast future values over time based on historical performance or data.

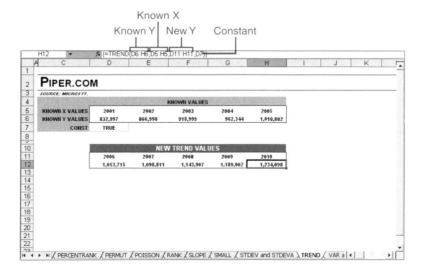

VAR

VAR returns an estimate for the variance of a population, based on a sample data set:

=VAR(number1,number2,…)

Figure 16.33 shows a sample data set of 20 people and the time they spend (one way) commuting to work from a specific suburb. The VAR function provides an estimate of the variance for all the commuters from that suburb.

- **number** *n*—You can specify up to 30 arguments for the VAR function. The arguments can be cell references, arrays, or range names. Blank cells or cells containing text are ignored. Cells that contain a zero (0) are included in the VAR calculation.

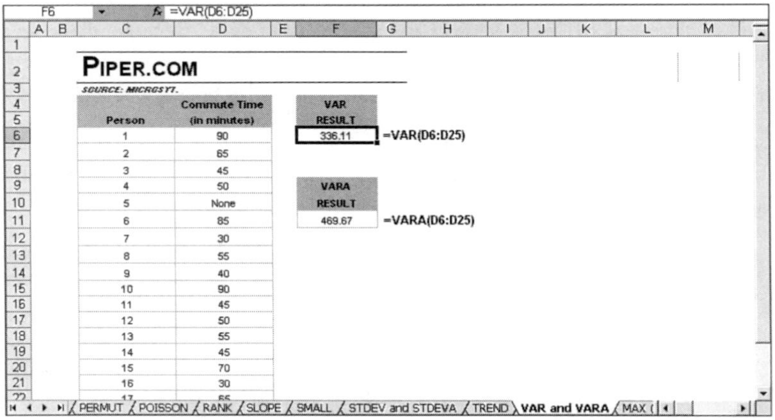

Figure 16.33
The VAR and VARA functions are used when you have only a sample of the entire population. If the data set is the entire population, use the VARP and VARPA functions.

VARA

VARA estimates variance based on a sample, including samples that contain text or logical values:

=VARA(value1,value2,...)

The VARA function differs from the VAR function in that it will also evaluate logical values such as TRUE and FALSE. TRUE evaluates to one (1); FALSE evaluates to zero (0). Arguments that contain text also evaluate to zero. Refer to Figure 16.33 for a comparison of VAR and VARA.

- **value** *n*—The cell reference(s), range name, text representations of numbers, array, or logical values that makes up the data set. Up to 30 arguments can be specified.

TROUBLESHOOTING

DO YOU HAVE A LARGE LIST WHERE YOU NEED TO FIND THE MOST COMMON OCCURRENCE OF A NUMBER?

Use the MODE function. MODE returns the value that appears the most times within the list or range

HOW DO I FIND THE LARGEST VALUE IN A RANGE?

Use the MAX function to return the largest value within a range.

EXCEL IN PRACTICE

If you structure your data in logical rows and columns, you can create dynamic lookups. Notice the MAX(IF formula in Figure 16.34. It looks up the year input in cell E7 from the date range C7:C17. It then looks up the month(1–12) in cell F7 from the same date range in C7:C17. If both conditions are met, the MAX formula returns the maximum value within that given year and month.

Figure 16.34
Use a conditional MAX formula to return the maximum value for a specified year and month.

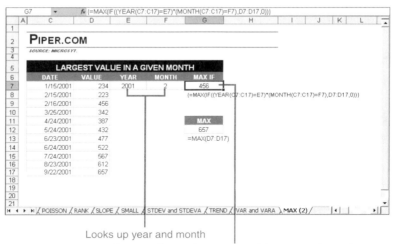

Looks up year and month

Returns the maximum value of the year and month

PART IV

USING EXCEL'S ANALYSIS TOOLS

17 Setting Up a List or Database in Excel   385

18 Using Excel's Data-Management Features   407

19 Outlining, Subtotaling, and Auditing Worksheet Data   439

CHAPTER 17

SETTING UP A LIST OR DATABASE IN EXCEL

In this chapter

Using Excel as a Database Program   386

Building an Effective List   386

Creating Structured Lists from Data Contained in One Cell   394

Working with the Data Form   396

Viewing and Printing the List   399

USING EXCEL AS A DATABASE PROGRAM

Although "number crunching" is Excel's primary purpose, the row-and-column format lends itself to creating and storing databases (called *lists* in Excel). Generally, a good general rule is that if your list grows to more than 2,000 rows, you should consider storing the information in a data warehouse or relational database such as Microsoft Access. Whether you need to store a product catalog for quick lookups or employee information for use with your accounting software, you can create, edit, sort, analyze, and filter your data with the options located in the Data menu.

This chapter begins with discussions of various methods of data entry and options for viewing, printing, and reporting on the list data. The following chapters explore additional options for sorting, filtering, grouping, consolidating, outlining, and auditing lists and tables; using tools and form controls to analyze data; and PivotTables, an important and useful feature of Excel for use in summarizing and manipulating the structure of your lists.

BUILDING AN EFFECTIVE LIST

Structuring a list is the most important part of the creation process because it ultimately determines what you'll be able to extract from the list and how effectively you can manage the list after it's created. Too much time is wasted in business today restructuring lists that were improperly set up.

Before you start to lay out a list, determine what data you will need to compile after the list is created. For example, will you need to compare page views versus the number of people who actually went there or clicked on an ad banner by year, month, and day? After you know what information you need to extract, laying out the list becomes simple. In the list in Figure 17.1, for example, each category has its own heading—Date, Product, Process, and so on. With this layout, data can be extracted as a whole or by individual categories.

When building the list, you can look at the list structure in terms of an outline; classify the outline from most important "topics" to least important. This provides a guideline in structuring the information. In Figure 17.2, the most important topic is product; the second is process.

When building the list, keeping things constant is extremely important. When you start to filter lists or extract information from lists using functions as discussed in later chapters, spelling is critical.

TIP FROM

To determine whether your list is structured effectively, ask yourself whether someone else could take over managing the list and understand its logic without assistance.

Figure 17.1
The structure of a list or database determines what you can extract from the list.

Field names in header row

Record

Field

17

Excel lists are generally made up of a hierarchical structure. So, think in terms of the lowest common denominator in your database or list. If you're setting up a list to track quantities or dollar amounts for the year by code, for example, the lowest-level item might be the actual cost or quantity, then the code, and finally the week or other timeline. The field names (headings) would be placed at the top of each field's column (working from right to left in this example), and beneath this header row would be the body of the list—the actual list data. The first field would be the week; second, the code; third, the cost or quantity. If you already understand how to use PivotTables, you know the importance of information leveling.

→ For details on creating and manipulating PivotTables, **see** Chapter 24, "Using PivotTables and PivotCharts."

CAUTION

Don't separate your list with blank columns or rows! Blanks create a mess when you try to manipulate data. Every level of information should have its own column, and there's no need to apply spacing between the rows. If you must add space between rows, use the row height feature to adjust the vertical size of each row. Also, adjusting a column width will remove the necessity of having to "skip a column" in your design because the contents of the first column spread over into the second.

CAUTION

Don't combine the names of employees, users, clients, and so on into a single cell. Separate first and last names so that each name has its own column for use in sorting or filtering the list by name or creating a PivotTable.

The following list summarizes some important list terminology:

- A *header row* at or near the top of the worksheet contains the field names for the list. This is not a requirement, but many list features won't work correctly (or at all) if the list isn't set up with one.

- *Field names* describe each category of data. These headings usually are positioned as column headings in the header row, but can take the form of row headings for lists in which the data is stored horizontally rather than vertically.

- Each cell containing data is called a *Data Field*.

- Data Fields are combined into a single row or column that comprises all the data for that particular item or person. This group of fields is called a *record*.

- All the records in a database combine to form the *body* of the list.

Table 17.1 describes some suggested formats for the individual parts of the list. These formats help create a clean, uncluttered list. When uppercase, lowercase, and initial caps are all used in the same list, the list is difficult to read. You should follow a standard format in all your lists. It's also good practice to create clean, short headings; the longer the heading, the more difficult the list is for others to review.

TABLE 17.1 STANDARD LIST LAYOUT

Item	Suggested Format
Horizontal field names	Bold type, uppercase, and 12-point font
Left column vertical field names	Bold type, uppercase, and 12-point font
Body text	All caps or initial caps and 10-point font, regular style
Font style	Arial, Tahoma, Courier, Garamond

By default, Excel 2003 extends the formatting of the list to any new list entries typed at the end of the list, including any formulas that are part of previous entries. (This assumes that at least three of the previous five entries used that formatting and/or formula, for which Excel establishes a usage pattern.) To turn off this feature—for example, if you want to customize certain types of entries within an individual list—choose Tools, Options, click the Edit tab, and deselect the Extend List Formats and Formulas option.

It's important to establish field names that match the category. Lists usually grow with time, and new field names are created as the list grows, so try to break down the description of the field name to its most detailed level from the beginning.

The format for the body of the list (the actual data) is the most critical part of your standardization process. The data should maintain consistency with like or similar text formats. Consistency here determines the manageability of the list.

In many cases, you'll inherit someone else's list and have to manipulate some of the current structure. Figure 17.2 demonstrates changing an existing list from lowercase to uppercase for consistency in this particular list. (You can change from uppercase to lowercase with the LOWER function, which is covered in Chapter 15, "Text Functions.")

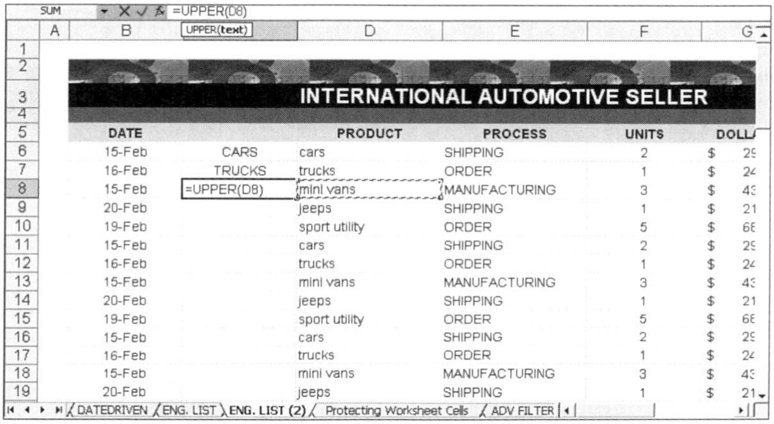

Figure 17.2
You can use the UPPER function to convert lowercase text to uppercase, and the LOWER function to convert uppercase text to lowercase.

After you convert the lowercase entries to uppercase with formulas for this example, you'll want to return the converted—now uppercase—text to its original column. To do this, follow these steps:

1. Select the converted range (column of formulas).

2. Choose Edit, Copy.

3. Select the first cell in the range to paste.

4. Choose Edit, Paste Special.

5. In the Paste Special dialog box, select Values (see Figure 17.3). This option converts all the formulas to their resulting values. (Table 17.2 describes the options in the Paste Special dialog box.)

Figure 17.3
The Paste Special dialog box enables you to paste ranges of formulas as values.

6. Click OK. The values are copied to the target cells, as shown in Figure 17.4.

7. Delete the formula column.

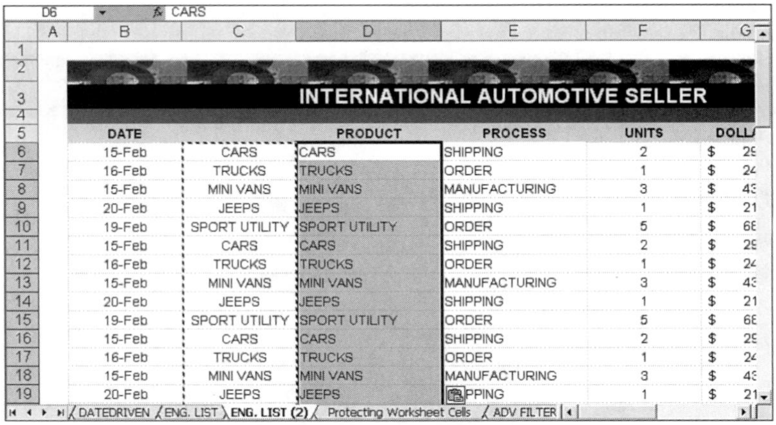

Figure 17.4
After you convert the text from lowercase to uppercase and paste the converted text in the original column, you can delete the formula column.

TABLE 17.2 PASTE SPECIAL COMMANDS

Paste Special Command	Result
Paste	
All	Pastes all contents including all cell formats.
Formulas	Pastes the formula from the copied cell or range without formatting.
Values	Pastes the values from the copied cell. No formats are pasted.
Formats	Pastes only the formats from the copied cell or range.
Comments	Pastes only comments from the copied cell or range.
Validation	Pastes all validation associated with the copied cell or range.
All Except Borders	Pastes all cell contents and formats excluding borders.
Column Widths	Pastes the column width of the selected or copied column to the desired destination column.
Formulas and Number Formats	Pastes the formulas and the number formats from the copied cell or range.
Values and Number Formats	Pastes the values and the numbers formats.

Paste Special Command	Result
Operation	
None	Default mathematical calculation is set to none.
Add	Adds the copied cell or range to the new cell or range.
Subtract	Subtracts the copied cell or range from the new cell or range.
Multiply	Multiplies the copied cell or range by the new cell or range.
Divide	Divides the copied cell or range by the new cell or range.
Skip Blanks	Avoids copying blank cells from a range to the new location.
Transpose	Changes the copied layout from a vertical format to a horizontal format and vice versa.
Paste Link	Links the pasted information from the copied cell or range to the new cell or range.

NOTE

> You can also access the Paste Special command by selecting the drop-down list on the Paste button in the Standard toolbar.

TRANSPOSING LIST DATA WITH THE PASTE SPECIAL COMMAND

Many times you'll either inherit a list of information or need to view it in a different layout. You can transpose lists from vertical to horizontal and vice versa with the Paste Special command. To transpose a table or list, follow these steps:

1. Select and copy the data table or range you want to transpose.
2. Select the cell in which you want to start the new transposed table.
3. Choose Edit, Paste Special or click the drop-down arrow next to the Paste button on the Standard toolbar.
4. Check Transpose and click OK or click Transpose on the Paste button's drop-down list. Notice the final transposed result in Figure 17.5.

TRANSPOSING TABLES WITH FORMULAS (WITHOUT ABSOLUTE REFERENCING)

Many times, you'll have tables that reference lists of information and the formulas don't have absolute referencing. In the likely event that you'll have to view the information in a new layout, you might have to spend countless hours applying an absolute reference to all the formulas—or you can use this trick. Select the region with the formulas as shown in Figure 17.6.

1. Choose Edit, Replace.

2. Under Find What, type =.

3. Under Replace With, type <.

4. Click Replace All, then click OK and close.

Figure 17.5

The vertical table is now transposed in a horizontal format.

Select upper-left cell where transposed table will begin

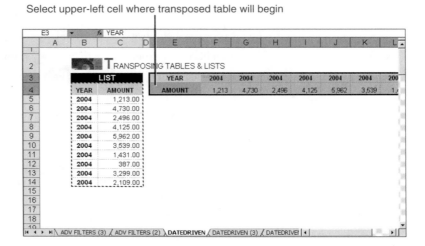

Figure 17.6

Select the region with the formulas to transpose the table.

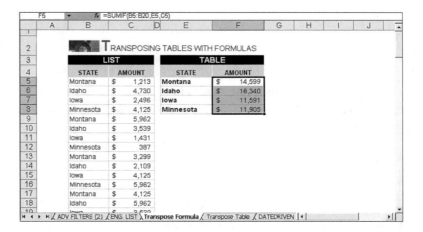

Select and copy the entire table to transpose the table as shown in Figure 17.7.

Select a cell or destination where you want the transposed table to be placed. Choose Edit, Paste Special dialog box, select Transpose. Now select the transposed formula cells as shown in Figure 17.8.

Figure 17.7
Copy the entire table to transpose the table.

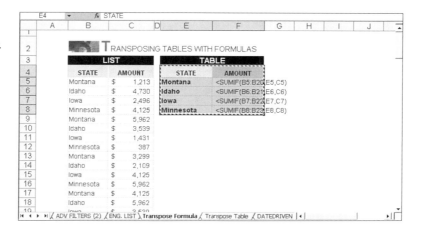

Figure 17.8
Select the formula cells in the transposed table to replace the < sign with =.

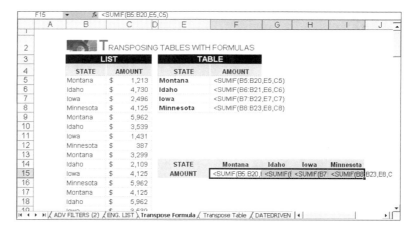

Choose Edit, Replace. Under Find What, type <. Under Replace With, type =. Click replace all then click OK and close. The transposed table now reflects the original referencing without using absolute as shown in Figure 17.9.

SETTING UP DATE-DRIVEN LISTS

Date-driven lists are among the most common types of lists used. All too often people try to combine information related to time in the same column, meaning quarter and date, for example. Never, ever do this, because it makes for difficult data or summary extraction given the tools available in Excel. If you have a list that you've inherited that was created with these errors you can clean the list up using "Text to columns" or Text functions and formulas. See also Chapter 15. If you have to make sense of the data with filters, formulas, or PivotTables down the road, set up your list or data in a similar fashion to that shown in Figure 17.10.

Figure 17.9
The result of replacing the < sign with the = sign reactivates the formula with the same referencing.

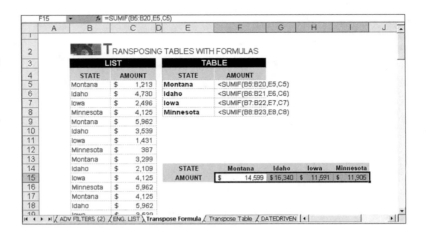

Figure 17.10
Establish your list with the time periods from biggest to smallest as shown.

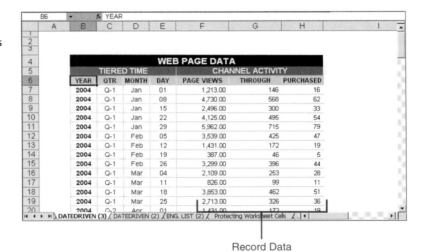

Record Data

In this example, the largest to smallest denominator is Year, Qtr, Month, and Day followed by the data. Not only does this give organizational appeal but it will allow you to group, summarize, filter, extract with formulas, and use PivotTables to their fullest. Itemizing data to their smallest levels will allow you to manipulate or slice the data in multiple ways.

CREATING STRUCTURED LISTS FROM DATA CONTAINED IN ONE CELL

If you have multiple bits of data in one cell, you might want to separate the bits into separate columns. You could copy the information from the formula bar bit by bit, and paste them into new columns, or you could use the automated text-to-columns approach.

Consider this: You get reports sent to you via email on a weekly basis containing the following Internet channel (page) information. First, the channel (page) name, then the number of page views (times viewed), the click-through number (number click on the link), and last, the number of people who actually click a certain feature within the final page. You copy the information from the email and paste it into Excel. Your table would look similar to the table in Figure 17.11.

Figure 17.11
Notice the information for each record is combined into one cell.

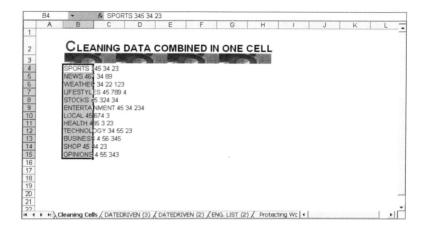

To clean this list and separate the four bits of data from one cell to four separate cells, follow these steps:

1. Select the list range as shown in Figure 17.11.
2. Choose Data, Text to Columns.
3. Select Delimited as shown in Figure 17.12.

Click Delimited...

Figure 17.12
Select Delimited when the data is separated by characters such as tabs, commas, or, in this example, spaces.

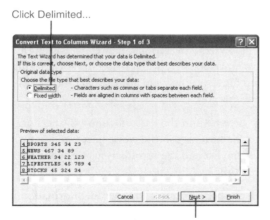

...Click Next and choose Space

4. Click Next.

5. Check Space Under Delimiters.

6. Click Finish to see the result as shown in Figure 17.13.

Figure 17.13
The final and cleaned-up result places the data bits in separate columns.

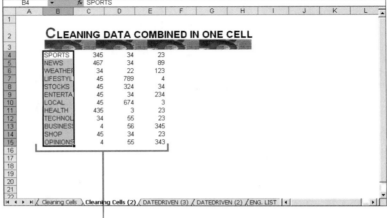

Final results separate the contents of one cell into multiple columns

WORKING WITH THE DATA FORM

People who work with Excel on a regular basis usually are comfortable with the row-and-column structure and have no difficulty entering list data directly into the appropriate cells. However, the ongoing data entry and maintenance of a list might be handled by someone who is less familiar with Excel. For those users—and even experienced Excel users who prefer a simpler data-entry method—Excel provides the *data form*. The data form works like a dialog box; it floats over the worksheet and includes buttons and other form controls to enable the user to enter one record at a time into the list.

You also can use the data form to search for specific records in the list, using specified criteria, or even to delete records. *Filters* (covered in Chapter 18, "Using Excel's Data-Management Features") are more effective when searching for information, but if your list is long and you're searching for a specific element, the data form does a good job of finding that particular record of information.

To use the data form, click anywhere in the list and choose Data, Form. Excel displays a data form, customized with the headings in the worksheet (see Figure 17.14). The data form displays the record count of the list and the scrollbar enables you to scroll the list, record by record, or many records at a time.

To enter new records, click the New button and type the information in the appropriate text boxes. (Notice that the record indicator in the upper-right corner of the dialog box changes to display the words New Record.) The data form works as a multipurpose form for data entry, searching, and viewing the list; the message in the upper-right corner indicates how the form is currently being used. Use the Tab and Shift+Tab keys, the underlined hotkeys, or the mouse to move from one text box to another. When the record is complete, press Enter or click the New button to enter the new record at the end of the list and start another new record.

Figure 17.14
Use the data form to enter or find records in a list.

CAUTION

Premature use of the Enter key will cause an incomplete record to be entered into the list and you'll need to use the Up arrow on the scrollbar (in the dialog box) to access the record again. This is a very common mistake.

TIP FROM

Although the data form simplifies the process of entering list data, it doesn't offer the advantage of auto-repeating information you have already typed once. If your list includes the same information in multiple records—for example, each new employee record will list one of a set of five orientation and training classes—you probably won't want to type that information repeatedly when entering data. Enter the data directly into the cells—where you can take advantage of the Copy and AutoComplete features—instead of using the data form, or skip those fields and enter that information later.

TIP FROM

Unless the list is sorted chronologically or by a customized account or part number, you probably will want new records to be sorted from the end of the list to their appropriate positions alphabetically or numerically.

→ For details on sorting and filtering lists, **see** "Sorting a List and Filtering a List," **p. 413 and 416**

To find a specific record in a list, follow these steps:

1. Click the Criteria button.

   Notice that the record indicator in the upper-right corner of the dialog box changes to display the word Criteria (see Figure 17.15).

Figure 17.15
Search for specific information within a list by typing the description in the corresponding text box.

2. Enter any known information from the record you're seeking and choose Find Next or press Enter.

   The search function works the same as the Find dialog box; you can search for just the first few characters of an entry or type the whole entry.

> **NOTE**
> Typing the first few characters works only on non-numeric data. To search for salaries, dates entered as dates, and so on, you must include the entire number or date.

   Excel searches the list and finds the first record that matches the specified criteria. Note that searches are not case sensitive.

3. To continue searching, click Find Next again. To search in the reverse direction, click Find Prev. Note that either method continues searching from the most recent record found, rather than starting at the top of the list.

   When you reach the last record to match the specified criteria, Excel beeps if you try to continue searching in that direction.

4. To enter another set of criteria, click the Clear button and type the new criteria. To return to data entry, click the Form button. To enter another set of criteria first click Criteria THEN click the Clear button.

VIEWING AND PRINTING THE LIST

The following sections provide a number of helpful suggestions for organizing the view of your list. Aesthetics aside, making your list attractive and readable can actually help with the data-entry process and make the list easier to use. It's important that a list be understandable, especially when someone else has to use the list.

CAUTION

> Don't get too carried away with these viewing options. As your data list grows, simple backgrounds and views become more desirable. The more complex the view, the less data you can see or comprehend onscreen.

KEEPING THE FIELD NAMES FROM SCROLLING

When scrolling down large lists in Excel, you'll notice that the headings and field names scroll off the screen. To keep the headings or field names on the screen as you scroll, *freeze* the headings onscreen. Select the range below the heading or to the right of the headings and choose Window, Freeze Panes, as shown in Figure 17.16. In this example, rows 1 through 4 will remain onscreen as you work with the list. To unfreeze the panes, choose Window, Unfreeze Panes.

Figure 17.16
Freezing the pane enables you to scroll the body of the list while keeping headings or field names visible.

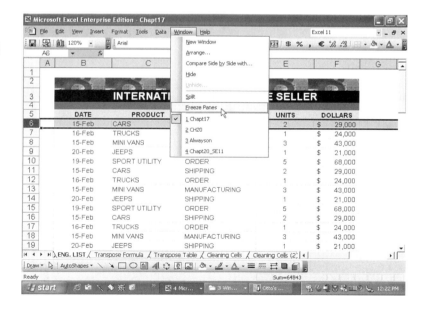

→ To learn more about freezing panes in Excel, **see** "Freezing Columns and Rows," **p. 42**

Splitting the window is much like freezing the panes, but the difference is the capability to intersect a row or column. For example, Figure 17.17 shows the same worksheet as in

Figure 17.16, but with the window split, intersecting column D, meaning that the *split bar* splits right through the cell. Freezing panes freezes to the right or left, or top or bottom of a cell. When panes are frozen, you can't move the frozen sections; you have to unfreeze the panes to adjust them. Split bars, on the other hand, can be dragged anywhere on the screen, which makes them more useful when working with lists. Split screen also allows you to scroll each side of the split screen.

Figure 17.17
Splitting the window is similar to freezing panes; however, with the split window, you can intersect a column or row, and also adjust it with your mouse.

Split box

Split bar

You can split the window by selecting a row or column and choosing Window, Split. To adjust the split, drag the split bar to the desired location. Another way to split the window is to drag one of the split boxes by the scrollbars to the desired location. You can split the window both horizontally and vertically. To remove a split, double-click the split bar or drag it to the edge of the window.

→ For more details on working with split windows, **see** "Splitting the Screen," **p. 43**

ARRANGING MULTIPLE WINDOWS

When creating lists to store your data, you might need to work with several workbooks at the same time or multiple sheets within the same workbook. For example, you might do this when copying and pasting information from one list to another, or when writing formulas that correspond from one workbook or worksheet to another.

NOTE

When establishing multiple lists within a workbook, if possible, start your lists on the same line and cell to make managing your workbook more efficient. Also, try to make the lists as similar in type and style as possible for consistency within the workbook.

To view multiple windows or sheets at one time within the same workbook, perform the following steps:

1. Select one of the sheets in the workbook you want to view.

2. Select Window, New Window. Excel adds a colon and the number 2 to the workbook title in the title bar of the second window and the number 1 to the title bar in the first window.

3. In the new window, select another sheet in the workbook.

4. Choose Window, Arrange.

5. In the Arrange Windows dialog box, select the desired window arrangement. If you want to arrange only the windows in the currently active workbook, be sure the Windows of Active Workbook option is checked.

6. Click OK.

Although Figure 17.18 seems to show two workbooks open, you actually are seeing two sheets within the same workbook. Any changes to either workbook are saved to the original workbook. In this example, the upper window and the lower window show two different worksheets in the same workbook.

Figure 17.18
By creating a new window in a workbook, you can view several sheets in the same workbook at the same time.

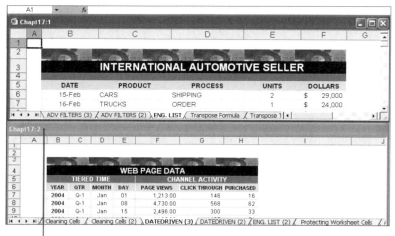

A number after the workbook title indicates that you're viewing the same workbook in multiple windows

Using the same method, you can view multiple workbooks or multiple windows showing the active workbook. When arranging multiple workbooks, be sure that the Windows of Active Workbook option in the Arrange Windows dialog box is not checked.

INSERTING DATA RANGES INTO A LIST

You probably are accomplished at cutting or copying a range and pasting it to an empty range. When working with lists, however, you often need to paste cut or copied records between existing records. Rather than using a simple paste operation, use the Insert menu.

TIP FROM

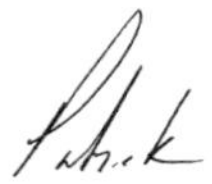

You can select multiple noncontiguous columns or rows and insert columns to the left of each or rows above each of them in the one step. For example, you can select row 6 and row 8 at the same time and insert one new row above each selected row by choosing Insert, Cells or Rows.

Figure 17.19 shows a selected group of records. In this example, the intention is to move the North Dakota records above the Minnesota records (assume that this list is not intended to be sorted alphabetically by project).

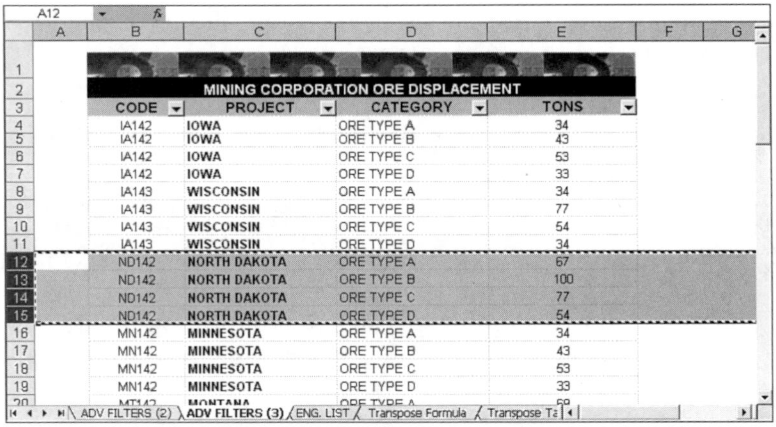

CODE	PROJECT	CATEGORY	TONS
IA142	IOWA	ORE TYPE A	34
IA142	IOWA	ORE TYPE B	43
IA142	IOWA	ORE TYPE C	53
IA142	IOWA	ORE TYPE D	33
IA143	WISCONSIN	ORE TYPE A	34
IA143	WISCONSIN	ORE TYPE B	77
IA143	WISCONSIN	ORE TYPE C	54
IA143	WISCONSIN	ORE TYPE D	34
ND142	NORTH DAKOTA	ORE TYPE A	67
ND142	NORTH DAKOTA	ORE TYPE B	100
ND142	NORTH DAKOTA	ORE TYPE C	77
ND142	NORTH DAKOTA	ORE TYPE D	54
MN142	MINNESOTA	ORE TYPE A	34
MN142	MINNESOTA	ORE TYPE B	43
MN142	MINNESOTA	ORE TYPE C	53
MN142	MINNESOTA	ORE TYPE D	33

Figure 17.19
Select and copy or cut the source records.

To move these records, you would cut them from their current location and insert them above the Minnesota records. After cutting the North Dakota records, select the target range, and choose Insert, Cut Cells. Excel repositions the existing data and inserts the cut cells (see Figure 17.20).

If you are inserting copied rather than cut cells, choose Insert, Copied Cells. The Insert Paste dialog box appears. Choose Shift Cells Down or Shift Cells Right to move the existing data in the target range out of the way of the incoming data.

Two drag-and-drop methods are also available:

- Position the mouse around the edge of the selection (just like the normal drag and drop), and drag the selection while holding down the Shift key. When the gray single-line-insert indicator appears in the desired location between rows/columns, release the mouse. The existing data is automatically shifted down/to the right, depending on the drag direction.

- Position the mouse in the same manner as the previous method, but drag with the right mouse button. When the gray border representing the data being moved is positioned in the desired location, release the mouse and choose Shift Down and Move (or Copy) from the shortcut menu.

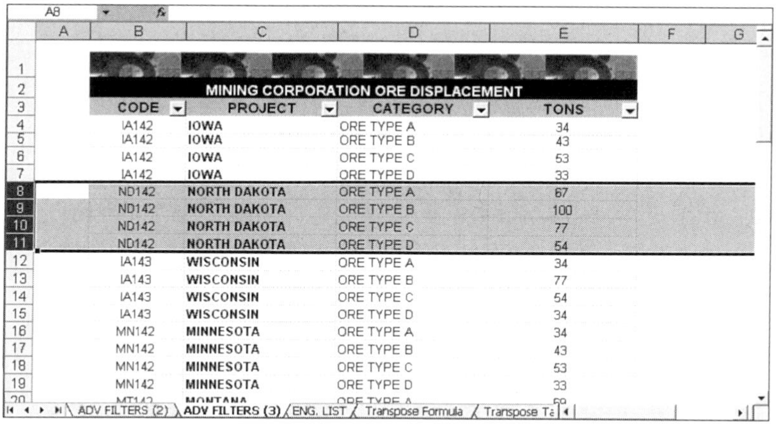

	CODE	PROJECT	CATEGORY	TONS
4	IA142	IOWA	ORE TYPE A	34
5	IA142	IOWA	ORE TYPE B	43
6	IA142	IOWA	ORE TYPE C	53
7	IA142	IOWA	ORE TYPE D	33
8	ND142	NORTH DAKOTA	ORE TYPE A	67
9	ND142	NORTH DAKOTA	ORE TYPE B	100
10	ND142	NORTH DAKOTA	ORE TYPE C	77
11	ND142	NORTH DAKOTA	ORE TYPE D	54
12	IA143	WISCONSIN	ORE TYPE A	34
13	IA143	WISCONSIN	ORE TYPE B	77
14	IA143	WISCONSIN	ORE TYPE C	54
15	IA143	WISCONSIN	ORE TYPE D	34
16	MN142	MINNESOTA	ORE TYPE A	34
17	MN142	MINNESOTA	ORE TYPE B	43
18	MN142	MINNESOTA	ORE TYPE C	53
19	MN142	MINNESOTA	ORE TYPE D	33

Figure 17.20 The cut range is pasted into place.

Because Excel doesn't allow you to insert copies of noncontiguous selections, you can use this feature only for a contiguous selection. To enter list data from noncontiguous areas, use Edit, Paste. In Figure 17.19, for example, you could select all the ORE TYPE A projects, copy them from the list, and paste them in a new location. The projects would appear in the order copied, with no additional spaces between them.

Establishing Custom Views

Because lists grow in size and only a certain amount of information needs to be viewed at one time, Excel enables you to create *custom views* that store just the relevant information displayed by the user, including print settings. You can even name the views to fit the situation. For example, Figure 17.21 shows an entire year of financial performance by job and month, but you might be interested in only the high-level totals by quarter. By applying a custom view, you can hide the information that is not relevant to you.

To hide the supporting information and show only the Quarter totals, follow these steps:

1. Establish the view you want saved as a custom view. In this example, you would hide rows 4 through 6, 8 through 10, and so on, until only the quarter totals are visible.
2. Choose View, Custom Views to open the Custom Views dialog box.
3. Choose Add to open the Add View dialog box.

4. Type a name for the new custom view.
5. Click OK.

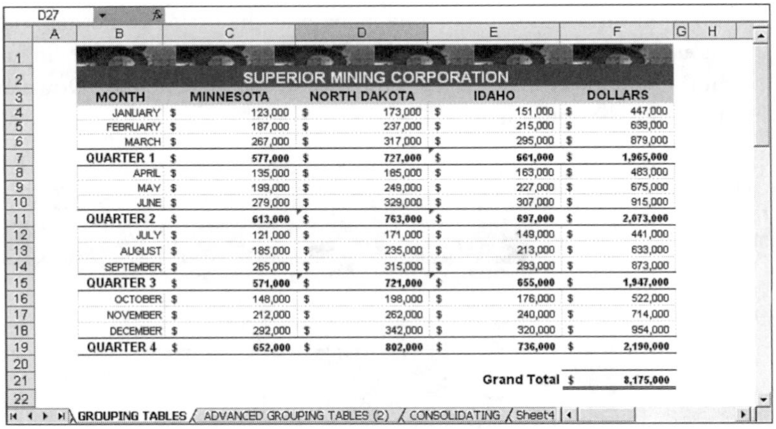

MONTH		MINNESOTA		NORTH DAKOTA		IDAHO		DOLLARS
SUPERIOR MINING CORPORATION								
JANUARY	$	123,000	$	173,000	$	151,000	$	447,000
FEBRUARY	$	187,000	$	237,000	$	215,000	$	639,000
MARCH	$	267,000	$	317,000	$	295,000	$	879,000
QUARTER 1	$	577,000	$	727,000	$	661,000	$	1,965,000
APRIL	$	135,000	$	185,000	$	163,000	$	483,000
MAY	$	199,000	$	249,000	$	227,000	$	675,000
JUNE	$	279,000	$	329,000	$	307,000	$	915,000
QUARTER 2	$	613,000	$	763,000	$	697,000	$	2,073,000
JULY	$	121,000	$	171,000	$	149,000	$	441,000
AUGUST	$	185,000	$	235,000	$	213,000	$	633,000
SEPTEMBER	$	265,000	$	315,000	$	293,000	$	873,000
QUARTER 3	$	571,000	$	721,000	$	655,000	$	1,947,000
OCTOBER	$	148,000	$	198,000	$	176,000	$	522,000
NOVEMBER	$	212,000	$	262,000	$	240,000	$	714,000
DECEMBER	$	292,000	$	342,000	$	320,000	$	954,000
QUARTER 4	$	652,000	$	802,000	$	736,000	$	2,190,000
						Grand Total	$	8,175,000

Figure 17.21
You can create custom views to show only relevant information.

Custom views are saved with the workbook. To show your custom view at any time, open the workbook and select View, Custom Views. The Custom Views dialog box opens. Select the desired view and click Show. To delete a custom view, open the Custom Views dialog box, select the view name, and choose Delete. When prompted, select Yes to confirm that you want to delete the view. The Print Settings option in the Add View dialog box allows you to store custom page setups for each view (such as different headers and footers, starting page numbers, print titles, and so on).

NOTE

> Set up custom views in workbooks that are shared between multiple users. Each user can store his or her favorite view and print settings.

Custom views store the following information:

- Window size/position, including splits or frozen panes
- Hidden columns, rows, and sheets in the workbook
- Most of the display options found on the View tab of the Option dialog box (choose Tools, Options)
- Selected cells, if any
- Filtered list criteria
- Page Setup settings

The Add View dialog box enables you to save print settings, hidden rows, and filter settings. The last is an important issue for working with lists; see the next chapter for details.

→ If you switch views often, add the Custom Views toolbar button to one of your toolbars. For details on customizing toolbars, **see** "Modifying Toolbars," **p. 714**

TROUBLESHOOTING

FREEZE PANES

How do I create Freeze Panes on both the columns and rows?

Select the cell in the upper-left corner of the range containing your data. Do not include your column or row headings. Then, choose Window, Freeze Panes to freeze your column and row headings.

UNIQUE RECORDS

I have a list of more than a thousand records, and I want to roll up only one of each record or show one occurrence of each record. Can Excel do this?

Yes, select the entire column range from 1 to 1010—for example, in column C. Then, select Data, Filter, Advanced filter. When Excel prompts you, click Yes or No depending on whether you want to include the header. From the Advanced Filter dialog box, check Unique Records Only. Click OK. Excel rolls up all records to one of each.

EXCEL IN PRACTICE

There are proper and improper ways to structure a list. Figure 17.22 shows a list with some problems:

- Mixed lowercase and uppercase text, which makes the list difficult to read and draws the audience's attention from the field names to the body of the list.
- The codes shouldn't be placed in separate rows; they should have their own field column and be associated with each record item in the list.
- First and last names are combined into one field, which means that you couldn't sort this list in order by last name.

A good test is to make sure that each line item can stand on its own, giving complete and accurate information per row.

Figure 17.23 shows a revised version of the list. The field divisions and formatting are consistent, and each record is complete—with date, code, first name, last name, project, and hours. You can now convert this list into a PivotTable for summation, or easily extract information with formulas.

YEAR	NAME	DAY	REG HOURS	OT HOURS	DT HOURS
	QUARTER 1				
2005	Sandy Ander	01	1,213.00	146	16
2005	John Ixter	08	4,730.00	568	62
2005	Lori Mathers	15	2,496.00	300	33
2005	Tim Valcon	22	4,125.00	495	54
2005	Steve Witmar	29	5,962.00	715	79
	QUARTER 2				
2005	Sandy Ander	01	1,431.00	172	19
2005	John Ixter	08	387.00	46	5
2005	Lori Mathers	15	3,299.00	396	44
2005	Tim Valcon	22	2,109.00	253	28
2005	Steve Witmar	29	2,713.00	326	36

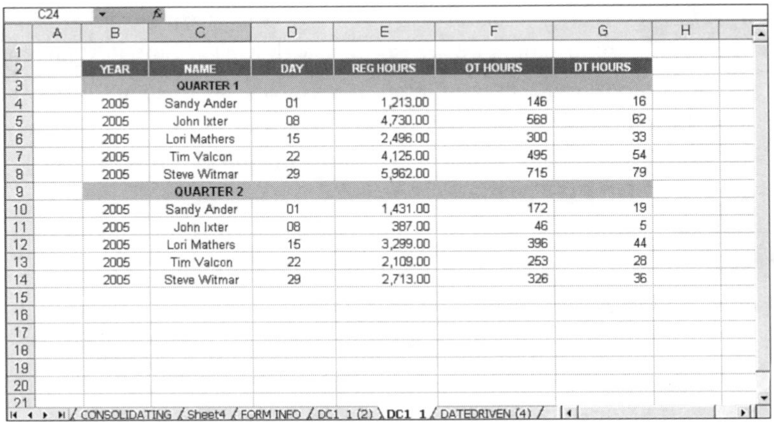

Figure 17.22
At first glance, this list might seem adequate, but the setup will make it difficult to use.

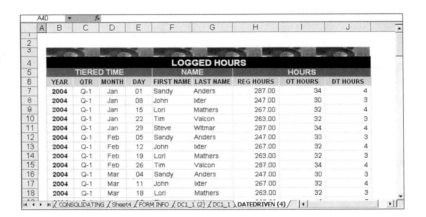

LOGGED HOURS

TIERED TIME				NAME		HOURS		
YEAR	QTR	MONTH	DAY	FIRST NAME	LAST NAME	REG HOURS	OT HOURS	DT HOURS
2004	Q-1	Jan	01	Sandy	Anders	287.00	34	4
2004	Q-1	Jan	08	John	Ixter	247.00	30	3
2004	Q-1	Jan	15	Lori	Mathers	267.00	32	4
2004	Q-1	Jan	22	Tim	Valcon	263.00	32	3
2004	Q-1	Jan	29	Steve	Witmar	287.00	34	4
2004	Q-1	Feb	05	Sandy	Anders	247.00	30	3
2004	Q-1	Feb	12	John	Ixter	267.00	32	4
2004	Q-1	Feb	19	Lori	Mathers	263.00	32	3
2004	Q-1	Feb	26	Tim	Valcon	287.00	34	4
2004	Q-1	Mar	04	Sandy	Anders	247.00	30	3
2004	Q-1	Mar	11	John	Ixter	267.00	32	4
2004	Q-1	Mar	18	Lori	Mathers	263.00	32	3

Figure 17.23
A clean, well-organized list improves the processes of both input and output.

CHAPTER **18**

USING EXCEL'S DATA-MANAGEMENT FEATURES

In this chapter

Data Management in Excel   408

Using Conditional Formatting with Lists   408

Using Formulas with Conditional Formatting   410

Using Formulas with Conditional Formatting to Create Timelines   411

Managing Data Using Text To Speech   413

Sorting a List   413

Filtering a List   416

Adding Form Controls to Your Worksheets   424

DATA MANAGEMENT IN EXCEL

Management of data in an Excel workbook shouldn't be time-consuming. For example, if you structure your data correctly and take advantage of functions, form controls, filters, and PivotTables you'll find data management to be less time consuming and more automated. This chapter discusses tools available within Excel that will enable you to manage both your time and data efficiently. From extracting and identifying information with formulas and formats, to using built-in sorting and filtering tools created specifically for managing worksheet data and lists, to tracking changes in worksheets shared among multiple users, Excel gives you every option necessary to effectively use your time and get the most out of your Excel data. This chapter also covers a topic close to the heart of any information manager—protecting workbook contents to prevent the loss of important data.

USING CONDITIONAL FORMATTING WITH LISTS

Conditional formatting is a tool in Excel that allows you to set formats to data if they meet a certain criteria. *Conditional formatting* can be a great way to call attention to specific information within a spreadsheet, or plot out timelines. The key when using conditional formats is to use a format to call out specific bits of information; for example, you can use it to call out "not to exceed" information or negative numbers.

The example in Figure 18.1 uses an interactive conditional format; when a state is entered in cell D3, the conditional format highlights the cells in the list that match the entry. When you enter a project name in this cell, the conditional formatting highlights the cells referring to that project within the list. Cell E3 contains a formula that then adds the numbers in column E (the Tons column) for the highlighted list entries. The key is to use the Excel tools in innovative ways to make your everyday tasks easier. By combining conditional formatting with a formula, a single entry in cell D3 yields two results: The specified project entries are highlighted in the list, and the tonnage for that project is totaled in cell E3. You can use up to three conditional formats within a list.

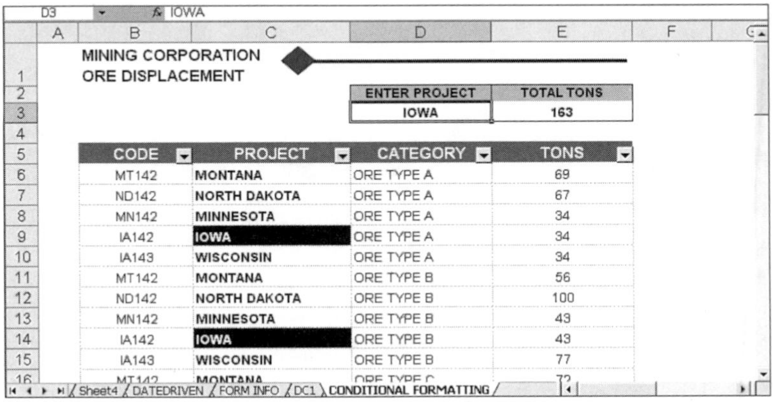

Figure 18.1
By knowing how to use conditional formats, you can call out all references to the information entered in one cell.

To create an interactive conditional format, follow these steps:

1. Select the range that you want to apply the conditional format. The range in Figure 18.1 is C6:C25.

2. Choose Format, Conditional Formatting.

3. In the Conditional Formatting dialog box, choose the first condition you want. For this example, you would choose Equal To from the middle drop-down list in the dialog box, as shown in Figure 18.2.

Figure 18.2
Setting the condition in the Conditional Formatting dialog box.

4. In the remaining condition box, select the cell to which you want to link your condition or type a value in the box.

5. Click the Format button in the Conditional Formatting dialog box.

6. Select the desired format from the three tabs in the Format Cells dialog box. For this example, black shading was selected on the Patterns tab, and the text was made bold and white on the Font tab (see Figure 18.3).

Figure 18.3
Format the cells in the list that meet the conditional-formatting criteria.

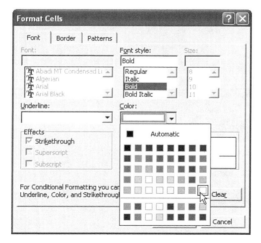

7. Click OK. The format is shown in the preview window.

8. If desired, add more criteria by clicking the Add button to add another condition.

9. Make any desired changes and then click OK.

In the example list, when you enter a project state in cell D3, the condition applies itself to the list. Any entry in the Project column that matches the value entered in cell D3 will get the formatting you set in the Conditional Formatting dialog box (see Figure 18.4).

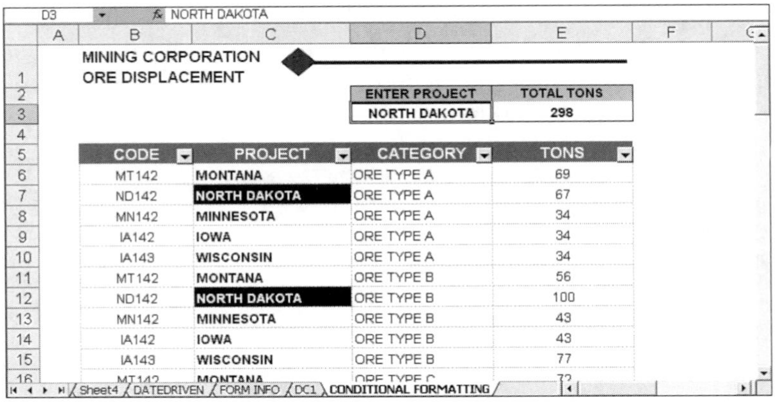

Figure 18.4
When a project state is entered, the conditional format operates based on the trigger cell D3.

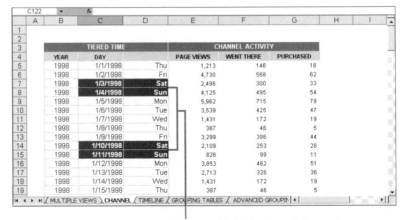

USING FORMULAS WITH CONDITIONAL FORMATTING

18

You can use formulas within the conditional format option to highlight the desired information. For example, if you have a list of days in your list or database, you can apply a simple weekday formula to call out any given day within a week. Notice the highlighted line items in Figure 18.5.

→ For more information on the weekday formula, **see** "Weekday," **p.210**

Figure 18.5
Use formulas as the criteria for the conditional format option to identify and highlight any given day of the week.

Use formulas with conditional formats to highlight days of the week

To apply a conditional format to call out a given day of the week, follow these steps.

1. Select the range of dates you want to apply a conditional format to. In the example in Figure 18.5 C5:D108 was selected.

2. Choose Format, Conditional Formatting.

3. In the Condition 1 section, select Formula Is in the drop-down list.

4. Type in the formula =weekday(c5)=1, where C5 is the first date cell in the range and 1 Sunday is considered the first day of the week. Notice the formula in Figure 18.6. To add another condition, select Add. In the example, we are looking to highlight Saturday and Sunday, which are represented by weekday values 1 and 7.

5. Click OK.

Type the weekday formula referencing the first date cell with the range highlighted

Figure 18.6
Add highlights to any given day of the week with the weekday formula applied to the conditional format.

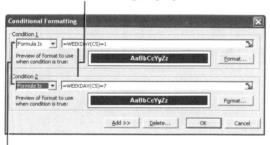

Make sure the condition is set to Formula Is

USING FORMULAS WITH CONDITIONAL FORMATTING TO CREATE TIMELINES

You can create seamless timelines that appear to have no formula in the cells with conditional formats. If you have to maintain schedules in business development, strategic planning, marketing, or production environments of any kind, this is one visual technique you can use. In Figure 18.7, the blocked timelines are really floating bars that reference the dateline across the top and the start and stop dates down the left.

The key in applying these formats is to effectively set up your timeline and your start and stop dates. Notice how the dateline starts from left to right every seven days in cell E6. The other key points of reference are the start and stop dates. The start dates are in column C and the stop dates are in Column D. You'll need to apply an AND formula to reference both the dateline and start and stop cells as shown in Figure 18.8. To create an automated timeline with conditional formats, follow these steps:

Dateline

Figure 18.7
Create floating timelines with conditional formats to manage time events.

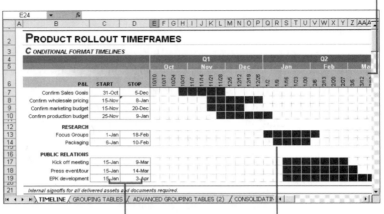

Start and stop dates   Floating conditional format bars

Figure 18.8
Apply an AND formula to create automated floating timelines.

18

1. First make sure you have a range for your timeline and start and stop dates similar to that shown in Figure 18.8.

2. Select the cell to which you want to apply the Conditional Format. Choose Format, Conditional Formatting. In the example, you would begin by selecting cell E7.

3. Select Formula Is in the drop-down list in the Condition 1 section of the Conditional Formatting dialog box.

4. Type in the formula =And(E$6>=$C7,F$6<=$D7), where E$6 is the beginning of the week, $C7 is the start date for that line item, F$6 is the end of the week, and $D7 is the stop date for that line item.

   The absolute references are applied to allow dragging the formula to the right and then copying the formula down. Click the Format button to apply a format.

5. Click OK.

CAUTION

> This formula will not work correctly for the last date in the dateline because the second part of the AND references a date one cell to the right of the date in its column—a date that doesn't exist when the current date is in the last column of the dateline. A different formula is needed to take this situation into account.
>
> For the conditional formats to work for the entire dateline, the following formula should be used:
>
> `=IF(LEN(F$6)>0,AND(E$6>=$C7,F$6<=$D7),E$6<=$D7)`
>
> This formula checks to see whether there's any date to the right of E6 on the dateline. If so, then your original formula is used. Otherwise, you must be at the end of the dateline and only need to check whether E6 is less than the stop date (D7).

MANAGING DATA USING TEXT TO SPEECH

Excel's new text-to-speech capabilities allow you to listen to your data, whether you're viewing a list and typing in cells or reviewing a sheet of information and want the values or titles read back to you. This is a great verification or auditing tool when reviewing your worksheet entries. The Text To Speech toolbar can be found by right-clicking any visible toolbar and selecting Text To Speech. You can also get to this toolbar, which is shown in Figure 18.9, by choosing View, Toolbars, Text To Speech.

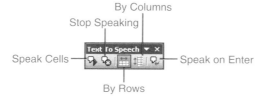

Figure 18.9
The Text To Speech toolbar allows Excel to read your data back to you.

Controls on the Text To Speech toolbar are as follows:

- **Speak Cells**—Reads the cells in the selected range.
- **Stop Speaking**—Stops the reading of the cells in the selected range.
- **By Rows**—Reads cells from left to right.
- **By Columns**—Reads cells from top to bottom.
- **Speak on Enter**—Reads cells upon pressing Enter.

SORTING A LIST

After you create a list, you'll want to view your information in different ways. Excel enables you to sort information in multiple ways and even create custom sorts. To sort a list or database, select the information and choose Data, Sort to open the Sort dialog box and specify your sort preferences (see Figure 18.10).

If you don't select anything before opening the Sort dialog box, Excel selects what it assumes is the list—all data contiguous to the active cell, minus the first row, which Excel assumes to be the header row. If your list contains possible blank lines or cells, select the list yourself before starting the sort process, or parts of the list might be excluded from the sort. Individual blank cells will not cause Excel to exclude data. Data gets excluded when the entire list is broken up by a row and/or a column of blank cells.

Figure 18.10
Use the Sort dialog box to specify the way you want to sort the list or selection.

If the cell pointer is in a list with no (apparent) header row, Excel selects the No Header Row option. If the list appears to include labels, Excel chooses Header Row and uses the labels as column indicators in the Sort By drop-down lists. When you manually select the data, the sensing feature is disabled. If the automatic selection includes your header row, specify the Header Row option in the Sort dialog box to avoid sorting your field names with the rest of the list (refer to Figure 18.5). If you accidentally end up sorting the field names into the list, use Undo immediately after the sort process to restore the list.

NOTE

> You can sort data in any column or row—it doesn't have to be a list. If you're just beginning a new worksheet, for example, you can start by entering a list of contact names, projects, inventory or catalog numbers, and so on. You can enter this information in random order and then sort it in the same way that you sort a list containing multiple columns/fields.

You can sort the list by up to three fields, in *ascending order* (0–9 and A–Z) or *descending order* (9–0 and Z–A). Excel can sort alphabetically, numerically, or by date. By selecting the Options button in the Sort dialog box, you can choose the left-to-right sort rather than the default top-to-bottom sort, in case your list has a horizontal rather than vertical orientation. You can also make the sort case sensitive—that is, sort such entries as *Oak* and *oak* separately because one is capitalized and the other isn't. In a case-sensitive ascending sort, all lowercase letters come before uppercase levels, so *oak* would come before *Ant*, for example. When running case-sensitive sorts, Ascending results in the lowercase text appearing first;

Descending places the lowercase text last (for details, see the later sidebar "Understanding Excel Sort Sequences").

If your list is located contiguous to other data that isn't part of the list, or if you're sorting selected data that isn't part of a list at all, Excel might warn you that you might not have selected the entire list and ask whether you meant to include all the contiguous data (see Figure 18.11). The assumption is that the entire list is contiguous, and that nothing else is located next to the list.

Figure 18.11
This dialog box indicates that the selection might not include the entire list.

If you meant to include all the contiguous data, accept the default setting, Expand the Selection; otherwise, choose Continue with the Current Selection.

Understanding Excel Sort Sequences

If you're unfamiliar with how computers "think," you might be surprised by how Excel sorts your data. Excel sorts left to right, character by character, beginning with numbers first, then spaces, symbols, and finally letters. If your list contains names that include spaces, Excel might not sort them the way you would expect (or prefer). For example, consider the following list of names:

List	Sorted Ascending
McArdle	Mc Ardle
Mc Ardle	Mc Lean
McCandle	McArdle
Mc Lean	McCandle

Because Mc Lean includes a space, it falls before any names beginning with Mc that don't include a space. When sorting, Excel ignores apostrophes (in names such as H'ailea, for example), but sorts words with hyphens (-) to last position after the same word with no hyphen. For example, consider the following list of names that differ only in that one includes a space and one includes a hyphen.

List	Sorted Ascending
Barkley-North	Barkley North
Barkley North	BarkleyNorth
BarkleyNorth	Barkley-North

18

The name with the space comes first, followed by the one with no space, and last of all the name containing a hyphen.

You also might be baffled by sorts that include numbers with letters. If your part numbers run from B1 through B102, for example, this is how Excel sorts them:

B1

B10

B100

B101

B11

B12

B2

B20

If you want the part numbers to sort correctly, insert zeros when numbering: B001, B002, and so on.

Excel uses the following sort sequence: 0–9 (space) ! " # $ % & ( ) * , . / : ; ? @ [\ ] ^ _ ` { | } ~ + < = > A–Z and a-z.

Blank cells or rows (depending on the sort selection) are sorted to the bottom of the list, whether you sort in descending or ascending order. When sorting values, note that FALSE comes before TRUE, and error values are all equal (but note that they appear in the original order in which they occurred). Ascending sorts place errors at the bottom; descending sorts place them at the top.

You can combine sorts to get the information the way you want it. For example, a common scenario would be sorting a customer list numerically by purchase, and then alphabetically by name, and perhaps including a third sort by contact name.

Because the Sort Ascending and Sort Descending buttons sort based on the position of the active cell, if you don't select any data—perhaps you merely clicked somewhere in the column by which you want the list sorted—the column containing the active cell becomes the sort key.

Reusing Sort Ascending and Sort Descending repeats any sorting options selected in the Sort dialog box.

FILTERING A LIST

Lists grow quickly, and soon locating a particular record in the list can take more time than you like. When you just want to view a particular record or records, *filtering* the list enables you to display only the selected information you want to see. The list itself is unchanged; you use the filter to specify exactly which data you want to see at that particular moment, and hide the remaining records. You can change the filter at any time to display a different set of records. The filtered records can be formatted, edited, and even charted. The active filter is saved with the workbook. (Note, however, that Excel allows only one list at a time to be filtered on a worksheet.)

Excel offers two types of filtering. An *AutoFilter* applies an automatic (simple) selection filter to a list, which you then can customize. An *advanced filter* enables you to specify more elaborate criteria for filtering.

CAUTION

Filtering demonstrates a major reason for making sure data is entered consistently. The filter treats entries that are typed inconsistently (for example, *Evans' Plumbing* and *Evans Plumbing*) as two different items. Excel does not treat them as one and the same.

TIP FROM

The fastest method of filtering a list is to use the AutoFilter button. You can add this button to any toolbar, as described in Chapter 27, "Customizing Excel to Fit Your Working Style."

MANAGING THE LIST WITH AUTOFILTERS

To apply an AutoFilter to a list, select a cell anywhere in the list and choose Data, Filter, AutoFilter. This command is a toggle; repeat it to turn off the AutoFilter at any time.

In a list with an AutoFilter, Excel displays arrow buttons for each entry in the header row (see Figure 18.12). These buttons activate pull-down menus that allow you to show individual records for viewing one at time or multiple records with the same entry in that particular field—for example, all records that list Minnesota as the project name or all records with ORE TYPE D as the category.

When you first set up an AutoFilter, Excel displays the AutoFilter drop-down buttons on the column headings but leaves the entire list displayed. To display a filtered list of records, use one or more drop-down buttons until the list narrows to the desired set of records. To display the records just mentioned, you would click the AutoFilter button in the PROJECT field name cell and select MINNESOTA, or use the CATEGORY button and select ORE TYPE D.

Using more than one AutoFilter button creates a combined filter. In the Mining Corporation example, selecting MINNESOTA in the PROJECT column narrows the displayed records to just those referring to the Minnesota project. If you then use the CATEGORY button to select ORE TYPE D, Excel displays only MINNESOTA records that list ORE TYPE D in the CATEGORY column, as shown in Figure 18.13. The arrows change color on the AutoFilter buttons that are currently in use—from black to blue.

18

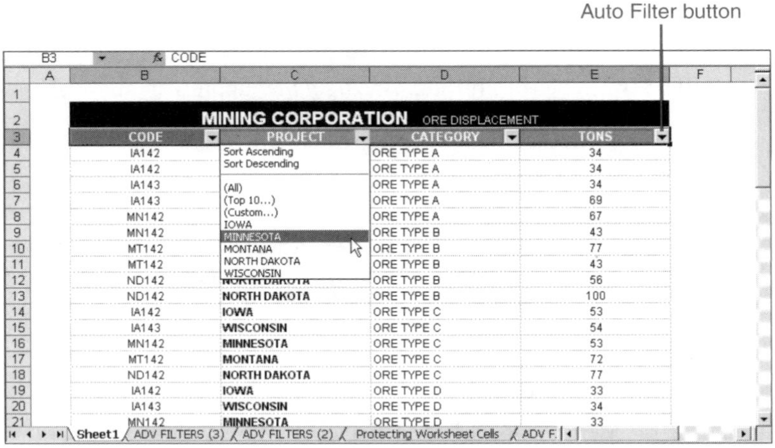

18

Auto Filter button

Figure 18.12
Use the AutoFilter button next to a column heading to open a drop-down list of choices for filtering that column.

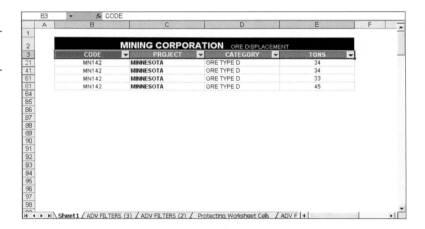

Figure 18.13
This AutoFilter combination displays only the single ORE TYPE D record for the MINNESOTA project.

The items at the top and bottom of the AutoFilter drop-down list provide special filtering options, as described in the following list:

- **(All)**—Lists all the records in that category. Use this option to redisplay the entire list for that column after filtering for specific records. The All option will not display all the records if other columns were also filtered.

- **(Top 10...)**—Applies only   to columns containing numbers or dates. Displays the Top 10 AutoFilter dialog box, in which you can specify records at the top or bottom of the list numerically (see Figure 18.14). You aren't limited to 10 records; you can specify that you want to see just the top or bottom (1) record, 50 records, or any number you prefer. To display the top or bottom 10% (or 15%, 50%, and so on) of your records, change the setting in the third combo box from Items to Percent.

Figure 18.14
Use the Top 10 AutoFilter dialog box to display a selected number of records.

NOTE

> The Top 10 AutoFilter doesn't sort the displayed records, but you can sort them after the filter using the Data, Sort command if you want to see them in numeric order—for example, to list former employees in order by termination date. Excel 2003 also allows you to sort ascending and sort descending.

- **(Custom...)**—Displays the Custom AutoFilter dialog box, in which you can specify a more detailed filtering option. (See the next section for details.)
- **(Blanks)**—Displays the records containing blanks in a particular field (column). Use this option to find records that have missing entries.
- **(NonBlanks)**—Displays all records containing any entries in that field (nonblanks). Use this option to display only records for which entries have been made in that field—for example, a nonprofit organization might enter contributions for the current year in a particular column. Records with such listings could then be displayed, sorted, and merged with an end-of-year letter to donors regarding tax deductibility of contributions.

The (Blanks) and (NonBlanks) entries appear only if the column contains empty cells.

CREATING A CUSTOM AUTOFILTER

If the default AutoFilter doesn't provide enough options, you can create a *custom AutoFilter*. Follow these steps:

1. From the drop-down AutoFilter list, choose (Custom...).
2. In the Custom AutoFilter dialog box, specify the custom criteria to use for filtering your list. Figure 18.15 shows the criteria for selecting records with values between two specified points—greater than 34 and less than 56.
3. Click OK.

Only records within the specified range show up in the filtered list (see Figure 18.16). You can customize the filtering even more by creating additional custom AutoFilters for other fields in the list.

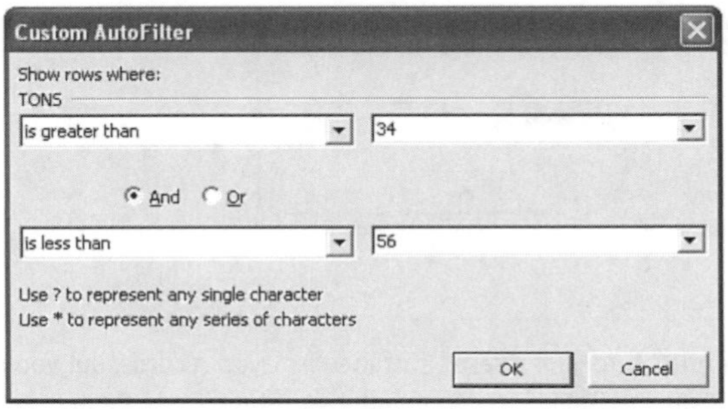

Figure 18.15
The Custom AutoFilter dialog box enables you to display only records that meet the specified criteria.

Figure 18.16
Only records matching the custom AutoFilter criteria are displayed.

Only records of the specified tonnage are shown

To display more than one type of entry in a particular field—for example, to display entries for two different projects in the Mining Corporation list—enter the first criterion (the *comparison operator*) in the first set of boxes in the Custom AutoFilter dialog box; then enter the value criterion in the second set of boxes. Select the And button if you want both sets of criteria met; select Or if you want records that meet either of the criteria. Figure 18.17 shows how to set the custom AutoFilter to display either the Minnesota or Wisconsin projects. For this example, you could use either contains or equals as the operator.

TIP FROM

You can use wildcard characters to select records in which the entries vary by a single character (?) or multiple characters (*). To find entries that begin with the same character(s)—for example, anyone named *Smith, Smithe, Smythe*, and so on—search for records that contain *Sm**. To find records in which the apostrophe is missing from *Evans' Plumbing*, search for *Evans?Plumbing*, which would display the incorrect *Evans Plumbing* but not the correct *Evans' Plumbing*.

Figure 18.17
Use the Or button if you want Excel to display records that meet either of the criteria in this dialog box.

USING THE ADVANCED FILTER

An *advanced filter* is similar to a custom AutoFilter. The difference is that you specify your *criteria* in a *range* outside the list—using the field names in the header row—and then specify the criteria under one or more field names on which you want the filter based. The Advanced filter was made to create criteria that the AutoFilter simply can't handle. For example, if you were looking for records whose project was IOWA, WISCONSIN, or MONTANA, the AutoFilter limits you to only two choices. With the Advanced Filter, you can type as many states under the PROJECT field (in the criteria range) as required. In addition, the Advanced Filter allows you to use the OR parameter across fields. This cannot be done using the AutoFilter. By placing IOWA under PROJECT on one row and >50 on a different row under TONS (in the criteria range), the Advanced filter will return records that either have IOWA PROJECTs OR TONS greater than 50. Figure 18.18 shows the Mining Corporation list with a criteria range set up in D3:E6. Notice that the criteria range includes the column heading (field name) above the specified criteria. To use an advanced filter, your list must include field names for use in the criteria range. The worksheet also must include at least one blank row between the criteria range and the list.

The field names in the criteria range must match the field names in the list exactly, except for case (*Category* and *category* will both work, for example).

TIP FROM

Copy the field names to the criteria range rather than typing them, to prevent errors.

Figure 18.18
The criteria range determines the displayed entries in the list.

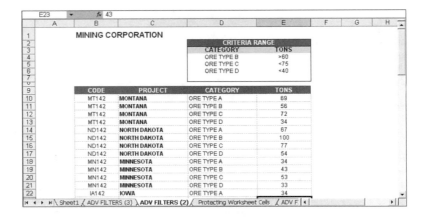

TIP FROM

Before starting the advanced filter, select the list and assign it the range name Database. If you plan to extract filtered records to a different area of the worksheet, select that area also and give it the range name Extract. Excel automatically uses these named ranges in the Advanced Filter dialog box. The Criteria range name is automatically created/redefined each time you specify a criteria range, so there's no need to name this range yourself. To access name range select Insert, Name, Define, to assign a name range.

To create an advanced filter, follow these steps:

1. Create the criteria range, specifying the field names in one row and the desired criteria directly below. If possible, place the criteria range above the corresponding columns that you plan to filter for easy viewing of both.

2. To specify multiple criteria, add more rows to the criteria range.

3. When the criteria range is complete, click anywhere in the list and choose Data, Filter, Advanced Filter to open the Advanced Filter dialog box (see Figure 18.19).

Figure 18.19
The Advanced Filter dialog box enables you to select the list range and criteria range.

4. Excel selects the list automatically if it's bounded by blank rows and columns. If the range in the List Range box is incorrect, select or type the correct range.

5. Specify the Criteria Range.

6. Click OK to run the filter. Figure 18.20 shows the result in the Mining Corporation example.

Figure 18.20
The results from the advanced filter match those specified in the criteria range.

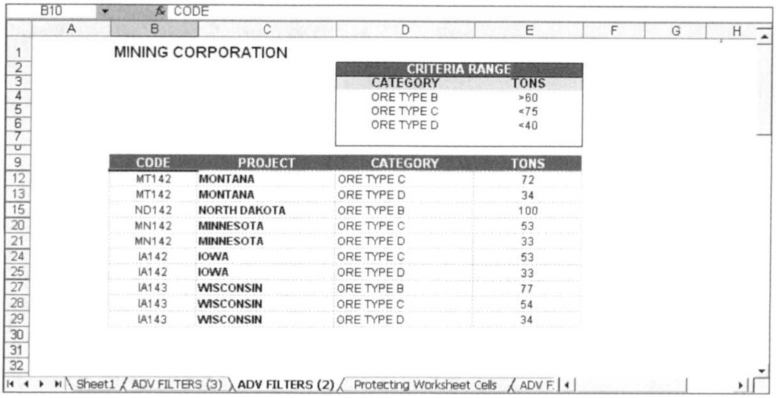

To show the entire list again, select Data, Filter, Show All.

Use the Advanced Filter when you need to do any of the following:

- Perform an OR condition across multiple fields.
- Specify more than two criteria in one field.
- Handle extremely complex criteria, requiring the use of functions/formulas, as well as multiple AND/OR criteria in one filter.

You can change the entries in the criteria range at any point to display a different set of filtered records. The list responds to the new criteria when you run advanced autofilter again.

COPYING RECORDS TO A NEW LOCATION

When you use an advanced filter, you can specify a separate location where you want the filtered records copied; for example, to create a separate list of former clients. Select the Copy to Another Location option in the Advanced Filter dialog box and specify the target cell or range in the Copy To box. Excel will copy just the filtered records to the new location.

SELECTING UNIQUE RECORDS

If your list contains names or records that appear repeatedly, you might want to extract just the unique records. For example, in a list that includes state information, you might want to know how many states are represented in the list. To display only the unique records (a single record of each type), select the Unique Records Only option in the Advanced Filter dialog box. Excel hides all the duplicates.

ADDING FORM CONTROLS TO YOUR WORKSHEETS

Form controls in Excel include check boxes, drop-down lists, spinners, and so on that you can add to charts, lists, and other areas of your worksheets to create custom forms for use in data entry and data management. There are multiple ways to use form controls, but the underlying premise is to use form controls in conjunction with formulas. Form controls can link to a cell, and then you can apply a formula that addresses the link to look up the information or calculate a value based on the information. For example, suppose you're creating a standard bid sheet for different types of construction equipment. A check box on the form could be set up so that if it's checked, Excel automatically includes a specific type of equipment with its rate in the bid.

You can use form controls with tables, lists, charts, and even PivotTables. The controls actually are simple to create and use. After you set up your worksheet, you then apply the controls from the Forms toolbar as needed to fit your situation. The form in Figure 18.21, for example, uses a simple drop-down list to extract an equipment number. Formulas tied to the cell link then extract the corresponding values. Some form controls can be tied to Excel macros or VBA programs to perform tasks. For information on writing Excel macros and simple VBA applications, see Chapter 31, "Recording and Editing a Macro," and Chapter 32, "Creating Interactive Excel Applications with VBA."

NOTE

If you have some experience writing Visual Basic code or Web scripts, you can use ActiveX controls from the Control toolbox in Excel to create custom applications for Excel. These topics are beyond the scope of this book, but Que Publishing (www.quepublishing.com) offers a wide variety of other books that specifically cover Visual Basic and ActiveX. You also can consult the Excel Help system for limited guidance on using the ActiveX controls with Excel.

Table 18.1 describes the form controls available from the Forms toolbar.

TABLE 18.1 CONTROLS ON THE FORMS TOOLBAR

Button	Name	Description
Aa	Label	Places a label in the worksheet for use in naming other controls.
abl	Edit Box	Creates a data-entry box for forms. (This control doesn't work on worksheets.)

Button	Name	Description
	Group Box	Groups option buttons together so they all refer to the same link cell. Using two groups allows additional cell links for additional groups of option buttons.
	Button	Runs a macro.
	Check Box	Produces a TRUE or FALSE response when selected or deselected.
	Option Button	When placed in a group with other option buttons, returns the number of the option button selected in the group. Use additional groups to generate a different set of options (new cell link).
	List Box	Returns the number of the item selected in the list.
	Combo Box	Combines a list box and an edit box.
	Combination List-Edit	A combined list and text box. This feature is not available on a worksheet.
	Combination Drop-Down Edit	A drop-down list with an edit box. This feature is not available on a worksheet.
	Scroll Bar	A draggable scrollbar that allows for high and low limits, as well as incremental change.
	Spinner	A counter that allows for high and low limits, as well as incremental change (a scrollbar control without the scroll box between the arrows).
	Control Properties	Displays a dialog box of options for the selected control.
	Edit Code	Enables you to edit or create VBA code associated with the selected control.
	Toggle Grid	Turns the grid lines of a worksheet on or off.
	Run Dialog	Displays the dialog box on the active dialog sheet. Used as a test or preview of the dialog box drawn. This feature is unavailable on a worksheet.

18

To apply form controls to a list or form, display the Forms toolbar (choose View, Toolbars, Forms), click the desired tool, and draw the control on the worksheet. After you create the control, you can format it and set its properties as desired.

Drop-down list form control

Figure 18.21
Form controls applied to lists allow for minimal formula writing and can serve as a great analytical tool.

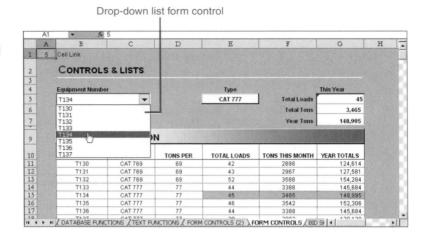

The following steps describe the process of creating the Equipment Number drop-down list shown earlier (refer to Figure 18.21):

1. On the Forms toolbar, click the Combo Box tool (see Figure 18.22).

Figure 18.22
The combo box control creates a drop-down list of entries from which you can choose.

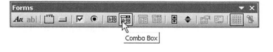

2. Draw the control on the worksheet by holding down the left mouse button and dragging the crosshair to the desired size (see Figure 18.23). To create a default-size control, just click in the worksheet. To modify the control size drag the sizing handles.

"Drawing" the control

Figure 18.23
Draw the form control to the desired size above the list. You can resize the control later, if necessary.

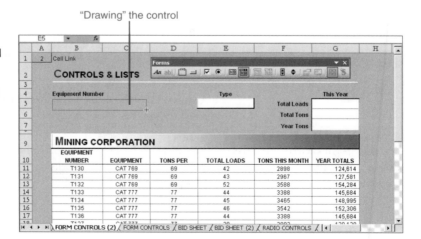

3. Right-click the form control, and select Format Control from the context menu (see Figure 18.24) or click the Control Properties button on the Forms toolbar. The Format Control dialog box appears.

Right-click the control to open context menu

Figure 18.24
Select Format Control from the context menu to establish the range and cell link for the control.

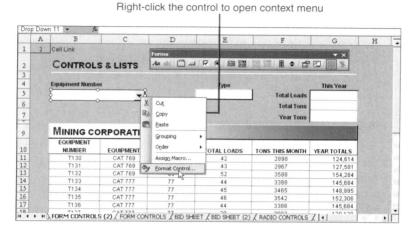

4. In the Format Control dialog box, select the Control tab. In the Input Range box, specify the range of the data you want to display in the drop-down list in the combo box. In Figure 18.25, the range is the Equipment Number column from the list.

Figure 18.25
In the Format Control dialog box, format the control and establish the cell link and list range.

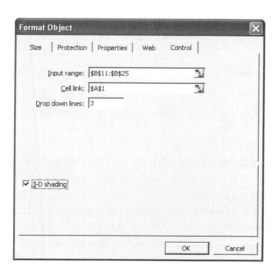

18

5. Input the cell link your formulas will reference in the Cell Link combo box. The cell link can be any cell on any worksheet in any workbook (although the current workbook is recommended). In the example, the cell link is in cell A1 on the worksheet containing the control. The cell link displays the item number of the chosen value on the list. A link value of 2, for example, would refer to the second item on the drop-down list.

6. Establish the number of drop-down lines you want to display in the Drop Down Lines combo box. If the number of items in the list exceeds the number of drop-down lines displayed, Excel displays a scrollbar that the user can click to scroll the list and display the rest of the entries. You need to use this option only if you want to restrict the number of lines shown in the drop-down list. By default, Excel automatically displays as many or as few lines as needed. In this example, the number of lines is set to three so the list won't cover the list below the control.

7. If desired, check the 3D Shading option to give the control a three-dimensional look.

8. Set additional options for the control as desired on other tabs in the dialog box. The following list describes some of the options:

   - **Colors and Lines (option and check boxes only)**—Determines the color, line, and arrow styles used for the control.
   - **Size**—Sets the control's size, scale, and so on.
   - **Protection**—Locks the object or its text to prevent changes by users when the worksheet is protected.
   - **Properties**—Manipulates the control's reaction to sizing, moving, adding, or deleting cells as well as printing the object with the worksheet.
   - **Web**—Specifies the alternative text you want to display on Web browsers when loading the object or when pictures are not displayed.

9. Click OK when the settings are complete.

10. Click anywhere on the worksheet to deselect the control.

11. To test the control, click the down arrow and select a record so that the cell link is activated (see Figure 18.26).

Now that you have created the control, create a formula that references the link cell to activate this model. So, if you want to find the Equipment type for the selected Equipment number then using this formula in cell E5 (=INDEX(C11:C25,A1,1)) checks the value in the Cell link cell (A1) and uses it to return the corresponding entry in the range C11:C25. You also can use =INDEX($C$11:$G$25,$A$1,2). Specifying the entire table (minus the equipment column) for the Reference argument and making the first two arguments absolute enables you to copy the formula to the other cells (G5:G7). All you would need to do then is change the Column argument in the pasted formulas.

Figure 18.26
Select a record from the new control to activate the cell link.

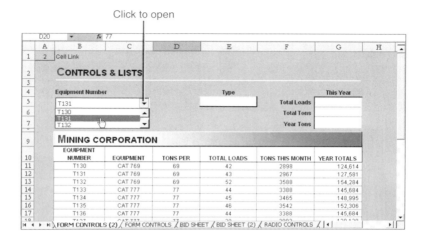

Click to open

Figure 18.27
Attach or reference formulas to the link and the list. The control then activates the cell link and the formula extracts the values.

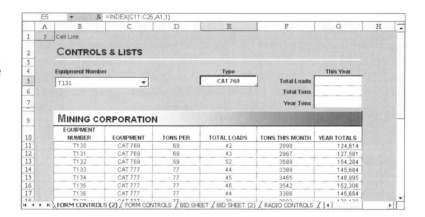

For each item you want to extract and or pull up, select a cell and create the index formula.

USING CONTROLS WITH CALCULATION TABLES

At this point, you might think form controls are a nice feature, but you may be unsure how you can really put them to good use. Think of using form controls in terms of a formula that's triggered by a form control's result. The result is an automated model.

Figure 18.28 shows a worksheet that uses check boxes, spinners, and text boxes to create a *calculation table* that determines whether certain criteria are met. In this case, the user selects the equipment to be used by way of the check boxes to the left of the Equipment column; the client is charged by the number of weeks using that equipment. Spinners to the left of the check boxes are used to determine the number of weeks for each of the different breakouts.

Figure 18.28
You can use check
boxes and spinners in
conjunction with cal-
culation tables to
automate bid sheets
or calculation tables
of any kind.

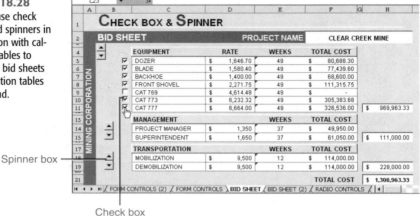

Spinner box

Check box

In this particular example, the check boxes are selected by default, as shown in Figure 18.29.
Thus, the check box control establishes a TRUE value in the linked cell. Using the Unchecked
option results in FALSE, and the Mixed option results in #NA.

NOTE

Mixed isn't a value that the user can select when clicking the control. It's the shading
effect that appears in the check box when #NA appears in the linked cell. It's normally
used to change the appearance of the control by changing the cell link value via programming. Formulas can't directly alter the contents of other cells, so there's no way to
change the value of the linked cell (to #NA) unless you manually type it in or change it
using VBA code.

Figure 18.29
A check box returns
the result FALSE if
unchecked, TRUE if
checked, and #NA if
mixed.

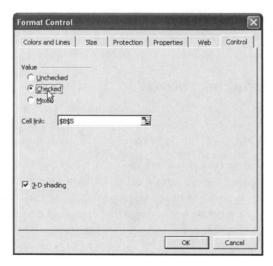

You can use a check box as an indicator only by placing a formula in the linked cell itself. For example, you can enter a nested IF formula in the linked cell that evaluates to TRUE, FALSE, or #NA. The formula's result then changes the look of the check box. To prevent users from using the check box (and thereby eliminating the cell link's formula), lock it (and its associated linked cell); then protect the worksheet.

The cell link for the row 5 check box is in cell B5, as shown in Figure 18.30. When checked, the check box returns the value TRUE, which is used by the IF statement in cell F5. Here is the syntax followed by an explanation:

=IF(*link_cell*,*true_result*,*false_result*)

- ■ ***link_cell***—The link cell in B5 returns the result TRUE if checked, FALSE if not. The IF statement refers to the link cell looking for a match.

- ■ ***true_result***—The TRUE result occurs if the box is checked. If TRUE is found in the link cell, the formula calculates the total cost.

- ■ ***false_result***—The FALSE result in the formula is 0. So, if there's no match between the statement and the link cell, the result posted is 0.

Figure 18.30
Use an IF statement to perform a calculation if the cell link is TRUE.

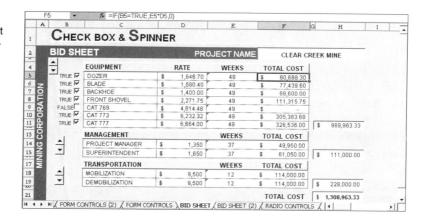

To hide the cell link value, format the cell so that the text color is identical to the background color. If the background is white, the text should be white. Alternatively, you can hide the column or row. Another way to handle this is to create Input Range data on one separate sheet, a sheet that serves as a central location for editing the lists, a sheet that can easily be hidden from users and does not require any special formatting. Text would, of course, be added to help identify each input range and cell link as well as the location where the input range/cell link was being used.

A spinner applies a number in a cell that incrementally increases or decreases, based on the specifications you provide on the Control tab in the Format Control dialog box (see Figure 18.31). Setting the minimum value of the spinner controls the lowest value the spinner will spin down to, and vice versa for the maximum value. The range is 0 to 30,000. Specifying an incremental change setting tells Excel to move the values up or down by the specified increment with each click of the spin arrows.

Figure 18.31
The spinner control enables you to apply maximum and minimum values and also apply an incremental change by which the spinner will increase or decrease the linked cell value.

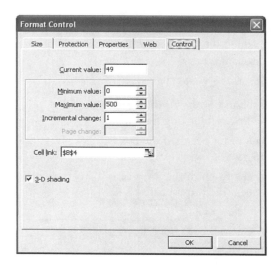

Setting the Weeks in the example equal to the value of the link cell for the spinner changes the Weeks to match the spinner (see Figure 18.32). For example, if the cell link to the spinner is in cell B4 (as in this example), apply =B4 to all the cells that you want to refer to the cell link. B4 drives the weeks of the equipment usage. In turn, this changes all the calculations for the final cost.

Figure 18.32
Make the Weeks equal to the spinner Cell Link, so that the Weeks change when the spinner is used.

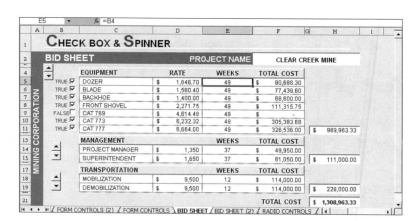

USING CONTROLS WITH CHARTS

You might never have thought of adding form controls to your charts, but the example in Figure 18.33 shows another way that form controls can be helpful. Here, a scrollbar controls the values displayed in the chart. The user can drag the scroll box, click the scroll track, or click the scroll arrows to change the quarter values displayed on the chart. The changes are incremental jumps you set when formatting the control. A drop-down list control also would work for switching between quarters.

→ For more information on creating charts with form controls, **see** Chapter 23, "Professional Charting Techniques."

Figure 18.33
You most often use scrollbars when you have large differences from the lowest value to the highest value. This example demonstrates scrolling through quarters.

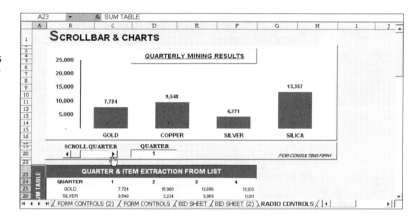

When drawing a scrollbar control, draw from left to right for a horizontal scrollbar or top to bottom for a vertical scrollbar. Set the value options to a desired high, low, incremental, and page change (see Figure 18.34). A *page change* is just an incremental jump when you click the scroll track.

Figure 18.34
Set the ceiling and floor that the scroll will reach up to and drop down to.

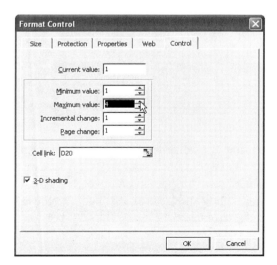

To create a chart that responds to the control, you'll need to create a table that references the cell link. Following is one way to do this:

1. For this example, please access the workbook on the CD. Create a SUM(IF formula that extracts the product by quarter from the list (see Figure 18.35). The formula shown here looks up the quarter in column B from the list against cell C$24, which is the quarter indicator 1. Then, it looks up the product in column C from the list against the product indicator in cell $B25, Gold. If these conditions are met, then the sum of column F—which is the total quantity for that quarter and product—is applied to the formula cell.

   The calculation could also be written this way:

   `{=SUM(($B$39:$B$86=C$24)*($C$39:$C$86=$B25)*($F$39:$F$86))}`

   Figure 18.35 shows the formula that references the cell link in cell D20. The IF statement just states that if the cell link equals 1, apply the value in cell C25, else FALSE (0). Notice the absolute referencing. When the formula is copied to the right, it references Q2, then Q3, and so on. This way, you need to create the formula only once. When it's filled to the right, the references adjust accordingly.

TIP FROM

For this tip, please refer to the workbook on the CD. If you prefer, you could combine this formula with the SUM(IF array used in the first table into one nested array formula, thereby eliminating the need for the SUM table.

Figure 18.35
Create a SUM IF table that extracts the product and quarter.

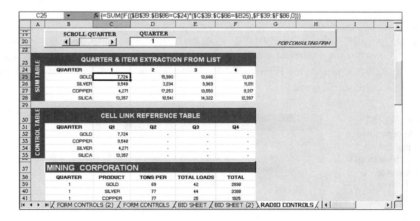

2. Create a column chart from the cell link reference table, setting the series to columns (see Figure 18.36).

   You set the series to columns to display the product rather than quarters on the category x-axis. The product will be displayed all the time, and the quarters respond to the selected quarter from the scrollbar.

Figure 18.36
Set the series to columns.

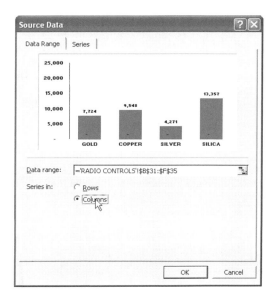

3. Select the data series in the chart, and choose Format, Selected Data Series.

4. Select the Options tab in the Format Data Series dialog box.

5. Set the overlap to 100 and the gap width to 80. This will place the columns over each other so that they don't move along the axis. The Y axis on the chart has been set to include a maximum/minimum value.

6. Click OK.

CONTROL CHARACTERISTICS

Form controls offer different results depending on the control. You'll notice that the check-box control shown in Figure 18.37 generates a true/false result based on whether the control is checked or not. The other controls result in numeric results. The control used should be dependent on the model you're creating. For example, Figure 18.32 uses a check box to include or eliminate a type of equipment being used in the bid sheet. The Spinner in the model generates a value that quantifies the amount of time the equipment will be used.

Figure 18.37 shows a variety of controls:

■ The List Box applies a cell link in the form of the number of the chosen record.

■ The Combo Box does the same, but uses a drop-down list instead of a scrolling list.

■ The Scrollbar and Spinner are similar controls, but the scrollbar allows for horizontal orientation, as well as page change scrolling—an incremental jump when the scroll track is clicked. You can also grab the scroll box and slide it along the scroll track.

■ The Check Box applies the cell link result of TRUE, FALSE, or #NA.

- The Option Buttons create stacked numbers associated with the number of option buttons. For example, Option Button 2 is stacked number 2 in the cell link. If you create a new group of option buttons, that group's cell link numbers start from 1 again.

Figure 38.37
Controls and their characteristics are shown here.

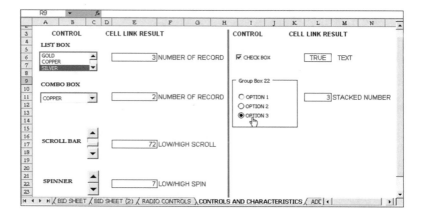

TROUBLESHOOTING

INTERSECTING POINTS IN LISTS OR TABLES

My index formula doesn't work when I try to pull up two intersecting points within a list.

Use the Lookup Wizard to help you rewrite formulas with complex INDEX(MATCH cases. (Use this tool as a way to learn indexing and matching formulas as well.)

COMPLEX FORMULAS

The formula has become too long to understand.

Use named ranges to simplify formulas. (But do this only for ranges that generally don't change.) You also can apply a range that's much longer than the list; as the list grows, the new cells with data will be included in the range.

FORMULAS ARE SLOWING DOWN THE WORKBOOK

How can I increase the performance of a workbook that seems lethargic?

One option is to turn off automatic calculation. Choose Tools, Options, click the Calculation tab in the Options dialog box, and select Manual. To then calculate the workbook, press F9. Another way to increase efficiency is to use form controls for looking up information. Finally, if possible, use PivotTables—the most efficient way to summarize large amounts of data in a workbook.

PARSING A LIST OF NAMES

I've inherited a list with first and last names combined and random capitalization. What's the best way to fix this problem?

To separate the combined names in a list, use the Text to Columns feature on the Data menu. To fix random capitalization, use the text `UPPER()` or `LOWER()` function in an adjacent row or column and then paste the final result back in the list as values (use Paste Special).

EXCEL IN PRACTICE

Formulas can be used alone or combined with form controls to become powerful extraction devices. Figure 18.38 shows a conditional sum formula that extracts the year totals for equipment number T133. However, by using a combo box form control, you can tie several index formulas to one cell link, as shown in cell A1 of Figure 18.39. This setup can pull up multiple bits of information at once. The worksheet is easier to use, and it's more efficient to hook formulas into a cell link and pull up line-item data with index formulas. (You could also use PivotTables to summarize this information.)

EQUIPMENT NUMBER	EQUIPMENT	TONS PER	TOTAL LOADS	TONS THIS MONTH	YEAR TOTALS
T130	CAT 769	69	42	2898	124,614
T131	CAT 769	69	43	2967	127,581
T132	CAT 769	69	52	3588	154,284
T133	CAT 777	77	44	3388	145,684
T134	CAT 777	77	45	3465	148,995
T135	CAT 777	77	46	3542	152,306
T136	CAT 777	77	44	3388	145,684
T137	CAT 777	77	39	3003	129,129
T138	CAT 777	77	42	3234	139,062
T139	CAT 777	77	22	1694	72,842
T140	CAT 777	77	32	2464	105,952
T141	CAT 777	77	25	1925	82,775
T142	CAT 777	77	32	2464	105,952

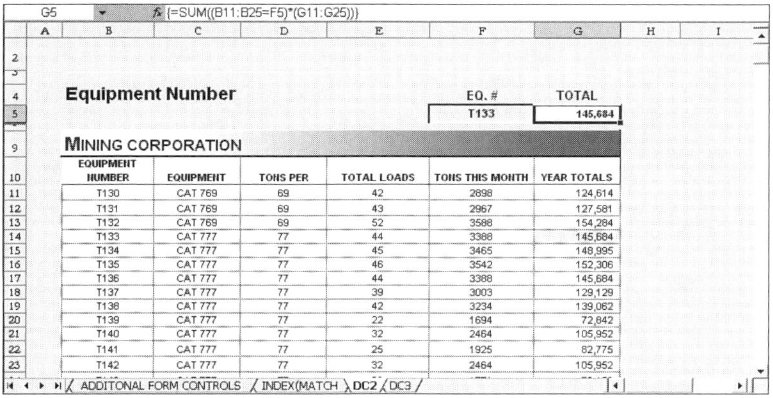

Figure 18.38
This SUM function works efficiently to total the amounts for a particular piece of equipment, but you must input the equipment number in cell F5 to look up a new piece of equipment's total, which could be subject to misspellings or wrong equipment numbers.

		TONS PER	TOTAL LOADS	TONS THIS MONTH	YEAR TOTALS
T130	CAT 769	69	42	2898	124,614
T131	CAT 769	69	43	2967	127,581
T132	CAT 769	69	52	3588	154,284
T133	CAT 777	77	44	3388	145,684
T134	CAT 777	77	45	3465	148,995
T135	CAT 777	77	46	3542	152,306
T136	CAT 777	77	44	3388	145,684
T137	CAT 777	77	39	3003	129,129
T138	CAT 777	77	42	3234	139,062
T139	CAT 777	77	22	1694	72,842

Figure 18.39
Form controls make lookups easy.

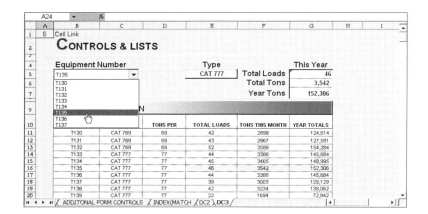

OUTLINING, SUBTOTALING, AND AUDITING WORKSHEET DATA

In this chapter

Organizing and Auditing Your Data   440

Grouping or Outlining Data   440

Consolidating Data   447

Creating Automatic Subtotals   450

Validating and Auditing Data Entry   453

ORGANIZING AND AUDITING YOUR DATA

As mentioned often in other chapters of this book, structuring the data in your workbooks is essential to using them effectively. Structure is particularly crucial if you plan to extract, chart, pivot, or create reports from the data. If the worksheet is put together randomly, without good planning, reorganizing, and reporting, it later can cost a lot of time and frustration. When a worksheet is well structured, on the other hand, you can take full advantage of Excel's data-management features to display, print, and report precisely what you want.

Chapter 18, "Using Excel's Data-Management Features," describes the Excel options for sorting and filtering. See Chapter 1, "Getting Around Excel," for protecting your workbook with passwords and file encryption. This chapter continues with data-management features by providing details on outlining and grouping, consolidating, and using data validation and auditing to help prevent, locate, and correct data errors.

GROUPING OR OUTLINING DATA

Outlining and *grouping* are two of Excel's data-management features. They're very similar. You can use grouping to effectively manage columns and rows with multiple levels of groups that display and hide information. Grouping data is different from outlining in that groups are defined to any depth, level, and location you want. An outline, on the other hand, is based on a structured list or table that has totals and subsets already built in.

TIP FROM

> When creating or establishing a workbook or database, don't move forward with the intention of just starting to create, and planning to incorporate the functionality as your needs grow. Outlines and groups are created from structure. If your list has no structure, your outline has little or no meaning for the user.
>
> To outline a list or table, consider working backward from the list and asking the question, "What information do I need to extract from the list?" If possible, write down the information and even how it's presented. This will help you work backward in planning the structure of the list.

Before launching into using the grouping and outlining features, you might want to create a custom toolbar for use with these features. Excel offers several useful outlining and grouping toolbar buttons that can be added to any toolbar or used as a separate custom toolbar. The custom toolbar includes buttons for creating, showing, and selecting visible cells in an outline or group. These buttons all come from the Edit category on the Commands tab in the Customize dialog box. Another helpful item that you could include is the Group and Outline menu from the Built-In Menus category on the same tab.

Table 19.1 describes the buttons on this custom toolbar. (You can include the buttons on any toolbar, of course, but it's helpful to combine these functions in one place.)

TABLE 19.1	OUTLINING/GROUPING TOOLBAR BUTTONS	
Button	**Name**	**Description**
	Show Outline Symbols	Shows the outline symbols along the rows and columns
	Group	Groups the selected rows or columns
	Ungroup	Ungroups the selected rows or columns
	Show Detail	Shows the detail by unhiding the hidden rows or columns for the selected group
	Hide Detail	Hides the detail of the selected group
	Select Visible Cells	Selects or highlights only the visible cells

→ For details on customizing the Excel toolbars, **see** "Modifying Toolbars," **p. 714**

GROUPING DATA

If Excel data contains common attributes, you can *group* the data to make it more readable. In the table in Figure 19.1, for example, the common groups are the months and then the quarters. This *hierarchical grouping* can be done with days, weeks, months, quarters, and years or any group of data with subsets. You also can reduce the list to lower levels, even minutes or seconds.

Figure 19.1
The table shown is known as a *hierarchical table*. The months are grouped by their respective quarters.

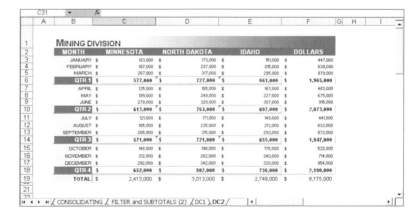

By creating a group, you can combine multiple rows or columns of information, enabling you to hide and show information with one click. To create a group, select the rows or columns you want to group and then choose Data, Group and Outline, Group. In the Group dialog box, specify whether you want to group Rows or Columns. (If you select the entire row/column, you won't get the Group dialog box; the grouping occurs automatically.)

Outline symbols appear on the left side of the worksheet for grouped rows and above the worksheet for grouped columns. Figure 19.2 displays the outline symbols for a group of rows. By clicking the outline buttons, you can hide or display the selected information, as shown in Figure 19.3. Excel calls these techniques *collapsing* and *expanding* the group. An outline button with a plus sign (+) indicates that the group is collapsed to show only the totals. A minus sign (–) indicates that the group is fully expanded.

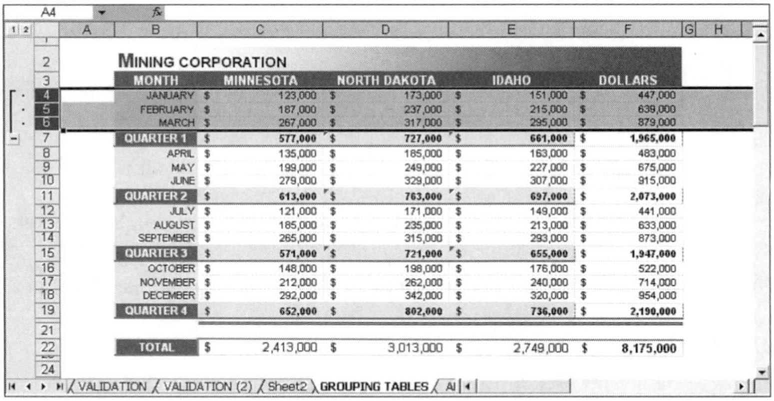

Figure 19.2
After you create a group, you can hide the group by clicking on the outline buttons shown on the left side of the worksheet.

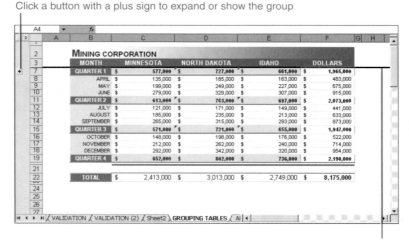

Click a button with a plus sign to expand or show the group

Figure 19.3
By creating a group, you can collapse (hide) the information so that the quarter is visible and the monthly information above it is hidden.

Rows 5 through 7 are collapsed to show only the total for Row 7

If you group the additional months (refer to Figure 19.1), you can show the quarters or the months by clicking the outline buttons. In addition, your list might contain additional levels, in which case *there will be additional* buttons numbered 3, 4, and so on. If there are more levels the buttons won't be numbered 3, 4, and so on, so much as there will be more buttons and the extra ones will be numbered 3, 4, and so on.

Notice how effective grouping can be after the groups have been created (see Figure 19.4).

Figure 19.4
Grouping the months enables you to view the summary of quarters, or the months if the groups are expanded.

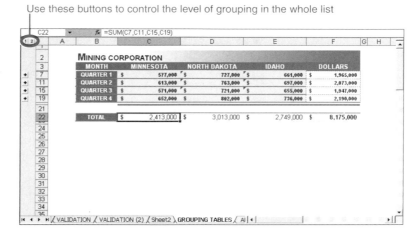

Use these buttons to control the level of grouping in the whole list

Not only can you group the rows but also the columns, as shown in Figure 19.5. By grouping the columns, you can collapse a view to the maximum—showing only totals for both rows and columns—as in Figure 19.6.

Figure 19.5
By grouping both rows and columns, you can collapse a list to show only totals.

Columns that will be hidden

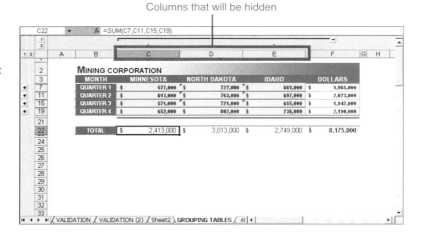

Excel enables you to add layers of groupings as well. This further enhances the capacity to create hierarchical groups. Notice the additional outline button added to the rows in Figure 19.7. To add an additional layer to the group, select the rows you want to hide, and choose Data, Group and Outline, Group (or click the Group button). Excel applies the group symbols and buttons for the additional layer.

Columns that are grouped or collapsed

Figure 19.6
The group now shows the lowest level of detail.

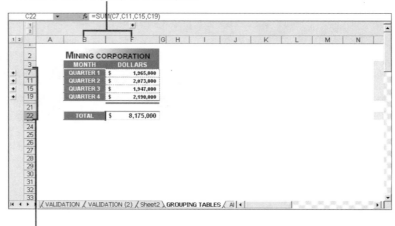

Rows that are grouped or collapsed

Figure 19.7
Excel enables you to create groups of groups for multiple-grouping scenarios.

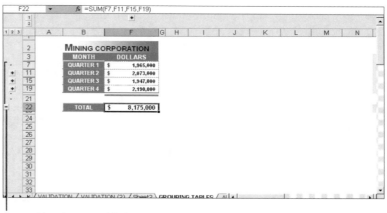

Second-level group added

After your list and groups are in place, you might want to restore the screen space lost to the outline symbols, while still keeping the grouping in place. Use the Show Outline Symbols toolbar button (refer to Table 19.1 in the preceding section) or press Ctrl+8 to hide and show the outline symbols. You also can turn the view of outline symbols off or on by choosing Tools, Options to open the Options dialog box, clicking the View tab, and selecting or deselecting Outline Symbols.

GROUPING SUMMARY TABLES

Now that you understand the basic logic of grouping, you can establish multiple summary tables on a single worksheet within a workbook and apply grouping symbols that apply to all the tables. If you have a workbook with several lists, for example, you might want to create one sheet that holds all your summary information. With this technique, you also can create custom views and reports easily and effectively. The key to creating summary tables on one worksheet with combined grouping is to establish similar setups for all the lists you plan to group. In Figure 19.8, for example, the geographic area tables—Australian and European, for example—are set up in similar fashion and the outline buttons apply to all.

Figure 19.8
By creating tables that are formatted consistently on a sheet within the workbook, you can apply groupings that apply to multiple tables.

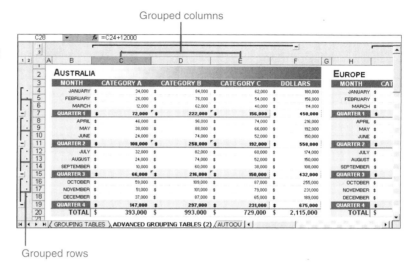

The groups summarize the information in an effective manner, as shown in Figure 19.9, and can be managed on a single screen at the highest level (see Figure 19.10).

Figure 19.9
The groups are collapsed by column.

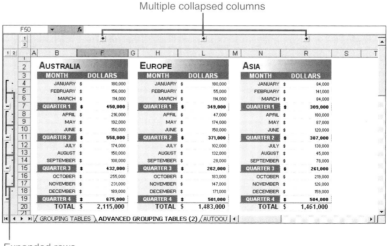

19

Figure 19.10
Collapsing the rows
brings all the tables
onto the screen at the
same time.

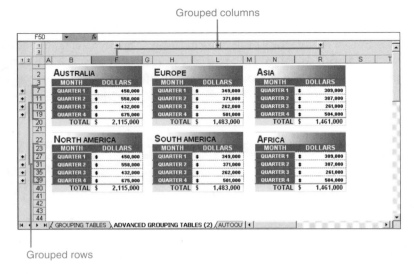

CREATING AN AUTO OUTLINE

Another way to outline a list is to use the *Auto Outline* feature. Auto Outline is a quick way to create an outline, but Excel first must understand the hierarchy of your list or database. You can apply all the groupings with one step if the list is structured in a manner that Excel understands. The information should be structured consistently throughout—for example, January, February, March, and then Q1 with no blank columns or rows as separators; then April, May, June, and Q2.

To create a multilevel Auto Outline, select Data, Group and Outline, Auto Outline. Excel applies outline symbols (see Figure 19.11). The active cell doesn't even need to be in the table/data set. You need only select the data if the worksheet includes more than one data set.

The Auto Outline feature depends on Excel's being able to detect the structure of your data automatically. If you get the error message Cannot create an outline, this means Excel doesn't see a logical structure to the data you're trying to outline. But you can place the outline symbols manually—to speed up the process, create the first outline, select the next range of data, and press F4 to repeat the last action.

CLEARING THE OUTLINE

To clear outline symbols, select the range of a single group or outline and use any of the following techniques:

- Choose Data, Group and Outline, Ungroup.
- Click the Ungroup button.
- Press Shift+Alt+left arrow.

- When eliminating all outlines, you can't have a range selected because it doesn't work properly if you do. For the previous three techniques, a range should be selected, but for this one, it shouldn't be.

Figure 19.11
The Auto Outline feature applies outline symbols to the list or table down to the lowest level defined by your list structure.

Select the range and choose AutoOutline

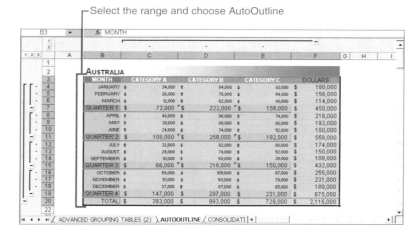

CHANGING THE OUTLINE SETTINGS

You can change the positioning of summary rows in the group or outline and apply Excel's built-in outline styles. Choose Data, Group and Outline, Settings to open the Settings dialog box. Specify whether you want summary rows placed below the detail and columns to the right of the detail (these are the default settings).

To apply Excel's built-in outline cell styles (RowLevel_1, ColLevel_1, and so on), select Automatic Styles in the Settings dialog box.

Clicking Create in the dialog box creates a new outline from the data on the active sheet with the settings you have specified in the dialog box. Clicking Apply Styles applies the settings to the existing outline.

CONSOLIDATING DATA

If you establish several lists or tables that have similar setups, you'll probably want to combine certain sets of data from these separate lists or tables into one consolidated list or table. Excel enables you to consolidate tables with the Consolidate command on the Data menu. Consolidation allows for analysis of the tables or lists with functions provided in the Consolidate dialog box.

The best way to consolidate a list or table is to set up a table that represents the format and layout of the original tables, like the example shown in Figure 19.12. Consolidation isn't limited to a worksheet or a workbook—you can consolidate data from the same worksheet, a different worksheet in the same workbook, other workbooks, or even from Lotus 1-2-3 files.

Figure 19.12
When consolidating a list or table, it's best to set up the consolidation destination with formats similar to those in the source tables.

Divisions to consolidate

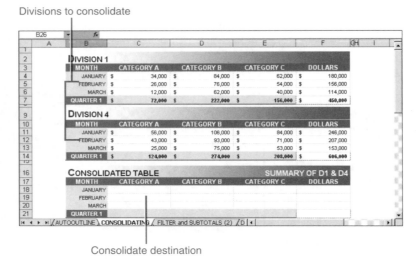

Consolidate destination

To create a consolidation table, follow these steps:

1. Select the destination for the consolidated data. In the example, the destination cell is C18.

NOTE

> Don't select multiple cells as the destination unless you're positive that the consolidated data will fit within the selected area; although other existing cells won't necessarily be overwritten, Excel might fail to consolidate parts of the source tables.

2. Choose Data, Consolidate to open the Consolidate dialog box.

3. Select the type of analysis you want to perform from the Function menu. In the example, the SUM function was used to add the data from the two worksheets

4. Under Reference, select the first range you want to include for consolidation. To select the range in the worksheet itself, use the Collapse Dialog button or just drag the dialog box out of the way and click in the worksheet. If the worksheet uses named ranges, you can type the range names in the dialog box, which saves time in selecting. In the example, the ranges are C4:F7 and C11:F14.

   Consolidation ranges are often found outside the active sheet. You can easily activate another sheet in the current workbook to get to a range there. If the ranges are located in one or more other workbooks, however, open the workbook(s) before starting the consolidation command, and then use the Window menu to switch to the desired workbook to access its ranges.

5. After you establish the range, click the Add button to add the range to the All References box (see Figure 19.13).

6. If you want the consolidation table to be updated automatically when its source data is changed, select Create Links to Source Data.

7. Click OK.

Type of analysis to perform

Figure 19.13
This example uses the SUM function to total the figures for January through March and the quarterly total for Divisions 1 and 4.

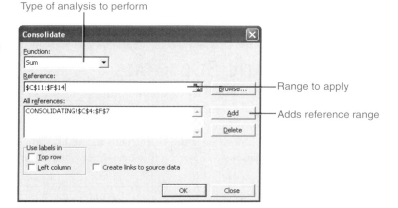

Range to apply

Adds reference range

The consolidated numbers in the example now reflect the addition of Division 1 and Division 4, as shown in Figure 19.14.

Figure 19.14
The result of the consolidated divisions is the addition of the tables because the SUM function was used for analysis.

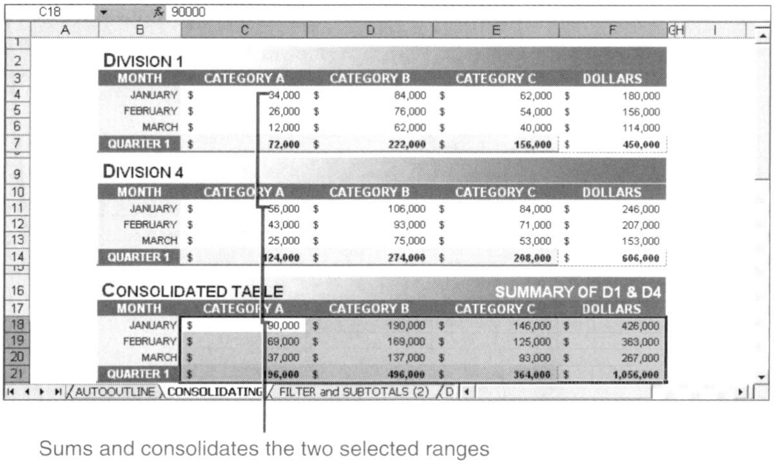

Sums and consolidates the two selected ranges

TIP FROM

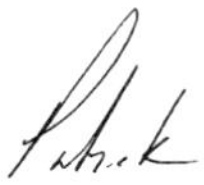

Although matching labels must be identical for the data to consolidate properly, sources that contain different column/row headings can easily be consolidated using the Use Labels In options in the Consolidate dialog box. Let's say your sources have different row and column headings. You include those labels when selecting each source range, turn on both Top Row and/or Left Column in the dialog box, and both the labels and consolidated data appear in the destination range.

Excel allows you to change the function with which you analyze the data; just open the Consolidate dialog box again, change the setting in the Function box, and click OK.

Consolidation ranges are saved with the workbook, making the refresh process easy. To refresh the consolidated table, just select the destination cell again (in this example, cell C22) and choose Data, Consolidate. Verify or change the ranges to consolidate and click OK.

CREATING AUTOMATIC SUBTOTALS

Excel provides an automatic subtotaling capability for use with any suitably organized data. Lists often lend themselves to subtotals because the most common question asked after filtering a list is, "How do I total just the visible cells?" In a *filtered* list, the Subtotals command on the Data menu subtotals only the visible cells in the list. You can also use subtotaling for other calculations—using the functions COUNT, MAX, MIN, and so on.

> **N O T E**
>
> To subtotal a filtered list, begin by filtering the list, if desired. For any other kind of subtotaling, skip this step. The procedure is the same otherwise.

To add a subtotal to a list, follow these steps:

1. Sort the list (and filter it, if desired), and then select the records. The first sort key you use should be the one you plan to select in the At Each Change In drop-down list in the Subtotal dialog box (see step 3). When selecting the records, include the row containing the column headings.

> **TIP FROM**
>
>
>
> If your list is surrounded by blank rows and columns, Excel selects the data to subtotal automatically; you don't need to select it before beginning the subtotaling process. The active cell must be somewhere in the list when you start this process.

2. Choose Data, Subtotals.
3. In the Subtotal dialog box, specify the subtotal criteria, function, and other settings you want to apply (see Figure 19.15).
    *   In the At Each Change In box, select the heading that indicates when you want Excel to perform a subtotal—for example, at each change in state, employee name, client, and so on. If you want to subtotal grouped items, sort the list on the column you select here *before* you subtotal the list.
    *   In the Use Function box, select the function you want Excel to use for the subtotals.
    *   In the Add Subtotal To list, select the column(s) that you want to subtotal.

- If you're performing a new subtotal function and want to replace the existing subtotals in the list, select Replace Current Subtotals. If you leave this unchecked, Excel adds additional subtotals to ones that might already exist in the list.

- Select Page Break Between Groups if you want Excel to start each new subtotaled group at the top of a clean page.

- If you want the subtotals and grand totals to appear below the data, select Summary Below Data. If this option is deselected, Excel places the subtotals above the first entry subtotaled in each group and places the grand total (or grand average, grand min, and so on, depending on the function you selected) at the top of the column, just below the row of headings.

In the example used here, subtotal is being used to subtotal the values for Tons for each Project—so there will be a subtotal for all the Montana projects, the IOWA projects, and so on.

Figure 19.15
The Subtotal dialog box enables you to subtotal records in a list.

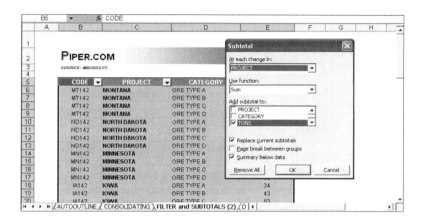

4. Figure 19.16 shows what happens when the reader runs the totals and then filters the result to show only Ore type B. also, an outline is created as a result of this process and the list was filtered.

The SUBTOTAL function uses the following syntax:

SUBTOTAL(*function_num*,*ref1*,*ref2*,...)

where *ref1*, *ref2*, and so on refer to the range(s) being calculated (up to 29 ranges), and *function_num* refers to a number from 1 to 11, with the following values:

Reference Number	Function
1	AVERAGE
2	COUNT
3	COUNTA
4	MAX
5	MIN
6	PRODUCT
7	STDEV
8	STDEVP
9	SUM
10	VAR
11	VARP

TIP FROM

You can build multiple layers of subtotals—using different functions and subtotaling different fields—by running the Subtotals feature multiple times and deselecting the Replace Current Subtotals option each time.

Figure 19.16
The subtotal function automatically places the subtotal function within the cells, so when you filter a list it subtotals the visible filtered cells only.

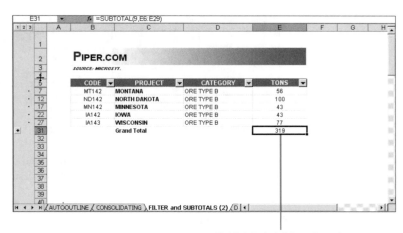

Subtotal of visible cells only

NOTE

Excel ignores any nested subtotals in the list, along with any hidden rows.

VALIDATING AND AUDITING DATA ENTRY

 Somewhere along the line, the data in every Excel workbook came from a human being. The process might have included typing data directly, downloading from a network or the Internet, importing from a database or data warehouse, and so on, but every bit of data can eventually be traced back to someone "filling in the blanks." Everyone makes mistakes at least *occasionally*, and the most complex formula is useless if its source data is wrong. On the other hand, accurate source data isn't very helpful if the formulas aren't constructed in a way that returns appropriate results. How can you prevent data errors and incorrect formulas from creeping into your Excel workbooks?

Excel offers some special features for dealing with the possibility of errors within a workbook:

- To prevent errors from being typed into a worksheet, the *data-validation* feature enables you to provide some guidance for the person entering the data (that might even be you!). You can tell Excel to accept only certain kinds of entries within a cell—for example, numbers or dates within a certain range—and specify a message for the user with instructions on filling in the information. With this feature, you also decide how you want Excel to respond to noncompliance: Display an error message and refuse the entry or accept the incorrect entry but warn the user that it's problematic?

- If invalid data already exists in the workbook, Excel can locate and circle those entries, using the same data-validation logic.

- To trace relationships between cells and formulas, you can use Excel's auditing feature to display the connection between formulas and their source cells (precedents) or between cells and their dependent formulas. You also can find the sources of error results in formulas.

The following sections describe these features.

As you might expect, Excel provides a special Formula Auditing toolbar for these functions. You can turn on the toolbar from the Toolbars list on the Toolbars tab in the Customize dialog box. Table 19.2 describes the buttons on the Formula Auditing toolbar.

TABLE 19.2 FORMULA AUDITING TOOLBAR

Button	Name	Description
![Error Checking]	Error Checking	Checks for errors within the selected work sheet.
![Trace Precedents]	Trace Precedents	Shows the preceding formulas or cell references that contribute to the cell. The cell being audited must be a formula.

continues

TABLE 19.2   CONTINUED

Button	Name	Description
	Remove Precedent Arrows	Removes the precedent auditing arrows.
	Trace Dependents	Shows the cell references with which the current cell is being used.
	Remove Dependent Arrows	Removes the dependent auditing arrows.
	Remove All Arrows	Removes all auditing arrows.
	Trace Error	Traces cells with error values.
	New Comment	Creates a comment for the active cell.
	Circle Invalid Data	Circles data outside the parameters set by validation.
	Clear Validation Circles	Clears the invalid data circles.
	Show Watch Window	Displays the watch window above the worksheet.
	Evaluate Formula	Evaluates formulas within the selected cell. Formulas containing nested calculations can be evaluated step by step.

DATA VALIDATION

For those who occasionally find that they have entered improper data, Excel has addressed this problem with data validation. Validation enables you to apply parameters to ranges or cells, keeping information within certain boundaries. For example, if your list applies to dates within a certain month only, you can specify parameters from the first of the month until month-end that allow the user to input only dates within that specified period of time. These parameters can be set up to prevent incorrect information completely, warn the user but allow the entry, and so on. (The next section describes how to come back and mark invalid data later.)

To apply validation parameters to a list, cell, or range, follow these steps:

1. Select the area where you want to apply validation. For example, for a range in which you want date validation, select the months, range of dates, and so on.

2. Choose Data, Validation.

3. If necessary, select the Settings tab in the Data Validation dialog box. In the Validation Criteria options, specify the parameters that will be acceptable when the user is entering data (see Figure 19.17).

   This example shows dates applied between two specified date ranges; the Ignore Blank option is selected so that the user can either enter an acceptable date or skip specifying a date in the input range.

Figure 19.17
The Settings tab in the Data Validation dialog box enables you to apply validation to dates, times, numbers, text, or even create a custom validation.

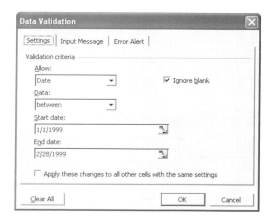

> **NOTE**
>
> Similar to customizing options for filters in lists, you can specify several characteristics on the Settings tab. Under the Data option, you can make the dates equal to, greater than, less than, and so on. Excel allows for flexibility to fit your specific requirements, and the options on the Settings tab change to reflect the selected data.
>
> Like Conditional Formatting, there is a Formula choice available (called Custom on the Allow drop-down list), allowing the user to use a custom formula (that evaluates to true/false) as the basis for the validation.

4. (Optional) You can provide an input message to help the user enter the correct data. Click the Input Message tab in the Data Validation dialog box, as shown in Figure 19.18. Whatever you specify in the Title box will appear in the title bar for the dialog box, and the Input message will be displayed in the box itself.

Figure 19.18
Providing clues *as to the type of data to be entered into a cell* can help the user avoid mistakes.

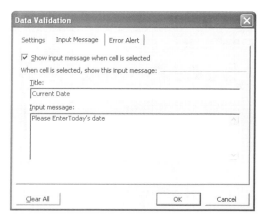

5. Next, specify what you want to happen if the user enters invalid data. Click the Error Alert tab (see Figure 19.19). Select a warning Style (the icon changes to match the style you select) and specify the Title you want the title bar of the message box to display. Finally, enter an Error Message to be displayed in the box.

6. After you enter all the information, click OK.

Figure 19.19
The Error Alert tab lets you specify three types of errors: Warning, Stop, and Information. You also can apply titles and text to the dialog box being created.

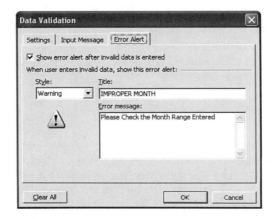

Figure 19.20 shows what happens when a user enters a date that's outside the specified parameters for this example. The user can choose Yes to accept the current date, No to correct the error, or Cancel to void the entry.

NOTE

Using the Stop style prevents users from entering invalid data.

Error indicator

Figure 19.20
The dialog box warns you when the data entered is outside the validation parameters set.

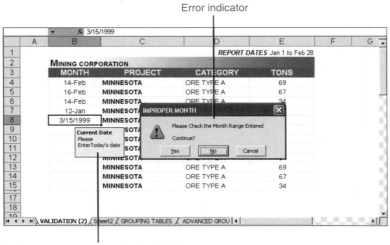

New input message pops up to help eliminate errors

You can change or remove the validation settings at any time by returning to the Data Validation dialog box. In most cases, you will just want to correct the settings, change the input or error messages, and so on. If you want to remove all the settings at once, however—all messages, alerts, and validation criteria—use the Clear All button at the bottom of the Data Validation box. (If you change your mind about this before closing the dialog box, clicking Cancel restores the settings.)

TIP FROM

You can make one set of changes on the Settings tab and tell Excel to apply those new settings to other comparable validated cells. Select the option at the bottom of the tab, Apply These Changes to All Other Cells with the Same Settings.

CIRCLING INVALID DATA

Excel includes a special validation feature to find and mark invalid data that was previously entered. You might use this feature for a number of reasons:

- Data was entered before you instituted validation, and you want to go back and fix existing errors.

- The validation you have in place allows the user to enter invalid data after displaying a warning. (Sometimes you want to be able to enter invalid information, but have it verified, corrected, or approved later.)

- You want to change the validation conditions.

To audit the worksheet and quickly display a circle around information that doesn't meet the data-validation conditions (up to 255 errors), click the Circle Invalid Data button on the Auditing toolbar. Excel circles the invalid data, as shown in Figure 19.21. If Excel finds 255 errors, you'll need to correct some of them and click the Circle Invalid Data button again before the program can mark any more.

Figure 19.21
Excel circles all information that doesn't fall within the specified validation parameters.

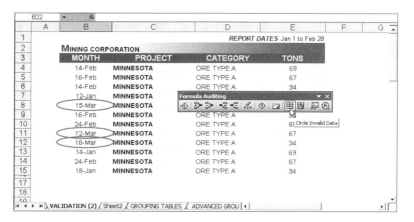

To remove the displayed circles, click the Clear Validation Circles button on the Auditing toolbar.

TIP FROM

> If validation wasn't applied to your list and you now want to highlight information that falls outside specified ranges, use conditional formatting and point to ranges and cells that establish parameters to meet your specifications.

AUDITING PRECEDENTS, DEPENDENTS, AND ERRORS

When inheriting a list of information or a workbook created by other users, the first thing you'll want to do is "check the wiring" of the workbook—how all the formulas and their data are connected. Excel's *auditing* feature can trace this information for you, as well as help you locate sources of errors returned by your formulas.

For each cell, auditing can trace the following information:

- If the cell contains a formula, auditing can trace its source cell(s), called *precedents*.
- If the cell contains data or formulas, auditing can trace any formulas that use the information from that cell, called its *dependents*.
- If the cell contains an error, auditing can trace the source of the error. For example, if a formula with a division operation returns #DIV/0, auditing can trace the source cell that either has no entry or evaluates to zero.

In each case, the relationships are pointed out with blue-colored *tracer arrows*.

> *If the auditing menu commands or buttons are disabled, the tracer arrows might be hidden. See "Displaying Tracer Arrows" in the "Troubleshooting" section at the end of this chapter.*

TIP FROM

> You can't audit a protected worksheet. To remove protection, choose Tools, Protection, Unprotect Sheet. If your workbook has more layers of protection, however, you'll have to get through those layers before you can even access the worksheet. Chapter 1 describes the various levels of protection available in Excel.

For example, if a cell contains a formula that sums a column of numbers, the formula's precedents would be the individual numbers being added. Each of those precedent cells would have the formula cell as one of its dependents. If that formula cell is itself included in a grand total somewhere else, the grand total would be a dependent of that formula cell.

The example in Figure 19.22 illustrates a simple scenario where both precedent and dependent cells are shown for two cells. When tracing the precedents for the formula in cell F16 (a SUM formula), Excel displays a blue border around cells F7:F15 with an arrow pointing to the formula. This indicates that the precedent cells are the cells in the range F7:F15. When tracing the dependents of cell G7, Excel displays a marker in cell G7 with arrows pointing to the cells that have dependent formulas (for example, cells G16 and H7). Notice that there is no border drawn around cells when you're tracing dependents, just arrows pointing to the dependent cells.

Figure 19.22
By displaying precedents, dependents, and errors, you can quickly see relationships between cells.

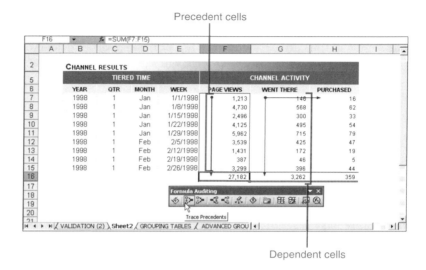

Precedent cells

Dependent cells

If the information originates from or points to a different workbook or worksheet, the tracer arrow is black and the icon resembles a small worksheet. To run or remove audits, you can use menu commands or the buttons on the Auditing toolbar, as described in the following list:

- **Trace a formula's precedents**—Select the cell containing the formula and choose Tools, Formula Auditing, Trace Precedents.

- **Trace a cell's dependents**—Select the cell and choose Tools, Formula Auditing, Trace Dependents.

- **Show multiple levels of precedents/dependents**—Repeatedly click the Trace Precedents or Trace Dependents button. If Excel beeps when you click one of these buttons, you have traced all levels of the formula, or you're trying to trace something untraceable (such as a graphic).

- **Track down the culprit cell leading to an error result**—Select the cell containing the formula with the error result and click the Trace Errors button or choose Tools, Formula Auditing, Trace Error. You might need to trace repeatedly to find all the errors involved.

- **Jump between dependents and precedents**—Double-click the tracer arrow. If the formula connects different workbooks, the workbook must be open to jump to it. If you jump to a different worksheet or workbook, Excel displays the Go To list; double-click the reference you want.

- **Remove tracer arrows**—To remove the tracer arrow from a cell to its dependents or precedents, select the cell and click the Remove Dependent Arrows or Remove Precedent Arrows button, respectively. To remove all tracer arrows, click the Remove All Arrows button on the Auditing toolbar or choose Tools, Formula Auditing, remove All Arrows.

Tracer arrows disappear when you save or close the workbook; you can't save an audit from one session to the next. Arrows also disappear if you insert or delete rows or columns, delete or move the cells involved in the formula, or change the formula itself.

→ Use comments to make notations as you explore the worksheet. For details, **see** "Using Comments to Explain Cell Content," **p. xxx** (Chapter 3)

TROUBLESHOOTING

DISPLAYING TRACER ARROWS

The Auditing toolbar buttons or menu options are unavailable.

If the worksheet isn't protected (you can't audit a protected worksheet), and the auditing features are unavailable, it might be because your Excel options are set up to hide graphical objects (which include tracer arrows). The auditing feature relies on tracer arrows to indicate errors, precedents, and dependents. To display the tracer arrows, choose Tools, Options to open the Options dialog box. Click the View tab, and select either Show All or Show Placeholders in the Objects section.

AUTO OUTLINE DOESN'T WORK

Why do I get the error message "Cannot create an outline"?

Excel understands only outlines that are set up consistently. Be sure you don't have inconsistent spaces between categories and totals, and that the rest of the list is organized in a consistent manner.

EXCEL IN PRACTICE

Figures 19.23 and 19.24 show two ways to structure a yearly list with quarters. Both worksheets use good overall structures with consistent titles and no extra spaces, but Excel can use the worksheet in Figure 19.24 to create an Auto Outline. With the grouping in this worksheet, you can roll up the data by quarter and then by year, and you can view grand totals by row and column. The worksheet in Figure 19.23 also can be summarized by quarter and then total, with two levels of grouping applied, but Excel can't understand the worksheet's layout automatically.

Figure 19.23
You can group this worksheet manually, but Excel can't apply a logical Auto Outline because the quarter totals all appear at the bottom of the columns rather than after their respective months.

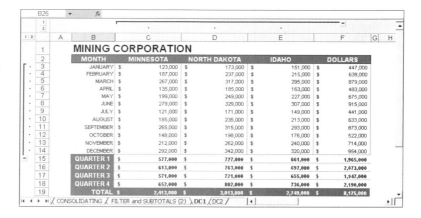

Figure 19.24
This worksheet uses the same data as the one in Figure 19.23, except that it uses a different layout to make it easier for Excel to understand and different formatting to make it easier for the user to understand.

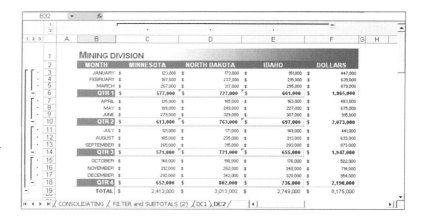

19

CREATING AND MODIFYING CHARTS

20 Building Charts with Excel   465

21 Modifying Excel Charts   505

22 Formatting Charts   533

23 Professional Charting Techniques   563

CHAPTER 20

Building Charts with Excel

In this chapter

An Overview of Excel Charts   466

Creating Charts with the Chart Wizard   469

Excel Chart Types   486

Printing Charts   500

AN OVERVIEW OF EXCEL CHARTS

Creating charts in Excel gives you the power to transform numbers into pictures that ultimately tell a story. All too often, charts are created "just because." But charts can be the basis of decision making in business; effective charts can ultimately express a business's current situation and future needs. In addition, charts presented and formatted properly can create impact. If done correctly, many charts can tell a story without any additional explanation. Also note, in many cases, less is better. Too much formatting can clutter the chart and deteriorate the intended message.

The interesting thing about Excel users I've noticed over the past years is how many of them spend their time. It's generally broken out into four categories:

- Setting up data
- Formatting Data
- Figuring out how to summarize the data
- Presenting the data

So why bring this up in a chapter about charts? Well, they're all related. Ultimately you have to make sense and come to decision based on the data collected, summarized, and then presented. If you have a firm grasp of the picture or decision that needs to be made it can drive how you set up, format, and present the data.

Before creating a chart, ask yourself what story you need to tell. The answer usually can help you decide what type of chart you need, as well as how to present it effectively. Also ask yourself, if someone views the chart in your absence, will the information present itself without narration? Consider the following examples:

- **You want to show the quarterly results of the previous year's performance against projected performance for this year**—Use a combination clustered column to show the actual sales and a line chart to show the projected sales.
- **You need to project the number of employees needed for the next three years**—Use a stacked column chart to show the base number of employees, with the projected future numbers stacked on top of the base.
- **You need a presentation that shows current market share**—Use a pie chart and show the percentages as data labels. Also consider using a Pie Overlay. See also, Pie Charts in this chapter.

CHART BASICS

Excel offers several ways to create charts. You can create a chart from the Insert menu with the Chart Wizard, from the toolbar with the Chart Wizard button, or by selecting the data and pressing F11 on your keyboard. You even can create a Microsoft Graph 2000 chart with the Insert, Object command.

You can embed your chart in the same worksheet with its source data or create the chart on a separate *chart sheet*. (By default, pressing F11 automatically creates the new chart on a new sheet.) See the later section "Choosing a Chart Location" for details on positioning charts.

Structuring Your Data for Automatic Charting

Excel makes it easy to create charts from information laid out in the proper manner. For example, structure your data in a simple grid, with titles along the left in the first column of the grid, and category information along the top in the first row. (Although category info isn't a requirement, it's usually helpful in charts.)

Make sure there are no blank rows or columns between the title and category headings and the body of the data, or Excel will plot the blank spaces. The cell where the headings cross—in the upper-left corner of the grid—should be blank.

If the data is formatted properly, as shown in later examples in this chapter, you can create an automatic chart instantly just by pressing F11. After you get the hang of the default Excel chart settings, you might find this feature to be a real timesaver.

By knowing all the chart elements and how to format your chart, you can create charts with visual impact rivaling that of high-priced drawing programs.

CHART TERMS

You should become familiar with the charting terminology so that you can respond appropriately to the Chart Wizard prompts, and you'll know what to look for when you want to edit a chart.

As shown in Figure 20.1, a basic chart offers a pictorial view of data, with the *y-axis* (usually vertical) indicating the amount or quantity of the information in the chart, and the *x-axis* (usually horizontal) showing the categories. For example, the quarters in a year might be the category for a company or a division of a corporation.

With multiple categories, a *legend* usually accompanies the chart. The *legend* provides a reference for the audience when viewing the charted information by illustrating what category each pattern or color represents in the chart with text and a small sample of the pattern or color.

Table 20.1 describes each basic chart element called out in this figure. In addition to these basic elements, certain chart types have other special features that you'll learn about later in the chapter.

20

TABLE 20.1   CHART ELEMENTS

Element	Description
Data point	An individually plotted value associated with a specific category.
Data labels	Text or values displayed at data points to indicate the specific value or category.

continues

TABLE 20.1   CONTINUED

Element	Description
Data series	A group of data points for a specific category.
Chart title	The title associated with the chart.
Value axis	The (usually vertical) axis that shows a scale of values by which the data series are measured.
Category axis	The (usually horizontal) axis that displays the category labels for all the data series.
Legend	A color, text, or graphics "key" identifying each series in the chart.
Tick marks	Separators on both the category ("x") and value ("y/z") axes. Tick marks act as guide markers for visual comparison.
Plot area	The area in the chart where data series are plotted.
Chart area	The total area of the chart. All elements are included in the chart area.
x-axis (category) title	Displays the category of the plotted data. For example, months.
y-axis (value) title	Displays a description for the scale of values against which the data is plotted.
z-axis (value) title	In 3D charts, displays a description for the scale of values against which the data is plotted.
Trendline	For certain chart types, displays a line across a specific data series identifying the pattern (trend) associated with the series.
Series Data labels	Labels the category name of the data on the plotted chart.

Figure 20.1
Standard elements in an Excel chart can be added, deleted, and formatted.

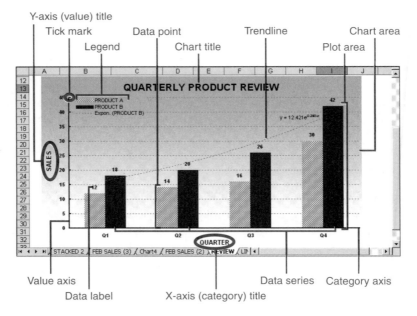

To minimize clutter on the chart, try to eliminate any information that just takes up space without adding anything helpful for the chart's audience. If the chart's categories are obvious without the legend, for example, perhaps you can live without it. You probably don't need both data points and data labels. This chapter and the next three show alternative ways to construct charts, with creative uses of color, pattern, text, and drawing tools.

CREATING CHARTS WITH THE CHART WIZARD

The Chart Wizard enables you to create a chart, step by step, and provides options along the way to help you tailor the chart. You can always go back in and modify the chart after it has been created, so don't worry if you've missed something. When creating the table that will be the source information for the chart, be sure to structure the data in a manner that Excel understands (see the earlier sidebar "Structuring Your Data for Automatic Charting"). For example, create the table with the row titles in the left column and the column titles across the top, or vice versa. Include the row and column titles in the selection when creating the chart.

Setting Up the Source Table for a Chart

Don't include cells containing totals in the selection when creating the chart. Unless you're showing a graph with categories as a percent of the total, this will create a distorted view of the data.

It's also a good idea not to place data in the upper-left cell of the selection you want to plot. Excel might interpret the data below or to the left of the upper-left cell as a series and plot it.

A trick exists for plotting row and column headings that are entered as numbers. For example, if you track sales over a period of years and enter year numbers for either the row or column headings, Excel plots the years as numbers. One way to avoid this problem is to place an apostrophe (') in front of each heading that Excel might interpret as a number.

After creating the source table—including the title and category information—open the Chart Wizard. The wizard defaults to certain chart types if you don't make a specific chart type selection, so you essentially can click Finish in step 1 and the default chart will appear as an object on the active sheet.

To create a chart with the Chart Wizard, follow these steps:

1. Create a table that contains the data you want to chart. See also Chapters 2 and 3 for setting up a table and editing spreadsheets.

2. Select the table.

3. Choose Insert, Chart, or click the Chart Wizard button on the Standard toolbar.

4. Follow the steps in the Chart Wizard dialog boxes, filling in any details as needed such as chart titles, gridlines, legends and so on. Click Finish when you're ready to create the chart.

20

TIP FROM

Sometimes, deleting a chart and starting over is easier than fixing it. You might see immediately after clicking Finish that you should have selected more or different options in the Chart Wizard. Unfortunately, you can't undo a chart insertion. However, if the chart is embedded and still selected, you can just press the Delete key. If the chart is placed on a chart sheet, delete the new chart sheet. Select the table, click the Chart Wizard button, and then begin again.

Another option is to select the chart (if it isn't still selected), click the Chart Wizard button to open the Chart Wizard, change the settings, and then click Finish.

You can also access the Chart (Wizard) Options by activating any part of the chart and choosing Chart, Chart Options.

SELECTING THE CHART TYPE

The first step in creating a chart with the Chart Wizard is to select a chart type and sub-type. (See the later section "Excel Chart Types" for details.) To use one of the default chart types, click the Standard Types tab, scroll the Chart Type list as needed, and click the desired chart type. As shown in Figure 20.2, the Chart Sub-Type list changes to provide variations of the chart type selected in the Chart Type list.

Figure 20.2
The first step in the Chart Wizard gives you the opportunity to select the chart type and sub-type. You also can select a custom type.

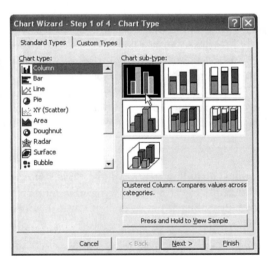

You can see a sample of the chart using the selected data by clicking and holding down the Press and Hold to View Sample button in the Chart Wizard dialog box under the Chart Sub-Type list. Although this is a small sample, it can help keep you from wasting time with a chart type that clearly won't give the audience the information you want to convey.

Clicking the Custom Types tab gives you an additional set of variations on the standard Excel charts (see Figure 20.3). For details on using custom charts, see the later section "Excel Chart Types."

After you make your selection, you can either go to step 2 of the Chart Wizard, or you can click Finish and Excel selects the default options for you.

Figure 20.3
The Custom Types tab enables you to select from predesigned custom charts or if you've already created a custom chart define your own by selecting User-Defined in the Select From section of the dialog box.

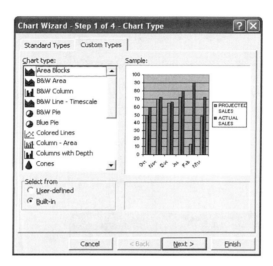

SPECIFYING THE CHART SOURCE DATA

Although you'll typically select the data that you want to *plot* (display in the chart) before starting the Chart Wizard, you might decide after starting the wizard that you need to change the *data range* you selected. Or, you might have forgotten to select the range before launching into chart creation. Step 2 of the Chart Wizard dialog box enables you to change the data range to be used in the chart (see Figure 20.4). The preview on the Data Range tab shows how the selected range will look in the chart. To adjust the range, change the settings shown in the fields on the Data Range tab.

By default, a *data series* is one category of your table. By selecting one of the columns in the chart, you've selected a data series. You can change the *orientation* of the data from rows (the default) to columns. Figures 20.5 and 20.6, for example, show two different versions of the same chart in the preview window. In Figure 20.5, the data is plotted in rows; in Figure 20.6, the data is plotted in columns. If you change a series to plot from rows to columns, Excel changes the data from a clustered series with no spaces between the columns to individual columns. Excel usually plots the orientation of your data correctly, but if it's incorrect or not what you were expecting, you can change it in this dialog box.

20

Figure 20.4
Use the Data Range settings to change category orientation from rows to columns.

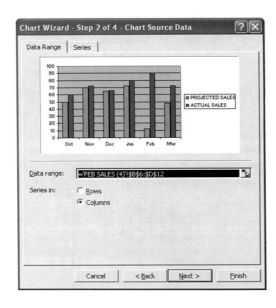

Figure 20.5
When the Series In option is set to Rows, Excel plots each row as a data series, with each row heading appearing in the legend. The column headings appear as category labels along the x-axis of the chart.

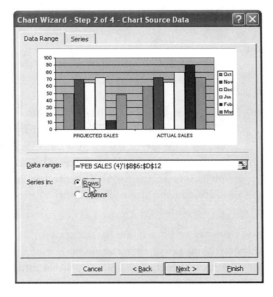

Figure 20.6
Setting the Series In option to Columns plots each column as a data series, with each column heading appearing in the legend. Row headings now represent the categories that appear along the x-axis of the chart.

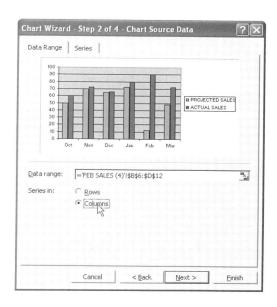

On the Series tab, you can manipulate the series in a chart by either adding or removing a series of a chart (see Figure 20.7). For example, if you've selected the entire range of a table and decide you want to view one data series only (to focus the audience), you can remove the data series by selecting it and clicking the Remove button. Conversely, you can add a series to the chart by clicking the Add button, and then specifying the details for the new series by using the other options on the Series tab.

Figure 20.7
The Series tab gives you the options of adding and removing data series. In addition, you can redefine the address from which Excel is retrieving names, values, and category labels.

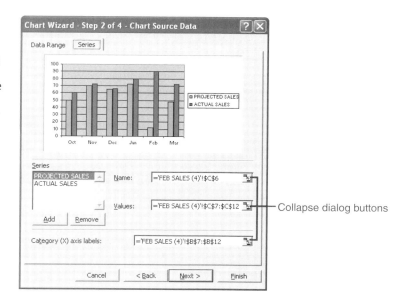

Collapse dialog buttons

20

The options in this dialog box change depending on the type of chart and the series selected in the Series list box. The following list describes the available options:

■ **Series, Add or Remove**—You can add a series to the chart by clicking the Add button. Then, you manually type the Series Label in the Name box or use the Range Finder (button with red arrow) to specify the cell containing the Series Label. Manually type the individual figures for the series (separating each figure with a comma or semicolon) in the Value box or use the Range Finder (button with red arrow) to specify the range of cells containing the Series' values.

Remove a series by selecting a series and clicking Remove.

■ **Name**—When you select a series in the Series list at the left side of the dialog box, this entry changes to show the address of the cell(s) containing the title for that series—for example, the name of a month or other time period, or the division or other category name used as a heading for that column or row.

In Figure 20.7, for example, the series name (PROJECTED SALES) comes from the heading in cell C6 on the Feb Sales (4) sheet, as indicated in the Name box. Don't be thrown by the ='Feb Sales (4)'! designation; for dialog box options that list cell addresses, Excel lists the entire address, including the worksheet name. For example, if the worksheet name were Sales and the category title were in cell A2, the location formula would look like this: =Sales!$A$2. If the sheet name contains more than one word, Excel encloses it in single quotation marks (').

■ **Values**—The Values box provides the address containing the values for the selected series. The values are the data used to build the columns.

For some chart types, the Chart Wizard displays an X Values box and a Y Values box.

■ **Category (X) Axis Labels**—This box shows the cell reference for the x-axis categories. In Figure 20.7, for example, the x-axis labels refer to the months listed in column B. As with the other options on this tab, you can select or type a different address or range for use as labels.

■ **Second Category (X) Axis Labels**—Specifies the location of cell(s) containing the labels to be used for the second x-axis—for example, in stock charts or column-area custom charts.

TIP FROM

If x-axis labels aren't located on a worksheet, you can type the labels in the Category (X) Axis Labels or Second Category (X) Axis Labels box, separating the labels with commas or semicolons. Excel converts the labels to a formula, placing each label in quotation marks (") and surrounding all the labels with a set of braces ({ }).

■ **Sizes**—In bubble charts, this option indicates the cells containing values indicating the size of the bubble markers.

You can also add a series by selecting the data on the worksheet and dragging it into the chart. You can remove a series by selecting it and using the Delete key.

For options in which Excel lists a range, you can change the range if Excel hasn't guessed the address correctly. Select the option by clicking in the text box. Then, use one of the following methods to change the range:

- Type the new range or name in the text box.
- Click outside the dialog box. Excel collapses the dialog box and enables you to select a new range.
- Click the Collapse Dialog button. This button squeezes the dialog box down to display just the option, as shown in Figure 20.8. Type or select the new range and then click the Collapse Dialog button again to return to the full-size dialog box.

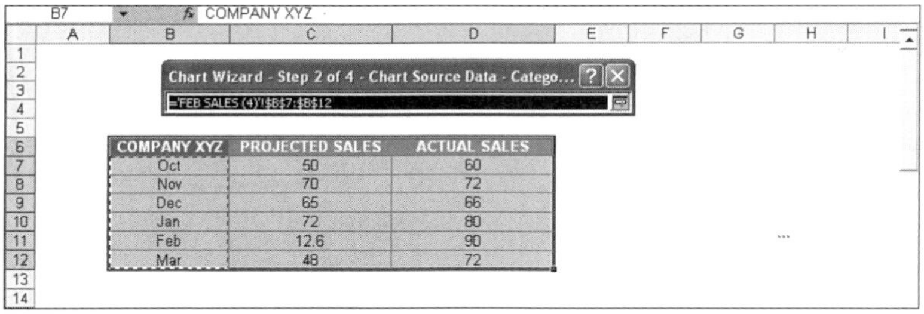

Figure 20.8
The collapsed dialog box activates the range represented and enables you to drag over a new location on the worksheet.

After you make your selections, you can either go back to step 1 of the Chart Wizard, go on to step 3, or click Finish and Excel will select the default options for you.

TIP FROM

If your column or row headings tend to be long, use an abbreviated version for titles, legends, and so on in the chart. You can change these items when you finish the chart, or create the abbreviations in a separate area of the worksheet and change the settings in the Series tab of the Chart Wizard to refer to these special cells. Conversely, if you tend to abbreviate column and row headings to squeeze as much information as possible into a worksheet, you can expand the titles and legends for use in charts.

CHOOSING THE CHART OPTIONS

Step 3 of the Chart Wizard dialog box enables you to tailor your chart in several ways. You can add and delete features at will; however, note that you must finish the chart before you can format the features added. (To learn about formatting parts of the chart, see Chapter 22, "Formatting Charts.") This dialog box also enables you to view the chart as you're adding the features to understand how the final chart will look with the changes you've made.

CAUTION

Keep the chart clean and drive home a point. Too much information on a chart detracts from the focus of the chart. All too often, people try to put everything on the chart; before long, the story they're trying to tell gets lost. Excel offers more features with each new edition of the program, but just because these features exist doesn't mean you should use them. As a test, show someone the information and see whether he can grasp the point within five seconds—ultimately, that's all the attention time you'll get for your chart. For example, if you have five or six callouts on a chart with multiple colors, the reader will need several minutes just to read through the data.

CHART TITLES

The Titles tab of the Chart Wizard—Step 3 of 4 on the dialog box—enables you to insert a chart title, name the category axis, and name the value axis, as shown in Figure 20.9. If you have a dual-axis chart, the dialog box also displays options for naming the second category x-axis and y-axis. The preview in the dialog box adds the new title a few seconds after you stop typing or click another option. Note, secondary titles show for only 2D charts.

Figure 20.9
The Titles tab enables you to add a chart title and provide titles for the chart's axes for easier reading.

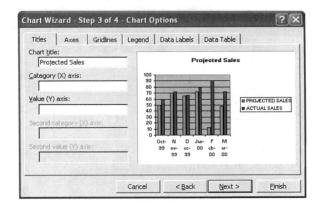

For most charts, you should add each of the elements listed in the Titles tab. The chart title represents the total picture of the information in the chart. In Figure 20.10, for example, an appropriate title that describes the information might be "Corporate Sales." This title clearly describes what the information represents. Keep the title short and to the point.

TIP FROM

After you complete the Chart Wizard, add a subtitle to the chart if needed; for this example, "Projected Six Month" would clarify further the information contained in the chart. You can add the subtitle within the chart title by pressing Return after the title or by adding a text box.

Figure 20.10
A chart without a chart title and x- and y-axis titles can draw blank stares.

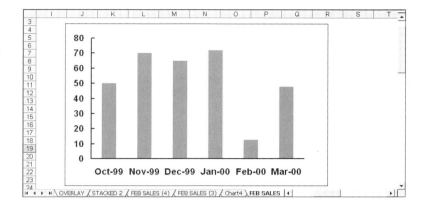

The importance of naming the value (Y) axis cannot be stressed enough. All too often, graphs are created with no y-axis title, and information that looks to be in the thousands of dollars can easily be misinterpreted as hundreds of thousands of dollars. In the previous Figure 20.10, are you measuring sales in units or dollars? This should be part of the value (Y) title. In many cases, the category (X) axis title is self-explanatory; however, for consistency, it's good practice to name that axis as well. Without the titles, what's the story?

Figure 20.11 shows another version of the same chart, with titles added to clarify the information.

Figure 20.11
With the proper titles in place, the chart now tells a clear story without any additional explanation.

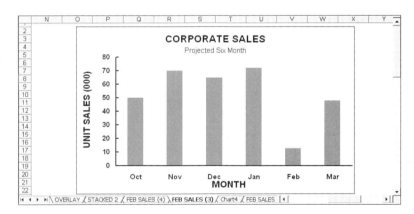

20

You can use the Display Units option in the Format Axis dialog box to specify the unit denomination you want to use, without adding a y-/z-axis title. The advantage to using this feature is that Excel automatically changes the values on the y-/z-axis to reflect the denomination you specify.

For example, if the source data contains values in millions, by default the scale values also appear in millions. However, if you specify millions for your display units, the word Millions will appear in the y-/z-axis title and all scale values will be divided by one million. Thus, 250,000,000 is displayed as 25 on the y-/z-axis.

To specify a display unit, finish creating your chart. Then, select the y-/z-axis and choose Format, Selected Axis, or right-click the axis and select Format Axis from the context menu. In the Format Axis dialog box, click the Scale tab, and select the desired unit from the Display Units list box.

You might have noticed and wondered why the examples to this point use all uppercase letters for titles. The simple reason is that it's clean. The subtitle, on the other hand, should have initial caps, and you should drop the font size by two points to draw attention first to the title and second to the subtitle. The x- and y-axis titles should be bold and two point sizes larger than the descriptions along the axis. (There's no absolute rule that says what's right and wrong, but experience has shown these practices to work well.)

AXES

The Axes tab in the Chart Wizard, as shown in Figure 20.12, automatically displays data with a time-scale format if the data is date formatted. By deselecting the Category (X) Axis option, you can remove the axis labels, as shown in Figure 20.13. If the Category (X) Axis option is selected, the selected radio button below the option indicates what the axis will display.

Figure 20.12
The Axes tab enables you to show or hide values and text associated with the corresponding axis. You can also change the category axis to time-scale display.

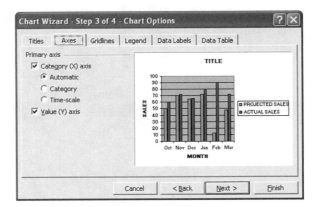

Figure 20.13
By deselecting the Category (X) Axis option, you can hide the x-axis labels.

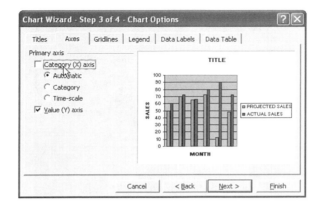

When the Time-Scale option is selected on the Axes tab, Excel converts the category from a text format to a date format. (If your date text crosses over year thresholds, convert the date format to time scale.) When the Time-Scale option is selected, Excel converts the text format to a date. If the date is formatted to show the month name in text, however, or you have data that crosses over years, you might want to convert the category to time-scale format to show the years. You can choose to remove the axis labels if they are not necessary.

CAUTION

> If the date text isn't in a specific date format, Excel might not initially display the dates in the desired format. For example, if dates consist of month and year only (such as 5/98), Excel might initially display the dates as years only.
>
> You can change the date format after finishing the Chart Wizard. (To learn about formatting parts of the chart, see Chapter 22.)

You also can add or delete the value (Y) axis. For example, if you're going to attach value labels to a data series, there's no need for the y-axis.

GRIDLINES

The Gridlines tab enables you to add major and minor axis gridlines (see Figure 20.14).

It's best to avoid gridlines to keep the chart clean. Normally, you would want to keep the major gridlines for the value (Y or Z) axis, but not apply additional gridlines. If formatted properly, however, gridlines can actually enhance, and not detract from or clutter, the chart.

Figure 20.15 shows major gridlines added to carry across and intersect the projected line when combining two chart types (this is a combination line chart and column chart).

20

Figure 20.14
The Gridlines tab enables you to apply vertical and horizontal gridlines to the plot area.

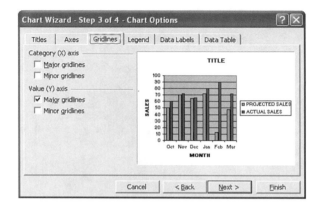

Figure 20.15
By adding only major gridlines to a chart, and creating a lighter tone for the format of the gridlines, you can add organization without creating clutter.

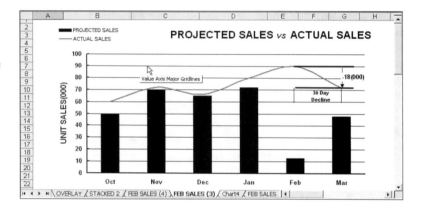

In Figure 20.16, minor value gridlines and major category gridlines have been added to create a grid effect when showing incremental shifts. You also can lighten the grid effect by selecting the gridline and choosing Format, Selected Gridlines. This example uses drawing tools to further illustrate the shift or decline over time on the chart.

→ To add drawing shapes to a chart, **see** "Enhancing Charts with Shapes," **p. 546**

The last example, in Figure 20.17, uses white gridlines to carry across and highlight a specific month of data. Drawing tools were also added to the chart to call out the month increase.

Figure 20.16
Minor value gridlines and major category gridlines can be used when highlighting incremental shifts in which callouts are needed.

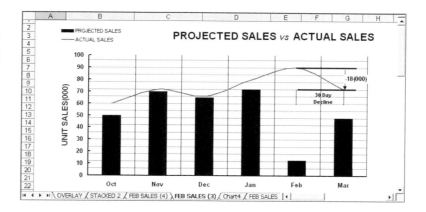

Figure 20.17
The gridlines in this example are actually white, and a text box sent to back was used to enhance the February sales increase. The chart area fill and the plot area fill are set to none.

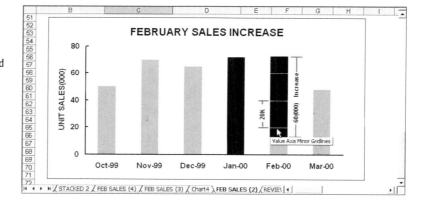

LEGEND

The legend in a chart acts like a "map," with callouts to the different data series in a chart. If the chart consists of several categories, a legend is needed to pinpoint the pattern or color of each series. The Legend tab in the Chart Wizard dialog box enables you to apply or delete a legend (see Figure 20.18). You also can place the legend in different locations on the chart. Placement options just specify where the legend appears initially; you can move and/or resize the legend after the chart is created. For example, if you want the audience to focus on the chart itself, you might want to reduce the font size of the legend and place it in an inconspicuous place on the chart.

20

Figure 20.18
The Legend tab enables you to delete the legend or place it in a different location on the chart.

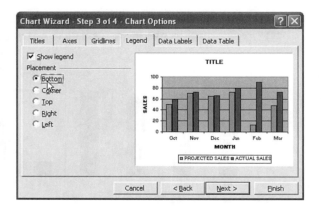

You can erase the borders of the legend to allow the legend to blend in with the rest of the chart. To erase the legend borders, select the legend after it's created on the chart (the sizing handles should be showing), choose Format, Selected Legend, and then set Border to None on the Patterns tab.

Legends don't always have to be on the perimeter of the chart. Formatted properly, a legend can be placed within the plot area. Notice that in Figure 20.19 the legend actually sits better in the plot area than it would in any other region on the chart. This strategy also allows you to use the total landscape of the chart area.

Figure 20.19
By dragging the legend to the plot area and erasing the legend borders, you can take advantage of the total landscape of the chart area.

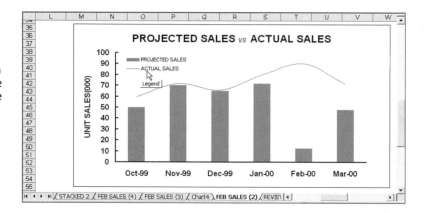

DATA LABELS

The Data Labels tab in the Chart Wizard dialog box gives you the option of adding labels and values next to each data point for every data series in the chart. The Label Contains option allows you to display stacked data per series. For example, by checking the Category Name, Value option and using the (.) period or semicolon as the Separator with the Separator drop down, you can add multiple sets of data to each column (data point) as shown in Figure 20.20.

Figure 20.20
The Data Labels tab enables you to attach multiple labels or values to the data series.

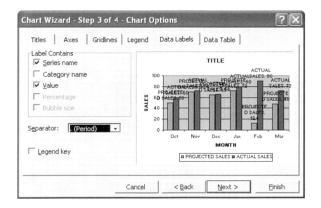

Figure 20.21 shows an example of using data labels.

Figure 20.21
Not shown in this figure but Excel now allows you to stack multiple labels per data series.

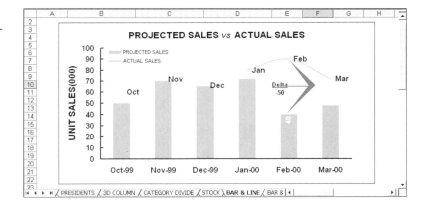

DATA TABLE

The Data Table tab in the Chart Wizard dialog box enables you to place a table below the x-axis (see Figure 20.22). This feature aligns the numeric data under the corresponding category. This is one way to display data labels without cluttering the plot area (see Figure 20.23). It's also a handy way to combine a chart and its data into a single compact form—for example, for embedding on a PowerPoint slide.

20

Figure 20.22
The Data Table tab places data series values under the x-axis.

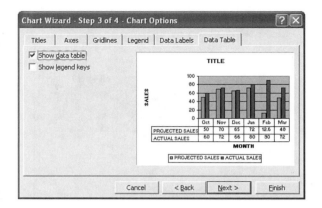

Figure 20.23
Notice that the data table aligns directly below the categories.

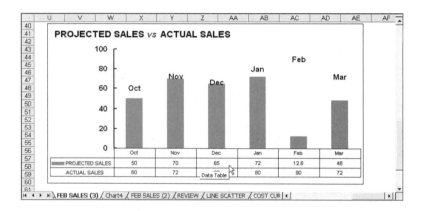

CHOOSING A CHART LOCATION

In step 4 of the Chart Wizard dialog box (the final step), you can use the following options to specify where you want to place the new chart (see Figure 20.24):

- **As New Sheet**—This option creates an independent *chart sheet* in the workbook (see Figure 20.25). With this option, the Chart Wizard automatically inserts a new sheet named Chart1. As with any other sheet tab, you can change this name to something more informative.

- **As Object In**—By default, this option embeds the chart in the worksheet containing the chart's source data (see Figure 20.26). You also can specify another sheet in the workbook by opening the drop-down list and selecting the sheet onto which you want to embed the chart.

Figure 20.24
Specify whether you want to create the new chart as a chart sheet or embedded on a worksheet you select.

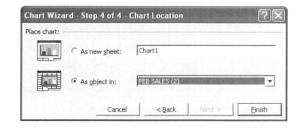

Figure 20.25
The chart on a separate worksheet created within the workbook.

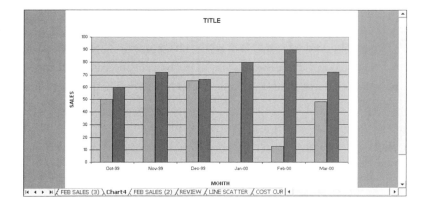

Figure 20.26
This chart is embedded at your specified location within the worksheet.

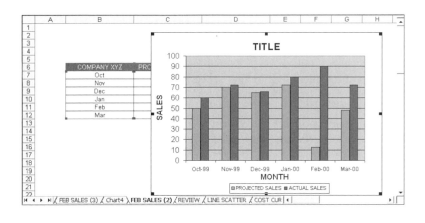

Although it might seem minor, the placement of the chart on the worksheet is critical. When combining a chart with additional data or tables on worksheets, it's important to place the chart in a manner that makes sense to the reader. The following sections describe the considerations for each placement.

20

EMBEDDED CHARTS

An embedded chart in a worksheet means the chart object is placed on the worksheet instead of as a separate chart sheet, so the chart object is essentially floating over the spreadsheet. There are many advantages to creating embedded charts:

- You can move and manipulate the size of the chart, as well as change locations by just cutting and pasting the chart.
- You can drag and size the chart and place it next to the source data. Changes in the data are immediately reflected in the chart, so you can experiment by watching the chart as you make changes.
- At times, you'll need to view or print multiple charts on the same sheet; with embedded charts you can size and place all the charts on the same sheet within a single window.
- An embedded chart enables you to easily print the data and chart together.
- You can connect the chart and data with drawing items and comments.

CREATING THE CHART ON A SEPARATE CHART SHEET

Creating a chart on a separate worksheet doesn't offer as many advantages as creating embedded charts, but here are a few:

- All the options for changing the chart's appearance are still available, except for being able to grab the chart itself and move it around the worksheet.
- A chart sheet gives the chart more room in the window so that you can view and edit it more easily.
- It makes for easy printing of the chart on its own page.

And, here are some disadvantages as well:

- When displaying a chart on a chart sheet, movement of the chart is limited.
- A chart sheet isn't as convenient as an embedded chart for viewing the chart with the data. It requires extra steps to see data changes reflected in the chart.

EXCEL CHART TYPES

Excel offers a wide variety of chart types because certain data works better with some chart types than others. For example, if you're plotting sales figures over a period of months, it's better to use a clustered column chart or line chart than a pie chart. The different chart types and the data that works best with the charts can be confusing, so it's important to understand which is the best chart for the information. The Chart Wizard suggests a certain type based on the data, but that doesn't mean that the suggested type is the best type to represent the data.

At some point, you'll probably want to experiment with each chart type to see how it plots data. This section shows the types that probably will be most beneficial in real-world use. After you become familiar with the different charts and what they're best suited for, you can even combine chart types for complex charting.

The following sections explore the various chart types. Rather than showing the standard version of each chart type (you can see these in the Chart Wizard dialog boxes), you'll get plenty of examples of how you can make your charts more interesting, readable, or effective with the special charting features available in Excel. These features are covered in detail in the next three chapters on charting (Chapter 21, "Modifying Excel Charts," Chapter 22, "Formatting Charts," and Chapter 23, "Professional Charting Techniques").

TIP FROM

Excel charts can be created in two-dimensional (2D) or three-dimensional (3D) format. (Many supposedly 3D charts actually are just 2D charts with perspective added to give a 3D effect. A true 3D chart has three axes.)

If you're not sure whether you want your data portrayed in 2D or 3D, or you have already created a chart and want to experiment with a different look, use the Chart Wizard to change the chart type or sub-type and watch the results in the preview window.

CAUTION

Adding a third dimension to a 2D chart makes it more visually interesting, but also can make it more difficult to understand or leave it open to interpretation. Frequent use of 3D charts also can dilute their effectiveness with your audience. Use 3D sparingly.

COLUMN CHARTS

A *column chart* has vertical bars and plots as separate points over time (noncontiguous). Column charts are good for showing value amounts and quantities over time (see Figure 20.27). Become familiar with this chart type—knowing it well can dramatically improve your communication of data to others.

In this example, the categories have been separated by displaying the value (Y) axis between categories on the x-axis. The method is simple: Right-click the x-axis, choose Format Axis, click the Scale tab in the Format Axis dialog box, and select the Value (Y) Axis Crosses Between Categories option. This is a good way to visually represent two distinct categories—by separating them with the value axis.

→ To learn more about axis positioning **see,** "Repositioning the Axes," **p. 521**

Figure 20.27
This column chart has the value axis repositioned.

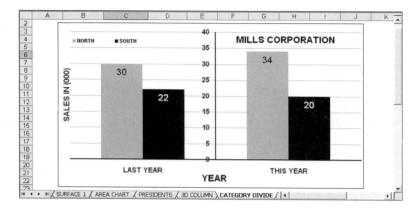

Another type of column chart is the *stacked column chart*. A stacked column chart would work well in the following situation: Your division must report personnel needs for the next two years to corporate headquarters, and a maximum headcount is in place that you can't exceed (see Figure 20.28). Notice that the additional personnel needed per department is called out in the dark stacked region, and a line chart is applied to show the maximum headcount per department.

Figure 20.28
A stacked column chart is a good way to show growth over current base.

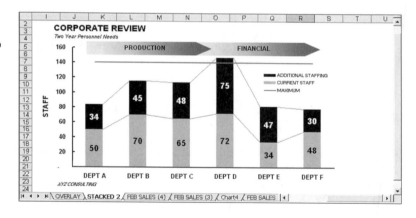

→ If you create 3D rather than 2D column charts, you have more formatting options to consider; **see** "Formatting 3D Charts," **p. 555**

BAR CHARTS

A *bar chart* is similar to a column chart in that it plots bars as separate points; however, it plots the bars in a horizontal format. The bars can be placed side by side, as a cluster, stacked, or 3D. The bar chart was the original chart used for data display in the 1700s; the column chart came shortly after. When Excel plots a bar chart from your data, you'll notice that information normally viewed right-to-left translates to bottom-to-top.

20

→ To reverse a bar chart for top-to-bottom viewing, **see** "Repositioning the Axes," **p.521**

→ To create thermometer charts see also "Working with the Secondary Axis, Overlap, and Gap Width" **p. 575**

Bar charts are great tools for showing measurement, such as the percentage of a project completed (see Figure 20.29). In this example, an overlay effect (also referred to as a thermometer effect) helps pinpoint actual results against projected results.

Figure 20.29
A bar chart plots bars horizontally as separate points.

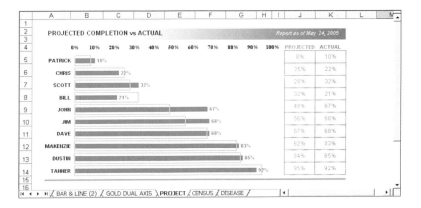

Bar charts can be used to display growth over time, as shown in Figure 20.30. Notice how data labels are applied to each series showing the online music spending growth over a six-year period. This chart form is used frequently throughout the analytical community.

Figure 20.30
Bar charts are great tools for showing growth over time.

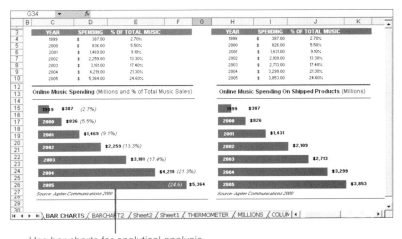

Use bar charts for analytical analysis

20

Bar charts originally were used to display events over time, and they're still great for that purpose, as shown in Figure 20.30. By adding a data label to the data series and applying proper formats to the bars, the events *become* self-explanatory within the chart.

LINE CHARTS

Line charts serve well for measuring or plotting continuously over time. They make a good combination with column charts, or in multiple-line fashion. Line charts also are great for showing information that involves trends or change over time with one or two sets of data.

TIP FROM

> If you have more than two sets of data in a line chart, you'll need to be creative with line styles; otherwise, they start to blend.

Figure 20.31 shows a typical line chart. Notice that the example shows the continuous trade price variance over time throughout the day.

Figure 20.31
Line charts work well when showing time analysis. Notice how drawing tools can be used to add time highlights and callouts within the chart.

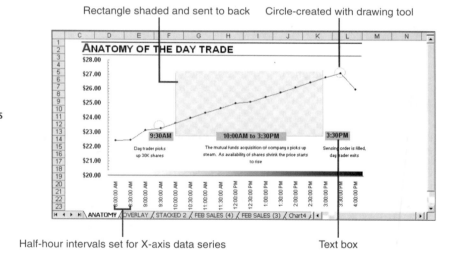

Rectangle shaded and sent to back   Circle-created with drawing tool

Half-hour intervals set for X-axis data series   Text box

PIE CHARTS

Pie charts are used for showing a percentage of the whole. The pie chart types available are the standard 2D pie chart; exploded 2D pie; 3D pie; exploded 3D pie; *pie of a pie*, which extracts a subset of a pie slice; and *bar of a pie*; which extracts a subset of a pie and plots it as a stacked column chart. Note that pie charts can plot only one series of data.

One of the great features Excel offers with pie charts is that you can select the data point and drag it away from the whole pie, thereby *exploding* the slice—also called a *piece* or *wedge*—to highlight a certain data point.

One of the drawbacks with charts in Excel is the limitation for modifying plot layouts. You can get creative to achieve your objective and still use pie charts. For example, if you have to give a presentation where you're showing market size comparisons over time, you may need to apply some overlay tricks to achieve a logical story for the presentation. In Figure 20.32, notice where the technology market size against the S&P 500 changed over the past eight years that you can visually depict this change by using pie charts. The issue: This chart cannot be created with the standard pie options or doughnut chart options. You'll need to create two charts embedded on a worksheet and then stack the technology chart on top of the S&P chart. Choose none for borders and backgrounds on the plot & chart areas.

→ See also Chapter 21, "Modifying Excel Charts".You can access this live chart example on the CD.

TIP FROM

> The key here is to understand that pies work well with market share and market size comparisons.

Figure 20.32
Use pie charts when you need to view market share.

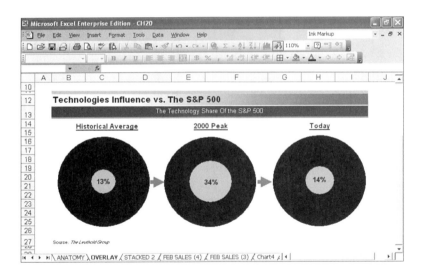

Pie charts are designed specifically for one set of data, and doughnut charts are for two sets of data compared in pie form. If you need to plot several data series and insist on using a pie shape, use a doughnut chart (see the next section for details).

CAUTION

> If you have more than 10 points of data in your data series, don't use a pie chart. With too much information, it's easy for the reader to become lost. If you exceed this number, you might want to consider a column or bar chart in place of a pie.

Excel also offers the capability to view pie charts with an option called Pie of Pie and Bar of Pie. The drawback here is the functionality is still limited in formatted capabilities. In cases where you have to create digestible presentations with large amounts of data you can combine chart types on one worksheet (see Figure 20.33).

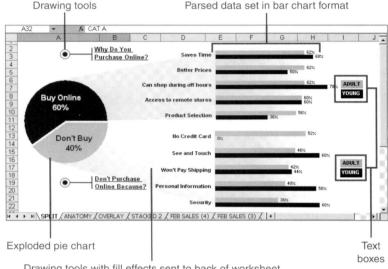

Figure 20.33
Use multiple chart objects on the same worksheet to combine and create sophisticated chart stories on one worksheet.

Drawing tools

Parsed data set in bar chart format

Exploded pie chart

Drawing tools with fill effects sent to back of worksheet

Text boxes

You can explode the pie slices then use bar charts to call out the independent line items behind the slice using independent chart objects embedded within the same worksheet. Note that this is an advanced example; see also modifying and formatting chapters for adding additional chart elements. The example shows a pie chart with two bar charts embedded as chart objects on the same worksheet. You can access the enclosed workbooks on the CD to dissect the actual objects within the worksheet.

DOUGHNUT CHARTS

Doughnut charts are variations of pie charts. The difference is that doughnut charts are for multiple sets of data—sort of like plotting several pie charts against each other. One way to use a doughnut chart is to compare a fiscal year cycle of projected sales versus actual sales. The doughnut chart is a natural choice for this type of data because a year cycle is often thought of as a circle.

In Figure 20.34, the doughnut chart represents actual sales vs projected for the fiscal year.

Figure 20.34
You can use dough-nut charts to compare sets of stacked data or data sets over time.

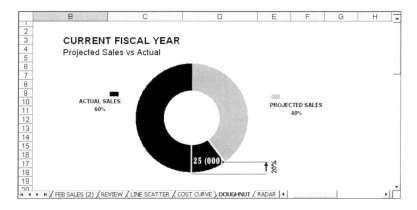

SCATTER CHARTS

Scatter charts are used for plotting data over uneven time intervals. This chart style is mostly seen in the scientific and engineering arenas. However, the use of scatter charts can defi-nitely cross over into other areas, as shown in Figure 20.35. This chart shows scatter charts plotted against industry averages. The industry average is in the form of a line chart (unchanging), and the names of the students are plotted in scatter form against time and against the industry average.

Figure 20.35
A scatter chart for competency scores is combined with a line chart displaying the industry average.

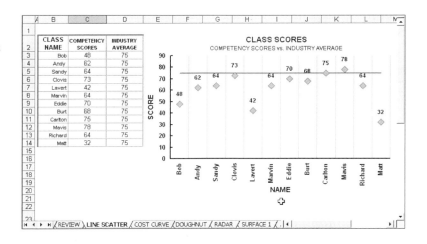

Using the same approach, notice that Figure 20.36 has the same chart types, but the data is sorted from lowest scores to highest scores. When creating charts with random plotted points, a better approach might be to sort the information from smallest to largest so that the audience can grasp the information in a shorter period of time.

Figure 20.36
Sort the scores in the worksheet from smallest to largest before creating the chart. This way, it's easier to compare the class scores against the industry average.

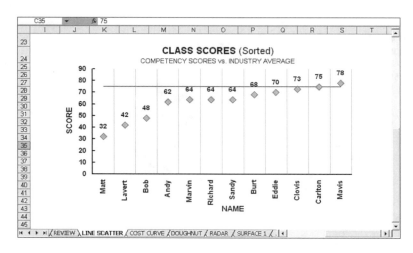

AREA CHARTS

Area charts are used much like line charts, in that area charts plot data over time in a continuous manner. The only difference is that the area is filled, hence the name area chart (see Figure 20.37).

Figure 20.37
When comparing global markets over time, area charts can effectively represent the differences between the markets.

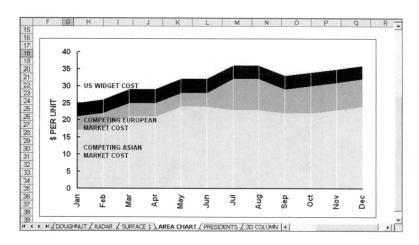

TIP FROM

When plotting multiple areas against each other on the same graph, consider using extreme differences in shading colors so the areas don't blend. An example of this would be to use the lightest shade of gray first and then darker and darker as the layers get deeper.

Avoid using more than five sets of data with this chart type. It's easy to lose the audience's focus if too much information is presented at once. It also helps if the data sets are sized so that one is smaller than the second which is smaller than the third—without this feature you get data areas crossing over each other making it impossible to read.

RADAR CHARTS

Radar charts show relationships between separate sets of data. The relationship is shown against the whole of a series, similar to the way a doughnut chart plots a data series against the whole of a series. Suppose that you want to compare the consumer spending in four categories of your market against your product distribution and focus. You can use a radar chart for market analysis in the form of a quadrant to analyze your current product focus against the consumer dollar spending, as shown in Figure 20.38. Radar charts help you establish market comparatives for quick decision making, as well as refocus your audience's efforts and business strategy.

Figure 20.38
Radar charts can be valuable tools in comparative analysis. This example helps the audience refocus its efforts and move its product focus closer to the consumer spending.

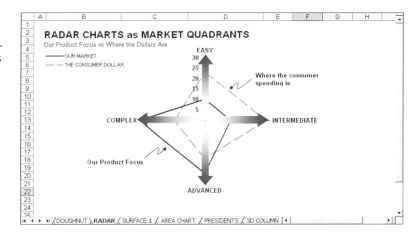

SURFACE CHARTS

Surface charts measure two changing variables in the form of a topographical map, providing a great 3D representation of the highs and lows. There are two types of surface charts, with two variations of each type. The *3D surface* provides variations in color, and the *3D wire frame* gives the topographical contour without color variations.

Assume that you have several variables that you want to display, such as time, profit, season, loss, breakeven, and so on. It can almost become confusing. However, with a 3D surface chart, you can measure certain sets of data and use drawing tools to analyze the rest. (Always think in terms of combining Excel's tools to enhance your graph. You'll run into situations that practically *require* chart embellishment.)

20

Figure 20.39 shows a surface chart and uses Excel's flexibility with drawing tools to tell the rest of the story. From this 3D view, you can see the average span of the season, the breakeven in mined ounces, and a profit scale above breakeven. A lot of information is crammed into this small chart.

Figure 20.39
You can use surface charts to show several levels of information that a 2D chart would convey only with difficulty.

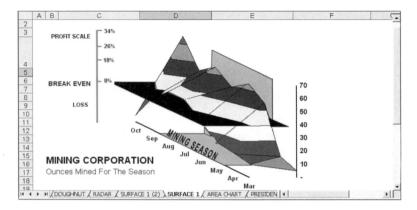

BUBBLE CHARTS

Bubble charts compare values in sets of three. The first two sets are actually used in the chart; the third value determines the size of the bubble markers. The bubble chart in Figure 20.40 represents the average ore mined per pod. In this example, you want to visually display the ounce concentration level per pod and show its respective location on the area map. If you have a picture of the map, you could paste it into the chart (in this case, however, it was drawn in). The highest concentration levels are formatted to be darker.

Figure 20.40
The bubble chart example shows the ounce concentration per pod and its respective location on the mining grid or area map.

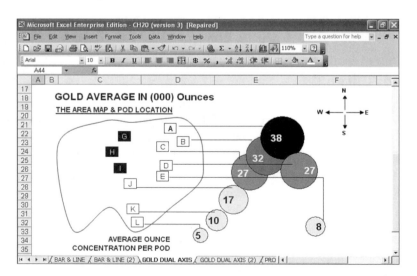

STOCK CHARTS

Stock charts are designed by default for the stock market and come in four varieties: high low close, open high low close, volume high low close, and volume open high low close. It might sound a little confusing; however, Excel indicates the order of the information in the chart sub-type in the Chart Wizard dialog box. For example, this type of chart can indicate the date and the high mark for the day, or the low mark and close for the day.

Often, you'll see *stock diaries* in publications that track information relative to the stock market's overall performance over the year or a specific period of time. The stock diary enables you to see the stock market's volume performance aligned against the high, low, and close for the specified period(s). You can create stock diaries in Excel as well. Notice the example in Figure 20.41, which consists of two charts: one for volume, and the other for the high, low, and close.

Figure 20.41
You can create stock charts in Excel to measure performance over time. You also can align two charts, one over the other, to create a stock diary.

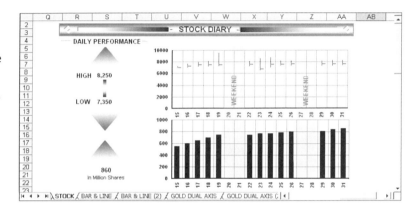

Rather than use two charts, you could plot this data on one chart with dual axes, but for simplicity it's easier to view it as two charts. Notice that the two charts have been aligned, using drawing tools to call out the key points for each day's performance, and the weekends have been blocked out.

TIP FROM

Stock charts are also handy for charting temperature variances for scientific or medical studies, crop yield projections, product analyses, and so on.

CYLINDER, CONE, AND PYRAMID CHARTS

Cylinder charts, *cone charts*, and *pyramid charts* are 3D charts with unique shapes. Where a standard column chart provides a rectangle effect in cluster column form, the cylinders, cones, and pyramids are shaped in the form of their names (see Figure 20.42). Sub-types include cluster column, stacked column, clustered bar, and stacked bar. If you like, you can create two forms of columns on the same chart—the example shows a column with a cylinder effect.

Figure 20.42
A formatted cylinder chart can be great when a presentation is as much about the graphics as the supporting data.

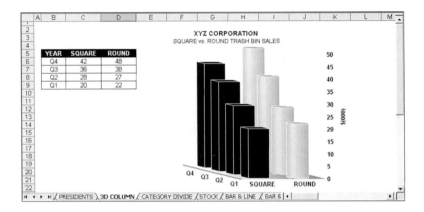

CUSTOM CHARTS

Excel offers many built-in custom chart types based on the standard chart types. Most of the custom chart types are formatted to add some pizzazz to a presentation or add a little variety into a basic, dull chart. To view what your data would look like as one of Excel's built-in custom chart types, select the Custom Types tab in step 1 of the Chart Wizard, or choose Chart, Chart Type from the menu bar.

Chances are you probably won't use any of the custom types; however, they can provide ideas on how you can format your chart. Remembering that charts are pictures that tell stories, it's easy to get carried away with all the tools and formatting options in Excel. Be cautious; you can easily lose focus with too much on the chart at once.

CREATING A PERSONALIZED CUSTOM CHART

After formatting a chart, you can save the format as a custom type. You'll probably save several types of charts as custom types, so be sure that your title description fits the chart. To save charts as a custom type, follow these steps:

1. Select the chart you want to save as a custom chart.
2. Choose Chart, Chart Type to open the Chart Type dialog box.
3. Click the Custom Types tab.
4. Select the User-Defined option in the Select From section (see Figure 20.43).

Figure 20.43
The Custom Types tab in the Chart Type dialog box enables you to save a chart as a custom type.

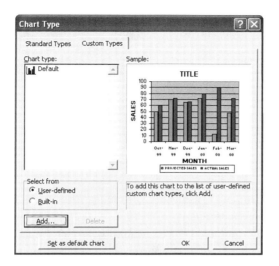

5. Click the Add button to open the Add Custom Chart Type dialog box (see Figure 20.44).

Figure 20.44
Name the custom chart type.

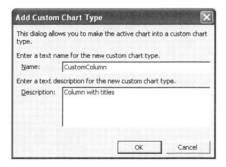

6. Type a name for the new chart type and supply a description, if desired. You can also uses spaces in the chart name.

7. Click OK. The custom type now appears on the Chart Type list on the Custom Types tab. If you want this custom chart type set as the default chart type for use in Excel, click the Set As Default Chart button and respond Yes in the message box that appears.

To delete a custom chart type, select it in the Chart Type list on the Custom Types tab, click the Delete button, and click OK when asked for confirmation.

20

NOTE

Certain formats are not retained in a custom chart (no border and no fill pattern for the chart area).

PRINTING CHARTS

Before printing a chart, it's good practice to preview the chart (see Figure 20.45). You can preview a chart in the following ways:

- If you created the chart on a chart sheet, activate or select the chart sheet. Choose File, Print Preview; a preview of the printed chart appears onscreen.

- If the chart is embedded on a worksheet, choose File, Print Preview to preview the entire worksheet with the chart on it.

- If the chart is embedded and you want to print just the chart, select the chart and choose File, Print Preview. Excel previews the selected chart and you can print it as you would a chart sheet.

Figure 20.45
The Print Preview feature enables you to review the chart on the embedded worksheet before you print it.

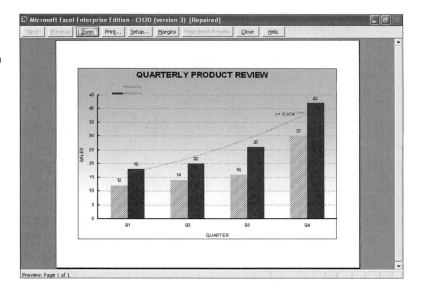

Whether you're printing on a color or a black-and-white printer (using *grayscale*), be sure to print a test copy and review it before distributing the chart. Remember that every printer is different, and Print Preview shows you only Excel's *projection* of how the printout will look. If you create the chart in color but are printing in grayscale, the different colors on the chart might appear similar in shade when printed. Data series should stand apart from each other; be sure to use contrasting shades or switch from using color to using black-and-white patterns. Even when printing in color, be aware that color monitors and color printers don't "think" in the same colors. The colors might turn out to be more red, blue, and so on than you expected. Also, note that the print quality of the printer, the paper, and the toner/cartridge/ribbon all affect the results you get.

TIP FROM

[signature]

> You can use the Options button in the Page Setup dialog box to access a color printer's settings. From there, you can switch from color to grayscale, then (from Print Preview) you can more accurately view how the printer will print the colors in shades of gray.

When printing a chart on a chart sheet or printing a selected chart embedded on a worksheet, you can click the Print button on the Standard toolbar to send the chart directly to the printer using the default print settings. Note that Excel resizes the chart as necessary to occupy the whole sheet of paper; this might not be exactly what you had in mind. Using the File, Print command, on the other hand, displays the Print dialog box as usual, but the Print What section of the dialog box gives you only one option: Selected Chart. While an embedded chart is selected, you can't opt to print the worksheet with the chart. If you want both, cancel the dialog box, deselect the embedded chart, and then issue the Print command from the menu or the toolbar button.

TROUBLESHOOTING

SELECTING A CHART ELEMENT

Excel won't let me select a specific chart element.

Excel gives you two ways to select chart elements:

- Click the element so the selection handles are showing.
- Click the Chart Objects button on the Chart toolbar and select the desired element from the drop-down list.

CHANGING A CHART SHEET TO AN EMBEDDED CHART

I can't move a chart sheet next to my data table.

Excel defaults to creating a chart as a worksheet, but you can change the chart worksheet to an embedded chart. Select Chart, Location to open the Chart Location dialog box. Select As Object In and use the drop-down list to specify the worksheet you want the chart to be embedded in.

ELIMINATING THE LEGEND BORDER

Can I eliminate the border of the legend?

Select the legend so the selection handles are showing. Choose Format, Selected Legend to open the Format Legend dialog box. Click the Patterns tab and select None for the Border setting; then click OK.

Saving a Formatted Chart As a Custom Chart

How can I save the formatting I applied to a chart so I don't have to re-create the formatting when new data is applied?

Select the chart. Choose Chart, Chart Type to open the Chart Type dialog box. On the Custom Types tab, select the User-Defined option and click the Add button to open the Add Custom Chart Type dialog box. Supply a name for the new custom chart and click OK twice.

Adding a Trendline

How do I add a trendline to a data series?

Trendlines can only be added to two-dimensional charts. To add a trendline, select the data series you want the trendline to represent. Choose Chart, Add Trendline to open the Add Trendline dialog box. On the Type tab, select the type of trendline you want and then choose OK.

Adding Data Labels

The chart is complete but I want to add data labels to a series.

Select the series of data for which you want to add labels. Then, choose Format, Selected Data Series to display the Format Data Series dialog box. On the Data Labels tab, select the Show Label option. To add data labels to all the series at once, click anywhere in the chart and choose Chart, Chart Options to open the Chart Options dialog box. Click the Data Labels tab and select the Show Label option. Click OK.

EXCEL IN PRACTICE

Choosing the correct chart type to display information is critical to comprehension. Figure 20.46 shows a typical clustered column chart that displays additions to each department's headcount as a separate column. Although the information being conveyed is clear, the ramifications aren't obvious; the audience must do a bit of quick calculating to figure out the results. In Figure 20.47, the stacked chart type displays additions to each department as stacks on top of the current headcount stack. When displaying information that's in addition to another column but within the same data set, stacked charts work much better for getting the point across.

Figure 20.46
Displaying the current and projected amounts in separate columns requires the audience to do a little math in their heads.

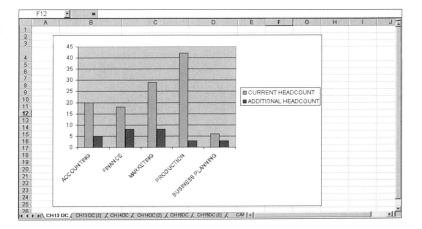

Figure 20.47
The stacked chart shows at a glance the contrast between current and projected counts, and makes it instantly obvious which department is hoping to gain how much additional staff.

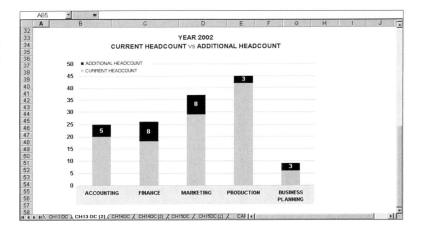

20

CHAPTER **21**

MODIFYING EXCEL CHARTS

In this chapter

Options for Improving Your Charts   506

Changing the Chart Type   508

Changing a Data Series   510

Adding a Secondary Axis to the Chart   514

Value Axis Scaling   516

Category Axis Scaling   521

Changing the Series Order   523

Adding a Trendline to a Data Series   525

OPTIONS FOR IMPROVING YOUR CHARTS

After you create a chart, you probably will want to add information or change elements of the chart. Excel enables you to manipulate any part of the chart as well as add elements to the chart. If you saved the chart as an embedded chart and now want to change it to a chart on a separate chart sheet, you can do that, too. Many times, however, you must go into an existing chart, delete a series of data, and replace it with data from a new location, or even change the chart type to give the chart a different look and feel.

Information in a newly created chart almost always will have to be modified to get your point across. The better you become at presenting information to achieve your goals, the better off you'll be.

Excel provides numerous tools and techniques to manipulate a chart to make it serve the specific needs of the audience. Some of these techniques are discussed in Chapter 22, "Formatting Charts," and Chapter 23, "Professional Charting Techniques." For now, it's important to learn the fundamentals of building and modifying charts. This section begins by discussing the fundamentals of adding information and changing existing information on a chart.

MOVING AND RESIZING EMBEDDED CHARTS

When an embedded chart is complete, you probably will want to move or resize the chart so that it fits better with the data on the worksheet.

To resize a chart, select the chart by placing the mouse pointer over the embedded chart and clicking. Small black boxes called *sizing handles* appear around the perimeter of the chart. Place your mouse over one of the handles. When the pointer changes to display a two-headed black arrow, click and drag away from the center of the chart to enlarge, or toward the center of the chart to reduce. Dragging a corner handle resizes height and width simultaneously. While resizing, Excel displays a dotted box to give you an indication of the final size of the chart.

You might decide at some point that an embedded chart should have been placed in a different location: somewhere else in the current worksheet, on a different worksheet entirely, or on a separate chart sheet. Perhaps you chose the wrong option in the Chart Wizard, or you just changed your mind and want to move the chart from one place to another. As usual, multiple methods are available; the following methods are the easiest:

- Move the chart from one worksheet location to another with a quick cut-and-paste operation. Select the chart, copy the chart, use the cut command, position the cell pointer in the new worksheet location, and paste the chart into place.

- To drag the chart elsewhere on the current sheet, select the chart so that the handles are visible. Then, click somewhere in the chart area (a ScreenTip says Chart Area), but not on any of the individual elements of the chart—in other words, don't click the title, axes, and so on—and watch for the mouse pointer to display the typical selection arrow. Drag the chart to its new position, and drop it there.

- To move the chart from one worksheet to another or to a separate chart sheet, select the chart and choose Chart, Location to open the Chart Location dialog box. Specify whether you want to place the chart on a separate chart sheet or as an object in another worksheet in the current workbook (select from the drop-down list).

SELECTING PARTS OF A CHART FOR EDITING

It's very likely that you'll need to change particular aspects of a new or existing chart—removing a particular data marker, adding text boxes, adjusting line size and color, and so on. The first step to changing features within the chart is to select the chart or an object in the chart such as a data series so that the sizing handles are showing. After the chart is selected, place the mouse pointer over almost any item in the chart to display a ScreenTip that indicates which object on the chart you're pointing to. To select the specified object, click it.

Chart objects such as data series and data points are grouped; clicking any one selects the entire set. If you need to change a particular one of the set, click it a second time to display handles around that item alone. Don't double-click; just click once to select the set, wait briefly, and then click the individual item.

TIP FROM

If the chart is small or somewhat crowded, you might find yourself squinting at the screen or increasingly frustrated as you attempt to click tiny elements in the chart. Instead, use the Zoom feature to enlarge the view so that you can see what you're clicking. If the chart is embedded, click outside the chart—anywhere in the worksheet—to enable the Zoom feature. Make your selections and changes, and then restore the original Zoom setting, if desired.

The Chart toolbar can be very helpful when you want to edit a chart—particularly if you're having difficulty selecting individual parts of a chart because you can't remember what they're called. Table 21.1 describes the buttons on the Chart toolbar. When you're working in the chart, the Chart toolbar should automatically display. If the toolbar isn't displayed while you are in the chart, right-click the menu or any toolbar and choose Chart from the context menu that appears.

TABLE 21.1   BUTTONS ON THE CHART TOOLBAR

Button	Name	Description
	Chart Objects	Displays a drop-down list of most of the objects and data points within the chart. Select the one you want from the list.
	Format *<object>*	Displays the Format dialog box for the selected object on the chart. (The ScreenTip name for this button changes to show the name of the selected object.)

continues

TABLE 21.1 CONTINUED

Button	Name	Description
	Chart Type	Displays a drop-down palette of chart types; click the type you want to apply to the current chart. The face of the button changes to show the last chart type selected.
	Legend	Toggles adding and removing a legend on the chart.
	Data Table	Toggles adding and removing a data table below the horizontal axis.
	By Row	Plots each row of data as a series in the chart.
	By Column	Plots each column of data as a series in the chart.
	Angle Text Downward	Changes the angle of selected text to 45 degrees downward. Use for data markers, axis labels, and so on.
	Angle Text Upward	Changes the angle of selected text to 45 degrees upward. Use for data markers, axis labels, and so on.

NOTE

You can often save time by right-clicking the item in the chart and using the context menu rather than the main menu. You also can double-click the desired element of the chart to display the Format dialog box for that element.

CHANGING THE CHART TYPE

No matter how much time you spend deliberating *before* creating a chart about what type of chart to use, occasionally the result just isn't what you need. You can change the chart type easily to some other type that works better for the data. Excel even lets you combine chart types by changing individual data series to a different type from the rest of the chart. For example, when comparing trends or different sets of data, it can be helpful to separate the data series with different chart types on the same chart to show distinct differences between two sets of information. Figure 21.1 shows projected sales in a line and actual sales in columns. In this example, displaying the projected sales as a line clearly emphasizes by how much sales fell short of projection.

The methods are basically the same for changing the chart type for the entire chart or for selected data series. The only difference is that if you want to change just a data series, you select the data series first. You can use any of the following methods to change the chart type:

■ Choose Chart, Chart Type to open the Chart Type dialog box, and then select the desired chart type and sub-type (see Figure 21.2).

Figure 21.1
It is possible to alter the chart type for a series to draw attention to different data.

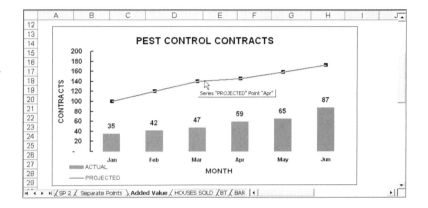

Figure 21.2
Use the Chart Type dialog box to select a different chart type and sub-type.

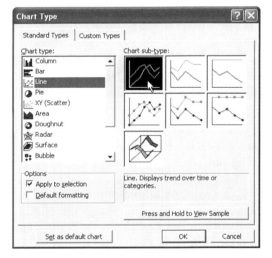

■ Right-click any data point in the series (or anywhere else in the chart if you want to change the entire chart) and select Chart Type from the context menu to open the Chart Type dialog box. Change the settings as desired.

■ Click the Chart Type button on the Chart toolbar and select a new chart type from the displayed palette.

■ Click the Chart Wizard button on the Standard toolbar to open the Chart Wizard - Step 1 of 4 - Chart Type dialog box. Select a new chart type and sub-type, and click Finish. This method changes the entire chart; it doesn't work for individual data series.

21

TIP

The advantage of using the Chart Wizard to change the chart type for an entire chart is that you can use the Press and Hold to View Sample button to preview the data in the new chart format. This can save some steps if you need to try several chart types before you find the best type.

CHANGING A DATA SERIES

A *data series* is represented by the bars in a bar chart, the columns in a column chart, and so on. For example, if you have a column chart and a set of the individual columns is one color, all the columns of that color together represent a data series.

In addition to formatting data series by changing the color, pattern, and so on, you can add or remove data series in the chart, as described in the following sections.

SELECTING A DATA SERIES OR DATA POINT IN A CHART

To modify or format a data series in a chart, you first must select the data series by clicking any one of the data points (a column, bar, and so on) in the series. You'll notice three things:

- When the mouse pointer is placed over the data series, a ScreenTip displays a description of the series and the particular data point's value under the mouse pointer.
- When a data point is clicked, the whole series is selected, and by clicking the data point again the sizing handles show up on the data point as square dots.
- When a data series is selected, its corresponding data in the worksheet is surrounded by colored Range Finder boundary lines. A purple boundary surrounds the axis labels, a green boundary surrounds the series labels (the ones normally found in the chart's legend), and a blue boundary surrounds the data series entries.

You also can change an individual data point in a data series. With the series selected, click the point you want to change (see Figure 21.3). To change the value of the data point and its corresponding value in the worksheet—remember that the two are linked—select the data point in the chart and drag it to the desired value.

One reason you might want to change values this way is for visual emphasis. If you're trying to drive home a point and the actual value isn't static or exact, you might want to drag the value or data point to look a certain way (for example, very low or very high) as opposed to registering an exact value.

REMOVING A SERIES FROM A CHART

When displaying information with charts, you often want to analyze the information with and without different sets of data. For example, in a chart that shows actual versus projected sales for the year, you might want to display just the actual sales and then just the projections. To remove a data series from a chart, select the data series so that the handles are showing, and then press the Delete key, or choose Edit, Clear, Series. To get the series to reappear, choose Edit, Undo Clear.

Figure 21.3
By selecting a single data point in a data series, you can format or change the value of the data point.

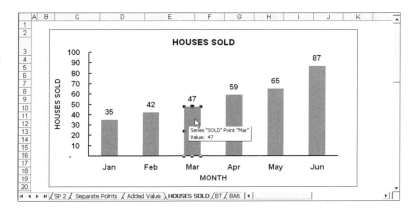

ADDING OR ADJUSTING SOURCE DATA

Because business needs change, you might sometimes have to add data series to a chart—for example, to include a new division or product—or adjust existing data series or data points to include new information. You can build a new chart or just add data to the existing chart, as described in the following sections.

ADDING DATA POINTS OR DATA SERIES

Excel gives you the flexibility of adding data to a chart in several ways:

- Adjust the source data, as described in the following section.
- Select the chart and choose Chart, Add Data to display the Add Data dialog box (see Figure 21.4). Specify the range of the data you want to add. You can use the Collapse Dialog button to reduce the size of the dialog box, or just drag the dialog box out of the way to see the worksheet. When the range is correct, click OK. You also can use this method to add data from a different worksheet.

Figure 21.4
Use the Add Data dialog box to add new series to an existing chart.

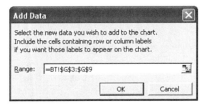

- Copy the data in the worksheet, select the chart, and paste the data into the chart. You can use the Paste command on the context menu; choose Edit, Paste; click the Paste button on the Standard toolbar; or press Ctrl+V. With the paste command, Excel selects the format for the new series automatically.

21

■ If you want more control over how Excel pastes the new data, choose Edit, Paste Special to display the Paste Special dialog box, in which you can indicate how you want the new data to appear (see Figure 21.5).

Figure 21.5
The Paste Special dialog box gives you options for plotting information as new points or in a new series, as well as by rows or columns.

In the example in Figure 21.6, the new data is added as a series and plotted in the form of columns along the y-axis—the same result as you would get with a simple paste. In Figure 21.7, on the other hand, the data is added as new points, thereby plotting the data separately, as a second category on the x-axis.

You can choose from the following options in the Paste Special dialog box:

- **New Series**—Adds the copied data to the chart as a new data series.
- **New Point(s)**—Adds the copied data to the chart as an additional data series along the same axis.
- **Rows** or **Columns**—Creates an additional data series from the contents of each row or column in the copied selection.
- **Series Names in First Row**—Uses the first row or column of the copied data as the label for the selected data series.
- **Categories (X Labels) in First Column**—Uses the first row or column of the copied data as category labels on the x-axis.
- **Replace Existing Categories**—Replaces the existing category labels with the category labels you want to paste in. For example, you could use this option to change existing labels January through December to 1 through 12.

Figure 21.6
The new information is pasted as a new series in columns.

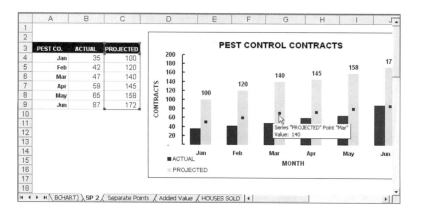

Figure 21.7
The result of pasting information in as new points along the same category-axis.

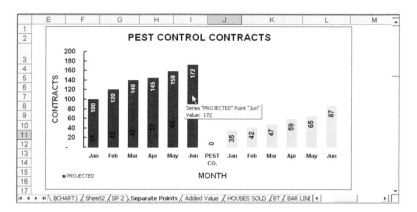

NOTE

Choose Undo if the results aren't what you had in mind. Also, certain options result in nothing happening, meaning that Excel cannot paste the data the way you want.

■ Use the drag-and-drop method to add data to a chart. Select the data you want to add. Move the mouse pointer over the edge of the selection until the pointer changes to an arrow with four smaller black arrows attached. Click and drag the data anywhere inside the chart; then release the mouse button.

If the data is on a different worksheet from the chart, hold down the Alt key and drag the data down to the tab for the worksheet containing the chart. When the destination worksheet appears, release the Alt key and drag the data into the chart.

If the data is in a different workbook, open the workbook and use the Window, Arrange command to display both workbooks onscreen. Display the worksheet containing the data and the worksheet containing the chart. Then, select and drag the desired data from the source worksheet window into the chart. Data added from another workbook creates links to that workbook in the destination chart.

NOTE

You might be prompted with the Paste Special dialog box if Excel can't define the new data automatically.

TIP FROM

Avoid adding too many data series to one chart. You can easily lose the point if too much information is presented at once. Another alternative is to create two charts and embed them on the same sheet, and then use drawing tools and/or text to help the reader compare them.

21

CHANGING THE DATA SOURCE

Sometimes you don't need to add a data series—just adjust some that are already included in the chart. You can change the source data for a chart in any of the following ways:

- Add data points or data series as described in the preceding section.

- With the worksheet data visible behind it, click an embedded chart (you might need to move the chart nearer to the source data for this method to work). Then, drag the selection handles for the colored lines that surround the source data, headings, and labels. If the mouse pointer is an arrow, you selected the corner handle. Dragging expands or contracts the selection. If the pointer is a black cross, dragging moves the selection rectangle. As you adjust the colored lines, the chart changes to reflect the new selection.

- Select the chart, start the Chart Wizard, and click Next in the Step 1 of 4 dialog box. In the Step 2 of 4 dialog box, change the data source as needed; then click Finish.

- Select the chart and choose Chart, Source Data, or right-click the chart and choose Source Data from the context menu. The Source Data dialog box opens (see Figure 21.8). Select the Data Range tab. From here, you can change the absolute address from which the data is derived.

Figure 21.8
The Source Data dialog box enables you to change the address of your chart data.

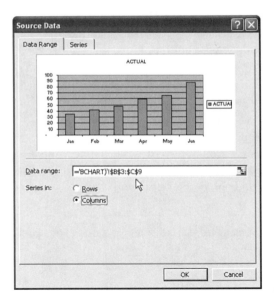

ADDING A SECONDARY AXIS TO THE CHART

More often than not, you'll run into a situation where you need to use a chart to compare two sets of data that are extremely different in value, such as unit output and dollars sold. One way to display this type of information is with a *secondary axis*. In most cases, the values would be extremely different, so you would want the units on one y-axis, and the dollars represented on another y-axis (see Figure 21.9).

Figure 21.9
You can plot series on two different y-axes.

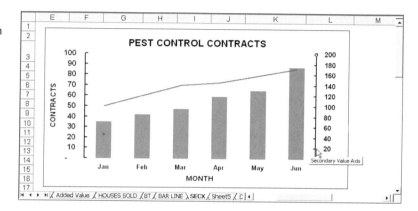

To create a dual-axis chart, follow these steps:

1. Select the data series that you want to plot on the secondary axis.

Figure 21.10
In this example, the line chart is plotted against the new secondary axis.

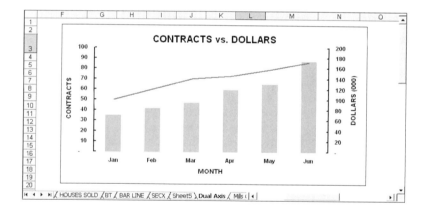

2. Choose Format, Selected Data Series to open the Format Data Series dialog box.
3. Select the Axis tab, as shown in Figure 21.11.
4. Under Plot Series On, choose Secondary Axis.
5. Click OK.

TIP FROM

Use a secondary axis when you have two types of information with extremely different low and high values. If plotted on the same axis, the category with the lower values might not be visible.

Figure 21.11
Use the Format Data Series dialog box to set up the secondary axis.

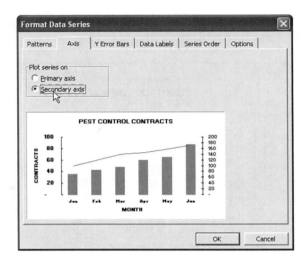

VALUE AXIS SCALING

The *scaling* of the axes in a chart can control the chart's visual characteristics, and thereby the assumptions that the audience makes based on viewing the chart. The x- and y-axes in a chart have different scaling options because they represent different things; usually, the x-axis represents categories of data, and the y-axis represents the values corresponding to those categories. You can adjust the scale of the axes by constraining visual highs and lows: the place where the two axes intersect (called the *origin*), the maximum value displayed, and the unit iteration between values.

The following sections describe scaling the value axis; see the later section "Category Axis Scaling" for details on adjusting the x-axis.

CHANGING THE MAXIMUM, MINIMUM, AND TICK MARK VALUES

Because the bars in Figure 21.12 take up most of the chart's axis, the sales represented look quite substantial (even if they're not). If you want to make the bars appear smaller, you can change the scale of the axis to reduce the visual size of the columns. Increasing the maximum value of the y-axis makes the columns look shorter; decreasing the maximum value makes them look taller. If the column value is 100, for example, and you set the maximum y-axis value at 100, the column extends to the maximum height of the y-axis, making it appear as if that data point is at peak value. Conversely, if you set the maximum value at 1,000, the column value of 100 is only one-tenth the height of the y-axis, minimizing the visual value of the column. In the example in Figure 21.13, the maximum value of the y-axis is constrained to 100, and the column sizes appear less substantial in size, giving the change from this year to last year less impact than in Figure 21.12, in which the maximum value is 40.

Figure 21.12
The default scale of
this y-axis is incre-
ments of 5.

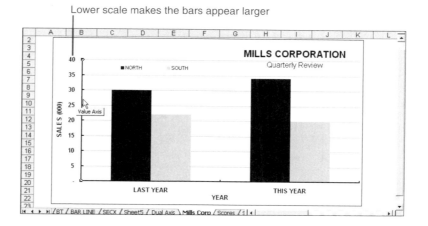
Lower scale makes the bars appear larger

Figure 21.13
By scaling the axis to
a maximum value of
100, you can control
the visual size of the
columns within the
chart.

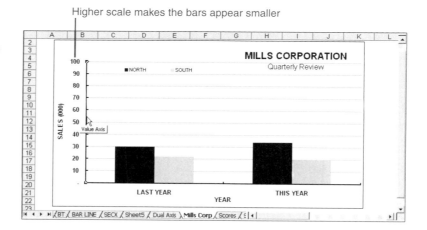
Higher scale makes the bars appear smaller

CAUTION

Obviously, skewing the visual elements in a chart also can skew the audience's percep-
tion of the chart's message. Be sure you understand exactly what information the chart is
conveying and that your data is represented in an appropriate perspective.

If the maximum value is 10 and for some reason the value changes to 20, Excel automatically adjusts the value axis to accommodate for the increase in value. By changing the
Maximum value setting on the Scale tab in the Format Axis dialog box, you can force Excel
to use a particular maximum value you prefer (see Figure 21.14). For example, changing the
maximum from the default of 40 to 100 for the chart in Figure 21.13 really diminishes the
results visually.

21

CAUTION

When you set the maximum value, the y-axis becomes static, showing plotted data series only to the maximum value that you specified.

Figure 21.14
The Scale tab in the Format Axis dialog box enables you to adjust the y-axis scaling.

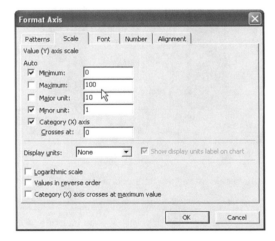

Figure 21.15
The result of applying a maximum value to the chart is a reduced column visual.

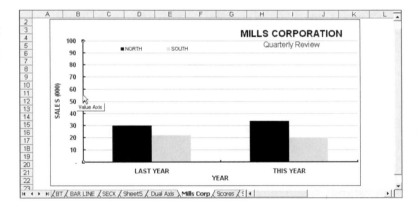

You also can use the settings on the Scale tab in the Format Axis dialog box to adjust the minimum unit to plot, as well as major and minor units that allow for interval adjustments. Suppose the y-axis plots every 20 units, but you want it to plot every 10 units. Just change the Major Unit setting from 20 to 10. The Minor Unit setting controls the unit interval of the tick marks on the minor gridlines. To space minor gridlines over three ticks, for example, set the Minor Unit setting to 3. The gridlines will appear at every third tick mark on the value axis.

If you're using the Logarithmic Scale option, the default origin is at 1, and the Minimum, Maximum, Major Unit, and Minor Unit settings are calculated as powers of 10 for the value axis, based on the data range plotted in the chart.

RESIZING THE PLOT AREA

In addition to axis scaling, you can resize the plot area—changing the height or width—to change the visual message of a chart. Suppose a line chart shows a certain amount of growth over a period of time, and you want the increase to look much steeper or flatter. Narrowing or reducing the height of the plot area might give you exactly the look you want.

In Figure 21.16, for example, the chart on the left shows three different versions of a line chart—all of which represent the same value, plotted against the same y-axis. The plot size in each case has been changed to give each line a different look. Figure 21.17 reverses this process; by adjusting the height of the plot area downward, you can visually lessen the growth line. To adjust the plot area downward simply left mouse-click over the plot area and then select the plot area sizing bar and drag it downward.

Figure 21.16
By adjusting the plot area, you can change the visual steepness of a line chart. This can give a false sense of growth, but also help in providing the right look for the audience in a given situation.

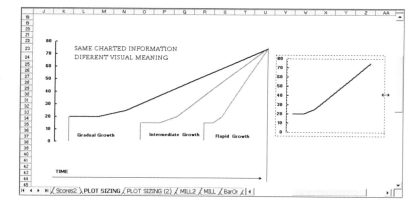

Figure 21.17
You also can adjust the height to a level that reduces the steepness of the line (which "planes" or levels it out) by adjusting the plot area height.

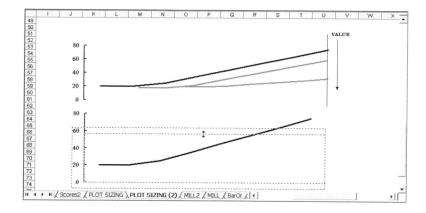

21

CHANGING THE ORIGIN

You can change where the category and value axis cross. By default, the value axis intersects the category axis at zero (the *origin*); however, you can adjust the origin by specifying the value at which you want the category axis to meet the value axis.

Suppose that you're showing scores in a competition for qualifying entrants for the current year and last year. The chart in Figure 21.18 shows a typical column chart setup (sometimes called a *waterfall* chart) that you might use. However, by moving the origin from 0 to 70, as shown in Figure 21.19, you can use the axis to display the breakeven point. In this case, 70 is the minimum qualifying score.

Figure 21.18
A typical column chart, also called a *waterfall* chart. Notice that the origin is positioned at 0 in this example.

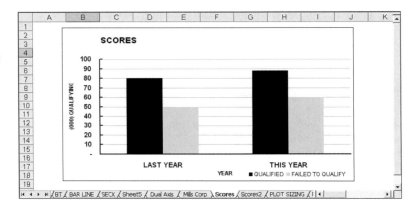

Figure 21.19
The category axis now takes on two roles: the year and the minimum qualifying score.

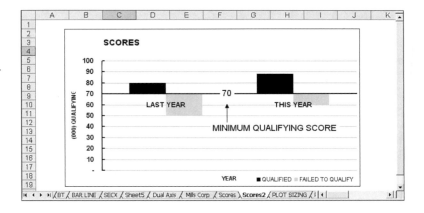

21

This technique is useful for any kind of pass/fail data. Charts like this are often used to represent value indexes with healthcare coverage plans, or other industries comparing corporate plans and their measured coverage. Even though the index reads positive, by placing the category axis at a certain point along the value axis, any value that reads below the line is viewed as less coverage, poor in rating, and so on.

To change where the category axis meets the value axis, select the y-axis and change the Crosses At setting on the Scale tab in the Format Axis dialog box (refer to Figure 21.14).

NOTE

> If you're using the Logarithmic Scale option, the default origin is at 1.

TIP FROM

> For an unusual look, you can set the x-axis to cross the y-axis at the maximum value rather than the minimum value. Select the option Category (X) Axis Crosses at Maximum Value on the Scale tab in the Format Axis dialog box. Because this chart arrangement is more difficult for the audience to interpret, however, you might need to add more explanatory text.

CATEGORY AXIS SCALING

The category axis scaling options act much like the value axis scaling options described in previous sections. You can adjust the settings to help define the story you're using the chart to tell.

To access the category x-axis settings, select the axis and choose Format, Selected Axis, or right-click the axis and choose Format Axis from the context menu. Either action opens the Format Axis dialog box. Click the Scale tab to display the scaling options for the x-axis. The following sections describe the options.

REPOSITIONING THE AXES

The y-axis doesn't have to cross the x-axis at the corner of the plot area; you can reposition the y-axis along the x-axis between categories. The example in Figure 21.20 shows a standard column chart. You could create more of a division between this year's numbers and last year's by positioning the y-axis between the two sets of columns, as shown in Figure 21.21. In this example, you set the y-axis to intersect at the second category of the x-axis.

Figure 21.20.
Standard positioning for the axes.

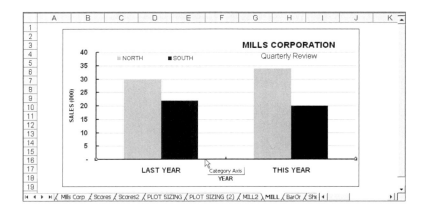

Figure 21.21
Change the position where the category axis and value axis cross to separate the years.

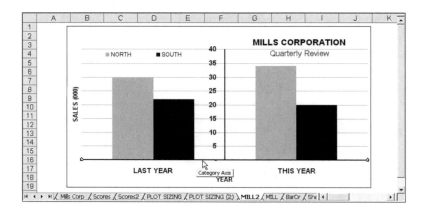

To change the position where the axes cross, change the setting for the option Value (Y) Axis Crosses at Category Number (see Figure 21.22). Two other options also affect the positioning of the y-axis on the x-axis:

- **Value (Y) Axis Crosses Between Categories**—This option places the y-axis to the left of the category indicated in the box for the option Value (Y) Axis Crosses at Category Number. If this option is selected, data points are plotted between tick marks; if not, points are plotted at the tick-mark positions.

- **Value (Y) Axis Crosses at Maximum Category**—This option places the y-axis after the last category on the x-axis, in effect placing the y-axis on the opposite side of the plot area.

Figure 21.22
Set the category number to move the value axis along the category axis. In this case it will appear between categories, to the left of category 2.

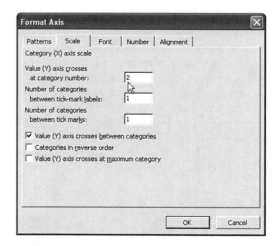

CHANGING TICK MARKS AND LABELS

The Number of Categories Between Tick-Mark Labels option on the Scale tab specifies the frequency with which you want category labels to appear on the x-axis. For example, if a chart showing 40 years of sales figures displays a label for every year, you might decrease the number of labels so that they appear every fourth or fifth year, or just mark the decades.

The Number of Categories Between Tick Marks option specifies the number of category labels displayed between each pair of tick marks. To place a minor tick mark between every category on the x-axis, set Number of Categories Between Tick Marks to 1.

TIP FROM

> If category labels are long, or the chart includes quite a few labels, they can become too crowded on the axis to be easily readable. You can adjust the angle of the category labels by setting the orientation on the Alignment tab in the Format Axis dialog box.

CHANGING THE SERIES ORDER

By changing the series order, you can manipulate the set of data the viewers' eyes will see first. Why do this? It's really a form of advertising—if you want to get a point across without getting lost in a conversation about all the other elements, you place the data in the most viewable place within a chart, which is normally the first series. Because people generally look at information from left to right or top to bottom, this naturally allows you to flow into a discussion about which data set is most important in the chart. There are ways to draw focus using formatting that far outweigh series order, but series order is an important tool to gain control over the chart and the audience.

REVERSING THE CATEGORIES

Reversing the data series is a trick that comes in handy from time to time, particularly with bar charts. For example, if you create a bar chart with quarters, Excel plots the last series of quarters at the top (see Figure 21.23). Because you naturally view information in a top-down manner, you'll probably want to reverse the order in which the series are viewed, so that Q1 appears at the top of the chart and Q4 at the bottom (see Figure 21.24).

To display categories on the x-axis in the opposite direction, select the axis, open the Format Axis dialog box, click the Scale tab, and select the Categories in Reverse Order option (see Figure 21.25).

Figure 21.23
The default category axis order clearly needs to be reversed because you view information from the top down.

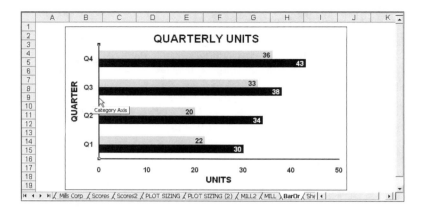

Figure 21.24
Reversing the categories.

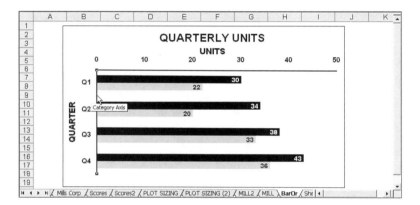

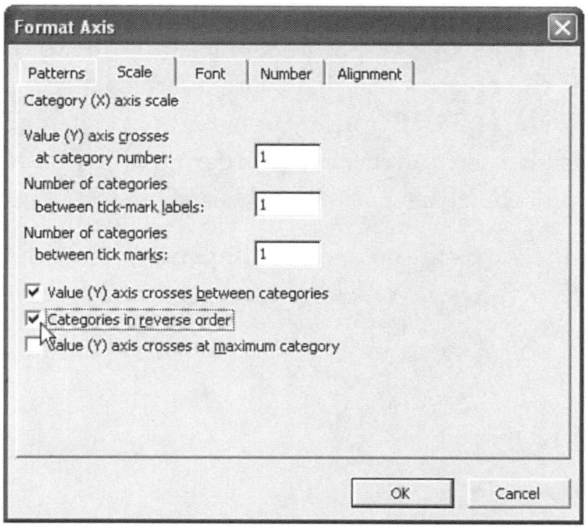

Figure 21.25
The Format Axis dialog box enables you to reverse the order of the plotted data series.

REVERSING THE VALUES

Sometimes less is better. Using golf scores as an example, you might want a player with a lower score to have a more prominent column on a column chart. In this case, you would want to have zero or negative values at the top of the value axis and the largest number crossing at the category axis. In this reversed approach, the player with the lowest score would also be perceived as having the most prominent column on the chart. Selecting the Values in Reverse Order option on the Scale tab in the Format Axis dialog box for the value axis reverses the direction of values on scatter, column, and bar charts. An alternative method of resorting data could be used.

ADDING A TRENDLINE TO A DATA SERIES

Adding *trendlines* in Excel helps you understand where you've been and where you're potentially headed. Using *regression analysis*, you can plot trends against a data series and plot out periods of time going forward. You can even specify the number of periods for which you would like to project.

> **NOTE** Trendlines can only be added to certain types of charts: area, column, line, bar, and scatter.

To add a trendline to your chart, follow these steps:

1. Select the chart or select the data series to which you want to add the trendline.

2. Choose Chart, Add Trendline to display the Add Trendline dialog box (see Figure 21.26).

Figure 21.26
The Add Trendline dialog box enables you to choose from six types of trends using regression analysis.

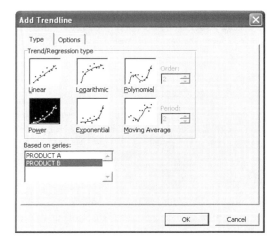

3. From the Type tab, select the type of trendline you want to add.

4. Click OK. Figure 21.27 shows a power trendline added to product B, showing the trend over fiscal quarters.

Figure 21.27
By adding a trendline, you can graphically display the trend of a series of information.

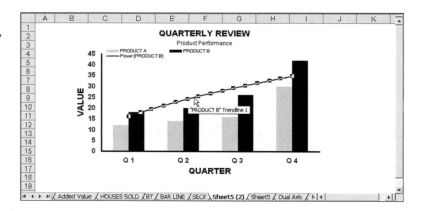

Table 21.2 describes the regression analysis trendline options available in the Add Trendline dialog box. The specific regression analysis equations and their explanations can be found by searching Excel's help for *Equations for calculating trendlines*.

TABLE 21.2 TRENDLINE SETTINGS

Setting	Description
Linear	Inserts a linear trendline.
Logarithmic	Inserts a logarithmic trendline.
Polynomial	Inserts a polynomial or curvilinear trendline.
Power	Inserts a power trendline using the Power Equation. When numbers are zero or less than zero, meaning a negative number, this option is unavailable.
Exponential	Inserts an exponential trendline. When numbers are zero or less than zero, meaning a negative number, this option is unavailable.
Moving Average	Inserts a moving average trendline. The number of points in a moving average trendline equals the total number of points in the series, minus the number you specify for the period.
Order	By entering a number in the Order box, you specify the highest polynomial order. The value is expressed as an integer between 2 and 6.
Period	By entering a number in the Period box, you specify the number of periods you want to use to calculate the moving average.
Based on Series	Selects the series in which the trendline will be displayed.

CAUTION

When you start to add elements to a chart, there's a point at which you must begin subtracting elements to eliminate the clutter. Be cautious when adding trendlines; avoid making your chart more difficult to interpret.

FORMATTING THE TRENDLINE

As with many other chart elements, quite often you'll want to format the trendline to fit within the visual aspects of the chart you're creating. Excel offers many options to create the look and feel you need for the trendline to fit into the picture. By selecting or activating the trendline, you can format the trendline as you would any other element of the chart (see Figure 21.28).

Figure 21.28
This trendline has a custom format.

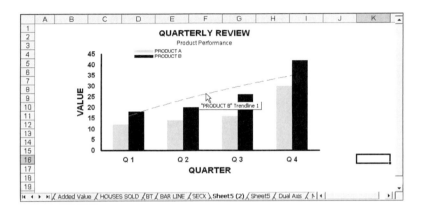

To format a trendline, follow these steps:

1. Select or activate the trendline.
2. Choose Format, Selected Trendline to open the Format Trendline dialog box.

TIP FROM

You can also double-click the trendline to access the Format Trendline dialog box or right-click the trendline.

3. From the Patterns tab in the Format Trendline dialog box, select formatting options to create the desired visual effect (see Figure 21.29).
4. Click OK.

21

Figure 21.29
On the Patterns tab, select the format style to apply to the trendline.

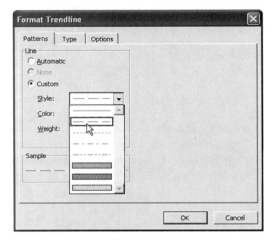

TIP FROM

> Trendlines should be formatted differently from other plotted data series to make the trendline stand out. It's also good practice to format trendlines as dotted. The dotted lines suggest that the data is forecasted or trend data; solid lines are viewed as real or actual data.

The following list describes some of the formatting options available for trendlines:

- **Automatic**—Applies the default Excel settings to the selected line or object.
- **Custom**—Enables you to customize the style, color, and weight of the selected trendline.
- **Style**—Specifies a style for the selected line or border.
- **Color**—Designates a color for the selected line or border.
- **Weight**—Indicates the weight (thickness) of the selected line or border.

As you make selections, watch the Sample box to see how the line or border will look with the options selected.

TRENDLINE OPTIONS

The settings on the Options tab in the Format Trendline dialog box enable you to further customize a trendline (see Figure 21.30).

21

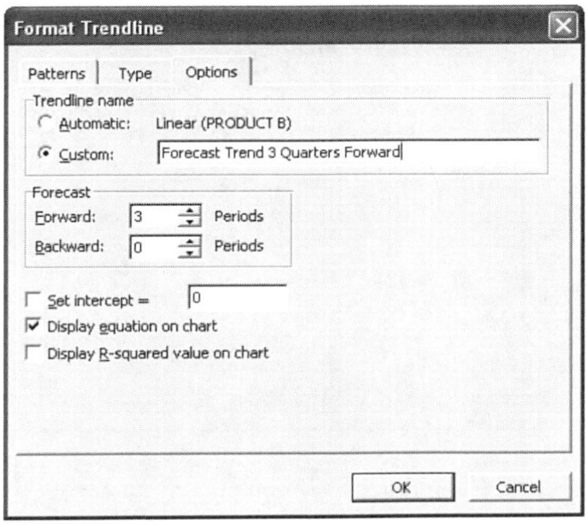

Figure 21.30
The Options tab in
the Format Trendline
dialog box enables
you to further cus-
tomize the trendline
with names and fore-
casting modes, as
well as display the
equations used.

The options are described in the following list:

- **Trendline Name**—Specify whether you want Excel to provide a name for the trendline, based on the trend chosen (Automatic), or select the Custom option and type your
own name.

- **Forecast**—Use the options in this section to specify the number of periods to chart,
going forward or backward. For example, based on the current or historical information
from the charted series, Excel can plot out the trend of future periods (see Figure 21.31).

- **Set Intercept = ___**—By setting the *intercept*, you specify where you want the trendline
to meet the y-axis.

- **Display Equation on Chart** and **Display R-Squared Value on Chart**—Use these
ooptions to post regression equations or R-squared values on the chart. If you have several scenarios of trendlines, for example, you might want to show the values for each
trendline.

TIP

By default, trendlines are not the same color as the data series they're plotted against.
Whenever possible, try to format the trendline to the color or shade of the series that the
trendline represents. Doing this helps the audience to understand instantly which series
the trendline is tied to, without additional explanation.

Figure 21.31
The trendline fore-casted out one period.

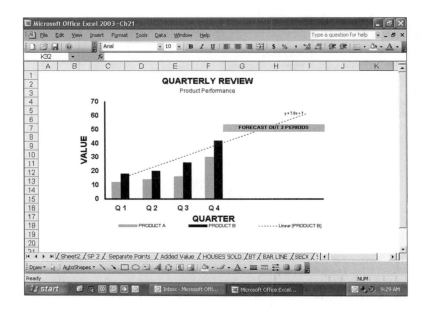

TROUBLESHOOTING

CHANGING THE MAXIMUM VALUE FOR THE VALUE AXIS

How can I make data appear smaller on the chart?

Select the value axis, choose Format, Selected Axis, select the Scale tab, and replace the Maximum value with a higher number.

CHANGING THE CHART TYPE OF A DATA SERIES

How do I change the chart type of just one of the data series in a chart?

Select the data series you want to change, choose Chart, Chart Type, select the desired chart type, and click OK. Note that some chart types can't be combined, but Excel will warn you if you choose a chart type that won't work with the existing chart.

ADDING DATA TO A CHART

I've added data to my data table; how do I apply it to my chart?

There are several ways to do this in Excel; here are the easiest. Select and copy the data you want to add, select the chart, and choose Edit, Paste. You also could choose Paste Special, or choose Chart, Add Data. You can also drag data onto a chart. Simply drag the data over the chart and drop it on the chart.

CHARTING DRAMATICALLY DIFFERENT VALUES ON THE SAME CHART

I have two data series on my chart with extremely different values. How do I compensate for this?

Use a secondary axis to plot one of the series. Select the data series to plot on the secondary axis. Then choose Format, Selected Data Series, click the Axis tab, and choose Secondary Axis.

CUSTOMIZING TICK MARKS

How can I customize the spacing of tick marks on the value axis?

Select the value axis, choose Format, Selected Axis to open the Format Axis dialog box, click the Scale tab, and type the spacing desired in the Major Unit option. The Minor Unit setting controls spacing for the minor gridlines.

EXCEL IN PRACTICE

When data series on a chart have extremely different values, as shown in Figure 21.32, but they still must be viewed on the same chart, use the secondary axis feature as shown in Figure 21.33. Select the data series to plot on the secondary axis and choose Format, Selected Data Series. Click the Axis tab and choose Secondary Axis.

Figure 21.32
The numbers for units and sales are widely divergent, making the chart look awkward and difficult to read.

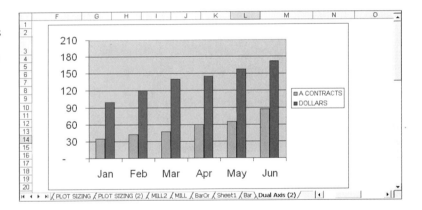

Figure 21.33
Plotting series on two different axes enables you to compare related series with different value sets.

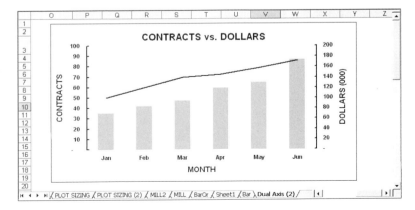

CHAPTER 22

FORMATTING CHARTS

In this chapter

An Overview of Formatting Charts   534

Formatting Lines: Axes, Tick Marks, High/Low Lines, and Error Bars   534

Formatting Text: Data Labels, Titles, Legends, and Text Boxes   540

Enhancing Charts with Shapes   546

Formatting Data Series   548

Changing the Border, Color, or Fill of a Chart Item   551

Formatting 3D Charts   555

AN OVERVIEW OF FORMATTING CHARTS

Formatting charts is as important as the data behind the chart. What you display says a lot about your skills and your ability to translate information to others. All too often, people clutter charts and the message gets lost in all the data. Because Excel offers such a wide variety of options, people want to use them all in graphic presentations. Remember, the less you try to cram onto the chart, the more easily understood your chart will be.

It's important to understand the characteristics and functions of the chart elements, as well as how to minimize or maximize their visual presence on a chart. Because you can format each chart element, you can fade in and fade out elements. *Fading in* means darkening and *fading out* means lightening the element. An *element* is anything that can be selected on the chart with your mouse. Fading just adds or reduces emphasis on a chart element, and because all chart elements can be selected individually, you can create or take away emphasis on any element.

NOTE

> Formatting options differ for different types of charts. For example, you can't format the axes of a pie chart, because it doesn't have any.

TIP FROM

> Use a standard format across all your charts. This will keep the focus on the information and away from trying to understand the new format with every chart presented. If the presentation is onscreen, the use of colors can be effective, but for most people, black and white is the standard form in which charts are presented.

FORMATTING LINES: AXES, TICK MARKS, HIGH/LOW LINES, AND ERROR BARS

Excel enables you to format just about any line element of a chart. The axes, for example, can be boldfaced and/or displayed with dots or dashes, colors, patterns, or different line weights. The same formatting options apply to high/low lines, tick marks, and error bars. Tick marks on the value or category axis can be removed from the axes altogether, placed inside the axes, crossed over the axes, or moved to the outside.

For radar, doughnuts, pies, and other nonrectangular charts, formatting options are available that don't apply to rectangular charts, such as *column charts* or *bar charts*. See the later section "Formatting Data Series" for details on these options.

FORMATTING THE Y-AXIS, SECONDARY Y-AXIS, AND Z-AXIS

Formatting value axes in different ways can either draw attention to or away from the axes (see Figure 22.1). Why would you want to change the format of the value axis? The default formats Excel chooses are fine; however, when presenting information, you might want to adjust the default formats for a more effective and clean presentation. For example, creating a bold Y-axis line without any tick marks looks much cleaner than the default thin line with tick marks outside.

TIP FROM

> Format primary and secondary y-axes to look at least somewhat alike, although the value, major units, and minor units can be extremely different.

Figure 22.1
These options are among the most common ways to format the value axis.

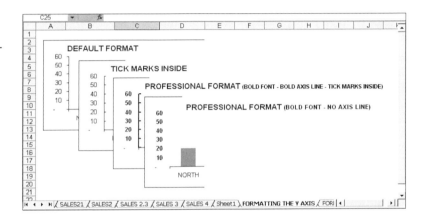

→ In most cases, you'll create a standard axis format that you'll use time and time again. Rather than reformat repeatedly, you can save the chart as a custom type. For details, **see** "Selecting the Chart Type," **p. 470**

TIP FROM

> The default setting automatically places *tick marks* outside the axis. The tick marks generally reference the numeric or text value on the axis, so the general direction of the tick mark points to the number or text. However, considering the information you're referencing is usually on the inside of the plot area, you'll probably want to change the direction of the tick marks in most cases.

To format the y-axis in the "professional" format shown in Figure 22.1, follow these steps:

1. Select the y-axis so that the selection handles are showing.
2. Choose Format, Selected Axis to display the Format Axis dialog box.
3. Select the Patterns tab.
4. Select the heavy-weighted line, as shown in Figure 22.2.
5. Under Major Tick Mark Type, choose Inside.
6. Select the Font tab in the Format Axis dialog box.

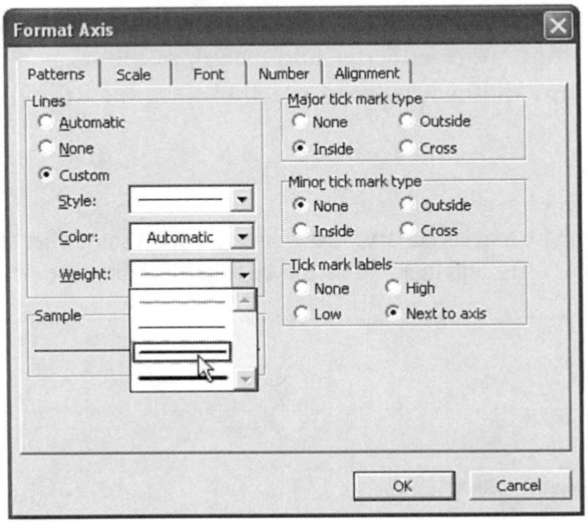

22

Figure 22.2
The Patterns tab in the Format Axis dialog box enables you to format the y-axis line type and style, as well as customize the tick marks.

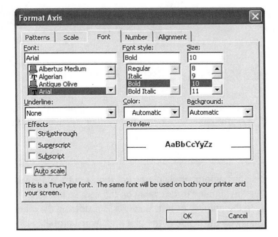

7. Under Font, choose Arial, as shown in Figure 22.3. (If Arial is your default font for Excel, this step can be skipped.)

Figure 22.3
The Font tab in the Format Axis dialog box enables you to change the font type, style, and size.

8. Under Font Style, select Bold.
9. Under Size, choose 10. (The size should be dependent on the size of the chart.)
10. Deselect Auto Scale.
11. Click OK.

TIP FROM

You should deselect the Auto Scale option because you'll be changing the chart size on many occasions. If Auto Scale is selected, all the fonts on that axis will change proportionally when you size the chart. This generally is a time-saving issue only.

FORMATTING AXIS LABELS

Besides changing the font style of the labels on an axis, you also can change the number style and alignment of the labels. In addition, Excel enables you to display the units on the axis with different measurement units (see Figure 22.4).

Figure 22.4
Excel enables you to display units in the measurement amounts shown in the Display Units drop-down list.

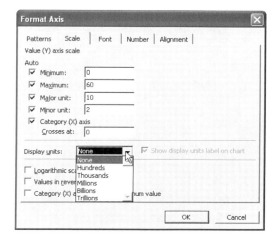

Figure 22.5 shows a comparison of some formatting options of the y-axis labels. Because there are so many variations, these are just a few of the option combinations available. To create the combination of settings that you want, select the axis and then use the options in the Format Axis dialog box, on the Format menu, and on the Chart and Formatting toolbars.

Figure 22.5
A comparison of value formats on the y-axis. Excel allows for multiple combinations.

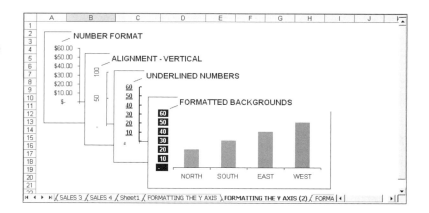

Figure 22.6 shows some additional comparisons in formatting of the x-axis labels. Try to keep the labels as clean as possible, because the labels act as the reference point for the

22

viewer. When you start combining the formatting techniques shown, you become more effective in presenting the information.

Figure 22.6
A comparison of category formats on the x-axis. These are just a few of the formatting options available in Excel.

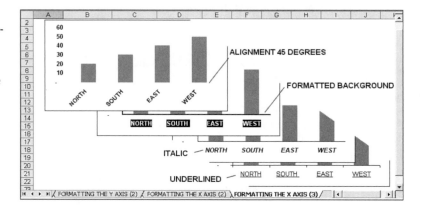

ADDING HIGH/LOW LINES

High/low lines generally are used for 2D stock charts that extend from the highest value to the lowest value in each category. High/low lines can help the chart reader distinguish the highs and lows of a data series. You can use 2D stock charts but you need to have a high and low value to do so. You need a second set of values for each entry set to 0. Select the data and the zero values before creating the chart as a line chart. Figure 22.7 shows high/low lines as a guide from the lowest score to the highest score extending to the category axis. You can use high/low lines even if you're not creating a stock chart. (All options can cross over into other categories, so be creative when working with charts.) To add high/low lines, follow these steps:

1. Select the data series.
2. Choose Format, Selected Data Series.
3. Select the Options tab in the Format Data Series dialog box.
4. Check the High-Low Lines check box.

ADDING ERROR BARS

The Y Error Bars tab in the Format Data Series dialog box enables you to show error amounts that you set, or you can use the standard error of the plotted values as the error amount for each data point. You most often see error bars associated with sample polls, where there's a possibility of error plus or minus. For example, a poll might indicate the number of people who drink milk on a daily basis, with a possibility of error plus or minus 3% from the results shown.

This option is not available for 3D charts (except for bubble charts), or for any pie, doughnut, or surface charts.

22

Figure 22.7
You can use high/low
lines in other ways
besides stock charts.
Here, they serve as
a guide to the
category axis.

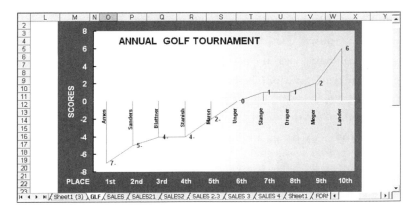

X-axis error bars also are available with scatter charts and bubble charts, where you have values that are horizontal as well as vertical.

To access the Format Data Series dialog box (see Figure 22.8), select the data series and choose Format, Selected Data Series. Figure 22.9 shows error bars added to a typical sales chart. You can format the error bars, just like any other line in a chart.

Figure 22.8
Y error bars enable
you to show plus or
minus errors or devi-
ations from the plot-
ted data point.

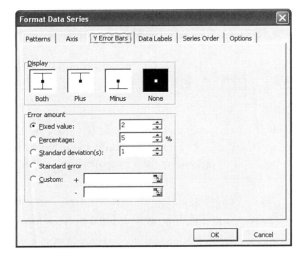

As with any element on the chart, by selecting the error bars, you can format them. The following list describes the options available on the Y Error Bars tab in the Format Data Series dialog box:

- **Both**—Displays both plus and minus error bars on the selected data series.
- **Plus**—Displays plus error bars.
- **Minus**—Displays minus error bars.

22

- **None**—Removes error bars from the selected data series.
- **Fixed Value**—Uses the value you input as the error amount.
- **Percentage**—Uses the percentage of each data point as the error amount.
- **Standard Deviation(s)**—Uses a fixed number of deviations from the mean of plotted values for the error amount.
- **Standard Error**—Uses the error of the values as the error amount for each data point.
- **Custom**—By typing a value in the plus (+) or minus (–) box or both, you set the error amount for the selected data series.

Figure 22.9
Error bars can help the audience see by what amount the results might be incorrect.

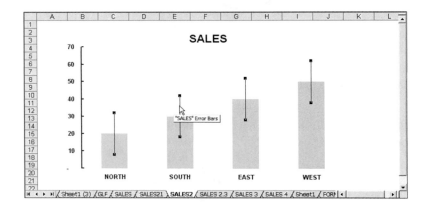

FORMATTING TEXT: DATA LABELS, TITLES, LEGENDS, AND TEXT BOXES

As mentioned earlier, all chart elements that can be selected also can be formatted. You can change the font, style, and color of the text as you would any other text in Excel. Select the text, title, legend, text box, and so on, and use the appropriate command on the Format menu, the Formatting or Chart toolbars, and so on.

→ For details on the techniques for formatting worksheets, **see** Chapter 5, "Formatting and Printing,"

The following sections provide some details on additional options for formatting the text in a chart.

ADDING AND FORMATTING DATA LABELS

Excel enables you to add information to a chart even after the chart is created (in case you don't get it right the first time). You can add data labels to a series of data, or you can add a data label to a single data point.

TIP FROM

In many cases, you'll want to point out a certain figure or data point in your chart. In this case, you can add a data label or value to a single data point. To do this, select only the data point. In addition, use the Separator option when including multiple data labels to a data set. This allows you to separate the labels with a space, comma, semicolon, period, or a new line.

To add data labels to a chart, follow these steps:

1. Select the data series.

2. Choose Format, Selected Data Series, or right-click the series and choose Format Data Series. You also can double-click the data series.

3. In the Format Data Series dialog box, click the Data Labels tab (see Figure 22.10).

Figure 22.10
To add labels or values to the desired data series, check the appropriate option under Data Labels.

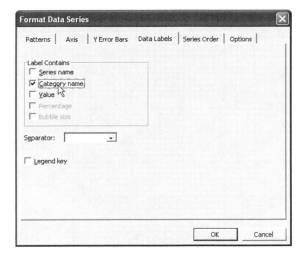

4. Under Data Labels, select Category name. You can also add data labels for values, percents, bubble size, and series name, or use the check boxes in combination.

5. Use the Separator option when including multiple data labels to a data set. This enables you to separate the labels with a space, comma, semicolon, period, or a new line.

6. Click OK.

NOTE

To add data labels to all data series at once, choose Chart, Chart Options to open the Chart Options dialog box. Click the Data Labels tab, select value, and click OK.

After creating data labels, you might want to change the location and appearance of the labels to match the rest of the chart. You can format the data labels by selecting the data label as you would a data value. After the data label is selected, choose Format, Selected Data Labels (or right-click the label and choose Format Data Labels); the Format Data Labels dialog box appears.

As with other text options, you can use the settings on the Alignment tab to change the alignment and orientation of the labels; you also can adjust the label position in relation to the data series (see Figure 22.11). As shown in Figure 22.12, you can use the Font settings to apply particular font styles, change the color and background, and add effects.

Figure 22.11
Excel enables you to align the data labels in several ways. Here, the label position is set to the inside end of the column and the orientation is at 90 degrees.

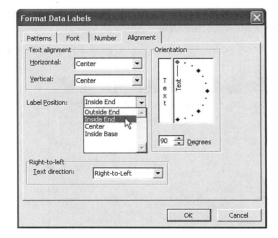

Figure 22.12
When a label is placed in a dark filled column, create a white-colored font and a transparent background to highlight the label.

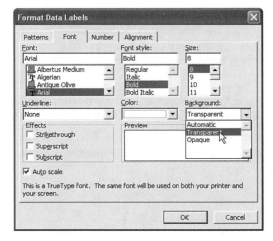

In this example, the labels will be formatted with a transparent (invisible) background and a white font, and then placed against dark columns in the data series (see Figure 22.13).

Aligning the labels within the data series can give you more room on the chart to call out other points of interest.

Figure 22.13
By placing the data labels inside the columns, you can create more land-scape on the chart.

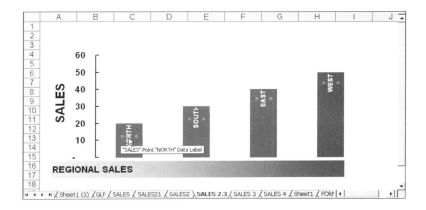

> In most cases, you should stay away from getting too creative with your data labels. Simple, clear, and concise is usually the best practice.

Moving or formatting a single data label is just as simple; after selecting the whole set of data labels, click the individual label you want to adjust. Then, move the label as desired, or use the Format menu to make changes to that specific label.

ADDING AND FORMATTING CHART TITLES

Chart titles consist of the title of the chart, the title of the y- or z-axis, and the title of the x-axis. You can add titles and elements to a chart using the Chart Options command on the Chart menu (see Figure 22.14).

Figure 22.14
You can add chart titles from the Titles tab in the Chart Options dialog box.

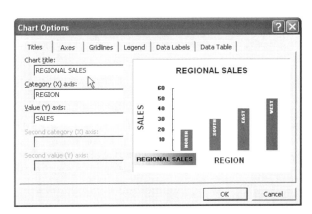

22

A fast way to add a "title" (or any text) is to select the chart, type the title text, and then press Enter. A text box appears in the center of the chart. You can select it and change the font style and size, and then place it in the desired location. Note that the text box doesn't contain the real title of the chart—for example, it doesn't show up in the Chart Options dialog box. This is just a quick way of creating text boxes in charts. This method also won't automatically resize the chart to accommodate the text. See the later section "Inserting and Formatting Text on a Chart" for details on working with text boxes.

When you have all the chart titles on the chart that you want, you'll probably want to change the size, font, style, or some other feature of the titles to fit your chart's appearance. Just select the title element and then choose Format, Selected Chart Title, or right-click the title and choose Format Chart Title. The Format Chart Title dialog box opens, as shown in Figure 22.15. Select the font settings, effects, and alignment you want, and click OK.

Figure 22.15
Format the chart title in the Format Chart Title dialog box. This example will show a black background and white text.

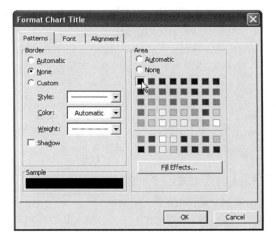

FORMATTING THE LEGEND

In most cases, you'll notice a legend takes up too much space in the chart. To move the legend, just select it and drag it to any location on the chart. Resizing is just as simple; click the legend and drag one of the handles either away from or toward the center.

The legend is just a descriptive reference to the data series on the chart. Don't draw too much attention to it. In most cases, it can be minimized by reducing the font size and moving it to an inconspicuous location on the chart. If you're using data labels for all of your series, or you're using the Data Table option, the legend is not needed at all.

INSERTING AND FORMATTING TEXT ON A CHART

Adding text to a chart is something you'll probably want to do on many occasions, not only for visual appeal (as shown in Figure 22.16), but also to call out certain aspects of your presentation. With proper formatting, adding text can be an effective way to help communicate your point. When adding text, remember, you can also format the text box to fit within the visual display of your charts.

Figure 22.16
By adding text to a chart, you can call out certain aspects of the chart or just add a creative touch.

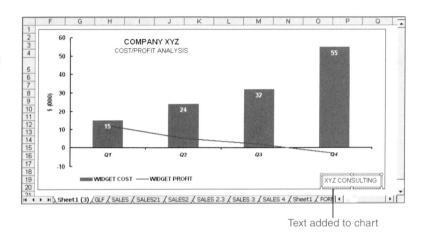

Text added to chart

NOTE

> You can also add text to the chart by using the Text Box tool on the Drawing toolbar. Make sure the chart is selected before using the text box; otherwise, the text won't be attached to the chart—when the chart is moved, the text won't move with the chart unless all items are selected.

To add text to a chart, follow these steps:

1. Select the chart so the selection handles are showing.
2. Type the text you want to display in the Formula Bar. You can also simply select the chart and start typing. You do not necessarily need to access the formula bar before typing the text.
3. Press Enter.

You format the text as you would any other chart element. Select the text box, and choose Format, Text Box. The Format Text Box dialog box appears with the font formatting options available.

22

ENHANCING CHARTS WITH SHAPES

Adding shapes to a chart enables you to provide additional visual interest and clarify data within the chart. Figure 22.17 shows how you can effectively use some of the drawing tools in a chart. In this example, the season was added across the charted time and the fiscal quarter names were applied between the x-axis and its labels. For more information, see Chapter 23, "Professional Charting Techniques."

Figure 22.17
You can add shapes to give several dimensions to your charts, including timelines and time spans that further tell the story of the chart.

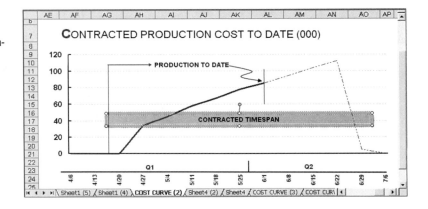

Shapes can be found on the Drawing toolbar (see Figure 22.18). Table 22.1 describes some uses for the drawing tools available.

Figure 22.18
AutoShapes enable you to further enhance charts, tables, and spreadsheets.

TABLE 22.1   SHAPES ON THE DRAWING TOOLBAR

Shape	Use
Lines	Used to point at or create specific cutoff points on a chart.
Connectors	Generally used for connecting shapes within flowcharts and can be used in Excel charts.
Basic Shapes	Applies basic shapes (triangles, circles, squares, and so on) for creating visuals.

Shape	Use
Block Arrows	Used to point at relevant information in a presentation, or to indicate a rise or decline in numbers by connecting one data point to another.
Flowchart	Can be added to graphic charts to further explain information plotted on the chart.
Stars and Banners	Used to create visual impact with a burst.
Callouts	Used to express ideas or call out points of interest. Points to specific information on the chart with a text message.
Text Boxes and Rectangles	Used for creating legends, keys, titles, and text messages.
Lines and Arrows	Points to different elements on a chart to draw attention.
More AutoShapes	Accesses clip art in the Insert Clip Art task pane.

Applying shapes to a chart enables you to call out elements of the chart to create direct focus, or to tell additional stories directly on the chart. After the chart is created, you can begin adding your drawing tools to the chart by selecting the chart and then selecting the shape you want to place on the chart. You can format the shape as you would other elements of a chart—by selecting the element and choosing the desired option(s) from the Format menu. In Figure 22.19, for example, the organizational chart was created with text boxes and connectors. Figure 22.20 shows the individual shapes, selected to make them more visible.

NOTE

Although some shapes are specifically designed to hold text (callout shapes, for example), you can convert almost any shape into a text box by selecting the shape and typing, or right-clicking the shape and choosing Add Text from the context menu.

Figure 22.19
Understanding how to use shapes with charts can establish visual impact, as well as tell the story behind the picture.

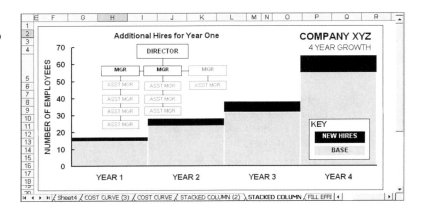

22

Figure 22.20
The highlighted shapes placed on the chart were boxes with text typed in the boxes.

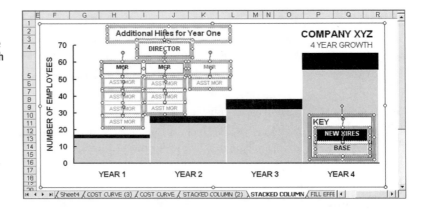

→ For details on working with shapes, **see** "Using the Drawing Toolbar," **p. 127**

FORMATTING DATA SERIES

Probably one of the most important aspects of formatting a chart is the formatting of the data series. You either call attention to or away from a series by how it's formatted. In addition to using the chart options provided specifically for formatting data series, you can add colors, fill effects, patterns, and even pictures, as described in the later section "Changing the Border, Color, or Fill of a Chart Item."

By changing the overlap and gap-width settings for the data series in Figure 22.21, a "stacked column" step chart was created. First, select the data series, then choose Format, Selected Data Series. From the Format Data Series dialog box choose the Options tab. For this chart, set the Overlap setting on the Options tab in the Format Data Series dialog box to 100 and the Gap Width setting to 0. The *gap width* is the gap or space between each category (for example, each set of columns on a column chart). The *overlap* is the amount of overlap of the individual data series (the individual columns in a column chart, for example). You can lay the columns of one data series slightly over the next column of data series by changing the gap width.

NOTE

If data series are stacked—for example, in a stacked column chart—there is technically only one column per category, so you would adjust gap width rather than overlap in this case. For charts with multiple series plotted separately, increasing the gap just changes the space between each category's group of columns.

CHANGING THE SERIES ORDER

You can change the series order in the Format Data Series dialog box. Click the Series Order tab and specify how you want the series to move by clicking the appropriate button.

In nonstacked charts, you can move data series left or right, and forward or backward; stacked charts move series up and down. The preview in the dialog box shows the result you'll get. This feature is particularly useful with area charts, in which a smaller set of data might be hidden when a larger set of data is positioned in front of it.

Figure 22.21
The Overlap and Gap Width settings can be a powerful tool for creating step charts.

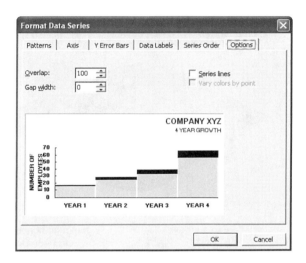

PLOTTING DATA ON THE SECONDARY AXIS

Use a secondary axis when comparing two sets of information that have totally different measurements, such as units sold for the year versus the revenue generated by those sales. If plotted on the same y-axis, the chart could effectively diminish one set of values visually. For example, suppose Units Sold for the year is 300, with Revenue totaling $4 million. In this case, you might plot the dollars on the secondary axis. To add a secondary axis, use the Axis tab in the Format Data Series dialog box.

EXPLODING PIE SLICES

Often, you'll see pie charts that have *exploded* slices of the pie to make them more noticeable. For example, your pie chart shows the division of Net users as shown in Figure 22.22. To explode a slice (ADULT), click the individual slice to display the selection handles; then drag it away from the center of the pie. Note, the triangles used on both sides of the chart were added using Autoshapes from the Drawing toolbar.

CHANGING THE DATA SERIES ANGLE IN PIE OR DOUGHNUT CHARTS

You might want to rotate a pie or doughnut chart to place particular data series at specific positions in the chart. You can rotate the chart with the Angle of First Slice option on the Options tab in the Format Data Series or Format Data Point dialog box. Specify the setting for Degrees, watching the preview, until the chart is positioned as you want it. The data

22

labels also move with the slices and can cause them to display off the chart, particularly when you increase the plot area, for example, to make the pie look larger in the chart.

Figure 22.22
Explode pie slices by selecting a data set from a series and dragging it away from the pie.

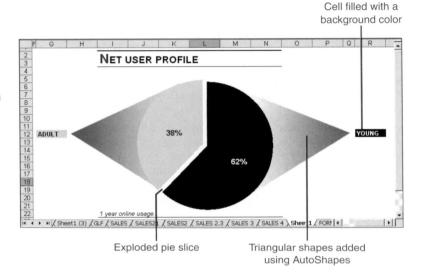

Cell filled with a background color

Exploded pie slice

Triangular shapes added using AutoShapes

FORMATTING A DATA POINT

Formatting an individual data point can be a great benefit in creating a focus. For example, if you have cost-to-date information in the form of a line chart as well as your projected future costs all in the same data series, you'll want to split the formatting of the line (see Figure 22.23). Notice the Actual Cost to Date appears in bold, and the Projected Cost is a dotted line. When you receive the cost for the next week, you'll change the format from projected to actual by selecting the single data point and adjusting the format. Notice the Actual Cost to Date appears in bold, and the Projected Cost is a dotted line. You achieve this by selecting each data point in the Actual Cost area and formatting it using the Pattern tab of the Format Data Point dialog to a heavy line weight. Format the remaining data points to dashed lines.

Another trick to attaining this result is to plot the same data in the form of two series that overlap one another, then format one line dotted (forecast), and the other line bold (Actual). Your forecast will be extended through the entire period as dotted and your actual will be added as the values are received in format of a bold line.

To adjust the format of a single data point, perform the following steps:

1. Select the data series so the selection handles are showing on the entire series.

2. Select the data point. Note, if you're selecting the data point correctly, the selection handles appear only around the data point.

3. Choose Format, Selected Data Point.

4. Adjust the format as you would a series.

5. Click OK.

Figure 22.23
By knowing how to format a single data series, you can create two stories on the same series.

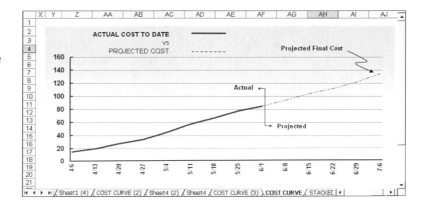

CHANGING THE BORDER, COLOR, OR FILL OF A CHART ITEM

You can format the backgrounds of the chart's data series, individual data points, plot area, chart area, and so on, by adding, altering, or removing borders and changing the color or fill effect used for the item. For example, a standard practice in formatting the background of the chart area is to create a white background with a white plot area. All the titles are black, as shown in Figure 22.24. You'll notice this standard approach to formatting in many publications and magazines.

Figure 22.24
You can format the plot area in any shade available in Excel. This example uses a sharp contrast to the white chart area color.

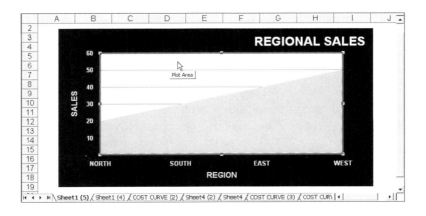

CAUTION

> Formatting the backgrounds can enhance the look of the overall chart; however, be careful not to overdo it. It's easy to get carried away and lose focus on what you actually want the picture to show.

CAUTION

> One good the practice for data series is to remove the standard borders on the series—unless the chart is a line chart, in which case this isn't an option. This is good practice because it cleans up the chart. There's no need to have borders around bars, columns, wedges, and so on. Try this, and you'll notice your charts will start to take on a more professional look.

To change the border or background of any chart item, select the item and use the Format menu to access the Format dialog box for that particular item. The options on the Patterns tab provide choices for borders, color, fill effects, and so on, as shown in Figure 22.25.

Figure 22.25
The Patterns tab provides plenty of options for selecting just the right border, color, pattern, and so on.

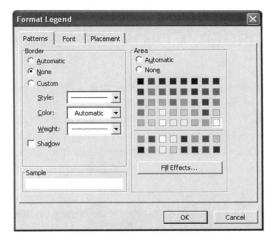

FILL EFFECTS

Fill effects enable you to use shading, gradients, patterns, and pictures within a data series, plot area, shape, and so on. Fill-effect options enable you to get creative with every element on the chart. Figure 22.26 shows just a few of the different fill options you can use.

The fill in the Picture column is actually a picture, stacked and scaled, as shown in Figure 22.27. The following section describes how to use this feature.

Now, notice the different fill on one column in Figure 22.28. This strong format draws the audience's eye to the specific chart element you want them to notice.

Figure 22.26
Shown are some of the different fill effects you can use to give a custom look to your charts.

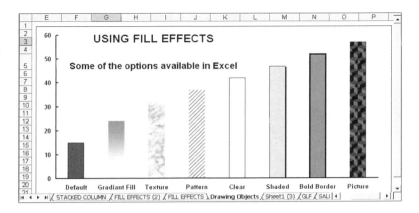

Figure 22.27
You can use a picture as a fill effect.

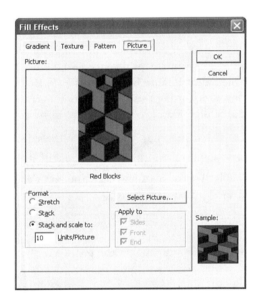

Figure 22.28
By applying a different format to one element, you call the attention of the audience to that element.

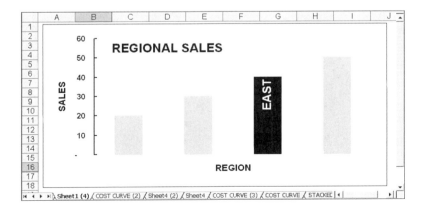

CAUTION

Be careful with fill effects! If you apply fills to too many elements of a chart, you can create confusion with all the colors and shades. One strategy is to apply fills only to every other series, with the remaining series using a solid background color.

To add a fill effect, click the Fill Effects button in the Area section of the Patterns tab. You can choose from four different types of fill effects: gradients, textures, patterns, or pictures.

NOTE

Gradient shades can be used to draw attention to or from a specified piece of data on the chart. Generally, attention is drawn to the lighter end of the shading effect.

Using Pictures as Backgrounds

The Picture tab in the Fill Effects dialog box enables you to apply a picture as a background (see Figure 22.29). You can use pictures in any of the standard picture formats: PCX, WMF, JPEG, GIF, and so on. Click the Select Picture button on the Picture tab, select the desired picture, and then adjust it as necessary, using the following options (see Figure 22.30). Note that some of the options might be disabled for certain picture formats.

- **Stretch**—Applies the picture and stretches it throughout the selected chart item.
- **Stack**—Stacks copies of the picture vertically and horizontally to fill the chart item.
- **Stack and Scale To**—Enables you to stack and scale the picture and adjust it to the size or units you select in the Units/Picture box.
- **Sides**—Used for 3D charts, this option applies the picture to the sides of the data series.
- **Front**—Used for 3D charts, this option applies the picture to the front of the data series.
- **End**—Used for 3D charts, this option applies the picture to the top end of the data series.

Does a chart seem to take forever redrawing when you change the underlying data? See "Reducing the Number of Units in a Picture" in the "Troubleshooting" section at the end of this chapter.

Figure 22.29
The chart shows the selected picture stretched in the columns.

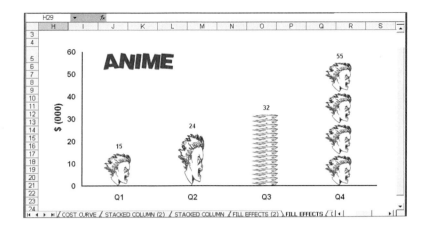

Figure 22.30
The Picture tab enables you to insert a picture and scale or stack the picture based on the settings you determine.

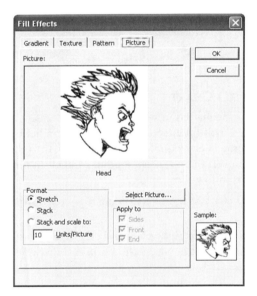

FORMATTING 3D CHARTS

Formatting 3D charts offers a few different options from 2D charts. On a 3D-column chart, for example, you can format the front, side, and top of the column because Excel allows you to fill flat surfaces. Figure 22.31 shows the default format of a clustered column with a 3D effect. This chart is used as the starting point to walk through some of the important elements in formatting a 3D chart in the following sections.

Figure 22.31
A 3D, clustered column chart in default format.

22

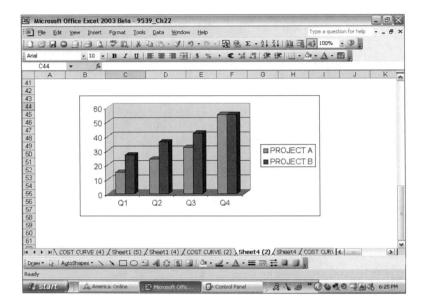

FORMATTING THE WALLS OF A 3D CHART

The walls of a 3D chart can be formatted in several ways, from erasing the walls completely to applying fill effects. As usual with fill effects, you can apply gradients, textures, patterns, and pictures. Note: Walls are the background of the chart (similar to the plot area on a 2D chart). As with all cautions on overdoing it, keep it simple and clean on these options. To format the walls of a 3D chart, follow these steps:

1. Select the walls of the 3D chart so the selection handles are showing at each corner of the wall.

2. Choose Format, Selected Walls, or right-click and choose Format Walls. You can also double-click the item on the chart to access the Format Data Series dialog box. Another way is to select it and press Ctrl+1.

3. The Patterns tab in the Format Wall dialog box enables you to apply fills to the area as well as outline the walls with border styles. To erase the walls, choose None under Area.

4. To get rid of the remaining gridlines, right-click the gridlines and choose Clear from the context menu, or select the gridlines and press Del.

You'll notice only the floor and axis are left. Many times, you'll find 3D charts work well as standalone (embedded in a worksheet) charts, and you can get rid of a lot of the fluff that makes up the standard default chart.

FORMATTING THE FLOOR OF A 3D CHART

You format the floor of a 3D chart similarly to how you format the other elements of the chart. The floor is actually the base the columns sit on. To format the floor, right-click and choose Format Floor, or select the floor and choose Format, Selected Floor. The Format Floor dialog box appears, and the standard options on the Patterns tab become available.

TIP FROM

> In most cases, the floor of a chart isn't an area of focus, so sometimes it's helpful to eliminate the floor.

Fill effects work well on 3D chart floors because you can use a gradient fill to create a light-to-dark effect—for example, placing light colors closer to the audience and gradually darkening to very dark colors at the back.

FORMATTING THE DATA SERIES OF A 3D CHART

More options are available when formatting a data series in a 3D chart. For example, you can apply different column shapes to a column chart and adjust the depth in which the series reaches back into the chart. The Shape tab isn't the only 3D format you can apply. On 3D charts, you have other formatting options, such as gap and chart depth and, when you use pictures for fill effects, the Apply To options are enabled. To use these 3D formatting features, follow these steps:

1. Select a data series on the 3D chart.
2. Choose Format, Selected Data Series.
3. In the Format Data Series dialog box, select the Shape tab (see Figure 22.32). Note, as mentioned earlier, that the Shape tab isn't the only 3D format you can apply.
4. Select the desired column shape.

Figure 22.32
The shapes available enable you to format the data series in the picture shape you select.

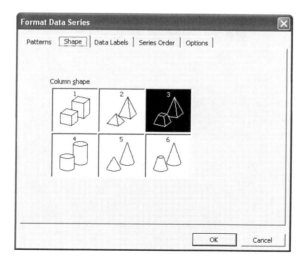

For a dramatic change in a column chart, choose a cone shape for one of the data series. Then, on the Options tab in the same dialog box, set the Gap Depth at 0, the Gap Width at 270, and the Chart Depth at 600, as shown in Figure 22.33.

22

Figure 22.33
You can set the width and depth to create a dramatic effect for a 3D chart.

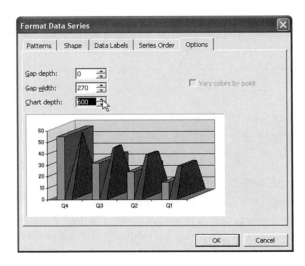

FORMATTING THE 3D VIEW

Now that you have the fundamentals of formatting the different elements of a chart, you can take the chart and create a view from any angle. By selecting the walls of a 3D chart, you can right-click to access the 3D view, or choose 3-D View from the Chart menu to access the 3-D View dialog box (see Figure 22.34).

Figure 22.34
The 3-D View options enable you to adjust the angle of the 3D chart as needed.

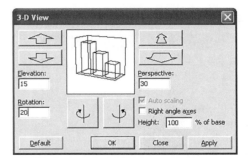

Options in this dialog box vary, of course, depending on the type of chart and the items in it, but the following list describes the major options:

- **Elevation**—Enables you to view the chart from a top-down manner, looking at the chart from above.

- **Rotation**—Changes the view in degrees, spinning the chart around the z-axis (or in simple terms, from left to right).

NOTE

> The arrows for elevation and rotation change the view from top-down and right-left of the 3D chart. Click the appropriate arrow and see the chart angle in the preview window change.

- **Auto Scaling**—Available only when the Right Angle Axes box is checked, this option creates a right-angle proportion. Often, when charts are created in 3D, depending on how you're elevating and rotating the chart, the chart size is reduced.

- **Height % of Base**—Controls the z-axis height relative to the length of the x-axis.

- **Right Angle Axes**—Independent of the chart rotation, this option sets right angles as opposed to seeing the chart in Perspective view. Making sure the Right Angle Axes box is checked usually creates a more uniform look to your chart, because the lines are displayed only in a vertical manner.

- **Default**—Use this button when your adjustments to the chart view have left it a hopeless mess. Excel restores the default settings.

NOTE

> You also can adjust the plot view of a 3D chart with the mouse. Click the floor or wall of the chart to display the sizing handles. Click one of the corner handles at the corner of the floor (the ScreenTip displays Corners) and drag. You might need to click twice (not double-click) before you can drag successfully. The plot is replaced with a wireframe image that you can drag to adjust the angle.

- **Perspective**—This option is available only when the chart includes two or more sets of data that compare values across categories and series. Perspective view changes the horizontal view of the chart, making the chart appear closer or further away. You can specify a particular Perspective setting, or use the arrow buttons above the option to make incremental adjustments. If the Right Angle Axes option is checked, Perspective view becomes unavailable, because right angles allow for perpendicular lines and right angles only.

TIP FROM

> Charts in Perspective view often take on a cluttered, unprofessional look, so use care when using angles other than right angles for 3D charts.

TROUBLESHOOTING

ELIMINATING THE AXIS WHILE KEEPING AXIS LABELS

Excel won't let me eliminate the axis line and keep the axis labels.

Select the axis and choose Format, Selected Axis to open the Format Axis dialog box. Click the Patterns tab, and choose None in the Lines section. You also need to set the floor border to none.

ELIMINATING BORDERS AND BACKGROUNDS

Why can't I chart information without the chart borders?

Select the chart and choose Format, Selected Chart Area. In the Format Chart Area dialog box, click the Patterns tab and choose None in the Border section. You also can choose None in the Area section to eliminate the area. This makes the chart area transparent so the underlying worksheet shows through.

FORMATTING A SINGLE DATA POINT

Why does Excel make me format all my data series at once?

You can format just one data point by selecting the data series and then clicking the individual data point until handles display around the single point. Then, format this data point as you would format a series, using the Format options.

OFFSETTING THE CATEGORIES

I need to add space between category labels and the axis line.

The Offset feature enables you to move data labels away from the axis line. Select the axis and choose Format, Selected Axis to open the Format Axis dialog box. Then, adjust the Offset setting on the Alignment tab.

ELIMINATING DATA LABEL BACKGROUNDS

The colored background on my chart conflicts with Excel's data label colors.

Select the axis with the labels and choose Format, Selected Axis. Select the Font tab in the Format Axis dialog box and choose Transparent under Background.

REDUCING THE NUMBER OF UNITS IN A PICTURE

Excel seems to take an eternity to redraw a chart that uses fill effects.

If you're using a picture with stacked units as a fill effect, and the number of units is fairly large, Excel might require additional memory and time to redraw the chart if you change the underlying data. You might be able to get away with a reduced number of repetitions, without changing the fill effect noticeably. Select the data point or series and open the Format Data Point or Format Data Series dialog box. Click the Fill Effects button, click the Picture tab, reduce the number in the Units/Picture box, and click OK.

EXCEL IN PRACTICE

By adding a few key titles and callouts to the standard chart in Figure 22.35, the chart can begin to speak for itself. Combining shapes, fill effects, and text boxes can create charts that not only look professional, but also tell a story without discussion, as shown in Figure 22.36.

Figure 22.35
This chart can get the point across.

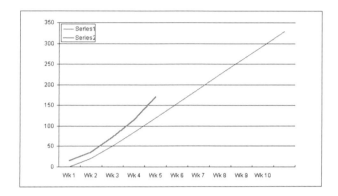

Figure 22.36
This chart provides more information in the same space, while simultaneously creating a positive impression on the audience.

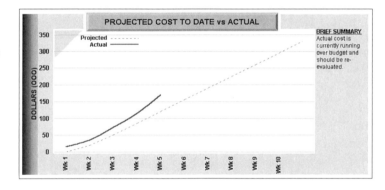

CHAPTER 23

PROFESSIONAL CHARTING TECHNIQUES

In this chapter

Formatting Charts for a Professional Look   564

Creating Column Depth   573

Pie Chart Techniques   5769

Using Fill Effects to Show Variance in 3D Charts   582

Using Form Controls with Charts   584

Stacking Multiple Charts   590

Creating Cost and Production Curves with Charts for Variance   591

Linking Chart Text to Worksheet Cells   592

Charting Hidden Data   592

Creating Effective Multiple-Combination Charts   594

23

FORMATTING CHARTS FOR A PROFESSIONAL LOOK

What are "professional" chart techniques? And who dictates what "professional" is? Professional techniques separate those who achieve and create impact from those who don't. To be able to say a thousand words with a single chart or a series of charts can be extremely important. There's a certain standard in the corporate world, as you might have noticed, but no one ever says what that standard is. In this chapter, you'll learn some of those basic "professional" elements that can help you achieve greater impact with your charts. In addition, you'll learn some new ways to combine charts with their source worksheets.

This chapter reviews several distinctly different chart types. Learning ways to mix and match information will help you become more creative in using the charting capabilities in Excel. You'll learn techniques such as erasing borders and backgrounds, which is one of the key elements in being able to combine and manipulate information on worksheets with charts. Another way to combine tools in Excel is to use form controls. Form controls are best used with charts when you have to continually extract to-date information, such as cost-to-date or production-to-date. This technique is also described.

The key is understanding the tools in Excel—not only how to combine them, but how to combine them effectively. Because Excel offers more tools with each new edition, the learning never stops.

KEY ELEMENTS IN PROFESSIONAL FORMATTING

In Figure 23.1, some of the key elements in professional techniques are pointed out. Table 23.1 describes professional standard formats that will help you create more effective charts in the future—the cleaner, the better, in most cases.

TABLE 23.1   SUGGESTED FORMATS FOR STANDARD CHART ELEMENTS

Chart Element	Suggested Format
Chart title size	Standard chart title, 16 point
Chart title style	Arial Bold
Y-axis title size	Standard y-axis title, 14 points
Y-axis title style	Bold
Y-axis tick marks	Inside or None
Y-axis line style	Bold
X-axis title size	Standard x-axis title, 14 points
X-axis title style	Bold
X-axis tick marks	None
X-axis line style	Bold

Chart Element	Suggested Format
Data series border	None
Data series (no emphasis)	Light fill
Data series (emphasis)	Dark fill
Trendlines	Same fill as the data series on which the trendline is based
Trendline style	Thin dotted
Legend border	None
Legend font style	Bold
Legend font size	Standard legend, 8 points
Legend placement	Best upper-right or right

Figure 23.1
Standard professional formats can create clean, effective presentations without clutter.

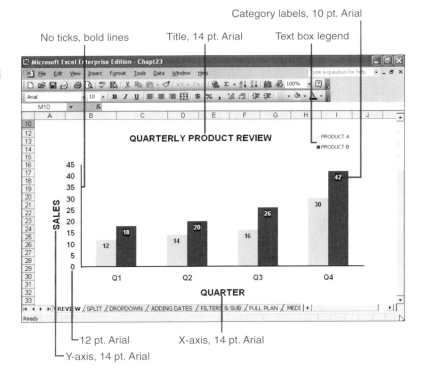

TIP FROM

After you have a group of chart types that are formatted with the proper font sizes, axis thickness, and data series formats, save them as custom chart types to save future time and effort in reformatting.

Whenever possible, it's good practice to differentiate the data series with light and dark shades and create a spectrum of emphasis from light (least emphasis) to dark (most emphasis). The audience's attention is drawn toward bold and dark.

TIP FROM

Excel offers so many options with callouts and drawing objects that it's easy to add elements and forget the focus. Objects such as bursts and stars can have appeal at times, but use restraint with fancy objects in charts. Don't use different font styles—keeping things constant creates a clean effect. Use consistent axis formatting; if you've created a bold y-axis, also create a bold x-axis. A constant line size is a good practice.

ADDING PICTURES AND SHAPES TO CHARTS

You can enhance your charts with pictures, AutoShapes, and WordArt. Figure 23.2 shows a column chart that could be improved by adding a picture to the background of the chart. To insert a picture, choose Insert, Picture, From File to display the Insert Picture dialog box, in which you can browse and select the desired picture (see Figure 23.3).

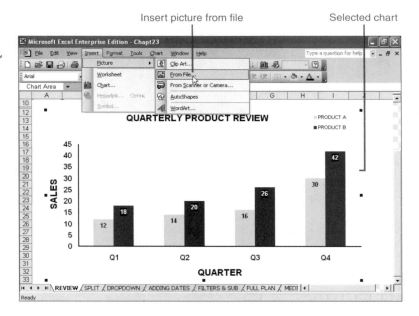

Figure 23.2
From the Insert menu, Excel enables you to insert shapes, pictures, and WordArt.

After you select the picture and click Insert in the Insert Picture dialog box, the image appears with the Picture toolbar. This allows you to manipulate the picture's brightness, shading, and so on (see Figure 23.4).

Figure 23.3
Select the stored picture you want to embed in the chart, and then click Insert.

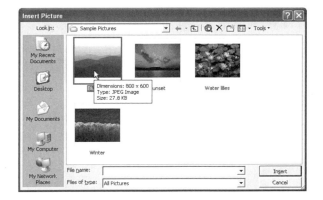

Inserted picture

Figure 23.4
By selecting the chart, you can insert a picture onto a chart and adjust the chart's characteristics with the Picture toolbar.

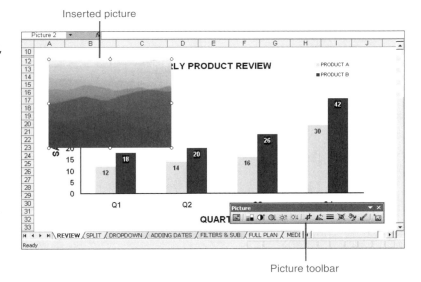

Picture toolbar

Table 23.2 describes the buttons on the Picture toolbar.

TABLE 23.2   BUTTONS ON THE PICTURE TOOLBAR

Button	Name	Description
	Insert Picture from File	Displays the Insert Picture dialog box
	Image Control	Enables the image to be displayed as grayscale, black and white, or watermark

continues

23

TABLE 23.2   CONTINUED

Button	Name	Description
	More Contrast	Increases the distinction between light and dark areas of the picture, sharpening the image
	Less Contrast	Decreases the distinction between light and dark areas of the picture, reducing the sharpness of the image
	More Brightness	Lightens the image
	Less Brightness	Darkens the image
	Crop	Hides the edges of the selected picture (but doesn't remove them)
	Rotate Left	Rotates the image to the left
	Line Style	Changes the style of the lines or borders to make them heavier, lighter, and so on
	Compress Picture	Compresses the picture to a lesser dpi resolution and reduces the file size
	Format Picture	Displays the Format Picture dialog box
	Set Transparent Color	Sets a pixel color within an inserted picture to transparent
	Reset Picture	Resets the picture to its original state

COMBINING CHARTS, PICTURES, AND DRAWING OBJECTS

Because Excel enables you to manipulate the backgrounds and styles of charts and their elements, you can combine charts with graphics, shapes, and worksheet elements. If you're in marketing or you plan to display your company's information in a presentation, for example, an image in the background of the chart can give it a certain look or feel. Figure 23.5 shows a chart/picture overlay. The chart in this figure doesn't have borders or backgrounds.

TIP FROM

If you insert a picture into a chart and then drag the picture and size it to the chart, it covers the plot area that contains the data. Insert a picture onto a worksheet, and then size the chart and picture to the same size. Drag the chart over the picture and bring it to the front (right-click and select Bring to Front). Last, select the chart and remove the borders and backgrounds to make the chart transparent so that the picture shows through.

A faster (but less flexible) method is to select the chart area and access the Fill Effects feature. There you can insert a picture and have it appear as a background image without changing any other part of the chart. The drawback is that you can't format the inserted picture.

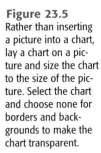

Figure 23.5
Rather than inserting a picture into a chart, lay a chart on a picture and size the chart to the size of the picture. Select the chart and choose none for borders and backgrounds to make the chart transparent.

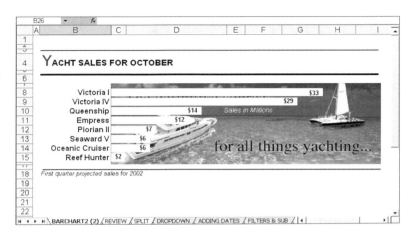

To lay a chart over a picture, perform the following steps:

1. Insert or Paste a picture onto the worksheet containing the chart.
2. Place the chart over the picture.
3. Size the chart so that the chart completely covers the picture. Or you could size the picture so it completely covers the chart.
4. Next, if your picture is on top of your chart you'll want to send the picture to the back. Simply select the Draw menu on the drawing toolbar and choose Order, Send to Back if your picture is on top.
5. Choose Format, Selected Chart Area.
6. Select the Patterns tab in the Format Chart Area dialog box.
7. Choose None in the Border area.
8. Choose None in the Area section of the dialog box.
9. Click OK.

The chart appears with the picture in the background.

When using several layers of objects, charts, and text, you'll need to become familiar with such tools as the Bring to Front and Send to Back buttons. By selecting an object and choosing Bring to Front, the object is placed on top of all the objects layered. You can add toolbar buttons for the Bring to Front and Send to Back commands (see the following Tip), or you can select these commands from the context menu. For charts, right-click the chart and select Bring to Front or Send to Back. For drawing objects, right-click the object, select Order, and then select Bring to Front or Send to Back. If you have multiple layers of objects, you can use the Bring Forward or Send Backward command on the Order submenu to move the selected object forward or backward one layer at a time.

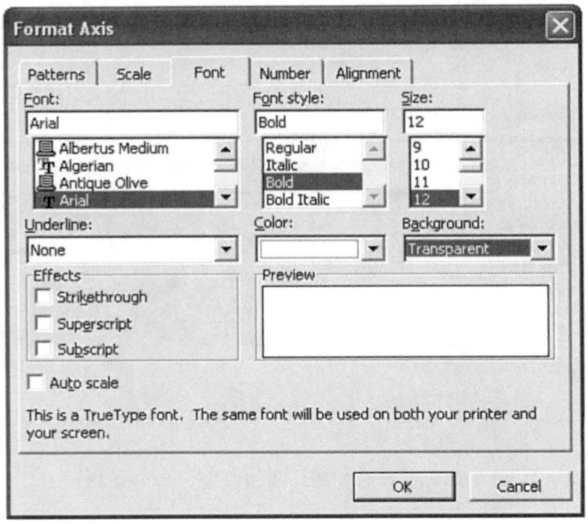

Figure 23.6
To erase the back-ground of fonts on the axis, select Transparent for the background.

Format Axis

Patterns | Scale | Font | Number | Alignment

Font:
Arial

Font style:
Bold

Size:
12

Albertus Medium
Algerian
Antique Olive
Arial

Regular
Italic
Bold
Bold Italic

9
10
11
12

Underline:
None

Color:

Background:
Transparent

Effects
☐ Strikethrough
☐ Superscript
☐ Subscript

Preview

☐ Auto scale

This is a TrueType font. The same font will be used on both your printer and your screen.

OK   Cancel

TIP FROM

If you use the Bring to Front and Send to Back buttons often, add them to your Drawing toolbar. Right-click the toolbar and select Customize to open the Customize dialog box. In the Categories list on the Commands tab, choose Drawing, and then scroll the Commands list to find the Bring to Front and Send to Back commands and drag them to the toolbar. Close the Customize dialog box when you're finished.

Another method is to open the Draw menu on the Drawing toolbar, select the Order option, and "tear off" the Order submenu as a floating toolbar with the Order buttons. You can use this toolbar as needed, or drag the buttons from the Order toolbar (hold down the Ctrl and Alt keys while dragging) to the desired position on any other toolbar.

ADDING A DRAFT STAMP OR WATERMARK WITH WORDART

You can create draft stamps or *watermarks* that you can place on charts or worksheets with WordArt. This is more of an aesthetic and formatting trick; however, it can add a nice touch for presentations. Figure 23.7 shows an example of a chart with a DRAFT stamp created with WordArt.

TIP FROM

With Excel's formatting capabilities, you can group objects with lines, creating stamps that show lines for signatures.

To create a transparent stamp, perform the following steps:

1. Click the WordArt button on the Drawing toolbar. Select the desired style for the text from the options included in the WordArt Gallery dialog box, as shown in Figure 23.8, and then click OK.

WordArt

Figure 23.7
A draft stamp can be used as an "onscreen stamp," as opposed to stamping a chart or document after printing.

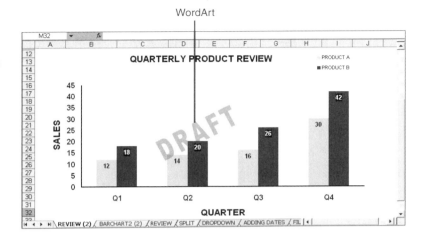

Figure 23.8
To create a transparent stamp, begin by selecting the WordArt style in the WordArt Gallery.

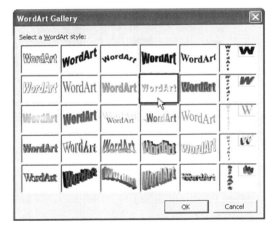

2. Type **DRAFT** in the Edit WordArt Text dialog box, as shown in Figure 23.9. Add boldface and/or italic, if desired, by clicking the Bold and/or Italic button.

3. Click OK to close the dialog box, and display the WordArt object in the chart.

4. On the Drawing toolbar, click the Shadow Style button and choose No Shadow (see Figure 23.10).

5. With the WordArt image still selected, choose Format, WordArt.

6. In the Format WordArt dialog box, select the Colors and Lines tab.

7. Under Fill, choose Gray-25%.

8. Check Semitransparent.

Figure 23.9
Type the draft text in the Edit WordArt Text dialog box. You can capitalize it or use a combination of cases.

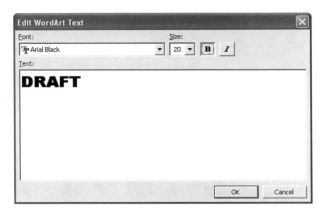

Figure 23.10
To eliminate the shadow on WordArt, select the Shadow Style button on the Drawing toolbar and choose No Shadow.

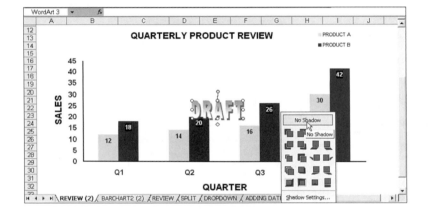

9. Click OK.

10. Rotate the text as desired by selecting the WordArt and then selecting the green rotate handle and dragging left or right (see Figure 23.11).

POSITIONING CHARTS OVER SHAPES

Not only can you place charts over pictures, but you can also place charts over drawing objects as shown in Figure 23.12. By creating a shape such as the 3D box shown, you can place a chart over the top of the box. Choose None for borders and areas as discussed in the previous example of Star Yacht Sales.

The arrows shown in this example are drawn from AutoShapes on the Drawing toolbar. The up arrow emphasizes the corrugate sales increase, and the down arrow emphasizes the chipboard decrease over the previous period. The arrow objects provide additional information that otherwise wouldn't be included in the chart.

Drag a rotate handle to change the position of the WordArt image.

Figure 23.11
Rotate the text with the Free Rotate command from the WordArt toolbar.

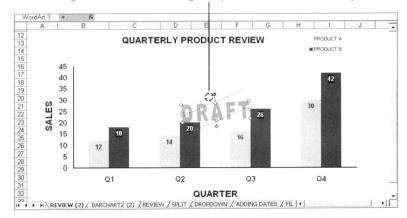

Drawing tools   Pie chart   3D box

Figure 23.12
By using fill effects, you can even create a gradient from the center of the pie to the edges.

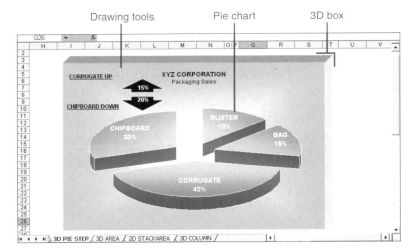

CREATING COLUMN DEPTH

After creating a default 3D column chart, you can either leave the chart in its default format, or you can take advantage of Excel's depth options. By understanding the value of 3D elevation and rotation in Excel's 3D charts, you'll be able to add the right perspective to a chart and create emphasis on certain areas.

CAUTION

Unless you have specific reasons to plot a chart in a 3D format, stay with 2D charts. A 3D chart might be more aesthetically pleasing, but remember that the audience should be able to determine what the chart says in seconds. If possible, use 2D charts.

By adding depth to a 3D column chart, you can dramatically change the shapes of the original columns, as shown in Figure 23.13. Applying gradient fills, drawing objects, and WordArt can further enhance the look of the chart.

Figure 23.13
Using Excel's depth capabilities with 3D charts can give charts more appeal.

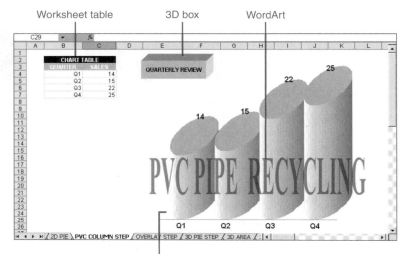

Worksheet table   3D box   WordArt

No background and no border

The following paragraphs highlight the important steps in creating a chart with depth and perspective similar to the chart shown in Figure 23.13. First, create a simple table like that in the figure. Then, create an embedded 3D column chart from the table, using the Cylinder chart type instead of the standard 3D column to give the data series the oval shape.

To add the perspective and depth, follow these steps:

1. Right-click the plot area of the chart.

2. Select 3-D View from the context menu to display the 3-D View dialog box.

3. Set the Elevation to 6 and the Rotation to 4. Be sure the Right Angle Axes option is checked (see Figure 23.14).

4. Click OK.

5. Select any data series.

6. Choose Format, Selected Data Series to open the Format Data Series dialog box. Click the Options tab.

7. Set the Gap Depth at 0, Gap Width at 10, and Chart Depth at 960 (see Figure 23.15). These settings change the width of the columns, the depth to which the columns reach "back" into the chart, and the distance between the columns.

8. Click OK.

Figure 23.14
Set the elevation, rotation, and right angles of the 3D column chart.

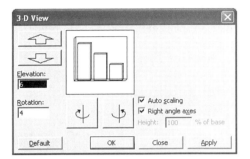

Figure 23.15
The Options tab in the Format Data Series dialog box enables you to change the width and depth of the data series.

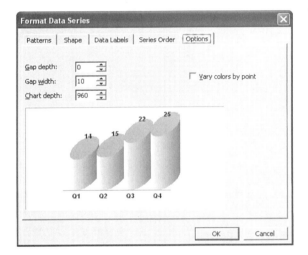

To add a 3D object as shown in the chart title (refer to Figure 23.13), select a drawing shape, draw the shape you want, and then select the 3D button from the Drawing toolbar. Then, apply the 3D perspective and depth you want.

To add the text, select the object and type the text you want. Excel automatically creates a text box that allows for text to be typed on the face of the 3D object.

To add WordArt, click the WordArt button on the Drawing toolbar and type the desired text. Place the WordArt over the chart.

If an object is hidden behind the chart, right-click the object and select Bring to Front, or right-click the chart area and select Send to Back.

WORKING WITH THE SECONDARY AXIS, OVERLAP, AND GAP WIDTH

Occasionally, you might need to measure two sets of data in a chart. By understanding how to create an overlay, you can compare data more effectively. A simple column chart with overlays (such as the one in Figure 23.16) can compare this year versus last year, but what if you need to show the status on multiple projects for your weekly production meetings? This same approach in the form of a bar chart instead of the column chart could be used to show projected completion versus actual completion by this point in time (see Figure 23.17). The key elements in creating charts like this are to select one of the data series and give it a secondary axis. Then, set the gap width and overlap, and set one of the data series fills to None.

Figure 23.16
By using the secondary axis and changing the overlap and gap width, you can create overlays.

23

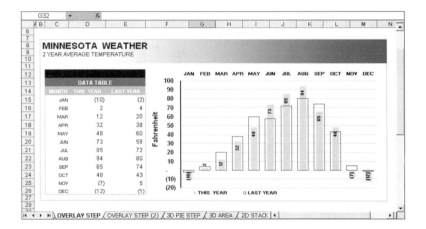

Figure 23.17
Using the same overlay approach, you can show projected versus actual on the same line.

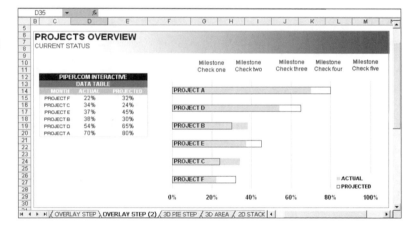

Excel enables you to align the data series one over another. By eliminating the background of one of the data series, you can create this "thermometer" effect. To create a column chart with a thermometer effect as shown previously in Figure 23.16, follow these steps:

1. Start with a clustered column chart.

2. Select the first data series.

3. Choose Format, Selected Data Series to open the Format Data Series dialog box.

4. Select the Patterns tab.

5. Under Area, choose None.

6. Select the Axis tab (see Figure 23.18).

7. Choose Secondary Axis.

Figure 23.18
Create separation of
the data series by
plotting one of the
series on a secondary
axis.

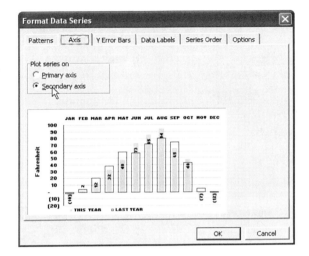

8. Select the Options tab (see Figure 23.19).

9. Set the Overlap to 0.

10. Set the Gap Width to 50.

Figure 23.19
Set the overlap and
gap width.

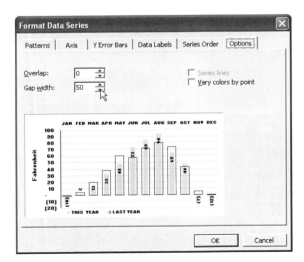

11. Click OK.

To add the gray corner shown previously in Figure 23.16, select AutoShapes from the Drawing toolbar, and then select Basic Shapes. Select a triangle and draw it on your chart to the desired size. While the triangle is still selected, flip and position it to match the corner of the chart. Choose Draw from the Drawing toolbar, then choose Rotate or Flip, and lastly, choose Flip Horizontal or Flip Vertical, as needed to position the triangle to match the corner. Place the triangle in the corner and fill with a desired fill.

SINGLE STACKED THERMOMETERS

Thermometer charts are seen most frequently in fundraising events. In addition to using thermometer charts to track progress and show changes over time, you can also create a single stacked thermometer chart as shown in Figure 23.20.

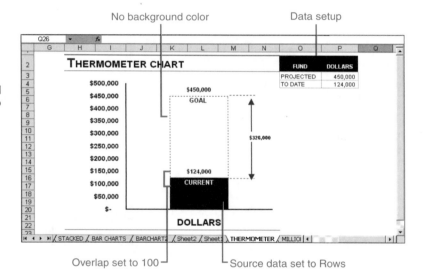

Figure 23.20
Create a single thermometer by setting the data series from columns to rows and changing the overlap setting.

To create a single stack thermometer, set up your table as shown in Figure 23.20. Then, follow these steps:

1. Select the data table.
2. Choose Insert, Chart.
3. Under Chart Types choose Column and under Chart Sub-Type choose Clustered Column. Click Next.
4. Select Rows from the Data Range tab on step two in the Chart Wizard. Click Finish.
5. Select the projected data column on the chart. Choose Format, Selected Data Series.

6. On the Options tab in the Format Data Series dialog box, set the Overlap to 100.

7. Format the projected series with a custom dotted blue line and no background to give it an empty effect and remove the legend by selecting it and pressing the Delete key.

PIE CHART TECHNIQUES

When creating pie charts, you'll want to bring focus to a certain category. You can focus the audience's attention on a certain pie slice in several ways. One is by formatting the slice to stand out. Another is by changing the angle of the first slice. The following sections describe these techniques.

→ To make a particular slice of the pie chart really noticeable, you can explode the slice. For details, **see** "Exploding Pie Slices," **p. 549**

SPINNING THE PIE CHART

Notice that Q4 in Figure 23.21 is angled to the top. This wasn't the default version of the chart. You can angle the first pie slice to make a particular slice appear on the top, side, and so on.

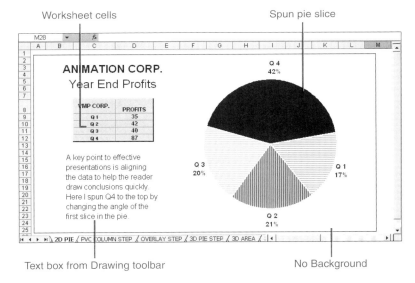

Worksheet cells   Spun pie slice

Figure 23.21
You can "spin" a chart by changing the angle of the first slice.

Text box from Drawing toolbar   No Background

To change the angle of the first slice, follow these steps:

1. Select the data series.

2. Choose Format, Selected Data Series to open the Format Data Series dialog box.

3. Choose the Options tab.

4. In the Angle of First Slice box, type in the desired degree or use the spinner buttons to enter it.

5. Click OK.

To create a table on a chart as shown in Figure 23.21, select the chart and choose None under Area in the Format Chart Area dialog box. Drag the chart over a table and then deselect the chart. The table shows through the transparent chart area. You'll have to move and format the different elements of the chart to get the exact appearance you're looking for. It also helps to have the data behind the percentages on the pie.

ORGANIZING PIE CHARTS TO TELL A STORY

The organization of charts is extremely critical when it comes to helping the audience understand the point. Figures 23.22 and 23.23 show two versions of a pie chart showing expenses for a physician. In both cases, sorting the underlying data in ascending order gives the chart structure. In the second version, custom formats and titles are key elements in getting the point across, and the angle of the first slice is adjusted to create further structure. An additional table to the right of the pie chart provides related details.

Figure 23.22
With the data series sorted in order, this pie chart is clear and informative.

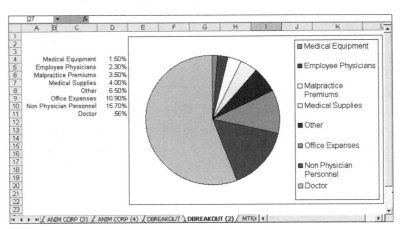

ADVANCED PARSING OF PIE CHARTS

Pie charts are often high-level pictures of detailed subsets of data. Most of the major analytical research firms use multiple charts together to do data set comparisons. This is a great way to tell complex stories that have massive amounts of information behind the scenes. For example, you might have to do a comparison of young versus adult consumers who buy and don't buy goods online.

First, answer the high-level key question: What percent purchase online versus what percent do not purchase? Of each pie slice, there are two variables behind the slice—Young and Old—as shown in Figure 23.24. Use drawing tools with fill effects sent to back with gradients for the parsing visuals to bar charts.

Figure 23.23
Another version of the chart in Figure 23.22 uses custom formats and a title to make the story clearer.

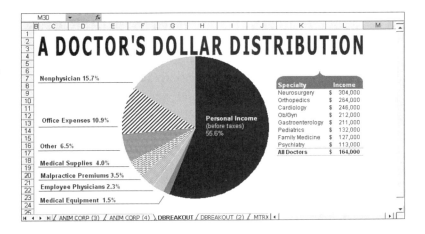

Figure 23.24
Use advanced chart techniques to parse data from pie charts into more detailed information.

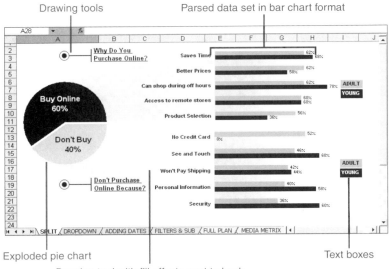

Second, of those who purchase online parsed from that pie slice, what variables or key drivers are behind their purchases (refer to Figure 23.24)?

Third, of those who do not purchase online parsed from that pie slice, what variables or key drivers are behind their decision?

USING FILL EFFECTS TO SHOW VARIANCE IN 3D CHARTS

One way to distinguish levels of data series is to apply a grade that reflects a series with colors or shades. Notice in Figure 23.25 that the different grades of stock are reflected by the gradient fills of the data series. Subtle visual tricks like these can work on the subconscious of the audience to help get the point across—for example, light color for less and darker colors for more if you're thinking in terms of numbers.

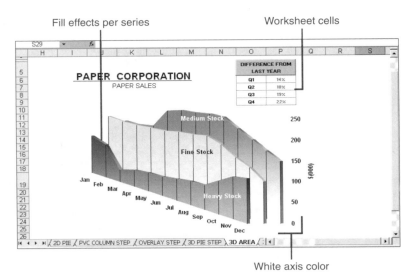

Figure 23.25
Data series are formatted to reflect the series grade.

To create a 3D area chart with gradient fills that separate products, follow these steps:

1. Create a table that distributes the sets of data, as shown in Figure 23.26.

Figure 23.26
This table distributes three sets of data over a period of time.

PAPER SALES

Month	Fine Stock	Medium Stock	Heavy Stock
Jan	136	125	90
Feb	135	128	80
Mar	138	135	30
Apr	142	182	40
May	146	195	45
Jun	155	200	46
Jul	160	208	52
Aug	168	212	58
Sep	158	195	59
Oct	138	180	80
Nov	125	165	102
Dec	100	150	108

2. Create an area chart with a 3D effect.
3. Right-click over the chart area and choose 3-D View.

4. Set the Elevation to 10 and the Rotation to 60.

5. Check the Right Angle Axes option.

6. Click OK.

7. Select the data series that you want to look heavy or dark. Choose Format, Selected Data Series to display the Format Data Series dialog box.

8. Select the Options tab. Set the Gap Depth to 500 and the Chart Depth to 60. Select the Drop Lines option.

9. From the Patterns tab, choose Fill Effects to open the Fill Effects dialog box. Choose Two Colors (see Figure 23.27).

Figure 23.27
Set the two-color gradients to reflect the grade of paper weight.

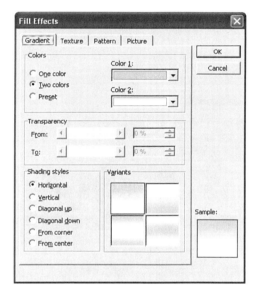

10. Choose Black for Color 1 and choose Gray-25% for Color 2.

11. Be sure that the shading style is Horizontal with the upper-left variant selected. Click OK twice.

12. Repeat the fill effect steps with each data series, selecting settings for medium and light shading.

13. Delete the chart wall, gridlines, and chart area.

To incorporate a table in the chart corner as shown, select the chart and be sure that Area is set to None on the Patterns tab in the Format Chart Area dialog box.

USING FORM CONTROLS WITH CHARTS

You might combine form controls and charts for several reasons. Based on a database from which the information is generated, you can use form controls to combine data into a single chart and make the chart active. (To learn more about combining charts with active tables, see Chapter 24, "Using PivotTables and PivotCharts.")

Figure 23.28 shows an example of a chart that uses option buttons to display the desired data. The user clicks the Wichita Plant button or the Middelton Plant button to change the displayed data in the chart. This combination of chart, tables, and form controls uses a formula to extract information from a large database and condense and display it in a small space. Form controls with charts can become powerful tools for accessing multiple data sets with just one click.

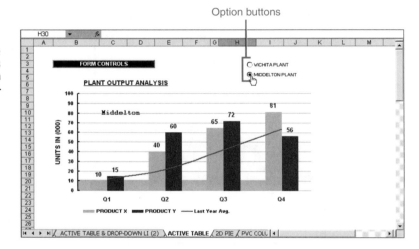

Figure 23.28
Form controls can be a great way to access and view information that must be continually regenerated.

For this example, you create an active table that's derived from two separate tables. Using a simple IF statement, you then create the chart from the active table. Finally, the form control toggles the set cell referenced by the IF statement.

→ To learn more about the IF statement, see "IF," **p. 280**

To access the form controls, right-click any toolbar and choose Forms, or select View, Toolbars, Forms.

To create an active chart with an option button, begin by setting up the information as described in the following steps:

1. Set up tables 1 and 2 as shown in Figure 23.29. These are the origin tables that the source table will reference.

Figure 23.29
It's important to set up the tables with the proper relative referencing.

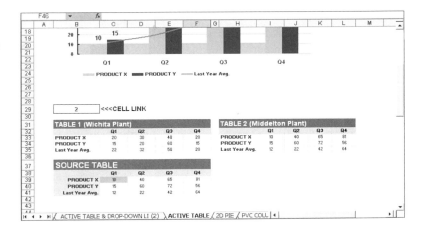

2. Set up the source table, formatted identically to the origin tables.

3. Create the chart from the source table, and select it. (If you create the option buttons before selecting the chart, the buttons will be attached to the worksheet rather than the chart. Consequently, the buttons won't move with the chart.)

4. Draw an option button, right-click it, and then choose Format Control from the pop-up menu (see Figure 23.30).

Figure 23.30
Format the option button and select a cell the source table will reference.

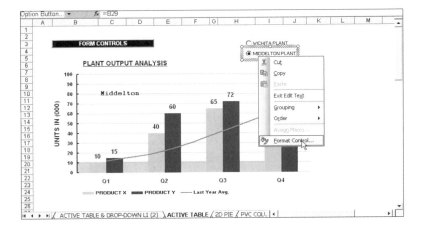

5. Select the Control tab in the Format Control dialog box.

6. Type the address for the cell link (for this example, in cell B29).

7. Click OK.

8. Select the option button and title the button.

23

9. Repeat steps 4 through 8 with the same cell link, but give the second option button a different name. To save time with the cell link and formatting, you can use Ctrl+D to duplicate the option button control. You still need to rename it, of course.

10. Now enter the formula. In this example, in cell C39 of the source table is the following formula: `=IF($B$29=1,C33,I33)`. Drag and fill to the right and then down. The statement will fill to the right and down to mirror that of the two tables. This statement reads from the cell to which the option button is linked. If it's 1, the result is that of the first origin table (Wichita, in this example) or the second origin table (Middelton) if 2.

When Middelton is selected, the source table values equal that of the origin table Middelton Plant. The chart changes to match.

To create a toggle name (such as Wichita or Middelton) that sits in the plot area, be sure you choose None for Area on the chart. Next, in a cell that won't get in the way of the data series, type a formula that references the cell link again. The formula in this example would reference the cell link B29 and reads as follows:

```
=If(B29=1,"Wichita","Middelton")
```

This basically says, if B29=1 then Wichita, else Middelton.

TIP FROM

If you expect the chart to move at some point, don't use a cell in the background to represent the label. (Should the chart be moved or resized, a new cell would have to be used.) Chart titles and labels as well as text boxes (or any shape) can contain a reference to any cell on your worksheet. Place the preceding formula in any cell outside the chart area (maybe near the source table). Then, select the chart and click the Formula bar. Type an equal sign; then click or type the cell address containing the preceding formula, and press Enter. A text box will appear in the center of the chart. You can then move, size, and format the text box to your liking. Unlike using a cell directly, this text box will move and size with the chart.

TIP FROM

You can add as many option buttons as you want and reference the same cell link. The number of the option button will continually increase, based on the number of option buttons you select and link.

If you don't anticipate moving or resizing a chart, you can create the option buttons on the worksheet behind the chart. Then, eliminate the borders and the backgrounds in the chart by selecting None under Area on the Patterns tab in the Format Chart Area dialog box.

You should also deselect the maximum value check box for the y- and z-axes on the Scale tab of the Format Axis command. If you do not do this, switching chart information using the option buttons can yield charts that look similar even when the figures are vastly different because Excel automatically changes the Scale values to match the data's maximum value.

CREATING CHART MODELS WITH FORM CONTROL COMBO BOXES

Another way to use form controls is with a combo box, also called a drop-down menu. With this control, you'll want to use an Index function to look up the cell link in cell A1 on this worksheet in Figure 23.31. The data list is in cells B21:G141 and the chart references the formula cells in C143:G144. This is a basic example, a more complex scenario with a multiple or weekly date lookup can be found in the next example.

23

Form control combo box

Figure 23.31
Create automated models from lists of information with combo box form controls and the index function.

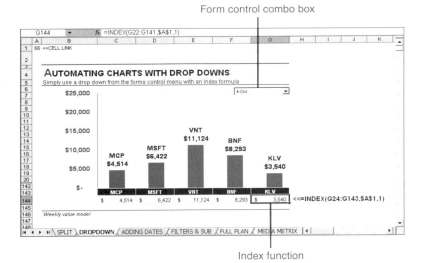

Index function

To re-create this model, do the following:

1. Create your list in cells B21:G141, where column B is the date column and Column C through G are the company data columns. Collapse or hide the rows between row 20 and 142, as shown in the figure.

2. Draw the combo box form control on the worksheet from the Form's toolbar. Size the combo box with the sizing handles and right-click and drag to move it to the desired location.

3. Right-click the combo box form control and select Format Control.

4. From the control tab on the Format Control dialog box, place the input range $B$22:$B$141 in the Input Range text box.

5. In the Cell Link box, type **A1**. The cell link will appear in cell A1. Another way to do this is by placing the cursor in the cell link box and then selecting cell A1 with your cursor. You can place the cell link on another sheet if you want. This is a common technique to house all of your cell links.

6. In the Drop Down Lines box, keep the default at 8.

7. Create the column company headings in cells C143:G143 for the chart table.

8. In the following cells, type the index formula to reference the list, cell link, and column number:

Cell C144	=Index($C$22:$G$141,$A$1,1)
Cell D144	=Index($C$22:$G$141,$A$1,2)
Cell E144	=Index($C$22:$G$141,$A$1,3)
Cell F144	=Index($C$22:$G$141,$A$1,4)
Cell G144	=Index($C$22:$G$141,$A$1,5)

9. Select a date from the combo box to activate the cell link.

10. Create the chart from the range C143:G144. Then, select a date from the form control and the chart is automated.

CREATING ADVANCED CHART MODELS WITH COMBO BOXES

Building on the previous example of creating a combo box form control to automate a chart, what if you were looking up weekly data from one form control? Say you wanted to select a day of the year and show the five days forward from the date you selected? In Figure 23.32, a cell link was created in cell B2. Directly below B2 in cell B3 type the formula **=B2+1**. The cell link range would be in cells B2:B8 and the Index formulas in the table B23:H27 reference each of the cell links in the cell link range.

NOTE

> For a cleaner, more professional look, the cell link with its additional row reference formulas, as well as the hidden raw data, can be easily placed on a separate sheet (and normally are in well-designed workbooks). For demonstration purposes, all the data is kept on the same sheet.

NOTE

> The chart references the table in C21:G27 and the vertical dates beneath the chart are linked picture objects from cells M2:Q2.

CREATING CHART MODELS WITH FILTERS AND SUBTOTALS

Another way to create automated charts is with simple filters and subtotals. The filters allow you to filter the desired information and the SUBTOTAL function summarizes the filtered information in which the chart references. The subtotal function ignores the hidden records of a filtered list (whereas most regular functions—Sum and Average, for example—do not).

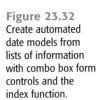

=Previous cell + 1

Only cell link in B2

Dynamic pictures change with selection

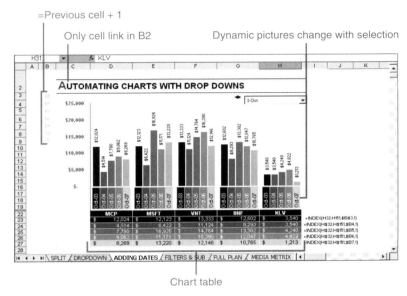

Figure 23.32
Create automated date models from lists of information with combo box form controls and the index function.

Chart table

23

To create an automated chart as shown in Figure 23.33, follow these steps:

1. Create your list and choose Data, Filter to select and apply filters.
2. Create a table above the filtered list that mimics the headings of the list as shown in Figure 23.33.
3. As shown in cell C21 of Figure 23.33, type the SUBTOTAL function with the analysis type 9—which means sum—and then the range of the list it's summarizing.

Chart reference table

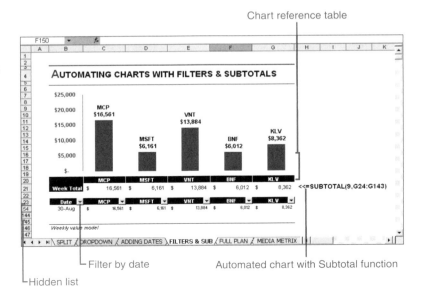

Figure 23.33
Automated chart models can reference lists of information by using a SUBTO - TAL function to summarize the fil- tered information.

Filter by date

Automated chart with Subtotal function

Hidden list

4. Create a chart from the subtotal table. Now, when you select a new filter, the SUBTOTAL function summarizes that data and the chart updates with the new information.

STACKING MULTIPLE CHARTS

If you have several bits of information to chart and are wondering how to effectively present it all together, the answer might be to separate the data into multiple charts and stack the charts. Because charts often are used to show historical information or projections over time, you can create multiple charts based on time frames, aligning the charts so each time period on one chart vertically aligns with the time period from the other charts.

In Figure 23.34, the unit output chart has been aligned directly above the associated cost chart, and the fourth quarter has been highlighted to draw attention. You can stack two, three, or more charts in this manner to create comparisons of multiple groups of data. Why not place them on separate sheets? You can place each chart on its own sheet, but viewing how all the data correlates can provide conclusions you might not normally derive by reviewing the data separately.

Figure 23.34
Stacking charts can combine several bits of information on the same sheet, while still showing all the data at the same time.

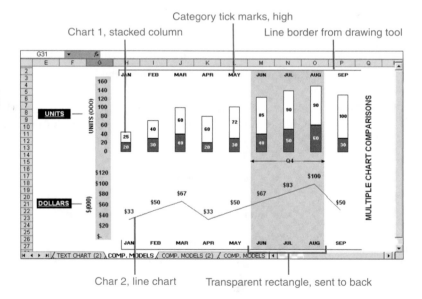

After the charts are aligned, you can add drawing objects, such as lines and semitransparent boxes. The semitransparent box highlights the quarter and is sent to the back with the Send to Back command. Be sure you've selected None for chart fills, so that the charts are transparent. Otherwise, the shape sent to the back will be covered by the chart's fill color.

CREATING COST AND PRODUCTION CURVES WITH CHARTS FOR VARIANCE

What is a *cost curve* or *production curve*? As a process happens over time, cost accumulates over time, as do production, percentages, and so on. All too often, people have difficulty measuring and understanding how to view information over time, especially when they need to draw some relevant conclusion from the data. This section begins by establishing a table that provides projected weekly costs, and then, as the costs are incurred, applies that information as well (see Figure 23.35). By knowing how to lay out the underlying data, you can create charts that have meaning, instead of charts that have only graphic appeal. (You can find more information in Chapters 20, 21, and 22.)

Figure 23.35
By setting up a cost curve table in this fashion, you can establish a usable measuring tool in the form of a line chart that gives a visual of what has occurred over time.

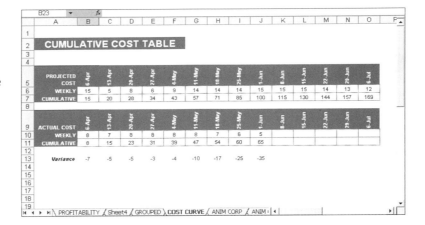

As costs are incurred, you add that data to the actual weekly cost row. To automate the cumulative cost, sum the previous cumulative week plus the current week. (By doing this, you won't have to add up the cumulative every time a week's cost is input.) To display the data in chart format, select the date range and the cumulative projected/cumulative actual cost range, and then create the chart. Figure 23.36 shows a cost-curve line chart, displaying the variance between projected and actual costs. It's quick-hitting and easy to understand.

Production curves are created in similar fashion. Because production occurs over time as well, you can cumulate widgets, time, and so on. The key here is to understand that everything is measurable. If it isn't, either you're not accomplishing anything, or you're not creating anything.

To add the text as shown, select the chart, select the text box from the Drawing toolbar, and type the desired text.

To add lines or arrows for callouts, select the chart, select the Line or Arrow tool from the Drawing toolbar, and then draw the desired line. Adjust the position as necessary.

Figure 23.36
Cost curves not only make great measuring tools with regard to variance, but also show historically what has happened.

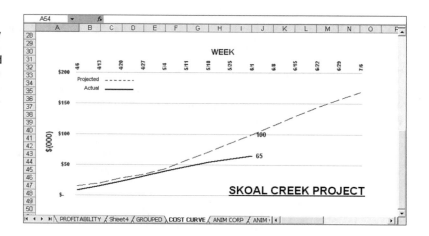

LINKING CHART TEXT TO WORKSHEET CELLS

When setting up workbooks that will be used by several people, you might want to link text or numbers from a cell in the workbook to a chart, so that when the chart is shown, it's representative of the worksheet. Suppose you have a worksheet that performs many calculations and the chart is the outcome of the calculations, but is titled differently every time a calculation is done. In this case, you'll want to see the different title in the chart for each scenario or calculation done on the spreadsheet. To link a cell to a chart, just select the chart and type the formula `=cell`, substituting the cell reference for `cell`. A text box shows up in the chart displaying the value of the referenced cell. The text box can be formatted like any other text box. When text or a number is generated in the cell, it shows up in the text box on the chart as well.

CHARTING HIDDEN DATA

You can maintain a chart's integrity even if you hide the data that the chart references. By default, Excel hides the information in a chart when the underlying data is hidden. Suppose you created an outline that sums up the quarters under the months, as shown in Figure 23.37. If you hide the monthly data, as shown in Figure 23.38 the chart displays only the quarterly totals.

To plot nonvisible cells on the chart, perform the following steps:

1. Select the chart.
2. Choose Tools, Options.
3. Select the Chart tab in the Options dialog box (see Figure 23.39).
4. Uncheck Plot Visible Cells Only.
5. Click OK.

Figure 23.37
A chart and its underlying monthly and quarterly data are shown here.

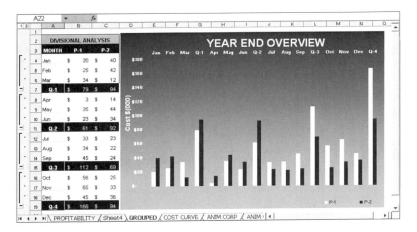

Figure 23.38
Notice that only the visible cells are shown on the corresponding chart.

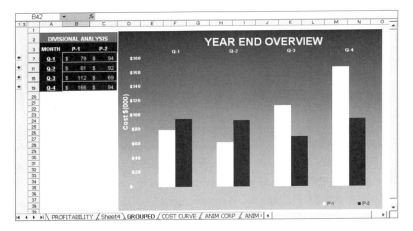

Figure 23.39
Hidden cells remain plotted on the chart when the Plot Visible Cells Only option is unchecked.

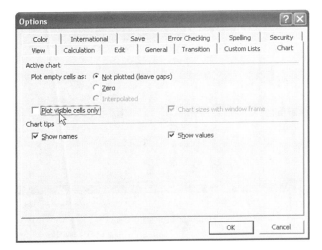

CREATING EFFECTIVE MULTIPLE-COMBINATION CHARTS

Multiple-combination charts are good for comparing two or more sets of data. Figure 23.40 shows the three sets of data used to create the chart in Figure 23.41. This example looks at the total contracted amount minus the monthly completed totals against the prior year's output. Charts can be a great way of showing depletion of total reserves.

Figure 23.40
You can create multiple sets of data to establish a multiple-combination chart.

For this example, you start by establishing three sets of data as shown in Figure 23.41. The Contracted Ore to Mine data series reduces total quantity remaining from the monthly ore amounts mined. The third column represents last year's monthly output as a comparison to this year's quantities.

Figure 23.41
Multiple-combination charts can separate several data series on the same chart.

Bevel from Drawing toolbar

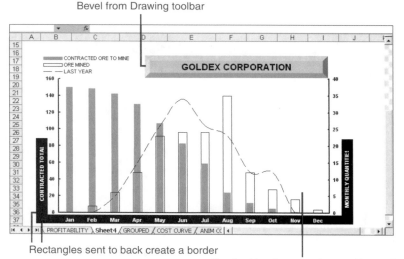

Rectangles sent to back create a border

No chart border or background is used

You can create multiple-combination charts in more than one way:

■ Select the entire table and create a chart with the Chart Wizard, and then select each data series and change them independently by choosing Chart, Chart Type.

■ Paste the data separately.

After formatting a multiple-combination chart, save the chart as a custom chart type to avoid having to reformat each new multiple-combination chart you create.

VISUAL DISPLAY IN EXCEL

Visual display isn't limited to charts. Visual display can include words, objects, lists, or a combination thereof. Take sounds, for example. Although sounds aren't visual, audible sounds can create a sense of calm or urgency. Remember the theme from *Jaws* and how it created a sense of urgency? The same is true when thinking in terms of visual display. Soft pastel colors evoke a calm feeling, while bright or fluorescent colors can evoke urgency or attention.

You see this all the time in finance—illustrations shown in the red or in the black. Everyone knows red is bad and black is good in finance, but because it's second nature, you don't think of it in terms of visual display. The same colors used in a different arena can have quite the opposite effect. Because this book is limited to displaying grayscale, the visual display must be created primarily with structure and layout.

COMBINING CHARTS, WORKSHEETS, TEXT, AND TIME

Now that you have some of the basics in combining charts with worksheets, you can start to embed charts into worksheets and lists. You see this all the time in magazines and newspapers; however, many people use graphic programs to create these charts and marry them to the spreadsheet. With Excel's flexibility, you can start to create lists that measure visually. Take Figure 23.42, for example. This is a list of information that provides several vehicles of measure or value in the form of a chart, drawing tools or shapes, and finally words (see Figure 23.43). Combine these elements with a list of information, and now you have one line in a list that provides multiple angles or views on product or competition.

Start to think outside the norm. Just because Excel is referred to as a spreadsheet program, doesn't mean that the word *spreadsheet* should limit how you use Excel.

In Figure 23.44, the formatting is removed to show how a bar chart is positioned on top of the grid. (Remove the borders and background fills to make the chart transparent.) In this example, the chart is constructed to cross the x-axis at 100, so the value index appears negative or less than average if the bar is to the left of 100.

CREATING A CUSTOM L-BAR AXIS

Excel enables you to create custom axes, as shown in Figure 23.45. Eliminate the original axis and background of the chart and replace it with a transparent shape, such as the rectangle from the Drawing toolbar. After the rectangle is placed over the corresponding x and y values, select a fill color on the Colors and Lines tab in the Format AutoShape dialog box, make the shape semitransparent, and then send the shape to the back, placing the object behind the values of the chart, and creating an *L-bar axis*.

Figure 23.42
By combining charts, drawing tools, and words with line-item information, you provide the audience with multiple views of the product or company.

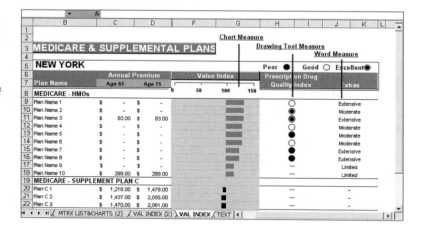

Figure 23.43
You can create measuring tools from charts, drawing objects, and even words.

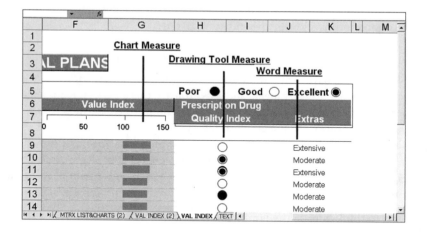

BUILDING SINGLE-STACK CHARTS

Single-stack charts designed with text boxes and drawing tools can be extremely effective when showing percentages between categories, as shown in Figure 23.46. You'll often see charts of this nature when comparing industry categories. (If you have too many categories, however, the stacked chart can become cumbersome.) The borders and backgrounds were eliminated in this example. By eliminating these features, you can make chart stacks stand alone, and then use text boxes, callouts, and lines to finish the chart.

Figure 23.44
The bar chart is placed on the grid and sized to fit within the line-item category.

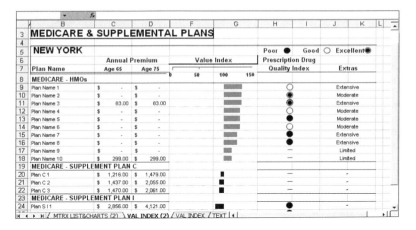

Figure 23.45
By eliminating the background and the axis of the chart, you can place a drawing object such as a rectangle over the values and send the object to the back, giving it the appearance of an axis.

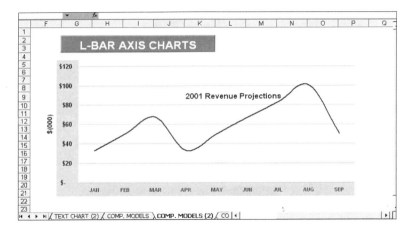

STACKED CHARTS WITH SERIES LINES

When comparing like sets of data over time periods, stacked charts can provide a good picture or comparative between the stacks. The key is to make sure the stacks are aligned in the same order and to apply series lines between the stacks. Series lines visually show variance between the sets of data. If possible, lighten or dot the series lines so the main emphasis stays on the stacked data. In Figure 23.47, the comparative data is over a two-year period and the stacked data is aligned with series lines. You can change the format of the series lines by selecting the series lines and choosing Format, Selected Series Lines as shown in Figure 23.48. To add series lines, double-click the data series, and check the Series Lines option from the Options tab.

Figure 23.46
Eliminate the chart borders and backgrounds to make the stacked chart stand alone. Use drawing tools and text boxes to call out the important elements of the chart.

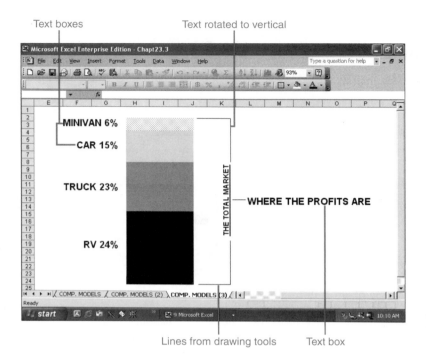

Figure 23.47
Use stacked charts with series lines to visually show variance between data sets over time.

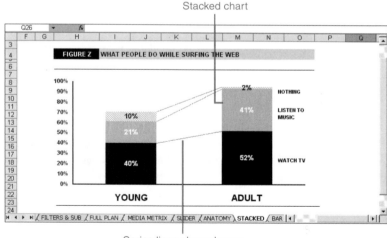

DETAILED TIME ANALYSIS WITH ANNOTATION

You can create detailed analysis over short time spans, such as hours in a day. When telling a story over a short period of time with charts, it's imperative that you use callouts of some type to clarify the picture. For example, Figure 23.49 shows the anatomy of a day trade.

Figure 23.48
Format the series lines by double-clicking the lines.

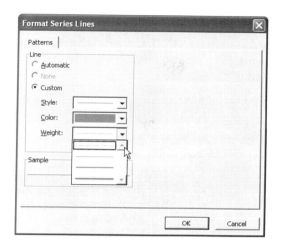

Figure 23.49
Use drawing shapes to highlight detailed information within a specified period of time.

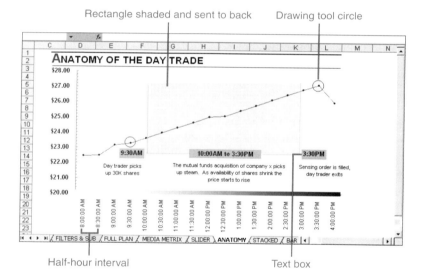

The day trade occurs over the course of one day and the day trader picks up the shares at 9:30 a.m., called out by an oval and two text boxes. The next annotation is with a transparent gray box sent to the back of the chart highlighting the mutual fund as it picks up steam over the course of the day. This is the key area of focus called out on the chart. And the last annotation is similar to the first in that an oval and text boxes are used to call out the endpoint.

ADVANCED BAR CHART FORMATS

When creating presentations for display, you'll want your charts to take on a professional, analytical look. Certain keys will help you attain this look for presentations. Figure 23.50 shows Web advertising revenue, for example.

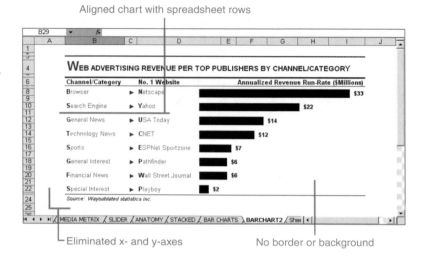

Aligned chart with spreadsheet rows

Figure 23.50
Combine bar charts with data on the spreadsheet by erasing the chart border and background.

Eliminated x- and y-axes

No border or background

Both the x- and y-axis are eliminated and the chart values are called out by applying the values to the bar chart data series. The borders and backgrounds on the chart are also eliminated and the categories are aligned with the rows on the worksheet. If you have to give a presentation in PowerPoint (see "Combining Excel with Word and PowerPoint"), you'll want to copy the whole area of the worksheet and chart, and you'll also want the background of the worksheet to be white. To create the white background, select the whole area of the worksheet and choose the white fill from the fill color palette.

ADVANCED ANALYTICAL CHART FORMATS

Professional research companies often provide reports that give the state of an industry or sector within an industry. These reports are often good reference material to see how to visually compare data and format bar charts together. If you practice the same formatting techniques throughout the different chart types that you employ, you'll notice a consistent look and feel to your PowerPoint presentations as well. Figure 23.51 is a great example of two professionally formatted bar charts combined.

Also, take into account the bordered headings above each chart and the reference to the source material called out beneath the charts.

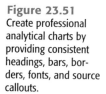

Figure 23.51
Create professional analytical charts by providing consistent headings, bars, borders, fonts, and source callouts.

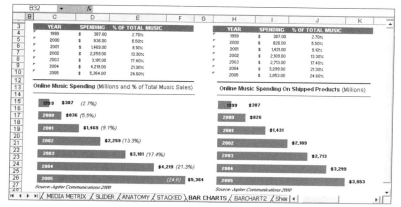

CREATING LIFETIME PROFITABILITY/BREAKEVEN CHARTS

Lifetime charts are great for showing the profitability of a product over time. Notice in Figure 23.52 how you can view loss, breakeven, and profit, all in the same chart. For simplicity, you could also separate these items into individual charts, showing net units, total profits, and so on. It's important to understand the audience and intent of the chart when making those decisions.

Figure 23.52
Use the line chart to establish lifetime profitability and breakeven analysis charts.

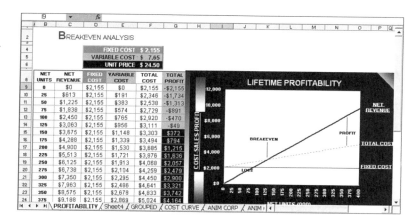

To set up a lifetime profitability chart, establish the table by following these steps:

1. Establish the net units in increments. In the example, the increments are set every 25,000 units in column B.

2. Set up the net revenue in column C, multiplying the net units by the unit price to calculate the net revenue.

3. Establish the fixed cost in column D. The example shows a fixed cost of $2,155.

23

4. Apply the variable cost in column E. Multiply the variable cost rate by the net units in column B to calculate the variable cost in column E.

5. The total cost column in column F combines the fixed cost and variable cost to reach the total cost.

6. To create the chart, select the net units, net revenue, fixed cost, and total cost data from the table. (Select just these columns by holding down the Ctrl key as you click.)

7. Use the Chart Wizard to create a line chart.

8. In Step 2 of the Chart Wizard dialog box, select the Series tab and supply the Net Units range for the Category (X) Axis Labels setting.

9. Click Finish.

10. Select the net units data series in the chart and delete it. The net units is now the category (X) axis.

TIP FROM

> You can automate the Net Units column with a formula. For example, in another cell (for example, B6), type the increment number. In cell B10, type the following formula: =$B$9+$B$6. Copy the formula down the column. This enables you to quickly view interval changes in both the table and the chart by changing only cell B6.

TROUBLESHOOTING

MOVING CATEGORY LABELS

Excel won't let me place my category labels in a different location.

You can move the x-axis on a column chart to the top of the chart. Select the axis and choose Format, Selected Axis to open the Format Axis dialog box. On the Patterns tab, choose High under Tick Mark Labels.

INVISIBLE DATA SERIES

When I create a secondary axis for the second data series of my column chart, the columns are hidden behind the first data set.

Select the data series in front of the other data series, and choose Format, Selected Data Series to open the Format Data Series dialog box. On the Patterns tab, choose None under Area.

MOVING A CHART WITH OBJECTS

When I move or resize a chart, the drawing objects don't move with the chart and I have to move and realign them.

There are two ways to fix this problem. You can select all the objects (including the chart) and group them. Or select the chart before you create an object, which makes Excel treat the object as part of the chart.

ALIGNING CHART LABELS WITH GRIDLINES

Excel doesn't allow me to align my chart labels to match the gridlines on the spreadsheet.

This can be tricky. Align the chart labels to match the gridlines as closely as you can. Then select the range of columns over the width of the chart and adjust the width to a larger size. Readjust the columns to a smaller size, and the category labels on the chart should then match.

EXCEL IN PRACTICE

By using the spreadsheet, drawing tools, and formats you can combine elements to make slider graphs, as shown in Figure 23.53. Notice the use of squares and ovals that act as placeholders for young, denoted by Y, and adult, denoted by A. This graph shows where the two age categories fare against each other as digital consumers.

Figure 23.53
Use shapes and spreadsheet formatting to create slider graphs.

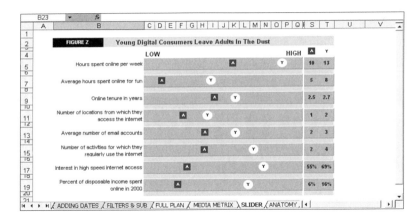

USING EXCEL IN BUSINESS

24 Using PivotTables and PivotCharts 607

25 Using Analysis Tools: Goal Seek, Solver, and Data Tables 645

26 Using Excel in Business 675

27 Customizing Excel to Fit Your Working Style 703

CHAPTER **24**

USING PIVOTTABLES AND PIVOTCHARTS

In this chapter

Understanding PivotTables   608

Using the PivotTable and PivotChart Wizard   611

Creating PivotCharts   623

Modifying PivotTables and PivotCharts   624

Working with Dates in PivotTables   633

Creating a PivotTable from Multiple Ranges   635

Saving and Editing PivotTables in HTML Format   636

UNDERSTANDING PIVOTTABLES

A *PivotTable* uses two-dimensional data to create a three-dimensional table—in essence, a summary table based on multiple conditions that have intersecting points. PivotTables are a great way to summarize large amounts of information in a small amount of space, with just a few short steps. They're interactive in that, after the PivotTable is created, you can drag a field to another location, thus *pivoting* the structure of the table with a single step.

PivotTables are often viewed as too complex to understand, but they're not that complicated if you think in terms of an automated summary table. You could write a formula to sum a quantity with multiple conditions, or you could use a PivotTable to summarize the data. Both are effective tools, but the advantages of the PivotTable is its flexibility to view the detail that makes up the total number and its ease in performing numerous calculations without your ever typing a formula.

PivotTables enable you to audit your data as well. If you must manage costs on a weekly basis—for example, costs of your employees and the hours they're generating—you should use PivotTables. (See the later section "Managing Employee Hours and Costs with PivotTables" for specific details.)

It's important to note the flexibility of PivotTables in Excel 2003. A PivotTable was a great way to summarize information in previous versions; however, it was so difficult to format and manipulate that it was easier to create your own tables and write formulas to extract the information. PivotTables are now a lot easier to format and can be used to their full potential. When you format the PivotTables, they stay formatted when refreshed, PivotCharts do not. They return to the default formatting when refreshed.

NOTE

> Although Excel maintains the refreshed data with the PivotTable format first introduced in Excel 2002, make sure you un-check the Autoformat table option in the PivotTable options dialog box. To access the Autoformat table select a cell within the PivotTable and right mouse click, then select Table Options.

Your data sources for PivotTables can also be queried through Microsoft Query if you're using a database or other data source.

→ For details on using Excel with database programs, **see** Chapter 29, "Using Excel with Access and Other Databases,"

The Excel list in Figure 24.1 shows the data for one division of a corporation. The structure of the list is important. In the example, there are three levels of information:

- The *highest level* of information being summarized is the mine site; the PivotTable will be based on the mine site.
- The *next level* is the code; the data will be organized and summarized by the code.
- The *third level* is the ore grade; the data will be structured and sorted based on the grade of the ore.

Figure 24.1
Organize your data list in logical structured columns.

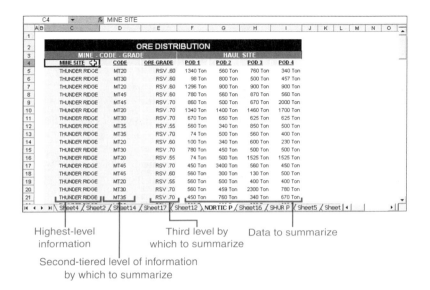

Highest-level information

Second-tiered level of information by which to summarize

Third level by which to summarize

Data to summarize

24

To summarize this information, you could create a table manually and use formulas, or you could create a PivotTable that summarizes all the information for you. The PivotTable in Figure 24.2 was created from this list. As you can see from the figure, when you create a PivotTable the PivotTable toolbar automatically appears. When you change the information in the list, you can use the Refresh Data command from tthe PivotTable toolbar to update the PivotTable. The refresh command looks like a exclamation mark.

Figure 24.2
A PivotTable quickly summarizes information in an interactive table by the categories you specify.

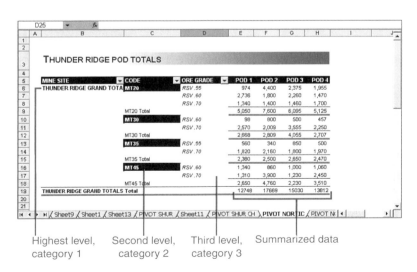

Highest level, category 1

Second level, category 2

Third level, category 3

Summarized data

The PivotTable toolbar shown here enables you to modify and refresh the selected PivotTable or PivotChart. Table 24.1 describes the options available on the toolbar.

TABLE 24.1   PIVOTTABLE TOOLBAR

Button	Name	Description
PivotTable ▾	PivotTable	Drop-down menu with options for further PivotTable or PivotChart enhancement.
	Format Report	Opens the AutoFormat dialog box for use in formatting the PivotTable.
	Chart Wizard	When in a PivotTable, automatically creates a PivotChart; when in a PivotChart, opens the Chart Wizard dialog box for use in formatting the PivotChart.
	Hide Detail	Hides the detail of a grouped range in a PivotTable.
	Show Detail	Displays the detail behind grouped ranges in the PivotTable.
	Refresh Data	Refreshes the data in the selected PivotTable.
	Include Hidden Items in Totals	Includes the values of the items that are hidden.
	Always Display Items	When clicked, hides the item headings or labels for the values. Unhides the item headings when clicked again.
	Field Settings	Allows for adjusting the summarization of the data in the field selected.
	Hide Fields/ Display Fields	Hides/displays the field buttons on the toolbar or he outlines tand labels in the PivotTable layout.

In its typical form, a PivotTable is the intersection of two columns of data in your list, with one column of information listed down the left side of the table and the other column's information "pivoted" to list its elements across the top of the table. The intersection of the two becomes the summary data.

What's unique about PivotTables is the capacity tto move fields by drag and drop. Excel summarizes the data in the new arrangement instantly. This is a bit tricky for those not familiar with PivotTable layouts so I'd suggest creating a practice PivotTable to get familiar with field layouts. Figure 24.3 shows the same PivotTable as in Figure 24.2, but with the MINE SITE field dragged to the inside. When you move a field, the PivotTable *pivots* the data to accommodate the field's new location. You don't need to write new formulas or refilter the data because the PivotTable recalculates automatically when you rearrange the fields.

Figure 24.3
When you drag a field to a new location, the PivotTable pivots the information to reflect the data's new location.

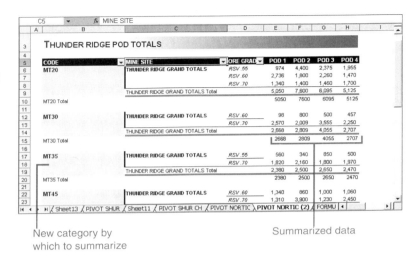

New category by which to summarize

Summarized data

24

USING THE PIVOTTABLE AND PIVOTCHART WIZARD

You can use the PivotTable and PivotChart Wizard to create a new PivotTable or PivotChart, or to edit an existing PivotTable. (The difference between a PivotTable and a *PivotChart* is that one summarizes the data in the form of a table and the other in the form of a chart.) Like other wizards in Excel, the PivotTable and PivotChart Wizard walks you step-by-step through the process. The PivotChart feature is also wizard-driven (see the later section "Creating PivotCharts").

To construct a PivotTable, follow these steps:

1. Select the information from the list you want to include in the PivotTable Or click somewhere inside your data first, which in most compact lists will allow Excel to automatically define the range in the wizard. Choose Data, PivotTable and PivotChart Report.

2. In the Step 1 of 3 dialog box of the PivotTable and PivotChart Wizard, indicate the source of the data that you want to use in the PivotTable (see Figure 24.4). For the data source to be analyzed, you choose from four options:

    • **Microsoft Excel List or Database**—Uses data organized by row labels and columns on a worksheet. This is the default setting.

    • **External Data Source**—Created from a file or database outside the current workbook.

    • **Multiple Consolidation Ranges**—Creates a PivotTable or PivotChart from multiple Excel worksheets.

    • **Another PivotTable Report or PivotChart Report**—Creates a PivotTable or PivotChart from another PivotReport in the same workbook.

Figure 24.4
Step 1 of 3 of the PivotTable and PivotChart Wizard enables you to choose from several data source options, as well as pivoting in the form of a table or chart.

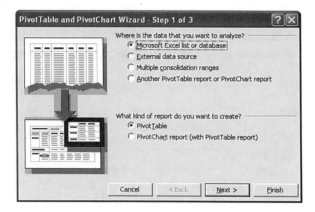

3. Specify the type of PivotTable you want to create: a table or a chart. Then click Next.

4. In Step 2 of the PivotTable and PivotChart Wizard, select a data source if none is selected, or if the data is in a different workbook or range from the one shown in the dialog box (see Figure 24.5). Figure 24.5 shows the selected list used for this example.

CAUTION

> If you didn't select the data to be pivoted before starting the PivotTable and PivotChart Wizard, be sure to check the default range that Excel selects for accuracy.

All columns must have headings

Figure 24.5
Step 2 of 3 of the PivotTable and PivotChart Wizard enables you to select a range and browse to a different document.

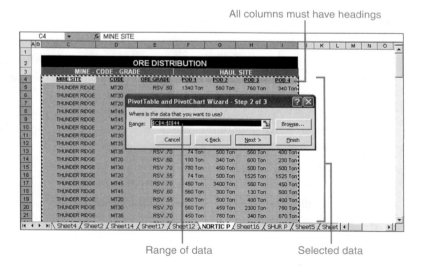

Range of data   Selected data

This list will be summarized into a PivotTable.

5. Step 3 of 3 of the PivotTable and PivotChart Wizard gives you multiple options to place and format your PivotTable (see Figure 24.6).

   The PivotTable can be placed on a new worksheet or on the existing worksheet next to the list; specify the location if you choose to place the PivotTable on the existing worksheet. You also can use the Layout and Options buttons to further specify the desired settings for the new PivotTable (see the following sections for details), or change these settings later, after creating the PivotTable or PivotChart.

6. When you're finished selecting the options you want, click Finish to create the table.

Figure 24.6
Step 3 of 3 of the PivotTable and PivotChart Wizard enables you to establish the location of the PivotTable and also customize the format and other settings.

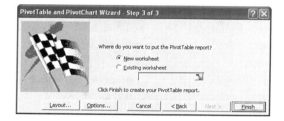

> **NOTE**
>
> If the active workbook contains at least one PivotTable, Excel enables you to create another PivotTable from that PivotTable by selecting Another PivotTable or PivotChart in Step 1 of the PivotTable and PivotChart Wizard. This saves on memory when creating large workbooks with multiple PivotTable reports. If another PivotTable already exists in the workbook, Excel will ask you whether you want to base the new PivotTable on one of the other PivotTables. If more than one PivotTable exists, you'll get another dialog box asking you to choose one of the PivotTables.

LAYING OUT THE PIVOTTABLE

Clicking the Layout button in the Step 3 of 3 PivotTable and PivotChart Wizard dialog box displays the PivotTable and PivotChart Wizard - Layout dialog box shown in Figure 24.7. You can use this dialog box to control the view of data displayed in a PivotTable. The fields from the selected data appear on the right side of the dialog box. Select and drag the desired fields into the area in the center of the dialog box and drop them in the ROW, COLUMN, PAGE, and DATA sections of the dialog box to create the desired layout. Descriptions of each section are coming up later in this section.

> **NOTE**
>
> Although Excel maintains the refreshed data with the PivotTable format first introduced in Excel 2002, make sure you un-check the Autoformat table option in the PivotTable options dialog box. To access the Autoformat table select a cell within the PivotTable and right mouse click, then select Table Options.

continues

continued

> Also, note that after a field is applied to a Row, Page, Column, or Data section, you can double-click the field to access and change the type of summary information, such as count, average, or sum. You can also customize the field name. Note that anything in the Page area creates a "filter" effect for those fields, allowing them to home in on one of the items in the field. The row area lists the items for the field down each row in the spreadsheet, whereas the column area lists items for a field across each column in the spreadsheet.

The following list describes the four areas that are available to apply fields:

- **Page**—Creates a drop-down menu above the table, enabling you to pull out or analyze a specific item from the field, such as a selected division or country. In this example, "Mine Site."

- **Row**—Applies a vertical format to the table, summarizing data from top down. The row drop area lists each item in the field down the left side of the PivotTable.

- **Column**—Applies a horizontal format to the table, summarizing the data from left to right; the column drop area lists each item in the field across the top of the PivotTable.

- **Data**—The data drop area is the summary of the numbers. This area adds, counts, or creates other analytical functions against the data dropped here. Double-click the field to access the desired function or summary type.

The following figures show the same data or list being summarized with different fields and layouts, to illustrate the change in PivotTable structure and analytical functions.

In Figure 24.7, the MINE SITE field is dropped in the page drop area. Figure 24.8 shows the resulting PivotTable.

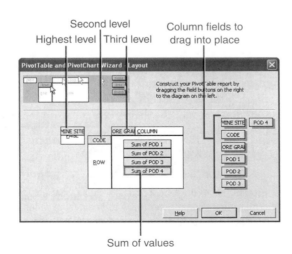

Figure 24.7
Specify the PivotTable layout with the wizard. In this example, the MINE SITE field was dropped in the page drop area.

PivotTable toolbar

Figure 24.8
This PivotTable was created from the layout in Figure 24.7.

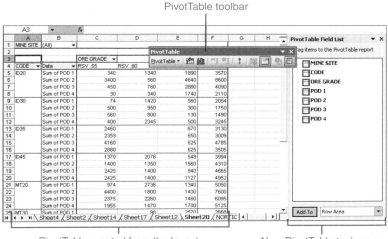

PivotTable created from the layout   New PivotTable task pane

In Figure 24.9, the MINE SITE field is dropped in the row drop area. The result is a summary of the total tonnage for the pods in each mine site (see Figure 24.10). Notice the PivotTable task pane shows in bold the fields included in the PivotTable while the fields not included appear in plain text.

Figure 24.9
In this table, the MINE SITE field is dropped in the row drop area, and will summarize the total tons for all the pods for each mine site.

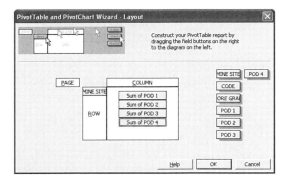

In Figure 24.11, fields are stacked in the row drop area, and the PivotTable summarizes the grades of ore by code within each mine site. Notice the COUNT function applied to the CODE field in the data drop area. Figure 24.12 shows the result after clicking OK on the PivotTable Wizard. The layout of the fields in the Row area in Figure 24.11 means that the MINE SITE field will list its items first down the left side of the report. Within each MINE SITE, a list of CODE items will appear. Finally, within each CODE item, a list of ORE GRADE items will appear.

Figure 24.10
This PivotTable was created from the layout in Figure 24.9.

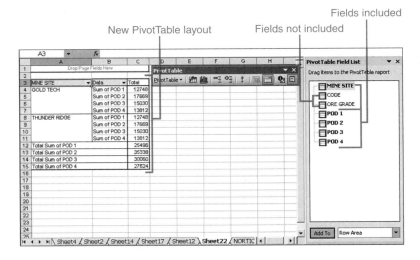

Fields included

Fields not included

New PivotTable layout

Figure 24.11
With fields stacked in the row drop area, the PivotTable will summarize the grades of ore by code within each mine site.

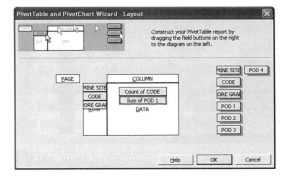

Figure 24.12
The stacked field result summarizes by priority of the field dropped in the row drop area, with the highest priority going to the topmost field in the row area of the PivotTable's layout.

SUM function

COUNT function

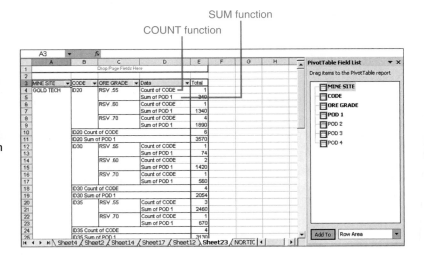

You can click Finish at any point in the PivotTable and PivotChart Wizard to create the PivotTable, and then use the PivotTable task pane to drag the fields to the drop zone areas on the PivotTable, as shown in Figure 24.13. This powerful feature (which also can be used with PivotCharts) enables you to view fields in the drop area as soon as you add them to the PivotTable. In essence, it's an interactive PivotTable builder, with onscreen viewing as it happens (see Figure 24.14). If you don't like the result, drag the field—the gray labels on the PivotTable—off the table and replace it with another field from the PivotTable Field List. To get back to the PivotTable Wizard click in the PivotTable, choose PivotTable on the PivotTable toolbar, and click PivotTable Wizard. Click Back to access the Layout and Options buttons for this PivotTable.

Code in row drop zone

Field in column drop zone

24

Figure 24.13
Start with an essentially blank PivotTable and use the PivotTable Field List to build the PivotTable.

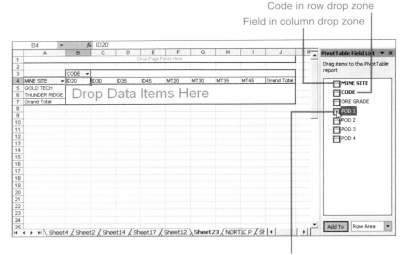

Select a field from the PivotTable task pane

Drop indicators

Summarized data

Figure 24.14
The result of dropping the Pod 1 field in the data drop zone.

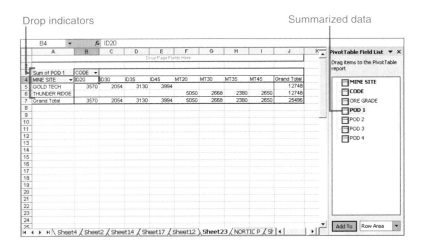

The function Excel chooses (COUNT, SUM, and so on) depends on the nature of the field you dropped. You can choose to apply different functions, such as averaging, showing the maximum or minimum, and so on. To change the function that Excel uses to summarize the data, double-click the field whose function you want to change in the DATA section of the PivotTable and PivotChart Wizard - Layout dialog box. You can access these options directly in the PivotTable by right-clicking the data and selecting Field Settings. The PivotTable Field dialog box opens; select the function you want to use (see Figure 24.15).

Figure 24.15
The PivotTable Field dialog box enables you to change how the data is analyzed.

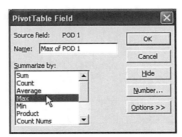

You can customize the summary functions by clicking the Options button to expand the PivotTable Field dialog box (see Figure 24.16). The additional options allow you to analyze data such as the difference from the Thunder Ridge Base Item, as shown. The *base field* is the comparison field in the custom calculation, and the *base item* is the field item in the custom calculation.

Figure 24.16
Click the Options button in the PivotTable Field dialog box to further analyze fields by base field and item.

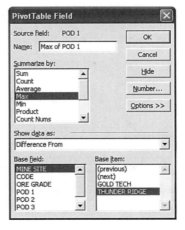

SETTING PIVOTTABLE OPTIONS

Clicking the Options button in the Step 3 of 3 dialog box for the PivotTable and PivotChart Wizard opens the PivotTable Options dialog box, in which you can further specify formats and data source options (see Figure 24.17). You can access this dialog box after completing the wizard by either clicking the PivotTable button on the PivotTable toolbar and selecting Table Options from the drop-down list, or by right-clicking a completed PivotTable and selecting Table Options from the context menu.

Figure 24.17
You can customize the PivotTable format and data options.

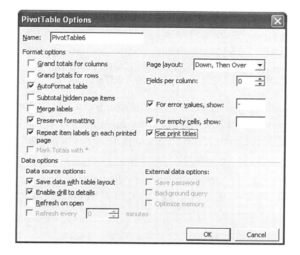

The following sections describe the options.

TIP FROM

> If your PivotTable still contains the row subtotals and you want all subtotals eliminated from your summary try the following: Double-click on the field title within your PivotTable. Under Subtotals, select the radio button None. Click OK.

NAMING THE PIVOTTABLE

The Name option in the PivotTable Options dialog box enables you to specify a name for the PivotTable. By default, Excel names new tables PivotTable1, PivotTable2, and so on, but you can type a different name. It's important to name the PivotTable something identifiable in case you have to start creating PivotTables from other PivotTables to save memory. If you haven't named your PivotTable, you'll find it hard to go back in and identify which PivotTable you want to re-create the PivotTable from.

ADDING TOTALS

The Grand Totals for Columns option in the PivotTable Options dialog box performs the analysis function and provides the grand totals for each column in the PivotTable. The Grand Totals for Rows option does the same for each row in the PivotTable. The default option selects the grand totals; however, you might want to always deselect these two options because they clutter the PivotTable with too many totals.

If your PivotTable contains hidden fields, you might want those fields subtotaled, but without displaying the field contents. If so, select the Subtotal Hidden Page Items option in the PivotTable Options dialog box.

APPLYING AUTOFORMATS

In previous versions of Excel, PivotTables were difficult to format and didn't allow for visual flexibility. Like Excel 2002, Excel 2003 enables you to manipulate and format a PivotTable similar to the way in which you format worksheets—changing the font, point size, colors, and so on.

Excel automatically applies a preset *AutoFormat* to new PivotTables. If you prefer to select a different format, you can turn off the AutoFormat Table option in the PivotTable Options dialog box, or just change the format after creating the PivotTable (see Figure 24.18).

By clicking the Options button in the AutoFormat dialog box (see Figure 24.19), you can determine exactly which type of formats from the selected AutoFormat will be applied to your PivotTable (see Figure 24.20). Note also that, in fact, Figure 24.20 shows an AutoFormat applied to a PivotTable.

Figure 24.18
Rather than keeping the default format, you can apply a new AutoFormat to your PivotTable.

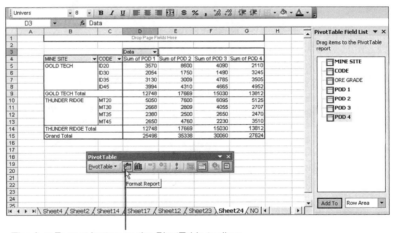

The AutoFormat button on the PivotTable toolbar

AutoFormats do more than apply the formats for color, font, and so on; they also adjust the fields and can pivot your information to display the information more effectively. After applying the new AutoFormat, if you don't like the result, just undo the change and try a different format. You can also manually reposition the fields after applying the AutoFormat, or repivot the fields by dragging their field labels into a different drop area.

Figure 24.20 shows a PivotTable with a new AutoFormat applied. Notice the difference between the PivotTable in this figure and the one shown earlier (refer to Figure 24.18).

Figure 24.19
Excel allows you to select from a variety of preset formats that can format and repivot the PivotTable.

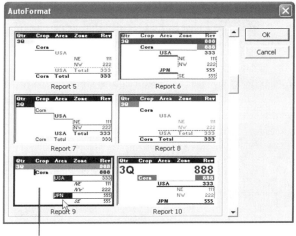

Reports and tables also change field locations

Figure 24.20
With the right AutoFormat, the table format helps tell the story of the data.

MINE SITE	CODE	POD 1	POD 2	POD 3	POD 4
GOLD TECH		12748	17669	15030	13812
	ID20	3570	6600	4090	2110
	ID30	2054	1750	1490	3245
	ID35	3130	3009	4785	3505
	ID45	3994	4310	4665	4952
THUNDER RIDGE		12748	17669	15030	13812
	MT20	5050	7600	6095	5125
	MT730	2668	2809	4055	2707
	MT735	2380	2500	2650	2470
	MT745	2650	4760	2230	3510
Grand Total		25496	35338	30060	27624

AutoFormatted PivotTable

An important improvement introduced in Excel 2002 that carries over into 2003 is Excel's capacity to preserve the formatting of a PivotTable when you refresh the data or change the PivotTable's layout. The Preserve Formatting option is selected by default in the PivotTable Options dialog box, but you can turn off this option if you prefer to revert to the original format.

NOTE

Manually applied inside borders (on right and left) are not preserved when the PivotTable is refreshed. Inside horizontal borders also disappear.

DISPLAYING LABELS

The Merge Labels option in the PivotTable Options dialog box enables you to merge column cells and row cells on the outer perimeter of the PivotTable. This is generally a formatting feature.

As with other printed reports, a PivotTable can run to multiple pages. Without labels for columns and rows, it can be difficult or impossible to determine what each individual item refers to. The Repeat Item Labels on Each Printed Page option in the PivotTable Options dialog box is set by default to repeat the item labels on each printed page. To print item labels on the first page only, deselect this option.

Another option in the PivotTable Options dialog box that relates to printing the labels is Set Print Titles. By default, this option is turned off. If you want to use the field and item labels in the PivotTable titles when printing the report, select this option.

TIP FROM

> For most printed reports, you probably use the first few rows of the worksheet as the title and print it on the top of each page. If you use the field and item labels of a PivotTable as print titles, be sure to prevent repeating other columns and rows. Choose File, Page Setup, click the Sheet tab, and clear any settings in the Print Titles section.

CONTROLLING THE LAYOUT

By default, the field order in the PivotTable layout is down and then over, setting precedent for the vertical format. If you prefer that the order be over and then down, change the Page Layout setting in the PivotTable Options dialog box. One example of when you would want to change this format is when you're dealing with dates and you want a left-to-right precedent.

You can change the number of fields per column or row in the layout by indicating a specific number in the Fields per Column box in the dialog box. By default, the number is 0.

HANDLING ERRORS AND EMPTY CELLS

Two options in the PivotTable Options dialog box enable you to control what Excel displays in cells that don't display values as expected. The For Error Values, Show __ option enables you to specify a character or a blank in place of the error values; the For Empty Cells, Show __ option enables you to specify a character or a blank in place of the empty cells. For example, if you have a report that shows an `#ERR` message, you might find it helpful to point your attention to the errors by typing the phrase **missing name** in the box next to the For Error Values, Show __ option. This setup will display that phrase in every cell containing an error. In addition, you can apply conditional formats to apply colors to highlight the cells containing the phrase.

Leaving both options enabled with nothing in their text boxes will display the cells as blank in the PivotTable. Disabling the For Empty Cells, Show __ option will display a zero for empty cells in the PivotTable.

> **NOTE**
> For PivotTable cells only, enabling the For Empty Cells setting overrides the Zero Values option found in the Window Options section of the View tab in the Options dialog box (choose Tools, Options).

SOURCE DATA OPTIONS

The Data Options section of the PivotTable Options dialog box provides a number of helpful features. The following list describes these options:

- **Save Data with Table Layout**—Saves a copy of the data used from an external data source. Selected by default.

  This option isn't only for external data sources. Deselecting this option saves on the workbook's size but also forces you to manually refresh the PivotTable(s) when opening the workbook (unless the Refresh on Open option is enabled). With this option disabled, you can't work with PivotTables until they've been refreshed.

- **Enable Drill to details**—Shows the detail when a field is double-clicked. Selected by default.

- **Refresh on Open**—Refreshes the PivotTable when the workbook is opened. By default, this option isn't selected; in most cases, you should select it unless the source data is extremely large and is located in an external data source on a distant server.

- **Refresh Every __ Minutes**—Allows for automatic refreshing based on the minutes set. By default, this option isn't selected. This option is available only for PivotTables based on external data sources. (It really should appear under the External Data Options section of the dialog box.)

- **Save Password**—Saves the password associated with the external data source where the information is derived. This option is deselected by default; enabling this option compromises database security.

- **Background Query**—Runs the query in the background while allowing you to continue to work. Turned off by default.

- **Optimize Memory**—Optimizes and manages the memory when using PivotTables; however, this option slows down performance. By default, this option is not selected.

CREATING PIVOTCHARTS

Figures 24.21 and 24.22 show data structured with the same criteria as a PivotTable versus a PivotChart. When a PivotChart is created, Excel creates both a chart sheet and a

24

PivotTable sheet within the workbook; because the chart information must be derived from a table, Excel automatically creates the table. The default action of the PivotChart feature is to create a chart as a worksheet, but you also can create an embedded chart on a worksheet in the last step of the "PivotTable Wizard" or by choosing Chart, Location and selecting the As Object In option after creating the PivotChart.

Figure 24.21
This PivotTable is based on a structured list.

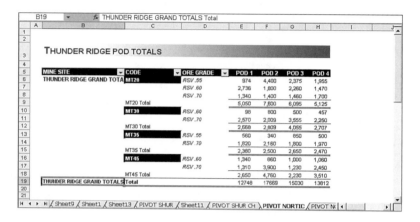

Figure 24.22
A PivotChart based on the same structured list used in Figure 24.21.

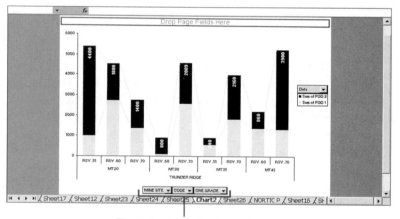

These fields can be dragged

PivotCharts can be formatted with worksheets to plot and show data in chart format and can be combined with other worksheet data, making this new feature flexible and powerful.

MODIFYING PIVOTTABLES AND PIVOTCHARTS

After you create a PivotTable or PivotChart, you can restructure the PivotTable or PivotChart to look different by dragging and dropping fields, or by using the options on the menus or the PivotTable toolbar. You also can change the look or structure of the PivotTable with formatting options (see the earlier section "Applying AutoFormats").

CAUTION

Don't waste your time formatting PivotCharts because when the data is refreshed it reformats the PivotChart back to the default format. Since the inception of PivotCharts, this has always been a huge flaw and it remains unfixed in Excel 2003.

You can adjust and manipulate just about all aspects of the PivotTable or PivotChart. You can apply colored fills, borders, and font colors just as you would a regular table on a worksheet. PivotCharts are a bit more difficult to format because of sizing limitations on the plot area and legend locations, but for the most part, they're as flexible as charts created with the standard charting features. When the structure of the PivotChart changes, so does its corresponding PivotTable (and vice versa).

DRAGGING FIELDS IN A PIVOTCHART

PivotCharts offer the power of PivotTables and normal charts combined in one interactive surface. You can select and drag fields to new locations on the chart, and Excel will pivot the chart to correspond to the new field location. For example, dragging the field out of the drop zone in the PivotChart in Figure 24.23 eliminates the field and changes the chart to correspond to the new pivoted information, shown in Figure 24.24. Changes to the fields in the PivotChart also are reflected on the corresponding PivotTable.

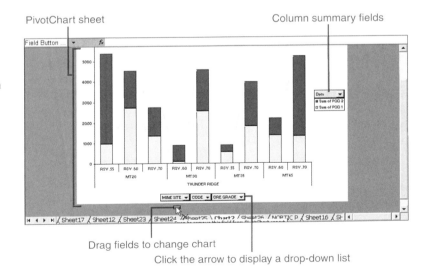

PivotChart sheet

Column summary fields

Figure 24.23
You can select and move the fields in a PivotChart, just as in a PivotTable.

Drag fields to change chart

Click the arrow to display a drop-down list

Move field location

Figure 24.24
By dragging the field to a new location or the drop zone, you can restructure the chart with one move.

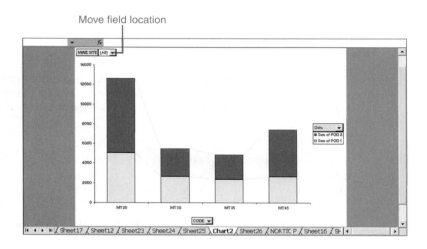

HIDING FIELD DATA

Clicking the arrow button shown on a field in the PivotChart or PivotTable displays a drop-down list from which you can select or deselect items (see Figure 24.25). The information will be removed from or added to the PivotChart or PivotTable (see Figure 24.26).

You can deselect items from the field list

Figure 24.25
Select or deselect items from fields by using the drop-down list on the field.

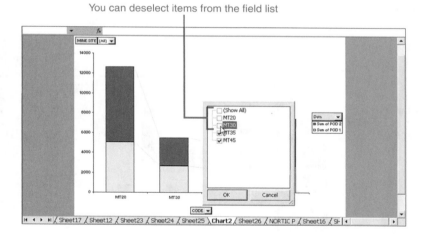

SHOWING AND HIDING DETAIL

You can show detail behind a field by double-clicking the field's heading and then clicking on the Show Detail button on the PivotTable toolbar. If lower-level information exists behind the field, the Show Detail button on the PivotTable toolbar is enabled (see

Figure 24.27). When you double-click a field label, you can gain detail. When you double-click a value, you get a list/subset of records on a new sheet that contributed to or made up that value. Select the category you want to show the detail for; Excel drills down to show the detail that makes up the total number. For example, if you have employees' hours summed for the week and you double-click the total number, Excel shows all the weekly information that creates the total number. In this case, the RSV .55 line was double-clicked to show the detail behind it (see Figure 24.28).

Figure 24.26
By deselecting categories from fields, you can eliminate data sets with one click.

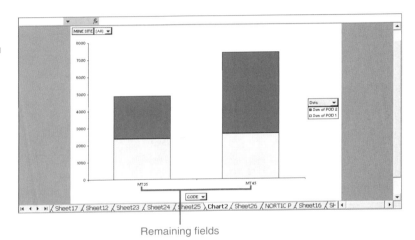

Remaining fields

Detailed information behind the field

Figure 24.27
Excel enables you to drill down to show the detail that makes up the summary information in the PivotTable.

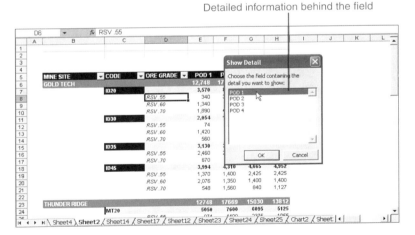

After detail is added, double-clicking RSV .55 again will hide the detail, and another double-click will show it again (without the dialog box appearing a second time). Along the same line, if you double-click the ID20 code, Excel hides the ore grades for that item (again, no dialog box would appear) because the CODE field already has ore grade details showing.

Detail

Figure 24.28
The detail behind the selected region is shown here. In this case, RSV .55 was double-clicked and POD 1 detail was chosen for viewing.

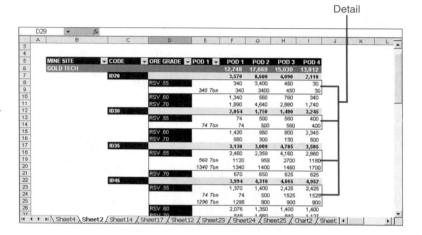

If you click the field label ORE GRADE and use the Show Detail button on the PivotTable toolbar (double-clicking won't display the Show Detail dialog box here), you can view or display details for all the ore grades at once.

PERFORMING CALCULATIONS ON A PIVOTTABLE

You can perform calculations on a field or multiple fields within a PivotTable. Click the PivotTable button on the PivotTable toolbar. Then choose Formulas, Calculated Field from the drop-down menu.

In Figure 24.29, the name of the calculated field to be added represents the overhead for the POD 4 region. The formula =SUM('POD 4')*.12 calculates the percentage of overhead for the region, calculated against the current field amount ('POD 4'). Single quotation marks always appear around a field name when it contains spaces.

TIP FROM

You also can create these calculations on the worksheet and reference them to the cells in the PivotTable. Just create a simple function that references the field column and row. Please note that such calculations can't appear inside the PivotTable, but can appear just outside it (although applying AutoFormats might delete such data if the format manipulates the fields). Calculations can also be done back at the original list (in the form of an additional column). The new column would then be one of the field names in the PivotTable and could be dragged onto a PivotTable as you would any other field.

Figure 24.29
Excel enables you to add field names and perform calculations against the PivotTable. The calculated field added now is part of the PivotTable.

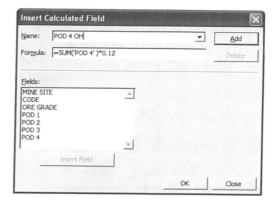

Notice the results in Figure 24.30 of the new calculated field in the PivotTable. It shows the percentage attributed to overhead for the region. Each time the table is refreshed, the calculations automatically update.

24

Calculated field added

Figure 24.30
By adding a calculated field to the PivotTable, Excel makes the addition part of the PivotTable. Each time the data is refreshed, the calculations are automatically updated.

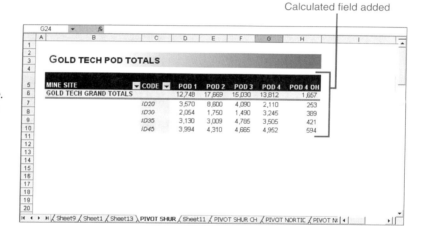

HIDING COLUMNS OR ROWS

For presentations or printouts, you might want to show only certain bits of information within the PivotTable. You can hide rows or columns that you don't want to show (see Figure 24.31) or unhide hidden rows or columns, just as you would in any other report.

→ For details on hiding and unhiding rows and columns, **see** "Hiding and Unhiding Rows and Columns," **p. 37**

DRILLING DOWN IN A FIELD

In the PivotTable in Figure 24.32, all the information is rolled up to its highest level, without the use of grouping or hidden rows. This shows the 3D element of PivotTables. To drill up and drill down, select a field that has a subset and double-click it. It's that simple. Notice the results of the code type in Figure 24.33 after you double-click the product field. For this drill-down effect to work, you first must show the detail for the field, as explained in "Showing and Hiding Detail," earlier in the chapter. If details for a field are not already listed in the PivotTable, a double-click will display the Show Detail dialog box.

Figure 24.31
By hiding columns or rows, you can focus on newly calculated fields that point out certain pieces of information that might get lost in the original table with all data showing.

Columns D through F are hidden

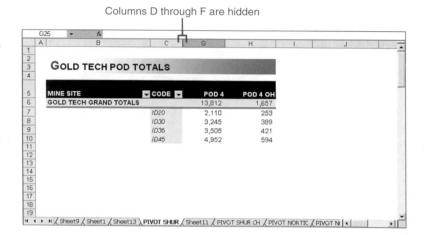

Figure 24.32
You can hide information by using the drill-down technique on PivotTables. Just double-click the field name.

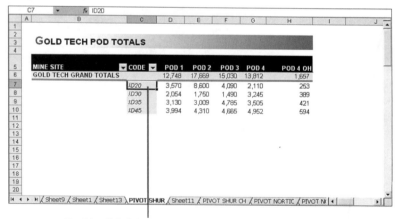

Double-click fields to hide the detail

 If double-clicking doesn't allow you to drill down, this feature might be disabled. See "Enabling Drilldown" in the "Troubleshooting" section at the end of this chapter.

DRAGGING A FIELD FOR A PAGE VIEW

The flexibility of dragging fields in PivotTables enables you to drag fields outside the table and create a *page view*. Select the field from the PivotTable and drag it above the table; the insert bar appears (see Figure 24.34). Drop the field and it becomes a drop-down list to manage the information, as shown in Figure 24.35. The mouse symbol has a small icon that represents a PivotTable. The blue part of the tiny PivotTable indicates where the field is currently located in the drag.

Double-click to expand or contract the detail   Detail behind ID20

Figure 24.33
Here are the results of managing the view of the PivotTable by drilling down or double-clicking. Notice how the information acts as though it's collapsed or expanded, similar to grouping.

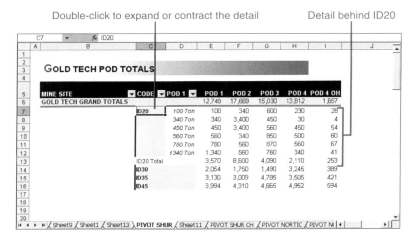

Drag the field to page view

Figure 24.34
You can drag the field outside the table to create a page view. You're not limited to one field outside the table; you can drag and create multiple drop-down lists.

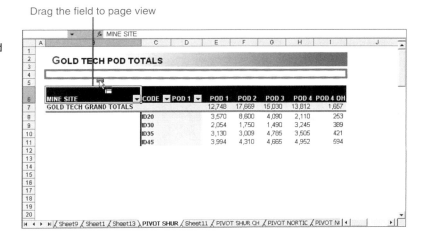

Page drop zone

Figure 24.35
By creating a page view with a PivotTable, you can manage the information from the PivotTable with a drop-down list.

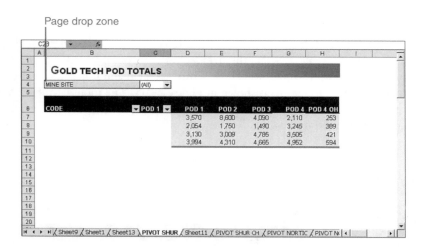

AUDIT YOUR TOTALS

If you want a quick summary breakout of a data set, double-click any value, as shown in Figure 24.36, and Excel automatically creates an independent breakout on a separate worksheet. The detail from double-clicking the value is shown in Figure 24.37. By double-clicking the data set, the subset of data that appears in that set will be displayed or hidden.

Double-click to audit

Figure 24.36
To create an automatic summary, just double-click the grand total.

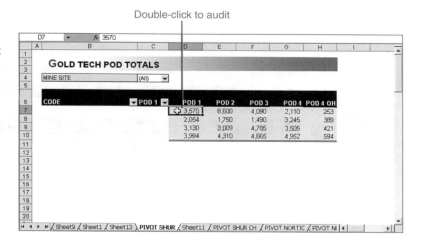

Figure 24.37
The result of double-clicking the grand total of a set in a PivotTable is a summary of that particular data.

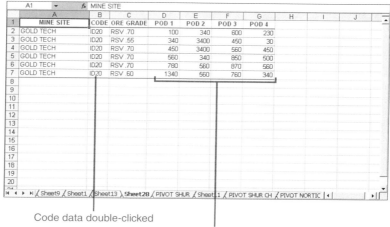

Code data double-clicked

Data audited behind the code

WORKING WITH DATES IN PIVOTTABLES

Quite often, you'll have information from lists that contain dates. To transpose it into a n understandable PivotTable, follow a few simple steps and you can create an effective summary of the information. Again, start with your list or database, like that shown in Figure 24.38.

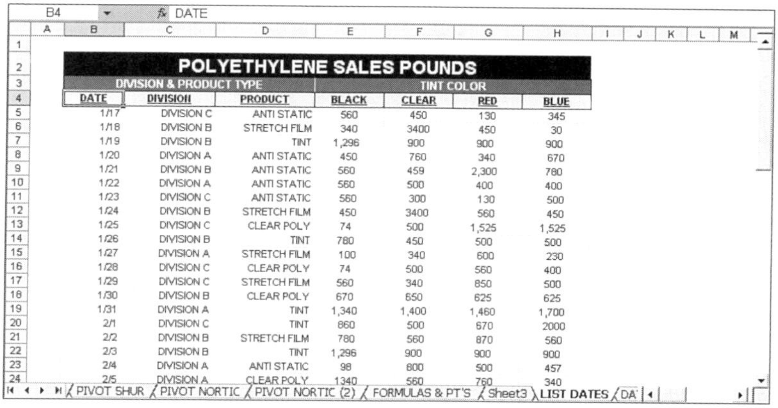

Figure 24.38
When working with dates, you can combine the dates to summarize by days, weeks, months, and so on.

When working with dates, many times it's easier to see and print the date information left to right rather than up and down, because most timelines are generated in this manner. Be sure to set the Page Layout setting in the PivotTable Options dialog box to Over, Then Down, as shown in Figure 24.39.

Figure 24.39
When working with dates, many times it works well to view the information left to right rather than up and down.

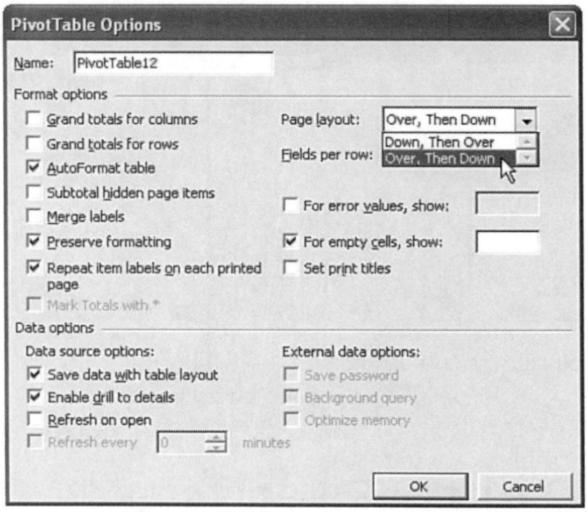

PivotTable Options

Name: PivotTable12

Format options

☐ Grand totals for columns
☐ Grand totals for rows
☑ AutoFormat table
☐ Subtotal hidden page items
☐ Merge labels
☑ Preserve formatting
☑ Repeat item labels on each printed page
☐ Mark Totals with *

Page layout: Over, Then Down

Fields per row:
Down, Then Over
Over, Then Down

☐ For error values, show: ____
☑ For empty cells, show: ____
☐ Set print titles

Data options

Data source options:
☑ Save data with table layout
☑ Enable drill to details
☐ Refresh on open
☐ Refresh every 0 minutes

External data options:
☐ Save password
☐ Background query
☐ Optimize memory

OK   Cancel

To group dates together, select the first date field in the PivotTable and choose Data, Group and Outline, Group. The Grouping dialog box appears enabling you to set parameters on the dates to be grouped (see Figure 24.40). Figure 24.41 shows the PivotTable grouped on a weekly basis (every seven days). You can do the same with numbers—for example, if you have average scores in a PivotTable and you want them grouped in ranges.

Figure 24.40
You can set the parameters on date ranges by using the Group option. This works well with summarizing data weekly and monthly.

Grouping

Auto
☑ Starting at: 1/17/1998
☑ Ending at: 3/18/1998

By
Seconds
Minutes
Hours
Days
Months
Quarters

Number of days: 7

OK   Cancel

Grouped every seven days

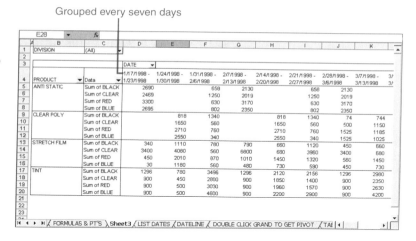

Figure 24.41
The result of setting the number of days to seven breaks out the groups by weeks.

24

CREATING A PIVOTTABLE FROM MULTIPLE RANGES

Excel enables you to create PivotTables from multiple consolidation ranges by selecting the multiple consolidation Ranges option from Step 1 of the PivotTable and PivotChart Wizard. For example, if you have two companies with product sales or two divisions with product sales, you can establish separate worksheets or databases to control the list and then combine into a multiple consolidated PivotTable. (The wizard walks you through step-by-step.) Figure 24.42 shows Step 2b of 3 of the PivotTable and PivotChart Wizard, which enables you to select lists or ranges in any open documents. Drag over the range of data you want to consolidate and click the Add button to add it to the All Ranges section of the dialog box (see Figure 24.43 for the result).

Figure 24.42
To consolidate lists into a PivotTable, select the Multiple Consolidation Ranges in Step 2b of the wizard and add the ranges together.

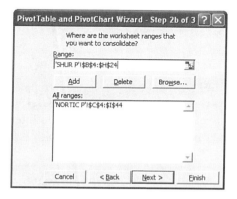

If your consolidation ranges are coming from multiple files (as opposed to sheets), you can use the Browse button to select unopened files. The problem is that the Browse button doesn't actually open the files. Unless you've memorized the data ranges (addresses or range names), it's better to open the files before starting the PivotTable and PivotChart Wizard. The only time this could be a problem is if you have numerous files to open and restricted computer memory. In such a case, name each consolidation range so that you can manually type it in the Range box after the name of the file.

Figure 24.43
Combine lists or ranges into one PivotTable.

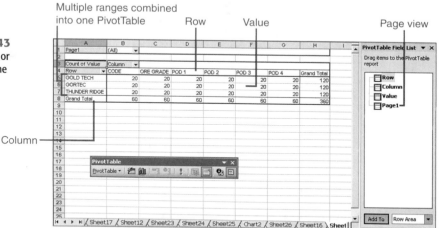

SAVING AND EDITING PIVOTTABLES IN HTML FORMAT

Excel 2003 enables you to save a PivotTable as an HTML document and modify HTML documents posted on an Internet or intranet site. The benefit of this feature is that you can manipulate the data fields while the document is posted and then print the changes. The drawback is that you can't save the changes in Excel format; changes made to the HTML document revert to the format in which the document was posted (HTML). The data can be refreshed, but formatting changes saved must come from the source document, thus making this feature a bit cumbersome.

To save a PivotTable as a Web page, follow these steps:

1. Choose File, Save As Web Page.

2. Specify whether you want to save the whole workbook or the selected worksheet, as shown in Figure 24.44. If you select Selection: Sheet, the Add Interactivity option becomes available. Select Add Interactivity and click Publish.

NOTE

> It's important to note that if the user selects a range (a PivotTable) before using the File, Save as Web Page command, the Selection option will reflect the selected range instead of the entire sheet.

Figure 24.44
Add interactivity to
your Web PivotTable
by selecting Selection:
Sheet and checking
Add Interactivity.

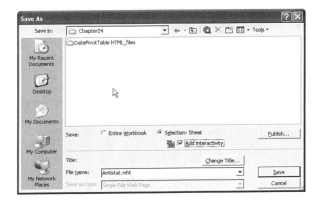

24

3. In the Publish As Web Page dialog box, select the sheet from the Choose list. Then select the entire sheet or just the PivotTable region.

4. The Add Interactivity With option enables you to create spreadsheet functionality (formulas and so on) or PivotTable functionality (which allows you to move fields). Select PivotTable Functionality (see Figure 24.45).

5. Specify a filename for the Web page and click Publish.

Figure 24.45
You can choose
spreadsheet function-
ality or PivotTable
functionality from the
Add Interactivity With
option.

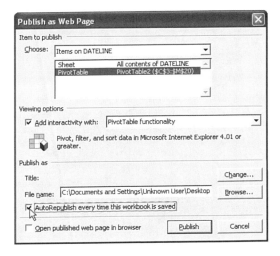

6. Select and open the HTML document from the folder where it was saved. You can deselect field items with the drop-down list from the field just as you would in a normal PivotTable. You can also expand and collapse fields, drag and drop fields, and add or remove fields.

CAUTION

> You will not be able to manipulate the published Excel data unless you have the Office XP Web components installed. Apparently, Office 2000 Web components are not compatible, which makes this useless unless you upgrade the components.
>
> Note that you don't need Office XP installed, just the components, which are separate entities. Office 2000-published data (PivotTables or otherwise) are compatible with the new XP components—in other words, Office 2000 data opens fine in the browser.

TROUBLESHOOTING

ENABLING DRILLDOWN

Why can't I drill down in my PivotTable?

To be able to drill down by double-clicking, the Enable Drill to details option must be selected in the Data Options section of the PivotTable Options dialog box.

GROUPING PIVOTTABLE DATES

How do I group PivotTable dates?

Select the first date cell in the PivotTable, and then choose Data, Group and Outline, Group. Enter the Starting At and Ending At date. Select the time measurement under By, and adjust the Number of Days setting if necessary.

VIEWING THE DATA BEHIND PIVOTTABLE SUMMARIES

How do I see the information behind PivotTable totals?

Double-click the total of the selected field item. Excel creates a separate sheet that lists the information that makes up the value you double-clicked on the PivotTable—a powerful auditing device.

EXCEL IN PRACTICE

For this Excel in Practice I show you two common uses of PivotTables: grouping data and managing employee costs and hours worked.

GROUPING DATA IN PIVOT TABLES

Notice the two PivotTable formats in Figure 24.46. The first format is the standard format when a PivotTable is created. The second, or the PivotTable to the right has custom formats applied as well as grouped dates by month. One of the unique features about PivotTables is that you can group dates by hour, day, month, Qtr, and so on from a list of dates. You could also create these summaries with formulas; however, PivotTables offer a much easier solution to the problem.

Standard PivotTable layout

Figure 24.46
Use grouping to group days into months and custom formats to create an organized look to your information.

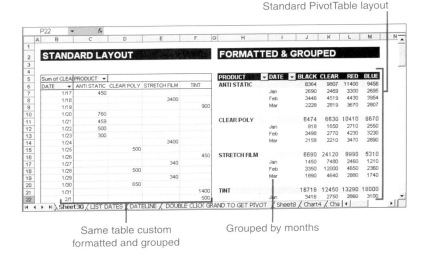

Same table custom formatted and grouped

Grouped by months

MANAGING EMPLOYEE HOURS AND COSTS WITH PIVOTTABLES

You can use PivotTables to manage employee hours and costs. After observing several attempts to manage employee hours and costs, the easiest solution is a combination of a table, list, VLOOKUP, and a PivotTable. After it's set up, such a table requires minimal effort to manage. If you have employee hours in one database or list, and in another area have a table that has the employee rates, use the VLOOKUP function to combine the two and then pivot the list. To build an employee cost-tracking PivotTable, first set up the information. Figure 24.47 shows a table that contains the employee base rate and overtime rate.

Figure 24.47
The first step in creating an employee cost-tracking PivotTable is to create the table with rates.

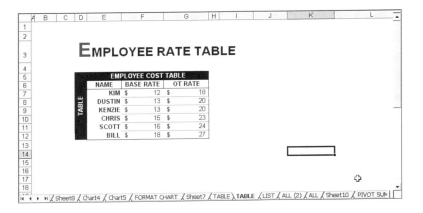

Combine the employee cost table with the list of hours an employee worked by using the VLOOKUP function. Notice in cell G15 of Figure 24.48, the VLOOKUP function searches for the employee name in cell D15 in the employee cost table. It refers to the table range C4:E10, and then the column number of the base rate. In this case, the column number of the base rate in the cost table is in column 2. Make sure the range referring to the cost table has absolute values, because you're going to be dragging the formula down and you want the table range to remain the same. The "FALSE" part of the VLOOKUP function instructs the function to locate an exact match for the employee name. Figure 24.49 shows the VLOOKUP referring to column 3, base rate for the employee in cell G15.

→ For details on VLOOKUP, **see** "VLOOKUP," **p.300**

Match the base rate from the table to the list with VLOOKUP

Figure 24.48
Use a VLOOKUP function to refer to the employee in the list and the cost associated with the employee from the cost table.

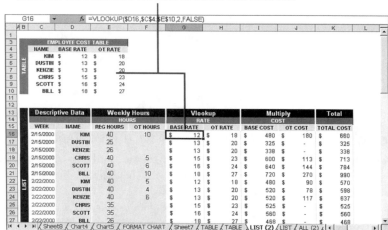

Match the overtime rate from the table to the list with VLOOKUP

Figure 24.49
Notice the difference in this VLOOKUP formula. It still refers to the same employee and table; but the column number is 3, referring to the overtime rate.

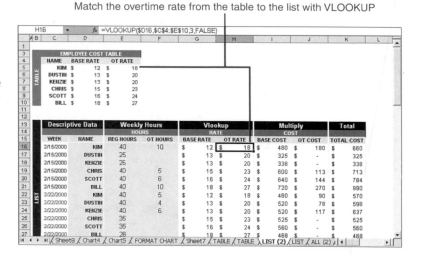

Multiply the regular hours by the base rate to find the base cost for the week for that particular employee. In Figure 24.50, cell I16, the formula reads =E15*G15. Drag the formula to the right to cell J15 to calculate the overtime costs. The total column in cell K15 adds the base cost and overtime cost in cells I15 and J15. Drag or fill cells G15:K15 down the length of the list.

Multiply the base rate times the regular hours to calculate the base cost

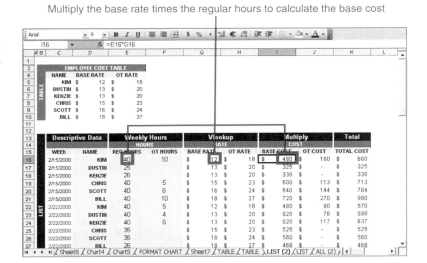

Figure 24.50
Multiply the base rate and the regular hours to get the base cost for the employee for that week.

Now that you have the base of information set up, you'll want to pivot the information to summarize the employee cost for the week. In addition, if you have codes and/or projects the employee is working on, you can include that information and break out the summaries in PivotTables by employee, project, week, and so on.

There is a trick to making this PivotTable effortless. In Step 2 of the PivotTable and PivotChart Wizard, the range selected is C15:K2100 (see Figure 24.51). Although the current range of the list only goes down to row 27, a range that the PivotTable will never actually reach has been selected; thus, the PivotTable range will always include all the new rows of information added.

NOTE

Although highlighting extra blank rows keeps the range updated, they are nevertheless included in the PivotTable calculations, which adds to the calculation effort and the PivotTable cache (memory). It also adds a blank listing to the PivotTable, which can be hidden by using the NAME field drop-down list.

To arrange the PivotTable in a logical fashion, set the fields in the following order (see Figure 24.52): the WEEK field in the PAGE section of the diagram and the NAME field in the ROW section. Place the regular hours, overtime hours, base cost, overtime cost, and total cost in the DATA section.

Figure 24.51
Select a range that the list will never grow to. This will ensure that when the PivotTable is refreshed, it's always selecting all the information in the list.

Page field layout

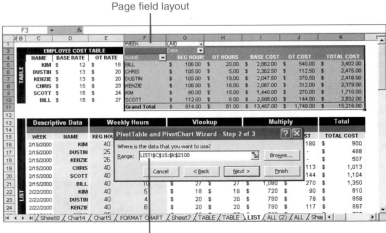

Extended range

Figure 24.52
Arrange the fields so that they present a logical flow. Place the WEEK field in the PAGE section so that you can pull up the costs for any week.

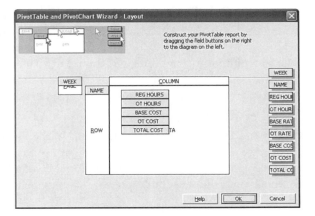

In the final step of the PivotTable and PivotChart Wizard, click the Options button and deselect Grand Totals for Columns and Grand Totals for Rows (see Figure 24.53).

The final setup of the PivotTable shows the Week pull-down at the top and the employees listed down the left column with the corresponding totals to the right (see Figure 24.54). The tables have been placed on the same sheet so you can understand how they work together.

24

Deselect the grant total options

Figure 24.53
Deselect the grand totals options to help create an easy-to-read PivotTable.

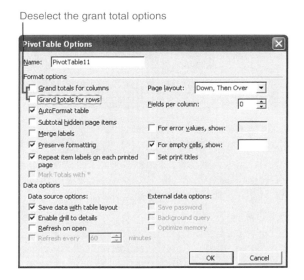

Rate table

Step 3 PivotTable

Figure 24.54
The final result shows the cost table, the list reference to the cost table, and the PivotTable derived from the list.

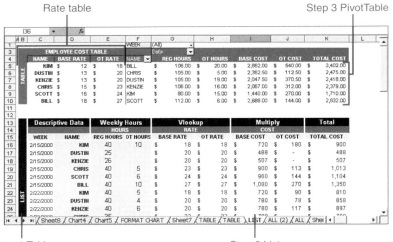

Step 1 Table

Step 2 List

24

CHAPTER 25

USING ANALYSIS TOOLS: GOAL SEEK, SOLVER, AND DATA TABLES

In this chapter

Analyzing Your Data with Excel   646

Using Goal Seek   646

Using Solver   650

Creating Amortization Tables to Calculate Mortgage Payments   662

Using the Analysis ToolPak Add-In   669

ANALYZING YOUR DATA WITH EXCEL

Many Excel users input data into a worksheet, use simple functions or formulas to calculate results, and then report those results to someone else. Although this is a perfectly legitimate use of Excel, it basically turns Excel into a calculator.

When you need to do more than just type data into a worksheet, you can use special Excel features to analyze your data and solve complex problems by employing variables and constraints. Goal Seek and Solver are two great tools included with Excel that you can use to analyze data and provide answers to simple or even fairly complex problems. Goal Seek is primarily used when there is one unknown variable, and Solver when there are many variables and multiple constraints. Although you might have used Solver in the past, primarily with complex tables for financial analysis, this chapter also shows you how to combine Solver with Gantt charts. Solver isn't just for financial analysis; it can be used against production, financial, marketing, and accounting models. Solver should be used when you're searching for a result and you have multiple variables that change (constraints). The more complex the constraints, the more you need to use Solver, as shown later in this chapter for resource loading.

Both Goal Seek and Solver enable you to play "what if" with the result of a formula when you know the result you're shooting for, without manually changing the cells that are being referenced in the formula.

→ For more on Gantt charts and Excel, **see** "Resource Pools," **p. 687**

Data tables in Excel provide a very important function: creating one- and two-variable tables for use in amortization and other tasks—allowing you to create a series of results based on one formula (such as cash flows). This chapter includes the details on how to set up your tables and shows a few tricks for these kinds of tables that can save you time and effort.

Whether you're manufacturing plastic cups, hauling quantities of material or dirt, or manufacturing digital assets in software development, Excel's powerful analytical tools combined with structured worksheet design can make your life easier and help you manage your time more effectively.

USING GOAL SEEK

The *Goal Seek* feature in Excel uses a single variable to find a desired result. To understand Goal Seek, consider this simple scenario. Suppose you're a sales representative for a packaging business. You must achieve $100,000 in sales this year to receive a bonus. Figure 25.1 shows a table that displays the current situation—you have sold 2,000 units of a product with a per-unit sales price of $3.46. How many units must you sell to achieve your $100,000 goal?

NOTE

The goal amount ($100,000 in this case) must be the result of a formula, not just plain data.

Figure 25.1
Use Goal Seek to find the unknown variable—such as how many boxes must be sold at a unit price of $3.46 to reach $100,000 in sales.

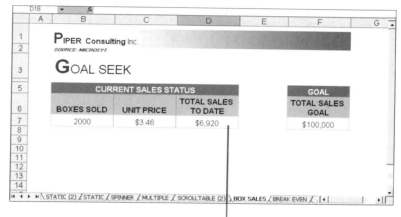

Cell D7 contains a formula

At this point, you've probably already set up the formula in your head: $(100000-6920)/3.46 = 26901.73$ units remaining to be sold. What would be the advantage of using a special Excel feature to calculate something so simple? Wouldn't you just create a formula in a cell and be done with it? The advantage of Goal Seek is that you can set up your formula just once, and then substitute different amounts to get quick alternative routes to your goal.

To use Goal Seek, select the formula cell (D7 in this example) and then choose Tools, Goal Seek to display the Goal Seek dialog box (see Figure 25.2). The following list describes the entries for each of the items in the dialog box:

- Set Cell specifies the location of the formula you use to get the end result. In this case, the formula is in cell D7, and multiplies the number of units sold by the unit price.

- Type the target value in the To Value box, which in this case is $100,000. Although you can type the figure using commas and a dollar sign, there is no need to use those extra characters. Note that Excel does not allow you to reference a cell containing your goal.

- In the By Changing Cell box, specify the cell location of the variable that you want to change to reach your goal—in this case, cell B7, the cell containing the amount of boxes you need to sell to achieve your $100,000 sales goal.

As soon as you click OK or press Enter, Excel begins seeking the specified goal. In this case, the solution indicated is 28901.7341 total units at the current price of $3.46 (see Figure 25.3). You probably would need to round the solution to the nearest integer (28,902), because units aren't generally sold in fractional amounts. To accept the proposed changes, click OK. To return the boxes sold amount to its previous value, click Cancel. When changing the variable table you need to restore the boxes sold cell to its initial value of 2000.

Figure 25.2
Specify the settings in the dialog box to begin the Goal Seek process.

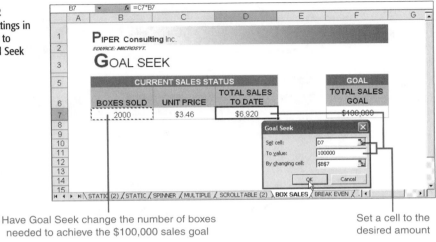

Have Goal Seek change the number of boxes needed to achieve the $100,000 sales goal

Set a cell to the desired amount

Figure 25.3
Goal Seek found the desired result.

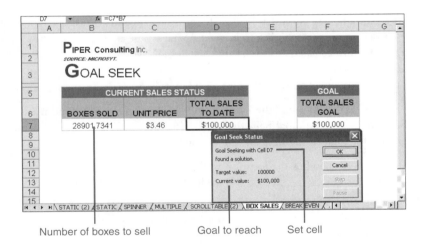

Number of boxes to sell   Goal to reach   Set cell

Now suppose you need to determine the unit price—the other variable in the total-sales-to-date formula. If you want to sell only 2,000 units of something, how high would the price need to be for you to reach the $100,000 target? To find out, you change the By Changing Cell setting in the Goal Seek dialog box to specify cell C7, the unit price (see Figure 25.4).

Figure 25.4
In this case, Goal Seek is adjusting the unit price to reach the target.

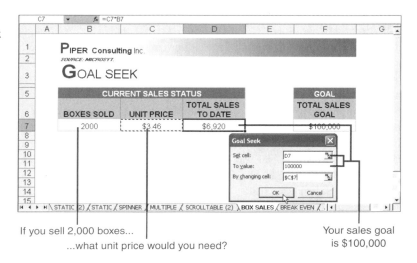

If you sell 2,000 boxes...
...what unit price would you need?

Your sales goal is $100,000

Here, Goal Seek will raise the price of the boxes to a dollar value that will equal $100,000 in sales but keep the units sold at 2,000. Figure 25.5 shows the outcome: To reach $100,000 by selling only 2,000 units, each unit must cost $50. Click OK to accept the new price, or Cancel to place the old one back in.

Figure 25.5
Goal Seek is finding a unit price to meet the target.

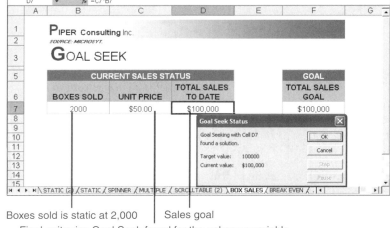

Boxes sold is static at 2,000   Sales goal
Final unit price Goal Seek found for the unknown variable

TIP FROM

You can use Goal Seek with complex financial models as well as with a simple solution. Link the final result cell to other cells within the model to drive the changes.

USING SOLVER

Goal Seek is an efficient feature for helping you reach a particular goal, but it deals with only a single variable. For most businesses, the variables are much more complex. How can you reach the profit goal if advertising expenses increase? What's the best mix of products to increase sales in the first quarter, when revenues traditionally decline for your business? Which suppliers give you the optimal combination of price and delivery? For problems like these, you can use *Solver*, an add-in program that comes with Excel. This powerful analysis tool uses multiple changing variables and constraints to find the optimal solution to solve a problem. Previously, Solver was a tool used primarily for financial modeling analysis. However, Solver can be used in conjunction with models of any kind that you build in Excel. Using Solver with Gantt charts is discussed later in this section.

NOTE

> Solver isn't enabled by default. To add it to the Tools menu, choose Tools, Add-Ins, select Solver Add-In in the Add-Ins dialog box, and click OK. If asked to confirm, choose Yes. (You might need the Office 2003 CD, depending on how you installed the software.)

TIP FROM

> The best way to learn how to work with Solver is to experiment with simple problems, using the Solvsamp.xls file on the Office 2003 CD. When you understand how to work with multiple variables and constraints to solve a problem, you can begin using your own data and solving real business problems.

The key to understanding complex analysis tools is to start with something relatively simple. The example in Figure 25.6 uses several variables to calculate a project's total cost. What if your total budget for the year is $500,000 (as shown in the constraints cell G20) and you were using only $377,670 (as shown in cell G16)? You want each project to have a total cost of $50,000 (G5:G14) and you want to optimize or add to your marketing and advertising dollars (columns E and F). Solver will add to the Marketing cost and Advertising cost for you, adjusting your total cost for a project to $50,000.

Quite often, companies must deal with projects that have total budget caps for the year. For this, Solver works well in adjusting variables within the projects to maximize dollar amounts in certain categories, while maintaining the budget cap.

To set up this Solver scenario, follow these steps:

1. Set up the table. In the example, the production costs are in C5:C14, the fixed costs in D5:D14, the marketing costs in E5:E14, the advertising costs in F5:F14, and the totals in G5:G14.

2. Set up the constraints. In cell G18 in the example, the constraint is $50,000 for the maximum cost per project. In cell G19, the constraint is marketing costs of no less than $6,000 per project, and the total maximum budget in cell G20 is set at $500,000.

Figure 25.6
A Solver scenario where you want all projects' total costs to equal $50,000, while optimizing marketing and advertising costs.

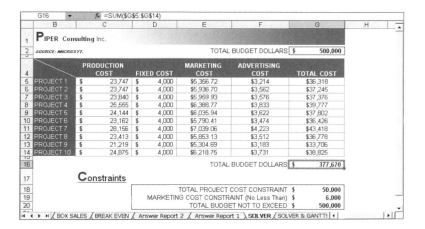

3. Select the target cell, G16, and choose Tools, Solver.

4. In the Solver Parameters dialog box, set the parameters you want to use for the problem (see Figure 25.7). For this example, you want the target cell to be the total dollars spent (cell G16), which you want to equal the budget maximum, $500,000 (specified in the Value Of box). Solver will calculate the best dispersion to achieve the optimal result by adjusting the amounts in the range E5:F14 (the changing cells).

25

NOTE

For many problems, the Guess button does a great job of selecting the cells needed to effect the result. It uses the auditing feature to locate the appropriate cells.

Figure 25.7
Establish the target cell, the target value, and the cells that can be changed.

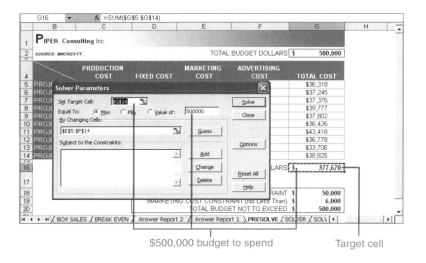

$500,000 budget to spend   Target cell

5. Next, you add constraints to the problem. Select Add to specify the first constraint. In this example, you want to spend exactly $50,000 total on each project. The constraint cell is G18, as shown in Figure 25.8.

The cell range for projects to include in the constraint

Figure 25.8
Add variable constraints you want Solver to adhere to.

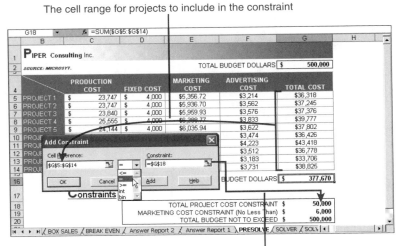

Can spend $50,000 per project (a constraint)

6. To add more constraints, click Add and specify the constraint. In this example, add another constraint, as shown in Figure 25.9. The marketing costs in the range E5:E14 must be greater than or equal to the constraint set in cell G19, $6,000. We still have one more constraint to enter, so click Add.

Figure 25.9
The second constraint ensures that the marketing dollars allocated to each project are greater than or equal to $6,000.

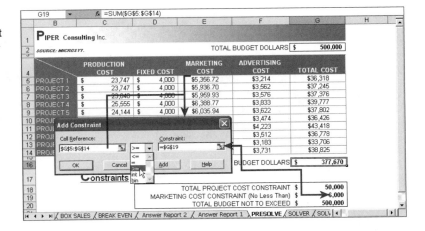

7. The last constraint is the total budget, $500,000, in cell G20 (see Figure 25.10). Don't click Add after entering the last constraint. Instead, when the constraints are complete, click OK to go back to the Solver Parameters dialog box. Notice that all the constraints added appear in the Subject to the Constraints list (see Figure 25.11).

Figure 25.10
The last constraint equals $500,000, or the sum of total projects.

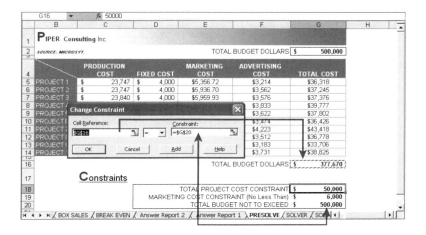

Figure 25.11
All the constraints appear in the Subject to the Constraints list. You can add more, change, or delete any of the constraints.

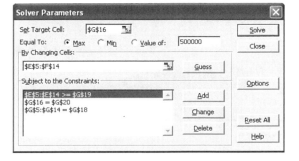

8. Click Solve or press Enter to start Solver on the problem. As Solver works, it displays a message in the status bar, as shown in Figure 25.12.

9. When Solver reaches a conclusion, it displays a dialog box that indicates the result and changes the specified values in the worksheet to reach the target. In Figure 25.13, notice the changed cells when Solver has created the optimal solution for the problem. The projects all equal $50,000 and the total budget now equals $500,000.

10. From here, you can save the Solver results and create an answer report that shows the original scenario of costs and the final result. Select Answer under Reports in the Solver Results dialog box, and click the Save Scenario button to display the dialog box shown in Figure 25.14.

Figure 25.12
The calculations appear in the lower left while Excel runs through all the constraints set.

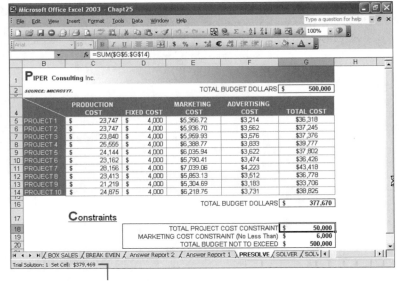

Current calculation appears in status bar

Values in these columns have changed

Figure 25.13
Solver enables you to create reports and save scenarios so that you can later view and recall scenarios you've run.

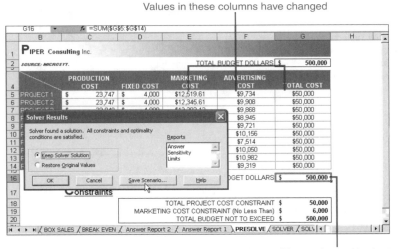

The total actual budget now equals $500,00

11. If you want to reset the worksheet to return to the original values, select the Restore Original Values.

Figure 25.14
Name the scenario.

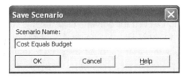

Excel automatically changes the data in the constraint cells referenced by the formula (clearing the original data). If the finished scenario isn't what you were looking for, click Restore Original Values to revert to the worksheet's original state before trying a new scenario.

12. Click OK and Excel will restore the values and create the answer report (see Figure 25.15). The answer report compares the original values with the changed values and indicates the cells that were changed. This way, you can compare scenarios.

TIP FROM

The answer report is created on a separate sheet. If you have multiple reports and scenarios, you might want to hide the report sheet(s).

25

Figure 25.15
The answer report shows original values against final values, along with the category name and the adjusted cell. The target cell is called out, separated at the top.

```
E8              ƒ× 500000
   A  B                C                  D         E        F    G    H
1  Microsoft Excel 10.0 Answer Report
2  Worksheet: [Chapt25.xls]SOLVER
3  Report Created: 2/18/2001 10:01:33 AM
4
5
6  Target Cell (Max)
7     Cell              Name         Original Value  Final Value
8     $G$16  TOTAL BUDGET DOLLARS TOTAL COST  $  377,671  $  500,000
9
10
11 Adjustable Cells
12    Cell              Name         Original Value  Final Value
13    $E$5   PROJECT 1 MARKETING COST      $5,356.72   $12,519.59
14    $F$5   PROJECT 1 ADVERTISING COST    $3,214      $9,734
15    $E$6   PROJECT 2 MARKETING COST      $5,936.70   $12,345.60
16    $F$6   PROJECT 2 ADVERTISING COST    $3,562      $9,908
17    $E$7   PROJECT 3 MARKETING COST      $5,959.93   $12,292.15
18    $F$7   PROJECT 3 ADVERTISING COST    $3,576      $9,868
19    $E$8   PROJECT 4 MARKETING COST      $6,388.77   $11,500.21
20    $F$8   PROJECT 4 ADVERTISING COST    $3,833      $8,945
21    $E$9   PROJECT 5 MARKETING COST      $6,035.94   $12,135.31
22    $F$9   PROJECT 5 ADVERTISING COST    $3,622      $9,721
23    $E$10  PROJECT 6 MARKETING COST      $5,790.41   $12,682.05
```

The constraints are saved with the workbook, so you don't have to retype them each time the workbook is opened.

If Solver can't reach a satisfactory conclusion with the data provided, a message box appears explaining Excel cannot reach a conclusion. Adjust the constraints or variables and click OK to continue attempting to solve the problem.

NOTE

Some problems are too complex even for Solver. For problems with too many variables or constraints, try breaking the problem into segments, solving each segment separately, and then using those solutions together in Solver to reach a final conclusion.

Solver's solution for a complex problem might be correct but unrealistic. Be skeptical; check the appropriateness of any adjusted amounts before reporting or implementing any suggestion from Solver.

Solver can be very useful, but you don't want it to run forever attempting to solve an unsolvable problem. You can change the Solver settings before starting on the problem if you suspect that the solution might take a long time or require too much computing power. Clicking the Options button in the Solver Parameters dialog box displays the Solver Options dialog box, in which you can set the number of iterations of the problem that Solver will run to search for an answer or the amount of time it will spend searching before giving up. Figure 25.16 shows the options available, and Table 25.1 provides descriptions of each option.

Figure 25.16
The Solver Options dialog box enables you to set parameters for Solver.

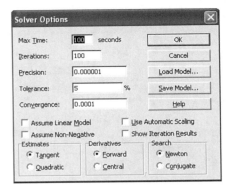

TABLE 25.1 SOLVER OPTIONS

Option	Description
Max Time	Determines the maximum amount of time Solver will search for a solution, in seconds, up to approximately nine hours.
Iterations	Determines the number of times Solver will run the parameters in search of a solution.
Precision	Determines the accuracy of the solution. The lower the number, the more accurate the solution.
Tolerance	When integer constraints are used, it's more difficult for Solver to solve the problem. Here, you can provide more tolerance and give up accuracy.

Option	Description
Convergence	For all nonlinear problems. Indicates the minimum amount of change Solver will use in each iteration. If the target cell is below the convergence setting, Solver will offer the best solution and stop.
Assume Linear Model	When checked, Solver will find a quicker solution, providing that the model is linear (using simple addition or subtraction). Nonlinear models would use growth factor and exponential smoothing or nonlinear worksheet functions.
Assume Non-Negative	Stops Solver from placing negative values in changing cells. (You also can apply constraints that indicate the value must be greater than or equal to zero.) The preceding example would use this option to prevent Solver from using negative amounts.
Use Automatic Scaling	Used when the changing cells and the target cell differ by very large amounts.
Show Iteration Results	Stops and enables you to view the results of each iteration in the Solver sequence.
Load Model	Loads the model to use from a stored set of parameters on the worksheet.
Save Model	Saves a model to a cell or set of cells and allows you to recall the model again.
Tangent	Select when the model is linear.
Quadratic	Select when the model is nonlinear.
Forward	When cells controlled by constraints change slowly for each iteration, select this option to potentially speed up the Solver.
Central	To ensure accuracy when constraint cells change rapidly and by large amounts, use this option.
Newton	Uses more memory but requires fewer iterations to provide the solution.
Conjugate	Use with large models because it requires less memory; however, it will use more iterations to provide a solution for the model. On complex models, if you decide to use the Conjugate set of equations, you might need to increase the Iterations box value.

USING SOLVER WITH GANTT CHARTS

Understanding the simple Solver scenario with constraints described in the preceding section can help you think in terms of combining Excel's powerful tools to solve real-world problems.

Although I've worked extensively with project-management programs, I've found that with the proper construction of workbooks in Excel, Solver can do the following:

- Forecast future costs
- Track actual costs against projected costs
- Forecast production plans
- Track actual production against projected production
- Forecast head count against production loads
- Run resource-loading models for maximum efficiency

When creating timelines in Excel, you can create variations on Gantt charts (visual charts that represent information over time). You can use Gantt charts in Excel with PivotTables, Solver, and formulas to manage production plans. The key here is proper worksheet format and workbook construction. If done correctly, the workbook can be completely automated to manage the most complex productions—from managing a construction site, where quantities and haul times are a factor, to manufacturing digital assets in software development.

Figure 25.17 shows a production model, with constraints indicated on the worksheet under the project's Gantt chart. In this example, a project must start on a certain day (cell O9) and be completed by a certain day (P11), and there is an average number of units or quantities not to exceed per week (Q9:Q11). The target cell is the maximum number of units on the project (Q7), or any quantity you specify. Figure 25.18 shows the parameters for the first problem in the Constraints box beneath the Gantt chart setup.

Figure 25.17
Using Solver to optimize production models can answer questions in seconds rather than running the scenarios manually.

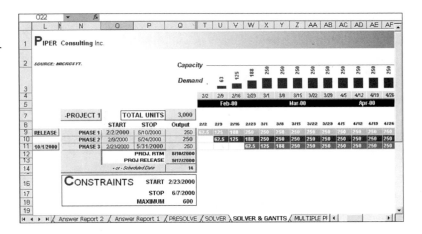

The following list describes the issues affecting the problem:

- The original planned start date was 2/2/00, but the constraint start date is 2/23/00, indicating that the project is starting later than planned.

- The original stop date was 5/10/00, but the project must be completed by the constraint set at 6/7/2000.

- The current weekly output is 250 units per week per phase, and the constraint is set not to exceed 600.

Start date

Figure 25.18
The Solver constraints give the project a start date, stop date (or at least completed by), total quantity of units to produce, and a maximum average weekly output.

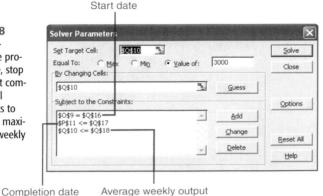

Completion date   Average weekly output

Figure 25.19 shows the solution. The weekly delivered average moved from 250 to 600 while still falling within the capacity of the resource. The completion date moved from 5/28 to 4/12 thus creating an earlier delivery by more than 1.5 months.

Completion date has been moved up

Figure 25.19
Excel optimized the result by using the 600 "not to exceed" per week output and maximized the use of time, thus showing a schedule that completes the project with almost two months to spare.

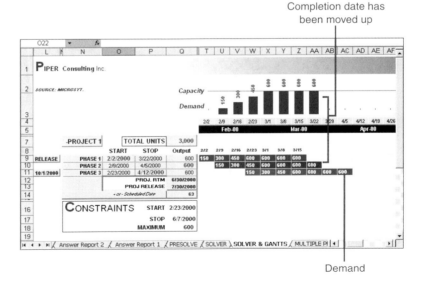

Demand

A MULTIPLE-PROJECT SOLVER SCENARIO

Based on the previous eexample and understanding how to apply constraints to production models, suppose that you have teams that have to be managed and quantities and dates you must adhere to. Solver can take multiple projects and multiple constraints and determine the optimal solution to the problem. In the example in Figure 25.20, the multiple projects overlap, and Phase 2 of each project is the critical path in the production of the project. The total units for both projects of Phase 2 are summed at the bottom, starting in cell T22.

The constraints are called out at the bottom as Start and Stop dates for each project and a maximum total output per week. On any given week, your total capacity to produce equals 600 units, but the example shows several weeks in excess of 1,000 units output in row 22. By applying the constraint to the total at the bottom, it will also take into account your capacity to produce, and find a solution. If the example isn't possible, Excel will still find the optimal solution, given the parameters of the constraints.

Figure 25.20
Excel can analyze critical-path production and cycle teams, phases, or machines by applying the right constraints with the production model.

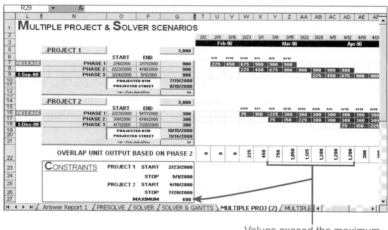

Values exceed the maximum of 600 units per week

Figure 25.21 shows the parameters used for this example. Notice how many cells are going to be changed based on the parameters or constraints supplied. All the start and stop dates have been established, as well as the maximum quantity per week not to exceed—not only per project, but also based on the overlap range starting in cell T22. This means the total capacity to output cannot exceed 600 per week for the company as a whole, so the projects' time and output will have to be modified to fit all these variables into the Solver parameters. Not all the ranges on the Change Cells line and the Constraints box are visible. To view all the ranges, scroll down in the Subject to the Constraints list.

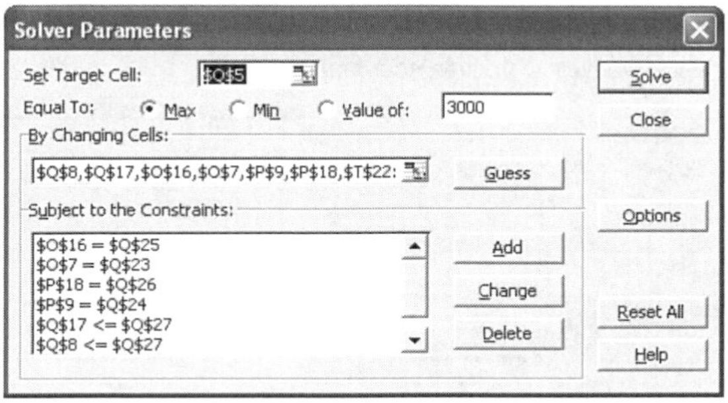

Figure 25.21
You can place multiple constraints of start and stop dates and quantities not to exceed, and Excel will find the optimal solution, taking all the variables into account.

The settings are as follows:

■ The original start date for project 1 is set at 2/9/00 and, based on the constraints, will start on 2/23 in cell Q23. The original stop date from 4/30/00 will be constrained to 5/1/00. The maximum not to exceed per week currently is 900 and will be constrained to 600 in cell Q27.

■ The original start date for project 2 is set at 2/23/00 and will be constrained to 4/10/00. The stop date from 6/30/00 will move to the constraint date of 7/28/00. The weekly not to exceed is constrained at no more than 600 per week in cell Q27.

■ The last constraint placed on the model will ensure that each weekly overlap unit output for Phase 2 (row 22) will not exceed the maximum output of 600 in cell Q27.

■ The change range is from T22:BB22, which is the sum of Phase 2 of both projects carried out through the length of the timeline.

Figure 25.22 shows overlap per week exceeding the weekly capacity to output in row 22. Figure 25.23 shows all the constraints placed on the project. Excel found the optimal solution.

Figure 25.22
Before Solver is used to apply constraints to the project's start and stop dates and overall capacity to produce, the total amounts for Phase 2 of each project greatly exceed the capacity to produce.

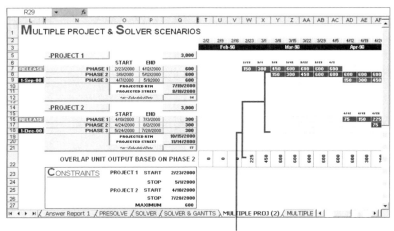

Total demand of Phase 2

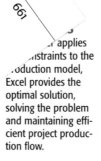

...r applies
...nstraints to the
...oduction model,
Excel provides the
optimal solution,
solving the problem
and maintaining effi-
cient project produc-
tion flow.

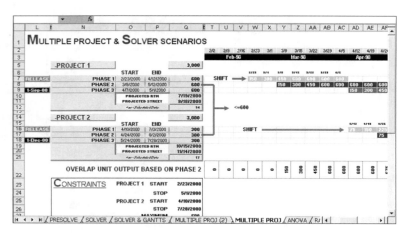

CREATING AMORTIZATION TABLES TO CALCULATE MORTGAGE PAYMENTS

Excel's Table feature helps you create structured tables for calculating mortgage and lease payments, depreciation, and so on. Suppose that you want to purchase a house; you need to see the mortgage rate based on variable percentages and mortgage amounts. Here, you would use the PMT function (see also Chapter 10 financial functions) to create a table to pro-vide the mortgage rate, as shown in Figure 25.24. The schedule in cells F5:F19 is calculated based on a total loan amount of $100,000 on a 30-year mortgage, with percentage rates starting at 5% and increasing in .5% increments.

Figure 25.24
A simple mortgage
table calculates the
mortgage payments
based on the interest
rate and the total
mortgage.

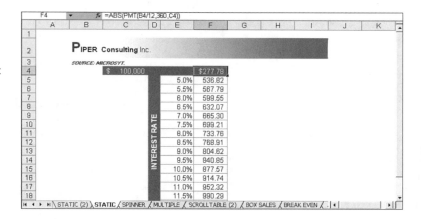

The PMT function calculates the loan payment for a loan based on constant payments and constant interest rates.

→ 'For more information on the PMT function and its syntax, see the "PMT" section of Chapter 10, "Financial Functions," p. 254

To set up a single-variable table, follow these steps:

1. In the first cell in the table, type the first interest rate percentage—for this example, you would type **5%** in cell E5.

2. In the next cell down, type a formula to increase the first percentage by the increment amount. In this example, the increment is .5%, so the formula in cell E6 is `=E5+0.005`. This will add .5 percent to the previous percentage. Then drag the formula down to the bottom row of the table (cell E19 in this case, which will equal 12%, which is the maximum interest rate you're willing to pay).

3. In the trigger cell (cell C4 in this case), type the mortgage amount—for this example, **$100,000**.

4. In the target cell (cell F4 in this case), type the payment function. Here, the formula is `=PMT(B4/12,360,C4)` where B4/12 is the monthly interest rate, 360 is the term (30 years is 360 months), and C4 equals the total mortgage. Where cell B4 is a placeholder of zero (Excel assigns a value of zero to a blank cell referenced in a numeric formula), Excel uses the placeholder to calculate the payment needed to amortize the loan at 0%.

   The reason you place the mortgage in a cell rather than in the formula is that all you have to do then is change the mortgage amount. The formula references the cell and the table automatically changes, instead of your having to go into the formula and change the mortgage every time. To maximize the flexibility, you could also place the period value in a cell.

5. Select the range you want to fill. The example uses cells E4:F19. In Figure 25.25, the previous table has been deleted to rebuild the example.

25

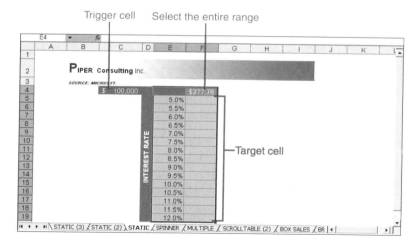

Figure 25.25
Select the total range to build the table.

Trigger cell   Select the entire range

Target cell

INTEREST RATE

6. Choose Data, Table. Excel displays the Table dialog box shown in Figure 25.26. Because the interest rates in this example are listed down a column, use the Column Input Cell box to look for the interest rate used in the PMT function. The input cell is

...ays one of the arguments in the single function used for the table and corresponds to the row/column headings in the table. For example, because we have interest rates going down a column, we look for the Interest argument in the PMT function and use its cell reference as the column input cell.

Figure 25.26
The input cell is the payment needed to amortize a loan, at 0% in this case.

7. Click OK to build the table (see Figure 25.27).

Notice that by changing the mortgage amount from $100,000 to $600,000, the table automatically responds (see Figure 25.28). The advantage of using a data table is that it refers to only one formula (F4, in this example). This increases calculation speed and reduces memory use.

Figure 25.27
The final result shows the mortgage payments in the body of the table, based on the corresponding percentage and mortgage amount.

25

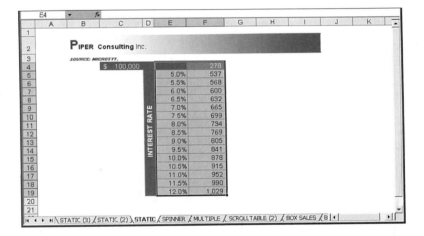

The new table is in the form of an array, which means that you can't change the table, although you can move or delete the table. You can apply tricks to get around this limitation, however. You could copy the table and paste it as values using Paste Special, or you could re-create the table with a mirrored table using =. Figure 25.29 shows a mirrored table. Using a simple formula that repeats the entries in the first table (starting with cell E5), you can drag the formula to pick up all the entries in the table, which you then can manipulate. The brackets around the table formula indicates an array formula (a formula that calculates on multiple rows or ranges of data).

Figure 25.28
By changing the mortgage, the table automatically responds.

Change the total value to establish mortgage payments

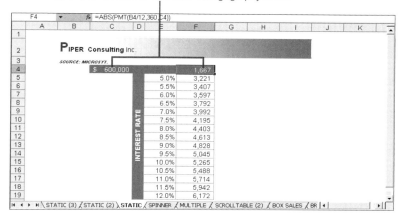

Figure 25.29
Create a mirrored table to get around the array formula, thus allowing you to manipulate the formula.

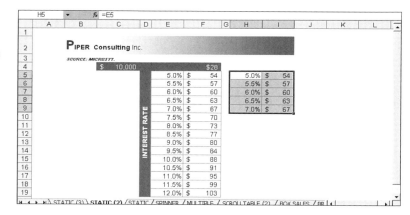

CREATING ACTIVE TABLES WITH SPINNERS

If your data tables are large, you can add special features such as form controls to make the tables easier to read and use. A spinner has been applied to the mortgage table in Figure 25.30. However, because the spinner control allows for a maximum value of 30,000, a multiplier is used in a different cell (cell C4 in this example) that multiplies the cell link in cell A1 times 50. Therefore, with every incremental change to the spinner control, it multiplies the cell link by 50.

→ For details on creating form controls, **see** "Adding Form Controls to Your Worksheets," **p 424**.

When creating the spinner, set the cell link to cell A1 in the Format Control dialog box (see Figure 25.31). Set the Maximum Value to **30,000** and the Minimum Value to **0**, and the Incremental Change to **1000**. This means the maximum value the spinner will go up to

⌐, and the lowest value is 0. By adding the multiplier, you can make the mortgage ⌐ more flexible; with each click of the spin arrow, the mortgage change will be 50,000.

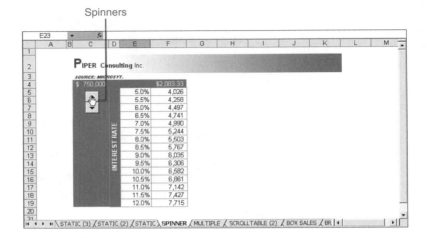

Figure 25.30
Use spinners with multipliers to drive tables.

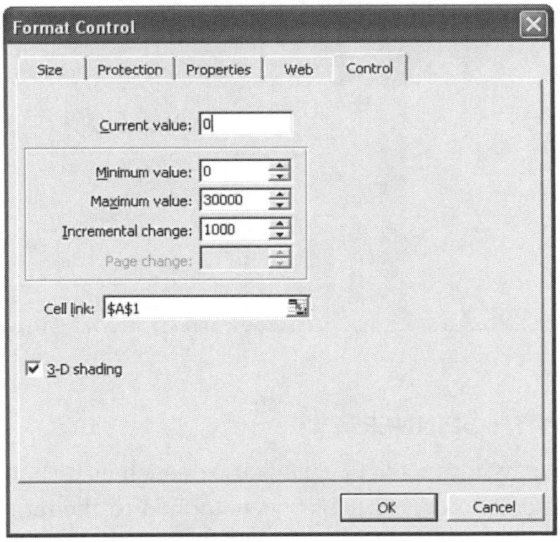

Figure 25.31
Set the cell link, mini-mum and maximum values, as well as the incremental change as shown.

25

Type the multiplier formula in the table reference cell (cell C4 in this example), as shown in Figure 25.32. The formula references the cell link—the current value of the spinner—and multiplies it by 50 to give you the current principal. You hide the spinner value in cell A1 by applying a white font color.

Clicking the spinner increases or decreases the mortgage amount.

Value in cell is hidden by using a white font

Figure 25.32
Type the multiplier formula in cell C4, the table reference cell.

Multiplier

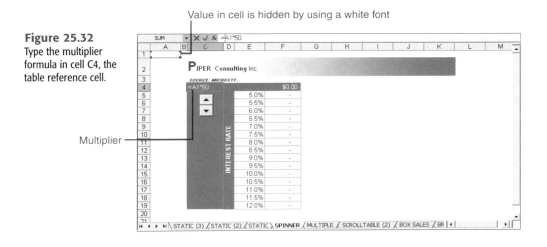

MULTIPLE-VARIABLE TABLES

After learning the basic one-variable table, you can apply multiple variables to make an expanded table, referenced to different mortgage amounts (see Figure 25.33). In the previous examples, you typed in the new mortgage amounts. In this instance, you reference the different cells across columns in the formula to create a broader-based table.

Figure 25.33
To create a broad-based table, the payment formula references cell F4.

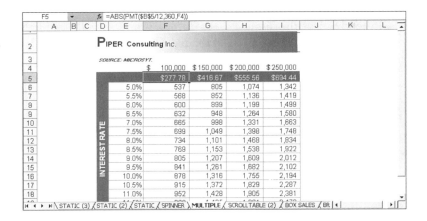

ADDING SCROLLBARS TO THE MORTGAGE TABLE

By adding scrollbars to a table, you can span hundreds of rows and columns in a window of a few rows and columns. In the example in Figure 25.34, the interest is scrolled down to 0% and the loan amount is scrolled back to 0 in the first column (cell F6). When you scroll up, the maximum interest rate in this example is 13.7% and the maximum mortgage is $1,150,000. It normally would take multiple rows and columns of information to span this list; however, with the proper use of scrollbars, you can create a window in which the table will scroll.

Figure 25.34
You can span the range of hundreds of rows and columns.

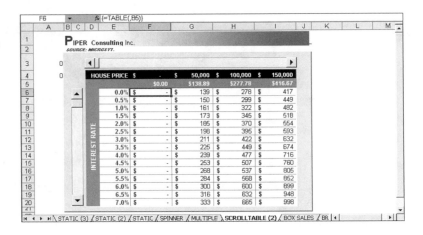

To create a scrolling window, follow these steps:

1. Create the same table setup as in the multiple-variable tables shown previously.

2. In cell E6, the beginning of the interest rate column, type the formula =A4/150, where A4 will equal the cell link for the vertical scrollbar form control.

3. In cell F4, type the formula =$A$3*10,000, where A3 is the cell link (note the absolute reference). Drag the formula to the right to I4.

4. Draw the scrollbar next to the interest rates, right-click it, and select Format Control (see Figure 25.35).

Figure 25.35
Draw the control and then right-click and select Format Control.

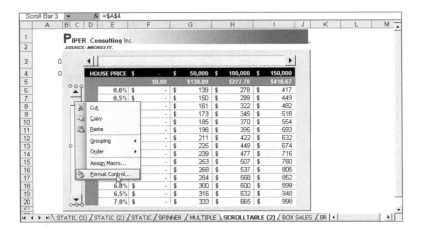

5. Format the control as follows:

    Current Value = **0**

    Minimum Value = **0**

    Maximum Value = **10**

    Incremental Change = **1**

    Page Change = **10**

    Cell Link = **A4**

These settings mean that the maximum value the scrollbar will reach is 10 and the lowest value is 0; each click will change the value by 1.

6. Click OK.

7. Draw the horizontal scrollbar above the house price. Right-click it and choose Format Control. Set the format control as follows:

    Current Value = **0**

    Minimum Value = **0**

    Maximum Value = **100**

    Incremental Change = **10**

    Page Change = **10**

    Cell Link = **A3**

8. Click OK to finish formatting the scrollbar.

USING THE ANALYSIS TOOLPAK ADD-IN

Excel's *Analysis ToolPak* (accessed by choosing Tools, Data Analysis) enables you to perform complex and sophisticated statistical analyses, with 17 statistical commands and 47 mathematical functions. From creating a random distribution of numbers to performing regression analysis, the tools can provide the essential calculations to solve just about any problem.

NOTE

> You might need to enable the add-in before you can use it (choose Tools, Add-Ins, and select the Analysis ToolPak in the list of add-ins).

Table 25.2 describes the various tools.

TABLE 25.2   TOOLS IN THE ANALYSIS TOOLPAK

Tool	What It Does
ANOVA: Single Factor	Simple variance analysis
ANOVA: Two-Factor	Variance analysis that includes more than one sample of data for each group
ANOVA: Two-Factor Without Replication	Variance analysis that doesn't include more than one sample of data for each group
Correlation	Measurement—independent correlation between data sets
Covariance	Measurement—dependent covariance between data sets
Descriptive Statistics	Report of univariate statistics for sample
Exponential Smoothing	Smooths data, weighting more recent data heavier
F-Test: Two-Sample for Variance	Two-sample F-Test to compare population variances
Histogram	Counts occurrences in each of several data bins
Moving Average	Smooths data series by averaging the last few periods
Random number generation	Creates any of several types of random numbers: **Uniform**—Uniform random numbers between upper and lower bounds. **Normal**—Normally distributed numbers based on the mean and the standard deviation. **Bernoulli**—Ones and zeros with a specified probability of success. **Poisson**—A distribution of random numbers given a desired lambda. **Patterned**—A sequence of numbers at a specific interval. **Discrete**—Probabilities based on the predefined percents of total.
Rank and Percentile	Creates a report of ranking and percentile distribution
Regression	Creates a table of statistics that result from least-squares regression
t-Test: Paired Two-Sample for Means	Paired two-sample students t-test
t-Test: Two-Sample Assuming Equal Variances	Paired two-sample t-test assuming equal means
t-Test: Two-Sample Assuming Unequal Variances	Heteroscedastic t-test
z-Test: Two-Sample for Means	Two-sample z-test for means with known variances
Fourier Analysis	DFT or FFT method, including reverse transforms
Sampling	Samples a population randomly or periodically

The analysis tools all work in basically the same way. Choose Tools, Data Analysis to display the Data Analysis dialog box (see Figure 25.36). Select the tool you want to use, and click OK to display a separate dialog box for that particular tool.

Figure 25.36
The Data Analysis dialog box allows you to access 20 analytical tools.

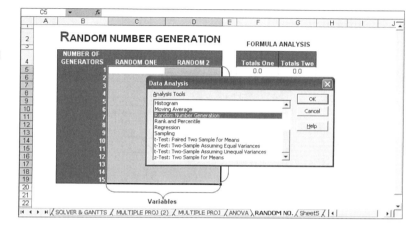

For example, suppose you want to generate random data sets to perform analysis of calls at your company's call center based on historical data. By far, the simplest method to achieve a random sampling is using the Random Number Generation tool, which creates realistic sample data sets between ranges that you specify.

To create a random sampling, select the Random Number Generation tool in the Data Analysis dialog box. When you click OK, Excel displays the Random Number Generation dialog box, in which you can specify the parameters for the data set you want. For the example in Figure 25.37, 2 columns of variables are needed, with each column containing 15 random numbers in uniform distribution between 50 and 100. (Seven different distribution generators are available; refer to Table 25.2 for descriptions.)

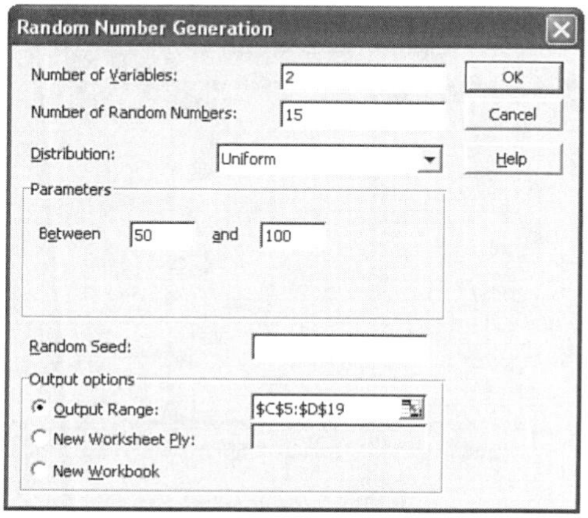

Figure 25.37
Use the Random Number Generation dialog box to set parameters for your data.

If you don't specify a particular number for variables or random numbers, Excel fills the cells in the Output Range.

Figure 25.38 shows the result. Figure 25.41 shows how you can use this data set for multiple analyses—just tie the analysis results to formulas, charts, and PivotTables.

Figure 25.38
Two sets of random numbers between 50 and 100.

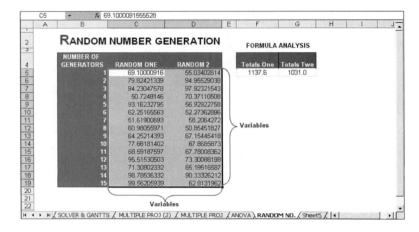

25

EXCEL IN PRACTICE

You can use tables and form controls to create automated scrolling tables. By adding scroll-bars to a table, you can span hundreds of rows and columns in a window of a few rows and columns. In the example in Figure 25.39, the interest is scrolled down to 0% and the loan amount is scrolled back to 0 in the first column (cell F6).

Figure 25.39
Use scrollbars to cre-ate scrolling windows.

Scroll dialed down

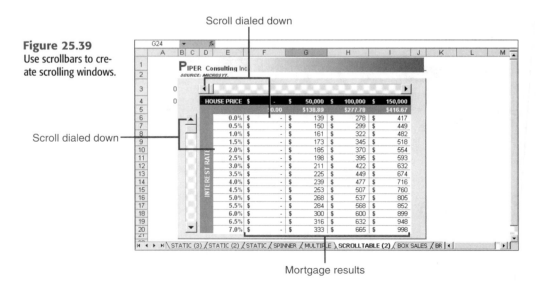

Scroll dialed down

Mortgage results

When you scroll up, the maximum interest rate in this example is 13.7% and the maximum mortgage is $1,150,000 as shown in Figure 25.40. It normally would take multiple rows and columns of information to span this list; however, with the proper use of scrollbars, you can create a window in which the table will scroll.

Figure 25.40
The scrollbar is dialed up to the maximum mortgage and interest rate.

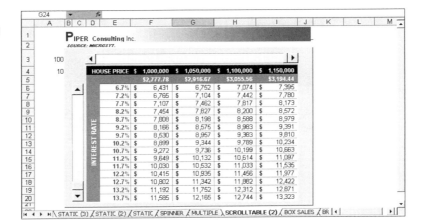

INTEREST RATE	HOUSE PRICE	$ 1,000,000	$ 1,050,000	$ 1,100,000	$ 1,150,000
		$2,777.78	$2,916.67	$3,055.56	$3,194.44
6.7%	$	6,431	$ 6,752	$ 7,074	$ 7,395
7.2%	$	6,765	$ 7,104	$ 7,442	$ 7,780
7.7%	$	7,107	$ 7,462	$ 7,817	$ 8,173
8.2%	$	7,454	$ 7,827	$ 8,200	$ 8,572
8.7%	$	7,808	$ 8,198	$ 8,588	$ 8,979
9.2%	$	8,166	$ 8,575	$ 8,983	$ 9,391
9.7%	$	8,530	$ 8,957	$ 9,383	$ 9,810
10.2%	$	8,899	$ 9,344	$ 9,789	$ 10,234
10.7%	$	9,272	$ 9,736	$ 10,199	$ 10,663
11.2%	$	9,649	$ 10,132	$ 10,614	$ 11,097
11.7%	$	10,030	$ 10,532	$ 11,033	$ 11,535
12.2%	$	10,415	$ 10,935	$ 11,456	$ 11,977
12.7%	$	10,802	$ 11,342	$ 11,882	$ 12,422
13.2%	$	11,192	$ 11,752	$ 12,312	$ 12,871
13.7%	$	11,585	$ 12,165	$ 12,744	$ 13,323

CHAPTER 26

USING EXCEL IN BUSINESS

In this chapter

Important Tools for Any Business   xx

Value Chains   xx

Value Matrixes   xx

IMPORTANT TOOLS FOR ANY BUSINESS

This chapter is specifically designed to break out certain tools, strategies, and functions as you apply to everyday business. Although daily business might differ from individual to individual (and business to business), you'll find problems and situations common to almost everyone. From creating tables and formulas, to presenting information graphically, Excel can handle just about any business problem.

SELL IN VERSUS SELL THROUGH

Sell-in versus sell-through is the important factor when running your business if you sell goods into a distribution channel. In addition, if your products aren't revolving off the shelf, the retailer will ultimately pull the product and find a product that generates revenues for the store or chain. PivotTables are great summaries of information for analyzing the marketplace and measuring product velocity per store, chain, sku, product type, and so on. However, you'll still need to view the product in a manner that allows you to see the product and the volume dollars per period that it is generating. Given this, you'll have to create a formula that shows velocity, or the rate at which the product is selling—which is viewed as a percentage and then take the average over the period and that achieves velocity. A conditional SUM formula is used in the following examples. The key is setup. Notice in Figure 26.1 that the conditional SUM formula in cell D4 is in the form of an array and looks up the date in cell D3 in the Date column in the In/Through table. The formula then looks up the product in cell C4 in the product column in the In/Through table. It returns the quantity for that date and product from the range D15 through D39, which is the sell-in column. The same formula is applied to the sold-through row (5); however, the return is from column E, which is the sell-through column. The array is activated by pressing Ctrl+Shift+Enter. The formula's syntax is as follows. This formula will achieve the same results without using the IF formula:

`=SUM(($C$15:$C$39=$C4)*($B$15:$B$39=D$3),$D$15:$D$39,0))`

Figure 26.1
Use a conditional SUM formula to set up sell in versus sell through.

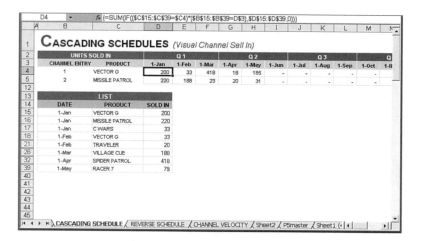

CHANNEL VELOCITY

Channel velocity is the rate at which your products are selling through a channel, store, or marketplace. This can be measured in the form of a percentage. The velocity is based on the amount of time the product will remain in the channel or the life of the product—the total unit sales expected for the product and the weekly projected flow or sell through for the product. However simple the formula might be, the structure and having all the components in place is important. The formula just divides the actual sell through by the weekly average. If your sales are seasonal and you have fluctuating performance, as most products do, find the velocity by dividing by that particular week. In the example the velocity is divided by the number of weeks calculated. Notice the model in Figure 26.2.

Figure 26.2
The velocity formula is the percentage sold through for the period of time–in this case, weeks.

Average values greater than zero

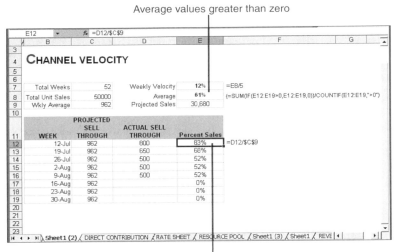

Percent sold through

CASCADING SCHEDULES

If you sell multiple products into a distribution channel and have to accumulate the sell in (products sold into a distribution channel) and sell through (products sold out of the channel to the consumer) numbers, you'll want to create a cascading schedule that reflects a product's performance. A cascading schedule gives you the information you need and helps you see when a product entered the channel and where its peak performance is. Many times, peak performance is seasonal, and if you sell toys, the winter holidays are going to be a big shot in the arm compared to July. Also, with a cascading schedule, you can create charts from the information for quick access to the product's sales velocity and peak performance. You'll definitely need to have a list or database set up for extracting the information. Based on receiving the data and pumping the data into a data-warehouse, database, or an Excel spreadsheet, you can create a cascading schedule that extracts the information. (PivotTables also work well for this.)

When creating a cascading schedule with ease, there are a couple of key elements. To create a cascading schedule follow these steps:

1. Sort the list or database by date in ascending order.

2. Select the product range and do not include the heading.

3. Choose Data, Filter, Advanced Filter.

4. Click No when Excel asks whether you want to include the row above the selection.

5. Select the Unique Records Only option, as shown in Figure 26.3.

Figure 26.3
To create the cascading schedule, sort the list by ascending date, and then filter the records by unique records only, giving you the cascading effect by order of occurrence.

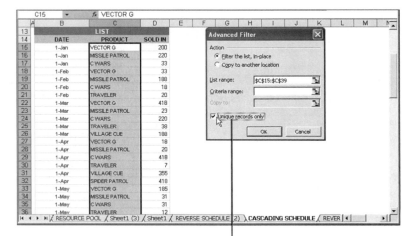

Consolidates duplicating records

6. Click OK.

7. Copy the unique records. In Excel 2003, copy the cells by selecting the range and pressing Ctrl+C. If you're using previous versions of Excel, follow these steps: In the Customize dialog box (accessed by choosing Tools, Customize), use the Select Visible Cells button on the Commands tab (see Figure 26.4). From the Categories list, choose Edit, under Commands, select and drag the feature to the toolbar.

8. Paste the copied visible cells to a new location. This creates the foundation for the cascading schedule. Now that the order of occurrence is sorted by date, all you have to do is create the same conditional SUM formula shown previously in Figure 26.1. However, be sure the absolute referencing is as follows so you can create the formula once and drag it the length of your table. Notice the formula with absolute referencing in place in the formula bar in Figure 26.5.

REVERSE SCHEDULES

Now that you've created a sell-in cascading schedule, you can easily create a reverse sell-through schedule that reflects the units sold through in order of occurrence. The key here is creating a channel entry number. Notice the channel entry number in column B in Figure 26.6. All you have to do is sort the table by entry number in ascending or descending order. Because the formula is set up with the proper cell referencing, it always reflects the dates and products referenced.

Figure 26.4
Select and copy visible cells only.

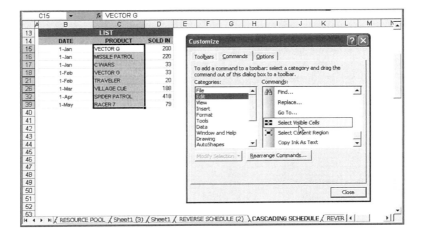

Figure 26.5
The cascading schedule helps you visualize your channel sell in.

SUMMING THE TOTAL VELOCITY

Now use the velocity formula as shown in Figure 26.7 that reflects total percentage of sales for the month.

AUTOMATING PROJECTED CASH FLOWS

Whether you're in business, finance, accounting, marketing, or production, you'll probably have to forecast project cash flows, units created, and so on. Here's an IF AND formula that

moves units, people, or money over time. Notice the formula in Figure 26.8:
`=IF(AND(M$5>=$G6,N$5<=$H6),$F6,"")`. The formula basically says, if the corresponding week is greater than or equal to the start date and the next week is less than or equal to the stop date, return the weekly cost in cell F6. In this example, conditional formatting is used to block off the timeline into boxes. As you change the quantity, weeks, rates, or start date, the timeline automatically moves to correspond with your changes.

Figure 26.6
Create a reversed schedule reflecting sell through.

Cascade effect →

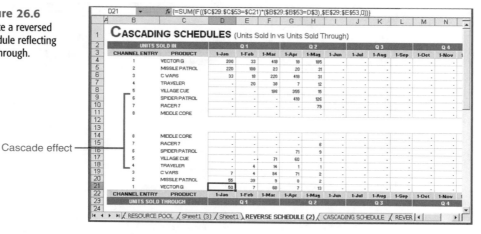

Figure 26.7
Insert the velocity between the schedules and calculate it by dividing the sold-through number by the sold in number.

26

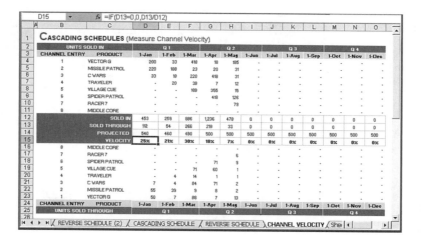

TRANSPOSING TABLES WITH FORMULAS (WITHOUT ABSOLUTE REFERENCING)

Many times, you'll have tables that reference lists of information and the formulas don't have absolute referencing. Now, in the likely event you'll have to view the information in a new format, you might have to spend countless hours applying an absolute reference to all the formulas—or you can use this undocumented trick. Select the region with the formulas as shown in Figure 26.9. Choose Edit, Replace. Under Find What, type =. Under Replace With, type <, and then click the Replace All button. The formulas have been temporarily converted to text.

Figure 26.8
Create automated timelines and cash flows with the combination of IF and AND.

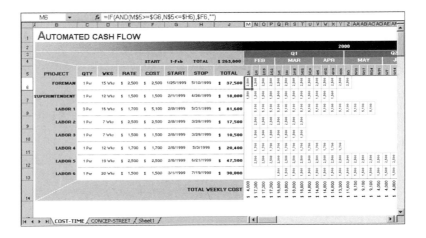

Figure 26.9
Select the region with the formulas to transpose the table.

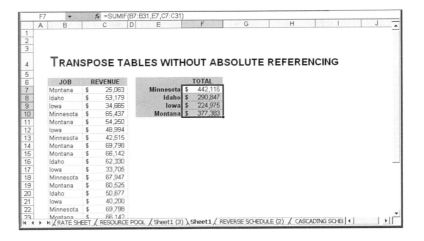

Select and copy the entire table to transpose the table as shown in Figure 26.10.

Select a cell or destination where you want the transposed table to be placed. Choose Edit, Paste Special. From the Paste Special dialog box, select Transpose. Now select the transposed formula cells as shown in Figure 26.11.

Choose Edit, Replace. Under Find What, type <. Under Replace With, type =. The transposed table now reflects the original referencing without using absolute referencing as shown in Figure 26.12.

Figure 26.10
Copy the entire table to transpose the table.

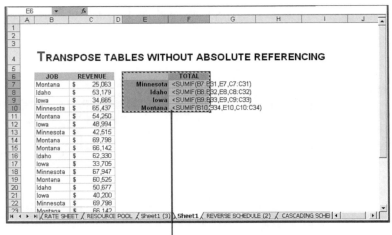

Copy the range to transpose

Figure 26.11
Select the formula cells in the transposed table to replace the < sign with =.

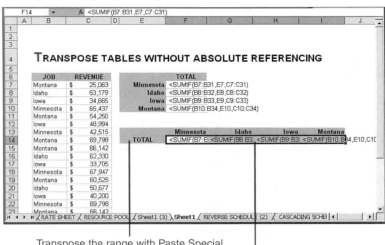

Transpose the range with Paste Special

Select the formula range

AVERAGING POSITIVE NUMBERS ONLY IN A RANGE

You'll often have a range of numbers that you want to average. However, sometimes not all the numbers are going to be positive. In that case, including zeros and negative numbers generates an inaccurate description of the average. What if you sell products globally and you have regions that sometimes select the product and other times you don't because it's not relevant to their culture? When regions aren't able to sell the product, you would only want the average of the positive cells rather than an average that includes regions that have not selected the product for their region. Using the SUM, IF, and COUNTIF functions in the form of an array will average just the positive cells. An alternative formula that would establish the same results is {=AVERAGE(IF(D4:D20>0,D4:D20))}. Notice the example in Figure 26.13.

Figure 26.12
The result of replacing the < sign with the = sign reactivates the formula with the same referencing.

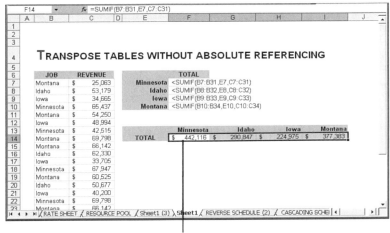

Replace the < symbol with = to reactivate the formula

Figure 26.13
Average only positive cells for a more accurate average.

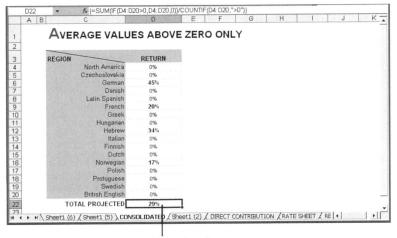

Average only positive values in a range

AUTO LOOKUP THE LAST NUMBER IN A COLUMN

When entering numbers into a list, you can create a formula that automatically looks up the last number entered. Use the OFFSET function combined with the COUNTA function to achieve the results (see Figure 26.14). The formula =OFFSET(C3,COUNTA(C:C)-1,0), where C3 is the Column Heading in the list or the start of the list, COUNTA counts all nonempty cells and -1 results in the last value. If you applied -2, it would result in the second-to-last value.

Figure 26.14
This formula automatically looks up the last value entered in a range.

Looks up last value in column

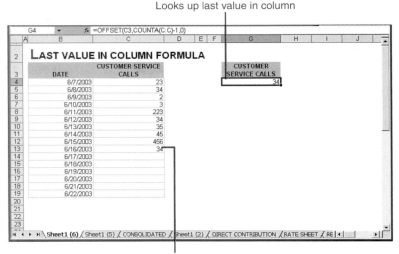

Last value entered

P&L—DIRECT CONTRIBUTION

When managing your business, you're going to need a certain amount of return on every investment to remain profitable. By creating a simple P&L layout, with the right formulas combined on the P&L, you can effectively forecast each project's contribution-margin ratio to your business. It's also important to know where your break-even points are for both total and monthly sales. In Figure 26.15, six formulas operate off each other and can effectively help you manage your projected return on investments. The key formulas and descriptions are

- **Contribution Margin Ratio =IF(C12<>0,C19/C12,0)**—The contribution margin dollar divided by the Projected Sales.

- **Break-Even Sales =IF(C4<>0,F25/F4,0)**—The Total Fixed Expenses divided by the Contribution Margin Ratio.

- **Monthly Break-Even Sales =IF(C11<>0,C5/C11,0)**—The Break-Even Sales dollar amount divided by Months. Months also can be described as the life of the product.

- **Contribution Margin =C12-SUM(C15:C18)**—The Projected Sales dollar amount minus the sum of the Variable Expenses (Materials, Labor, Variable Overhead, Other).

- **Total Fixed Expenses =SUM(F11:F24)**—The sum of the total Fixed Expenses.

- **Profit During the Period =(C12-C5)*C4**—The Projected Sales minus the Break-Even Sales times the Contribution Margin Ratio.

Figure 26.15
Establish a P&L to understand direct contribution and break-even sales.

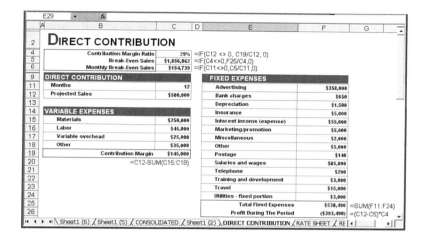

FINANCIAL RATIOS

Use the following formulas to determine financial ratios in Excel.

LIQUIDITY RATIOS

- **Current Ratio**—`Current Assets/Current Liabilities`—The current ratio shows the ratio of current assets to current liabilities as of the report date.

- **Gross Margin Percentage**—`Quick Assets/Current Liabilities`—Indicates what percentage of each dollar of sales is left over after paying the costs of sales amount for the period.

ACTIVITY RATIOS

- **Days Sales in AR**—`(Accounts Receivable Net*Days in Period)/Net Sales`—Shows how long it takes a business to collect receivables from its customers for the period.

- **Allowance for Bad Debt as % of AR**—`Allowance for Bad Debt/Accounts Receivables`—Shows what percentage of the accounts receivable balance is considered uncollectable for the period.

- **Bad Debt As % of Net Revenues**—`Bad Debt Expense/Net Sales`—Shows what percentage of revenue is considered uncollectable for the period.

- **Inventory Turnover**—`(Cost of Sales*Days in Year)/(Inventory*Days in Period)`—Shows how quickly a business sells its inventory by comparing the inventory balance to the cost of goods sold expense for the period on an annualized basis.

- **Days Inventory**—`(Inventory*Days in Period)/Cost of Sales`—Shows a ratio indicating how many days a business could continue selling using only its existing inventory as of the report date.

26

- **Net Sales to Inventory**—(Net Sales*Days in Year)/(Inventory*Days in Period)—Shows the size of annual net sales relative to inventory for the period on an annual basis.

- **Days Purchases in AP**—(Accounts Payable*Days in Period)/Cost of Sales—Indicates the size of the accounts payable relative to cost of sales for the period.

- **Net Sales to Working Capital**—(Net Sales*Days in Year)/(Working Capital*Days in Period)—Indicates the size of annual net sales relative to working capital for the period on an annualized basis.

- **Total Assets to Net Sales**—(Total Assets*Days in Period)/(Net Sales*Days in Year)—Shows how many dollars of assets are required to produce a dollar of sales for the period on an annualized basis.

- **Net Sales to AR**—(Net Sales*Days in Year)/(Accounts Receivable Net*Days in Period)—Indicates the size of annual net sales relative to accounts receivable for the period on an annualized basis.

- **Net Sales to Net Fixed Assets**—(Net Sales*Days in Year)/(Fixed Assets*Days in Period)—Shows the size of the annual net sales relative to the net fixed assets for the period on an annualized basis.

- **Net Sales to Total Assets**—(Net Sales*Days in Year)/(Total Assets*Days in Period)—Shows the size of the annual net sales relative to total assets for the period on an annualized basis.

- **Net Sales to Net Worth**—(Net Sales*Days in Year)/(Net Worth*Days in Period)—Shows the size of the net sales relative to net worth (Total Assets minus Total Liabilities) for the period on an annualized basis.

- **Amortization and Depreciation Expense to Net Sales**—Amortization and Depreciation Expense/Net Sales—Indicates what percentage of each dollar of sales pays noncash expenses such as amortization expense of intangible assets, such as copyrights and patents, and depreciation expense of fixed assets for the period.

PROFITABILITY RATIOS

- **Gross Profit Percentage**—(Net Sales-Cost of Sales)/Net Sales—Indicates what percentage of each dollar of sales is left over after paying the cost of sales amount for the period.

- **Operating Expense As a Percent of Net Sales**—Operating Expense/Net Sales—Indicates what percentage of each sale goes to pay operating expenses for the period.

- **Return on Total Assets**—(Net Income*Days in Year)/(Total Assets*Days in Period)—Indicates the size of net income after taxes relative to a company's total assets for the period on an annualized basis.

- **Return on Net Worth**—(Net Income*Days in Year)/(Net Worth*Days in Period)—Indicates the size of net income after taxes relative to a company's net worth (Total Assets-Total Liabilities) for the period on an annualized basis.

- **Return on Net Sales**—`Net Income/Net Sales`—Indicates what percentage of sales ends up as profit for the period.

- **Income Before Tax to Net Worth**—`(Income Before Tax*Days in Year)/(Net Worth*Days in Period)`—Indicates the size of net income before taxes relative to a company's net worth (Total Assets–Total Liabilities) for the period on an annualized basis.

- **Income Before Tax to Total Assets**—`(Income Before Tax*Days in Year)/(Total Assets*Days in Period)`—Indicates the size of net income before taxes relative to a company's total assets for the period on an annualized basis.

- **Retained Earning to Net Income**—`((Net Worth-equity)*Days in Period)/(Net Income*Days in Year)`—Indicates the size of the retained earning to net income for the period on an annualized basis.

COVERAGE RATIOS

- **Times Interest Earned**—`Interest Before Interest & Taxes/Interest`—Indicates the size of a company's interest expense relative to its operating profits for the period on an annualized basis.

- **Interest Expense to Net Sales**—`Interest/Net Sales`—Indicates what percentage of a company's net sales goes to pay interest expense on its debts for the period.

- **Current Liabilities to Net Worth**—`Current Liabilities/Net Worth`—Indicates the size of a company's current liabilities relative to its net worth as of the day of the report.

- **Current Liabilities to Inventory**—`Current Liabilities/Inventory`—Indicates the size of a company's current liabilities relative to its inventory as of the day of the report.

- **Accounts Payable to Net Sales**—`(Accounts Payable*Days in Period)/(Net Sales*Days in Year)`—Indicates the size of a company's accounts payable relative to its sales revenue for the period on an annualized basis.

- **Total Liabilities to Net Worth**—`Total Liabilities/Net Worth`—Indicates the size of a company's total liabilities relative to its net worth as of the report date.

- **Net Worth to Total Liabilities**—`Net Worth/Total Liabilities`—Indicates the size of a company's total net worth relative to its total liabilities as of the report date.

RESOURCE POOLS

At times, you'll have to schedule and manage resource pools. A resource pool is simply different groups of people within a business that may have direct implications on project release dates. There are several ways to do this. This resource pool takes into account international employee rates converted to U.S. dollar rates and applies the rates to a schedule that forecasts resource allocation over time, per employee. Use VLOOKUP to look up the rate of the employee, and then use the IF and AND functions to create the automated timeline.

The SUBTOTAL function summarizes the total for that employee over time when the list is fil-tered. You can create effective time-management tools for scheduling people using this or similar methods. First, establish a rate sheet. The example in Figure 26.16 shows the Canadian rates of the employees converted to U.S. currency.

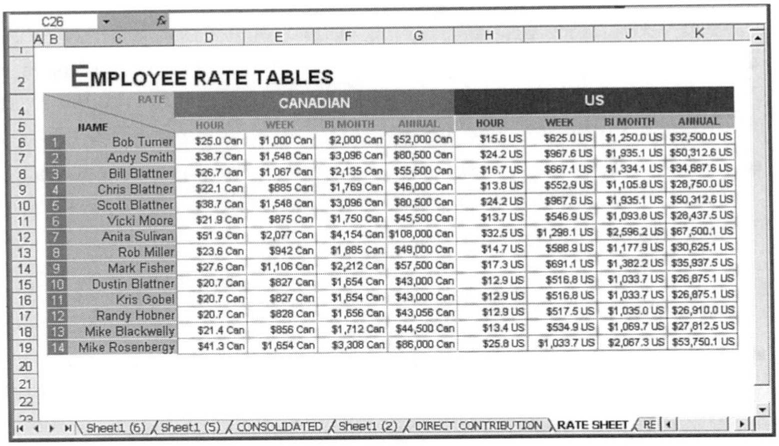

Figure 26.16
Establish the employee table from which to reference the dollar amount.

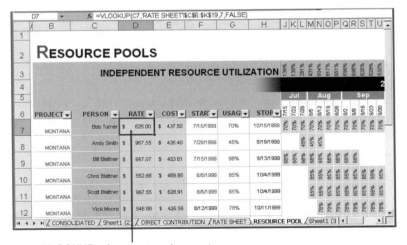

Establish the VLOOKUP formula as shown in Figure 26.17 to refer to the name on the Resource Pool Gantt chart worksheet: =VLOOKUP(C7, 'RATE SHEET'!$C$6:$K$19,7,FALSE). Where C7 refers to the employee in column C, the RATE SHEET range is C6:K19 and 7 is the seventh column over in the range.

Figure 26.17
Establish VLOOKUP to look up the employee rate.

VLOOKUP references employee rates

Create the IF and AND dynamic Gantt chart formula =(IF(AND(J$6>=$F7,J$6<$H7),$G7,"")) as shown in Figure 26.18.

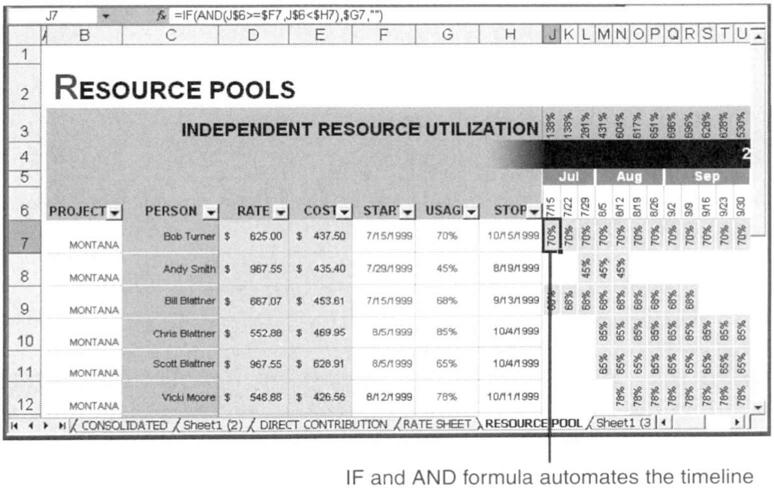

Figure 26.18
The dynamic Gantt chart formula will move and manage the percentage use over time.

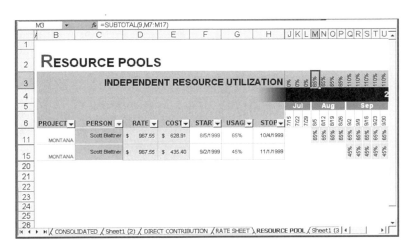

IF and AND formula automates the timeline

Use the SUBTOTAL function above each week to show the total for each employee when the list is filtered, as shown in Figure 26.19. Now, when you apply filters above the names, you can pull up individual names and see their total resource allocation.

Figure 26.19
The SUBTOTAL function can be placed above the corresponding weeks to subtotal individuals when filtered.

BUILDING CUSTOM FUNCTIONS

You might want to build your own custom function that does a calculation specific to your needs. For example, if you run a construction company and have several pieces of equipment with specific rates, you could apply the rates to the function and customize Excel to your needs, even nesting your own custom functions. You could establish your company's new rates at the beginning of the year and post the functions with syntax to all the estimators in the organization—then all you have to do is use the functions. To create this example—a custom function—follow these steps:

1. From the Visual Basic toolbar, select the Visual Basic Editor command or choose Tools, Macro, Visual Basic Editor; or press Alt+F11.

2. Choose Insert, Module. A new module opens.

3. In the first line of the module, enter the following code, also shown as Module 1 code in Figure 26.20. Use the Tab key to indent.

```
Function Cat769(hours, units)
        Cat769 = ((82.5 * hours) * Units)
End Function
```

Figure 26.20
Create custom functions where there is not an Excel function available and calculations are complex or repetitive.

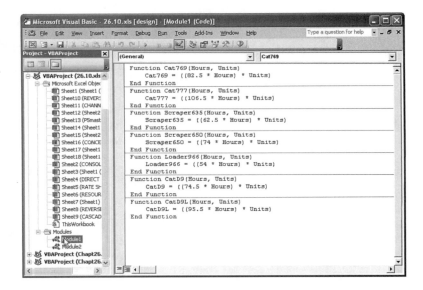

4. Click Save.

5. Switch back to the worksheet and create a column heading called Hours starting in cell D7 and then Units in E7.

6. Type **1250** in cell D8 and **5** in cell E8.

7. In cell F8, type the formula **=Cat769(D8,E8)**. The return result is $515,625 as shown in Figure 26.21.

Figure 26.21
Custom functions using your company's rates can provide accuracy throughout the company.

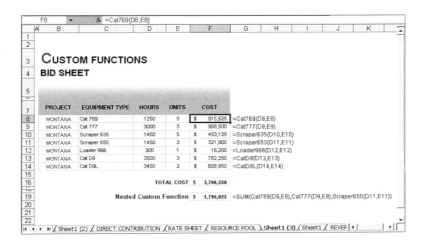

It's important to note the following points when creating custom functions:

- Custom functions can be used only by that workbook.

- To reuse the functions in any workbook, you must save it as an add-in, and then load the add-in whenever you want to use the functions or whenever you open another workbook that uses them.

  To create an add-in that will allow you to use the custom function in other workbooks follow these steps:

  1. Activate the VB Editor.

  2. Choose File and then select Properties. Click the Summary tab and enter a description for your function in the Title field and a longer comment in the Comments field.

  3. Select File, and then choose Save As.

  4. In the Save As dialog box choose the Save As Type drop down and then select Microsoft Excel Add-in.

  5. Click Save.

- You can store the add-in in your Add-Ins directory, and then select it using the Tools, Add-Ins command so it loads each time Excel loads.

- For the ultimate in share-ability, you can place the add-in on a share drive on the network, allowing anyone access to the functions.

- If you have it in a share drive, you can select Tools, Options and use the At Startup, Open All Files In line on the General tab to specify the shared folder path to the add-in, which will also allow the add-in to load every time Excel loads.

26

NOTE

Add-ins always load as read only, allowing multiple users to access the same add-in at the same time without getting a reservation or Already In Use message–that's a big advantage over regular Excel files. Only the first person to open the add-in can actually make changes to the original.

Producing a Line-Item Milestone Management Chart

On many occasions, you'll need to view multiple events on the same timeline. For reference, this worksheet example can be obtained from the CD in the back of this book. This can be achieved via one simple `IF(AND` statement nested several times. Notice the example in Figure 26.22; the original formula that would return one result for a date is `=IF(AND(X$7>=$B9,X$7<$C9),$P9,""))`. However, what if you need several results on the same line item? All you have to do is nest the function and refer the start and stop dates to a table of dates. The nested function begins after the first return results $P9. It is

`=IF(AND(X$7>=$B9,X$7<$C9),$P9,IF(AND(X$7>=$D9,X$7<$E9),$Q9,"")))`

All seven nested functions would be

```
=IF(AND(X$7>=$B9,X$7<$C9),$P9,IF(AND(X$7>=$D9,X$7<$E9),$Q9,
➡IF(AND(X$7>=$F9,X$7<$G9),$R9,IF(AND(X$7>=$H9,X$7<$I9),$S9,
➡IF(AND(X$7>=$J9,X$7<$K9),$T9,IF(AND(X$7>=$L9,X$7<$M9),$U9,
➡IF(AND(X$7>=$N9,X$7<$O9),$V9,"")))))))
```

Now, how do you return a conditional format that would highlight each result that's returned in a line item? Because conditional formats are limited to three conditions, you'll want to select the line range and from the Conditional Formatting dialog box, set the condition 1 to `Cell Value Is` - `greater than` - `="="`, and then set the format as shown in Figure 26.23. This will highlight any cell that has a return result in the line item.

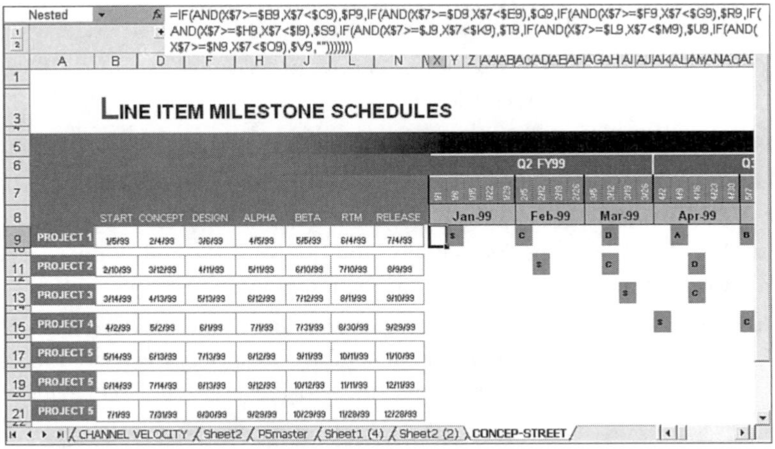

Figure 26.22
Use the nested
`IF(AND` function to
return multiple results
on a single line item.

Figure 26.23
Set the conditional formatting to return any result that occurs on a line item.

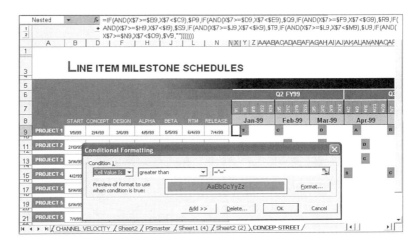

CONDITIONAL FORMATS TO SHOW PROGRESS AGAINST BASELINE

You can create baseline Gantt charts that show a phase of a project over time with the progress overlapped using conditional formats. As reference, you can access this workbook from the CD in the back of the book. In Figure 26.24, the baseline is created based on an IF(AND formula that operates off the dates in the table. The Percent Complete overrides the baseline with a conditional format formula shown in Figure 26.25. Reference the Web resource to access the workbook and to operate the model and see the results based on new dates and Percent Complete. Note that I used the hidden column N and the letter U formatted using the Wingdings font to create the diamond symbol.

Automated conditional format overlaps the baseline

26

Figure 26.24
Baseline items are dynamic based on dates. The Percent Complete shows progress and overrides the baseline with a conditional format formula.

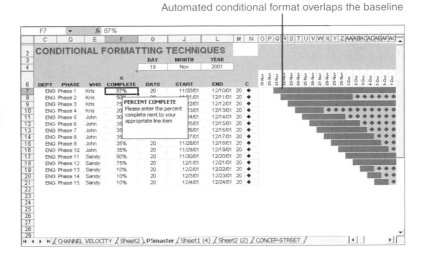

Format formula overrides baseline with Percent Complete

Figure 26.25
The conditional format formula is based on the AND formula in condition 1. Condition 2 is based on the cell value.

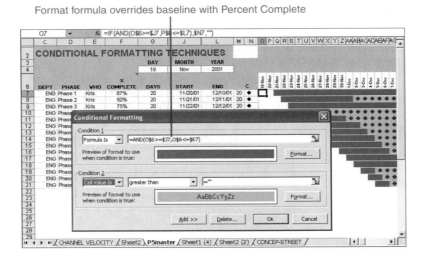

RAMPING UP PRODUCTION ON A SINGLE LINE ITEM

In the production world, moving into production mode usually takes a few weeks before production is running smoothly at 100%. In this case, you'll have to ramp up the production. Here's a formula that ramps the production after 21 days by 25% in week 4, 50% in week 5, and 75% in week 6, before reaching 100% or full capacity (see Figure 26.26). Please see the example on the CD as reference when recreating this setup.

```
=IF(AND(T$4>=$O10,T$4<$O10+$S10),IF(T$4-$O10<7,0*$Q10,
➡IF(T$4-$O10<14,0*$Q10,IF(T$4-$O10<21,0*$Q10,
➡IF(T$4-$O10<28,0.25*$Q10,IF(T$4-$O10<35,0.5*$Q10,
➡IF(T$4-$O10<42,0.75*$Q10,$Q10)))))),"")
```

This example actually tells you when you need to start a project based on a completion date with the following variables: Weekly Average, Total Output or Units, and Capacity to Deliver per phase.

Figure 26.26
This formula operates off a given completion date and three variables to tell you when to start production based on a six-week ramp-up time to 100% production.

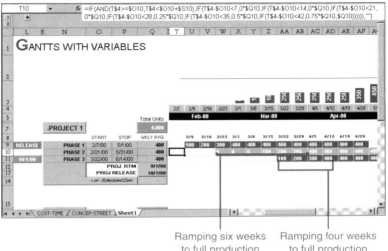

Ramping six weeks to full production

Ramping four weeks to full production

VALUE CHAINS

Value chains measure the value of process or products over a range of variables, such as steps in process or capabilities. You can use value chains to measure product coverage in the marketplace against competitors, or as a strategic business measure to understand the most logical approach in weighing risk factors.

CREATING A MARKET OPPORTUNITY VALUE CHAIN

A *market opportunity value chain* measures market coverage either internally—within an organization—or against competitors. Notice in Figure 26.27 that the market opportunity value chain for a small publisher measures the coverage of their books' accomplishment level and the company's coverage against it. By using Excel's formatting and drawing tools, you can create value chains for presentations or strategic initiatives for future approaches to the marketplace.

When creating a value chain, think in terms of the market or process as a whole with the different sections broken out from least to most, lowest to highest, easiest to hardest, and so on. Use the rectangle as the measurement tool that plots against the value chain.

To create the value chain shown in Figure 26.27, use the pentagon shape for the process or market analysis across the top of the sheet. The pentagon shape in the form of a chain represents the steps in the process, or the sectors in the marketplace. (Click the AutoShapes button and choose Block Arrows from the pop-up list; then click the Pentagon button as shown in Figure 26.28.)

Figure 26.27
By using drawing tools, you can create value chains to indicate market opportunity.

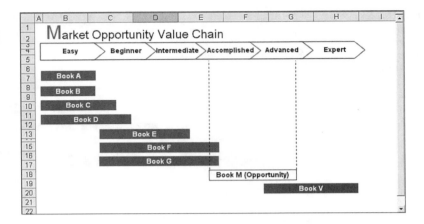

Figure 26.28
The pentagon shape is used to create the value chain.

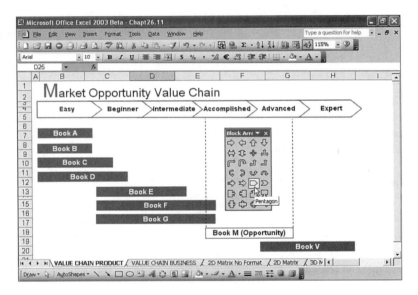

TIP FROM

You can duplicate the first pentagon by holding down the Ctrl key and dragging, or by pressing Ctrl+D. Pressing Ctrl+Shift and dragging creates a duplicate while keeping the horizontal alignment intact.

Use the Bring to Front or Send to Back buttons to create the overlap between the pentagons (the point of one pentagon placed on top of the next pentagon). To add text inside the shape, select the shape and type; then press Esc twice when you're done typing.

TIP FROM

> When adding drawn shapes to your charts and worksheets, you're likely to need four toolbar buttons quite often: Bring to Front, Send to Back, Bring Forward, and Send Backward. You can place these buttons on a toolbar within easy access by using one of these methods:
>
> - **Add the buttons to the Drawing toolbar**—Right-click the toolbar and select Customize to open the Customize dialog box. In the Categories list on the Commands tab, choose Drawing; then scroll the Commands list to find the commands for Bring to Front, Send to Back, and so on, and drag them to the toolbar. Close the Customize dialog box when you're finished.
>
> - **Tear off the Order toolbar**—Click the Draw button on the Drawing toolbar to open the pop-up menu. Click the Order option to display the submenu, and then drag the submenu's title bar away from the Draw menu to create a floating Order toolbar.

To create the product bars, use the Rectangle AutoShape from the Drawing toolbar. To create a white background, select the worksheet and use a white fill color (or just turn off the gridlines by choosing Tools, Options, clicking the View tab, and deselecting the Gridlines option in the Window Options section of the dialog box).

To create the dotted vertical lines shown on the sides of the opportunity block, click the Line button on the Drawing toolbar, draw the line, and then click the Dash Style button and select a style. You can draw an identical line on the other side, or Ctrl+Shift+drag to create the line and position it exactly parallel to the first line.

CREATING A STRATEGIC RISK FACTOR VALUE CHAIN

A *strategic risk factor value chain* enables you to measure business risks against different strategy approaches. In Figure 26.29, the solutions take a multiple-vendor approach against a single-source solution—the value chain measures the different steps in creating the product. Two approaches to producing the product are shown:

- Corporate Solution I shows multiple processes divided among several companies. This strategy creates dependencies on the other companies, thus creating greater risk, but lower cost in the short term; however, it ultimately will cost more in time and delivery risk.

- Corporate Solution II creates a single-source dependency with one company. The short-term cost might be a bit higher, but risk is minimized with sole control and single-source dependencies.

This example might seem a bit complex, but think in terms of your business and the different steps required to produce a service or product. Then, look at the opportunities available to create the same product or process, and the risks and cost associated with that opportunity.

Figure 26.29
A strategic risk factor value chain measures strategic approaches to arrive at a logical conclusion.

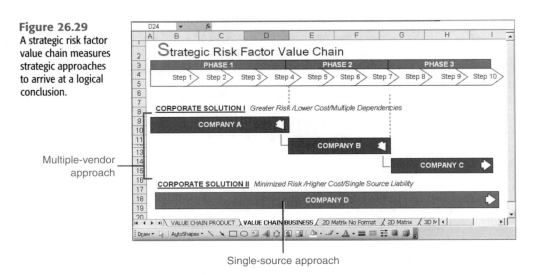

Multiple-vendor approach

Single-source approach

By using the pentagon shape, lines or connectors, arrows, and text, you can create strategic approaches to arrive at business conclusions.

VALUE MATRICES

You use a *value matrix* to measure multiple components of processes or products. A value matrix is created with two forms: two-dimensional and three-dimensional. Value chains are created primarily with drawing programs for presentations; however, considering that most number decisions are based in Excel, you also can create matrices and metrics in Excel for presentations or strategic cross sections of a market or business.

CREATING A 2D MATRIX

A *two-dimensional matrix* is a cross section between components where the equal components or intersections are checked. Figures 26.30 and 26.31 show two matrices: The first shows the structure on the worksheet, and the second illustrates a final form with formatting. In Figure 26.30, the 2D matrix measures the product and the components within the product. It provides a cross-section overview of the product's components as a whole. Figure 26.31 shows the matrix in final formatted form.

Suppose that your business distributes 10 different types of products throughout the United States. The 10 products could be listed across the top and the states along the left side, and the products distributed within the states would then be checked at the intersections. A matrix creates a simple intersecting picture that helps visualize complex cross sections of data.

Intersecting point

Figure 26.30
An unformatted, 2D matrix shows the simple layout required.

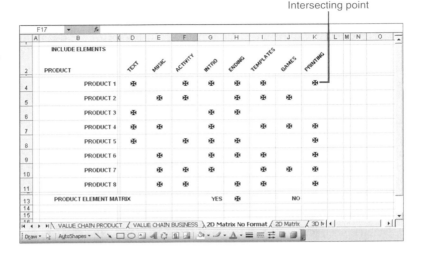

Figure 26.31
The final formatted 2D matrix.

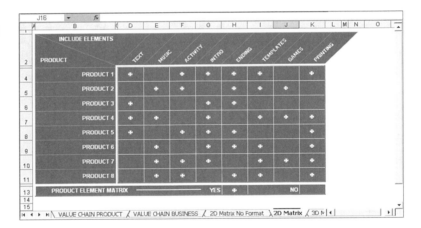

To create a 2D matrix, follow these steps:

1. Align the products or companies in the first column.
2. Align the components across the top in one or more rows.
3. Add an X, check mark, or other graphic where categories cross.

By adjusting column and row heights and centering text horizontally and vertically, you can establish a balanced matrix that resembles one created in a drawing program.

CREATING A 3D MATRIX

A *three-dimensional matrix* is used when levels of complexity are involved, adding a depth measure to the 2D matrix. Depth can include performance, perceived value, cost associated with like items, and so on. For example, if you have three cars with like components, but the cost associated with the components is extremely different, the depth could be measured in cost as inexpensive, moderate, and expensive. In Figure 26.32, the 3D matrix measures several components, as well as the value of items associated with the vehicle type. The structure of the matrix is the same as the 2D matrix covered previously; however, the 3D component is created with shapes from the Drawing toolbar to display depth: the level of performance.

Figure 26.32
A 3D matrix can provide levels of depth and complexity across a cross section of products and components.

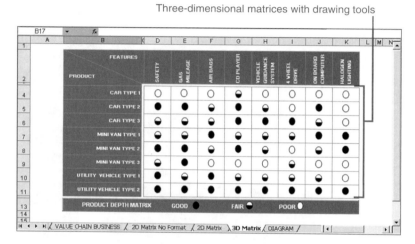

Three-dimensional matrices with drawing tools

EXCEL IN PRACTICE

Excel's new diagrams can be used to create presentations whether you use the presentation in Excel or export it to PowerPoint (see Figure 26.33). From the Drawing toolbar, the Insert Diagram or Organization chart button was clicked and the Cycle diagram was selected. After the diagram has been inserted, you can change the formatting of the diagram to include sections or change the format layout from 2D to 3D. The example shows the cyclical process of how jet engines work on airplanes.

Figure 26.33
Use the cyclical diagram chart from the Drawing toolbar to show cyclical processes.

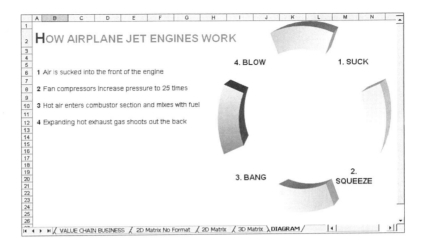

CHAPTER **27**

CUSTOMIZING EXCEL TO FIT YOUR WORKING STYLE

In this chapter

Why Customize Excel?   704

Changing the Default Excel Settings   704

Web Options Button   706

Changing Workbook Settings   706

Changing the Excel Window Settings   710

Recent Option Tabs   712

Modifying Toolbars   714

Customizing the Excel Menus   723

WHY CUSTOMIZE EXCEL?

Microsoft designed Excel to be powerful and yet easy to use, but every user is different. You might manage a number of small lists in Excel and need frequent access to the data tools on a toolbar. Perhaps your job requires building charts every day, and you want to add options to the Chart menu for this purpose. Maybe you create custom workbooks for other users and need special tools constantly at hand.

You can tailor Excel to look and work the way you want. If you want a certain type of font, worksheet color, and number of sheets within each workbook you open, Excel enables you to adjust such components and tools to fit your style. If you create workbooks that other people will use, you can tailor the workbook environment to protect your original information. You can even create custom toolbars and menus for yourself and your business.

This chapter reviews a number of options for customizing Excel so that it works the way you prefer to work. It's important to note, however, that Excel—particularly in conjunction with the other Microsoft Office products—is nearly infinitely customizable. No single chapter or even a whole book can provide all the details on all the changes you can make. You don't need to feel limited by the features and suggestions of this chapter; the Excel Help system can help you explore a wide range of other options.

CHANGING THE DEFAULT EXCEL SETTINGS

Excel enables you to customize many of the default settings for the program. Each of these features is controlled by settings in the Options dialog box. To open this dialog box, choose Tools, Options. The following list describes some suggested changes:

- **Move data entry in a different direction**—By default, when you press Enter after typing a cell entry, Excel accepts the entry and moves down to the next cell in that column. In many workbooks, however, moving to the next cell to the right, left, up, or even disabling this option completely would be more useful. You can change the direction that the cell pointer moves. Click the Edit tab in the Options dialog box. In the Direction box, select the direction you want the cell pointer to move, as shown in Figure 27.1. To prevent the cell pointer from moving, deselect the Move Selection After Enter option.

NOTE

> When entering data using the Enter key, you can control direction in a limited area of the worksheet by selecting that area first. As you enter the data, Excel moves down until you reach the bottom of the first column in the selection and then moves to the top of the next column, and so on. You can also use Tab and Shift+Tab to move left and right instead of changing the direction option to right or left.

- **Control the default number of sheets in a workbook**—By default, Excel creates new workbooks with three blank worksheets. You might prefer to start with fewer sheets or more sheets. To change the default number of worksheets in a new workbook, click the General tab in the Options dialog box. In the Sheets in New Workbook box, type or select the number of sheets you want (see Figure 27.2).

Figure 27.1
Change the direction of data entry so that pressing Enter moves the active cell right one cell instead of down one cell.

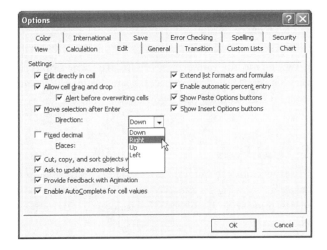

Changes column references from alphabetical to numerical. Cells are then referenced by R (row) and C (column), R24C2, for example.

Figure 27.2
You can customize the number of sheets that appear in a new workbook by changing the Sheets in New Workbook setting. Also, notice what the R1C1 Reference Style option does to a worksheet's column headings. Although available, it is not recommended.

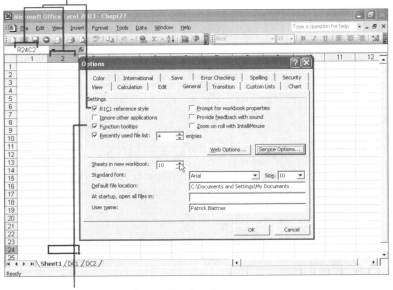

Causes function syntax to appear on-screen when writing functions

- **Set the default font and point size**—Excel defaults to a standard Arial font, but you can change the default font settings to something more appropriate. Click the General tab in the Options dialog box, and change the settings for Standard Font and Size. A warning will display before changes take effect. The warning you get states "For your changes to the standard font to take effect, you must quit and restart Microsoft Excel." It also gives you no Cancel option.

- **Function ToolTips**—The function ToolTips were new to Excel 2002 and appear again in Excel 2003. By default, the function ToolTips are turned on (on the General tab). When you start to write a function in Excel, a small pop-up appears with the syntax to help you understand the order of the arguments.

WEB OPTIONS BUTTON

The Web Options button from the General tab enables you to specify options you want saved with a workbook for viewing on the Web. You can change encoding, font styles, font language character sets, and target browsers. The following tabs contain options in the Web Options dialog box:

- **General**—This tab allows you to choose options that enable formulas on the Web page and determine how pictures not embedded in Excel will load.

- **Browser**—Lets you choose the target browser that people will use to view the workbook as well as which graphic and font displays to use, such as VML.

- **Files**—Allows you to specify filename length, folder organization, updating links, and so on.

- **Pictures**—Allows you to select target picture screen size and pixels per inch.

- **Encoding**—Allows for language encoding.

- **Fonts**—Allows you to establish font character sets, styles, and sizes (for example, Greek, Hebrew, Japanese, and so on).

CHANGING WORKBOOK SETTINGS

In addition to changing the overall settings that apply to all new workbooks, you can make changes within specific existing or new workbooks, as described in the following sections.

CHANGING THE COLOR PALETTE

For any open workbook, you can change the colors available on color palettes and customize the default palette by selecting and changing the colors on the palette. Note that this change applies only to the active workbook, not to Excel as a whole.

TIP

> When you copy or move a sheet to another workbook, the colors on the source sheet change to reflect the color palette in the target workbook. Excel replaces your custom colors with the colors in the corresponding positions on the color palette in the target workbook. To solve this problem, try the following techniques:
> - To retain your custom colors when copying worksheets to other workbooks, copy the color palette from the customized workbook to the other workbook before you copy the worksheet. It's important to note that copying the color palette will change all the customized colors used in the target workbook, which might be something you didn't expect (or want).
> - To copy the color palette, open both the source and the target workbooks. If necessary, switch to the target workbook. Open the Options dialog box (Tools, Options), and click the Color tab. In the Copy Colors From box, specify the source workbook. Then choose OK.
> - To use your custom colors in new workbooks, customize the palette for a blank workbook, save the workbook as a template, and use the template to create new workbooks.

To change a color on the palette, follow these steps:

1. Choose Tools, Options. In the Options dialog box, select the Color tab (see Figure 27.3).
2. Select the color you want to change on the Standard Colors, Chart Fills, or Chart Lines palette.

Figure 27.3
Select the color you want to change.

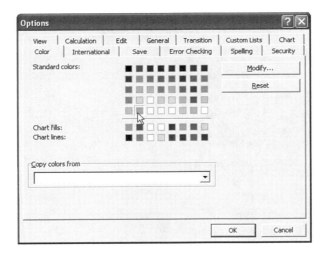

3. Click the Modify button to open the Colors dialog box (see Figure 27.4).
4. If the color you want to use is shown in the Colors palette, click it. The indicator in the lower-right corner displays a sample of the old and new colors.

Figure 27.4
Select the color you want from the color palette.

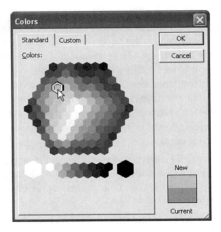

5. If you need a custom color, you can modify the existing color or create your own color. Click the Custom tab (see Figure 27.5). Here, you can click the desired color in the Colors box, or drag the slider to the right of the Colors box to modify the existing color visually. You also can adjust the settings at the bottom of the dialog box to change the red/green/blue mix or customize the color to a specific level of luminance, saturation, and hue.

6. When the color is correct (whether you're working on the Standard or Custom tab), click OK.

7. Click OK in the Options dialog box. Note that you must save the workbook to save the new color setting(s).

Figure 27.5
The Custom tab in the Colors dialog box enables you to adjust colors to specific levels of HSL (hue, saturation, luminance) and RGB (red, green, blue).

27

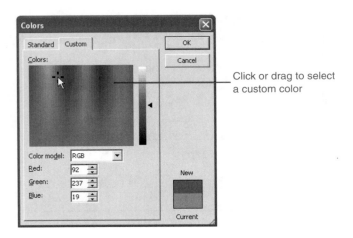

Click or drag to select a custom color

The default colors have ScreenTips that display the color name. Your custom color won't have such a ScreenTip; instead, Excel displays Color Scheme when you point to that color on a palette or in a dialog box.

To restore the original factory settings for the colors in a workbook, open the Options dialog box again, click the Color tab, and click the Reset button. Be sure you want to do this, however; Excel doesn't ask you to confirm this change. Note that making this change resets any modified colors in the workbook—wherever those colors were used.

HIDING PARTS OF THE WORKBOOK

For various reasons, you might want to hide parts of a worksheet. You probably are already familiar with hiding and unhiding columns and rows. The following sections provide other options for hiding parts of a workbook.

→ For details on how to hide and unhide columns and rows, **see** "Hiding and Unhiding Rows and Columns," **p. 45**

HIDING SHEETS

If you send out a report every week that contains summary information, you might want to display the backup data for the summary info only when you need to add more data. When you want to keep information in a workbook but also keep it out of view for the sake of confidentiality, privacy, or simplicity, you can hide the worksheet with that information.

You can hide a single worksheet at a time or hide multiple worksheets simultaneously. To hide a single worksheet, begin by displaying that worksheet. To hide multiple worksheets, hold down the Ctrl key and click additional sheet tabs until you have gathered all the applicable worksheets into a group. If the sheets you want hidden are consecutive, click the first sheet you want hidden, and then hold the Shift key and click the last sheet you want hidden. All sheets between the two clicks will be selected. With the worksheet(s) selected, choose Format, Sheet, Hide. The Unhide command becomes available when sheets are hidden within the workbook; to unhide sheets, choose Format, Sheet, Unhide. Excel displays a dialog box where you can specify which sheet to restore to view. You must unhide each sheet separately. You can also prevent hidden sheets from appearing in the Unhide dialog box by using the Very Hidden option. You can hide sheets this way by accessing the VBE, selecting the sheet you want hidden in the Project Explorer, press F4 to bring the sheet's properties up, and then selecting 2—xlSheetVeryHidden from the Visible property's drop-down list. This change is saved with the workbook.

→ You can prevent hidden worksheets from being unhidden by protecting the workbook with a password. For details, **see** "Password-Protecting a Workbook," **p. 35**

27

HIDING OR CHANGING THE DISPLAY OF ZERO VALUES

By deselecting the Zero Values option on the View tab in the Options dialog box, you can make all cells containing a zero on the active sheet appear blank. This helps keep spreadsheets with a lot of zero values from looking cluttered.

HIDING CELL ENTRIES

You might have cell content that you want to hide, without hiding the whole column or row. Excel offers a trick for this, as described in the following steps:

1. Select the cell(s) you want to hide.
2. Choose Format, Cells to display the Format Cells dialog box.
3. Click the Number tab.
4. Click Custom in the Category list. Type three semicolons (;;;) in the Type box.

    The value disappears from the worksheet and doesn't print. Of course, you can still see the value in the Formula bar when the cell is selected or in the cell if you edit the entry.

→ For details on how to create custom number formats, **see** "Creating Custom Formats," **p.97**

This trick works for any kind of entry. To view the cell value again in the worksheet, select the cell and change the format to General, Currency, or some other format.

CHANGING THE EXCEL WINDOW SETTINGS

You can customize the Excel program window to look a certain way for your own use or to prevent other users from moving to different worksheets or scrolling the worksheet. You can show or hide the horizontal and vertical scrollbars and the status bar, as described in the following sections.

ADDING AND REMOVING SCROLLBARS

Excel enables you to remove the vertical and horizontal scrollbars from the Excel window. If you have a document that contains information in a specific location on a worksheet, for example, and you don't want users to scroll this information off the screen, you might want to eliminate the scrollbars. (Note that they are easily restored by experienced users, however.)

To remove or restore the scrollbars, choose Tools, Options to open the Options dialog box, and click the View tab. To remove the horizontal scrollbar, deselect the Horizontal Scroll Bar option. To remove the vertical scrollbar, deselect the Vertical Scroll Bar option. To restore the scrollbar(s) at any point, open the Options dialog box again and select the option(s). Figure 27.6 shows the Excel window with the scrollbars removed.

NOTE

Removing just the horizontal scrollbar doesn't restore any usable screen space, but you regain an extra line if you also remove the sheet tabs (see the later section "Hiding the Sheet Tabs" for details).

Figure 27.6
The Excel window will have scrollbars removed and grid-lines changed to green.

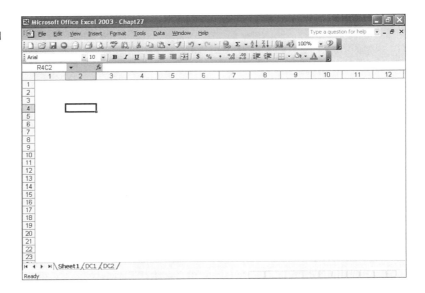

CUSTOMIZING THE STATUS BAR FOR QUICK ANALYSIS

If you're not currently showing the status bar onscreen, consider adding it. In addition to indicating the edit mode, providing quick instructions, and displaying messages, the status bar offers another quietly efficient feature: AutoCalculate. This is a great tool for quick analysis. If you have a list of costs associated with months, for example, you can highlight certain months—without summing or subtotaling—and see the total cost for those months. Any time you have a range of numbers for which you want to know the total value, average, count, and so on, just select the individual cells/ranges and look at the AutoCalculate section of the status bar. As the example in Figure 27.7 shows, you can select ranges to be calculated (just hold down Ctrl as you click and drag over the additional cells or ranges). In this example, AutoCalculate is showing the sum of February for Minnesota, North Dakota, Idaho.

27

Figure 27.7
When you drag ove
the range(s) or select
multiple individual
cells, the status bar
displays the total.

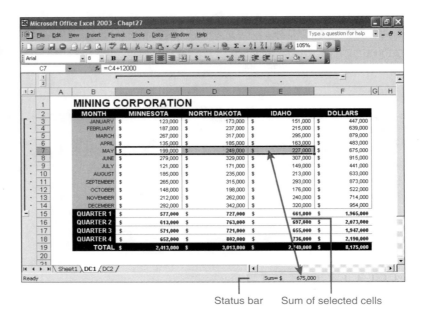

Status bar   Sum of selected cells

RECENT OPTION TABS

The following option tabs were added in Excel 2002; there are no new tabs for 2003.

- **International**—The International tab allows you to create number-handling separators different from the default system settings found in the Windows Control Panel. When different separators are chosen, they apply to every workbook until changed again. You can also allow for printing resizing, and viewing specific options from right to left. Notice Figure 27.8. When the View Current Sheet Right-to-Left option is checked, the rows, columns, and worksheet tabs are viewed from the right. When the Right-to-Left option is chosen, each new workbook created from that moment on is viewed right to left. This setting does *not* affect the currently open workbooks or any previously saved workbooks.

- **Save**—The Save tab allows you to set the AutoRecover feature every x minutes and also turn the AutoRecover feature off with the Disable AutoRecover option. AutoRecover saves the latest revision of your workbook and recovers crashed files. You also have the option to choose the path where all AutoRecovered files are kept. Should Excel crash, all AutoRecovered files appear in a Document Recovery pane the next time you start Excel. You then have the option of opening, saving, deleting, or displaying the repairs of each workbook on the list. The Display Repair option also opens the workbook.

- **Error Checking**—The Error Checking tab allows you to enable background error checking and view rules associated with the workbook. Background error checking displays an error indicator—a small triangle (green by default)—in the upper-left corner of each cell containing an error. When a cell containing an error is activated, Excel

displays an error symbol—a black exclamation mark inside a yellow diamond—to the
left of the cell. Clicking the error symbol displays choices for handling the error.

Figure 27.8
Check the View
Current Sheet Right-
to-Left option to view
the worksheet in the
opposite direction.

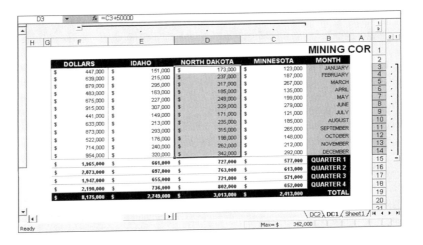

- **Spelling**—The Spelling tab allows you to specify which language to use each time the
  spelling feature is used. It also allows you to change which dictionary you want added
  words stored in as well as options for ignoring uppercase text, words with numbers, and
  Internet and file addresses. Note that Excel cannot create or edit custom dictionaries.
  To create or edit them, use the Custom Dictionaries button on the Spelling and
  Grammar tab in Microsoft Word's Options dialog box. It also accounts for language-
  specific spelling.

- **Security**—The Security tab allows you to create passwords for both Opening and
  Modifying the Current Workbook. You can also choose to mark the current workbook
  as read only and attach digital signatures. These features (except for digital signatures)
  were previously accessible through Excel's File, Save As command sequence and for
  compatibility reasons can still be found there.

The Advanced button allows you to choose which type of encryption method to use for
the Open Password option. Note that if the Office 97/2000 Compatible encryption
method is not chosen, users of those versions of Office will not be able to open the
workbook, even if they know the password.

Digital signatures are a way of authenticating workbooks. Signatures inform other users
that the current revision of the workbook was completed by the author of the signature.
Any attempt to alter and save the workbook results in the removal of the signature.

An example would be if you were in charge of preparing and sending a proposal workbook to a client. You want to ensure that the client does not attempt to alter any of the
data prior to approval. You also want the client to know that you were the last person to
edit the workbook of prospective clients. For both reasons, you attach your digital signature before sending the workbook to the client. If the client edits and saves the

workbook, which removes the signature, and then sends it back to you, you will know the client altered the workbook in some way when you see no signature.

Finally, the Macro Security button takes you to a dialog box that allows you to choose the level of security you want when workbooks containing macros are opened. This feature can also be found by choosing Tools, Macro.

MODIFYING TOOLBARS

Many tools are available on the default Excel toolbars, but you're likely to find that you use certain tools repeatedly, and others rarely or never. You're probably already comfortable with turning the various toolbars on and off with the View, Toolbars command, and have undoubtedly noticed that Excel displays certain toolbars automatically when you work in certain modes—the Chart toolbar appears when you're creating or editing charts, and so on. But you might not have thought about customizing those default toolbars to fit your specific needs. Excel enables you to add and remove buttons on any of the default toolbars, move buttons from one toolbar to another, and even create custom toolbars for various purposes.

To begin customizing toolbars, start by opening the Customize dialog box. Choose View, Toolbars, Customize, or right-click any toolbar and select Customize from the pop-up menu to open the Customize dialog box. With this dialog box open, you can right-click any toolbar button to display a special pop-up context menu for customizing that button, as shown in Figure 27.9. You can also access the Customize command from the Tools menu. This option appears just below the other command that controls Excel—the Options command. You can also access the Customize command from the Tools menu.

Figure 27.9
Right-click the toolbar, choose Customize, and then right-click a button on the toolbar to access this context menu to customize the button.

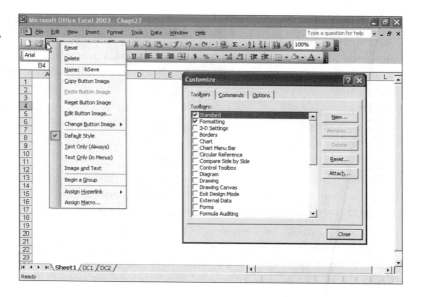

With the options on the pop-up menu, you can copy the images on the button faces and paste them on other buttons, create your own button names, display text on the buttons—even change the images on the button faces completely. The following sections describe how to use these options.

NOTE

For most of these operations, the Customize dialog box must be open. However, you can move, copy, and delete menus and buttons without the Customize dialog box visible by holding down the Alt key for moving (or Alt+Ctrl key for copying) as you drag the menu/button.

DELETING BUTTONS FROM TOOLBARS

Suppose that you want to delete a toolbar button you never use, just to get it out of the way (and maybe use that space for a different button that might be more helpful to you). To delete an existing button on a toolbar, open the Customize dialog box and then drag the button off the toolbar—being careful not to drop it over a menu or another toolbar, in which case Excel would move the button to that menu or toolbar. (It's safe to release the mouse when the pointer displays a large black X attached to the arrow pointer.) Another method is to right-click the button and select Delete.

DISPLAYING TEXT ON BUTTONS

By default, the buttons on the toolbars don't display any text, but you might find it helpful to display text on certain buttons, along with or instead of the button images. Change buttons to display text only, for example, if Excel users are unfamiliar with using toolbar buttons, or if they have a difficult time remembering what command an image represents. To make the Save button more obvious, for example, you can display the word Save on the button instead of or in addition to the button image. Begin by displaying the Customize dialog box as usual. Then right-click the button you want to change and select the appropriate text option. The Default style will display Image & Text when the button is on a menu and will display only the image when on a toolbar.

Figure 27.10 shows buttons customized to show the button image with text, the image alone, the text alone, and customized text.

27

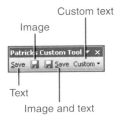

Figure 27.10
Keep in mind that showing text, or image and text, takes more space than just showing the button image.

Excel supplies text to go with every default button; the text is displayed in the ScreenTip when pointing to that button. Sometimes the button name isn't enough information to help the user figure out how or when to use the button, but you can customize the text to say whatever you want. To change the text, open the Customize dialog, right-click the button you want to customize, click in the text box next to the Name option on the pop-up menu, and type the desired text. If you want to use a hotkey (underlined letter) to activate a button, type an ampersand (&) before the letter that you want to underline.

The Name setting is what appears on the button when you choose any customizing option that includes text. The Name setting is also how you create custom text on a button face (such as the Save Workbook button shown earlier in Figure 27.15).

CHANGING THE BUTTON IMAGES

Sometimes the image on a button doesn't help you figure out what the button does. If you want to change the button image, you can add text or replace the image with text, as described in the preceding section, or you can modify the button image. With the Customize dialog box open, right-click the button you want to change to display the pop-up customizing menu. You have the following choices for changing the button image:

■ **Replace the image with one from the set of extra images supplied with Excel**— Select Change Button Image from the pop-up menu and then click one of the images on the submenu (see Figure 27.11).

Figure 27.11
You can apply these predesigned images to buttons on the toolbar.

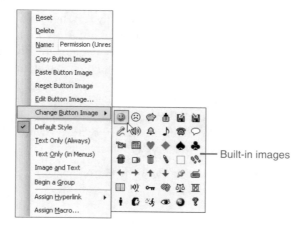

Built-in images

■ **Copy and modify an existing toolbar button image**—Display the Customize dialog box, right-click the source button, and choose Copy Button Image. Then right-click the target button and choose Paste Button Image. Finally, edit the image as described in the following item.

■ **Edit a default image or one of the extra images**—With the image in place on the button, select Edit Button Image to display the Button Editor, as shown in

Figure 27.12. Then edit the button as desired. (To edit one of the extra images, you must display that image on the button before selecting Edit Button Image.) By selecting the Color Picker you can modify the details of the colors as shown in Figure 27.12.

Figure 27.12
Use the Button Editor to modify or draw an image.

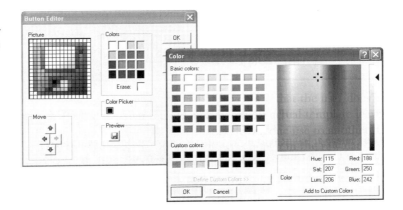

- **Copy an image from an image file**—Open the image file in Paint, Microsoft Photo Editor, or some other image-management program. Copy the image and switch back to Excel. Right-click the button whose image you want to change and choose Paste Button Image. Excel replaces the original image with the copied image. Note that scaling an image down to button size might cause distortion; start with a simple image or edit the image with the Button Editor.

- **Create your own image, using the Button Editor**—Right-click the button, choose Edit Button Image, and then create the desired image. You also can start from an existing image and edit it in the Button Editor to get the desired effect (see the preceding item).

To change an image with the Button Editor, click a color and then click a pixel in the Picture box. The image changes to reflect the new color. The Move buttons adjust the location of the image up, down, left, or right on the button face. The Erase feature sets the image to the background color.

The following are some other things to keep in mind when you're customizing buttons:

- Any button that uses a drop-down menu (such as the Font list button) cannot be assigned a macro, nor can its image be copied or changed.

- You can resize buttons containing a text box with a drop-down list (such as the Font list button) like any worksheet column by dragging its left or right border.

- You can customize most of the buttons that contain just a drop-down but no text box, such as the Border and Fill Color buttons, by adding additional commands to their drop-down lists. A great example of this is to add additional border choices to the Border button's drop-down list (such as the Inside Vertical, Inside Horizontal, and

27

Apply Inside Borders buttons). In fact, you can add the Line Style and Line Color buttons to the Border button's drop-down list, so you'll rarely need to access the confusing Borders tab in the Format, Cells menu.

This method of customizing a button's drop-down list also works for the new Paste and AutoSum buttons, which now have their own drop-down lists. For example, you can add the Paste Formatting, Paste As Hyperlink, and Across Worksheets buttons to the Paste button's drop-down list.

ASSIGNING HYPERLINKS

In addition to being able to insert hyperlinks directly into worksheets, you can create toolbar buttons that let you jump quickly to other places in the current worksheet, other worksheets, or workbooks, or even hop over to Web sites that you often use in your business. For example, if you often jump to a certain financial Web page or check stocks regularly, you might want to add a link to a custom button that takes you directly to that financial page.

With the Customize dialog box open, right-click the button to which you want to assign a hyperlink. Select Assign Hyperlink, and then Open to display the Insert Hyperlink: Open dialog box (see Figure 27.13).

Figure 27.13
Apply or select the
Web site you want to
assign to a button.

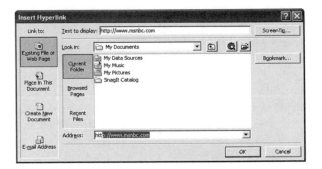

This dialog box enables you to assign a hyperlink to an e-mail address, a new document, an existing file, or a Web page. Select one of the buttons in the Link To list to indicate the target for the new link. The dialog box changes to display options associated with the destination you chose. You then can type the path to the file or Web site using the text box, or click the appropriate button to select the path from a list (Inserted Links, Browsed Pages, or Recent Files). You also can browse for the file or Web page.

ASSIGNING MACROS

To create efficient toolbar buttons that provide options you use frequently, you can assign macros to toolbar buttons. If you often need to adjust column width to provide room for lengthy text, for example, you can create a macro that AutoFits all the columns, and then assign the macro to any button on any toolbar.

To assign a macro to a toolbar button, you first create the macro as described in Chapter 31, "Recording and Editing a Macro." Then, create the button you want to use, right-click it, and select Assign Macro from the pop-up customizing menu to open the Assign Macro dialog box (see Figure 27.14). In the Macros In box, specify the location of the macro you want to use. Then, select the name of the macro in the list in the center of the dialog box, type its name in the Macro Name box, or click the Collapse Dialog button and select the macro from the open workbook where it's stored.

NOTE

> Macros stored in the Personal Macro Workbook begin with PERSONAL.XLS! in the list box. See Chapter 31 for details on using the Personal Macro Workbook. Note also that any macros not found in the currently active workbook start with their workbook name.

Select the recorded macro to assign

Custom toolbar with custom button

Figure 27.14
Use the Assign Macro dialog box to apply a macro to a toolbar button.

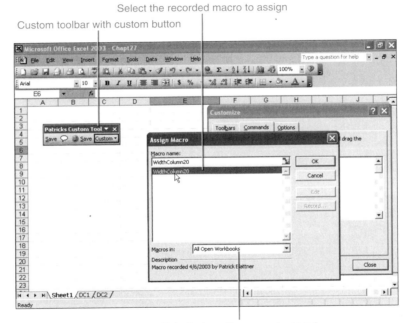

Select where the macro is stored

TIP FROM

> If you created the macro and will be the only user of the new toolbar button, the macro name might suffice as the text on the button, and you might not even want an image. For other users, try to assign text that's not as cryptic as the typical macro name, and/or use an appropriate button image to suggest the function of the button.

BUILDING CUSTOM TOOLBARS

Sometimes customizing the default buttons and toolbars isn't quite enough. For those instances, you can build custom toolbars that supply the exact combination of buttons that you need. To create a custom toolbar, open the Customize dialog box and click the New button to display the New Toolbar dialog box (see Figure 27.15). Type a name for the toolbar; this name will appear in the list of toolbars in the Customize dialog box and in the title bar of the toolbar (see Figure 27.16).

NOTE

> Unfortunately, Excel automatically resizes toolbars to accommodate the exact size of the buttons on the toolbar. You can't widen the toolbar to display the whole toolbar name in the title bar. Unless you have sufficient buttons on the toolbar to widen it, the name will be truncated. You sometimes can solve this problem by changing the toolbar name to something shorter, adding separators (described shortly), displaying the button text instead of or in addition to the button images, or reshaping the toolbar (drag the sides or corners as you would to resize a window).

Click to create a new toolbar

Figure 27.15
Assign a name to the custom toolbar.

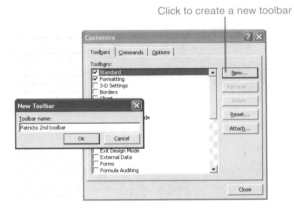

The toolbar appears with no buttons. To add buttons, you can use either of the following methods:

- **Copy buttons from other toolbars**—The source toolbar must be displayed to use this method. To copy a button from an open toolbar, hold down Ctrl+Alt and drag the button from its original toolbar to the custom toolbar. If the Customize dialog box is open, you can just hold down Ctrl.
- **Add buttons from the Commands tab in the Customize dialog box**—Click a category in the Categories list and then scroll the Commands list until you see the command, macro, shape, and so on, for which you want to add a button. Drag the item from the Commands list to your custom toolbar and drop it into position (see Figure 27.17).

Custom toolbar

Figure 27.16
The new toolbar
shows up in the list of
toolbars.

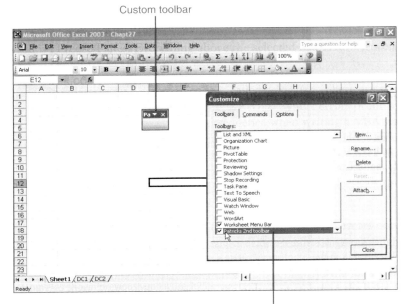

Custom toolbar appears in the toolbar list

With either method, Excel displays an I-beam on the toolbar to indicate where the button will be placed when you drop it.

Figure 27.17
Drag the button to
the desired location
on your custom
toolbar.

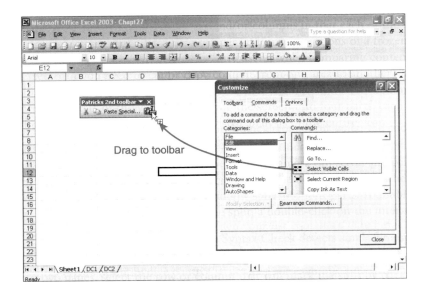

27

You might have noticed that toolbars in Windows programs generally are separated into *groups* with vertical markers (called *separator bars* or just *separators*) that group similar toolbar buttons together. You can add separator bars to your custom toolbar or any default toolbar. Right-click the button that you want to be first (reading from left to right) in the group and select Begin a Group from the pop-up customizing menu. Excel displays a separator bar to the left of the button.

TIP FROM

> You can move buttons anywhere on the toolbar without displaying the Customize dialog box. Just hold down the Alt key, left-click the button, and drag the button to the desired location.

To attach custom toolbars to specific workbooks, start by opening the workbook to which you want to attach a toolbar. Open the Customize dialog box and click the Attach button on the Toolbars tab. In the Attach Toolbars dialog box, select the toolbar in the Custom Toolbars list and click the Copy button to copy the toolbar name to the Toolbars in Workbook list (see Figure 27.18). Close the Customize dialog box and save the workbook. Now every time the workbook is opened, the attached toolbars appear in the workbook.

Figure 27.18
Attach custom toolbars to a workbook to provide specific tools for that workbook.

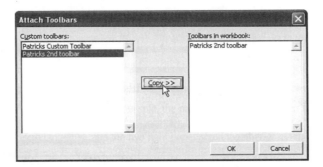

Considerations When Attaching Toolbars

When you attach a toolbar, Excel makes a separate copy of the toolbar just for that workbook. In effect, you now have two copies of the toolbar on your machine: the one you created, which appears on the toolbars list (let's call it the global toolbar for simplicity), and the one attached to the workbook, which we'll call the custom toolbar. The one on the toolbars list (global) takes precedence. If you hide the global toolbar, Excel won't display the attached toolbar when the workbook is opened. If no such toolbar name appears on the toolbars list when the workbook is opened, however, the custom toolbar appears. In the latter case, Excel adds a (global) separate copy of the custom toolbar to the list. If you delete your custom toolbar, and then open the workbook containing the attached toolbar, the toolbar should still appear.

One more point: Because the global and attached toolbars are separate entities, if you customize the global toolbar after adding the attached toolbar, the attached toolbar doesn't update to show the changes. You must delete the old attachment and reattach the new modified toolbar.

In short, attached toolbars can cause havoc, particularly when sharing workbooks with attached toolbars with unsuspecting/inexperienced users. It's perplexing for users to see five or six custom toolbars appear on their list that they never created themselves, but were the result of attached toolbars being added to their global list. The custom (attached) toolbars are not automatically removed when the workbook containing the attached toolbar is closed or deleted.

DELETING AND RESETTING TOOLBARS AND BUTTONS

You can delete custom toolbars and buttons or restore customized default toolbars and buttons to their original forms. Start by opening the Customize dialog box as usual. Then use the following methods:

- To delete a custom button, drag the button off the toolbar or right-click it and select Delete.

- To delete a custom toolbar, select the toolbar in the Toolbars list on the Toolbars tab in the Customize dialog box and click the Delete button. When Excel asks you to confirm this action, click OK.

- To restore a default toolbar to its original form, select it in the Toolbars list and click the Reset button. When Excel asks you to confirm this action, click OK.

- To restore a default button to its original form, right-click it and select Reset. Be sure that you want to do this, however: Excel doesn't ask you to confirm this change.

CUSTOMIZING THE EXCEL MENUS

With all the options available in Excel, people can get carried away and add or change things in the setup or a workbook. By knowing how to change the environment, you can eliminate this risk by customizing the Excel environment on your computer or those of other users. Changing the menus also can simplify or improve your own use of Excel. Customizing the menus and customizing the toolbars in Excel are closely related operations—both are fairly simple tasks that use the Customize dialog box.

Suppose you have a worksheet that you want someone to use only to input information, but you don't want that user to be able to manipulate the file in any way. Figure 27.19 shows a custom setup for this type of situation—providing a single menu item, File, and removing the Standard and Formatting toolbars.

Customized menu

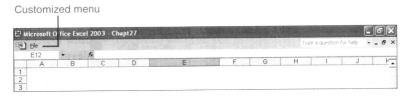

Figure 27.19
Minimize your risk for error by changing the environment so that a small number of options (if any) are available.

CAUTION

An experienced user might reset the menus or use shortcut keys to access hidden commands, unless you program Excel to generate and maintain the custom environment.

To change menu names, delete menus, change hotkeys, or change the location of the menus, begin by right-clicking the menu bar or a toolbar and selecting Customize from the pop-up menu to open the Customize dialog box. With the Customize dialog box open, you can customize any of the standard menus or create your own menu.

TIP FROM

When creating or customizing menus, be sure to assign unique hotkeys (the underlined letters in the menus) for use with the Alt key. If a hotkey is used more than once on a particular menu or submenu, the first use of the hotkey by the user selects the item closest to the top of the menu or dialog box. The user then must press Enter to execute the command. Pressing the hotkey a second time highlights the next command with that underlined letter, and so on.

The following list describes how to customize existing menus. For details on creating custom menus or menu items, see the next section.

- To delete a menu, right-click the menu and select Delete from the pop-up customizing menu, as shown in Figure 27.20.
- To move the menu item to a new location, drag it to the desired location, as shown in Figure 27.21.

Figure 27.20
Use the context menu to change the menu name or location, or to delete the menu.

TIP FROM

Excel's menu bar works like a toolbar in that you can drag it to a different position on the screen. Keep in mind, however, that most users expect the menu to be at the top of the screen and might find it disconcerting to see it positioned elsewhere.

Left-click and drag menu to its new location

Figure 27.21
You can reposition a
menu or even drag it
onto another menu.

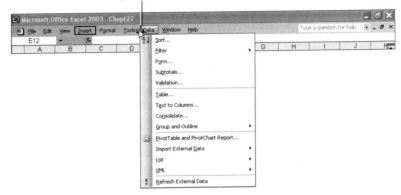

CREATING A CUSTOM MENU

You can create your own menus in Excel to reflect custom macros and commands. For a
workbook with different summary tables, for example, you might create a menu with
options to print the specific tables.

TIP FROM

If you frequently go to specific Internet sites to download or review information, create a
custom menu with submenus hyperlinked to those sites. See the earlier section
"Assigning Hyperlinks" for details on hyperlinking.

To create your own custom menu, open the Customize dialog box, click the Commands
tab, and select New Menu at the bottom of the Categories list. Click the New Menu item
in the Commands list (see Figure 27.22). Drag it to the menu bar or toolbar on which you
want to place the menu. As you drag, Excel displays a button and a black plus sign (+) with
the pointer. Drop the new menu in the desired place, right-click it, and name it with the
Name option in the pop-up customizing menu, as shown in Figure 27.23.

To create the items in your new menu, you can Ctrl+drag existing items from other menus
or toolbars, drag commands from the Commands list on the Commands tab in the
Customize dialog box, or create new items. To create new items, click Macros in the
Categories list on the Commands tab in the Customize dialog box. Then, drag the Custom
Menu Item from the Commands list to the new menu and drop it in place (see Figure 27.24). When the custom menu is in place, assign a macro to it, as described in the earlier section, "Assigning Macros."

27

Left-click and drag menu

Figure 27.22
Create your own menu with the New Menu option in the Commands list.

Figure 27.23
Name the custom menu to reflect the submenu items you plan to place in the menu.

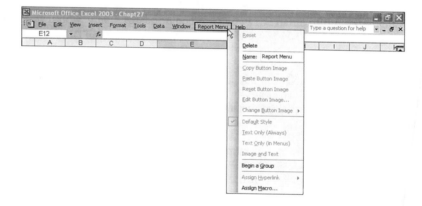

TIP FROM

There's little difference between a custom menu item and a custom toolbar button. Dragging a button onto a menu displays both the image and text; a menu item displays only text (and has no image by default). If you want an image on a menu item, just add a custom button with text instead of a custom menu item.

To remove a custom menu or menu item, open the Customize dialog box and then drag the menu or menu item off the menu bar. You can also move, copy, or remove a menu using the Alt+left-click and drag technique without displaying the Customize dialog box. However, you cannot Alt+left-click and drag an individual menu item using this technique.

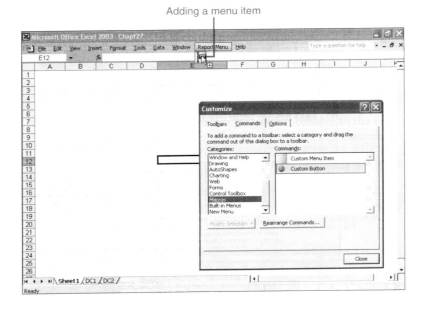

Adding a menu item

Figure 27.24
Figure 27.24
Create the custom menu subitems by dragging a Custom Button Item to the custom menu.

TURNING PERSONALIZED MENUS ON AND OFF

Excel 2000 included a new feature, personalized menus, which allowed the user to see the most recently used commands first and temporarily hid commands that hadn't been used or were used less frequently. Personalized menus were the default menu setup when Excel 2000 was installed. This feature has been continued in Excel 2002, and also 2003 although the command used to turn this feature on and off has changed slightly. To revert the menus to the older Excel 97 style (displaying the entire menu when opened), choose Tools, Customize and click the Options tab in the Customize dialog box. Select the Always Show Full Menus option. The menu and toolbar customizations are saved in the Excel11.xlb file. On Windows XP, the file is located in C:\Documents And Settings\Username\Application Data\Microsoft\Excel.

NOTE

Custom menu items added to the default menu bar (which is actually a toolbar called Worksheet Menu Bar) will always appear. The personalized menu feature never hides them.

TROUBLESHOOTING

RETRIEVING DELETED MENUS

How can I get the menus back after deleting them?

Right-click where the toolbars should be. Choose Customize from the pop-up menu to open the Customize dialog box. Click the Commands tab and select Built-In Menus in the Categories list. Then, select and drag the menu you want from the Commands list to the menu bar.

To get all menus back (and, unfortunately, delete any custom menu items added to the default menu bar), you can reset the Worksheet Menu Bar. Click the Toolbars tab in the Customize dialog box, select Worksheet Menu Bar in the Toolbars list, click the Reset button, and confirm that you want to reset the menu bar.

EXCEL IN PRACTICE

By using Excel's customizing features, you can eliminate, move, or change the Excel menus to make the best use of a shared workbook, or to customize the tools you use most often. In Figure 28.25, the menus and toolbars are in default form. The scrollbars along the side and bottom are visible, and the worksheet tabs are visible as well. Figure 28.26 shows the same worksheet, but with the Excel environment changed. The toolbars are not displayed. Menus have been eliminated except the one in the upper-left corner of the window. The scrollbars and status bar are turned off, and worksheet tabs are hidden.

Figure 27.25
In the default window format, you can see the Standard and Formatting toolbars, the menu bar, the worksheet tabs, and so on.

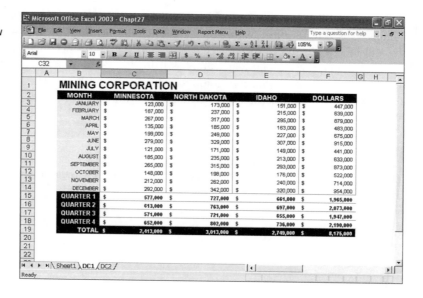

Deleted menu items

Figure 27.26
Customizing the Excel environment can dramatically simplify the window for new or inexperienced users.

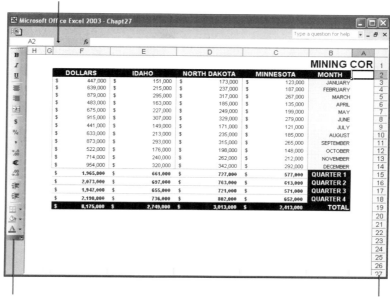

Format toolbar

View current sheet from right to left

27

INTEGRATING EXCEL WITH OTHER APPLICATIONS

28   Building Presentations With Excel   733

29   Using Excel with Access and Other Databases   755

30   Retrieving Data from OLAP Servers   789

31   Recording and Editing a Macro   809

32   Creating Interactive Excel Applications with VBA   837

CHAPTER 28

BUILDING PRESENTATIONS WITH EXCEL

In this chapter

Using Excel with Other Microsoft Office Programs   734

Copying Excel Data to a Word Document   734

Copying Excel Data to a PowerPoint Presentation   736

Copying Word and PowerPoint Data to an Excel Worksheet   744

Combining Word, Excel, and PowerPoint Files with Hyperlinks   746

USING EXCEL WITH OTHER MICROSOFT OFFICE PROGRAMS

Interoperability is probably the main reason that users purchase a suite of products rather than buying word-processing programs, spreadsheet software, and presentation products individually. The pricing of suite software is generally attractive, but the capability to share content between applications easily, with predictable results, is a powerful incentive.

Office 2003's focus on Web-enabled collaboration improves upon previous versions' collaborative tools. Microsoft's vision for the workplace requires that everyone's efforts be shared, and toward that end, HTML becomes the common file format among applications. The result? Through the Clipboard and Insert menu, you can insert as much or as little as you like of one application's content into another application's file quickly and easily, retaining as much or as little as you like of the source application's formatting.

COPYING EXCEL DATA TO A WORD DOCUMENT

You can add Excel content to a Word document to save time and effort in reentering existing text and/or numbers, and to ensure consistency between files. If your Word document discusses numbers already entered into an Excel worksheet, don't create a Word table and reenter the numbers—copy them from Excel and paste them into the Word document. The result is an instant table, containing the numbers as they appeared in Excel.

Using Excel for tables that contain numeric data also gives you access to Excel's tools for calculation and numeric formatting, which you don't have to the same extent in Word. Therefore, you should try to create, format, and add formulas to the table in Excel—before you copy the table into a Word document.

Figure 28.1 shows the Word and Excel application windows tiled, with a selection in Excel pasted into a Word document as an Excel Object by using Paste Special.

TIP FROM

> If you can't see the table's gridlines, choose Table, Show Gridlines in Word. Nonprinting gridlines such as those in Excel will appear.

If you create charts in Excel, you can also copy those charts to a Word document (for instance, to support data presented in a written proposal). Excel provides extensive charting capabilities, whereas Word provides only limited chart features through the use of Microsoft Graph.

You can add Excel content to a Word document in one of two ways:

- Copy the Excel source content (such as a range of cells or a chart) to the Clipboard, and paste it into the Word document.
- Insert an Excel workbook in its entirety or select an individual worksheet to insert.

Figure 28.1
The chart and data on the Excel worksheet was pasted into Word using Paste Special and pasting as a Microsoft Excel Worksheet Object.

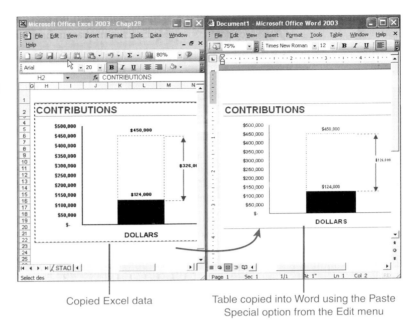

Copied Excel data

Table copied into Word using the Paste Special option from the Edit menu

PASTING EXCEL DATA AS A WORD TABLE

One of the simplest ways to take Excel content and place it in a Word document is to use the Clipboard.

To paste Excel data into a Word document, follow these steps:

1. In an Excel worksheet, select the cell or range you want to copy.
2. Choose Edit, Copy, or press Ctrl+C.
3. Switch to Word, and click in the document to position the insertion point where you want to place the Excel data.
4. In Word, choose Edit, Paste, or press Ctrl+V.

The Excel content appears as a table, in Arial, 10-point text (or whatever default font you have set in Excel).

TIP FROM

If you want to copy all the data in a worksheet, press Ctrl+A in the Excel worksheet to select all the cells. Only the range of cells that contain data will be pasted in Word.

28

FORMATTING EXCEL DATA IN A WORD DOCUMENT

Excel workbooks, worksheets, or cell ranges by default appear in Word in the form of a Word table—a collection of columns and rows, forming cells. Word provides a significant set of tools for adjusting the dimensions of table columns and rows, and visually formatting table cells and their content.

You can use Word's formatting tools to format the inserted Excel content in the Word document:

- **Change the width of columns and height of rows**—Click anywhere inside the table and choose Table, Table Properties. Using the Row and/or Column tabs, adjust the measurement of selected sections of the table. You can also click and drag one of the table's borders to resize a column or a row, or double-click a vertical border to size a column automatically.

- **Apply paragraph formatting**—If you want space above or below the cells' text, select the cells and then choose Format, Paragraph. Enter a point measurement in the Before and/or After boxes in the Spacing section of the Paragraph dialog box. Alternatively, you can vertically align text in a cell or cells by choosing Table, Table Properties and on the Cell tab selecting one of the three Vertical Alignment choices.

- **Format the text**—Select individual cells or columns/rows, and change alignment, fonts, font sizes, and font styles (such as Bold, Italic, and Underline). You can use the Formatting toolbar or the Font dialog box (choose Format, Font).

Unless you don't need or want any formatting of the data in Excel (perhaps the worksheet requires a plain appearance), it might be easier to format the cell content in Excel and use the Paste Special procedure to preserve formatting.

COPYING EXCEL DATA TO A POWERPOINT PRESENTATION

PowerPoint presentations often contain numeric data in the form of tables and charts. Charts are perhaps the more prevalent form in which numeric data is presented—they're highly graphical, and if set up properly, easy to interpret. Because presentations are generally best when they contain more pictures than words, charts are an important component.

PowerPoint presentations can display Excel data as cell blocks (which appear as tables) and as charts. You can build the chart in Excel and then copy it to the presentation slide, or you can use Excel data to build the PowerPoint datasheet, which in turn produces a PowerPoint chart.

Deciding which Excel content to use (cell ranges or an Excel chart) depends on what already exists in Excel—if you have only Excel data and haven't created a chart, you can use the data and create the chart in PowerPoint. However, keep in mind that Excel provides more extensive charting capabilities than PowerPoint. You might prefer to complete the chart in Excel and then transfer it to PowerPoint.

28

USING EXCEL RANGES IN A POWERPOINT SLIDE

Assuming Excel is your primary tool for storing statistical, financial, and list data, it's very likely that the information you want to use in your PowerPoint presentation already exists in an Excel worksheet. Rather than risk a typo or waste time retyping it into a PowerPoint table, why not use the Clipboard and/or Office's OLE tools for placing the Excel data into your PowerPoint slide?

It's a simple procedure to take a range of cells from your Excel worksheet and paste them into a PowerPoint slide. Somewhat more complex methods can be employed to insert the Excel content and at the same time create a link between the worksheet and the slide, enabling you to keep the slide updated when changes are made to the worksheet. The approach you take depends on whether or not you need such a relationship between the source file (Excel worksheet) and the target file (PowerPoint slide).

PASTING EXCEL RANGES INTO A POWERPOINT SLIDE

To paste a range of cells from an Excel worksheet into your PowerPoint slide, follow these steps:

1. In your Excel worksheet, select the contiguous range of cells that you want to use in your PowerPoint slide.
2. Choose Edit, Copy or press Ctrl+C.
3. Switch to or open your PowerPoint presentation, Select the slide and press Ctrl+V or paste from the Edit menu.
4. If the Clipboard pane is displayed, click the icon that represents your Excel content.

Your Excel range appears as a table in your PowerPoint slide, and it can be formatted by moving, resizing the object as a whole, or by adjusting the dimensions of columns and rows using PowerPoint's table tools (which are taken from Word's table tools). To find out more about PowerPoint, check out Que's *Special Edition Using Microsoft PowerPoint 2003*, ISBN 0-7987-2957-1.

LINKING EXCEL DATA TO YOUR POWERPOINT SLIDE

To create a relationship between your Excel source range and the copy of it pasted on a PowerPoint slide, you must link the two files. After the files are linked, moving or renaming either the Excel workbook or the PowerPoint presentation severs the link. You can update and break links later should you need to.

To paste Excel content into your PowerPoint slide and establish a link between the source and target files, follow these steps:

1. In your Excel worksheet, select the contiguous range of cells that you want to use in your PowerPoint slide.
2. Choose Edit, Copy, or press Ctrl+C.

28

3. Open or switch to your PowerPoint presentation, and use Slide view to display the slide into which you want to paste the Excel content.

4. In the PowerPoint window, choose Edit, Paste Special.

5. In the Paste Special dialog box, choose the Paste Link option (see Figure 28.2).

Figure 28.2
Your copied Excel content will now be linked to the PowerPoint presentation, and you can keep the data between source and target in sync as needed.

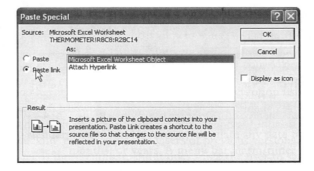

6. Choose Microsoft Excel Worksheet Object from the As box, and click OK.

Your linked Excel content appears in the form of an Excel worksheet object, which looks like a table. It can be moved or resized. To edit the object's content, double-click it. The Excel worksheet from which it came opens, and any edits you perform there are updated in the slide. Make your changes, and then switch back to the PowerPoint slide (use the taskbar or Alt+Tab) and you'll see the changes reflected there.

TIP FROM

Each time you open the target presentation in the future, you can choose whether or not to update the link—if changes have been made to the source Excel content, you can opt to have them reflected in the presentation. If you choose not to, you can always update them later by choosing Edit, Links and selecting the Update Now button.

Excel content can also be embedded in your PowerPoint slide, which will give you not only the existing Excel content, but when the Excel object is active, the tools of Excel as well, right within your PowerPoint window.

PASTING A PIVOTTABLE INTO POWERPOINT

When tables created in Excel have to be presented in a PowerPoint presentation, they can often create problems. There are many workarounds to these problems using the Paste Special option. Take, for example, PivotTables; if you copy a PivotTable to Excel using

28

simple Copy and Paste commands, the data format is changed. To apply a PivotTable maintaining the original format as shown in Figure 28.6, follow these steps:

1. In your Excel worksheet, select the PivotTable range and choose Copy, as shown in Figure 28.3.

Figure 28.3
Copy the PivotTable range.

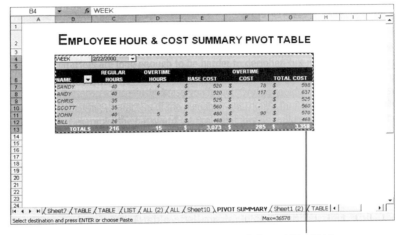

Selected PivotTable range

2. In the PowerPoint window, choose Edit, Paste Special. Choose Microsoft Excel Worksheet Object and click OK.

The resulting table appears as shown in Figure 28.4.

Figure 28.4
Select Paste Special to paste the PivotTable into your slide.

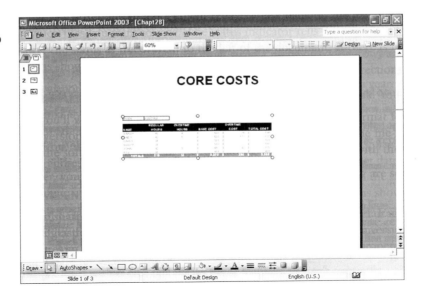

28

Evenly size the object by selecting the object, holding down the Shift key, and dragging the sizing handle as shown in Figure 28.5. The result appears in Figure 28.6.

Figure 28.5
Evenly size the slide by holding down the Shift key and dragging the handles.

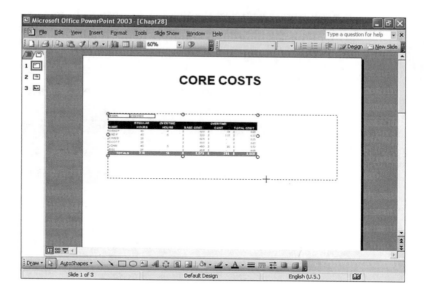

The PivotTable pasted as an Excel object is still fully functional. You can double-click the pasted object, and that will allow you to edit it as a PivotTable just as you would in Excel.

Figure 28.6
The final-sized PivotTable appears intact in the PowerPoint slide.

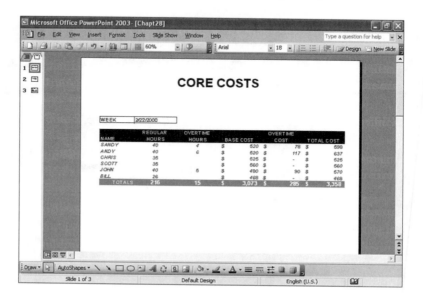

PASTING A CHART OVER IMAGES IN POWERPOINT

All too often, charts are pasted over corporate logos or background images in PowerPoint so that the chart covers those objects instead of allowing those objects to be seen through the chart. If you want to paste a chart into a slide where watermarked or background images appear through the background of the chart, follow these steps:

1. Select the chart in Excel and choose Format, Selected Chart Area.
2. From the Format Chart Area dialog box, select the Patterns tab.
3. Under Border choose None and under Area choose None. Click OK.
4. Now you can copy the chart and paste it into the PowerPoint slide, and then size it.

The template or images in the background will appear through the chart as shown in Figure 28.7. I recommend you repeat the process for any objects in the chart, such as the chart title and particularly the legend, which contains a border and white background by default.

NOTE

> If you want the Excel data that was used to create the chart to remain linked to this copy of the chart, use Paste Special and choose the Paste Link option on the chart. If the chart is linked and not pasted, changes to the Excel data will update the chart in PowerPoint.

Figure 28.7
Give charts invisible borders and backgrounds that allow other images to appear through.

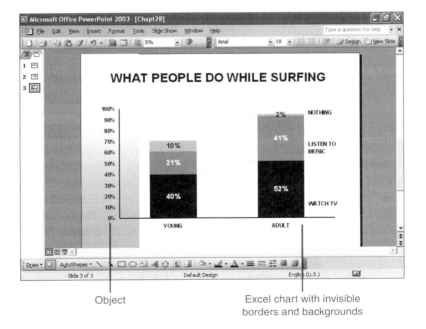

Object

Excel chart with invisible borders and backgrounds

28

PASTING EXCEL IMAGES AND OBJECTS IN POWERPOINT

Presentations using charts or objects are often created and combined in Excel. You can copy both cell data and objects—drawing objects, pictures, charts—by selecting the entire range of cells that encompass both the cell data and the objects, as shown in Figure 28.8. When pasting the data into a PowerPoint slide, choose Edit, Paste Special, Microsoft Excel Worksheet Object.

Figure 28.8
Select the entire range of objects and images.

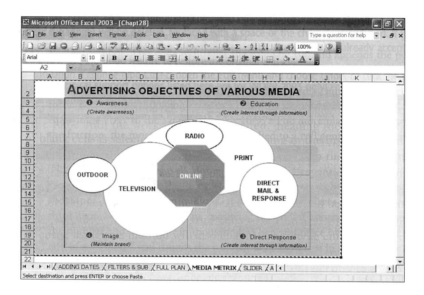

By pasting the presentation in with Paste Special, the integrity of the original Excel information is maintained. The final-sized presentation as it appears in PowerPoint is shown in Figure 28.9.

PASTING EXCEL DATA IN A POWERPOINT DATASHEET

Although not recommended, if you *must* use the Excel data sheet to create data or charts in PowerPoint, here's how. In addition to using existing Excel data directly on a PowerPoint slide, you can use it to fill in your PowerPoint datasheet when creating a PowerPoint chart. To use Excel data in a PowerPoint datasheet, follow these steps:

TIP FROM

> It's good practice not to use the datasheet or create charts with PowerPoint charting capabilities. Create your data or charts in Excel and then paste the information into PowerPoint using Paste or Paste Special.

1. With both the PowerPoint presentation and Excel worksheet open, select the Excel content you want to use (see Figure 28.10).

Figure 28.9
The final-sized Excel object as it appears in PowerPoint.

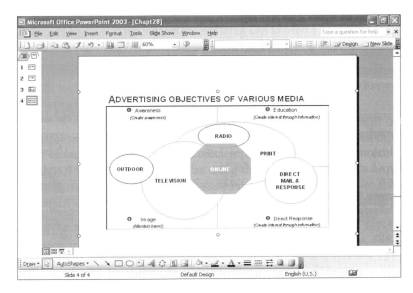

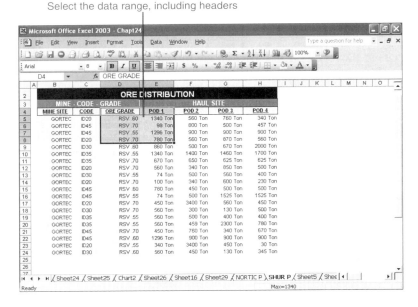

Select the data range, including headers

Figure 28.10
Keep the chart's content in mind when selecting the range of cells to paste into the PowerPoint datasheet.

2. Choose Edit, Copy.

3. Switch to the PowerPoint presentation, and go to the slide in which you'll be using the data.

4. Double-click the chart placeholder to display the datasheet. The datasheet appears with sample data inside it.

5. In the PowerPoint datasheet, click the upper-left gray cell to select all the cells in the datasheet (see Figure 28.11).

Figure 28.11
Selecting all cells before deletion enables you to be certain that all the sample data is removed.

Click here to select all the cells in the datasheet ───

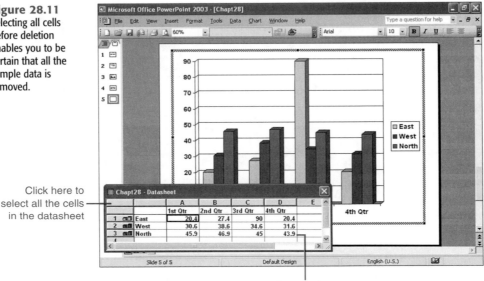

Sample data

6. Press Delete to remove the datasheet's sample data.

7. Click in the first cell in the datasheet (above row 1, in the blank column to the left of column A).

8. Choose Edit, Paste. The Excel content appears in the datasheet, and you'll see a chart form behind the datasheet Continue the chart-creation process in PowerPoint.

NOTE

> You use the first blank column instead of column A in the datasheet because the first blank column contains the chart's legend data. The row above row 1 contains the category axis information. PowerPoint's charting tools will enable you to switch these two groups of data as needed.

COPYING WORD AND POWERPOINT DATA TO AN EXCEL WORKSHEET

Whereas Excel data can be a valuable addition to Word documents and PowerPoint presentations, the reverse also is true—you can realize significant savings of time and effort by using existing Word and PowerPoint content in Excel worksheets. Following are some examples of how you can use Word and PowerPoint content:

- If the data's first appearance is in a PowerPoint datasheet, copy it to an Excel worksheet to avail yourself of Excel's superior formatting and calculation tools. If the data is valuable beyond the scope of the presentation, you'll get much more out of it in Excel.

- If a table containing a valuable list already exists in Word, bring it into Excel for quick sorting and filtering. Although these features are available in Word, their Excel equivalents are much more powerful and easier to use.

- Reuse clip art or drawn objects from PowerPoint or Word in an Excel worksheet. If the graphic images you need already exist in another file, don't reinsert or redraw—paste them!

- Copy an individual PowerPoint slide into your Word document. If you've created a visually pleasing slide that conveys something valuable for your document, don't waste time re-creating it. Using slide content in your Word documents also contributes to an overall visual consistency between your files.

ADDING WORD TEXT TO AN EXCEL WORKSHEET

Word text appears in two formats that you can use in Excel—paragraph text and table text. Obviously, Word tables are a natural for placing in an Excel worksheet—the data is already arranged in cells. Paragraph text is best used when it appears in the form of short phrases or titles. Unless the Excel cells are formatted for text wrapping, a long sentence or paragraph can cause problems fitting into an existing Excel worksheet. If you insert paragraph text as an object into a worksheet, it will appear as a text box, obscuring worksheet cells.

TIP FROM

> Your paragraph text can be parsed (separated) into individual cells through Excel's Data, Text to Columns feature. See also Chapter 17.

You can add Word content, regardless of form, to an Excel worksheet in one of the two following ways:

- **Use the Clipboard**—Copy the Word text and paste it into the Excel worksheet. You can use this method for tables or paragraph text. When pasting, be sure to click in the cell that should contain the text or that will serve as the first cell in the pasted range.

- **Insert a Word object**—In this case, the text is typed into the object after it's inserted (see Figure 28.12). It is placed in a floating object window, which, when active, causes Word's tools to take over the Excel toolbars and menus.

SORTING AND FILTERING TABLE DATA

One of the primary reasons for bringing Word table data into an Excel worksheet is to avail yourself of Excel's sorting and filtering tools. Although you can perform simple sorts in Word, Excel's sorting tools are faster and easier to use, and provide additional sort options.

28

Figure 28.12
Choose Insert, Object,
Microsoft Word
Document. Type the
text into the Word
window that opens
on the worksheet.

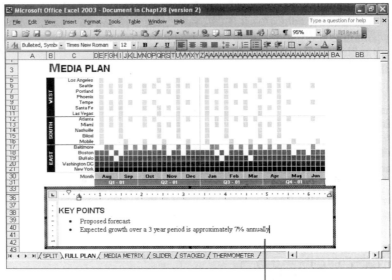

Word window on top of worksheet

Sorting and filtering commands are found in the Data menu in Excel. Sorting can be performed on up to three fields, and filtering can be performed on as many fields as you desire.

TIP FROM

If you still need to use the table data in a Word environment, paste it back into the Word document after you've sorted and/or filtered it in Excel.

→ For more information on sorting and filtering Excel lists, **see** "Sorting a List," **p. 413** and "Filtering a List," **p. 416**

COMBINING WORD, EXCEL, AND POWERPOINT FILES WITH HYPERLINKS

A powerful way to use Office 2003 applications together is to use hyperlinks. A *hyperlink* is a selection of text or a graphic image that is associated with another file, a Web page on the Internet, or your company's intranet. You can link Word, PowerPoint, and Excel files quickly and easily with hyperlinks, making it possible to open a workbook from within a Word document, a Word document or Excel workbook from within a PowerPoint presentation, or a PowerPoint presentation from within a Word document or an Excel workbook. There is no limit to the number of hyperlinks you can insert into a single file, nor is there a limit to the relationships that hyperlinks can create—for example, a hyperlink in a Word document can point to a presentation that contains an Excel chart, thus combining two applications in a single link.

Following are some ideas for using hyperlinks with Office XP:

- **Access supporting data**—Create a hyperlink in a PowerPoint presentation that opens a workbook containing the data that a PowerPoint chart reflects. If someone asks to see the supporting data, you can get to it quickly, but you haven't wasted space on the slide displaying the data.

- **Refer to related documents**—If you're sending a memo that refers to an Excel list (database), include a link to that workbook. This is more efficient for the memo recipients than merely telling them where the database is stored. If the hyperlinked workbook is not in a location available to the recipients of the memo, the hyperlink won't work.

- **Display a chart on command**—What if you don't want to waste space on the worksheet with a chart or have a sheet within the workbook used for the chart? Copy the chart data to another workbook, create a chart from it, and then create a hyperlink in the original workbook that points to the chart. If the chart is of interest, it's accessible, but it's not taking up valuable space. You can also create hyperlinks in Word, Excel, or PowerPoint that link to Outlook items such as contact cards, email addresses, and calendar entries.

CREATING A HYPERLINK

Hyperlinks can be represented by text or graphics. The procedure you use to create hyperlinks is the same for Word, Excel, and PowerPoint.

To create a hyperlink in Word, Excel, or PowerPoint, follow these steps:

1. In the open file, select a single word, short phrase, or a graphic object that you want to use as a hyperlink.

2. Choose Insert, Hyperlink or right-click the selection and choose Hyperlink from the shortcut menu.

3. In the Insert Hyperlink dialog box, enter or select a folder and filename (or Web page name) for the file the hyperlink should point to (see Figure 28.13).

Figure 28.13
It's a good idea to browse for the file if you're not absolutely sure of the path and filename.

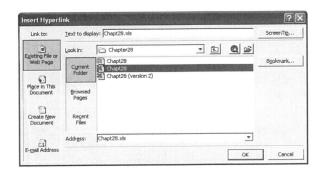

4. If you don't know the exact folder path to the file or the full filename, choose the Browse for file button on the right.

5. After entering or selecting the file for the hyperlink, click OK.

In the file that contains the hyperlink, test it by pointing to it with the mouse—the mouse pointer should turn into a pointing hand (see Figure 28.14). The file referenced in the link appears in a ScreenTip beside the pointing hand. Click the hyperlink to verify that the link points to the appropriate file.

Figure 28.14
When you see the pointing hand, click once to go to the hyperlinked location.

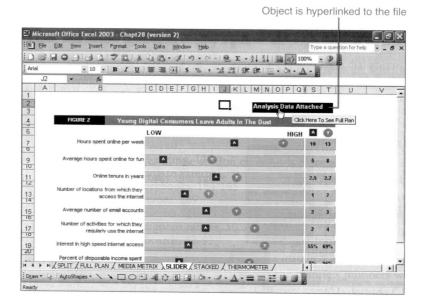

Object is hyperlinked to the file

In the destination file (the file that the hyperlink jumps to), you might choose to include another hyperlink that returns the reader to the previous file (the source file containing the first hyperlink). Use the same procedure detailed previously to add the second hyperlink, and then reference the original file in step 3. You also could instruct readers to click the Back button in the Web toolbar (if it appears onscreen) to return to the previous file.

CAUTION

If others within your organization will use the file containing hyperlinks, be sure that the files the hyperlinks point to are available to those users. The hyperlinked files should be on network drives to which everyone has access. If the hyperlink is for your own use, the linked files can reside anywhere you have access to.

If you want a different ScreenTip (other than the filename) to appear onscreen when you point to a hyperlink, choose the ScreenTip button in the Insert Hyperlink dialog box. Type the ScreenTip text in the resulting dialog box, and click OK.

TIP

> If you want the person reviewing the file to be able to easily email you with comments or questions, add a hyperlink that points to an email address. When the link is clicked, a new message window will open, automatically addressed to the address you specify. Choose the E-Mail Address button on the left side of the Insert Hyperlink dialog box and supply all requested information.

USING HYPERLINKS TO ACCESS A RANGE OF CELLS

You also can use hyperlinks to navigate within an open Excel workbook. Working similarly to named ranges, hyperlinks can be established in a worksheet, pointing to other cells within the workbook. This quick navigation/access method eliminates the need to create names for the ranges, and makes it possible to create the look and feel of a Web page within the workbook.

To create a hyperlink to access a specific range of cells, follow these steps:

1. In the open workbook, click the cell or graphic image that will serve as the hyperlink.
2. Choose Insert, Hyperlink (or right-click the selection and choose Hyperlink from the shortcut menu); and then choose the Place in This Document button on the left side of the dialog box.
3. Type the cell address. It can be a single cell or a range of cells (see Figure 28.15). You also can select a named range from the Defined Names list.
4. Choose the ScreenTip button, type the pop-up text that will appear when pointing to the link (see Figure 28.16), and click OK.
5. In the list box, select the worksheet that contains the specified cell or range.
6. Click OK.

TIP FROM

> You can nest links by creating a hyperlink in Word or PowerPoint that points to an Excel workbook that contains its own hyperlinks to important locations within its own worksheets.

UPDATING HYPERLINKS

Over time, hyperlinks can become invalid—perhaps the file to which the hyperlink points has been moved or deleted, or the information considered important enough to link to is no longer of interest. For a multitude of reasons, you'll want to update the hyperlinks.

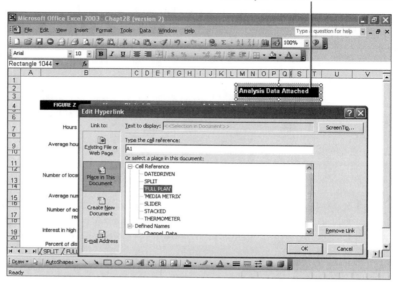

Figure 28.15
Create hyperlinks to cells within the workbook.

This object will link to the destination

Figure 28.16
Type the name of the cell range or a description of the information the hyperlink points to.

To edit the hyperlink, follow these steps:

1. Right-click the hyperlink you want to edit.

2. From the shortcut menu, choose Edit Hyperlink (see Figure 28.17).

3. The Edit Hyperlink dialog box opens, which looks very similar to the Insert Hyperlink dialog box. Click the appropriate Link To button (on the left side of the dialog box) to choose the type of link.

4. Make the desired changes to the link, and click OK.

DELETING HYPERLINKS

If a hyperlink is no longer of use, you can delete it. Deleting a hyperlink doesn't delete the text or graphic that currently serves as a hyperlink—deleting the link merely eliminates the text or graphic's role as a pointer to another file or range of cells within the workbook.

28

Figure 28.17
Select the Edit Hyperlink option to edit the hyperlinks.

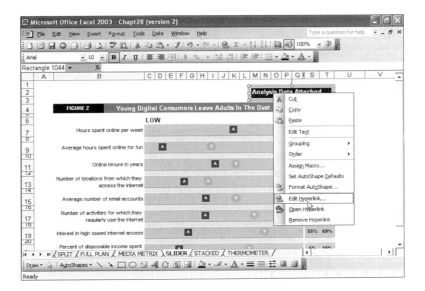

To delete the hyperlink, follow these steps:

1. Right-click the hyperlink text or graphic.
2. From the shortcut menu, choose Hyperlink, Remove Hyperlink.

TIP FROM

> You can delete a hyperlink from within the Edit Hyperlink dialog box by clicking the Remove Link button.

TROUBLESHOOTING

UPDATING LINKS BETWEEN FILES

The Excel data that I linked to a PowerPoint slide seems to be broken. Whenever I change the data in Excel, these edits aren't reflected in PowerPoint. How do I fix the link?

Switch to the application containing the link (PowerPoint, in this example), and choose Edit, Links. Then, select the link you want to reconnect from the Links list box and choose the Change Source button. In the Change Source dialog box, select the file you want the linked object to connect to (select another folder from the Look In list, if necessary). Choose the Open button. The file you chose appears in the Links dialog box; choose Close to close the dialog box. The updated link information appears in the application.

EDITING AN EXISTING HYPERLINK

I need to make changes to an existing hyperlink, but when I try to click the hyperlink to select it, I jump to the file referenced in the hyperlink. How do I edit the hyperlink?

Right-click the hyperlink. Then, choose Edit Hyperlink from the shortcut menu. Make the desired changes in the dialog box, and then choose OK.

If you just want to make simple formatting changes to the hyperlink (such as using a different font or adding italic), right-click the hyperlink and choose Edit Hyperlink; then either edit the address in the Address bar or change the name of the hyperlink by typing a name in the Text To Display bar. Then, use the menus or toolbars to format the text, as usual. Click outside the hyperlink to deselect it.

FIXING INVALID HYPERLINKS

The hyperlink I created in an Excel workbook no longer works. How do I fix this?

Most likely, the file referenced in the hyperlink was moved or deleted, or you moved the Excel file itself. To update the hyperlink, right-click the hyperlink and choose Edit Hyperlink. Click the appropriate Link To button, edit the location of the destination file, and choose OK.

If this doesn't seem to be the source of the problem, and the hyperlink references files on a network, be sure you have proper access to those files.

EXCEL IN PRACTICE

Creating consistency between data sources as well as visual consistency is essential to the effective distribution and presentation of data in any business. Providing a similar look and feel to your documents, worksheets, and presentations helps your audience see the connection between them. In addition, ensuring that the source of the data is updated in a timely fashion (and updated to all relevant files) helps the audience feel confident in the data's accuracy and reliability.

Figure 28.18 shows a PowerPoint presentation with an Invisible chart border and background to allow images or watermarks in the background to peer through. This makes charts appear seamless in the slide.

Figure 28.18
Create invisible bor-
ders and back-
grounds on Excel
charts to create a
seamless presentation
in PowerPoint.

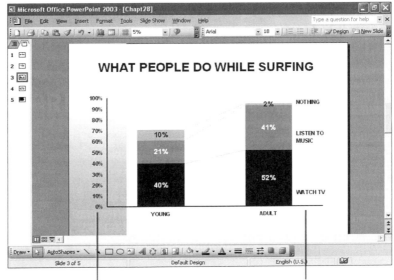

Object peers through chart

No borders or background
on the Excel chart

CHAPTER 29

USING EXCEL WITH ACCESS AND OTHER DATABASES

by Bill Bruns

In this chapter

Using Excel with Database Software   756

Using Access to Complement Excel   757

Exporting Excel Data into Other Databases   766

Retrieving Data from Access and Other Relational Databases   767

Importing Data from Text Files   783

USING EXCEL WITH DATABASE SOFTWARE

Excel is no slouch at handling data. With its sophisticated list-handling capabilities (which you can read more about in Part IV, "Using Excel's Analysis Tools"), you can easily sort or filter data to find key values, as well as create subtotals and custom formulas to see the big picture.

However, if you want a more comprehensive and multifaceted way to keep track of your data, you might be interested in looking at a relational database. Relational databases allow you to link more than one table (such as a worksheet in Excel) and manage separate lists when querying and reporting data. Excel would have much more difficulty accomplishing this.

The obvious choice for Excel users is to use Microsoft's desktop database, Microsoft Access. If you have Microsoft Office 2003 Professional or Professional Enterprise edition, you already have Microsoft Access. Other editions of Microsoft Office 2003 will not come with Access. Excel and Access have been designed specifically to work together, so Access is the natural choice for Excel users.

This chapter discusses when you should make the switch from Excel to Access, and how to move your data seamlessly between the two programs. I also include some pointers on how to move data from Excel into databases other than Access, should you prefer to go that route. Finally, you'll learn how to retrieve financial data directly from the World Wide Web.

NOTE

> Although this chapter covers specific techniques for getting Excel data into Access, it doesn't cover how Access itself works or how Access databases should be designed. If you need to learn more about Access, see Que's *Special Edition Using Microsoft Access 2003* (ISBN 0-7897-2952-0).

Although you might keep most of your data in Excel, if you work in a business, it's a sure bet most of the business's data is stored in a corporate database somewhere. If you work in a large company, that data may be stored on a mainframe system running a database such as IBM's DB2, a Linux, Unix, or NetWare system running Oracle Corporation's Oracle, or a Windows-based server with Microsoft's own server database, Microsoft SQL Server. If you are really lucky, your company has recently purchased an Enterprise Resource Planning System (ERP), which purports to be the soup-to-nuts data storage and retrieval solution for your company.

This chapter also shows you how to access the entire world of data outside your PC without leaving Excel's familiar environment. As you'll see, Excel can be used to get at the data you need, wherever it might be stored.

If you work with large amounts of data, you'll also want to check out the next chapter to learn how to use Excel 2003's analytical data processing features. They'll be a big help on tough data-analysis jobs.

USING ACCESS TO COMPLEMENT EXCEL

Access and Excel do a good job of filling in each other's rough spots. If you need to work with long lists of data, for example, you'll appreciate the built-in Access tools that help make sure your information is entered without mistakes.

The following sections cover how to decide when to stay with Excel and when to use Access. You'll also learn how to move your Excel data over to Access painlessly, and how to create Access forms and reports that work with Excel data.

WHEN TO USE ACCESS INSTEAD OF EXCEL

The single biggest difference between Access and Excel is that Access is a relational database, whereas Excel's database features are nonrelational ("flat-file"). To put that in practical terms, let's say you're a sales manager and have built up a list of customer contacts over the years. The list contains information about each contact's name, address, credit limit, and so on. When a contact places an order, you naturally have to track the associated invoice number; you place it in a spare column at the end of your list. So far, so good.

However, because customers were so pleased with their purchases (and because you were doing such a fine job staying on top of each account!), they place a few more orders.

At this point, Excel puts you in a bind. You must keep all the invoice numbers around for historical order tracking, yet you need to track new orders as they occur. One solution is to keep adding new columns to the table as needed, as shown in Figure 29.1.

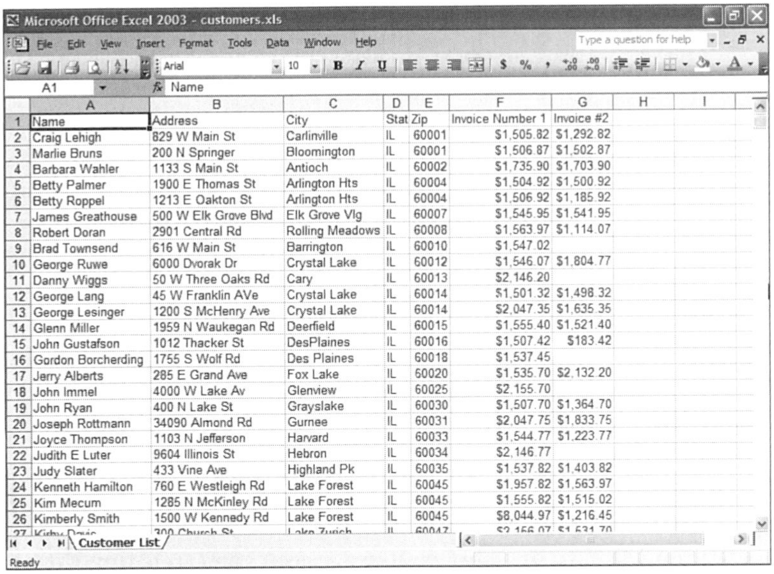

	A	B	C	D	E	F	G
1	Name	Address	City	Stat	Zip	Invoice Number 1	Invoice #2
2	Craig Lehigh	829 W Main St	Carlinville	IL	60001	$1,505.82	$1,292.82
3	Marlie Bruns	200 N Springer	Bloomington	IL	60001	$1,506.87	$1,502.87
4	Barbara Wahler	1133 S Main St	Antioch	IL	60002	$1,735.90	$1,703.90
5	Betty Palmer	1900 E Thomas St	Arlington Hts	IL	60004	$1,504.92	$1,500.92
6	Betty Roppel	1213 E Oakton St	Arlington Hts	IL	60004	$1,506.92	$1,185.92
7	James Greathouse	500 W Elk Grove Blvd	Elk Grove Vlg	IL	60007	$1,545.95	$1,541.95
8	Robert Doran	2901 Central Rd	Rolling Meadows	IL	60008	$1,563.97	$1,114.07
9	Brad Townsend	616 W Main St	Barrington	IL	60010	$1,547.02	
10	George Ruwe	6000 Dvorak Dr	Crystal Lake	IL	60012	$1,546.07	$1,804.77
11	Danny Wiggs	50 W Three Oaks Rd	Cary	IL	60013	$2,146.20	
12	George Lang	45 W Franklin AVe	Crystal Lake	IL	60014	$1,501.32	$1,498.32
13	George Lesinger	1200 S McHenry Ave	Crystal Lake	IL	60014	$2,047.35	$1,635.35
14	Glenn Miller	1959 N Waukegan Rd	Deerfield	IL	60015	$1,555.40	$1,521.40
15	John Gustafson	1012 Thacker St	DesPlaines	IL	60016	$1,507.42	$183.42
16	Gordon Borcherding	1755 S Wolf Rd	Des Plaines	IL	60018	$1,537.45	
17	Jerry Alberts	285 E Grand Ave	Fox Lake	IL	60020	$1,535.70	$2,132.20
18	John Immel	4000 W Lake Av	Glenview	IL	60025	$2,155.70	
19	John Ryan	400 N Lake St	Grayslake	IL	60030	$1,507.70	$1,364.70
20	Joseph Rottmann	34090 Almond Rd	Gurnee	IL	60031	$2,047.75	$1,833.75
21	Joyce Thompson	1103 N Jefferson	Harvard	IL	60033	$1,544.77	$1,223.77
22	Judith E Luter	9604 Illinois St	Hebron	IL	60034	$2,146.77	
23	Judy Slater	433 Vine Ave	Highland Pk	IL	60035	$1,537.82	$1,403.82
24	Kenneth Hamilton	760 E Westleigh Rd	Lake Forest	IL	60045	$1,957.82	$1,563.97
25	Kim Mecum	1285 N McKinley Rd	Lake Forest	IL	60045	$1,555.82	$1,515.02
26	Kimberly Smith	1500 W Kennedy Rd	Lake Forest	IL	60045	$8,044.97	$1,216.45

Figure 29.1
Bad design alert! Mixing two types of information in the same table (in this case, customer information and invoice information) is a recipe for trouble and a sure sign a relational database is needed.

Seeing the same column repeated over and over to track the same type of information (such as the Invoice Number columns in this example) is a dead giveaway that your needs exceed Excel's capability to track your data.

TIP FROM

Bill

> Do you find yourself tacking extra data columns onto the ends of lists because you need to track more information than really fits? Are you continually adding the same information (such as the client's information on each new order)? These are sure signs that you should be switching to a relational database.

The real limitation is the fact that a spreadsheet is a two-dimensional surface. After you've used the horizontal dimension (the columns) to label your fields, only the vertical dimension (the rows) is left for data. As a result, lists can effectively manage only one type of data—customer information, order information, or product information, for example, but not two or more at once.

You could have customer information in a list on one worksheet and put invoice information in a second list on a separate worksheet. That strategy keeps the information grouped properly, but it introduces a new problem: You must duplicate some customer information in the second list (such as the customer ID number) so you'll know which customers are connected with which invoices. Keeping duplicated information synchronized between the two lists is going to be a painful job. If you add a third list (for example, invoice line items) and then must keep invoice numbers in two places, you'll wish you had never heard of Excel.

TIP FROM

Bill

> Don't mix more than one kind of information in a list at once. Keep the structure of your lists focused on a single type of data, and you'll avoid big growth problems later.

Tracking multiple kinds (or dimensions) of data is just what a *relational database* does. The name "relational" comes from the fact that tables in a database often contain some duplicated data (such as customer IDs, which are stored both in a customer table and in an invoices table). This information is stored twice so the database knows which records in one table are "related" to which records in the other table.

Relational databases can track hundreds of these relationships at once and have sophisticated ways of guaranteeing that if information is updated in one place, all related information is updated as well.

Needing to store multiple types of (still related) information at once is the major reason a database like Access should be used rather than Excel, but there are other reasons as well:

■ **You must have multiple people accessing and updating the same information at once**—If you require more than one person to enter data at once (for example, a group of data-entry clerks entering data from a stack of paper invoices), you'll want to use Access. Excel has some simple facilities for tracking multiple users working on the same worksheet, but Access is built from the ground up for this job.

- **You would like to use your own data-entry forms to get more flexibility in how you enter data (as well as use more professional-looking forms)**—Unlike the "one size fits all" Excel data-entry form, Access provides a graphical development environment for building completely customizable forms. These forms can contain pictures and other graphic elements to look professional and simplify the data-entry process and can include information from more than one table at the same time on the same form.

- **You want to be able to automate forms to provide additional information from a single entry**—Access can automate the entry of information in a form (without VBA). For example, picking a client ID number from a drop-down list in an Access form can automatically fill in the rest of that client's info (such as the address and phone number) in other parts of the form. Performing a comparable action in Excel would require programming with VBA.

- **You need to store more than 65,536 records (Excel's limit)**—Access can store much larger data sets than Excel can, while still doing so very quickly. Excel worksheets can have up to 65,536 rows of data, but Access databases can have an unlimited number of rows, as long as the total database doesn't get larger than 2GB (Access 97 databases can't be larger than 1GB). Access also can build special database structures called *indexes* that make searching through a few hundred thousand rows a quick operation, and Access databases of this size are common.

- **You must produce professional reports presenting and summarizing your data**—If you need professionally formatted reports for summarizing and presenting data, Access has much better tools for the job than Excel. Excel has terrific formatting capabilities for one-of-a-kind printouts but has trouble with multiple pages.

  Access also separates the format of a report from its data—you can use the same data to produce many different kinds of reports. In Excel, you would have to copy the data to a new sheet or link from the new sheet back to the original each time to get the same result.

When you reach the point where it's necessary to move some of your Excel data over to Access, the following section shows how to do it.

SENDING EXCEL DATA TO ACCESS FOR FURTHER ANALYSIS

Several methods for transferring Excel data into Access are available. As you might expect, the tried-and-true copy-and-paste technique works fine (even better than in previous versions, in fact). You also can choose to use the Import Spreadsheet Wizard in Access if you want more control over the resulting Access database, or you can leave your data in Excel and just link to it from Access by using the Link Spreadsheet Wizard.

29

COPYING DATA USING COPY AND PASTE

As you might expect, the simplest way to copy data from Excel to Access is by using the Clipboard and a simple copy and paste.

Access understands Excel's row-and-column format and can automatically turn Excel data into a new table when the data is pasted into Access. For a simple transfer of an Excel list into Access, select the entire list, including the column headings; then copy the data to the Office Clipboard by choosing Edit, Copy or pressing Ctrl+C. Column headings will become the names of the fields in the new table.

TIP FROM

Bill

> If you have a long list of data items, let Excel select the list for you. Place the cell pointer somewhere in your list and press Ctrl+Shift+* (asterisk) or choose Edit, Go To, click the Special button, select the Current Region option, and click OK. Excel will highlight the contiguous group of cells containing the active cell (out to the first column and row of blank cells found).

Now start Microsoft Access. Choose Blank Database from the task pane, type a filename for the new database, and choose Create.

The main database management window opens for the new database. Choose Edit, Paste or press Ctrl+V to paste in the data. Access then will ask whether the first row of your data contains column headings. If you selected column headings in Excel (a smart thing to do), choose Yes. You'll then see Access create a new table containing the pasted data. The table will have the same name as the name of the Excel worksheet you have open.

NOTE

> Copied columns that contain formulas are converted to values when pasted into Access.

What you've done here is a straight copy of Excel data into Access. The data isn't linked in any way, and the two files (the Excel file and the Access file) are completely independent. Sometimes (if you'll send the file to someone else, for example), independence is exactly what you want. If not, you can link the data from one program to the other. See the later section "Linking Data Using the Link Spreadsheet Wizard."

 If the source list is AutoFiltered, you might be surprised to see that the new Access table contains the entire list rather than the filtered version. For details on solving this problem, see "Copying Visible Cells Only" in the "Troubleshooting" section at the end of this chapter.

TIP FROM

Bill

> If you're pasting a whole Excel list into Access, paste it into the main database window, not in a blank database table window. You'll preserve the column names that way.

If you already have a table created and are pasting more rows into it, be sure to select the entire final row in Access (by clicking on the asterisk next to the bottom row) before you paste the data. The pasted data will all appear jammed together in one field if you don't select the whole row.

When pasting additional rows into an existing table, be sure not to select the column labels (fields) in Excel when copying.

IMPORTING/EXPORTING EXCEL DATA WITH THE IMPORT SPREADSHEET WIZARD

If you plan to move a large set of Excel rows permanently into Access, you're better off using the Import Spreadsheet Wizard in Access instead of a copy-and-paste operation. This technique takes a little more work but enables you to do more, such as create indexes and a primary key for your new table, and thus produce a better-designed Access database.

On the other hand, if you need to keep the data up to date in Excel and merely use Access for its querying and reporting capabilities, linking the Excel list to an Access database might be a better plan. See the later section "Linking Data Using the Link Spreadsheet Wizard" for details.

To start the Import Spreadsheet Wizard, start Access and create (or open) a database file. Then choose File, Get External Data, Import to open the Import dialog box. Select Microsoft Excel in the Files of Type drop-down list, and choose the Excel workbook you want to import. Then, click Import.

1. The Import Spreadsheet Wizard opens and asks which worksheet or named range you would like to import. (The wizard can import only one of either at a time.) A preview of the data appears in the lower half of the dialog box, which makes it easier to choose the data you want to import (see Figure 29.2). If the workbook doesn't contain additional sheets or named ranges, this step may be skipped. Specify the worksheet or range you want to import, choose Next to continue.

TIP FROM

Bill

Creating a named range for the list in Excel makes this first step much easier, especially if the worksheet contains more than just the list (such as titles or queried data).

2. Step 2 of the wizard asks whether the first row of data you're importing contains column names or whether all the rows are data (see Figure 29.3). Check First Row Contains Column Headings, if appropriate, and choose Next.

   If the first row contains data that can't be used as field names, Access presents a warning message. Click OK; the wizard will make up valid field names, which you can review and edit later in the wizard as needed.

Figure 29.2
The Import Spreadsheet Wizard can import only one worksheet or range at a time. Choose which one you want to import in the first step of the wizard.

Figure 29.3
Look in the data preview area to double-check whether the data has column headings. In this example, the data does have column headings.

3. The wizard next asks whether Access should put your data into a new table by itself—you specify the name later—or add the data to an existing table. If you choose to add data to an existing table, you'll skip right to the last step of the wizard.

TIP FROM

Bill

> If you don't have column headings in your data, you won't have the option of putting your imported data into an existing table. Access must know column names to match new data to columns in an existing table.

4. Step 4 of the wizard asks whether you would like to add indexes to particular columns as part of the data-import process. Remember that indexes are special database objects that make searching for data in that column very fast. If your database will be larger than a few hundred rows, you definitely should add an index for each column containing key search information. For example, if you'll probably search for customers based on their customer code, ZIP code, or state, all three of these columns should be indexed.

In this step, you can also rename the field labels and skip certain columns.

To add an index to a column, click anywhere in the column in the wizard dialog box to select the column, and then choose to index the data using the Indexed drop-down list (see Figure 29.4).

Figure 29.4
Adding indexes to your data really speeds up database searches. Add an index to each column in your database you will use in later searches.

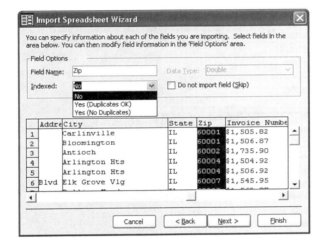

You can choose two kinds of indexes: those that allow the same data to be entered more than once in the column, for which you choose Yes (Duplicates OK), and those that guarantee that each field entered in the column is unique, for which you choose Yes (No Duplicates). If you don't know for certain that all the records in a given column are in fact unique, pick the Yes (Duplicates OK) option. Unique indexes are faster than indexes that allow duplicates, so use unique indexes when you can.

If you make a mistake and choose no duplicates, you will not get an error until the end of the wizard. The table will be imported, but without the creating the desired indexes.

CAUTION

> Keep in mind that, although indexes speed up searches, they can slow record updates performed with operations such as append queries. Index fields only if necessary.

When you're finished creating indexes, choose Next.

The next-to-last step of the wizard asks you to define a *primary key* for the table (see Figure 29.5). A primary key isn't anything mysterious; it's just a special name for a selected column that has no duplicates in its data (and has a unique index defined on it).

If you already have such a column in your data—for example, a customer code column—select it as the primary key. If you don't, let Access add a primary key to the table for you.

Access will create a new column of ascending numbers (the first data row will be number 1, the next number 2, and so on) as a primary key column.

Each table can have either one primary key, a primary and a secondary key, or none. When you've selected one (or asked Access to add one), choose Next.

TIP FROM

Bill

A primary key isn't required for each table, but the primary key (and other columns with no-duplicate indexes) are really important database building blocks. When the database grows and you begin to combine information from multiple tables, having a primary key for each of your tables will become very important.

Figure 29.5
Using a primary key index can speed up your database considerably. If you don't have any columns with all unique entries in them, Access can add a special primary key column to your database.

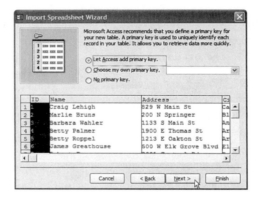

Finally, you'll be asked to name the new table. Access defaults to the name of the worksheet or named range you selected earlier, but you can type in any name you want. Click Finish, and Access will perform the import operation.

 You might get an error if you select a primary key that contains null (empty) values or if duplicates exist in the key column (in which case no key is applied). See "When Access Can't Create an Index" in the "Troubleshooting" section at the end of this chapter.

LINKING DATA USING THE LINK SPREADSHEET WIZARD

Linking the Access database to the source Excel spreadsheet is a good idea if you want to use the data-entry and reporting capabilities in Access while still keeping the source data in only one place. The easiest way to have Access link its database back to the Excel file is to just open the Excel file in Access. This feature was new in Access 2000. Just choose File, Open (or press Ctrl+O) in Access, select Microsoft Excel in the Files of Type box, and choose Open. Access then launches its Link Spreadsheet Wizard.

NOTE

This method automatically creates a new Access database file and places it in the same folder as the Excel file. If you want to place the link in an existing Access database file, open the file and choose File, Get External Data, Link Tables to open the Link dialog box. Specify Microsoft Excel in the Files of Type box, select the workbook you want to link, and click the Link button or press Enter to open the Link Spreadsheet Wizard. After this point, the steps are the same.

Choose which workbook or named range you would like to link to, as shown in Figure 29.6. Then choose Next to continue. (If you don't have multiple workbooks or named ranges, you won't see this first wizard screen.)

Figure 29.6
If you have multiple worksheets or named ranges in the linked Excel workbook, you'll be asked to choose which worksheet or named range you want to use.

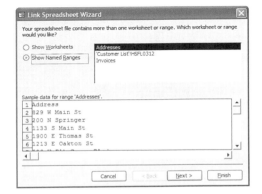

In the next step, Access asks whether the first data row of the workbook contains column headings. The data is conveniently displayed so you can double-check (see Figure 29.7).

Figure 29.7
Open an Excel file in Access, specify whether or not the first data row contains heading names, and click Finish. You've just linked Access to Excel!

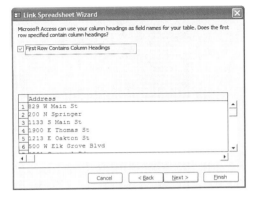

Click Next, give the new table a name, and click Finish. A message box appears, indicating that the database table is linked to the Excel workbook. Click OK. When the wizard closes, you'll see that Access uses a special icon in the database window to indicate that the table has a live link back to the Excel file (see Figure 29.8).

Figure 29.8
Access uses a special icon (an arrow pointing to the Excel symbol) to indicate that a table is getting its data directly from an Excel workbook instead of storing the data in Access itself.

Icon indicates linked data

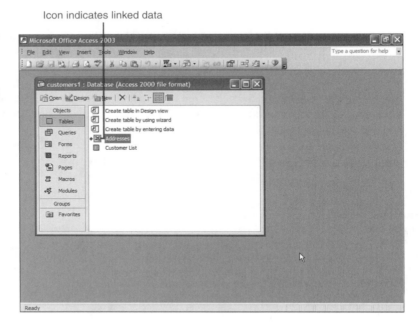

Linked tables are really convenient because you can modify data in either Access or Excel (but not at the same time) and see changes from either program.

Two important drawbacks must be mentioned. First, although you can modify and add records to your Excel data list from Access, you can't delete them! Access displays a message saying that deleting records isn't supported.

Also, you shouldn't have both the Excel table and Access database open at the same time. If you have the linked table open in Access, you won't be able to open it in Excel—you'll get a dialog box saying that Excel can't access the file. As long as Access has the table window open, you won't be able to use Excel to open the workbook. This happens even if you've made your workbook multiuser-capable by choosing Tools, Share Workbook.

These negatives also affect Access forms and reports created from Excel data, because they use linked workbooks behind the scenes to get their data.

EXPORTING EXCEL DATA INTO OTHER DATABASES

Moving Excel data into databases other than Access (for example, dBASE or Corel Corporation's Paradox) isn't as easy, but it isn't rocket science, either.

The way most sure to work the first time is to save your Excel data as a *comma-delimited file* (a file in which each column is separated from the next by a comma). Comma-delimited format is a standard way to pass data around in the database world, and all the major database products support importing comma-delimited data.

You can create a comma-delimited file by choosing File, Save As and then selecting CSV (Comma delimited) (*.csv) in the Save As Type box in the Save As dialog box. CSV is the standard extension for comma-delimited files. Check your database program's help file to find out how to import .csv format files—you may be able to simply open them or you may need to import the data from them, depending on your requirements and how the other program works.

TIP FROM

Bill

> Use comma-delimited files to transfer data to and from databases that don't support cutting and pasting the data. Comma-delimited files are understood by every database program.

RETRIEVING DATA FROM ACCESS AND OTHER RELATIONAL DATABASES

Moving data from Excel into Access is obviously the right move if the data started its life in Excel in the first place. But what if you didn't type the data yourself, or if it's not in an Excel workbook?

This section describes how to get at database data wherever (and however) it might be stored.

WHERE CORPORATE DATA IS FOUND: RELATIONAL DATABASES AND ODBC

In most companies, the most likely place for important data is in corporate databases. These databases might be Access databases, but they're more likely to be server databases, such as Oracle, DB2, or Microsoft SQL Server, running on large servers and managed by professional database administrators.

The standard way Microsoft products access database data is through a database industry standard called *ODBC*, which stands for *Open Database Connectivity*. ODBC allows database clients such as Excel to log into, select, and retrieve data from a database server without having to know how that particular database handles those tasks (and each database program handles them differently).

Microsoft is currently promoting the OLE DB standard at the expense of ODBC. The ODBC standard is mature and entrenched, but OLE DB is better suited than ODBC to handle unusual data types, such as images and sounds. ODBC is so widely used that this might take many years before it is completely replaced by OLE DB, however.

29

Office uses OLE DB internally; in fact, Excel actually accesses ODBC through OLE DB. The database drivers included with Excel are also OLE DB drivers, although they're used in exactly the same way as ODBC drivers.

The key piece of magic that makes ODBC or OLE DB work is a *database driver*, which is a file containing software (usually written by the database vendor) that lives on your computer system and translates standard ODBC or OLE DB programming calls into whatever format the particular database is expecting. With an ODBC database driver, any ODBC-enabled software package on your system can access data from that database without having to know all the gnarly details involved.

Excel is most definitely a database-enabled software package, and so, with the right database drivers installed, a whole new world of data opens up. In fact, Excel includes a set of Microsoft-written drivers for a set of common desktop databases plus two server databases—Microsoft SQL Server and Oracle. You can retrieve data from any of the following databases (drivers are included with Excel:

- Excel files
- Web pages
- XML files
- Text files
- Access databases
- Access projects
- Database queries
- Lotus 1-2-3 files
- Quattro Pro/DOS files
- Microsoft Works
- dBASE files
- Data Interchange Format files

You can also use the Data Connection Wizard to connect to remote data sources, such as a Microsoft SQL Server, OLAP Services, and ODBC DSN, Oracle, or many other OLE DB providers. You access the Database Connection Wizard by clicking the New Source button within the Select Data Source dialog box. To get to the Data Connection Wizard, on the Data menu, point to Import External Data, and then click Import Data. Then open an existing data source or create a new data source connection.

TIP FROM

Bill

Notice that Excel includes an ODBC database driver for itself. This enables you to access Excel data lists from any ODBC-enabled software package, even if the application doesn't know how to read Excel files. You can set up an ODBC link to Excel data in the same way you set up ODBC links to other databases. The next section shows how.

QUERYING THE DATABASE WITH THE QUERY WIZARD

The mechanism by which you retrieve data from a database is called a *database query*. Like other multiple-step tasks, Excel walks you through the process of retrieving database data using a wizard: the Query Wizard.

CHOOSING THE DATA SOURCE

To kick off the querying process, choose Data, Import External Data, New Database Query in Excel. The Choose Data Source dialog box opens (see Figure 29.9).

NOTE

If you don't have the database query components installed on your system, you'll get a message from Excel saying that it can't start Microsoft Query and asking whether you want to install it. If you see this message, go ahead and choose Yes. You'll need the Office 2003 CD.

Figure 29.9
If you're accessing a database for the first time, choose <New Data Source>; otherwise, choose a data source you've already created.

NOTE

This figure does not contain all the database choices. The list depends on the drivers installed on your system as well as which database sources users have already created sources for (using the New Data Source option in the dialog box).

If the data is a dBASE, Excel, or Access database, select one of those types. Otherwise, choose New Data Source, and click OK. This last approach is more general and will handle any kind of database, so the following sections describe how that procedure works.

The Queries tab is discussed later in this chapter; the OLAP options are covered in Chapter 30, "Retrieving Data from OLAP Servers."

CREATING AN ODBC DATA SOURCE DEFINITION

For this example, I'll use the sample Access database called Northwind (it's included with Access) as the data source. When you're first working with Excel's query tools, it's a good idea to use a sample database such as Northwind rather than your live data. Any errors in your procedure won't damage the real data, and you can experiment until you get the hang of the querying process.

Type a name for the data source in step 1 of the Create New Data Source dialog box (see Figure 29.10). The name can be anything that makes sense to you and helps you remember which data tables this data source accesses.

Figure 29.10
Type a data source name and select the right driver from the drop-down list to start defining a new data source.

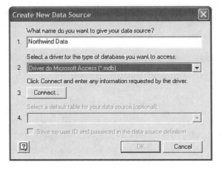

Next, select a database driver to use for this data source. It should be a driver that matches the database you're going to use: the Microsoft Access Driver (*.mdb) for Access databases, the SQL Server driver for Microsoft SQL Server, and so on. If you don't see the driver you need in this list, you must install it (or have your database administrator install it) before you can continue.

Click the Connect button to continue the process.

The next screen you see differs according to the specific database driver you selected. In general, all drivers require you to identify which database file or server you want to access, and many drivers request a database username and password. (Get these from your database administrator.)

To complete the dialog box in this example (ODBC Microsoft Access Setup), you need to tell the driver which database to access. Click Select in the Database group of buttons, and browse to find the Access database (see Figure 29.11).

Figure 29.11
Click Select to indi-cate from which Access database you want to get in formation.

To use the Northwind database, browse to C:\Program Files\Microsoft Office\Office11\ Samples and select the Northwind database (Northwind.mdb). If you don't see the database there, you'll need to install it from the Office CD-ROM, using the Add/Remove Programs option in the Windows Control Panel.

After you select an MDB file and click OK, you should return to the ODBC Microsoft Access Setup dialog box and see the path and filename of the database listed there. That's all you need to do here, so click OK to return to the Create New Data Source dialog box.

The last step is to choose a default table to use when selecting which data to retrieve. You don't have to decide now if you're not sure which table you really want, but if you do know, it will save some time later on. For this example, we'll choose the table Customers.

NOTE

> Not selecting a default table forces a prompt each time you access the source using Microsoft Query. This might be a better setup if you're a novice, because you won't have to go hunting for the command after the default table already exists.

TIP FROM

Bill

> By this point, some databases already will have asked you to log in with your database username and password. You can choose to save the database user ID and password with the data source definition, which saves you from having to type this information each time to use this data source.
>
> However, note that this option compromises database security. Anyone who can access Excel on your system can then retrieve data using that data source as if they were you! In addition, the password itself is easily visible in the data source definition file.
>
> Excel will warn you about these facts before it lets you save your database ID and password with a data source definition.

When you click OK in the Create New Data Source window, you'll be returned to the Choose Data Source window. The Northwind Data source is now listed in the Databases tab, and you're finished creating the new source! The good news is you have to create a data source only once, and then you can use it over and over again.

SELECTING THE RIGHT INFORMATION: CHOOSING COLUMNS

After the data source is created, it should be selected in the list. If not, select it by clicking its name (in this case, click Northwind Data). Then click OK. This launches the actual Query Wizard (see Figure 29.12) if the Use the Query Wizard to Create/Edit Queries check box is enabled in the Choose Data Source dialog box.

When the Query Wizard's Choose Columns dialog box appears, it might look like you have the whole world to choose from. In the left pane is a list of all the tables and columns in the source database. On large databases, this might be a very long list.

29

Figure 29.12
This is the heart of the data-retrieval process. Select which columns from which tables you want to retrieve by clicking selected column names and then clicking the > button to place them into the query.

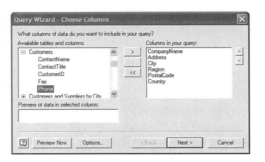

TIP FROM

Bill

You can sort the list alphabetically by clicking the Options button to open the Table Options dialog box, selecting the option List Tables and Columns in Alphabetical Order, and clicking OK.

You also can jump quickly to a particular table by typing the first few letters of its name.

Select the columns you want to retrieve from the data source by clicking their names. You might need to click the plus (+) symbol in front of the selected table first to expand its column list. Then, click the > button to place the selected column in the query. You should select the columns in the order that you want them to appear (left to right) in Excel. If you want to change the order, you can click on a column name you want to move, and then click the up and down arrows on the right side of the Query Wizard dialog box.

If you make a mistake and select something you don't want, just click the column name in the right pane and click the < button to remove it from the query.

TIP FROM

Bill

To copy all the columns in a table at once, highlight the table name itself and click the > button.

If you aren't sure exactly what information is in a particular table column, highlight the column and click the Preview Now button to display a few rows from the column in the Preview of Data in Selected Column box.

You're free to select columns from more than one table, but remember that Excel must be able to find a relationship between the two tables for this kind of database query to work. If Excel can't do that, you'll get the warning shown in Figure 29.13.

NOTE

Queries that involve more than one table use database links called *joins*. Normally, Excel creates joins automatically. If Microsoft Query can't find shared information required to create a join, double-check the query to be sure that it only uses columns from related tables and that these columns contain the same data (a customer ID field in both a customer list table and customer order list table, for example). If a relationship genuinely exists between the two (or more) tables you're using, and Microsoft Query can't detect it, you'll need to manually create the join yourself. See the later section, "Creating Joins."

Figure 29.13
You'll get this warning if Excel can't figure out how to join information from more than one table into a single query. If you really meant to create this query, you must create the join yourself.

When you're finished selecting the columns you want, click Next to continue to the next step in the Query Wizard.

SELECTING THE RIGHT INFORMATION: FILTERING DATA

The next step in the Query Wizard is the Filter Data dialog box. Here you can limit how many rows of data you'll retrieve in the final query. It's easy to pull down 10,000 rows of data from a server database unexpectedly; this is where you fix the problem.

The Query Wizard provides a wide range of conditions you can add to restrict the query. To add a rule that limits how much data is returned (*filtering* the data), click one of the columns in the Column to Filter box, select a condition (or, in database terminology, a *constraint*) from the first box on the Only Include Rows Where section, and select or type a data value in the second box. Microsoft Query looks up all the possible values for that field, so you don't have to type a value if you don't want to. The filtering process here should be familiar if you have filtered Excel database lists.

You can have from zero to three conditions on the query, and they can be combined by AND (in which case, all constraints apply simultaneously) or by OR (in which case, each acts independently of the others). Figure 29.14 shows an example in which records will be filtered to include only those where Region is either Isle of Wight or County Cork. In short, AND will include records where all the conditions are satisfied. If you use OR, then satisfying any single condition results in the record being returned.

When you're finished adding conditions, click Next.

Figure 29.14
You can limit the number of records you retrieve by adding conditions to the query.

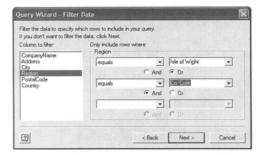

SORTING THE DATA

The next-to-last step is quick. You can choose to sort the rows returned by up to three columns, each of which can be sorted in ascending or descending order. You can sort the data later in Excel, if you prefer, but it saves time to do it now (it might also be faster, because the database server, instead of your PC, will do the sorting). The sort order is saved as part of the query; each time you use the query, your preferred sort will be applied.

To add a sort, select the columns you want to sort, and then choose Ascending or Descending. When you get that step out of the way, click Next.

THE LAST STEP: SAVING THE QUERY FOR REUSE

The query is now complete, and Excel wraps everything up by presenting three final options. You can just return the query's data to Excel (the default option), or send the query to Microsoft Query for further fine-tuning (which I'll discuss shortly). You also can save the data as an OLAP cube (OLAP is explained in Chapter 30).

It's a good idea to save your query at this point by clicking on the Save button in the toolbar and giving it a name. I cover how to run it again, as well as edit it, in the following sections.

After making your selection, click Finish. If you have made the choice to return the query's data to Excel, then Excel will then ask whether you want to put the returned data in the current worksheet (and if so, starting in what cell), in a new worksheet, or directly into a PivotTable (you can create a PivotTable later, if you prefer).

If you choose the Properties button, you'll be able to set various advanced settings on your query, including whether your database password should be saved with the query and how often it should be refreshed. We'll visit this window again in the section "Refreshing Data," later in this chapter.

Make your choice, click OK, and you'll see the data appear like magic!

USING MICROSOFT QUERY

As you might expect, the Query Wizard doesn't have the flexibility to deal with special situations or ones where you want to have complete control. For that, you must use Microsoft Query.

Microsoft Query is a full-fledged database query tool included with Excel that lets you take advantage of all that your database has to offer. It also lets you use SQL (Structured Query Language) to write queries, if you know how to do that. You don't have to use any SQL if you don't want to, though—Microsoft Query has graphical tools that will write SQL for you behind the scenes.

NOTE

> Structured Query Language (SQL, usually pronounced *sequel*) is a specialized computer language developed just for writing database queries. It's based on mathematical set theory and is an extremely powerful way to specify which records you want and which you don't. As you might expect, many books are available on SQL, and database administrators are expected to live and breathe the stuff.
>
> At the same time, basic SQL isn't hard to understand, and you'll get an immediate feel for it by seeing how Microsoft Query writes your SQL query for you.
>
> If you need a more detailed view of SQL, see Que's *Special Edition Using Microsoft SQL Server 7.0*, ISBN 0-7897-1523-6.

You can see (and change) the SQL commands Microsoft Query writes for you by clicking the View SQL button in Microsoft Query.

WHEN TO USE MICROSOFT QUERY

Microsoft Query is a much more powerful interface into a database than the Query Wizard, for the following reasons:

- Although you can retrieve columns from different tables by using the Query Wizard, the process is easier to understand in Microsoft Query because you can see table relationships graphically and preview the data.
- You can add more criteria (and more complex criteria) using Microsoft Query to restrict which rows are returned to Excel.
- With Microsoft Query, you can perform calculations on the query, such as counting or summing the records returned, or retrieving only the largest or smallest values in a column.
- Finally, you can write database queries directly in SQL with Microsoft Query.

The following list describes the circumstances in which you should use Microsoft Query instead of the Query Wizard:

- You want to work with multiple tables.
- You need to create your own joins (table relationships).
- You need to add complex criteria to filter returning records.
- You need to see calculations such as counts or sums.
- You want to write your own database query using SQL.

29

STARTING MICROSOFT QUERY

You start Microsoft Query the same way you start the Query Wizard: Choose Data, Import External Data, New Database Query. Select a data source from the Choose Data Source dialog box (if you want, go back to a database you used before), or create a new query.

Before clicking OK, be sure to deselect the option Use the Query Wizard to Create/Edit Queries. Deselecting this option tells Excel that you want to use Microsoft Query, not the Query Wizard (refer to Figure 29.9). Then click OK, and Microsoft Query will start.

> **NOTE**
>
> Microsoft Query does the work, regardless of how the option Use the Query Wizard to Create/Edit Queries is set. Deselecting this option simply gives you full access to the interface/tools of Microsoft Query. Even if you forget to deselect this option, you can still invoke Microsoft Query by clicking Cancel anywhere in the wizard and answering Yes to the prompt to continue editing the query in Microsoft Query.

CHOOSING WHICH DATABASE TABLES TO USE

If you didn't select a default table when defining the data source, the first thing you're asked when Microsoft Query starts is which tables you want to use in the query.

Notice that, whereas the Query Wizard jumps immediately to selecting columns within a table, Microsoft Query is designed to work with multiple tables from the beginning. It's part of the difference between the Query Wizard and Microsoft Query—Microsoft Query assumes that you want the bigger picture and will be ranging more widely over the database than possible with the Query Wizard.

To select the additional tables you want to access, if the Add Table dialog isn't already open, then click the Add Table(s) button in the middle of the toolbar (the one with the plus sign). The Add Tables dialog box appears. Select the first table you want from the Table list in the dialog box and click the Add button, or just double-click the desired table. Microsoft Query displays a small window in its query pane, listing the name of the table you've just selected, along with the columns in that table (see Figure 29.15).

> **TIP FROM**
>
> *Bill*
>
> This table list can be quite long on a large database system. If you know the table name you want, you can jump right to it by starting to type its name.

Notice that the Add Tables dialog box remains open after you've added the first table. You can close the dialog box, but you can also select more tables to include in the query—and you'll probably want to. Why? Remember that proper database design says that each table should have only one kind of information in it. An Employees table should only have information about the employee that normally doesn't change or accumulate over time. So, if you want to just get a list of employee names and addresses, the base Employees table should have that information.

Figure 29.15
Select the tables you want to use in the Add Tables dialog box.

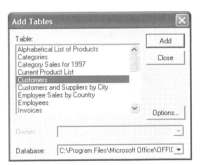

However, if you want to find out which of your customers are handled by which employees, you'll need information from both the Customers and Employees tables. If you're in this kind of situation, select each table you need to include in the query and click Add.

If you accidentally add the wrong table, click the table in the query pane and press Delete.

Choose Close when you're finished adding tables.

> **CAUTION**
>
> Although you can do so, I advise against clicking the Options button and making selections in the Table Options dialog box unless you know what you're doing. The default settings in Table Options really shouldn't be changed. It's easy to get really confused by turning System Tables on, for example—there are hundreds of them in server databases.

CREATING JOINS

To combine information from several tables, you must connect the tables using relationships called *joins*. (If you just need to access information from one table, you can go straight to the next section, because you won't need any joins.)

Microsoft Query connects the tables together using a line between tables. The lines represent joins (see Figure 29.16).

Microsoft Query automatically creates joins between two tables when it notices that one table has a column with the same name as a special index column in another table called a *primary key*. (Microsoft Query marks primary keys in bold.) This is a guess on its part, but it's a pretty safe guess and will be right most of the time.

If Microsoft Query can't find joins between your tables, you'll have to add them yourself. Select a column in one table and drag and drop that column name onto the matching column name in another table (in the database world, this column is called a *foreign key*). You'll see a join line appear.

Column names need not have the same names to participate in a join; they just have to contain the same data. It's good database design to give columns containing the same information the same name, because identical names are a good tip-off that the two columns can be

29

joined together. It's not a sure thing, though; your database administrator might have decided to break the same-name rule for some reason.

Figure 29.16
The lines between columns in each table are called *joins* and are needed to retrieve information from more than one table. Create them by dragging a column name from one table and dropping it onto the same column in another table.

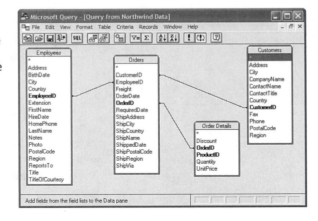

TIP FROM

Bill

> Microsoft Query will warn you if you try to join two columns with different data types. This is a sure sign that you shouldn't be joining those two columns!

You don't need to create more than one join between tables—one is enough. If you accidentally create a join you don't want, double-click the join line to display the Joins dialog box. Correct the join as needed, or select it in the Joins in Query list and click the Remove button.

TIP FROM

Bill

> If you're having a hard time finding the right columns in a big table, you can make the table windows bigger (I always find they start out too small) and drag the table windows around into more convenient places.

SELECTING WHICH TABLE COLUMNS TO USE

Now that you've selected the right tables (and created relationships between them, if you're accessing more than one table), you need to select which actual columns you want to return to Excel.

All you need to do is drag and drop the column names you want into the lower half of the Microsoft Query window (see Figure 29.17). You also can select column names by double-clicking them.

If you want to remove a column from your query, move the mouse pointer over its column name. In the data pane, the pointer will turn into a down arrow if you're in the right area.

Click to select the column, and then press the Delete key. Be careful not to try to get rid of a column in your query by highlighting its name in the table pane and pressing Delete! You'll actually delete the whole table from the query, which will really set you back.

Figure 29.17
Mark the columns you want to retrieve by double-clicking their names. The first few rows of actual data will show up in the lower half of the Microsoft Query window.

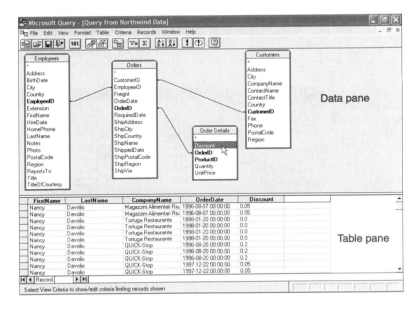

What we're getting in this example is a list of employees, the customers they handled, and the dates those customers placed their orders.

The column order in Microsoft Query is the same column order that will appear in Excel. You can drag and drop added fields to rearrange the column order. Click the field name to select it; then, drag the field name and drop it in the desired position.

If you scroll to the bottom of the list of data and click on the last record, you'll see how many rows will be returned to Excel.

TIP FROM

Bill

You can click anywhere in the sample data and press Ctrl+End to jump to the last record.

LIMITING WHICH INFORMATION IS RETURNED

You can restrict the records returned to Excel by adding *criteria* (various restrictions) to the query. Click the Show/Hide Criteria button (with the eyeglasses and a funnel) to show the criteria grid window.

You add criteria by selecting which field you want to limit in the Criteria Field drop-down list and then adding a value to which you want to limit that field in the Value box under the

Criteria Field. In Figure 29.18, the data returned is limited to records with the value .05 in the Discount field.

TIP FROM

Bill

> If the Criteria Field drop-down list contains too many field names to scroll through comfortably, drag the desired field from the table above and drop it into the Criteria Field box.

Figure 29.18
Specify filter criteria to indicate which records you want returned to Microsoft Excel.

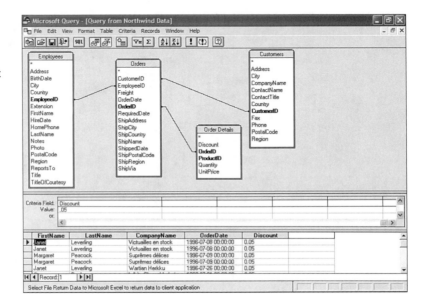

Now you can just type a value or double-click the Value box to display the Edit Criteria dialog box, which presents a long range of conditions you can add, including some very handy conditions such as begins with, contains, and is between (see Figure 29.19). The Values option enables you to pick one of the values from the field without having to type it (which could lead to spelling errors).

Figure 29.19
Double-click the Value edit box to display this handy Edit Criteria dialog box, which simplifies handling complex criteria.

Don't worry about the strange characters—the percent and pound (#) signs—that Microsoft Query might put in the Value box when you use the Edit Criteria dialog box; it's all valid SQL syntax and needed by the database.

TIP FROM

Bill

> If you specify criteria including a phrase surrounded by brackets ([ ]), Excel will ask you to fill in that value when the query is run. For example, if you want to use the same query to get data for different cities, type **What city do you want to use?** in the criteria Value box with the city field in the Criteria Field box. You'll immediately be asked to answer the question (you can type any value or just choose OK at the Enter Parameter Value box for now).
>
> When you return to Excel (and every time you refresh the query later), a box will pop up asking you for a new city name to use as a filter in place of this parameter. This is called a *parameter query*.

ADDING COUNTS AND TOTALS

Suppose you don't want to see just the raw data, but some "big picture" information, such as the total number of orders per customer, or which salesperson sold more dollars' worth of product. Microsoft Query can automatically perform five kinds of calculations on your data: sums, averages, counts, minimums, and maximums.

To add these calculations, click in the data column to which you want to add a calculation, and then click the Cycle Through Totals button—the one with the Greek Sigma (Σ). Microsoft Query will cycle through all the available calculations; just stop clicking when you get to the one you want. You can add a specific field more than once and use a different calculation on each one.

You also can sort the data before returning it by clicking anywhere in the column of data you want to sort, and then clicking either the Sort Ascending or Sort Descending buttons in the toolbar.

When you have the final query you want, click the Return Data button (the one with the door) to close Microsoft Query and send the data to Excel. Specify where you want to place the data, and after you've clicked OK again, you're finished!

MANAGING DATABASE DATA IN EXCEL

Creating a database query is most of the work when accessing database data from Excel, but there are still some tricks to learn that will really make Excel hum.

The following sections cover how to set advanced query properties to make sure your query is always showing the latest data. You'll also learn how to rerun and modify existing queries so you don't have to create a new query from scratch each time you want to see what's changed in the database.

29

REFRESHING DATA

Now you're looking at the product of your hard work: an Excel worksheet filled with up-to-the-minute data from your corporate database. But what if you come back to the file tomorrow or next week? How will you know whether the data is still current? If you queried historical data, there's little reason to think it will change in the database. But if you're looking at operational data—for example, orders this week—the data will be changing hour by hour.

There isn't any way to know whether the data in your Excel worksheet matches what's currently in the database, but it's easy to refresh the worksheet so that it has the most recent data. Just choose Data, Refresh External Data; right-click anywhere in the returned data set and choose Refresh External Data; or click anywhere in the data and click the Refresh External Data button on the External Data toolbar.

You can also configure Excel to update a query for you automatically. Choose Data, Import External Data, Data Range Properties while the cursor is in the query data (that's important—the option won't be activated otherwise). Alternatively, you can right-click and choose Data Range Properties on the shortcut menu or click in the data and click the Data Range Properties button on the External Data toolbar. The Data Range Properties button on the External Data toolbar runs the same command. You'll see the External Data Range Properties dialog box shown in Figure 29.20. You can configure the Refresh Control settings to tell Excel to refresh the query every so many minutes, refresh it each time you open the Excel file, or both.

Figure 29.20
You can configure Excel to automatically refresh the query for you.

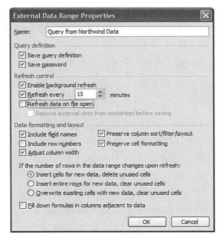

RERUNNING AND MODIFYING QUERIES

After working with Excel's query tools for a while, you'll build up a sizable collection of saved queries. You can easily run any of these again from another workbook by choosing Data, Import External Data, selecting the saved query from the file list that appears and click Open.

And what if you've gone through all this work and then discovered that there was really one more column you should have included in the query? No problem. You just need to edit the query to make the change.

Choose Data, Import External Data, Edit Query while the cursor is in the query data set (or click the Edit Query button on the External Data toolbar) and Excel will launch the tool you used to create the query (either the Query Wizard or Microsoft Query) with the query definition ready to be edited.

You can edit a saved query by choosing Data, Import External Data, New Database Query, and then choosing the Queries tab of the Choose Data Source window. You'll see your saved queries listed. Click the one you want to edit, and then choose Open, and it will be opened up for editing.

You also can right-click any query data cell and choose to edit the query, bring up the External Data Range Properties dialog box, or refresh the data.

IMPORTING DATA FROM TEXT FILES

In addition to database server access, Excel also can access data stored in plain text files. You probably won't do this as often as you access data on a corporate database, but it's still a handy option for special circumstances.

NOTE

If you want to learn how to access data stored on a Web page, see Chapter 33, "Using Excel on the Web."

While not as common as the need to retrieve database files, if you regularly analyze data from other sources in Excel, it's a sure bet you're going to eventually get a file sent to you in raw text format. Text files are the lowest common denominator for data files because they can be handled by just about any program on any platform. For example, mainframe data is often distributed in text file format.

If you do get a text file from someone, Excel has special tools to help you import successfully. If the file is in Excel's standard text format (comma-delimited format), you can open the file using the standard File, Open command without another thought. However, if it isn't, Excel will notice and you'll see the Text Import Wizard start up (see Figure 29.21). More commonly, you can invoke the Text Import Wizard by choosing Import External Data, Import Data from the Data menu, and selecting your text file.

Step 1 of the wizard asks whether the text file is delimited or fixed width. *Delimited* means that data elements in the file are separated by some special character, usually a comma or tab. *Fixed-width files* don't use a separator; they just use spaces to guarantee that every field always starts at the same column number. For example, the first field always starts at column 1 and the second field always starts at column 16. The wizard shows you a preview of the file to help out and sets the default choice to its best guess.

29

Figure 29.21
The Text Import Wizard helps you tell Excel how to interpret text data files. In this case, the file I'm importing is delimited using tab characters.

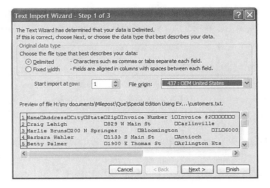

TIP FROM

Bill

Here are some rules to tell the two types apart visually. If the fields in each row of the file are packed together without any space between them, the file is probably delimited. If the fields in the file appear to line up nicely in the preview, it's a fixed-width file. The file in Figure 29.21 is delimited with tabs.

Choose either Delimited or Fixed Width, and then click Next.

If you chose Delimited in step 1, the wizard now asks what character acts as the delimiter (separator) between fields. You can tell by looking in the Data Preview box. Tab characters look like little boxes in the Data Preview. If you see small boxes regularly appearing between fields in each row of text, it's a dead giveaway that the file is delimited with tabs.

Select the delimiter character (or type it into the Other box if Excel doesn't have the right option presented in a check box). You'll see the Data Preview box update itself immediately after you make your choice. You may also use Text qualifiers. Comma-delimited files are often qualified by quotation marks in case there is actually a comma inside the fields.

If the file now looks correctly separated into columns, click Next to continue.

If you chose Fixed Width in step 1, the wizard asks you to confirm its guess as to where each column starts. Check the file over in the Data Preview. The Text Import Wizard might have gotten a column boundary wrong or missed a few (see Figure 29.22).

You can add, delete, or move column boundaries by clicking and dragging in the Data Preview. When the column boundaries look correct, choose Next to continue.

Step 3 of the Text Import Wizard asks you to confirm the data type of each column—that is, which are numbers, which are dates, and so on. The wizard is really good at figuring this out for itself, so you usually can just click Finish to complete the import.

29

Figure 29.22
Sometimes you have to help the Text Import Wizard. Here I'm importing a fixed-width text file, and the wizard missed the start of the Zip field.

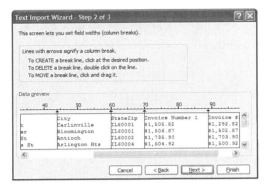

[ic318]If you regularly import the same file, set up a database query definition for the text file. Choose Data, Import External Data, Import Data, and then choose which file you want to import. After you're finished with the import (and any time later); you can right-click anywhere in the data and choose Refresh Data.

USING THE CONVERT TEXT TO COLUMNS WIZARD

The Convert Text to Columns Wizard enables you to use the power of the Text Import Wizard on data that's already in your worksheet. If you paste data by hand from a text file, for example, or retrieve long text fields from a database you would really rather have broken up into separate columns, you can use the Convert Text to Columns Wizard.

Highlight the cells you want to break apart and choose Data, Text to Columns to start the wizard. The key thing to remember when starting the wizard is that you need to have high-lighted all the text cells you want to break apart into separate columns (see Figure 29.23).

If you don't have any other data in that column, just highlight the whole column as a shortcut.

Figure 29.23
Turn unseparated text values like this into nicely separated columns using the Convert Text to Columns Wizard.

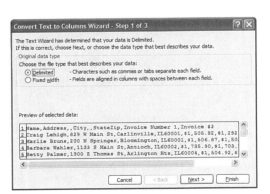

What you see now is basically the Text Import Wizard with a different name. The process is identical: Identify the data as delimited or fixed width and continue through steps 2 and 3 of the wizard. When you click Finish, your data will be properly separated into columns.

TROUBLESHOOTING

COPYING VISIBLE CELLS ONLY

I copied a filtered Excel list to an Access table and got the entire list rather than the filtered version. How can I copy just the filtered records?

If you want just the filtered data, two methods are available:

- Copy the filtered data to a separate section of the worksheet, and then copy that new section to Access.
- Select and then paste only the visible cells. First create a blank Access table. Then, go back to Excel and use Edit, Go To to open the Go To dialog box. Click the Special button, select Visible Cells Only in the Go To Special dialog box, and click OK. Then, copy the selection and paste it into the blank Access table. Or, to quickly select visible cells only, highlight the data and press Alt+; (semicolon).

WHEN ACCESS CAN'T CREATE AN INDEX

I was using the Import Spreadsheet Wizard, and Access says that it can't create an index.

If you get this message, double-check that the data is actually unique in the column you specified for the primary key. Telling Access to build a unique index on a column that actually has a few sneaky duplicate values (which are probably data-entry errors) is the most common problem when running this wizard.

EXCEL IN PRACTICE

Excel's data-entry forms are plain and just not very functional. Searching for data and checking that entered data is correct is difficult. By using Excel's data together with the Microsoft Access Form feature, you can use Access instead of Excel for data entry. Figures 29.24 and 29.25 show data forms in Excel and Access for you to compare.

Figure 29.24
This plain-Jane data
form in Excel is func-
tional, but that's it.

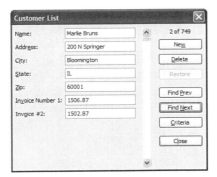

Figure 29.25
With its graphics,
formatting, and better
organization, this
Access form is much
easier to read
and use.

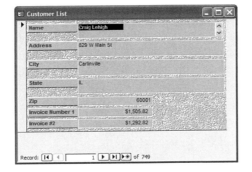

The Access form is a dressed-up version of the Excel data form, adding graphics and formatted text. I've also really made the form more useful by organizing it more logically and
by converting some fields to drop-down lists. These fields can be restricted by Access so that
users can enter only valid data. For example, with a bit of configuring, I set the State field to
show only U.S. states when the Country field is set to United States.

CHAPTER 30

RETRIEVING DATA FROM OLAP SERVERS

by Timothy Dyck and John Shumate

timothy_dyck@dyck.org, jcshumate@starpower.net

In this chapter

What Is OLAP?   790

Server Versus Client OLAP   791

Creating an OLAP Data Source Definition   794

Creating an OLAP PivotTable   794

Using OLAP PivotTables   795

Using OLAP PivotCharts   798

Saving Offline Cubes from Server Cubes   799

Performing OLAP Analysis on Database Data   801

WHAT IS OLAP?

Excel 2003's *On-line Analytical Processing (OLAP)* features enable you to quickly sift through large amounts of information to get the answers you need to solve business problems and make well-informed decisions. OLAP (pronounced (OH-lap) techniques are especially suited to help you see long-term trends and discover hidden relationships and causal factors in business performance.

OLAP views the world in two categories, *measures* and *dimensions*. Measures represent things that you can count or measure in numeric terms. The number of units sold, sales revenues, gallons of fuel, pounds of cargo, and number of employees are examples of typical measures. Dimensions are nonnumeric things that give relevance to measures. A salesman's name, date of sale, location of sale, and type of product sold are examples of dimensions that describe a sales revenue measure.

Dimensions typically are organized into hierarchies. For example, sales for all the sales persons at a store summarize to the store total; all the stores in a sales district summarize to the district total; all the districts in a sales region summarize to the region total; and all sales regions summarize to the corporate total. In this example, measures are aggregated at each level in the sales organization dimension hierarchy. Another example of a dimension hierarchy is a time dimension where daily sales summarize to a monthly total, monthly sales summarize to a quarterly total, and quarterly sales summarize to an annual total as shown in Figure 30.1.

Figure 30.1
Measures are aggregated at each level of detail in a dimensional hierarchy.

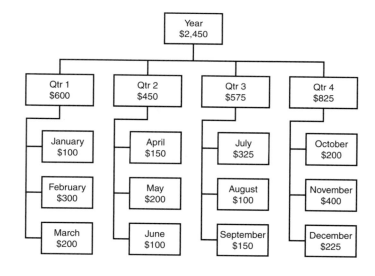

With OLAP, you are freed from the drudgery of entering values into your worksheet. Excel retrieves data values from a database at your request and inserts them into PivotTables. Measures are placed in the inner cells of the PivotTable, and dimensions are placed in the column and row headers, as shown in Figure 30.2. Excel maintains a connection to the data source (hence the term *online*) as you rearrange and requery the data through a series of exploratory views in an interactive dialogue with the computer. You may choose to change the dimensions displayed in the PivotTable's header rows or the measure displayed in the data cells, or you may drill down within a dimension to explode the view to the next level of detail within the dimension hierarchy. Excel quickly refreshes the PivotTable with the new values from the data source. Each view yields information from a different perspective and influences the path you take to create the next view.

Figure 30.2
Excel's OLAP PivotTables display measures in the data cells with corresponding dimension values in the row and column headers.

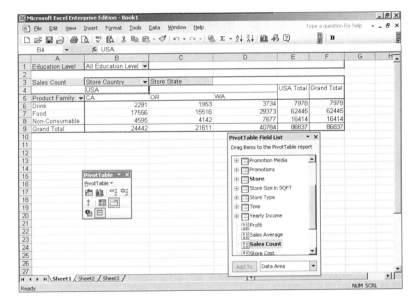

SERVER VERSUS CLIENT OLAP

OLAP depends on a special database structure called a *multidimensional cube* to provide fast response when you drill and change dimensions and measures. The cube organizes the data into dimensions and precalculates the aggregates at each of the dimension hierarchy levels. The decisions about which measures, dimensions, and dimension levels to include in a cube when it is created limit what you can view in an Excel OLAP PivotTable.

With Excel, you can choose to build your own cubes from a relational database, such as Microsoft Access or Oracle, or you can connect to cubes prebuilt by a database administrator and stored in Microsoft SQL Server version 7 or later (see Figure 30.3). With server-based cubes, you can connect to the server and immediately begin pivoting and drilling through cube data. With self-built cubes, first you must run Excel's wizard to define the cube structure and then wait for Excel to process data from the source into the cube. You then can browse the cube's data in an OLAP PivotTable and save the cube to disk for later reuse in PivotTables. Because cubes contain snapshots of the source data from which they are built, whenever data in the underlying source database changes, the cube must be reprocessed to include the new or changed data.

Figure 30.3
Excel can build offline cubes from relational databases. Excel PivotTables can work with offline cubes or connect to OLAP server cubes.

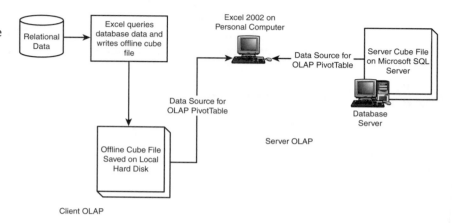

Processing cubes can be very time consuming. Smaller cubes can be built in a matter of minutes, but if the source data has millions of rows or the cube has many measures and dimensions with many hierarchy levels, loading and calculating the data in the cube could take hours. Larger, more complex cubes are best left to SQL Server database administrators who have powerful multiprocessor servers and scheduling software at their disposal. They can automate cube update processing and manage cube refresh schedules to ensure server-based cubes are always up to date. The size and complexity of the cubes you build yourself with Excel will be limited by the power of your personal workstation and your patience.

CREATING AN OLAP DATA SOURCE DEFINITION

Microsoft provides the offline database drivers with Office 2003 to connect to SQL Server OLAP cubes. The first step in connecting to cubes is to define a data source connection. After it is defined, you can reuse data source connections in future Excel sessions. You must define a data source connection for each OLAP source you intend to use in Excel. To do so, follow these steps:

1. Choose Data, Import External Data, New Database Query to open the Choose Data Source dialog box shown in Figure 30.4.

Figure 30.4
This is the same dialog box you use to create a query with the Query Wizard or Microsoft Query.

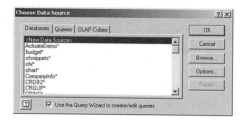

2. Click the OLAP Cubes tab, select <New Data Source> in the list, and click OK to open the Create New Data Source dialog box (see Figure 30.5).

Figure 30.5
Give your OLAP data source any name you want, and then select which type of OLAP server you want to use.

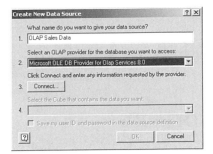

3. Type a name for your new data source. In the future, you will select this name from the Choose Data Source dialog box to connect to the data source.

4. Select an OLAP provider from the drop-down list. To connect to Microsoft SQL Server 2000 OLAP cubes, select Microsoft OLE DB Provider for OLAP Services 8.0.

5. Click the Connect button to open the Multidimensional Connection dialog box (see Figure 30.6).

Figure 30.6
The Analysis Server option accesses cubes in Microsoft SQL Server 2000; the Cube File option accesses offline cubes stored on your hard disk.

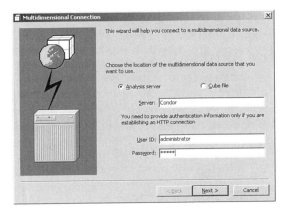

6. Click the Analysis Server radio button. Type the server name, your user ID, and password in the spaces provided. Click Next.

7. Select the OLAP database from the list of available databases and click Finish to return to the Create New Data Source dialog box.

8. Select the desired cube from the drop-down list of cubes in the database you connected to in the previous step. Select the check box at the bottom of the Create New Data

Source dialog box if you want to save your user ID and password as part of the data source definition—keep in mind that this might pose some security risk.

9. Click OK to save the OLAP data source definition and return to the Choose Data Source dialog box.

You could immediately start to use your new data source by selecting it in the Choose Data Source dialog box and clicking OK, but you learn another path to using OLAP data sources in the following section. Click Cancel to close the Choose Data Source dialog box.

CREATING AN OLAP PIVOTTABLE

To retrieve data from an OLAP cube, you create an OLAP PivotTable in your Excel worksheet. Follow these steps:

1. Choose Data, PivotTable and PivotChart Report to start the PivotTable and PivotChart Wizard (see Figure 30.7).

Figure 30.7
OLAP data access starts with the PivotTable and PivotChart Wizard. OLAP server data is defined as an external data source.

2. Click the External Data Source and PivotTable radio buttons, and click Next.

3. Click the Get Data button in Step 2 of the wizard (see Figure 30.8) to open the Choose Data Source dialog box.

Figure 30.8
Click the Get Data button to specify the location of the external data for the PivotTable.

4. Click the OLAP Cubes tab and select the data source you created previously.

5. Click OK to return to Step 2 of the wizard, and click Next to proceed to Step 3 of the wizard.

6. Choose to put the PivotTable in your current worksheet or in a new worksheet the wizard will create for you (see Figure 30.9). Click Finish to create the OLAP PivotTable.

Figure 30.9
Choose whether you want your new OLAP PivotTable to go into its own worksheet or into the one you're currently using. Click Finish to create the PivotTable.

USING OLAP PIVOTTABLES

Excel's OLAP PivotTable contains four drop areas for you to place data elements (see Figure 30.10). The center drop zone, labeled Drop Data Items Here, is reserved for placing measure fields from your cube. You place dimension fields in the Page, Row, and Column drop areas. While working with OLAP PivotTables, Excel also displays a dockable PivotTable toolbar and a PivotTable Field List. If the PivotTable Field List is not visible, you can click the Show Field List button on the PivotTable toolbar.

Figure 30.10
The empty PivotTable contains drop areas for you to place fields from the OLAP data source. You select measure and dimension fields from the PivotTable Field List.

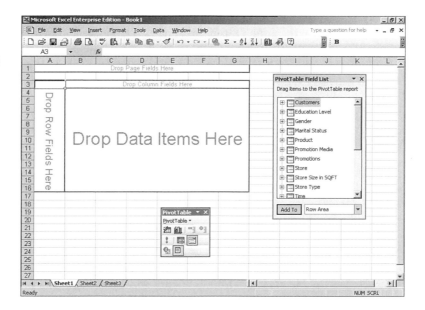

NOTE

> The PivotTable Field List disappears and the PivotTable toolbar becomes disabled if you click in any spreadsheet cells outside the borders of the PivotTable. Click any cell within the PivotTable to restore the Field List and toolbar to their previous states.

30

To have a meaningful view, you must place at least one measure field in the Data Area and one dimension field in either the Page, Row, or Column area. You do not have to use all three dimension drop areas. To place a field in the PivotTable, select the field in the PivotTable Field List and use the mouse to drag and drop it on the desired drop area. You also can select the desired drop area from the drop-down list at the bottom of the PivotTable Field List window and click the Add To button to place the selected field in the PivotTable. Excel will retrieve the selected data elements from the cube and refresh the PivotTable view.

The numbers displayed in the Data Area are those values that occur at the intersection of the dimensions displayed on the PivotTable. You can trace a cell value back to its row and column headers to see which dimensions are relevant to that data cell. Note that, although multiple dimension values can be displayed across multiple row and column headers, only a single value can be displayed for each dimension in the Page Area. You can think of the Page Area as a data filter. All the data values in the cells of the Data Area are filtered to match whatever dimension values are displayed in the Page Area.

You can place more than one measure field in the Data Area and more than one dimension field in each of the Page, Row, or Column Areas. Excel will nest the display of multiple fields within a single drop area, as shown in Figure 30.11. Each dimension or measure placed in a drop area displays a shaded PivotTable button. After you place a field on the PivotTable, you can drag and drop PivotTable buttons between the drop areas to rearrange the view. Right-click a PivotTable button, and choose Hide Dimension from the pop-up menu to remove a dimension from the PivotTable. Dimensions can also be removed from the PivotTable by dragging the PivotTable button outside the PivotTable until the mouse pointer displays an "X."

To drill down in a dimension hierarchy, double-click a dimension header cell in the Row or Column Area. If a lower-level hierarchy exists below the dimension level, Excel will explode the PivotTable view to show the details of the lower level. If the exploded level is already visible, Excel will collapse the view and remove the lower-level detail from the PivotTable. For example, double-clicking Drink in the PivotTable in Figure 30.11 expands the view to show the drink categories Alcoholic Beverages, Beverages, and Dairy, as shown in Figure 30.12. Double-clicking Drink in Figure 30.12 will return to the original view in Figure 30.11. You can also click the Show and Hide Detail buttons on the PivotTable toolbar to expand and collapse dimension hierarchies.

Click the drop-down arrow on a dimension PivotTable button to open a tree view of the dimension, as shown in Figure 30.13. Click the plus and minus signs to expand and collapse branches of the dimension hierarchy in the tree. You can pick and choose which elements of the dimension to display in the PivotTable by clicking to toggle a check mark on or off in the box to the left of the element. Elements with a check mark will display. Elements without the check mark will be hidden.

Figure 30.11
You can add multiple dimensions to the same drop area. Here the Store Type dimension is nested within the Product Family dimension in the Row Area of the OLAP PivotTable.

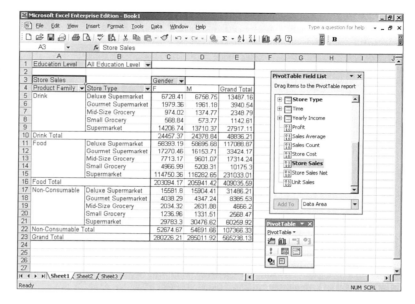

Figure 30.12
You expand and collapse the level of detail in a PivotTable by drilling into dimension hierarchies. Double-click a dimension header cell or use the Hide and Show Detail buttons on the PivotTable toolbar to drill up and down hierarchies.

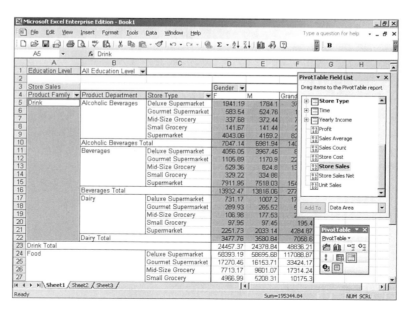

Figure 30.13
Clicking the drop-down arrow of a shaded PivotTable button opens the tree view of a dimension hierarchy where you can check off the individual dimension items you want displayed in the PivotTable.

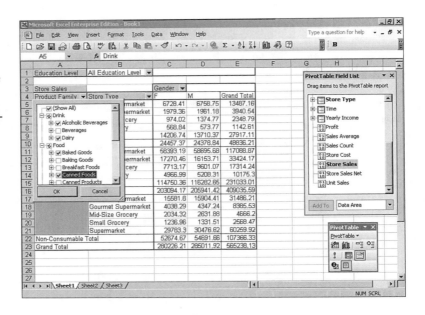

TIP FROM

John

When you hide items, they will not be displayed in the total lines of the PivotTable. Choose the Include Hidden Items in Totals button on the PivotTable toolbar if you want the totals to reflect hidden values.

USING OLAP PIVOTCHARTS

A PivotTable full of numbers is a good way to see details but is not always the best way to see the big picture. Excel charts are a great way to get an overview of your data at a glance and to reveal hidden information. Pie charts, bar charts, and area charts are good for demonstrating proportions and contributions to the whole of individual dimension elements. Bar charts and line charts are good for revealing trends, particularly across a time dimension. Excel PivotCharts complement PivotTables to provide advanced visual analysis of OLAP data.

NOTE

For more information on charts, see Chapters 20–23. For more on PivotTables, see Chapter 24.

 Choose the Chart Wizard button on the PivotTable toolbar to add a PivotChart to your workbook. The chart will appear on a new worksheet. The PivotChart is based on the dimensions and measures in the PivotTable and maintains a link to the PivotTable. Changes made to the PivotChart will be reflected in the PivotTable, and vice versa.

NOTE

> When you first run the PivotTable and PivotChart Wizard, you can choose to create a PivotChart report. Excel will automatically build a PivotChart and PivotTable. A PivotChart must always have an underlying PivotTable. You can create a PivotTable without a PivotChart, but you can't have a PivotChart without a PivotTable.

A PivotChart has the same Data Area and Page Area as the PivotTable, but maps the PivotTable's Row and Column Areas to the PivotChart's Category Axis and Series Axis. The PivotTable toolbar, PivotTable Field List, and PivotTable buttons all work the same on PivotCharts. However, in a PivotChart, you cannot drill down a dimension hierarchy by double-clicking. A double-click on a PivotChart opens a Format dialog box instead. You must use the PivotTable toolbar or drop-down arrow on PivotTable buttons to expand and collapse dimension hierarchy levels.

 Excel displays the Chart toolbar with the PivotChart. Use the Chart Type button on the toolbar to choose between Excel's various chart types for your PivotChart. Note that not all of Excel's standard chart types are supported with OLAP PivotCharts; for example, you cannot select Scatter or Bubble charts.

TIP FROM

John

> By default, Excel places the PivotChart on a separate chart sheet in your workbook. To place the PivotChart on the same worksheet with the PivotTable, right-click the PivotChart and select Location from the pop-up menu to open the Chart Location dialog box. Click the As Object In radio button and select the worksheet that contains the PivotTable from the drop-down list. Click OK.

SAVING OFFLINE CUBES FROM SERVER CUBES

When connected to a server-based cube with Excel, you can save subsets of the cube's data to local cubes on your hard disk. You can reload data from the local cubes into Excel PivotTables without connecting to the server. This pack-and-go option enables you to connect your laptop computer to the server while you are in the office, download OLAP cube data, and perform OLAP analysis sessions while on the road or include OLAP analysis as part of offsite presentations. You also can save and send local cube files to other Excel users who don't have access to your OLAP server. Follow these steps to create an offline cube from a server cube:

1. Create an OLAP PivotTable as you normally would, using an OLAP server as your data source.

2. In the PivotTable toolbar, open the PivotTable drop-down menu and choose Offline OLAP to open the Offline OLAP Settings dialog box. (This option won't be available unless you have one or more fields displayed in your OLAP PivotTable.)

3. Click the Create Offline Data File button to display the Create Cube File Wizard. The first wizard screen is an information-only screen. Click Next to proceed.

4. Step 2 of the wizard displays a tree of the server cube's dimensions (see Figure 30.14). Check off the dimension levels you want to include in your offline cube. Click the plus and minus signs to expand and collapse dimension hierarchies to select different detail levels in the dimension, and then click Next.

Figure 30.14
The server cube might contain too much data for an efficient offline cube. Just check off the parts of the server cube you really need.

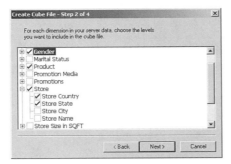

5. Step 3 enables you to select the measure fields and dimension data values from the dimension levels you chose in the previous step (see Figure 30.15). Click the plus and minus signs to expand and collapse the tree view and check off the items you want to include in the offline cube. Be sure to select at least one item from each dimension level. Click Next.

Figure 30.15
You can limit offline cube size by choosing certain measures and only some data values from the dimension levels you previously selected.

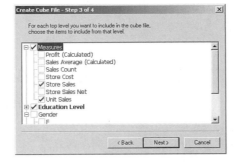

6. The last step is to tell Excel where to save the offline cube file. Type the filename or click the Browse button to open the traditional Windows Save As dialog box.

7. Click Finish to begin saving the cube file. Excel displays the Create Cube File - Progress dialog box while it is copying the data. You can click the Stop button to abort the process if it's taking too long.

When Excel is finished creating the local cube file, you are returned to the Offline OLAP Settings dialog box (see Figure 30.16). The Offline OLAP radio button is selected. When you click OK, your PivotTable will be disconnected from the server and working with data from the offline cube file.

Figure 30.16
The Offline OLAP Settings dialog box lets you switch back and forth between using an OLAP server or an offline cube file as your data source.

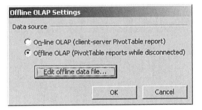

If you want to switch back to using the server cube, go back to the Offline OLAP Settings dialog box, select the On-Line OLAP radio button, and click OK. You will reconnect to the server cube from which the offline cube was created. You can also return to the Offline OLAP Settings dialog box and choose the Edit Offline Data File button to go back through the Create Cube File Wizard to change the dimensions or measures you included in the offline cube.

PERFORMING OLAP ANALYSIS ON DATABASE DATA

You can use Excel PivotTables and PivotCharts to analyze relational database data that has not been loaded into cubes on an OLAP server. For example, you might have your own Microsoft Access database that you want to analyze, or perhaps you need to work with data in an Oracle database that wasn't defined with the requirements when the database administrator built server-based cubes. If you have been using regular Excel PivotTables with a relational data source, you might find that you get better performance if you first build a cube from the data and then use OLAP PivotTables.

STARTING THE OLAP CUBE WIZARD

Choose Data, Import External Data, New Database Query, and create a new query or edit one that's already saved. Be sure the check box to Use the Query Wizard to Create/Edit Queries is selected in the Choose Data Source Dialog. See Chapter 29, "Using Excel with Access and Other Databases," for details on using the Query Wizard. In the Choose Columns step of the Query Wizard, be sure you include all the database columns from your data source that correspond to the measures and dimension levels you want to include in your cube. When you get to the final step of the Query Wizard (see Figure 30.17), choose Create an OLAP Cube from This Query, and click Finish to launch the OLAP Cube Wizard.

TIP FROM

John

If you are making a query specifically to support cube building, you will get the best performance if you omit any database columns that will not be part of the cube. Also, consider adding a filter to your query so it returns only the data you are interested in analyzing in PivotTables.

Figure 30.17
You'll get much faster PivotTable performance by creating an OLAP cube from database data.

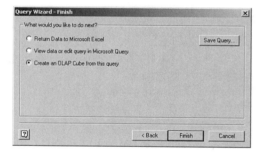

The OLAP Cube Wizard starts with a welcome message. After reading this message, click Next to proceed to the first step of the wizard. You can disable the welcome screen for future use by selecting Don't Show This Screen Again before you click Next.

SELECTING CUBE MEASURES

Step 1 of the OLAP Cube Wizard (see Figure 30.18) lets you select the source fields that will be summarized data fields (measures) in your cube. By default, the numeric columns in your query are preselected with the Sum aggregate operator. Deselect any numeric fields that are not truly measures. For example, a store number column might be stored as a numeric data type, and it would be nonsense to sum up the values of the store number in each database record.

Figure 30.18
Check off the fields you want summarized by the OLAP Cube Wizard. You also can choose how Excel will summarize this data by changing the contents of the Summarize By column.

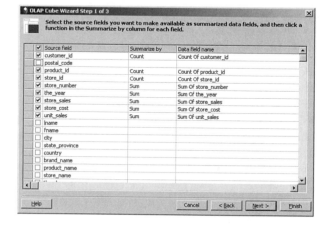

You also can decide here whether you want to aggregate your measures with the default Sum operator or if you would rather see the minimum value, maximum value, or count of values when details are rolled up to the next level in dimension hierarchies. For example, if the sales value of quarters 1, 2, 3, and 4 are $100, $200, $300, and $100, respectively, the sum at the year level will be $700, the minimum for the year would be $100, and the maximum for the year would be $300. To change the summarization type, click the word *Sum* in the Summarize By column and choose Count, Min, or Max from the drop-down list.

You can turn nonnumeric fields into measures by using the Count summarization. For example, counting customer IDs creates a measure field that represents the number of customers. Click the check box to the left of a nonnumeric source field and Excel automatically sets the Summarize By type to Count. Choose Next when you have finished selecting and setting options for all of your cube's measures.

ORGANIZING DATA INTO HIERARCHIES

Step 2 of the wizard requires you to arrange the remaining source data fields into one or more dimension hierarchies, as shown in Figure 30.19. Group fields logically according to the type of information they contain. For example, a set of fields describing a customer's address should be grouped into a dimension called customer location, or a set of fields describing various product data should be grouped into a product dimension.

Figure 30.19
Group all remaining source fields into dimensions by dragging and dropping. Note that date/time fields automatically expand into full-date dimensions.

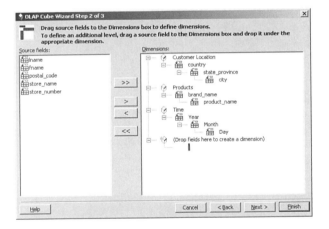

Drag and drop each field from the Source Fields window into the Dimensions window. If you drop the field onto the (Drop Fields Here to Create a Dimension) item, it becomes a new dimension. If you drop it onto an existing dimension, it becomes a level in the dimension hierarchy. Be sure you group your dimension hierarchy levels in the proper order from summary level on top to lowest detail level on bottom. For example, in the Customer Location dimension, Country is the highest summary level, with State_Province coming below and City on the bottom.

When you're finished creating dimensions, click Next.

TIP FROM

John

> You can rename a dimension element by right-clicking its name and choosing Rename. Naming your dimensions with proper names makes using the cube a lot easier, particularly if you send the cube to someone else to use.

SAVING THE CUBE

Congratulations! You've done pretty much what a database administrator does when setting up an OLAP server database for the first time.

Step 3 of the wizard just asks how you would like to save the cube (see Figure 30.20). You can choose to rebuild the cube each time you open a worksheet that references it, or you can build it once and then rebuild it as needed (which is important to do when the source database data is updated).

Figure 30.20
After you've built your new cube database, save it with its data to your local hard disk.

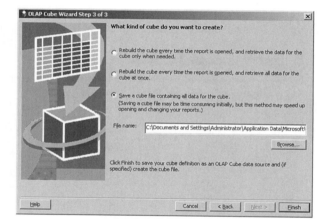

In most cases, you'll want to choose Save a Cube File Containing All Data for the Cube, because this maximizes the speed benefits of using an OLAP cube in the first place.

Type a name for the cube data file (it has a .cub extension), and then click Finish. You'll be asked to save the OLAP query definition (.oqy extension). Give it a name and click Save. You'll need to use this query definition file when you want to use the cube.

Next, you'll see the OLAP Cube Wizard running the query and creating the cube. A status box appears, saying that Excel is creating an offline cube.

NOTE

> It's normal for this process to take a few minutes, particularly if you're summarizing a large query.

After the local cube has been created, Excel pops you into Step 3 of the PivotTable and PivotChart Wizard so you can immediately create an OLAP PivotTable based on your new cube (refer to Figure 30.9).

USING THE CUBE

If you chose not to create an OLAP PivotTable as part of the process of creating your local OLAP cube, or if you want to reuse the same cube in another PivotTable, you'll need to tell Excel to use the cube for OLAP data. If you think back to when you first created an OLAP PivotTable, you'll probably remember that the PivotTable and PivotChart Wizard gives you the option of using a local OLAP cube instead of an OLAP server.

To take advantage of this option, follow these steps:

1. Choose Data, PivotTable, and PivotChart Report to start the PivotTable and PivotChart Wizard.

2. In the Step 1 of 3 dialog box, choose External Data Source and click Next.

3. In the Step 2 of 3 dialog box, click the Get Data button.

4. When the Choose Data Source dialog box opens, click the OLAP Cubes tab. There you'll see listed the OLAP query definition you created when you built the cube in the OLAP Cube Wizard. Select it and click OK. You'll then be back in the PivotTable and PivotChart Wizard, Step 2 of 3.

5. The rest of this should be old hat to you. Click Next; then decide where you want the OLAP PivotTable to go and click Finish.

EXCEL IN PRACTICE

OLAP PivotTables can display an enormous amount of detail—sometimes too much. For example, it's hard to see in the promotions analysis in Figure 30.21 what data is really important and what's just background noise. One of the goals of OLAP is to help you quickly find the hot spots in your data. You can apply Excel features to OLAP PivotTables to zero in on the important information and reveal hidden treasure in your data.

To turn the raw data into useful information, you can use several techniques:

■ Discover the top performers by placing the cell pointer in the Promotion Name column and choosing PivotTable, Field Settings, Advanced from the PivotTable toolbar (or right-clicking anywhere in the column and choosing Field Settings, Advanced) to open the PivotTable Field Advanced Options dialog box (see Figure 30.22). Choose Descending under AutoSort Options and select Store Sales from the Using Field drop-down list to sort promotions by descending store sales.

Figure 30.21
This table's immense amount of data makes it too complicated to comprehend.

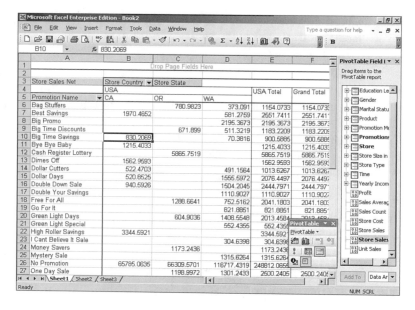

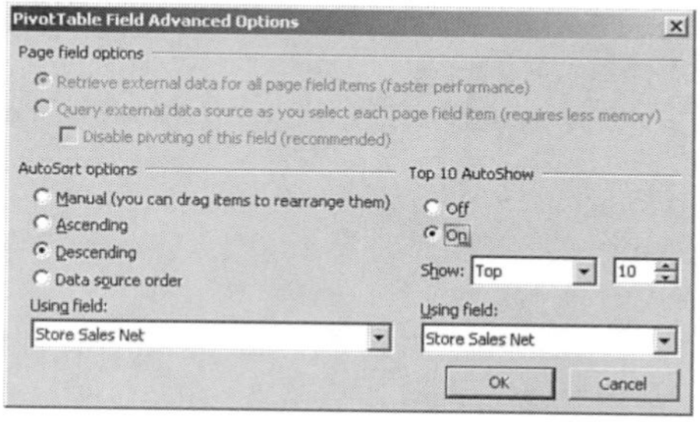

Figure 30.22
Setting advanced field options enables you to create ranking reports to remove clutter from your PivotTable.

- Cut down on the number of promotions by again opening the PivotTable Field Advanced Options dialog box and choosing On under Top 10 AutoShow to limit the list to the top 10 promotions. Now you know which promotions were the top 10 revenue earners.

- Place the cell pointer in a Store Sales data cell, and then choose PivotTable, Field Settings, Options, Show Data As. Set Store Sales to display as % of row, instead of an absolute value.

- Finally, select the entire PivotTable (PivotTable, Select, Entire Table) and use the Format, Conditional Formatting command to mark values between 50% and 99% in red font with shaded background. Now, out of the top promotions, you instantly can tell where each worked the best.

For example, it's now easy to see in Figure 30.23 that You Save Days is a promotion to repeat in California but not worth running again in Oregon or Washington. However, Washington customers responded extremely well to the Super Savers promotion, making it a winner in that state. Note that the formatting changes made previously will persist as you continue to slice and dice through the data in your OLAP PivotTable. Excel will automatically reapply the formatting whenever the PivotTable data is refreshed.

Figure 30.23
Sorting, limiting the list, using conditional formatting, and other techniques produce a much more useful report.

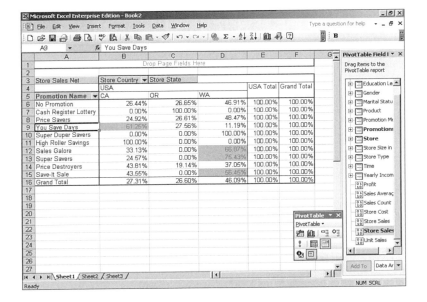

CHAPTER 31

RECORDING AND EDITING A MACRO

by Bill Bruns

In this chapter

Create Your Own Commands with Macros   810

Creating a Macro with the Macro Recorder   811

Macro Playback   817

Editing a Macro   828

Deleting Macros, Custom Buttons, and Custom Menu Items   831

Macros to Help You Work Faster   832

CREATE YOUR OWN COMMANDS WITH MACROS

Have you ever wished that you could create your own commands in Excel? Perhaps you print the same report every month. To print that report, you must follow the same 10 steps. Wouldn't it be nice to click a button or press a keyboard shortcut and have the report print automatically? For operations like these, you can create a macro—a mini-program that performs a specific task—to repeat the steps perfectly and with much greater speed each time. Macros are written in a programming language called *Visual Basic for Applications* or *VBA*.

Fortunately, you don't have to be a programmer to create a macro. Excel provides the *Macro Recorder*. The Macro Recorder works like an audio tape recorder. Rather than recording sound, however, the Macro Recorder records keystrokes and mouse actions. In this chapter, you'll learn how to create macros using the Macro Recorder. You'll also learn how to play and edit macros.

WHAT IS A MACRO?

A macro is a VBA procedure. A *procedure* is a group of VBA statements that either performs a specific task or returns a result. You can create two types of procedures in Excel: subroutines and functions. *Subroutines* are procedures that perform a specific task. The code for subroutines begins with the word Sub and ends with the words End Sub (see Listing 31.1 for an example). A macro is a subroutine-type procedure. For the purposes of this chapter, macro and subroutine are interchangeable terms.

LISTING 31.1 THIS MACRO SELECTS AND PRINTS THE CURRENT REGION

```
Sub PrintRegion()
    Selection.CurrentRegion.Select
    Selection.PrintOut Copies:=1, Collate:=True
End Sub
```

In Listing 31.1, the caveat will be that CurrentRegion will refer to the solid block of data where the cursor currently is. If you do not have a solid block of data, this macro may provide unexpected results.

TIP FROM

Bill

> A nice feature of recording macros in Excel is that the program automatically adds some comment information about the recording process: the macro's name and date, who recorded it, and any shortcut key(s) assigned to the macro. (For the sake of space, these comments aren't shown in the examples in this chapter—just the macro code itself appears in the examples.)

Functions are procedures that return a result. You are undoubtedly familiar with Excel's built-in functions, such as SUM and AVERAGE. VBA gives you the power to create custom functions that can be used like Excel's built-in worksheet functions. Functions begin with the word Function and end with the words End Function. Listing 31.2 shows a function that calculates income tax for a given income, deductions, and tax rate, for example.

LISTING 31.2 FUNCTION TO CALCULATE INCOME TAX

```
Function INCOMETAX(Income , Deductions _
, Rate)
    NetIncome = Income - Deductions
    INCOMETAX = NetIncome * Rate
End Function
```

TIP FROM

Bill

> When you record macros, the Macro Recorder automatically indents procedures for easier readability. When executed, Excel will ignore these indents or spaces before a statement. If you create rather than record a macro, you'll need to add your own indenting (Excel doesn't do it automatically).

WHY CREATE YOUR OWN COMMANDS?

Macros give you the power to create your own commands, which can save you time. Think of some of the tasks that you perform repeatedly in Excel. Macros can do these tasks for you. Following are some typical repetitive tasks that can be automated with macros:

- Format and print a report.
- Assist in the completion of an Excel form, such as an expense report.
- Consolidate data from several workbooks into a master workbook.
- Import and plot data to a chart.
- Apply your favorite AutoFormat to a range of cells.
- AutoFit all columns on the current worksheet.
- Create your own custom spreadsheet application.

→ Macros also can be assigned to custom toolbar buttons and shortcut keys. For details, **see** "Modifying Toolbars," **p. 714**.

CREATING A MACRO WITH THE MACRO RECORDER

The Macro Recorder records all your keyboard and mouse actions to a VBA subroutine. You use it like a tape recorder. Turn it on, execute the Excel task that you want to automate, and then turn it off.

TIP FROM

Bill

> Before you begin to record a macro, ensure that you are familiar with the steps involved with the task to automate. A good practice is to write them down on a piece of paper, as

continues

in the following example, which details the steps required to print two copies of the entire workbook:

1. Choose File, Print.
2. Type **2** in the Number of Copies box.
3. Choose Entire Workbook from the Print What option group.
4. Click OK.

Remember that the Macro Recorder records everything you do, whether it's an intended step or an unintended step. The only exception to this rule is the recording of dialog box commands. The Macro Recorder records the results of your selections when you click OK, and not everything you do while the dialog box is open. Knowing the steps to record before beginning makes the macro easier to record and play back faster.

WHAT YOU SHOULD CONSIDER BEFORE RECORDING

Before you begin recording, you must decide where to store the macro and how to record it. The following sections discuss the options to consider when making these decisions.

MACRO STORAGE OPTIONS

Excel provides the following three options for storing your macro:

- Current workbook
- Personal Macro Workbook
- New workbook

If you choose to store the macro in the current workbook, you can play back that macro when this workbook is open. Suppose you're recording a chart macro that will create a series of expense analysis charts in a workbook called Expenses.xls. It would make sense to store the macro with the Expenses.xls workbook. You wouldn't want to play back the macro in another workbook that doesn't contain expense data. The charts would be incorrect.

If you store the macro in the Personal Macro Workbook, it will be available to any workbook. Suppose you frequently must save some of your workbooks as text files for export to another program. You want to automate this process with a macro. If you store the export macro in the Personal Macro Workbook, you can run it regardless of which workbook is open. If you store the macro in another workbook, you have to open that workbook each time you want to run the macro.

TIP FROM

Bill

If you attach a macro to a workbook and then assign the macro to a toolbar button, clicking that button from a different workbook automatically opens (if necessary) the workbook containing the macro.

The *Personal Macro Workbook* is a hidden workbook that Excel creates the first time you choose this option for storage. It's saved to the XLStart folder—a subfolder that the Office install application creates. When you launch Excel, this workbook is opened automatically (although it's hidden, so you're not aware that it's open), thus making its macro content available to any other workbook.

NOTE

> The location of the XLStart folder can vary depending on your operating system. If you are using Windows 2000 or XP, it is probably in your personal profile, located under the Documents and Settings folder.   To locate the folder on your system, use the Search/Find command on the Windows Start menu.

CAUTION

> The Personal Macro Workbook is a file called Personal.xls. Use the Windows Search command on the Start menu to locate this file on your system. Be careful not to delete or move this file accidentally. If you record macros frequently, or record complex macros, back this file up occasionally to protect it.
>
> When upgrading from Office 2000, 97, or 95, the Office installation program will make a second copy of your Personal.xls file (if you have one) and add it to the Excel 2003 XLStart folder. Any additional globally recorded macros will be stored in this duplicate copy, Personal.xls, in the new Excel 2003 XLStart folder.

The option to store a macro in a new workbook is the least common storage option. It usually is used when you want to begin recording with no workbooks open. For example, you might want to record creating a new workbook as part of the macro process.

ABSOLUTE VERSUS RELATIVE RECORDING

A macro reference can be recorded relatively or absolutely by turning the Relative Reference button (found on the Stop Recording toolbar, which is discussed later in this chapter) on or off. If you choose to record *relatively*, the macro always plays back from the current position of the cell pointer. If you choose to record *absolutely*, the macro always plays back on the range used when you recorded the macro. Depending on the purpose of the macro, this can be important. As a general rule, if you want the macro to play back on a different range of cells each time, record it relatively. If you want it to play back on the same range of cells each time, record it absolutely. If the macro's purpose does not require modifying or selecting a range of cells, don't worry about relative or absolute recording.

RECORDING A MACRO

After you decide what to record, how to record it, and where to store it, you can begin the macro-recording process.

In most cases, you'll want to select cells or objects that the macro will affect before you begin the recording process. To illustrate the point, suppose that you're recording a macro to freeze panes. If you start recording, select cell B4, and then freeze panes, the macro will always freeze panes at cell B4. If you select cell B4 before you start recording, on the other hand, the macro will freeze panes at the current position of the cell pointer during playback. This makes the macro more versatile.

The exception to this rule is if you want the macro to affect the same cells or objects every time it plays back. For example, if you want a macro that always places the date in cell A1, you should record the process of selecting cell A1 as part of the macro.

To record a macro, follow these steps:

1. Choose Tools, Macro, Record New Macro to open the Record Macro dialog box (see Figure 31.1).

Figure 31.1
Use the options in this dialog box to set up the new macro's background information.

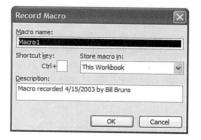

2. Type a name in the Macro Name text box. Macro names can contain letters, numbers, and underscores, but no spaces. They must begin with a letter and be no more than 64 characters in length.

Keep macro names short (20 characters or less) and make them descriptive of the task they will perform. Separate each word in the name with an underscore or use capitalization to differentiate each word. Structure the names—for example, Print_Expense_Rpt or PrintExpenseRpt.

3. (Optional) Select the storage location for the macro from the Store Macro In combo box. The default setting stores the new macro in the current workbook.

    If you're recording more than one macro in a session, you'll notice that the Store Macro In drop-down list displays whatever choice you made in the previous recording attempt. The setting here remains for each new Excel session as well.

4. (Optional) If you want to play back the macro by pressing a shortcut key, type the letter that you want to use as part of the shortcut key in the Shortcut Key text box.

CAUTION

> Macro shortcut keys override Excel's built-in shortcut keys. If you choose Ctrl+P as the shortcut key for a macro, for example, Ctrl+P will no longer open the Print dialog box. This isn't a good practice, especially if you're creating macros in a workbook that other people will use. Imagine opening a workbook created for you. You press Ctrl+P to open the Print dialog box and instead a 10-page report prints! Excel already uses most of the Ctrl+<letter> key combinations as keyboard shortcuts. Try using Ctrl+Shift+<letter> key combinations instead.

5. (Optional) Type in the Description text box a brief description of what the macro does. The description can be seen in the Macros dialog box at playback time. Descriptions help you to remember what task each macro performs, especially if you plan to record a lot of macros.

   Figure 31.2 shows the completed Record Macro dialog box.

Figure 31.2
When the Record Macro dialog box is complete, you're ready to begin recording.

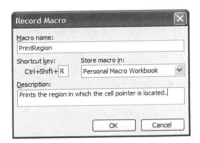

6. Click OK to close the Record Macro dialog box. The status bar displays the word `Recording` and the Stop Recording toolbar appears (see Figure 31.3).

Figure 31.3
Use the Stop Recording toolbar to record relatively and to stop recording.

CAUTION

> Don't hide the Stop Recording toolbar. You'll need it to stop the Macro Recorder! If you do accidentally hide it, choose Tools, Macro, Stop Recording.
>
> To get the Stop Recording toolbar to reappear after you've hidden it, you must start recording a macro, use the View, Toolbars command, and select the Stop Recording toolbar. Because this becomes part of the macro recording you must then end the macro recording and delete it, or edit it to remove the step that redisplays the toolbar.

7. To record the macro relatively, click the Relative Reference button on the Stop Recording toolbar.

8. Perform each step that's part of the task you are recording.

9. Click the Stop Recording button on the Stop Recording toolbar.

CAUTION

It's easy to forget that the Macro Recorder is on. It will keep recording until you tell it to stop, so be sure that you turn it off when the task at hand is recorded, or you'll get unexpected results at playback time! If you do forget to stop the recorder, you don't have to record the entire macro again; you can just edit it to remove the extra steps. See the later section "Editing a Macro" for details.

WHERE ARE MACROS SAVED?

A workbook is composed of objects such as worksheets, chart sheets, and modules. A *module* is an object that holds VBA code. Collectively, a workbook's objects are called a *project*. When you save a workbook, you're really saving the project that contains all the workbook's objects.

If you're storing a macro in the current workbook, save the workbook after recording. If you're storing a macro in the Personal Macro Workbook, you'll be prompted to save it when you exit Excel. Choose Yes when prompted to save the Personal Macro Workbook, or you'll lose any new macros you designated for storage there.

CAUTION

If you're recording or creating lengthy or complex macros, save the Personal Macro Workbook (Personal.xls) from the Visual Basic Editor immediately after completing each macro. A power loss may result in your losing any unsaved macros.

OPENING WORKBOOKS THAT CONTAIN MACROS

When you open a workbook that contains a macro, you might see the message box shown in Figure 31.4.

Figure 31.4
This message box appears when opening a workbook that contains macros and the macro security level is set to high (the default).

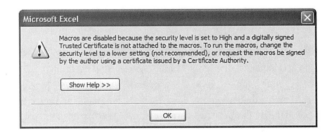

Some macros contain viruses that can corrupt workbooks or Excel itself. For this reason, all macros of unknown origin are disabled by default. As the message box in Figure 31.4

indicates, you must change the security level before you can run your macros. To do so, choose Tools, Macro, Security to open the Security dialog box (see Figure 31.5). Select Medium to have Excel prompt you to enable macros each time you open a workbook that contains macros. Choose Low if you know that the source of your macros is always reliable (you open only workbooks that contain macros you have created yourself, for example).

Figure 31.5
Use the Security dialog box to disable macro warning-message boxes.

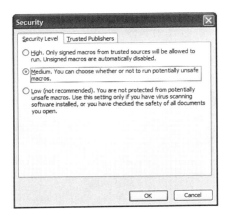

CAUTION

If you download sample workbooks from the Internet or receive them via e-mail from unreliable sources, don't choose the Low security setting. You could expose Excel and your workbooks to potentially damaging macro viruses.

NOTE

Excel 2003 allows you to digitally sign your macros. By doing so, other users of your macro workbooks can bypass the security message, yet keep security in place for workbooks from less-reliable sources. For more information on digital signatures, choose Help and search for "digital signatures" on Microsoft.com. Look for an entry called "Add a digital signature to a file or macro project."

TIP

To learn more about Excel macro viruses, search for Macro Viruses in Microsoft's Knowledge Base at http://support.microsoft.com.

MACRO PLAYBACK

Excel provides a variety of ways to play back a macro:

- Select the macro from a list in the Macro dialog box.
- Give it a keyboard shortcut.

- Attach it to a toolbar button.
- Assign it to a menu.
- Assign it to a graphic object on a sheet.

CAUTION

> Always save a workbook that contains a macro before you test the macro. If the macro contains errors, you might lose data when it plays back! If you find that data loss occurs after playback, close the workbook without saving and open it again to restore the lost data.

Table 31.1 lists each method's pros and cons.

TABLE 31.1   MACRO PLAYBACK METHODS

Playback Method	Pro	Con
Macro dialog box	No additional setup for playback required.	Longest method of playback.
Keyboard shortcut	Fast and easy. Can be assigned at the time of recording or by clicking the Options button in the Macros dialog box. Access to the macro from anywhere in the workbook.	Must memorize the shortcut. Could inadvertently overwrite system keyboard shortcuts.
Toolbar button	Macros can be grouped by function. Quick access to the command. Access from any part of the workbook.	Buttons are small and sometimes hard to understand. They also require additional work to set up and maintain.
Menu command	Macros can be grouped by function. More familiar to new and casual users. Easy access to macros from any part of the workbook.	Menus aren't used as often by frequent or power users.
Graphic object	Large surface area to click for playback. Space for typing a longer text description directly on the object. Can beplaced directly in a workbook.	Too many objects can clutter the worksheet. Object available to only one sheet in the workbook. Easy to lose the object when scrolling and when rows and columns aresized and deleted.

How should you decide which method is best? If the workbook that contains the macros is for your own personal use, select the method that you find easiest. Avoid graphic objects if the macro will be used in a large, multiple-sheet workbook.

If you're designing a workbook that other people will use, find out the users' likes, dislikes, and skill levels. If they're casual or inexperienced users, use menus and graphic objects. If they're experienced or power users, assign a toolbar button and a keyboard shortcut to each macro. Give the inexperienced users fewer options to minimize confusion and give the experienced users more options so they can choose their own method of playback.

TIP FROM

Bill

> Menus can't be attached to a workbook as can toolbars, but you can create a custom toolbar that consists of menus and looks and works like a menu bar, which can then be attached to a workbook. See Chapter 27, "Customizing Excel to Fit Your Working Style," for details on creating custom toolbars.

USING THE MACRO DIALOG BOX

Playing back a macro using the Macro dialog box requires the least amount of effort by the macro's creator; however, it's also the least convenient method of playback. It's used mostly in the testing phase of macro creation. Use the command as follows:

1. Choose Tools, Macro, Macros or press Alt+F8 to open the Macro dialog box (see Figure 31.6).

Figure 31.6
The Macro dialog box displays a list of macros from all open workbooks for playback or editing.

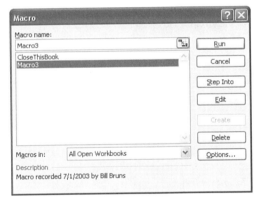

2. Select the macro you want to play back. As you click a macro name in the Macro Name list, note that the description for the macro appears at the bottom of the dialog box.

TIP FROM

Bill

> If you are selecting from a long list of macros, use the Macros In list to help you locate a macro. The Macros In list displays all open files that contain macros. Select a filename from the list, and only macros from that file will display.

3. Click the Run button or press Enter.

ASSIGNING A KEYBOARD SHORTCUT

A keyboard shortcut can be assigned to a macro at the time of recording (see the earlier section "Recording a Macro"). There are times, however, when you will want to assign or change a keyboard shortcut after the macro has been recorded. Keyboard shortcuts are easy to use provided that you can remember them! If your macro is part of a workbook that will be used by others, consider another method of playback, such as a button or menu command. Most users find these methods easier than remembering a keyboard shortcut. As mentioned earlier, keyboard shortcuts can also surprise the user—even you—if they replace the Excel default shortcuts, or if they use a key combination that can easily be pressed by accident.

To assign a shortcut to a macro after recording is complete, follow these steps:

1. Choose Tools, Macro, Macros, or press Alt+F8.
2. From the Macro Name list in the Macro dialog box, select the macro to which you want to assign a keyboard shortcut.
3. Click the Options button to display the Macro Options dialog box.
4. Place the insertion point in the Shortcut Key text box (see Figure 31.7).

Figure 31.7
Assign a shortcut key to an existing macro with the Macro Options dialog box.

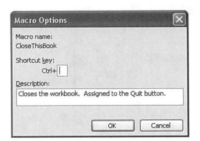

5. Press the desired shortcut-key combination.

> **NOTE**
>
> You don't have to press the Ctrl key when entering a shortcut-key combination. Instead, press the remaining key or keys. For example, to assign Ctrl+Shift+P to a macro, just press Shift+P.

6. Choose OK, and then close the Macro dialog box.

> **TIP FROM**
>
> *Bill*
>
> You also can add or change the description of a macro in the Macro Options dialog box.

ASSIGNING A MACRO TO A TOOLBAR OR MENU

In Excel, toolbars and menus are very similar. Both consist of button groupings. The only real difference between the two is the way menus and toolbars appear onscreen. When assigning macros to toolbar buttons or menu commands, the same procedures are followed.

You might want to assign a macro to a menu or toolbar to provide for easier playback, especially if you're mouse-oriented. You also might want to make the commands available to other people in a familiar way if you're designing a workbook that they'll use.

→ To learn more about assigning macros to toolbars, **see** "Assigning Macros," **p. 718**

To attach a macro to a toolbar button or menu, follow these steps:

1. Right-click any toolbar button or menu command.
2. Choose Customize from the shortcut menu to open the Customize dialog box.
3. Choose the Commands tab.
4. Select Macros from the Categories list (see Figure 31.8).

Figure 31.8
Drag Custom Button to add a new toolbar button or Custom Menu Item to add a new menu command.

5. To add a new toolbar button, drag Custom Button from the Commands list to the desired location on the existing toolbar and release it.

    To add a new menu command, drag Custom Menu Item to an existing menu. For example, if you want to place the new command on the File menu, drag Custom Menu Item on top of the File menu. Don't let go of the mouse button yet! The entire File menu will appear. Drag down the File menu until you have the new command positioned properly on the menu; then release the mouse button. If you opened the wrong menu by accident, just continue dragging the Custom Menu Item button, placing it over the correct menu, and position it.

6. Right-click the new button or command.
7. Choose Assign Macro from the shortcut menu (see Figure 31.9).

Figure 31.9
Right-click a custom
menu command or
toolbar button, and
choose Assign Macro.

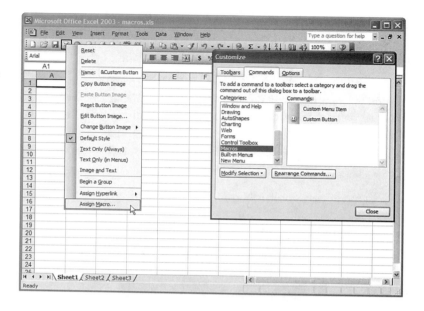

8. Select the macro that you want assigned to the button or command from the Macro
   Name list in the Assign Macro dialog box (see Figure 31.10).

Figure 31.10
Select a macro from
the Assign Macro dia-
log box to assign to a
toolbar button or
menu command.

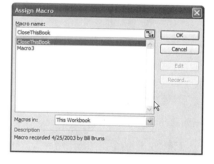

9. Click OK.

TIP FROM

Bill

A faster way to assign the macro to the button is to double-click it from the Macro Name
list in the Assign Macro dialog box.

10. Close the Customize dialog box.

ScreenTips can be assigned to toolbar buttons. The name you assign to the button appears as its ScreenTip. The name also functions as the button's text if you choose one of the text-display options. Here's how to assign a name to a toolbar button or menu command:

1. Right-click any toolbar button or menu.

2. Choose Customize.

3. Right-click the button or command to which the macro was assigned. From the resulting shortcut menu, type a name for the command in the Name text box. If desired, you can use spaces. Keep the name as succinct as possible. Long names don't work well as ScreenTips or button-display text.

NOTE

> The ampersand (&) in the Name box signifies where the underscore will appear on the menu command. Therefore, if the new command is called Print Region and you want the e to be underscored, you would type **Print R&egion** in the Name box.
>
> As a reminder, menus can be operated from the keyboard by pressing Alt and the underscored letter of the command (as in Alt+F to access the File menu). It's good practice to provide this functionality for consistency with other Excel menu commands.

31

CAUTION

> Before you assign an underscore to the new command, be sure that the letter you choose doesn't conflict with the letter of any other command on that same menu. If two or more commands on the same menu contain the same letter, Excel cycles through, selecting the commands that share the same letter. When the desired command is selected, you must press Enter to execute the command.
>
> If you assign the command to the File menu, for example, place it below the Print command, and give it an underscore of P. When you press Alt+F+P on the keyboard, Excel selects the Print command on the menu. Press P a second time, and Excel selects your command. Press P a third time, and Excel goes back to selecting the Print command. Press Enter, and the Print dialog box appears because Print is the currently selected command. If this happens to you, return to the custom command, and change the underscored character to a unique one for the menu command in question.

4. Press Enter to lock in the new name.

5. Close the Customize dialog box.

Excel enables you to control how the button or command displays on the toolbar or menu. You can display an image, text, or both for either a toolbar button or a menu command. To change how a menu or button displays, use the context menu that pops up when you right-click the custom menu item or the button with the Customize dialog box open.

Table 31.2 shows the display commands and their meanings.

TABLE 31.2   TOOLBAR BUTTON AND MENU COMMAND DISPLAY OPTIONS

Display Option	On a Toolbar, Displays...	On a Menu,Displays...
Default Style	Image only	Both image and name
Text Only (Always)	Name only	Name only
Text Only (In Menus)	Image only	Name only
Image and Text	Both image and name	Both image and name

TIP

Assign images to toolbar buttons that will be used for your personal use. If the toolbar is part of a workbook that will be used by other people, consider displaying text on the button instead of or in addition to the image.

→ For more information on customizing toolbars and buttons, see Chapter 27, "Customizing Excel to Fit Your Working Style."

CREATING A NEW TOOLBAR OR MENU FOR MACROS

Sometimes it's more convenient to have all your macros on a new custom toolbar or menu. You might do this to organize and categorize your macros. It's also wise when you're creating a workbook for other users. Such a workbook can be designed to display custom menus and toolbars upon opening. There are a couple of reasons for this approach:

→ To learn more about custom toolbars, **see** "Building Custom Toolbars," **p. 720**

- **Making the workbook easier to use**—If you're designing a workbook for other people to use, it's likely that the majority of these people don't know much more than the basics of Excel. Your first goal is to make the workbook as easy for them to use as possible.

- **Preventing the user from modifying the workbook**—If you remove commands that allow the user to modify the workbook, you won't have to worry about seeing your workbook in several different versions. Custom toolbars and menus allow you to control the commands to which you want the user to have access and, sometimes more importantly, the commands to which you don't want them to have access.

NOTE

If the user is familiar with the Customize command, he can easily alter your custom menu and toolbar scheme. To truly prevent the user from altering your changes, VBA is needed.

TIP FROM

Bill

Although this section discusses placing buttons and menu items on custom toolbars and menus, it's important to note that you can edit any of the Excel menus to add, change, or remove items as desired.

A custom menu is simply a custom toolbar to which menu commands are added. To create a custom menu, follow these steps:

1. Right-click an existing toolbar.

2. Click Customize to open the Customize dialog.

3. Click the Commands tab in the Customize dialog box.

4. Select New Menu from the Categories list.

5. Drag New Menu from the Commands list up and drop it into position on the menu bar (see Figure 31.10).

Figure 31.11

Create a new menu by dragging a New Menu command from the Customize dialog box to the menu bar.

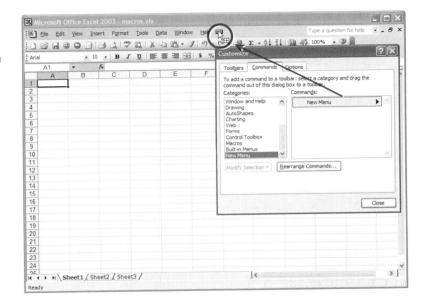

6. Right-click the New Menu button on the menu bar.

7. Type a name for the menu in the Name text box. Keep the name short and descriptive of the type of commands the menu will display. Place an ampersand (&) in front of the letter that you want underscored for keyboard access to the menu (for more on the ampersand and its usage, see the earlier section "Assigning a Macro to a Toolbar or Menu").

8. Press Enter to lock in the new name.

9. To assign commands to the new menu, see the earlier section "Assigning a Macro to a Toolbar or Menu."

ASSIGNING A MACRO TO A GRAPHIC OBJECT

The last method of macro playback is the graphic object. The most common graphic object used is a button, but macros can be assigned to most graphic objects created with the Drawing and Forms toolbars.

TIP FROM

Bill

> Use a graphic object if you have only a few macros to assign or if you want a large object with a long name. Avoid them in large workbooks. They're hard to access when scrolling great distances and when frequent switching between sheets is required.

To assign a macro to a button on a worksheet, follow these steps:

1. Right-click an existing toolbar and choose Forms from the shortcut menu to display the Forms toolbar.
2. Select the Button tool from the toolbar (see Figure 31.12).

Figure 31.12
Create a worksheet button with the Button tool on the Forms toolbar.

3. Move the mouse to the position on the sheet where you want the button to appear and drag in a diagonal direction. Release the mouse button when the worksheet button is drawn to your liking. (To create the button in a default size, you can just click, rather than drag.) The Assign Macro dialog box appears.
4. Select the macro to assign to the button from the Macro Name list.
5. Choose OK.
6. Drag across the name on the button to select it. Type a name descriptive of the macro the button will play (see Figure 31.13).
7. Click any cell in the current sheet to deselect the button. After the button has been deselected, it becomes active. An active button plays when it's clicked. Excel changes the mouse pointer to a hand when it's placed over an active button.

TIP FROM

Bill

> You might need to reselect the button to change its name, appearance, size, or location; assign a new macro to it; or delete it. Press and hold down the Ctrl key before you click the button to select it, or right-click the button.

Assigning a macro to a graphic object other than a macro button is very similar. The only difference is that the Assign Macro dialog box won't appear after you draw the graphic object. If you want to assign a macro to a rectangle, for example, draw the rectangle, right-click it, and choose Assign Macro from the shortcut menu. Select a macro from the Macro Name list and choose OK.

Figure 31.13
Apply a descriptive name to a worksheet button by selecting and typing over the generic name given by Excel.

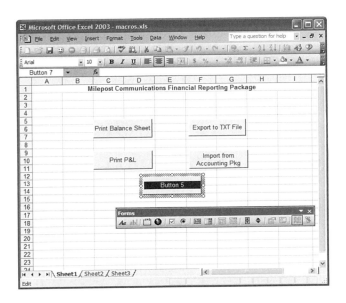

If you need to assign a macro to a graphic object that contains text and you have just finished entering or editing text but have not yet clicked off the object, right-click anywhere on the border of the object to access the Assign Macro command (see Figure 31.14).

Figure 31.14
Right-click a graphic object's border to access the Assign Macro command.

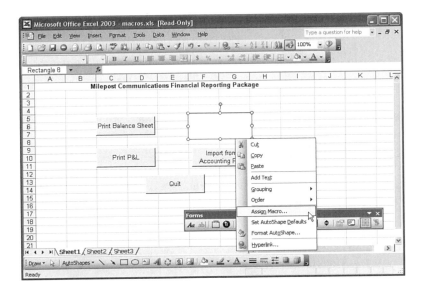

EDITING A MACRO

Editing a macro can be intimidating the first few times you try it. Macros are edited in the Visual Basic Editor. The Editor is a sophisticated program that contains multiple windows (see Figure 31.15). Don't worry! You don't have to know much about the Editor to make a simple macro edit.

Figure 31.15
Don't let this picture scare you. You don't have to know much about the Visual Basic Editor to edit a macro.

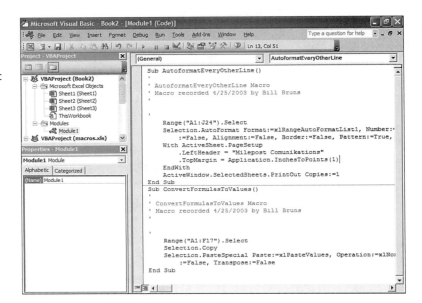

Notice the right side of the Editor screen. The right side displays the Code window. Macros are edited in the Code window. If you don't know VBA, you won't be able to edit much. Following are some typical edits that you can make:

- Change the spelling of text that was incorrectly typed during recording.
- Remove a command that was recorded but isn't required for proper playback, such as an accidental scrolling command.
- Correct an erroneously recorded number, such as a margin or column width.
- Delete a command that's no longer required in the macro.

Macros are composed of VBA statements. You can edit these statements just as you would edit text in a word-processing document. You can get a sense of what most statements do by looking at them. Following are some sample VBA statements that need editing, followed by a description of the edit that needs to be made:

- .LeftHeader = "Milepost Comunikations"

  Communications is misspelled.

- `ActiveWindow.SelectedSheets.PrintOut Copies:=1`

  The number of copies to print should be 2.

- `Range("A1:F17").Select`

  A4:F17 is the cell range that should be selected.

- `.TopMargin = Application.InchesToPoints(1)`

  The top margin was supposed to be 1.5 inches, not 1 inch.

NOTE

> These examples involve corrections that are not a must for a macro using them to execute properly. Each line of code would execute properly as is. However, they are changes you might want to make to improve the result of the macro.

CAUTION

> Literal text always appears between quotation marks (" "). If you remove one or both of the quotation marks during editing, the macro will generate an error.
>
> Don't delete a VBA statement if you're not sure what it does. This might result in the macro's not playing back properly.

To edit a macro, follow these steps:

1. If the macro you want to edit is stored in the Personal Macro Workbook, you must unhide the workbook before you can edit the macro. To unhide the Personal Macro Workbook, choose Window, Unhide (see Figure 31.16). Choose Personal.xls from the Unhide dialog box and then click OK.

Figure 31.16
Unhide the Personal Macro Workbook to edit the macros it contains.

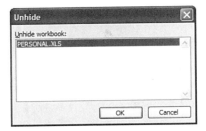

2. Choose Tools, Macro, Macros, or press Alt+F8.
3. Select the macro to edit from the Macro Name list (see Figure 31.17).
4. Click Edit. The selected macro opens in the Visual Basic Editor.
5. Edit the macro in the Code window.
6. Close the Visual Basic Editor by choosing File, Close and return to Microsoft Excel.
7. Save the workbook.

Figure 31.17
To edit a macro, select a macro name and click Edit.

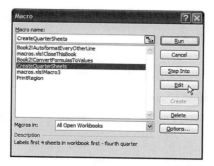

NOTE

> When you have completed editing a macro in the Personal Macro Workbook, hide the workbook by activating its window and choosing Window, Hide. If you don't hide the Personal Macro Workbook, it will be the first workbook you see every time you launch Excel.

EXAMPLE: EDITING A SHEET-NAMING MACRO

Consider the situation where you have a macro named CreateQuarterSheets that is stored in the Personal Macro Workbook. The macro names the first four sheets in the current workbook First Quarter, Second Quarter, Third Quarter, and Fourth Quarter, respectively. Suppose that after recording, you found the names were too long. You decide to edit the word Quarter to the abbreviation Qtr. Here's how you would make the change:

1. Unhide the Personal Macro Workbook. Open the macro CreateQuarterSheets in the Visual Basic Editor.
2. Double-click the first instance of the word Quarter in the Code window to select it (see Figure 31.18).
3. Type **Qtr** in its place, as shown in Figure 31.19.
4. Repeat this edit for the other three quarters.
5. Close the Visual Basic Editor.
6. Save and hide the Personal Macro Workbook.
7. Upon exiting Excel, be sure to choose Yes when prompted to save the Personal Macro Workbook. What you're saving here is the setting that the workbook is hidden. You'll always see this prompt after hiding the Personal Macro Workbook and exiting Excel. Always choose Yes, or the Personal Macro Workbook will be the first workbook to appear each time you start Excel.

Figure 31.18
Select the word Quarter in the Code window of the Visual Basic Editor.

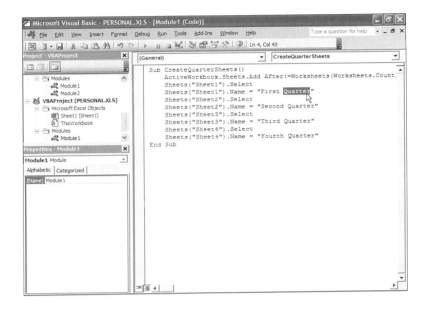

Figure 31.19
Type over the old text with the word **Qtr**. Be sure to leave the quotation marks.

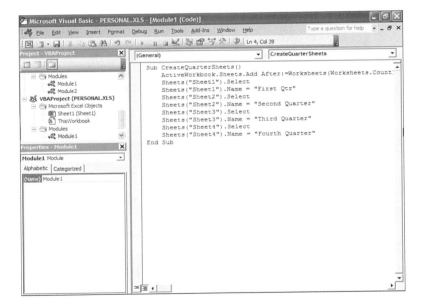

DELETING MACROS, CUSTOM BUTTONS, AND CUSTOM MENU ITEMS

From time to time, you might need to delete a graphic object, macro, custom toolbar button, or custom menu item, usually because the item is no longer needed or was created in error. The easiest object to delete is a graphic object, such as a worksheet button. Click on the object while holding Ctrl, and press the Delete key.

Other objects require a little more work to remove.

To delete a macro, follow these steps:

1. Open the workbook that contains the macro to remove. If the macro resides in the Personal Macro Workbook, you must first unhide that workbook.
2. Choose Tools, Macro, Macros or press Alt+F8.
3. From the Macro Name list, select the macro that you want to delete.
4. Click the Delete button and answer Yes at the prompt asking you whether you want to delete the macro.
5. Click Cancel to close the Macro dialog box.
6. Save the workbook and hide it again, if necessary.

To delete a custom toolbar button or menu item, follow these steps:

1. Right-click any toolbar button or menu command, and choose Customize from the shortcut menu.
2. To remove the button or command, do one of the following:
   - Drag the button or menu command that you want to remove from the toolbar or menu away from the toolbars and menus (so you don't accidentally drop it on a different toolbar or menu). When the mouse symbol shows a black X, release the mouse. The button or command is deleted.
   - Right-click the toolbar button or menu command that you want to delete. Choose Delete from the context menu.
3. Click Close, and the Customize dialog box closes.

NOTE

To remove (or move) a toolbar button (but not a command on a menu) without opening up the Customize dialog box, hold down the Alt key and drag the desired button.

MACROS TO HELP YOU WORK FASTER

This section provides some helpful suggestions for macros that can speed up your work. Be sure to store them in the Personal Macro Workbook so that they'll be available for playback in all your workbooks. Consider assigning each a keyboard shortcut or toolbar button for faster playback.

- **Print the current region**—This macro selects all the cells in the current region and prints them. The *current region* is defined as a range of contiguous cells bounded by blank columns and blank rows (or positioned at the edge of the worksheet). When recording this macro, choose Edit, Go To, click the Special button, and select Current Region to select the current region.

> To take full advantage of the "print current region" macro, don't include any blank spacing rows or columns between titles, subtitles, or within the data. If you need to add spacing, change row heights and column widths instead.

- **AutoFormat**—Record a macro to apply your favorite AutoFormat for quick and professionally formatted worksheets (see Listing 31.3). You can record the macro one of two ways: It can apply an AutoFormat to the current selection or apply it to the current region. If a range of cells is selected, the AutoFormat command applies the AutoFormat to the selection. If a single cell is selected, the AutoFormat command applies an AutoFormat to the current region. Regardless of how you choose to record it, select a range or a single cell, which is part of a larger block of cells, before you turn on the recorder.

31

LISTING 31.3   THIS MACRO AUTOFORMATS THE CURRENT REGION USING THE SIMPLE AUTOFORMAT STYLE

```
Sub ApplyAutoFormat ()
    Selection.AutoFormat Format:=xlRangeAutoFormatSimple, Number:=True, _
        Font:=True, Alignment:=True, Border:=True, Pattern:=True, Width:=True
End Sub
```

TROUBLESHOOTING

INCREASING MACRO PLAYBACK SPEED

My macros play back slower than I like. How can I get them to play back faster?

When played back, any recorded macro will show screen motions such as scrolling. In some instances, this can significantly increase playback time. To turn off screen updating and thereby decrease playback time, open the VB Editor, and add the following line of code directly under the Sub <macro name> line of the macro:

```
Application.ScreenUpdating = False
```

RUNTIME ERRORS

I keep getting a runtime error during playback and can't determine why. What should I do?

A *runtime error* indicates that some part of the code no longer makes sense in the current playback environment. For example, perhaps as part of the original macro recording, you selected a sheet called Expenses. Later, after recording, you rename the sheet Current Expenses. A runtime error is generated because the macro is attempting to select a sheet called Expenses that no longer exists.

Of course, finding and correcting runtime errors (known as *debugging*) isn't always easy. So, you have two choices. You can record the macro again from the beginning or use the VB Editor's debugging tools to find the bug. If you don't have the time or desire to learn more about macros beyond recording them, recording the macro again is the fastest solution. However, if you know you'll work with macros often or will have to create complex macros in the future, you should learn more about debugging with the VB Editor. This will be covered in the next chapter.

EXCEL IN PRACTICE

APPLYING CUSTOM HEADERS

A common task in Excel is applying custom headers and footers to a sheet in a workbook. To record the macro, follow these steps:

1. Turn on the Macro Recorder. Store this macro in the Personal Macro Workbook, and call it CustomHeaderFooter or something similar.

2. Choose File, Page Setup to open the Page Setup dialog box. Click the Header/Footer tab to select it and use the Custom Header and Custom Footer buttons to set the headers and footers (see Figure 31.20). Click OK when you're done.

Figure 31.20
Set the header and footer using the Custom Header and Custom Footer buttons.

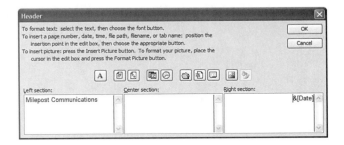

3. Stop the recorder.

CAUTION

If you select all sheets in the workbook as part of a recorded page setup macro, the macro will alter the Page Setup settings for only the active sheet when played back. To alter Page Setup settings for multiple sheets simultaneously, you must write some VBA code.

CREATING AN AUTOFIT COLUMN MACRO

A simple and time-saving macro to record will AutoFit every column on the active worksheet. The following macro selects every column on the current sheet, AutoFits each column, and then selects cell A1. (If you prefer your worksheets to have custom column sizes, of course, you can record something else for practice, or just delete this macro—or never use it—after recording.) To record the AutoFit macro, perform the following steps:

1. Be sure that cell A1 is visible onscreen.
2. Display the Record Macro dialog box by choosing Tools, Macro, Record New Macro. Store the macro in the Personal Macro Workbook so that it will be available to any workbook. Name it FitColumnWidths (or some other appropriate name). Assign a keyboard shortcut of Ctrl+Shift+C. Choose OK to start recording.
3. Press Ctrl+A to select all the cells on the current sheet.
4. Choose Format, Column, AutoFit Selection.
5. Select cell A1 on the current sheet.
6. Stop the Macro Recorder by clicking the Stop Recording button.
7. Now test the new macro. Switch to a new sheet or workbook that requires column-width adjustments. Press Ctrl+Shift+C to AutoFit the column widths.

31

CREATING INTERACTIVE EXCEL APPLICATIONS WITH VBA

by Ken Cook

In this chapter

Why Write Macros Rather Than Record Them?   838

Introduction to Object-Oriented Programming   839

Variables and Constants   842

Understanding the Visual Basic Editor   845

Getting Help with Visual Basic   847

VBA Procedures   848

Control Structures   856

Code-Writing Tips   861

Debugging   865

Automatic Execution of VBA Code   871

WHY WRITE MACROS RATHER THAN RECORD THEM?

The Macro Recorder enables you to create your own command macros in Excel by recording menu selections, keystrokes, and mouse movements. Recorded macros have their limitations, however. Following are a few things that can't be recorded:

- **Interaction**—You want the user to have input into how the macro will play back. Suppose that you create a workbook that charts sales data for 20 product segments. Rather than force users to print a chart for each segment (in this case 20 charts), you would have them select which segments they want to print.

- **Decisions**—You want the macro to make decisions on how to play back based on what it encounters when playing back. Suppose that you have a worksheet with one thousand rows of product sales data at the product level. Your sales data provider gave you the data in Excel workbook form. The file contains some products with sales amounts equal to zero interspersed among the data rows. You want to eliminate these products.

- **Custom functions**—You continually perform the same complex or lengthy calculation in your spreadsheets. Suppose that you have several worksheets that require you to display the number of year-to-date days. Rather than entering that complex formula every time you need the current number of year-to-date days, you want a simpler way to enter the calculation.

- **Efficiency**—The Macro Recorder can be inefficient. For example, in most cases you don't have to select a range of cells to do something to it, yet because the Macro Recorder can only record keystrokes, it knows of no other way to refer to a range. For this kind of operation, writing the macro yourself with VBA is much more efficient.

Visual Basic for Applications (VBA), Excel's programming language, provides the tools to create solutions to scenarios that can't be recorded. Through VBA you can create a solution to virtually any problem that you encounter in Excel. You can make using Excel more efficient for yourself and, sometimes more importantly, for other users who don't know much about the application but are required to use it. You can completely customize Excel through VBA to perform a specific task. You can even change the entire Excel interface.

The goal of this chapter is to provide you with a basic VBA foundation. With that foundation, you can take your recorded macros to the next level. Due to the enormous scope of VBA, of course, this chapter can't possibly provide more than a brief overview of the possibilities for programming Excel procedures with VBA. You should consult other resources to become highly VBA proficient.

The first part of this chapter explains some VBA terms and concepts and shows code samples that help define the concepts. The latter part of the chapter explains how to use the tools that Excel provides to write VBA code. By gaining an understanding of these VBA concepts, your code writing will come easier.

NOTE

For more in-depth information on VBA, see Que's *Special Edition Using Visual Basic 6*, ISBN# 0-7897-1542-2.

INTRODUCTION TO OBJECT-ORIENTED PROGRAMMING

VBA is a structured programming language just like English is a structured communication language. English sentences are constructed of building blocks such as nouns, verbs, and adjectives; VBA sentences (called *statements*) are constructed of building blocks such as objects, methods, and properties. English sentences are grouped in larger blocks of related information called paragraphs; similarly, VBA statements are grouped in larger blocks called procedures. A *procedure* is a set of VBA statements that performs a specific task or calculates a specific result. If you want to learn how to construct VBA statements and procedures, you first must learn more about the building blocks. This section provides some background information on VBA's building blocks.

OBJECTS

VBA is an object-oriented programming language. Excel is made up of a series of objects that you can manipulate through code. Think of some of the objects that make up your office. You probably have a desk, chair, computer, and telephone. You use these objects to complete the various tasks that your job requires.

Similarly, when using Excel to complete a task, you're manipulating Excel objects to complete the task. For example, when you complete an Excel expense report form, you might open the workbook containing a worksheet with the expense report form, and then enter data in a range on that form and save the workbook. The workbook, worksheet, and range are all Excel objects. VBA can be used to manipulate such objects, making it easier for you to complete the task of submitting an expense report. Emailing the report to the Finance department, for example, is a process that could be automated. (For a complete list of Excel objects, see the Object Browser located in the Visual Basic Editor.) To learn more about the Visual Basic Editor, see "Understanding the Visual Basic Editor," later in this chapter.

COLLECTIONS

Some objects are collection objects. A *collection* is a group of similar objects that are treated as one. Suppose that in your office, you have a desk with three drawers. You call them the top, middle, and bottom drawers. Together, you could say that they make up the "drawers collection." You refer to each drawer by its name when completing a task that involves that drawer. You might say to your co-worker, "Please get the Murphy account folder from the bottom drawer of my drawers collection."

The Workbooks collection is an example of an Excel collection object. The Workbooks collection consists of each workbook object that you have open and at your disposal. You refer to a workbook in the Workbooks collection by enclosing its name in parentheses. The following VBA snippet refers to the Expenses workbook:

```
Workbooks("Expenses.xls")
```

METHODS

A *method* is an action that can be performed by an object. Think once again of the desk drawers in your office. They can be opened and closed. So, you could say that each has an open method and a close method. When you open a drawer to get a file, you are using the open method of the drawer.

An Excel object has methods as well. Excel's workbook object has an Open method and a Close method. You can use Excel's File menu to manually manipulate the workbook object with the Open and Close commands, or you can use VBA to programmatically manipulate the workbook object with the Open and Close methods. Excel objects are separated from their methods by a period. The following VBA snippet uses the Close method to close the Expenses workbook:

```
Workbooks("Expenses.xls").Close
```

PROPERTIES

Properties are used to describe an object. You could describe your office desk drawer as brown and made of wood. You could say that these are its color and material properties, respectively.

Some properties are read-only; others are read/write. Read-only properties can't be changed; read/write properties can. Your desk drawer's color property would be read/write. You can always pull out your paintbrush and change the color of the drawer. However, you can't change the material from which it's made without changing the drawer entirely, so the material property would be read-only.

Excel properties describe Excel objects. For example, the workbook object has a Path property. It describes the complete path to the referenced workbook. The Path property is read-only. You can't change the path of a workbook without first saving it to a different folder. Just as methods are separated from objects by periods, so are properties. The following code snippet uses the Path property of the workbook object to display the path of a workbook called Expenses.xls in a message box onscreen:

```
Msgbox Workbooks("Expenses.xls").Path
```

> **NOTE**
>
> Msgbox is a function that displays a small message dialog box onscreen to alert or inform the user of something. For more information on functions, see the later section, "Functions."

If you set a read/write property equal to something, it will change the current value. If you don't set a read/write property equal to something, it will tell you (also known as *return*) its current value. The Name property of the Sheet object of the Sheets collection is a read/write property. It can return the name of a sheet or set the name of a sheet.

This code snippet sets the name of Sheet1 to January:

```
Sheets("Sheet1").Name = "January"
```

The following code snippet returns the name of the active sheet (the one with the white sheet tab) in the current workbook in a message box onscreen.

```
Msgbox ActiveSheet.Name
```

FUNCTIONS

A VBA *function* is similar to a workbook function. It performs a calculation and then returns a result. Functions provide information that can assist you in building VBA procedures. Suppose that you want to ask the user a question. The InputBox function displays a dialog box onscreen, with a prompt and text box. Figure 32.1 shows an input box.

Figure 32.1
This input box prompts the user for a title.

When the user types a response in the input box and closes it with the OK button, the function returns whatever was typed in the box. If you typed **Sales** in the input box displayed in Figure 32.1, it would return the word Sales to your VBA code. You could then write code to place the word in a cell, use it as a header on a report, or make it the title of a chart—just to name a few uses. For a complete list of functions, including what they return and how to use them, see "Functions" under "Visual Basic Language Reference" on the Visual Basic Help Contents tab. For more information on accessing Visual Basic Help, see the section "Getting Help with Visual Basic," later in this chapter.

PUTTING IT ALL TOGETHER

Objects, methods, and properties are the building blocks of VBA code. Understanding what they are and how they're put together will give you a head start when writing VBA code. There will be times, especially in the beginning, when you know what should be done next but you don't know the correct VBA statement you need to complete your task. That's when you should ask yourself the following questions:

- What object am I trying to manipulate?
- Do I want to change the way the object is described?
- Do I want to do something to the object or have it do something?

If you know the answers to these questions, you can search the Help system for the statement you'll need. For example, if you want to use VBA to determine whether the current workbook is saved, start with the workbook object. Whether it's saved or not is descriptive. This tells you to look for a property. Each object's help page provides a link to the methods and properties of that object. Through that link, you can obtain information on various properties and methods of an object, including examples of how to use them.

When you query the Help system for the workbook object and then click its properties link, you'll see the Saved property.

VARIABLES AND CONSTANTS

During code playback, there are times when information that's gathered from the user, returned by a function, or defined by the programmer must be stored temporarily for use later on. Sometimes, this information will change as the code is running. Other times, it will stay the same the entire time the code is running. Variables and constants are used to store this type of information during code playback.

WHAT IS A VARIABLE?

A *variable* is a temporary storage location in your computer's memory for a piece of information used by a procedure. Certain procedures obtain different data each time they run. Suppose that you've written a procedure that asks the user for his or her name and places it in the footer of the current workbook. If many people use this procedure, the name will be different every time the procedure is run. These are the logical steps such a procedure would follow:

1. Ask the user for his or her name.
2. Store it somewhere temporarily.
3. Place it in the footer.

Although it is possible to place the results of an input box function directly in the footer, the most efficient way is to have a place to store the answer temporarily—in a variable. By placing it in a variable first, you can analyze the result before using it. For example, you might want to check the variable to see whether the user actually typed anything in the input box and place it in the footer only if he did. A variable name can be anything you want it to be; subject to these rules which apply to variable names.

- The name can be from 1 to 255 characters in length.
- It must begin with a letter.
- It can't contain spaces or periods.
- It must be unique among all other variable names within the same procedure.

TIP FROM

Ken

> Try to keep your variable names to 20 characters or less. For multiple-word variable names, capitalize the first letter of each word for better readability. Following are some sample variable names:
> - CompanyName
> - ShippingDate
> - ReportTitle

The code in Listing 32.1 shows how the variable UserName is employed in a procedure. The procedure uses the InputBox function to query the user for a name, and then places that name in the left section of the footer. It also adds the page number to the right section of the footer and clears all header sections. (Creating this type of procedure is discussed in detail later in this chapter.)

LISTING 32.1   THE AddNameToFooter PROCEDURE

```
1 Sub AddNameToFooter()
2    UserName = InputBox("What is your name?", "Add Name to Footer")
3    With ActiveSheet.PageSetup
4        .LeftHeader = ""
5        .CenterHeader = ""
6        .RightHeader = ""
7        .LeftFooter = UserName
8        .CenterFooter = ""
9        .RightFooter = "Page &P of &N"
10   End With
11 End Sub
```

Let's look at the procedure line by line. The first and last lines of the procedure define its starting and ending points. In addition, the first line defines the procedure's name, AddNameToFooter. Every command procedure begins with the word Sub followed by the name of the procedure and ends with the words End Sub.

Line 2 uses the InputBox function to ask the user for his or her name and then stores that name in a variable called UserName. Lines 3 and 10 begin and end a With statement that executes a series of statements (in this case, properties) on an object (in this case, the PageSetup object). The use of the With statement saves you the time of having to type the word PageSetup in front of each PageSetup property you want to set. Every use of With must have the phrase End With to complete it, as in line 10 in the previous listing.

Lines 4–9 use the header and footer properties of the PageSetup object to set the text of the header and footer. In particular, line 7 sets the left section of the footer equal to the value of the UserName variable and line 9 sets the right section of the footer equal to the current page number and the total number of pages. Lines 4, 5, and 6 clear all three parts of the header and line 8 clears the center section of the footer by setting those properties equal to "".

NOTE

An empty set of quotation marks (" ") in VBA represents what's called a *zero-length string*. A zero-length string is equivalent to nothing. Therefore, if you set a property or variable equal to " ", you erase its current value.

WHAT IS A CONSTANT?

Like a variable, a *constant* is a temporary holding area for a piece of information used in a procedure. Unlike a variable, however, a constant, as its name implies, never changes. Suppose that you have a procedure that uses your company name multiple times. Further suppose that the company name is a long one, such as Widget Manufacturing & Development, Incorporated. Rather than typing that text in your procedure each time it's needed, you can assign it to a much shorter constant name. That way, when you need your company name, you don't have to type out all that text. Instead, you can type the constant name. Plus, should the value of the constant (in this case, the name of the company) change at some point in the future, you only have to change the definition of the constant and not the multiple lines of code that refer to it.

Constants must be declared. A *declaration statement* in VBA is used to define the value of a constant. Each constant declaration begins with the word Const. Constants should be declared at the top of a procedure, usually right under the Sub or Function statements. They often are named using caps for easy identification from variable names. Each word of a multiple-word constant usually is separated from the next with the underscore character (_), again, to help identify a constant from a variable. Listing 32.2 shows what the company name constant might look like in a procedure. Notice that the CO_NAME constant on line 2 is used to place the company name in cell A1 and in the left footer (lines 3 and 8, respectively).

LISTING 32.2   THE DECLARATION AND USE OF A CONSTANT IN A PROCEDURE

```
1 Sub SetCoTitleToPage()

2    Const CO_NAME = "Widget Manufacturing & Development, Incorporated"

3    Range("A1").FormulaR1C1 = CO_NAME
4    With ActiveSheet.PageSetup
5       .LeftHeader = ""
6       .CenterHeader = ""
7       .RightHeader = ""
8       .LeftFooter = CO_NAME
9       .CenterFooter = ""
10      .RightFooter = "Page &P or &N"
11   End With

12 End Sub
```

NOTE

> The company name is enclosed in quotation marks. All *literal text* (this is what VBA calls a string) placed in a procedure must be surrounded by quotation marks or an error will occur when running the procedure. VBA will interpret any text without quotation marks as a constant, variable, or VBA programming language word.

A closer look at the procedure in Listing 32.2 reveals that line 2 declares the constant CO_NAME equal to the string Widget Manufacturing & Development, Incorporated. Line 3 uses the FormulaR1C1 property of the Range object to set the value of cell A1 equal to the value of the CO_NAME constant. This line is the VBA equivalent of typing text in a cell.

Lines 4 through 11 use With to set the header and footer properties of the PageSetup object. The CO_NAME constant is used in line 8 to set the left footer equal to Widget Manufacturing & Development, Incorporated.

UNDERSTANDING THE VISUAL BASIC EDITOR

The Visual Basic Editor is the tool used to display VBA code in Excel. All VBA code is accessed through the Editor.

Before you look at the Editor, here's a little background on what it displays. Every workbook is made up of a series of Visual Basic objects, as mentioned earlier. Each sheet in a workbook is an object, as is the workbook itself. If a workbook contains a VBA procedure, it will have a *module* object. A module looks and acts like a word processing document. It contains the VBA instructions or code that make up procedures. The collection of all objects that make up a workbook is called a *project*. The Editor displays projects and their associated objects.

The Visual Basic Editor can be intimidating when first examined. To view it, choose Tools, Macro, Visual Basic Editor from the menu or press Alt+F11. The Standard toolbar contains tools required to manage your project.

Table 32.1 shows the Editor's Standard toolbar buttons.

TABLE 32.1   VISUAL BASIC EDITOR STANDARD TOOLBAR BUTTONS

Button	Name	Description
	View Microsoft Excel	Returns you to Excel.
	Insert Object	Adds a new object to the current project.
	Save	Saves the workbook that contains the current project.
	Cut	Cuts selection so that it can be moved elsewhere.
	Copy	Copies selection so that it can be duplicated elsewhere.

continues

TABLE 32.1   CONTINUED

Button	Name	Description
	Paste	Pastes cut or copied selection to the location of the insertion point.
	Find	Finds a word or phrase within the project.
	Undo	Reverses previous actions.
	Redo	Reverses the Undo command.
	Run	Plays the current macro. Place the insertion point in a macro's code to make it the current macro. It also displays custom forms.
	Break	Pauses macro execution. Continue a paused macro from the breakpoint with the Run button.
	Reset	Stops macro execution.
	Design Mode	Toggles design mode on and off. Macro code doesn't run in design mode.
	Project Explorer	Shows the Project Explorer window if it's hidden. The Project Explorer enables you to browse the objects that make up a project for each open workbook.
	Properties Window	Shows the Properties window if it's hidden. Properties describe an object. For example, a worksheet object has a Name property.
	Object Browser	Shows the Object Browser. The object browser displays all the objects that can be manipulated through VBA code.
	Toolbox	Shows the Toolbox. The Toolbox is used during the design of a custom form.
	Microsoft Visual Basic Help	Accesses the help system.

By default, the Editor is divided into three windows (see Figure 32.2). The *Project Explorer* displays all open projects and their associated objects. You use this window to browse modules, which contain VBA code, when attempting to locate a particular procedure.

The *Properties window* displays the properties of the selected object in the Project window. If a module is selected in the Project window, for example, the Properties window will display the only property of a module—its Name property. Read/Write properties of selected objects can be changed directly in the Properties window.

The *Code window* displays the code that is associated with the object selected in the Project Explorer. Because all procedures appear in the Code window, this is the window that you will use most often in the Editor.

Figure 32.2
Three windows displayed by the Visual Basic Editor.

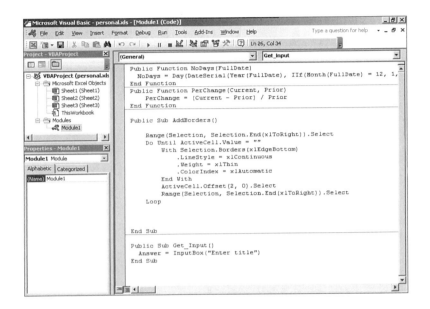

TIP FROM

If you inadvertently close any of these windows, you can reopen them in the Editor by choosing the window name from the View menu.

GETTING HELP WITH VISUAL BASIC

The fastest and cheapest VBA help resource is Excel's online help system. It contains the entire VBA language reference. Even experienced programmers find themselves using the Help system on a regular basis.

There are several ways to access the help system. The easiest is to use the Type a question for help box located in the upper-right corner of the Editor. Follow these steps:

1. While in the Editor, click in the Type a question for help box.
2. Formulate a question for the topic for which you need help and type it in the box. It uses Microsoft's Natural Language feature, so you can use sentencelike text or type the word or phrase that you feel will yield the topic you are interested in.
3. Press Enter to display a list of possible matching help topics (see Figure 32.3).

Figure 32.3
Use the Type a question for help box for help on VBA topics.

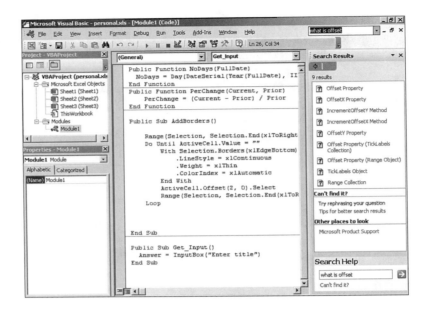

4. Choose a topic from the list to display a help screen about the topic you selected. If the desired topic doesn't appear on the initial list, you can click the See More phrase to get additional suggestions.

Another method is to press the F1 key. While working on a module in the Editor, select or type the VBA word for which you want help. Make sure that the insertion point is somewhere in the word or that the word is selected. Then press F1. The Help system displays the help topic for the selected word.

VBA PROCEDURES

A procedure is a block of VBA code that either performs a specific task or returns a result. Procedures come in two flavors:

- Subroutines are procedures that perform a specific task. Macros recorded with the Macro Recorder are subroutines. (For more on the Macro Recorder, see Chapter 31, "Recording and Editing a Macro".)

- Functions are identical to subroutines, but they also return a result.

The following sections show you how to use the Editor to create both types of procedures.

CREATING A NONRECORDED PROCEDURE

Whether you're creating a subroutine or a function, you can follow these general guidelines to get you started:

1. Open the workbook to which you want to add the new procedure.

2. Choose Tools, Macro, Macros from the menu or press Alt+F8 (see Figure 32.4).

Figure 32.4
Use the Macro dialog box to create a new nonrecorded procedure.

3. Type a name for the procedure in the Macro Name box.

TIP FROM

Procedure names must begin with a letter and can contain letters, numbers, and the underscore character. They cannot contain spaces.

4. Decide where you want to store the procedure and select the appropriate option from the Macros in: drop-down list. You can choose among All Open Workbooks, This Workbook, or Personal.xls.

5. Click the Create button. The Visual Basic Editor opens with the new procedure displayed in the Code window (see Figure 32.5). The Sub statement is followed by the procedure name, a set of parentheses, and the End Sub statement. The parentheses are used if the procedure requires one or more parameters. A *parameter* is information that can be passed to the current procedure from another procedure.

6. If you want to create a function, change the word Sub to Function on the first line of the new procedure. The last line will change automatically from End Sub to End Function.

7. Type the VBA statements required to create the new procedure.

TIP FROM

Type all VBA statements (objects, methods, properties, built-in functions) in lowercase. By doing so, you can catch your mistakes as you type. When you move off the current line, the Editor capitalizes at least one letter in each word if you have typed the word

continues

continued

correctly. The Editor also appropriately capitalizes the names of the variables and constants. If no capitalization takes place, check the word in question. Is it spelled correctly? Is it an actual Excel object, method, property, or VBA function?

Suppose that you type the following line:

```
range("A1").formular1c1 = co_name
```

When you move off it to the next line, the Editor changes it to this:

```
Range("A1").FormulaR1C1 = CO_NAME
```

So far, so good. Now what if the Editor displays this?

```
rane("A1").FormulaR1C1 = CO_NAME
```

The first word has no capital letters, so you know that you made some kind of typing error that must be corrected. In this case, *range* is misspelled at the beginning of the line.

Figure 32.5
A new procedure named `ChartData` is displayed in the Code window of the Visual Basic Editor.

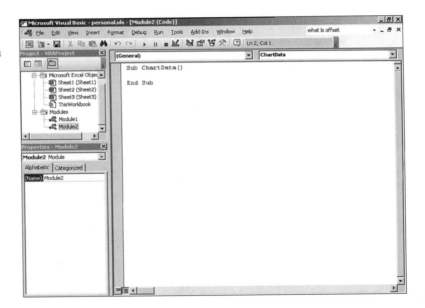

After you create your first procedure in the Editor, you might need to add more procedures. A module can, and typically does, contain multiple procedures. The `Sub` or `Function` statement denotes the beginning of a procedure and the `End` statement marks the end of a procedure. To add procedures you can use the Macros command on the Tools menu of the Editor; however, it's easier to add the new procedure using another command in the Editor window itself, especially if you're adding a function. Here's how:

1. Make sure that the module to which you want to add the new procedure is selected in the Project Explorer and is displayed in the Code window to its right. If it isn't, look for an entry such as `VBAProject (<filename.xls>)`. Expand the project (if necessary) to

reveal its Microsoft Excel Objects and Modules folders. Expand the Modules folder if necessary to reveal the modules for the selected workbook. Then, double-click the module name (most likely Module1) in the Modules folder to open the module in the Code window.

2. Choose Insert, Procedure from the menu. The Add Procedure dialog box appears (see Figure 32.6).

Figure 32.6
Use the Add Procedure dialog box to add a new procedure to the currently displayed module in the Code window.

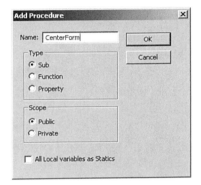

3. Type a name for the procedure in the Name text box.

4. To create a new subroutine, select Sub from the Type section of the dialog box. To create a function, select Function.

5. Leave the default scope of Public. *Scope* refers to the availability of the procedure to other procedures in the current project that aren't in the same module. Public procedures can be accessed by any other procedure in a project. For more information on scope, search the Help system for the word *scope*.

CAUTION

> You can't have two public procedures with the same name in the same project. To be on the safe side, always use a unique name for each procedure within the same project.

6. Choose OK to add the new procedure to the selected module.

7. Type the VBA code required of the new procedure in the Code window.

TIP FROM

Ken

> A faster way to create a new procedure is to type **Sub** or **Function** directly in the Code window, followed by the name of the procedure. When you press Enter, the Editor automatically adds the set of parentheses and the End Sub or End Function statement to the end of the new procedure. Make sure the cursor is not inside another procedure when you type Sub or Function. You can only insert procedures after the End statement from one procedure and before the Sub or Function statement of another procedure.

32

There might be times when you need to add a new module to a VBA project. Usually, this is done to organize procedures in some way. Perhaps you want to place all your functions in one module and your subroutines in another. This makes individual procedures easier to find when browsing for them in the Editor. To add a new module, use the following steps:

1. Choose Tools, Macro, Visual Basic Editor from the menu or press Alt+F11.
2. Select Insert, Module from the menu.

Similar to sheets in a workbook, after you have several modules in a project, you might want to name each module with a more meaningful name than the default for easier identification of the type of procedures the module contains. Without intervention the editor will name modules Module1, Module2, and so on. Here's how to name a module in the Editor:

1. Select the module to name in the Project Explorer. It will be in the Modules folder under the project that contains it.
2. Double-click the default name next to the Name property in the Properties window. If the Properties window is not currently visible, click View, Properties Window or press F4.
3. Type the new name and press Enter. Module names must begin with a letter, cannot contain spaces and certain other special characters, and cannot exceed 255 characters in length.

If you added a module in error or want to delete it for some other reason, perform the following steps:

1. Right-click the module to delete in the Project Explorer window.
2. Choose Remove *<module name>* from the shortcut menu.
3. Select No when asked whether you want to export the module before removing it (see Figure 32.7).

> **NOTE**
>
> The Editor enables you to export a module. This means that you're saving the module and all of its code. By doing so, you can import the module to another workbook. In effect, by exporting and importing, you're copying a set of procedures between workbooks. If you want to move a module to another workbook, make sure you export it before you remove it from the source workbook.

Creating a Function Procedure

As mentioned previously, a function is a type of procedure that returns a result. For example, the built-in Excel SUM function returns the total of a range of numbers that you supply to it. There might be times when you want to create your own custom functions, usually when the calculation you're attempting is complex or lengthy and you would like to simplify its entry. This section details some scenarios for creating a custom function and explains how to create one.

Figure 32.7
Choose No in this message box when deleting a module unless you want to keep a copy of the code in a text file for use in another project.

CREATING A FUNCTION TO CALCULATE THE NUMBER OF DAYS IN A MONTH

You can use custom functions to automate the process of entering a complex or frequent calculation in Excel. Suppose that you often must calculate the number of days in a given month. Listing 32.3 shows a formula that supplies this number. Try opening a new workbook. Enter a date in A2 of sheet 1 and the formula in A3. The formula returns the total number of days in the month of the date you entered.

LISTING 32.3   A FORMULA THAT CALCULATES THE TOTAL NUMBER OF DAYS IN A MONTH

```
=DAY(DATE(YEAR(A2),IF(MONTH(A2)=12,1,MONTH(A2)+1),1)-1)
```

32

It might be difficult to remember this calculation or too time consuming to enter it repeatedly in each new worksheet that requires it. So, as an alternative, you can create a function. The function requires you to enter the formula one more time. In the future, however, when you need your calculation, all you have to enter is the name of the function, just as you would any other Excel function (plus any required arguments).

Most functions require at least one argument. An *argument* is a piece of information that the function needs so that it can perform its calculation correctly. In this case, the information the function needs is a date so that it can determine the number of days in the month referenced by the date.

Here's how to create and use this function:

1. Navigate to an existing or insert a new module in the Personal Macro Workbook.

> **NOTE**
>
> When you use the record macro feature Excel automatically creates a Personal Macro Workbook named personal.xls. If available, you will find personal.xls in the object browser's project list.

2. Type the code in Listing 32.4 at the end of the module.

LISTING 32.4   CALCULATE THE NUMBER OF DAYS IN A GIVEN MONTH

```
Function NoDays(FullDate)
    NoDays = Day(DateSerial(Year(FullDate), IIf(Month(FullDate) = 12, 1,
    ➥Month(FullDate) + 1), 1) - 1)
End Function
```

NOTE

Some worksheet functions have VBA equivalents with slightly different names. The VBA function equivalent of the worksheet function DATE is DATESERIAL. The VBA equivalent of the worksheet function IF is IIf.

3. Click the Save button on the Editor's Standard toolbar.

4. In a new workbook, type **2/15/00** in cell A1.

5. Select cell A2 and choose Insert, Function from the menu.

6. From the Function Category list, select User Defined.

7. Choose PERSONAL.XLS!NoDays from the Function Name list and Click OK.

8. Type **A1** in the FullDate text box.

9. Click OK. The custom function returns 29—the year 2000 was a leap year, so February contained 29 days. Figure 32.8 displays the function in use in a simple worksheet.

Figure 32.8
The NoDays function in use in a simple sales analysis worksheet.

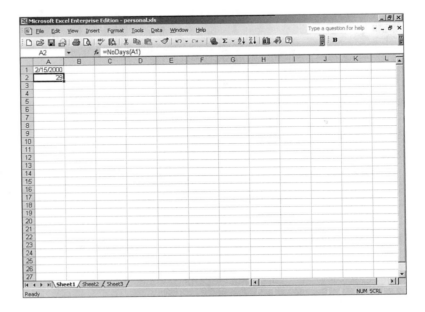

CREATING A PERCENT CHANGE FUNCTION

A difficult calculation for some to remember is the percentage change between two numbers. Do you divide by the first number or the second? A custom function can help here as well. Although this is a simple calculation, you have to remember it only once if you make it into a custom function.

Here's how to create the function:

1. Open the Visual Basic Editor and open a module from the Personal Macro Workbook (Personal.xls).
2. Place the cursor at the desired insertion point inside the module and choose Insert, Procedure from the menu. The Add Procedure dialog box opens.
3. Type **PerChange** in the Name box.
4. Select Function from the Type list.
5. Click OK.
6. Modify the new function so that it matches Listing 32.5.

LISTING 32.5   THE COMPLETED PERCHANGE FUNCTION

```
Function PERCHANGE(Current, Prior)
    PERCHANGE = (Current - Prior) / Prior
End Function
```

32

To use the function, follow these steps.

1. Enter numbers in two cells in a worksheet or identify two numeric cells in an existing worksheet. The first will be the current value and the second will be the prior value. Place the cell pointer in the cell where you want the answer to appear.
2. Choose Insert, Function from the menu.
3. From the Function Category list, select User Defined.
4. Select Personal.xls!PerChange from the Function Name list and click OK.
5. Select a cell for the Current value and a cell for the Prior value.
6. Click OK. See Figure 32.9 for an example of the function in use in an actual worksheet.

NOTE

You can type out the entry of a custom function that's stored in another open workbook (such as the Personal Macro Workbook) by entering the workbook name followed by the exclamation point and the procedure name into a cell formula like this:

```
=PERSONAL.XLS!perChange(A1, A2)
```

In this example A1 and A2 are the cells containing the current and prior values.

Figure 32.9
The PerChange function in use in a simple sales analysis worksheet.

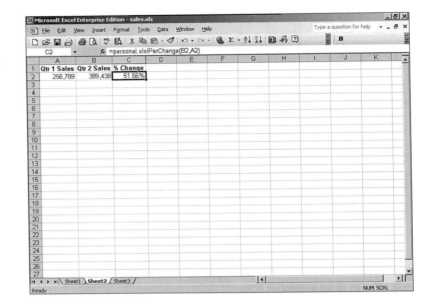

CONTROL STRUCTURES

Control structures give your procedures more power and efficiency by allowing them to make decisions or perform repetitive tasks. Think of how powerful your VBA procedures could be if they could make decisions. If the user chose hardware from a product list, for example, you could show a graph of hardware sales. If the user chose software, you could show a software sales graph. Without a decision structure, providing for and acting on user choices wouldn't be possible.

Repetition is another common scenario in VBA procedures. If you record enough VBA procedures, you'll eventually encounter repetition. It will be in the form of a lengthy procedure that repeats the same several lines of code over and over again. Loops help you make this type of procedure much more efficient.

DECISION-MAKING STRUCTURES

Decision structures are commonly used to check user-supplied data entry. In Listing 1, earlier in this chapter, the InputBox function was used to gather the username so that it could be placed in the footer of the current workbook. The InputBox function provides a spot for the user to enter data along with OK and Cancel buttons. One of the problems with this procedure is that, regardless of which button the user chooses from the InputBox, a footer will be inserted into the current sheet of the current workbook. If the user clicks OK, the name and page number are inserted into the footer. If the user clicks Cancel, the name is ignored but the page number is still inserted into the footer.

Usually, when you click OK you want the procedure to continue, and when you click Cancel you want it to stop. Decision structures can test for which button was chosen and act accordingly. The most common decision structure is the If-Then structure. Listing 32.6 shows the syntax used for the If-Then structure.

LISTING 32.6   THE If-Then DECISION-MAKING STRUCTURE

```
If <condition1> Then
     <code if condition1 is true>
Else
     <code if all other conditions are false>
End If
```

N O T E

> The InputBox function returns nothing, indicated by an empty set of quotation marks (""), if the Cancel button is clicked or if the user clicks the OK button but does not type anything in the text box.

Listing 32.7 shows how to use If-Then in the footer procedure to make it cancel properly. The condition is indicated by the test for the value of the variable UserName. If the variable is equal to nothing, exit the procedure. Otherwise, set the left side of the footer equal to the value of the variable UserName and put the page numbers on the right side of the footer.

32

LISTING 32.7   THE REVISED AddNameToFooter PROCEDURE

```
Sub AddNameToFooter()

    UserName = InputBox("What is your name?", "Add Name to Footer")
    If UserName <> "" Then
        With ActiveSheet.PageSetup
            .LeftHeader = ""
            .CenterHeader = ""
            .RightHeader = ""
            .LeftFooter = UserName
            .CenterFooter = ""
            .RightFooter = "Page &P of &N"
        End With
    End If

End Sub
```

N O T E

> Comparison operators are used quite often in VB decision-making structures. Not all operators are represented in computer programs the way they are on paper. All computer programs use >= to represent greater than or equal to, <= to represent less than or equal to, and <> to represent not equal to.

> **NOTE**
>
> If the `If-Then` decision structure is making only one comparison, the `Else` keyword is not required.

As mentioned earlier, the `With` control structure applies a number of statements to the same object, thus saving you from having to type the name of the object repetitively. The Macro Recorder often uses the `With` control structure as you record a procedure. In the `AddNameToFooter` procedure, the `With` control structure is used to set several properties of the `PageSetup` object.

LOOPS

Suppose that you have a list containing 1,000 rows of data and you want every other row to have a border under it. This process would use the same lines of code over and over. A *loop* would allow you to run those same lines of code multiple times. This dramatically cuts down on the length of your procedures and improves their readability and playback speed.

If you were to record this process, you would have quite a long macro. Listing 32.8 shows just a small part of what such a macro would look like. Notice the same general pattern to the macro:

- Select four cells in a row.
- Place a thin border across the bottom of the selection.
- Move down two rows and start all over again.

LISTING 32.8   A RECORDED PROCEDURE WITH REPETITIOUS CODE

```
1 Sub AddBorders()

2     ActiveCell.Range("A1:D1").Select
3     With Selection.Borders(xlEdgeBottom)
4         .LineStyle = xlContinuous
5         .Weight = xlThin
6         .ColorIndex = xlAutomatic
7     End With
8     ActiveCell.Offset(2, 0).Range("A1:D1").Select
9     With Selection.Borders(xlEdgeBottom)
10        .LineStyle = xlContinuous
11        .Weight = xlThin
12        .ColorIndex = xlAutomatic
13    End With
14    ActiveCell.Offset(2, 0).Range("A1:D1").Select
15    With Selection.Borders(xlEdgeBottom)
16        .LineStyle = xlContinuous
17        .Weight = xlThin
18        .ColorIndex = xlAutomatic
19    End With

20 End Sub
```

A closer look at Listing 8 reveals that the procedure is divided into three sections of repetitive code: lines 2–7, 8–13, and 14–19. The first line of each section (2, 8, and 14) uses the Select method to select a range of cells. So, in effect, these lines are selecting a certain number of cells from the current position of the cell pointer (the active cell).

Line 2 selects the active cell plus the three cells directly to its right. Note the A1:D1 range is not an absolute reference. In this usage A to D means select four columns starting from the current column and 1 means stay on the same row. Lines 8 and 14 are slightly different in that they use the Offset property to select a range of cells that's a designated number of rows and columns from the active cell. In this case, the Offset property is used to designate a range of cells that's two rows down and zero columns over from the active cell. Once located in the new cell both of these lines then use the Select method to actually select the new range of cells. Again the A1:D1 range is a relative reference meaning select a range of cells starting with the current cell that is four columns wide and one row deep. So lines 8 and 14 select four cells in the row that's two cells directly below the active cell.

The code in lines 3–7, 9–13, and 15–19 actually draws the border under the range of cells that the corresponding previous line of code selects. The Borders object is a collection object. It refers to all six borders of a cell. The constant xlEdgeBottom designates which border in the collection to change (in this case, the bottom border). LineStyle, Weight, and ColorIndex are properties of the Border object. They describe the type of border that the code will create.

There are two problems with this procedure. First, if it were to run for 1,000 rows, its length would be somewhere around 6,000 lines of code! Imagine trying to edit or modify that procedure. Second, it can only be used on a listing of 1,000 rows. Wouldn't it be nice if it ran on any number of rows, not just 1,000?

This is where looping can help. The most commonly used looping structure in VBA is the Do loop. Do loops repeat the same lines of code until a particular condition occurs that you define as part of the loop. For example, you might want the loop to continue on a list until it encounters a blank cell (a blank cell would indicate the end of the list).

TIP FROM

Ken

To test a cell for a value of nothing (an empty cell) in VBA, use an empty set of quotation marks (" ").

The AddBorders procedure can be written more efficiently with a loop, as shown in Listing 32.9. The loop will continue until the active cell is empty, indicating the end of the list. This new procedure places a border under every other row, regardless of the length of the list. So, not only is the procedure more efficient, it's also more flexible.

32

LISTING 32.9   THE AddBorders PROCEDURE REWRITTEN USING A Do LOOP

```
Sub AddBorders()

    ActiveCell.Range("A1:D1").Select
    Do Until ActiveCell.Value = ""
        With Selection.Borders(xlEdgeBottom)
            .LineStyle = xlContinuous
            .Weight = xlThin
            .ColorIndex = xlAutomatic
        End With
        ActiveCell.Offset(2, 0).Range("A1:D1").Select
    Loop

End Sub
```

To make this procedure even more efficient, you can have it determine the number of cells in each row to select. Listing 32.10 shows how.

LISTING 32.10   THE AddBorders PROCEDURE MODIFIED TO SELECT TO THE END OF THE DATA IN EACH ROW

```
Sub AddBorders()

    Range(Selection, Selection.End(xlToRight)).Select
    Do Until ActiveCell.Value = ""
        With Selection.Borders(xlEdgeBottom)
            .LineStyle = xlContinuous
            .Weight = xlThin
            .ColorIndex = xlAutomatic
        End With
        ActiveCell.Offset(2, 0).Select
        Range(Selection, Selection.End(xlToRight)).Select
    Loop

End Sub
```

Many built-in VBA function parameters and object settings use numbers that are really only meaningful to the computer or are hard for users to remember. For example, the LineStyle setting for a continuous border is 1. Instead of having to memorize a series of numbers for settings and write code full of numbers that are hard to interpret, Excel provides a set of constants to be substituted in procedures where the numbers would usually be placed. These constants all begin with the xl prefix as used in Listing 32.10. Unlike variables, constants have pre-assigned values that never change. xlContinuous has a pre-assigned value of 1, so instead of typing .LineStyle = 1 you can type .LineStyle = xlContinuous which is much easier to remember and clearer to read.

Keys on the keyboard are also assigned numeric values. The value for the right arrow key is -4161. Thus the function End(-4161) tells Excel to simulate pressing the End key followed by the right-arrow key which moves you to the last filled cell in a row. We used the constant xlToRight in place of -4161 in Listing 32.10 to make this more readable as follows:

```
Selection.End(xlToRight)
```

CAUTION

> It's possible—even easy—to create an infinite loop. If you've done so, you'll know it; your code won't stop running after a lengthy period of time and an hourglass remains onscreen. To stop any code during its execution, press Ctrl+Break.

CODE-WRITING TIPS

There are some general rules to follow when writing code that make it easier to read and understand. The Editor has some options that you can use to your advantage in this area.

USING THE AUTO LIST MEMBERS AND AUTO QUICK INFO

As you type statements in the Editor, you might notice a pop-up list box will appear after you type an object name followed by a period. This is called the *List Members list* (see Figure 32.10). It normally displays a list of methods and properties appropriate for the object that preceded the period. This list can help you complete the VBA statement you're typing. Select a method or property from the list, using the mouse or by typing the first few letters of the method or property name. Press the next appropriate character (like a space, a period, or the Enter key) to have the Editor place the selection in your statement.

Figure 32.10
The List Members list box for the Range object.

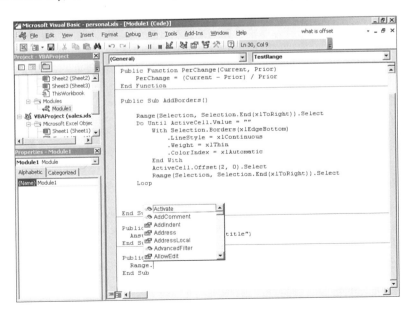

32

When typing the name of a function or method that contains arguments, Auto Quick Info will display the arguments required by that function or method in a ScreenTip box (see Figure 32.11). This helps cut down on syntax errors. For example, if you were to type **ActiveWorkbook.SaveAs** followed by a space, a Quick Info ScreenTip would appear, displaying the arguments for the SaveAs method.

Figure 32.11
The Quick Info box for the VBA InputBox function.

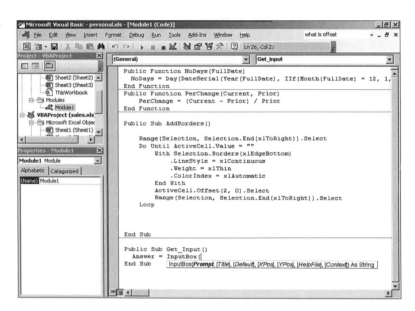

TIP FROM

Ken

Use the Editor Tab in the Tools, Options menu command in the Visual Basic Editor to enable or disable Auto List Members and Auto Quick Info. By default, each feature is enabled.

WRITING EASY-TO-READ CODE

When writing code, adding indents in the proper areas makes the code easier to read. Indents are usually added to control structures to indicate that they go together. All the previous code listings in this chapter contain indents to group control structures.

NOTE

Although indents make code easier to read and understand, they aren't required. Excel ignores indents when running code that contains them.

Listing 32.11 shows the AddNameToFooter macro without indents. Notice how hard it is to see where the If-Then and With control structures begin and end. Listing 32.12 contains the same procedure with indents. Notice how much easier it is to read and understand.

Use the Tab key at the beginning of a line to indent a line of code and Shift+Tab to remove an indent. Be sure to position the cursor just in front of the first character in the code line before you press the keys.

> You can indent a group of statements simultaneously by selecting the statements in the Editor before pressing Tab. Conversely, you can remove the indent from a group of statements by selecting the group and pressing Shift+Tab.

LISTING 32.11   THE AddNameToFooter MACRO BEFORE INDENTS HAVE BEEN ADDED

```
Sub AddNameToFooter()

UserName = InputBox("What is your name?", "Add Name to Footer")
If UserName <> "" Then
With ActiveSheet.PageSetup
LeftHeader = ""
CenterHeader = ""
RightHeader = ""
LeftFooter = UserName
CenterFooter = ""
RightFooter = "Page &P of &N"
End With
End If

End Sub
```

LISTING 32.12   THE AddNameToFooter MACRO AFTER INDENTS HAVE BEEN ADDED

```
Sub AddNameToFooter()

    UserName = InputBox("What is your name?", "Add Name to Footer")
    If UserName <> "" Then
        With ActiveSheet.PageSetup
            .LeftHeader = ""
            .CenterHeader = ""
            .RightHeader = ""
            .LeftFooter = UserName
            .CenterFooter = ""
            .RightFooter = "Page &P of &N"
        End With
    End If

End Sub
```

> The length of the indent (measured in spaces) can be changed using the Tab Width option on the Editor tab in the Visual Basic Editor's Tools, Options dialog box.

COMMENTING CODE

You've probably noticed by now that the Macro Recorder places green text at the beginning of each procedure it records. This text is called a *comment*. You can add comments to your code so that you and others can better understand it in the future.

Here's a common scenario. You wrote a procedure eight months ago. It needs to be updated. You view it in the Editor, ready to make the change, look at it for a few minutes, and can't remember how it works. You spend the next several minutes or even hours reviewing the procedure before you can make your changes.

Procedures that are commented are easier to understand, and therefore easier to change. Excel ignores comments when playing back a procedure.

Placing an apostrophe in front of a line of text in the Code window of the Editor creates a comment. When you move the cursor off a commented line, the Editor changes the color of that line to green. Listing 32.13 shows the AddNameToFooter procedure with comments.

LISTING 32.13   **THE AddNameToFooter PROCEDURE WITH COMMENTS ADDED TO UNDERSTAND THE PROCEDURE**

```
'Procedure - AddNameToFooter
'Created By - Ken Cook on 9/29
'Purpose - Prompt the user for a name and add it to the footer
'          for the current sheet

Sub AddNameToFooter()
'Displays input box prompting for username
    UserName = InputBox("What is your name?", "Add Name to Footer")
'If no name was typed or Cancel was selected, exit the procedure
    If UserName <> "" Then
'Otherwise, create the footer
        With ActiveSheet.PageSetup
            .LeftHeader = ""
            .CenterHeader = ""
            .RightHeader = ""
            .LeftFooter = UserName
            .CenterFooter = ""
            .RightFooter = "Page &P of &N"
        End With
    End If

End Sub
```

TIP FROM

Ken

> When writing code for other people, always comment your code. This can help them understand your code should they need to make a change.

You also can add comments at the end of code lines by typing an apostrophe followed by the desired comment text. This technique is good for adding brief comments without taking up extra lines. Typically, the Tab key is pressed after the last character of code and before the apostrophe is typed to separate the code from the comment.

DEBUGGING

The process of finding and correcting errors in code is called *debugging*. There are several types of errors that can occur in code. The first is a *syntax error*. Syntax errors occur when you misspell a word or don't follow the proper word sequence when writing a VBA statement or series of statements. An If statement without the word Then at the end is an example of incorrect word sequence. The Editor has a feature called Auto Syntax Check that checks a line of code for syntax errors when you move off the line. Whenever an error is detected, it's displayed in a message box, and the Editor applies a red color to the line of code containing the error. Then it's up to you to correct the error.

The second type of error is a runtime error. As the name suggests, runtime errors occur when the code is running. Even if the syntax is correct, the code might be attempting to perform a task that's impossible, such as saving a file to a folder that doesn't exist. When a runtime error occurs, the code stops running, and a message box displays the nature of the error (see Figure 32.12). This message box gives you the option of stopping the code from running with an End button or viewing the line of code causing the error with the Debug button.

Figure 32.12
This message box is displayed when a run-time error occurs. This particular error occurred because an incorrect sheet name was referenced (Sheet4 instead of Sheet4).

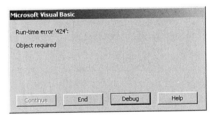

The third type of error that can occur is a *logic* error. Logic errors occur when the code runs properly but doesn't do what you intended it to do. It might select the wrong cells to delete or chart the wrong data.

Excel provides tools to help you correct all these types of errors.

COMPILING A PROJECT

VBA's compiler checks code for syntax errors. Auto Syntax Check detects single-line syntax errors as they occur. However, some syntax errors occur across multiple lines of code. These types of syntax errors often involve control structures; for example, a Do without a Loop or an If-Then without an End If. To have the Editor check for all these types of syntax errors in all the code in the active project, choose Debug, Compile VBAProject. If an error is found, a message box displays the type of error that occurred (see Figure 32.13) and the line containing the error is highlighted. After you correct an error found by the compiler, you must compile the project repeatedly until all errors are corrected.

Figure 32.13
This message box appears when a compile error occurs. This particular error occurred because an End If statement was omitted from the end of the procedure.

STEPPING THROUGH CODE USING THE STEP COMMAND AND BREAKPOINTS

The process of running VBA code one line at a time is called *stepping*. Stepping is used to correct logic and runtime errors. It's not always possible to look at a procedure and determine how to fix what's wrong with it. Sometimes you have to slow down the procedure as it plays back so that you can see what it's doing step by step. This strategy often sheds light on how to correct the problem. You can step through the procedure from its very first line or by using a *breakpoint*.

Here's how to step through a procedure from the very beginning:

1. Choose Tools, Macro, Macros from the menu or press Alt+F8.
2. In the Macro Name list, select the macro that you want to step through.
3. Click the Step Into button. The Editor appears with the first line of the procedure colored in yellow.
4. (Optional) Minimize all application windows except the Excel and Editor windows. Then tile the two windows.
5. Press the F8 key to step through each subsequent line of the procedure. The F8 key works as long as the insertion point is anywhere in the routine.

TIP FROM

Ken

Watch what the procedure is doing in the Excel window as you step through each line of code in the Editor window. When the procedure does something incorrectly, take note of the line of code that's executing. This will pinpoint the area of your procedure that needs correcting. If you are confident that you have found all errors and you have not yet stepped through the entire procedure, cancel stepping through the remainder of the procedure using the Reset button on the Editor's Standard toolbar or by choosing Reset from the Editor's Run menu.

If your procedure contains the line `Application.ScreenUpdating = False`, you should disable this line by placing an apostrophe in front of it before stepping through the procedure. If you do not disable this line, you will not be able to see each line of code execute in the Excel window.

If you have a lengthy procedure that contains errors, you can waste plenty of time stepping through lines of code, waiting to reach the point in the procedure that requires scrutiny. This is where a breakpoint can help. A breakpoint is used to mark a specific line of code as a stopping point during playback. After you reach the stopping point, you can step through the remaining lines of code.

Here's how to step through a procedure using a breakpoint:

1. Place the insertion point on the line at which the procedure should pause.
2. Choose Debug, Toggle Breakpoint from the menu or press F9. The Editor will enclose the line in a dark red rectangle and place a dark red circle on the Margin Indicator Bar (see Figure 32.14).

Figure 32.14
The AddBorders procedure with a breakpoint on the active cell `Select` code line.

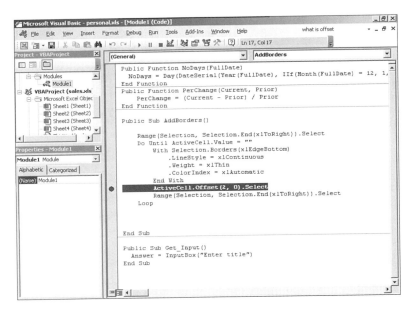

3. Return to the Excel window (optional) and run the procedure. The procedure will run until it reaches the breakpoint and the Editor will open displaying the procedure.
4. Press F8 to step through the rest of the procedure.

The breakpoint command is a toggle between on and off. To remove a breakpoint, follow the same steps that you used to add it.

32

TIP FROM

Ken

> You can add and remove a breakpoint using the mouse by clicking the Margin Indicator Bar in front of the line for which you would like to add or remove the break.

When you close a workbook that contains procedures with breakpoints, the breakpoints are automatically removed.

The Immediate Window

The *Immediate window* displays the result of a function or property and also allows you to run individual lines of code without creating a function or subroutine. To display the Immediate window in the Editor, choose View, Immediate Window, or press Ctrl+G. To display a function result or property result in the Immediate window, perform the following steps:

1. Type the function or property name, preceded by a question mark. Be sure to use the proper syntax for the function or property.

2. Press Enter. The current value of the function or property appears below the line of text that you typed (see Figure 32.15).

Figure 32.15
The Immediate window, displaying the results of the custom NoDays function and the `active-workbook` path property.

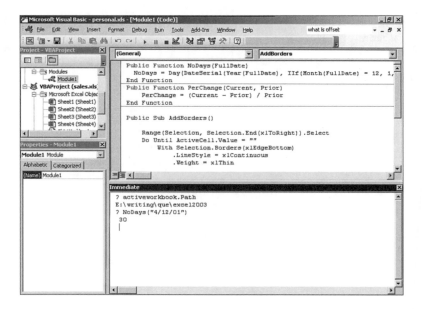

So, how can the Immediate window help you? You can use it to test custom functions. For example, you can test the NoDays function created earlier in this chapter (see "Creating a Function to Calculate the Number of Days in a Month") by typing ?NoDays("4/12/01") in the Immediate window (the project containing the NoDays function must be active in the

Editor for this to work). If you get the correct answer (30), you know the function was written properly. If you get the wrong answer, you know that more work needs to be done.

You also can use the Immediate window to experiment with and test individual lines of code. If you type **?Activeworkbook.Path** in the Immediate window, you'll see the path of the active workbook in the Excel window. This type of experimentation can help you become more familiar with objects and their properties. This type of testing can help you identify errors before runtime. The more familiar you become with objects and properties, the easier it will be to write code. The more testing you do beforehand, the fewer errors you will have to find later.

WATCHING VARIABLES AND EXPRESSIONS

Sometimes, during the debugging process, you need to know the value of a variable or property. Suppose that you wrote the procedure in Listing 32.14. You run it and it doesn't stop when it passes the last row of your list. The loop is supposed to stop the procedure when the value of the active cell equals zero. To help you determine the problem, you can place a watch on the `ActiveCell.Value` statement to see what the value property of the active cell is as the procedure loops through the rows of data.

LISTING 32.14 **PLACE A WATCH ON THE VALUE PROPERTY OF THE** `ActiveCell` **AND THE** `NewHeight` **VARIABLES**

```
'****************************************************************
' SUB: AddRowSpacing()
' PURPOSE:
'    Add double spacing to every fifth row in a list
' ARGUMENTS:
'    None
'****************************************************************

Sub AddRowSpacing()

    Do Until ActiveCell.Value = 0
        X = X + 1
        If X = 5 Then
            CurrentHeight = ActiveCell.RowHeight
            NewHeight = CurrentHeight * 2
            ActiveCell.RowHeight = NewHeight
            X = 0
        End If
        ActiveCell.Offset(1, 0).Select
    Loop

End Sub
```

To place a watch on a statement or variable, perform the following steps:

1. In the Editor's Code window, select the variable or property statement whose value you want to watch.

CAUTION

When testing a property, you must select the object name and its property before invoking the Quick Watch command. If you don't, the command won't work properly.

2. Choose Debug, Quick Watch from the menu or press Shift+F9. The Quick Watch dialog box appears (see Figure 32.16).

Figure 32.16
Click Add from the Quick Watch dialog box to watch the value of the currently selected statement or variable.

3. Click Add.

4. The Watch window appears (see Figure 32.17). Note the Expression and Value columns in the Watch window. The Expression column shows the name of the statement or variable being watched. The Value column shows the value of the statement or variable as you step through the procedure.

Figure 32.17
Use the Watch window to display and track the value of a VBA property or variable.

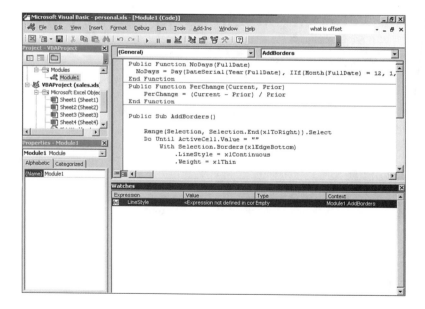

5. Step through the procedure that contains the watch.

6. Note the value of the property or variable after you step past it in the Code window.

To display the value of a property statement or variable temporarily, place the mouse over the statement or variable after you have stepped past it (see Figure 32.18). A ScreenTip appears, displaying the value of the statement or variable. In this case we revealed the value of xlToRight to be -4161, which is the internal number assigned to the right-arrow key on the keyboard. This works only if you're stepping through a procedure.

NOTE

The content of the Watch window is cleared when you exit Excel.

Figure 32.18
The mouse was placed over the constant xlToRight to display a ScreenTip of its current value as the procedure is running.

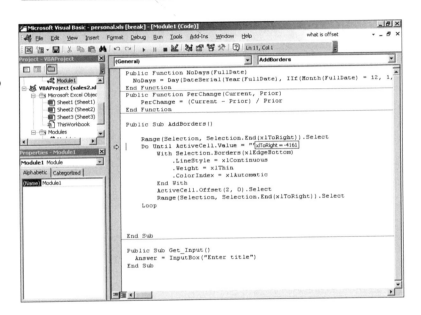

AUTOMATIC EXECUTION OF VBA CODE

In some instances, you might want Excel to start your code when you open the workbook that contains it. Perhaps the workbook is an expense report form that contains some VBA code to help the user complete the form. When the workbook opens, you might want the code to start so that the user doesn't have to start it separately.

Some procedures can run automatically through the use of events. An *event* is a predetermined occurrence to which you can attach code that will run when that occurrence takes place. For example, each workbook has an Open event. Code that's attached to the Open event will run when the workbook is opened. Here's how to make your code run automatically using the Open event:

1. Open the Visual Basic Editor. In the Project Explorer window, expand the desired workbook's VBA Project object by clicking the plus sign (+) next to the object's icon.

2. Right-click the ThisWorkbook object and select View Code (see Figure 32.19). Each object has an associated module. This step opens the module of the ThisWorkbook object.

Figure 32.19
Access the ThisWorkbook object's module to add your Open event procedure.

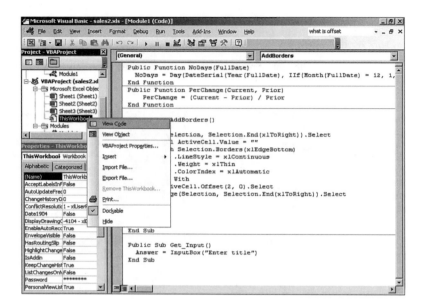

3. Use the Object drop-down list in the upper-left corner of the Code window to select the Workbook object. The Procedure drop-down list in the upper-right corner of the Code window will automatically select Open. The Workbook_Open procedure will appear in the module (see Figure 32.20).

CAUTION

> It is important that you place the Open event code in the ThisWorkbook object's module and that you name the procedure Workbook_Open. If you don't, your procedure won't run automatically when the workbook is opened.

4. Enter the code that you would like to execute automatically when the workbook is opened.
5. Save and close the workbook.
6. Reopen the workbook to test. Your code in the Workbook_Open procedure should run automatically.

NOTE

> To disable the Workbook_Open event, press and hold down the Shift key as you open the workbook that contains the event.

Figure 32.20
Insert a procedure in the `ThisWorkbook` module called `Workbook_Open`.

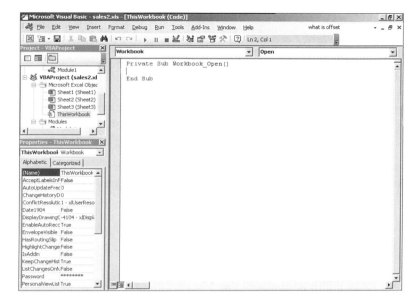

EXCEL IN PRACTICE

A common spreadsheet problem that relates to macros and VBA is having to loop through a variable number of rows of data and do something to rows that meet certain criteria. For example, the worksheet in Figure 32.21 (Sales.xls) contains sales data for more than 400 products. Notice that some of the products in the current year have zero sales values. These are discontinued products.

Figure 32.21
The first few rows of the Sales.xls worksheet. Notice the zero values in the Current Year Sales column.

	A	B	C	D	E	F	G
1	**Product Name**	**Sales (x 1,000,000)**					
2	Consolidated 200 MG Acetominifen	5.49					
3	Gorilla String Cheese	5.37					
4	Gorilla Chocolate Milk	0					
5	Musial Spicy Mints	8.76					
6	Monarch Thai Rice	6.22					
7	Red Wing Copper Pot Scrubber	0					
8	Gorilla Havarti Cheese	10.02					
9	Ebony Lettuce	10.53					
10	Even Better String Cheese	10.5					
11	Bird Call 200 MG Acetominifen	0					
12	Gauss Monthly Home Magazine	6.44					
13	Bird Call Conditioning Shampoo	11.72					
14	Tell Tale Honey Dew	8.4					
15	Red Spade Potato Salad	0					
16	BBB Best Regular Coffee	4.48					
17	Gulf Coast Bubble Gum	0					
18	Even Better 1% Milk	13.16					
19	Bravo Chicken Noodle Soup	10.96					
20	Urban Large Eggs	2.62					
21	Horatio Dried Apricots	3.04					
22	Genteel Extra Lean Hamburger	3.8					
23	Black Tie City Map	3.14					
24	Landslide Corn Oil	3.69					
25	Tell Tale Cantelope	11.46					
26	Fast Raspberry Fruit Roll	2.72					

Suppose that you're going to export this data to another program and you want to export only viable products, not discontinued ones. You could work your way through the list and manually delete the rows that contain discontinued products. With more than 400 products, however, this could take quite some time! So, as an alternative, you can use VBA to remove the unwanted rows. Here's how:

1. Open the workbook that contains the rows to be deleted. You can try this on one of your existing worksheets or enter the data that you see in Figure 32.21 into a new worksheet.

CAUTION

> If you're going to try this on one of your existing worksheets, make a backup copy of it before you continue.

2. Choose Tools, Macro, Macros from the menu or press Alt+F8.
3. Type `RemoveDiscontinuedProds` (or something similar) in the Macro Name box.
4. Click the Create button. The Visual Basic Editor opens with your new procedure displayed in the Code window.
5. Type the code that you see in Listing 32.15 into the new procedure. When finished, your procedure should look exactly like the one in Figure 32.22.

LISTING 32.15   TYPE INTO THE NEW `RemoveDiscontinuedProds` **PROCEDURE (OMIT THE LINE NUMBERS)**

```
1 Application.ScreenUpdating = False
2 Do Until ActiveCell.Value = ""
3    If ActiveCell.Value = 0 Then
4        ActiveCell.EntireRow.Delete
5    Else
6        ActiveCell.Offset(1, 0).Select
7    End If
8 Loop
```

6. Close the Editor and save the file.
7. Place the cell pointer on the first number in the column that contains the zero values (in the Sales.xls example, use cell B2).
8. Run the `RemoveDiscontinuedProds` procedure. Verify that the rows with the zero values have been removed.

Line 1 of the code in Listing 32.15 turns off the updating of the screen display. This makes the code play back faster because Excel doesn't have to refresh the screen during playback. Line 2 of the code initiates a loop that runs until a cell with a value equal to nothing is encountered (in other words, an empty cell). Line 3 tests whether the value of the active cell is equal to zero. If so, line 4 deletes the row that contains the zero with the result that the current cell is now the one that was in the row immediately below the one you just deleted. If not, as indicated by the Else in line 5, line 6 moves to the next cell. Line 7 marks the end of the VBA decision-making structure. Line 8 loops back to line 1.

Figure 32.22
Compare your
RemoveDiscont-
inuedProds pro-
cedure to this one.

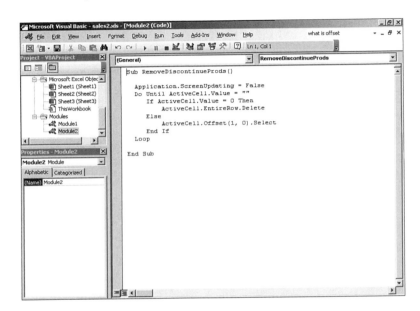

32

PART VIII

APPENDIX

A   What's on the CD   879

WHAT'S ON THE CD

This book includes a fully licensed copy of Woody's Office POWER Pack 2003, the legendary collection of Office add-ins that will help you work faster, smarter, and more productively. This latest version of WOPR includes updates of your favorite features from previous versions, plus a handful of indispensable new tools that you'll use every day.

The copy of WOPR 2003 on the CD is fully licensed at no additional cost to you. This isn't shareware, freeware, trialware, demoware, or limited in any other way. Previous versions of WOPR cost more than the price of this book, and now you are getting WOPR and this book for less than the cost of the software.

As with any other software, however, WOPR 2003 does have a license agreement. Be sure to read that and agree to it before using the software.

WHAT IS WOPR?

For more than a decade, WOPR (pronounced "whopper") has led the way with incredibly useful extensions to Office—in fact, many of the features you see in Office today originated as WOPR utilities. If you rely on Office, you should be using WOPR, the one truly indispensable addition to your Office bag o' tricks.

WOPR 2003 brings dozens of new capabilities to Office 2003:

WOPR COMMANDER

In order to reduce the user interface clutter normally associated with having such a large and complex add-on package like WOPR installed into Microsoft Word, we've created the WOPR Commander. The WOPR Commander removes all of WOPR's user interface elements out of Microsoft Word's menus, toolbars, and so on. and places them on one convenient popup menu that is accessed via clicking on the WOPR Commander icon down in the Microsoft Windows Taskbar's system tray area (that is, the tray notification area located down by your system clock).

Each time Microsoft Word is started, the WOPR Commander's icon is automatically placed into your system tray. To access any of the WOPR utilities, simply *right or left mouse-click* on the WOPR Commander's icon (or use the *CTRL+ALT+W* hot key), and a popup menu will appear allowing you to control all aspects of the WOPR program (such as displaying the *WOPR Tools* or *Lil'WOPR Tools* toolbars, adding or removing the various WOPR components, running each of the WOPR utilities, and so on.).

ENVELOPER

Replace that wimpy Word envelope printer with an industrial-strength one-click wonder! Enveloper works in Excel, Access, and Outlook, too.

Print logos/graphics, notes, and bar codes on your envelopes. Maintain multiple customized envelopes. Each envelope may be customized for a different situation: envelope size, return address, note, logo, fonts, and so on....

Enveloper lets you create custom envelopes and call them up when you need them. You can position the return address, addressee, bar code—even a logo or a note line—with a simple click and drag. One more click sets the font, and the whole process unfolds right before your eyes, so you can see how your envelopes will look before you print them. Most of all Enveloper fits right into Office. There's no need to shell out to another program, or mess around with copying and pasting—Enveloper "grabs" addresses from your documents, worksheets, or Outlook Contacts, and churns out gorgeous envelopes in no time at all. You can pull addresses from Outlook or the address book of your choice, and even look up ZIP+4 codes on the U.S. Postal Service Web site, with a couple of clicks. Whether you print one envelope at a time, churn out thousands of envelopes for mass mailings, or just run the occasional holiday card mail merge, Enveloper helps every step of the way.

WorkBar

WorkBar gives you a one-click listing of your key working documents right on Word's menu bar (or on a toolbar—it's your choice), automatically sorts the document list as you add documents, supports a variety of file formats (it will launch a file's parent application for you automatically so you're not limited to only Word documents on your WorkBar), and gives you control over how the document is opened in Word.

FileNew Popup

This feature displays a list of useful commands that help you create new documents and interact with those documents' parent templates. It can

- Display the fully qualified filename of the current document's parent template, and allows you to open it with just a click.
- Create new documents or templates based on the current document, the current document's template, Word's global template (Normal.dot), or any existing user or workgroup template.
- Quickly find and open any user or workgroup template.

FloppyCopy

Working with documents on removable media (such as a floppy or Zip disk) can be a real pain—it's just plain slow. WOPR FloppyCopy makes working with documents on removable media easy. FloppyCopy steps in after you open a document from a removable media disk with Word's open file dialog box, and gives you the option of copying the document to your hard drive during editing. When you close the document, it is copied back to the removable media drive. You also have the option of keeping a copy on your hard drive for future editing.

LOOKUP ZIP+4

A utility for looking up ZIP+4 codes from the United States Postal Service (USPS) Web Site. Have you ever sent off a letter only to have it returned due to no ZIP code or an incorrect ZIP code? Have you ever wondered what the ZIP code for a particular city was or just wanted to find the ZIP+4 code for your own or someone else's address? Well wonder no more; WOPR Lookup ZIP+4 comes to the rescue! WOPR Lookup ZIP+4 is a unique "ZIP Finding" utility that was designed to run exclusively from within Word. Simply enter an address (or partial address) into your document, fire up WOPR Lookup ZIP+4 and it will automatically grab the address, start your Dial-Up Internet Connection, retrieve the correct ZIP+4 code, and insert it into your document. WOPR Lookup ZIP+4 will even automatically disconnect from your Internet Provider after a set amount of time or you can choose to remain connected. WOPR Lookup ZIP+4 has also been hooked into Enveloper's "Find Zip" button for easy access from within your envelopes.

INSERT PICTURE

Gives you quick access to all of your graphic images, with more options and flexibility than Word's insert picture tool. With WOPR Insert Picture you can:

- Insert an image in its original size.
- Specify an exact size for the image before inserting it.
- Scale an image by any percentage before inserting.
- Insert an image into the drawing layer, where you can float behind or on top of your text.
- Insert multiple images by telling Insert Picture to remain open on your screen after each insertion.

TASK PANE CUSTOMIZER

A powerful tool that lets you customize the New Document, New Workbook, New Presentation, New File, and New Page or Web Task Panes in Microsoft Word, Excel, PowerPoint, Access, and FrontPage. With the Task Pane Customizer you can add files or hyperlinks to, or remove files or hyperlinks from, any of the host Office application's New... Task Panes, rename existing files or hyperlinks, quickly move your files or hyperlinks to any of the four different Task Pane sections, and even clear the Task Pane's most recently used (MRU) document and template lists.

IMAGE EXTRACTOR/EDITOR

Ever want to grab the small 16x16 pixel icon out of an EXE file, DLL file, or from an Office application's command bar/toolbar? Well, WOPR Image Extractor lets you do just that. With Image Extractor, you can extract the small icons from any EXE, DLL, ICO, or BMP file, or from any Office command bar (toolbar or menu), edit them and use them in any Office application such as Word, Excel, PowerPoint, Access, FrontPage, and Outlook.

DOCUMENT NOTES

The electronic equivalent of paper sticky notes for all of your Word documents. The notes travel along with each of your documents and can even be password protected.

DATE AND TIME TOOLS

Insert monthly calendars into your documents, calculate any date by selecting a start date and adding days, weeks, months, or years. A menu bar alarm/timer and much more!

POPUP CONTACTS LIST

Lets you access all of your Microsoft Outlook contacts from within Microsoft Word, and insert various information about the contacts (such as their addresses, phone numbers, and so on) into your documents with just a couple of mouse clicks.

QUICKMARKS

One-key navigator for big documents. QuickMarks turns your number key pad into an instant document navigator.

SHOW/HIDE ALL

Transforms Word's built-in Show/Hide ¶ command found on the Standard toolbar into a fully customizable Show Whatever You Want powerhouse. Without having to write a single line of code, WOPR Show/Hide All allows you to choose which View options to show or hide and which View State to display when Show/Hide All is toggled on or off.

FORMATTING TOOLBAR

The WOPR Formatting Toolbar is simply a better way to access your most-used formatting tools. The WOPR Formatting Toolbar features are

- **Enhanced Styles Menu**—Gives you quick access (via a plain text preview) to all available styles, plus organizational fly-outs for Recently Used Styles, User-Defined Styles, In-Use Styles, Built-In Styles, and All Styles. You can even manage your styles.

- **FastFonts**—Makes it fast and easy to find just the right font for your documents. FastFonts displays all available fonts on your system, with the font name in its actual typeface. You can even generate a printed sample of every available font! Very slick.

- **Format Font and Format Paragraph Menus**—Makes it easy to access commonly used font or paragraph formatting attributes.
- **Insert Symbol Menu**—Instant access to any available symbol. With just a couple of clicks, you can insert Math, Greek, Wingdings, and International symbols. There's also a Miscellaneous Symbols library that includes currency symbols (and the new Euro currency symbol tool), dots and daggers, publishers quotes, em and en dashes, trademarks and copyright symbols, and much, much more.
- **SuperSub**—Makes working with superscripts and subscripts fast and easy.

MODULE TOOLS

A custom toolbar containing a collection of tools for working with forms, modules, and macros in Microsoft Word. Features of WOPR Module Tools are

- **All Keys**—Generates a table of all available key assignments.
- **Rebuild File**—Rebuilds corrupted documents or templates. A real life saver!
- **Import/Export**—Imports or exports multiple VBA project components (forms, classes, and modules) in a single shot!
- **All Command Bars**—Generates a table of all available command bar controls (that is, menu bars, toolbars, and toolbar buttons).
- **FixXlate**—Fixes line-continuation characters problems in WordBasic macros that have been translated into VBA by Microsoft Word.
- **Button Face IDs**—Displays all available button images for the built-in face ID numbers. You can copy the images to the Clipboard, or print them out in a document.

CITY2AIRPORT SMART TAGS

Recognizes common city names as you type them into your documents and presents you with a popup menu that allows you to insert the city's airport name or code into your document, view an online map of the city or the city's airport region, get driving directions TO or FROM the city's airport, and much more!

WOPR UPDATER!

The absolutely easiest way to make sure that you have the latest most up-to-date version of WOPR.

A

LITTLE WOPRs LIBRARY

Small, fast tools that you'll use everyday:

- **Active File Manager**—Gives you quick file management tools for working with the active document or template—move, copy, rename, or delete the active document/template with a few clicks. You can even create a shortcut to the active document/template on your desktop, Start menu, favorites folder, and more.

- **Digital Signatures**—Provides easy access for working with digital signatures in the active document or template. You can quickly add digital signatures to or remove digital signatures from the active document or template, and easily import digital certificate files (using Microsoft's PVK Import tool) for use in signing your documents/templates.

- **Print Selector**—Gives you quick access to all of your printer's settings, and makes printing only the portions of your documents that you what you want, a snap!

- **Calculator**—Takes whatever values are currently selected, calculates a result, and places the result immediately after the selection in your document. There's even a stand-alone toolbar based calculator that will paste the calculation result into your document in a variety of different formats.

- **Normal Quotes**—Converts Microsoft Word's "smart quotes" back into "normal quotes."

- **Fix Line Breaks**—Removes extra line breaks from imported ASCII text files.

- **Duplicate Style**—Lets you quickly make an exact copy of any existing style in the active document or template.

- **View Characters**—Tells you exactly what ASCII codes lie behind your inscrutable characters.

- **View Header/Footer**—Brings back the ol' Word 2.0 header/footer functionality.

- **Remove Personal Information**—Provides easy access to Microsoft Word's Remove Personal Information feature that removes all personal information from the active document or template's comments, revisions, and File Properties dialog box.

- **Change Date/Time Stamp**—Provides a quick and easy way to change any file's creation, last modified, and last accessed date and time stamps.

- **Toggle Showing Windows in Taskbar**—Provides easy access to toggling on or off Microsoft Word's Show Windows in Taskbar feature that displays a separate icon on the Microsoft Windows taskbar for each open window in Microsoft Word.

- **Edit Replace**—Allows you to kick off the find and replace process with the currently selected text.

- **Fast Find**—Finds the current selection *quickly*; just highlight your text and press the quick-keys.

A

INSTALLING WOPR 2003

To install WOPR 2003, make sure that you have Office 2003 installed, shut down all Office 2003 applications, insert the CD in this book into your CD drive, and run the WOPR2003.EXE program directly from the CD.

You must run the installer directly from the CD. If you copy all the files on the CD to your hard drive and run WOPR2003.EXE from your hard drive, you'll need to insert the original CD into your CD drive before the installer will proceed.

The installer asks you to select which WOPR components you want to install. By default, all options are selected. (You might want to go ahead and install all WOPR tools because you can easily remove any unneeded components later.) Click Next to finish the first stage of the installation.

The Install Wizard starts Word to finish the installation. After it has completed the installation, Word will close. Most of the WOPR components install with no further prompts, but some, such as Enveloper, have their own additional installers, which run when you first attempt to use them.

If you have an Internet connection active, WOPR 2003 can automatically check to see whether there are any updates at the end of the installation.

If you performed a partial installation, and you want to install any component that you missed, select Add/Remove WOPR Components from the WOPR Commander's system tray menu (down by the Windows system clock). Select any component that wasn't installed, and follow the prompts.

If you want to install WOPR on multiple PCs, please send an email to mike@wopr.com for site licensing terms.

SECURITY CONSIDERATIONS

Because of the security model in Microsoft Office 2003, it is possible that the security settings in Office might prevent some of the WOPR applications from running. Many of these applications are based on macros in templates. Although all the macros and templates on the CD are virus-free, Office security settings might prevent them from running anyway. If your Office security settings are set to High, unsigned macros will not run and you will not be given a prompt to change them. You can change this option by following the directions discussed in this book. If your company has "locked" your copy of Office to prevent you from changing this setting, you will need to contact your Office 2003 administrator to change this setting to allow these to run.

CAUTION

> Some of the macros have been signed with a digital certificate to authenticate who the creator was. With these, you might be prompted whether or not to run them and asked whether you "trust" the signer. You should accept the prompt to allow the template or macro to work correctly.

To uninstall WOPR 2003:

1. Close all the host Office applications (Word, Excel, PowerPoint, Access, FrontPage, and Outlook).
2. Select the Add or Remove Programs applet from the Windows Control Panel.
3. Scroll down to WOPR 2003 and click the Add/Remove or Change/Remove button. Follow the on-screen prompts.

TECH SUPPORT

NOTE

> The technical support options listed here are for WOPR 2003 only! For support with the other items on this book's CD, contact support@quepublishing.com.

For technical support:

- Visit the FAQ (Frequently Asked Questions) page on our Web site at `http://www.wopr.com/wopr-xp/support/woprsupportfaq.htm`, and you'll likely find your answer.
- Visit our Online Technical Support page at `http://www.wopr.com/wopr-xp/support/woprsupport.shtml`.
- Post a message to your WOPR-using peers on the WOPR Peer-to-Peer forum in the WOPR Lounge located at `http://www.wopr.com/lounge`.

A

INDEX

Symbols & Numbers

+ (addition) operator, 161

& (adjoining) operator, 161

' (apostrophe) character, 469

* (asterisk) character, 420

/ (division) operator, 161

= (equal to) operator, 160-161

> (greater than symbol) operator, 161

< (less than symbol) operator, 161

<=(less than or equal to) operator, 161

- (minus) character, 442

* (multiplication) operator, 161

- (negation) operator, 161

? (question mark) character, 420

% (percent) operator, 161

, (separation reference) operator, 161

- (subtraction) operator, 161

3-D View dialog box (Chart menu), 558-559

3-D View dialog box (chart shortcut menu), 574

3D button (Drawing toolbar), 129

3D charts, formatting, 555
3D views, 558-559
data series, 557
floors, 556-557
walls, 556

3D view (charts), 558-559

24-hour time format, 96-98

A

A4 paper size, 144

abbreviating column/row headings, 475

ABS function, 304, 307-308

absolute referencing, 178, 680-683
anchoring references, 179-180
keyboard shortcuts, 323

absolute value (Modulus), 217, 304-308

accepting/rejecting edits and changes, 77-78

ACCRINT function, 234, 238-239

ACCRINTM function, 234, 239-240

accrued interest, calculating, 238-240

ACOS function, 304, 308-309

ACOSH function, 304

active cells, 28-29, 50

active charts, adding form controls, 584-587
combo boxes, 587-589
option buttons, 586
text boxes, 586

active tables
adding spinners, 665-666
multiple-variable tables, 667-669

ActiveX controls, 424

activity ratios, 685-686

actual page count (ACT), 273

adaptive menus, 20

Add Data dialog box (Chart menu), 511

Add option (Paste Special dialog box), 391

Add Procedure dialog box, 851

Add Tables dialog box, 776

Add Trendline dialog box (Chart menu), 525-527

Add-Ins (Tools menu), 206

AddBorders procedure
Do loop, 859-860
listing, 858-859
modified, 860

AddIns dialog box (Tools menu), 293

addition
database functions for, 197-198
formulas, 162
operator, 161
SUM function for, 320-323
SUMIF function for, 321-322

AddNameToFooter procedure, 862-864

ADDRESS function, 286

Address info type, 267

adjoining operator, 161

Advanced Filter, 421-423
copying records, 423
selecting unique records, 423-424

Advanced Filter dialog box (Data menu), 422

Align Left button (Formatting toolbar), 18, 110

Align Right button (Formatting toolbar), 18, 110

aligning
cells, 119-121
chart labels with gridlines, 603
text
in cells, 29, 111
in data labels, 542

Alignment tab (Format Cells dialog box), 111, 120-121

All Except Borders option (Paste Special dialog box), 390

All option (Paste Special dialog box), 390

alpha (significance level), 352

alphanumeric keys, 64

Always Show Full Menus option (Customize dialog box), 727

Always Show Full Menus option (Tools menu), 20

AMORLINC function, 234

amortization payments, 667-669

amortization tables, creating, 662-665

ampersands, 148

Analysis Server option (Multidimensional Connection dialog box), 793-794

Analysis ToolPak, 669
adding EDATE function, 206
enabling
GETSTEP function, 224
HEX2BIN function, 225
tools, 669-672

analytical charts, formatting, 600

analytical tools, 646
Analysis ToolPak, 669-672
Goal Seek, 646-649
Solver, 646, 650-655
analysis options, 656-657
Gannt charts, 657-659
limitations, 656
multiple projects, 660-662

analyzing data, OLAP, 790
dimensions, 790
measures, 790
SQL Server for, 792

anchoring
cell references, 179-180
date references, 283

AND formulas, timelines, 412-413

AND function, 278-280

Angle of First Slice option (Format Data Series dialog box), 549

Angle Text Downward button (Chart toolbar), 508

Angle Text Upward button (Chart toolbar), 508

angles, measuring. *See* math; trigonometric functions

annuities, rate of interest per period, 257-258

ANOVA tools (Analysis ToolPak), 670

apostrophe (') character, in chart source tables, 469

Arabic numerals, converting to Roman numerals, 306, 317-318

arccosine, calculating, 304, 308-309

arcsine, calculating, 304, 309-310

arctangent, calculating, 304

area charts, 494-495

AREA function, 286

arguments, 160. *See also* functions
date functions
DATE, 204-205
DAYS360, 205-206
EDATE, 206-207
MONTH, 207
NETWORKDAYS, 208-209
TODAY, 209-210
WEEKDAY, 210-211
YEAR, 211-213
defined, 160
GETPIVOTDATA function, 198-199
functions, 160

arithmetic means, calculating, 349-350

arithmetic operators, 161-163
  formulas, 162-163
  in nested calculations, 163-164

Arrange option (Window menu), 401, 513

Arrange Windows dialog box (Window menu), 182

Array form (INDEX function), 286, 290

Array form (LOOKUP function), 287, 294-295

arrays
  activating, 275
  indexes for searches, 290

Arrow button (Drawing toolbar), 128

Arrow Style button (Drawing toolbar), 129

ascenders, 113

ascending sorts, 414-416

ASIN function, 304, 309-310

ASINH function, 304

Assign Hyperlink, Open dialog box (Customize dialog box), 718

Assign Macro dialog box, 718-719, 822

Assume Linear Model option (Solver Options dialog box), 657

Assume Non Negative option (Solver Options dialog box), 657

asterisk (*) character, 420

ATAN function, 304

ATAN2 function, 304

ATANH function, 304

Attach Toolbar dialog box (Customize dialog box), 722

audio effects in charts, 595

auditing
  data
    accessing audit tools, 460
    protected worksheets, 458
  data entry, 453-454
    auditing options, 458-460
    marking invalid data, 457-458
  protected worksheets, 458
  workbooks, 28

Auditing toolbar
  Circle Invalid Data button, 457
  Clear Validation Circles button, 458

Auto Lookup, 683-684

Auto Outline feature, 446-447, 460

Auto Quick Info, description, 862

Auto Scale option, 536

AutoCalculate feature
  Average function, 177
  Count function, 177
  CountNums function, 177
  formulas, 175-176
  including on status bar, 711
  Max function, 177
  Min function, 177
  status bar, 712
  Sum function, 177

AutoComplete feature, 30, 397

AutoCorrect feature, 30

AutoFill feature, copying formulas, 173-174

AutoFill Option button, creating data series, 70

AutoFilter, 417
  customizing, 419-421
  filtering options, 418-419

AutoFit feature, 32-34

AutoFormat feature, 126

AutoFormat option (PivotTable and PivotChart Wizard), 620-621

automatic subtotaling, 450-452

automating PivotTable summaries, 632-633

AutoRecover feature (Save tab), 712

AutoShapes, 566

AutoShapes button (Drawing toolbar), 128, 546-547

AutoSum button (Standard toolbar), 17, 166

AutoSum feature, 166, 186
  SUM function, 166-168
  SUMIF function, 168-170

AVEDEV function, 344

AVERAGE function, 344, 349-350

Average function (AutoCalculate), 177

AVERAGEA function, 344

averages
  calculating, 190-193, 349-350
  comparison with medians, 370
  positive numbers only, 682-683

axes (charts)
adding secondary axis, 514-515
formatting, 478-479
custom formats, 595-597
handling problems with, 560
naming, 476-478
origin with, 516
repositioning, 521-522
scaling X-axis, 521-523
scaling Y-axis, 516-521
secondary axes
adding to charts, 575-578
when to use, 549
X-axis, 467-468
Y-axis, 467-468
Z-axis, 468

Axes tab (Chart Wizard), 478-479

Axis tab (Format Data Series dialog box), 549, 576

B

backgrounds, charts
adding graphics to, 568-569
formatting options, 551-554
pictures as, 554-555
troubleshooting, 560

bar charts, 488-489
formatting, 600
reversing, 489

base 10 logarithms, calculating, 305

base field (PivotTables), 618

base item (PivotTables), 618

Based on Series setting (Trendline dialog box), 526

baseline charts, 693-694

Basic Shapes button (Drawing toolbar), 546

Bernoulli trials, 350-351

BESSELI function, 216-218

BESSELJ function, 216

BESSELK function, 216

BESSELY function, 216

best-fit regression lines, 366-367

BETADIST function, 344

BETAINV function, 344

Bevel tool (Drawing toolbar), 134-135

bevels, adding to charts, 133-135

BIN2DEC function, 216, 219

BIN2HEX function, 216

BIN2OCT function, 216

binary numbers, conversions
decimal numbers to, 216-219, 223
hexadecimal numbers to, 216-217, 225
octal numbers to, 216-218, 230

BINOMDIST function, 344, 350-351

Blank Worksheet option (Start menu), 10

blanks
displaying using AutoFilter, 419
in lists, 387

Block Arrows button (Drawing toolbar), 547

blocks of cell, keyboard shortcuts, 52-53

body (of list), description of, 388

body text (hierarchical lists), layout for, 388

Bold button (Formatting toolbar), 18, 109

bolding cell contents, 114

borders
active cells, 28-29, 50, 122-125
chart legends
eliminating borders, 501
formatting options, 482
charts, 560
deleting, 122, 125

Borders button (Formatting toolbar), 19

Borders toolbar, Eraser button, 122

boundaries, 32

Boxes and Ovals button (Drawing toolbar), 547

boxes, three-dimensional (3D), placing charts in, 572

breaking links, 85-86

breakpoints
debugging, 867-868
description, 866

Bring Forward (Draw menu), 131

Bring to Front button (Drawing toolbar), 569-570

broken links, redirecting, 85

Browser Tab (Web Options button), 706

browsers, selecting for Web pages, 706

bubble charts, 496

budget caps, maintaining, 650-655

Built-In Menus category (Custom dialog box), 440

business concepts
cascading schedules, 677-679
cash flows, 679-680
channel velocity, 677
financial ratios
activity ratios, 685-686
coverage ratios, 687
liquidity ratios, 685
profitability ratios, 686-687
line item milestone management charts, 692-693
P&L, 684-685
POS (Point of Sale), 679
ramping up production, 694-695
resource pools, 687-689
reverse schedules, 678-680
sell in versus sell through, 676
value chains
market opportunity value chain, 695-697
overview, 695
strategic risk factor value chain, 697-698
value matrixes, 698-700

Button control (Forms toolbar), 425

Button Editor, 717-718

buttons, toolbars
adding
hyperlinks, 718
macros, 718-719
changing icons, 716-718
deleting, 715-716
displaying text, 715
moving, 722

By Column button (Chart toolbar), 508

By Row button (Chart toolbar), 508

C

calculations
arithmetic operators, 161-163
AutoCalculate feature, 175-177
AutoSum feature, 166-170
SUM function, 166-168
SUMIF function, 168-170
comparison operators, 161
complex tools
Analysis ToolPak, 669-672
Goal Seek, 646-649
Solver, 650-662
date of maturity/date due, 206
engineering functions, 216
error messages, 177-178
financial functions, 234-243, 263, 662-669
accrued interest, 238-240
days in coupon period, 240-242, 263
mortgage amortization payments, 662-665
multiple-variable active tables, 667-669
next coupon date, 242-243
in PivotTables, 628-629
math and trigonometry functions, 304-307
nested, 163-164
number of days between two dates, 208-209
number of days in a month, 853-854
percent change, 855
queries, 781
reference operators, 161
statistical functions. *See* statistical functions
tables, 429-432
text operators, 161

callouts, 598

Callouts button (Drawing toolbar), 547

capitalization,
function, 327, 335-336
random, 437

cascading schedules, 677-679

cash flows, 679-680

categories (charts), 523-525, 560

Categories in Reverse Order option (Scale tab), 523

category (X) axis (charts), 468
formatting, 478-479
naming, 476-477
scaling, 521-522

category labels, moving, 602

category orientation (charts), changing, 471

CEILING function, 304

CELL function, 266-269

cells, 28
activating, 275
active, 28-29, 50
applying color and patterns to, 125-126
AutoSum calculations, 168
blank, entering content, 52
capacity of, 28
comments
adding, 79-80
displaying/hiding, 80-81
printing, 80

content
   alignment options,
      119-121
   deleting, 29
   editing, 29-30
   hiding/displaying, 710
copying, 69-70
creating structured lists
  from single cells, 394-396
data series, 70-71
   AutoFill options, 70
   custom fill series, 71-75
deleting content, 64
dependents, 458
editing
   drag and drop, 68
   Formula bar, 66-67
   formulas, 171
   keyboard, 64-65
   undoing changes, 65
empty, 266, 269-270
entering data, 29-33
exiting without making
   changes, 172
filling with AutoSum
   formulas, 168
formatting
   alignment, 111
   borders and shading,
      122-125
   contents, 111
   font, 111-113
   individual characters,
      115
groups
   editing contents of,
      65-66
   Formula bar, 66
hierarchical lists, 387
links
   adding to form controls,
      427-428
   calculation tables,
      430-432
   referencing in charts,
      434-435

merging, 119-120, 153
multiple, copying identical
   formulas into, 174
pointers, 28-29, 50,704-705
precedents, 458
ranges, 57-60
   accessing with hyper-
      links, 749-752
   AutoSum formulas, 170
   copying, 737-738
   editing, 171-172
   named ranges, 164-166
   selecting, 50
   testing, 272-273
references, 160, 178,
   680-683
   ACCRINT function,
      238-239
   advantages over hard
      coding, 200
   anchoring references,
      179-180
   hard coding, 170
   linking to external
      workbooks, 184-185
   return types, 269
   selecting, 50-54
      contiguous ranges, 50
      keyboards, 52-53
      noncontiguous ranges,
         54
      vulnerability, 52
   testing return results for,
      272-273
Center Across Selection
** alignment option, 120**
Center button (Formatting
** toolbar), 18, 110**
centering
   cell content, 120
   worksheets, 146
Central option (Solver
** Options dialog box), 657**
changing fonts, 112
channel velocity, 677

CHAR function, 326
characters
   individual, formatting, 115
   nonprintable, removing,
      326
   styles, 114
   symbols
      currency, 101
      formatting code, 99-102
      repeating characters, 104
chart area (charts), 468
Chart menu
   3-D View dialog box, 558-
      559
   Add Data dialog box, 511
   Add Trendline dialog box,
      525-527
   Chart Options, 470, 543
   Chart Type dialog box, 508
   Source Data dialog box, 514
Chart Objects button (Chart
** toolbar), 507**
Chart Options dialog box,
** 543**
Chart tab (Option dialog
** box), 592**
Chart toolbar
   changing chart type, 509
   editing embedded charts,
      507-508
Chart Type button (Chart
** toolbar), 508-509**
Chart Type dialog box
** (Chart menu), 508**
Chart Type dialog box
** (Chart Wizard), 502**
Chart Wizard, 469
   accessing, 466-469
   Axes tab, 478-479
   chart type options
      accessing, 470-471
      changing, 509
      viewing samples, 470

Collapse Dialog button, 475
creating charts, 469, 595
Custom Types tab, 498-499
customizing charts, 475-476
Data Labels tab, 482-483
Data Range tab, 471
Data Table tab, 483-484
deleting charts, 470
editing charts, 514
exploring chart types, 487
Gridlines tab, 479-481
identifying
  data series, 471
  source data, 471
Legends tab, 481-482
placing finished charts, 484-486
selecting
  existing charts, 470
  orientation, 471
Series In option
  Columns setting, 473
  Rows setting, 472
Series tab, 473-475
specifying source data, 475
Titles tab, 476-478

Chart Wizard button
PivotTable toolbar, 610
Standard toolbar, 17, 469, 509

charts, 466
automatic charting, 467
baseline, 693-694
copying
  PowerPoint presenta-tions, 736
  Word documents, 734-735
creating (Chart Wizard), 469
  adding/removing series options, 474-475
  chart type options, 470-471

column-based data series, 473
identifying data series, 471
identifying source data, 471
row-based data series, 472
selecting orientation, 471
specifying source data, 473-475
customizing (Chart Wizard), 475-484
  adding gridlines, 479-481
  axes, 478-479
  chart titles, 476-478
  data labels, 482-483
  data tables, 483-484
  legends, 481-482
  naming axes, 476-478
data entry, 530
data series
  adding, 511
  changing chart type for, 530
  removing, 510
  selecting, 510
  trendlines, 527-529
deleting, 470
editing
  adding data series/data points, 511-513
  adding secondary axis, 514-515
  chart type, 508-510
  data series, 510
  data source, 514
  origin, 520-521
  resizing plot area, 519
  scaling category (X) axis, 521-523
  scaling value (Y) axis, 516-521
  series order, 523-525

elements, 467
  adding and deleting, 468
  category axis, 468
  chart area, 468
  chart titles, 468
  data labels, 467, 502
  data points, 467
  data series, 468, 471
  legends, 467-468
  plot area, 468
  selecting, 501
  series labels, 468
  tick marks, 468
  trendlines, 468, 502
  value axis, 468
  X-axis, 467-468
  Y-axis, 467-468
  Z-axis, 468
embedded, 506-508
forecasting, Gantt charts, 657-659
formatting, 534
  3-D views, 555-559
  adding bevels, 133-135
  adding filters and subtotals, 588-590
  adding graphics, 566-569
  adding shapes, 546-548
  adding text, 545
  analytical charts, 600
  axis labels, 537
  axis lines, 560
  backgrounds, 551
  bar charts, 600
  borders, 560
  chart titles, 543-544
  column depth, 573-575
  cost/production curves, 591
  customizing axes, 595-597
  data label backgrounds, 560
  data labels, 540-543
  data points, 550, 560

data series, 548-549
design considerations, 534
draft stamps/watermarks, 570-573
embedding in work-sheets/lists, 595-596
error bars, 538-540
exploded pie chart slices, 549-550
fill effects, 552-554, 560
form controls, 584-589
gradient fills, 582-583
graphics, 566
hiding/displaying data in, 592-593
high/low lines, 538-539
in PowerPoint, 741
layering objects, 569-570
legends, 501, 544
lifetime profitability/breakeven charts, 601-602
linking text to worksheet cells, 592
multiple-combination charts, 594-595
offsetting categories, 560
overlays, 575-578
pie charts, 579-581
placing charts over shapes, 572
professional design features, 564-566
secondary axes, 575-578
single-stack charts, 596-599
slider charts, 153-155
special effects, 595
stacking techniques, 590
tick marks, 535-536
time analyses with annotations, 598
value axes, 534-535
Gantt charts, 693-694
identifying using ScreenTip, 507

intercept calculating, 364-365
line item milestone management charts, 692-693
minimizing clutter, 469, 476
pasting over PowerPoint images, 741-742
printing, 500-501
saving, 484-486, 501-502
secondary axis, 531
selecting, 470, 507
sheets
    changing to embedded charts, 501
    creating charts from, 467
    moving charts to, 507
    saving charts as, 484-486
source tables, 469
sources of data for, 467
tick marks, 531
titles, 468
    customizing, 476-477
    uppercase letters in, 478
trendlines, 525-527
types, 486-487
    2D versus 3D, 487
    area charts, 494-495
    bar charts, 488-489
    changing, 508-509
    column charts, 487-488, 502
    custom charts, 498-499
    doughnut charts, 491-493
    line charts, 490
    of bubble charts, 496
    of cone charts, 497
    of cylinder charts, 497-498
    of pyramid charts, 497
    of stock charts, 497
    of surface charts, 496
    pie charts, 490-491
    radar charts, 495
    scatter charts, 493-494
    surface charts, 495

updating with OFFSET function, 298-299
value axes, formatting, 530-535
viewing, Zoom feature, 507
waterfall charts, 520-521
Word, creating from Excel data, 734-735

Check Box control (Forms toolbar), 425, 435

check boxes, 431

chi-squared distribution, calculation, 351-352

CHIDIST function, 344, 351-352

CHIINV function, 344

CHITEST function, 344, 352

Choose Columns dialog box, 771

Choose Data Source dialog box, 769, 792-794

CHOOSE function, 287-288

Circle Invalid Data button, 454, 457

Circular error message, 178

CLEAN function, 326

Clear All button (Data Validation dialog box), 457

Clear Validation Circles button (Auditing toolbar), 458

Clear Validation Circles button (Formula Auditing toolbar), 454

clip art
    accessing, 15
    adding to charts, 547
    copying into Excel, 745

Clipboard
coping noncontiguous data to, 55
task pane
Insert Clip Art option, 15
viewing contents, 13-15
viewer, 64

Close button, 11, 140

closing
Excel, 11
workbooks, 11

Clustered Column chart type, 578

code
debugging, 865-870
breakpoints, 866-868
compiling projects, 865
expressions, 869-870
Immediate window, 868
Step command, 866-868
variables, 869-870
starting automatically, 871-872
writing
Auto Quick Info, 862
commenting code, 864
indents, 862
List Members list, 861

CODE function, 326

Code window (Visual Basic Editor), 847

coefficients, converting into complex numbers, 216-220

Col info type, 267

Collapse Dialog button, 475, 511

collapsing group views, 442-443

collating during printing, 137

collections, 839

Color info type, 267

Color tab (Options dialog box), 707-709

colors
adding to worksheet tabs, 23-24
applying to cells, 125-126
applying to trendlines, 529
customizing palettes, 707-709
formatting code for, 101
formula references, 171
workbooks, customizing palettes, 706-707
troubleshooting, 53

Colors tab (Options dialog box), 707

COLUMN function, 286

Column Hide option (Format menu), 45

Column Widths option (Paste Special dialog box), 390

column-based data series (charts), 473

columns
adjusting width, 31-32
blank, 387
charts, 487-488
formatting, 736
freezing, 42-43
grouping by, 443
headings, 388, 475
hiding/displaying, 45
in PivotTables, 629
labeling, 30-31
queries, 771-773
selecting, 53-54

COLUMNS function, 286

COMBIN function, 304, 310-311

Combination Drop-Down Edit control (Forms toolbar), 425

Combination List-Edit control (Forms toolbar), 425

combinations (numbers), 310

Combo Box control (Forms toolbar), 425-428, 435

combo boxes, adding to charts, 587-589

Comma Style button (Formatting toolbar), 18, 92

comma-delimited files, 767

comma-separated values (CSV), 767

commands. *See also* macros
Data menu, 446
Insert menu (Visual Basic Editor), 851
Tools menu, 814-819

Commands tab (Custom dialog box), 440

Comment box (Insert menu), 79

Comment button (Reviewing toolbar), 81

comments
adding to cells, 79-80
deleting, 80
displaying/hiding, 80-81
editing, 80
macros, 810
printing, 80
writing code, 864

Comments option (Paste Special dialog box), 390

comparison operators, 161, 420-421

compiling projects, 865

complementary ERF function, 216

complex conjugate, 217, 225-226

complex formulas, simplifying, 436

COMPLEX function, 216-220

complex numbers
  adding, 218, 229
  calculations
    absolute values (Modulus), 217
    coefficients, 217
    common logarithms, 217
    complex conjugates, 217, 225-226
    cosine, 217
    exponentials, 217
    logarithm base 2, 217
    natural logarithms, 217
    sine, 217
    square root, 217
  creating function, 216
  dividing function, 217
  multiplying function, 217, 227-228
  raising to a power function, 217, 226-227
  subtracting function, 218, 228-229

Compress Picture button (Picture toolbar), 568

CONCATENATE function, 326-329

concatenating text strings, 328-329

conditional formatting, 408, 622
  codes, 103-104
  dialog box (Format menu), 409
  formulas, 410-413
  interactive approach, 408-410

cone charts, 497

CONFIDENCE function, 344, 352

confidence intervals, calculating, 352

Conjugate option (Solver Options dialog box), 657

conjugates, 217, 225-226

Connectors button (Drawing toolbar), 546

Consolidate dialog, 447-449

consolidating
  data, 447-449
  ranges, PivotTables, 635
  tables, 448-449

constants, 844-845

constraints
  formulas, 652-653
  Solver, 660-662

Contents info type, 267

context menus, 20, 427-428

contiguous cells, 68

contiguous ranges, 50, 55-57

Control Properties control (Forms toolbar), 425

control structures, 856-860

Control tab (Format Control dialog box), 585

controls
  ActiveX controls, 424
  form controls, 424-427, 584-589
    calculation tables, 429-432
    charts, 433-435
    control characteristics, 435
    creating, 428-429

Convergence option (Solver Options dialog box), 657

CONVERT function, 216, 220-222, 230

Convert Text to Columns Wizard, 785-786

copy and paste method, 102

Copy button (Standard toolbar), 17

copying
  cells, 69-70
  formulas, 173-174
  links, 82
  records, 423

corrections, unwanted, 86

CORREL function, 344, 353-354

correlation coefficients, calculating, 353-354

Correlation tool (Analysis ToolPak), 670

corrupted worksheets/data, recovering after crashes, 37

COS function, 304, 311

COSH function, 304

cosines of complex numbers, 217, 304

cost curves, creating, 591

COUNT function, 177, 344, 354-355

COUNTA function, 345, 354-356

COUNTBLANK function, 266, 269-270, 345, 356-357

COUNTIF function, 304, 311-313, 345, 356-357

counting
  blank cells, 356-357
  cells, 354-357
  last record entered, 355-356

CountNums function (AutoCalculate), 177

COUPDAYBS function, 234, 240-241

COUPDAYS function, 234, 241-242, 263

COUPDAYSNC function, 234

COUPNCD function, 234, 242-243

COUPNUM function, 235, 243-244

coupons, calculations
days in settlement period, 241-242, 263
Macauley duration, 246-247
next coupon date following settlement, 242-243
number of coupons to be paid, 243-244
period settlement date, 240-241

COUPPCD function, 235

COVAR function, 345, 358

Covariance tool (Analysis ToolPak), 670

covariance, calculating, 358

coverage ratios, 687

Create Microsoft Outlook Task button (Reviewing toolbar), 81

Create New Data Source dialog box, 793

CRITBINOM function, 345

criteria
argument (DFUNCTION), 191-192
filtering, 417
ranges, 190

Criteria button, 398

critical path production analyses, 660

Crop button (Picture toolbar), 568

CSV (comma-separated values), 767

cubed formulas, 183

cubes, multidimensional (OLAP), 791
offline cubes, 801-803
data sources, 791-794
PivotCharts, 798-799
PivotTables, 794-797
processing, 792
saving locally, 799-801, 804-805

CUMIPMT function, 235, 244-245

CUMPRINC function, 235

currency
formatting options, 92
custom codes, 101

Currency Style button (Formatting toolbar), 18, 92

current cells. See active cells

current date, function for, 209-210

current day of week, function for, 210-211

cursors
movement direction, 704-705
point hands, 748

curves, calculating exponentials, 368

Custom category (Format Cells Number tab), 97, 103-105

Custom Header dialog box, 148

Custom Header/Footer field buttons, 148-150

Custom Types tab (Chart Wizard), 471, 498-499

Custom Views option (Views menu), 403

Customize dialog box
adding buttons to custom toolbars, 720-721
Always Show Full Menu option, 727
Assign Hyperlink, 718
Assign Macro, 718-719
Attach Toolbars, 722
Commands tab, 440
creating custom menus, 724-725
deleting custom toolbars, 723
New Toolbar dialog box, 720
retrieving deleted menus, 728
Toolbars menu, 714-717

customizing. See also editing
axes, 477-478
charts (Chart Wizard), 475-484
adding gridlines, 479-481
chart titles, 476-478
data labels, 482-483
data tables, 483-484
formatting axes, 478-479
legends, 481-482
defaults, 704-706
hyperlinks, 718
list formatting, 388
macros, 718-719
menus, 723-727
PivotCharts, 610, 624-625
PivotTables, 610, 624-625
status bar settings, 711-712
toolbars, 714-723
window settings, 710-711
workbook settings, 706-710

cut and paste, copying
charts into Word documents, 734-735
Excel data into PowerPoint, 737, 741-742
PivotTables into PowerPoint presentations, 738-739

Cut button (Standard toolbar), 17

Cut Cells option (Insert menu), 402

cut ranges, 402

cylinder charts, 497-498

D

Dash Style button (Drawing toolbar), 129

data
automatic charting, 467
charts
comparing with multiple-combination formats, 594-595
hiding/displaying, 592-593
conditional formatting, 408
formulas, 410-413
interactive approach, 408-410
copying
cut and paste method, 737
into PowerPoint slides, 737
linking method, 737-738
PivotTables, 738-739
corrupted, recovering, 37
dependents, 458
editing
AutoCorrect feature, 30
find and replace actions, 75
spell checking, 30

extracting from tables, 194-195
filtering lists, 416
Advanced Filter, 421-424
AutoFilter, 417-421
forms
controls, 428-435
lists, 396-397
searching records, lists, 398
formatting
PowerPoint, 740-741
Word documents, 736
grouping in PivotTables, 638-639
hiding/displaying, 45
labels (charts), 467
adding to charts, 502, 541
formatting, 482-484, 540-543
lists, transposing, 391-393
management
auditing data. 457-460
automatic subtotaling, 450-452
consolidating data, 447-449
grouping data, 440-445
outlining data, 440, 446-447
performance issues, 436
validating data entry, 453-457
pasting into PowerPoint datasheets, 742-744
PivotTables/PivotCharts
hiding/displaying, 626-627
viewing, 638
points (charts), 467
adding, 511
formatting, 550
selecting, 507
precedents, 458

ranges
inserting in lists, 402-403
modifying, 475
specifying for charts, 471
referencing, 181-182
links, 183-185
updating values, 185
saving, 34-38
encryption, 35-37
file formats, 37-38
first-time saves, 34-35
passwords, 35-37
selecting for sorting, 415
series (charts)
adding, 473-475, 511-513
AutoFill Option series, 70
category data, reversing order of, 523-525
changing, 510
charts, 511
column-based, 473
custom fill series, 71-75
data labels, 541-543
formatting, 548-550, 557, 582-583
hiding/displaying, 602
identifying, 471
pie charts, 580-581
removing, 473-475, 510
row-based, 472
selecting, 507, 510
trendlines, 502, 525-529
sets, 369-377
shading, 566
single cells, creating structured lists from, 394-396
sort options, 413-416
source data, PivotTables, 611, 623
sources
changing/editing, 514
creating consistency between, 752
OLAP cubes, 791-794

summarizing, PivotTables, 608-611, 618-619, 632-633
text to speech features, 413
validation feature, 453-458
warehouses, 386

data analysis
OLAP, 790-792
tools, 646-672
Analysis ToolPak, 669-672
Goal Seek, 646-649
Solver, 650-662

Data Area (OLAP PivotTables), 796-797

Data category (Customize dialog box), button options, 440

Data Connection Wizard, 768

data entry, 29
auditing, 457-460
charts, 530
cursor movement, customizing, 704-705
editing, AutoCorrect feature, 30
forms, adding to charts, 584-589
importance of consistency, 417
lists, 396-398
text, 29-30
validating, 453-457
Data Validation dialog box options, 454-457
Formula Auditing toolbar, 453-454

Data Fields, 388

Data Labels tab (Chart Wizard), 482-483

Data Labels tab (Format Data Series dialog box), 541-543

Data menu
Advanced Filter dialog box, 422
AutoFilter, enabling/disabling, 417
commands, 446
Consolidate dialog box, 447-449
Data Validation dialog box, 454
Form option, 396-397
Group and Outline submenu
Group dialog box, 441
Setting dialog box, 447
Import External Data, Choose Data Source dialog box, 792-793
Sort dialog box, 413-415
Subtotals dialog box, 450-451
Text to Columns option, creating lists using, 395

Data Options section, 623

Data Range tab (Chart Wizard), 471-472

Data Table button (Chart toolbar), 508

Data Table tab (Chart Wizard), 483-484

Data Validation dialog box, 454-457

database argument (DFUNCTION), 191

Database range, 422

databases, 386. *See also* **lists**
Access
importing Excel data, 759-764
integrating with Excel, 756-759
linking Excel data, 764-766
accessing
Data Connection Wizard, 768
database drivers, 768
ODBC (Open Database Connectivity), 767
OLE DB, 767-768
drivers, 768
Enterprise Resource Planning System (ERP), 756
exporting Excel data into non-Access databases, 766-767
functions, 190-199
DAVERAGE, 190-193
DCOUNT, 190, 193-194
DCOUNTA, 190
DFUNCTION syntax, 191-192
DGET, 190, 194-195
DMAX, 190, 195-196
DMIN, 190, 196
DPRODUCT, 190, 197
DSUM, 191, 197-198
DVAR, 191
DVARP, 191
GETPIVOTDATA, 191, 198-199
querying, 777
calculations, 781
choosing columns, 771-773
data sources, 769
editing queries, 782-783
filtering data, 773-774
joins, 777-779
limiting information returned, 779-781
Microsoft Query, 774-777
ODBC data source definitions, 769-771
Query Wizard, 769
saving queries, 774
sorting data, 774
totals, 781

relational databases, 756-758
sorting data, 774
structuring, 440
subtotals, 319-320
troubleshooting, 786

datasheets (PowerPoint), 742-745

date and time codes (formatting codes), 97

Date button (Custom Header/Footer dialog boxes), 149

Date category (Format Cells Number tab), 95

date functions, 202-213
DATE, 202-205
DATEVALUE, 202
DAYS360, 202-206
EDATE, 206-207
EOMONTH, 202
MONTH, 203, 207
NETWORKDAYS, 203, 208-209
NOW, 203
TODAY, 203, 209-210
troubleshooting errors with, 213
WEEKDAY, 203, 210-211
WORKDAY, 203
YEAR, 203, 211-213
YEARFRAC, 203

date systems, 211

date-driven lists, 393-394

dates
displaying in headers and footers, 149
formatting options, 94-99
grouping in PivotTables, 633-634, 638
timelines, 283
viewing with ScreenTips, 70

DATEVALUE function, 202

DAVERAGE function, 190-193

DAYS360 function, 202, 205-206

DB function, 235

DCOUNT function, 190, 193-194

DCOUNTA function, 190

DDB function, 235

debugging code, 865
breakpoints, 866-868
compiling projects, 865
expressions, 869-870
Immediate window, 868
Step command, 866-868
variables, 869-870

DEC2BIN function, 216, 223

DEC2HEX function, 216

DEC2OCT function, 216

decimal numbers
conversions
binary numbers, 216, 219, 223
hexadecimal numbers, 216-217
octal numbers, 216-218
formatting
code, 100
decrease decimal option, 92
fractions, 96
increase decimal option, 92
percentages, 92

decision-making structures, If-Then, 856-858

declaration statements, 844

Decrease Decimal button (Formatting toolbar), 19, 92

Decrease Indent button (Formatting toolbar), 19, 120

defaults
AutoCalculate settings, 175
column widths, 32
currency delimiters, 92
customizing
cursor movement, 704-705
fonts, 706
function ToolTips, 706
hiding/displaying cell contents, 710
status bar settings, 711-712
toolbars, 714-718
Web options, 706
window settings, 710-711
workbook colors, 706-709
workbook sheets, 704-705
worksheet displays, 709
zero value displays, 710
date formats, 94
folder for saved files, 35
fonts, 111
changing, 152
resetting, 115
list formatting, 388
margins, 144
number formats, 92
number of worksheets, 23
PivotChart placement on worksheets, 799
PivotTable
data ranges, 612
names, 619
printer setting, 136
styles, 116-117
text
alignment, 29
fonts, 30
time formats, 95
worksheet displays, 108, 709

definitions
absolute referencing, 178
arguments, 160
body (of list), 388
breakpoint, 866
cell, range referencing, 178
Code window, 847
collection, 839
comment, 864
constants, 844
contiguous ranges, 50
cost/production curves, 591
declaration statements, 844
element, 534
event, 871
external worksheet
 references, 181
fading out, 534
formatting codes, 97
formula, 160
functions, 386, 841
grouping, 56
hard coding, 170
Immediate window, 868
links, 183
List Members list, 861
literal text, 845
logic error, 865
loops, 858
Macro Recorder, 838
method, 840
modules, 845
nested calculations, 163
noncontiguous ranges, 54
operators, 160
procedures, 839
Project Explorer window,
 846
projects, 845
properties, 840
Properties window, 846
relative referencing, 178
return, 841
runtime error, 865
scientific notation, 32
scope, 851

source workbooks, 183-185
statements, 839
stepping, 866
syntax error, 865
variables, 842
zero-length string, 844

degrees
converting radians to, 305,
 313
converting to radians, 306

**DEGREES function, 305,
313**

degrees of freedom (df), 351

**Delete Comment button
(Reviewing toolbar), 81**

deleting
axis labels in charts,
 478-479
borders, 122, 125
buttons from toolbars, 715
cell contents, 29, 64
chart elements, 468
charts, 470
comments, 80
custom menus, 726
custom toolbars, 723
from multiple worksheets
 simultaneously, 56
hyperlinks, 750-751
macros, 831-832
modules, 852
named ranges, 59

delimiters
currency, 92
data, 395
files, 783

**DELTA function, 216,
223-224**

**dependent workbooks,
updating values in, 185**

dependents, 458-460

descenders, 113

descending sorts, 414-416

**Descriptive Statistics tool
(Analysis ToolPak), 670**

design
data sources, creating
 consistency between, 752
menus, 728
pie charts, 580-581
VBA, removing unwanted
 rows, 873-874

desktop, shortcut icons, 10

DEVSQ function, 345

DFUNCTION syntax
criteria argument, 191-192
database argument, 191
field argument, 191

**DGET function, 190,
194-195**

diagrams, presentations, 700

dialog boxes
Add Data, 511
Add Tables, 776
Add Trendline, 525-527
Advanced Filter, 422
Assign Macro, 822
Chart Type, changing chart
 type, 508
Choose Columns, 771
Choose Data Source, 769
Colors, 707
Conditional Formatting,
 409
Consolidate, 447-449
Data Validation
 Clear All button, 457
 Error Alert tab, 456
 Input Message tab, 456
 Settings tab, 454
Format Axis, Scale tab,
 517-518, 523
Format Cells, 93-97, 103-
 105, 409
Format Data Series, adding
 Secondary Axis, 515
Format Trendline, 527-529
Function, 169

Group, 441
Insert Function, 169
Insert menu, 58
Macro Options, 820
Macros, 815, 819
Name Define, 165
Options, Color tab, 707
Page Setup, Header/Footer tab, 147
Paste Special
  adding data to charts, 512
  modifying lists, 389-391
PivotTable Field, 618
Print, 136-137
Random Number Generation, 671
Record Macro, 814-815
Security, 817
Settings, customizing outline settings, 447
Sort, 413-415
Source Data, changing data source, 514
Subtotals, 450-451
Top 10 AutoFilter, 418
Unhide, 829
Visual Basic Editor
  Add Procedure, 851
  Quick Watch, 870

digit placeholders, formatting code, 99

digital signatures
enabling, 713
macros, 817

dimension hierarchies (OLAP), 790
building in PivotTables, 796-797
drilling down, 796-797
OLAP Cube Wizard, 803
tree view, 796

Directory text type, 271

disabling Clipboard viewer, 64

DISC function, 235, 245-246

discount rate, calculating, 245-246

displaying
comments, 80-81
custom toolbars, 720
dates in headers and footers, 149
Drawing toolbar, 129
menus, 20
multiple workbooks, 513
OLAP PivotTable items, 798
values, 871

distance units, 221

distributions, calculating
exponential distributions, 358-359
F probability distributions, 359-360
inverse normal distributions, 372
normal distributions, 371-372
Poisson distributions, 374-375

Divide option (Paste Special dialog box), 391

division, 161-162, 306
formula, 162
functions, 306
operator, 161

divisor, calculating greatest common divisor, 305

DMAX function, 190, 195-196

DMIN function, 190, 196

documents
formatting Excel data in, 736
Word, copying Excel charts to, 734-735

DOLLAR function, 326

dollar sign ($) symbol, anchoring cell references, 179-180

DOLLARDE function, 235

DOLLARFR function, 235

dots-per-inch (dpi). *See* dpi

double-clicking, 629-631

doughnut charts, 491-493, 549

dpi (dot-per-inch) setting, print quality, 144

DPRODUCT function, 190, 197

draft stamps, 570-573

drag and fill feature, AutoSum formulas, 168

drag-and-drop
adding features
  buttons to custom toolbars, 720-721
  charts to pictures, 568
  data to charts, 513
cell range changes, 172
copying cell contents, 69-70
creating PivotTables with, 614-617
customizing menus, 725
enabling, 68
fields, PivotCharts, 625
inserting data ranges into lists, 402
moving features
  cell contents, 68
  fields in PivotTables/PivotCharts, 625-626
  fields outside PivotTables, 631-632
  worksheets, 25
selecting cell ranges, 50
PivotTables, 610

Draw and Autoshapes button (Drawing toolbar), 130

Draw Borders button (Formatting toolbar, 122-125

Draw button (Drawing toolbar), 128

Draw menu, 131-132

Drawing button (Standard toolbar), 17

Drawing toolbar, 129-130
  adding features
    buttons, 569-570
    cost/production curves to charts, 591
    shapes to charts, 546
  AutoShapes option, 546
  Bevel tool, 134-135
  buttons, 127-130, 546-547
  displaying/hiding, 129
  Text Box tool, 545
  WordArt button, 570

drawing tools
  activating, 130
  inclusion matrices, 154
  media matrices, 153-154
  slider charts, 153-155

drilling down
  OLAP dimension hierarchies, 796-797
  PivotTables, 626-631, 638

drivers, database drivers, 768

drop areas, OLAP PivotTables, 795-797

drop-down menus (combo boxes), adding to charts, 587-589

DSUM function, 191, 197-198

dual-axis charts
  creating, 515
  naming axes, 476-477

DURATION function, 235, 246-247

DVAR function, 191

DVARP function, 191

dynamic charts, creating, 584-589
  combo boxes, 587-589
  option buttons, 586
  text boxes, 586

E

E-mail button (Standard toolbar), 17

EDATE function, 206-207

Edit Box control (Forms toolbar), 424

Edit Code control (Forms toolbar), 425

Edit Hyperlink dialog box (hyperlink shortcut menu), 750-751

Edit menu
  Go To Special dialog box, 28
  Links dialog box, 84
  Paste dialog box, 511
  Paste Special dialog box, 82
    adding data to charts, 512
    linking, 82-83
  PowerPoint, pasting PivotTables, 739
  Replace dialog box, 75

edit mode, 171

Edit WordArt Text dialog box (Drawing toolbar), 571

editing
  accepting/rejecting edits, 77-78
  cells
    adding comments, 79-81
    content, 29

    deleting comments, 80
    drag and drop, 68
    Formula bar, 66-67
    groups, 65-66
    keyboard, 64-65
    undoing edits, 65
  charts
    category (X) axis, 521-523
    chart types, 508-510
    data series/data points, 510-513
    embedded, 507-508
    origin, 520-521
    secondary axes, 514-515
    series order, 523-525
    source data, 514
    plot area, 519
    value (Y) axis, 516-521
  data, find and replace actions, 75
  formulas, 170-172
    changing cell ranges, 164-165, 172
    pasting named ranges into, 165-166
  hyperlinks, 749-752
  macros, 828-830
  multiple worksheets simultaneously, 56
  PivotTables
    adding interactivity, 636-637
    HTML format, 636-638
  queries, 782-783
  tracking edits, 75-77
  undoing edits, 513

editors, Visual Basic Editor, 828-830

EFFECT function, 235

elapsed time, formatting options, 99

elements (charts), 534

How can we make this index more useful? Email us at indexes@quepublishing.com

embedded charts, 484-486
    changing chart sheets, 501
    editing, Chart toolbar
        buttons for, 507-508
    lists, 595-596
    moving and resizing,
        506-507
    worksheets, 595-596

employee hours and costs,
    managing with
    PivotTables, 639-643

empty cells
    counting number of, 266,
        269-270
    handling in PivotTables,
        622-623
    obtaining information
        about, 266, 272-274

enabling
    Clipboard viewer, 64
    Solver add-in, 650

encoding Web pages, 706

Encoding Tab (Web Options
    button), 706

encryption, applying to
    worksheets, 35-37

energy units, converting
    between, 221

engineering functions,
    216-231
    BESSELI, 216, 218
    BESSELJ, 216
    BESSELK, 216
    BESSELY, 216
    BIN2DEC, 216, 219
    BIN2HEX, 216
    BIN2OCT, 216
    COMPLEX, 216, 219-220
    CONVERT, 216, 220-222,
        230
    DEC2BIN, 216, 223
    DEC2HEX, 216
    DEC2OCT, 216
    DELTA, 216, 223-224
    ERF, 216

ERFC, 216
GESTEP, 217, 224
HEX2BIN, 217, 225
HEX2DEC, 217
HEX2OCT, 217
IMABS, 217
IMAGINARY, 217
IMARGUMENT, 217
IMCONJUGATE, 217,
    225-226
IMCOS, 217
IMDIV, 217
IMEXP, 217
IMLN, 217
IMLOG10, 217
IMLOG2, 217
IMPOWER, 217, 226-227
IMPRODUCT, 217,
    227-228
IMREAL, 217
IMSIN, 217
IMSQRT, 217
IMSUB, 218, 228-229
IMSUM, 218, 229
OCT2BIN, 218, 230
OCT2DEC, 218
OCT2HEX, 218

Enter key, 50
    cursor movement, cus-
        tomizing default direction,
        704-705
    data entry, 29
    navigating tables, 52
    navigating worksheets, 27

entering numbers in cells,
    32

Enterprise Resource
    Planning System. See ERP

EOMONTH function, 202

equal sign (=), 160

equal to operator, 161

erasing borders, 122

ERF function, 216

ERFC function, 216

ERP (Enterprise Resource
    Planning System), 756

Error Alert tab (Data
    Validation dialog box), 456

error bars (charts),
    formatting
    X error bars, 539
    Y error bars, 538-540

Error Checking button
    (Formula Auditing
    toolbar), 453

Error Checking tab (Options
    dialog box), 712

ERROR.TYPE function,
    266, 270-271

errors
    formulas, troubleshooting,
        186
    functions
        error type numbers, 266,
            270-271
        information functions,
            275
        ISERR, 266, 273
        ISERROR, 266, 273
        ISLOGICAL, 266, 273
        ISNA, 266, 273
        ISNONTEXT, 266, 273
        logical, 283
        lookup and reference
            functions, 301
        NA, 267
        TYPE, 267
    handling
        auditing tools, 458
        Auto Outline feature,
            446
        data entry, validating
            entries, 453-454
        date functions, 213
        formulas, 177-178
        PivotTables, 622-623
    macros, 833-834
    range naming., 59-60
    undoing edits, 513

Evaluate Formula button (Formula Auditing toolbar), 454

EVEN function, 305

even numbers, identifying, 266, 273

events, starting code automatically, 871-872

EXACT function, 326, 329-330

Excel
closing, 11
customizing, 704-723
integrating with Access, 756-759
integration with other Office programs, 734
copying data from Word/PowerPoint to Excel, 744-746
copying Excel tables/charts into PowerPoint, 736-742
copying Excel tables/charts into Word, 734-735
hyperlinks for, 746-752
starting, 10-11

Exit option (File menu), closing Excel, 11

EXP function, 305

expanding group view, 442-443

exploded pie chart slices, 490, 549-550

EXPONDIST function, 345, 358-359

Exponential setting (Trendline dialog box), 526

Exponential Smoothing tool (Analysis ToolPak), 670

exponentials
calculations
curves, 368
distribution, 358-359
growth, 363-364
complex numbers, 217
formulas, 162
operator, 161

exporting Excel data into non-Access databases, 766-767

expressions, debugging, 869-870

Extend Lists Formats and Formulas option (Tools menu), enabling/disabling, 388

external links, locking, 85

external references, 181-182

external workbooks
linking to, 183-185
references, syntax, 184

Extract range, 422

F

F probability distribution, calculating, 359-360

F-Test, Two-Sample for Variance tool (Analysis ToolPak), 670

F1 keystrokes, 12

F2 button, 171

F5 key, 28

FACT function, 305

FACTDOUBLE function, 305

factorials, calculating, 305

fading in/out, 534

FALSE function, 278

FDIST function, 345, 359-360

field argument (DFUNCTION), 191

Field List (OLAP PivotTables), 795

field names
hierarchical lists, 388
preventing from scrolling, 399

Field Settings button (PivotTable toolbar), 610

fields
hidden, including in PivotTable subtotals, 620
hierarchical lists, 388
OLAP PivotTables, accessing, 795-797
PivotCharts
hiding/displaying, 626-627
layout options, 613-617
rearranging, 610, 625-626
PivotTables
dragging outside table, 631-632
drilling down, 629-631
layout options, 613-617
rearranging, 610

file formats, saved worksheets, 37-38

File menu
Exit option, closing Excel, 11
New dialog box, accessing templates, 40
Page Setup dialog box, 141-143
Page tab, 143
Set Print Area feature, 151
Sheet tab options, 150

Print dialog box, 137-138
Print Preview feature, previewing charts, 500
Print Setup dialog box, Header/Footer tab, 147-150
Save As command, 34
Save As dialog box, 39
Save as Web Page command, 636
Save command, 34

File Name button (Custom Header/Footer dialog boxes), 149

Filename info type, 267

filenames, stored macros, 719

files
comma-delimited files, 767
identifying versions of, 46
printing worksheets to, 137
Web files, setting defaults, 706

Files Tab (Web Options button), 706

Fill Color button
Drawing toolbar, 128
Formatting toolbar, 19, 126

fill color, applying to cells, 126

fill effects, charts, 552-554, 560, 582-583

Fill Effects dialog box
Format Data Series dialog box, 583
Picture tab, 554-555

fill handles, 172
AutoFill series, 70, 173-174
custom fill series, 71-72
linear/growth trend series, 72-73
organization-specific lists, 73-75

Fill Series menu, creating custom fill series, 71-72

filtering
data entry forms, 396
imported Word tables, 745-746
lists, 397, 416-424
Advanced Filter, 421-424
AutoFilter, 417-421
automatic subtotaling, 450-452

filters
adding to charts, 588-590
queries, 773-774

financial calculations
mortgage payments, multiple-variable active tables, 667-669
Solver tool, 646

financial functions, 234-263
ACCRINT, 234, 238-239
ACCRINTM, 234, 239-240
AMORLINC, 234
COUPDAYBS, 234, 240-241
COUPDAYS, 234, 241-242, 263
COUPDAYSNC, 234
COUPNCD, 234, 242-243
COUPNUM, 235, 243-244
COUPPCD, 235
CUMIPMT, 235, 244-245
CUMPRINC, 235
DB, 235
DDB, 235
DISC, 235, 245-246
DOLLARDE, 235
DOLLARFR, 235
DURATION, 235, 246-247
EFFECT, 235
FV, 235, 247-248
FVSCHEDULE, 235
INTRATE, 236
IPMT, 236, 248-249

IRR, 236
MDURATION, 236, 249-250
MIRR, 236
NOMINAL, 236
NPER, 236, 250-251
NPV, 236, 251-252
ODDFPRICE, 236
ODDFYIELD, 236
ODDLPRICE, 236
ODDLYIELD, 237
ODDPRICE, 252-254
PMT, 237, 254-255
PPMT, 237
PRICE, 237, 255-256
PRICEDISC, 237
PRICEMAT, 237
PV, 237, 256-257
RATE, 237, 257-258
RECEIVED, 237, 258-259
SLN, 237
SYD, 237
TBILLEQ, 237
TBILLPRICE, 237, 259-260
TBILLYIELD, 237, 260-261
VDB, 238
XIRR, 238
XNPV, 238
YIELD, 238, 261-262
YIELDDISC, 238
YIELDMAT, 238, 262-263

financial ratios
activity ratios, 685-686
coverage ratios, 687
liquidity ratios, 685
profitability ratios, 686-687

find and replace, editing data, 75

FIND function, 326, 330-331

finding text strings, 330-331

FINV function, 345

FISHER function, 345

FISHERINV function, 345

FIXED function, 326, 331-332

fixed-width files, 783

floating timelines, 411-413

floating toolbars, 129, 570

FLOOR function, 305

floors (3D charts), formatting, 556-557

Flowchart button (Drawing toolbar), 547

FNUM arguments (SUBTOTAL function), 319-320

folders
    subfolders, 35
    Templates folder, 46
    XLStart folder, 813

Font button
    Custom Header/Footer dialog boxes, 148
    Formatting toolbar, 18, 109

Font Color button
    Drawing toolbar, 129
    Formatting toolbar, 19, 110

Font Size box (Formatting toolbar), 18

Font Size button (Formatting toolbar), 109

Font tab (Format Cells dialog box), 111

fonts
    ascenders/descenders, 113
    AutoFormat feature, 127
    changing, 112-113
    defaults, 111
        changing, 152
        customizing, 706
        resetting, 115

formatting in cells, 112
hierarchical lists, 388
size options, 113-114
styles, 112-114
text, defaults, 30
viewing font names, 113
Web pages, setting defaults for, 706

Fonts Tab (Web Options button), 706

footers
    creating, 147-150
    setting margins, 145

force units, measurements, converting between, 221

FORECAST function, 345, 360-361

forecasting tools, 646, 657-659

form controls
    active tables
        adding scrollbars, 667-669
        multiple variables, 667
        spinners, 665-666
    adding to charts, 584-587
        drop-down menus, 587-589
        text boxes, 586
    adding to worksheets, Combo Box example, 426-428
    charts, 433-435
    Check Box, 435
    Combo Box, 435
    formulas
        calculation tables, 429-432
        referencing cell links, 428-429
    List Box, 435
    Option Button, 436
    Scrollbar, adding to charts, 433-435
    Spinner, 435

Form option (Data menu), 396-397

Format Axis dialog box
    Patterns tab, 535
    Scale tab, 517-518, 523

Format button (Chart toolbar), 507

Format Cells dialog box (Format menu), 111
    adding borders and shading, 122-125
    Alignment tab, 120-121
        Merge Cells option, 121
        Shrink to Fit option, 121
        text wrapping option, 121
    Conditional Formatting dialog box, 409
    creating custom styles, 117
    hiding/displaying cell content, 710
    Number tab, 93-94
        Custom category, 97, 103-105
        custom characters and symbols, 102
        Date category, 95
        Fraction category, 96
    Patterns tab, 125-126

Format Chart Title dialog box (Format menu), 544

Format Column Width dialog box (Format menu), 32

Format Control dialog box (Forms toolbar), Control tab, 585

Format Control option (form control context menu), 427-428

Format Data Labels dialog box, 542-543

Format Data Point dialog box (Format menu)
angling data series, 549
formatting individual points, 551

Format Data Series dialog box
File menu
Axis, Secondary Axis option, 576
Data Labels tab, 541
Format menu
adding Secondary Axis, 515
Axis tab, 549
Data Labels tab, 541-543
Fill Effects, 583
Options tab, Angle of First Slice option, 549
Series Order tab, 548
Shapes tab, adding 3D shapes, 557
X-axis Error Bars tab, 539
Y-axis Error Bars tab, 538-540

Format dialog box (Format menu), Patterns tab, 552

Format Floors dialog box (Format menu), Patterns tab, 556-557

Format info type, 267

Format menu
AutoFormat feature, 126-127
Column/Row Hide option, 45
Conditional Formatting dialog box, 409
Format Axis dialog box, Selected Axis option, 535

Format Cells dialog box, 111
adding borders and shading, 122-125
hiding/displaying cell content, 710
Patterns tab, 125-126
Format Chart Title dialog box, 544
Format Column Width/Row Height dialog boxes, 32
Format Data Point dialog box, 549-551
Format Data Series dialog box, 515
Axis tab, 549
Data Labels tab, 541
Format Data Labels dialog box, 542-543
Series Order tab, 548
X-axis Error Bars tab, 539
Y-axis Error Bars tab, 538-540
Format Floor dialog box, 556-557
Format Series dialog box, Options tab, changing angle of pie slices, 579
Format Trendline dialog box, 527-529
Format Wall dialog box, 556
Hide/Unhide dialog boxes, Sheet submenu, 709
Style dialog box, 116-118

Format Object button (Picture toolbar), 568

Format Painter button (Standard toolbar), 17

Format Picture button (Custom Header/Footer dialog boxes), 149

Format Report button (PivotTable toolbar), 610

Format Row Height dialog box (Format menu), 32

Format Series dialog box (Format menu), 579

Format Tab Color dialog box, 24

Format Trendline dialog box (Format menu), 527-529
Options tab, 528-529
Patterns tab, 527

Format Wall dialog box (Format menu), Patterns tab, 556

Formats option (Paste Special dialog box), 390

formatting
AutoFormat feature, 126
cells
alignment options, 119-121
applying colors and patterns, 125-126
borders and shading, 122-125
fonts, 112-114
individual characters, 115
charts, 534
3D effects, 555-559
analytical charts, 600
axes, 478-479, 595-597
axis labels, 537
backgrounds, 551-555
bar charts, 600
bevels, 133-135
borders, 560
chart types, 508-509
chart titles, 476-477
column depth, 573-575
cost/production curves, 591

data labels, 482-483, 540-544, 560
data points, 550, 560
data series, 548-549
data tables, 483-484
design considerations, 534
draft stamps/watermarks, 570-573
embedding in lists/ worksheets, 595-596
error bars, 538-540
exploded pie chart slices, 549-550
fill effects, 552, 560
filters and subtotals, 588-590
form controls, 584-589
gradient fills, 582-583
graphics, 566-569
handling problems with, 560
hiding/displaying data in, 592-593
high/low lines, 538-539
layering objects, 569-570
legends, 481-482, 501, 544
lifetime profitability/breakeven charts, 601-602
linking text to worksheet cells, 592
multiple-combination charts, 594-595
option buttons, 586
overlays, 575-578
pie charts, 579-581
placing over shapes, 572
professional design features, 564-566
secondary axes, 575-578
shapes, 546-548
single-stack charts, 596-599

slider charts, 153-155
source tables, 469
special effects, 595
stacking techniques, 590
text, 545
tick marks, 535-536
time analyses with annotations, 598
trendlines, 527-529
value axes, 534-535
codes, 97-104
conditional codes, 103-104
currency formats, 101
custom characters, 102
date and time formats, 98-99
large numbers, 102
number and text formats, 99-101
repeating characters, 104-105
conditional formats, 408, 622
formulas, 410-411
timelines, 411-413
interactive approach, 408-410
Excel objects in PowerPoint, 740-741
charts, 741
PivotTables, 740
fonts, resetting default, 115
form controls, 428
lists
custom layouts, 388
modifying legacy lists, 388
Paste Special dialog box options, 389-391
standard layouts, 388
media matrices/plans, 153-154
multiple worksheets simultaneously, 55

numbers, 92
comma style, 92
conditional formatting codes, 103-104
currency, 92, 101
custom characters, 102
custom formats, 93-97
dates, 94-99
decrease decimal option, 92
fractions, 96
increase decimal option, 92
large numbers, 102
numbers and text, 99-101
percent style, 92
repeating characters, 104-105
scientific notation, 93
specialized formats, 96
time, 95-99
viewing built-in codes, 97
PivotTables/PivotCharts, 608
AutoFormat option, 620-621
label display options, 622
layout options, 613-617
page layout, 622
PivotChart Wizard formatting options, 613
styles, 116-118
creating custom styles, 117
editing Normal style, 116-117
merging styles among workbooks, 118
titles, 119-120, 153

worksheets, 108
   advantages, 108
   Format Cells dialog box, 111
   Formatting toolbar, 109-110
   page setup options, 141-142
   tips, 156
   Word documents, 736

Formatting toolbar, 109-110
   Align Left button, 18
   Align Right button, 18
   Bold button, 18
   Borders button, 19
   Center button, 18
   Comma Style button, 18
   Currency Style button, 18
   customizing, 110
   Decrease Decimal button, 19
   Decrease Indent button, 19, 120
   display options, 15-16, 110
   Draw Borders button, 122-125
   Fill Color button, 19, 126
   Font button, 18
   Font Color button, 19
   Font Size box, 18
   Increase Decimal button, 19
   Increase Indent button, 19, 120
   Italic button, 18
   Merge and Center button, 18, 119-120
   number formats, 92
   Percent Style button, 18
   Underline button, 18

forms
   controls, 424-427
   data forms
      data entry, 396-397
      searching, 398
   Microsoft Access forms, 786-787

Forms toolbar
   activating, 584
   controls, 424-427

Formula Auditing toolbar, 453-454

Formula bar, 28
   editing
      cell contents, 66-67
      cell groups, 66
      formulas, 171
   linked-cell displays, 84
   Name box
      creating named ranges, 58
      viewing cell addresses, 50
   viewing cell contents, 30

formulas
   absolute cell references, 680-683
   active tables
      multiple-variable tables, 667-669
      multiplier formulas, 665-666
   adding to PivotTables, 628-629
   arithmetic operators, 161-163
      handling multiple operators, 163
   AutoCalculate feature, 175-177
   AutoSum feature, 166-170
      SUM function, 166-168
      SUMIF function, 168-170
   built-in, 160
   cell referencing
      absolute versus relative, 178-180
      adding to chart controls, 434-435
   comparison operators, 161

   conditional formatting, 410-413
      timelines, 411-413
   copying, 173-174
   cubed, summarizing multiple worksheets, 183
   drag and fill feature, 168
   editing, 170-172
      changing cell ranges, 164-165, 172
   enabling on Web pages, 706
   error messages, 177-178
   financial calculations, 662-665
   finding missing parentheses, 163
   form controls
      calculation tables, 429-432
      referencing cell links, 428-429
   Goal Seek dialog box, 647-649
   handling during transpose operations, 391-393
   nested calculations, 163-164
   order of operations, 161-163
   parentheses, 162
   pasting named ranges into, 165-166
   precedents and dependents, 458
   reference operators, 161
   referencing data from other workbooks
      links for, 183-185
      updating values, 185
   referencing external worksheet data, 181-182
   Solver, 650-654
      analysis options, 656-657
      limitations, 656
      resetting values, 654-655
   SUM IF, chart controls, 434-435

text operators, 161
text, 341
transposing ranges, 186
troubleshooting
    complex formulas, 436
    errors, 186
    index formulas, 436
    performance issues, 436
Watch Window, 180
Formulas and Number Formats option (Paste Special dialog box), 390
Formulas option (Paste Special dialog box), 390
Forward option (Solver Options dialog box), 657
Fourier Analysis tool (Analysis ToolPak), 670
Fraction category (Format Cells, Number tab), 96
fractions, formatting options, 96, 100
Freeze Panes command (Window menu), 43
freezing
    panes during scrolling, 399
    rows or columns, 42-43
FREQUENCY function, 345, 361-362
FTEST function, 345
Function dialog box, 169
functions
    arguments, 160
    AutoCalculate feature, 175-177
    COLUMN, 286
    COUPDAYS, 234
    custom functions, 164, 689-691

databases, 190
    DAVERAGE, 190-193
    DCOUNT, 190, 193-194
    DCOUNTA, 190
    DFUNCTION syntax, 191-192
    DGET, 190, 194-195
    DMAX, 190, 195-196
    DMIN, 190, 196
    DPRODUCT, 190, 197
    DSUM, 191, 197-198
    DVAR, 191
    DVARP, 191
    GETPIVOTDATA, 191, 198-199
date, 202
    DATE, 202-206
    DATEVALUE, 202
    DAYS360, 202
    EDATE, 206-207
    EOMONTH, 202
    MONTH, 203, 207
    NETWORKDAYS, 203, 208-209
    NOW, 203
    TODAY, 203, 209-213
    WEEKDAY, 203
    WORKDAY, 203
    YEAR, 203
    YEARFRAC, 203
description, 841
engineering, 216-231
    BESSELI, 216-218
    BESSELJ, 216
    BESSELK, 216
    BESSELY, 216
    BIN2DEC, 216, 219
    BIN2HEX, 216
    BIN2OCT, 216
    COMPLEX, 216, 219-220
    CONVERT, 216, 220-222, 230

DEC2BIN, 216, 223
DEC2HEX, 216
DEC2OCT, 216
DELTA, 216, 223-224
ERF, 216
ERFC, 216
GESTEP, 217, 224
HEX2BIN, 217, 225
HEX2DEC, 217
HEX2OCT, 217
IMABS, 217
IMAGINARY, 217
IMARGUMENT, 217
IMCONJUGATE, 217, 225-226
IMCOS, 217
IMDIV, 217
IMEXP, 217
IMLN, 217
IMLOG10, 217
IMPOWER, 217, 226-227
IMPRODUCT, 217, 227-228
IMREAL, 217
IMSIN, 217
IMSQRT, 217
IMSUB, 218, 228-229
IMSUM, 218, 229
OCT2BIN, 218, 230
OCT2DEC, 218
OCT2HEX, 218
equal sign (=) in, 160
financial, 234-263
    ACCRINT, 234, 238-239
    ACCRINTM, 234, 239-240
    AMORLINC, 234
    COUPDAYBS, 234, 240-241
    COUPDAYS, 241-242, 263
    COUPDAYSNC, 234

COUPNCD, 234, 242-243
COUPNUM, 235, 243-244
COUPPCD, 235
CUMIPMT, 235, 244-245
CUMPRINC, 235
DB, 235
DDB, 235
DISC, 235, 245-246
DOLLARDE, 235
DOLLARFR, 235
DURATION, 235, 246-247
EFFECT, 235
FV, 235, 247-248
FVSCHEDULE, 235
INTRATE, 236
IPMT, 236, 248-249
IRR, 236
MDURATION, 236, 249-250
MIRR, 236
NOMINAL, 236
NPER, 236, 250-251
NPV, 236, 251-252
ODDFPRICE, 236
ODDFYIELD, 236
ODDLPRICE, 236
ODDLYIELD, 237
ODDPRICE, 252-254
PMT, 237, 254-255, 662-665
PPMT, 237
PRICE, 237, 255-256
PRICEDISC, 237
PRICEMAT, 237
PV, 237, 256-257
RATE, 237, 257-258
RECEIVED, 237, 258-259
SLN, 237
SYD, 237

TBILLEQ, 237
TBILLPRICE, 237, 259-260
TBILLYIELD, 237, 260-261
VDB, 238
XIRR, 238
XNPV, 238
YIELD, 238, 261-262
YIELDDISC, 238
YIELDMAT, 238, 262-263
IF, embedding date functions in, 211-213
information, 266-276
CELL, 266-269
COUNTBLANK, 266, 269-270
ERRPR.TYPE, 266, 270-271
INFO, 266, 271-272
IS, functions, 272-273
ISBLANK, 266, 273-274
ISERR, 266, 273
ISERROR, 266, 273
ISEVEN, 266, 273
ISLOGICAL, 266, 273
ISNA, 266, 273
ISNONTEXT, 266, 273
ISNUMBER, 266, 273-275
ISODD, 266, 273
ISREF, 266, 273
ISTEXT, 266, 273
N, 267
NA, 267
troubleshooting, 275
TYPE, 267
logical, 278-283
AND, 278-280
FALSE, 278
IF, 278-281
NOT, 278, 281-282
OR, 278, 282-283
troubleshooting, 283
TRUE, 278

lookup and reference, 286-301
ADDRESS, 286
AREA, 286
CHOOSE, 287-288
COLUMNS, 286
HLOOKUP, 286-289
HYPERLINK, 286
INDEX, 286, 290-292
INDIRECT, 287
LOOKUP, 287, 294-295
MATCH, 287
OFFSET, 287, 296-299
ROW, 287
ROWS, 287
TRANSPOSE, 287, 299-300
VLOOKUP, 287, 300-301
math and trigonometry, 304-323
ABS, 304, 307-308
ACOS, 304, 308-309
ACOSH, 304
ASIN, 304, 309-310
ASINH, 304
ATAN, 304
ATAN2, 304
ATANH, 304
CEILING, 304
COMBIN, 304, 310-311
COS, 304, 311
COSH, 304
COUNTIF, 304, 311-313
DEGREES, 305, 313
EVEN, 305
EXP, 305
FACT, 305
FACTDOUBLE, 305
FLOOR, 305
GCD, 305
INT, 305
LCM, 305
LN, 313-314
LOG, 305

LOG10, 305
MDETERM, 305
MINVERSE, 305
MMULT, 305
MOD, 305
MROUND, 305
MULTINOMIAL, 305
ODD, 305
PERMUT, 305, 315
PI, 306, 316
POWER, 306
PRODUCT, 306
QUOTIENT, 306
RADIANS, 306
RAND, 306, 316-317
RANDBETWEEN, 306
ROMAN, 306, 317-318
ROUND, 306
ROUNDDOWN, 306
ROUNDUP, 306
SERIESSUM, 306
SIGN, 306
SIN, 306
SINH, 306
SQRT, 306, 318-319
SQRTP1, 306
SUBTOTAL, 306, 319-320
SUM, 307, 320-323
SUMIF, 307, 321-322
SUMPRODUCT, 307
SUMSQUARES, 307
SUMX2MY2, 307
SUMX2PY2, 307
TAN, 307, 322
TANH, 307
TRUNC, 307
PivotTables
changing, 618
VLOOKUP, 639-640

statistical, 344-381
AVEDEV, 344
AVERAGE, 344, 349-350
AVERAGEA, 344
BETADIST, 344
BETAINV, 344
BINOMDIST, 344, 350-351
CHIDIST, 344, 351-352
CHIINV, 344
CHITEST, 344, 352
CONFIDENCE, 344, 352
CORREL, 344, 353-354
COUNT, 344, 354-355
COUNTA, 345, 354-356
COUNTBLANK, 345, 356-357
COUNTIF, 345, 356-357
COVAR, 345, 358
CRITBINOM, 345
DEVSQ, 345
EXPONDIST, 345, 358-359
FDIST, 345, 359-360
FINV, 345
FISHER, 345
FISHERINV, 345
FORECAST, 345, 360-361
FREQUENCY, 345, 361-362
FTEST, 345
GAMMADIST, 345
GAMMAINV, 345
GAMMALN, 346
GEOMEAN, 346, 362-363
GROWTH, 346, 363-364

HARMEAN, 346
HYPGEODIST, 346
INTERCEPT, 346, 364-365
LARGE, 346, 365, 377
LINEST, 346, 366-367
LOGEST, 346, 368
LOGINV, 346
LOGNORMDIST, 346
MAX, 346, 368-369
MAXA, 347
MEDIAN, 347, 369-370
MIN, 347, 370
MINA, 347, 371
MODE, 347, 371
NEGBINOMDIST, 347
NORMDIST, 347, 371-372
NORMINV, 347, 372
NORMSINV, 347
PEARSON, 347
PERCENTILE, 347, 373
PERCENTRANK, 347, 373-374
PERMUT, 347
POISSON, 348, 374-375
PROB, 348
QUARTILE, 348
RANK, 348, 375-376
SKEW, 348
SLOPE, 348, 376-377
SMALL, 348, 377
STANDARDIZE, 348
STDEV, 348, 378
STDEVA, 348, 378-379
STDEVP, 348
STDEVPA, 348
STEYX, 348
TDIST, 349
TINV, 349
TREND, 349, 379
TRIMMEAN, 349
troubleshooting, 381

TTEST, 349
VAR, 349, 380
VARA, 349, 380
VARP, 349, 380
VARPA, 349
WEIBULL, 349
ZTEST, 349
SUBTOTAL, syntax for, 451-452
SUM, embedding date functions in, 211-214
text functions, 326-340
CHAR, 326
CLEAN, 326
CODE, 326
CONCATENATE, 326-329
DOLLAR, 326
EXACT, 326, 329-330
FIND, 326, 330-331
FIXED, 326, 331-332
LEFT, 326
LEN, 326, 332-333
LOWER, 326, 333-334
MID, 327, 334-335
PROPER, 327, 335-336
REPLACE, 327
REPLACEB, 327
REPT, 327
RIGHT, 327, 336-337
SEARCH, 327
SEARCHB, 327
SUBSTITUTE, 327, 338-339
T, 327
TEXT, 327
TRIM, 327, 339-340
UPPER, 327, 340
VALUE, 327
Time, 203
ToolTips, enabling/disabling, 706
future value, calculating, 247-248
FV function, 235, 247-248
FVSCHEDULE function, 235

G

GAMMADIST function, 345
GAMMAINV function, 345
GAMMALN function, 346
Gantt charts, 646, 657-659, 693-694
gap width (charts), 548-549, 575-578
GCD function, 305
General tab
Tools menu, resetting font defaults, 115
Web Options button, 706
GEOMEAN function, 346, 362-363
geometric means, calculating, 362-363
GESTEP function, 217, 224
GETPIVOTDATA function, 191, 198-199
Go To shortcut, navigating worksheets, 28
Go To Special dialog box (Edit menu), 28
Goal Seek dialog box, 647-649
Goal Seek tool, 646-649
gradient fills (3D charts), 582-583
gradient shading (adding to charts), 554
Grand Totals for Columns option (PivotTable and PivotChart Wizard), 619

graphics
charts
adding, 566-569
backgrounds, 554-555
column depth, adding 3D effects, 573-575
draft stamps/watermarks, 570-573
drawing shapes, 572
layering, 569-570
macros, 826-827
toolbar buttons, customizing, 716-718
Web pages, 706
gray corners, adding to overlays, 578
grayscale, printing charts in, 500
greater than operator, 161
greater than or equal to operator, 161
greatest common divisor, calculating, 305
gridlines
adding to charts, 479-481
charts, aligning labels with, 603
displaying in Word documents, 734
Gridlines tab (Chart Wizard), 479-481
Group Box control (Forms toolbar), 425
Group button (Outlining/Grouping toolbar), 441
Group dialog box (Data, Group, and Outline menu), 441

grouping
 data, 440-445
  column-based groups, 443
  creating groups, 441
  creating toolbar for, 440
  hierarchical grouping, 441
  layered groupings, 443-444
  multiple summary tables, 444-445
  overview of, 442
  PivotTables, 638-639
  viewing groups, 442-443
 dates
  PivotTables, 634
  troubleshooting, 638
 objects
  charts, 602
  shapes and lines, 132-133
  stacking and ordering, 131
 worksheets, 23-27, 56
  selecting and naming ranges, 61
  selecting cells, 55-57

Grouping dialog box (PivotTables), grouping dates, 634

GROWTH function, 346, 363-364

growth
 calculating exponential growth, 363-364
 trends, custom fill data series, 72-73

H

handles, grouped objects, 132-133

hard coding, 170

HARMEAN function, 346

header margins, setting, 145

header row, hierarchical lists, 387-388

Header/Footer tab
 Page Setup dialog box, 142, 147
 Print Setup dialog box, 147-150

headers
 creating, 147-148
 custom fields, 148-150
 setting margins, 145

headings
 columns and rows, abbreviating for charts, 475
 consolidated tables, matching labels, 449

height, rows
 adjusting, 31-32
 locking, 33

Help button (Print Preview toolbar), 140

Help system
 accessing, 12
 Microsoft Help, 13
 ScreenTips, 11
  chart elements, 507
 VBA, 842, 847

Help window, 12

HEX2BIN function, 217, 225

HEX2DEC function, 217

HEX2OCT function, 217

hexadecimal number, converting
 binary numbers into, 216
 decimal numbers into, 216
 octal numbers into, 218
 to binary format, 217, 225
 to decimal format, 217
 to octal format, 217

Hide Detail button (Outlining/Grouping toolbar), 441

Hide Detail button (PivotTable toolbar), 610

Hide dialog box (Format Sheet menu), 709

Hide Fields/Display Fields button (PivotTable toolbar), 610

hiding
 cell contents, 710
 chart data, 592-593
 columns in PivotTables, 629
 comments, 80-81
 custom menus, 727
 data series in charts, 602
 Drawing toolbar, 129
 report sheets, Solver, 655
 rows and columns, 45
 worksheets, 709
 zero values, 710

hierarchical groups
 data groupings, 441
 layered groupings, 443-444
 multiple summary tables, 444-445

hierarchical lists, 387-388

hierarchies, dimensional (OLAP), 790
 OLAP Cube Wizard, 803

high/low lines (charts), adding, 538-539

Highlight Changes dialog box (Track Changes feature), 76-77

Histogram tool (Analysis ToolPak), 670

HLOOKUP function, 286-289

Home key, 27, 50

horizontal alignment options, 120

horizontal axis. *See* X-axis

horizontal field names (hierarchical lists), 388

horizontal lists/tables, transposing to vertical, 391-393

horizontal lookups, 286-289

Horizontal option (Window menu), 42

horizontal ranges, returning as vertical ranges, 287, 299-300

horizontal scrollbars, adding/removing, 710-711

hot keys, customizing, 724

HOUR function, 203

HTML file format, saving and editing (PivotTables), 636-638

hyperbolic cosine, 304-306

hyperbolic sine, 304-306

hyperbolic tangent, calculating, 304, 307

Hyperlink button (Standard toolbar), 17

HYPERLINK function, 286

hyperlinks
accessing cell ranges, 749
assigning to objects, 718
deleting, 750-751
editing and updating, 749-752
integrating Office applications, 746-752
nesting, 749

HYPGEODIST function, 346

icons
desktop, launching Excel, 10
menus, 20
toolbar buttons, changing, 716-718

IF function, 278-281
AND function, 279-280
IS BLANK function, 274
ISNUMBER function, 274
OFFSET function, 296-297
YEAR function, 212-213

IF statement
cell links, syntax, 431
creating dynamic chart entry, 584-587

If-Then structure
footer procedure, 858
listing, 857

IMABS function, 217

Image Control button (Picture toolbar), 567

images, toolbars, 716-718, 824

IMAGINARY function, 217

imaginary/real coefficients, converting into complex numbers, 216, 219-220

IMARGUMENT function, 217

IMCONJUGATE function, 217, 225-226

IMCOS function, 217

IMDIV function, 217

IMEXP function, 217

IMLN function, 217

IMLOG10 function, 217

IMLOG2 function, 217

Immediate window, 868

Import Spreadsheet Wizard, 759-764, 786

importing
data from text files, 783-785
Excel data into Access databases, 759-764
text files, 785-786

IMPOWER function, 217, 226-227

IMPRODUCT function, 217, 227-228

IMREAL function, 217

IMSIN function, 217

IMSQRT function, 217

IMSUB function, 218, 228-229

IMSUM function, 218, 229

Include Hidden items in Totals button (PivotTable toolbar), 610

inclusion matrices, creating with Webdings, 154

inclusion reference operators, 161

Increase Decimal button (Formatting toolbar), 19, 92

Increase Indent button (Formatting toolbar), 19, 120

indents, writing code, 862

INDEX formula
form controls, 428-429
troubleshooting, 436

INDEX function
Array form, 286, 290
combining with MATCH function, 292
Reference form, 286, 290-291

index numbers, 288

INDIRECT function, 287

INFO function, 266, 271-272

info types, 267-269

information functions, 266-276
CELL, 266-269
COUNTBLANK, 266, 269-270
ERROR.TYPE, 266, 270-271
INFO, 266, 271-272
IS... functions, 272-273
ISBLANK, 266, 273-274
ISERR, 266, 273
ISERROR, 266, 273
ISEVEN, 266, 273
ISLOGICAL, 266, 273
ISNA, 266, 273
ISNONTEXT, 266, 273
ISNUMBER, 266, 273-275
ISODD, 266, 273
ISREF, 266, 273
ISTEXT, 266, 273
N, 267
NA, 267
troubleshooting, 275
TYPE, 267

information leveling, 387

inherited lists. *See* legacy lists

Input Message tab (Data Validation dialog box), 456

Insert Clip Art button (Drawing toolbar), 128

Insert Clip Art option (Clipboard task pane), 15

Insert Diagram or Org Chart button (Drawing toolbar), 128

Insert Function dialog box, 169

Insert Hyperlink dialog box (Insert menu), 747-749

Insert menu
Chart Wizard, 469
Chart Wizard option, 466
Comment box, 79
Cut Cells option, 402
Insert Hyperlink dialog box, 747-749
Insert Picture dialog box, adding graphics to charts, 566
Name Define dialog box, 165
Visual Basic Editor, Procedure command, 851
Worksheet option, 23

Insert Picture button (Custom Header/Footer dialog boxes), 149

Insert Picture dialog box (Insert menu), adding graphics to charts, 566

Insert Picture from File button (Picture toolbar), 567

Insert WordArt button (Drawing toolbar), 128

INT function, 305

integrating Office programs, 734
copying data from Word/PowerPoint to Excel, 744-746
copying Excel tables/charts into PowerPoint, 736-742
copying Excel tables/charts into Word, 734-735
hyperlinks, 746-752

interactivity
adding to PivotTables, 636-637
conditional formatting, 408-410
presentations, OFFSET function, 296

INTERCEPT function, 346, 364-365

interest payments, calculations
accrued interest, 238-239
accrued interest at maturity, 239-240
annuity returns, 257
cumulative interest payments, 244-245
payment amounts, 254-255
per-period annuity returns, 258

International tab (Options dialog box), 712-713

INTRATE function, 236

invalid data, marking, 457-458

inverse hyperbolic cosine, calculating, 304

inverse hyperbolic sine, calculating, 304

inverse hyperbolic tangent, calculating, 304

inverse tangent, calculating, 304

investments, calculations
amount due at maturity, 258-259
net present value, 251-252
odd first periods, 252-254
present value, 256-257
T-bill prices, 259-260
T-bill yields, 260-261
total number of accounting periods, 250-251
total value, 255-256
yields, 261-263

IPMT function, 236, 248-249

IRR function, 236

ISBLANK function, 266, 273-275

ISERR function, 266, 273

ISERROR function, 266, 273

ISEVEN function, 266, 273

ISLOGICAL function, 266, 273

ISNA function, 266, 273

ISNONTEXT function, 266, 273

ISNUMBER function, 266, 273-275

ISODD function, 266, 273

ISREF function, 266, 273

ISTEXT function, 266, 273

Italic button (Formatting toolbar), 18, 110

italicizing cell contents, 114

Iterations option (Solver Options dialog box), 656

J-K

joining. *See* concatenating

joins (database queries), 777-779

keyboard
  alphanumeric keys, 64
  editing cell content, 64-65
  navigating worksheets, 65
  numeric keypad, 64
  shortcuts
    absolute/relative referencing, 323
    accessing GoTo menu, 28
    accessing help system, 12
    adding buttons to custom toolbars, 720-721

adding data to charts, 513

adding titles to charts, 544

aligning cell contents, 120

closing Excel, 11

closing workbooks, 11

creating charts, 466

customizing menu hot keys, 724

customizing menus, 725

data forms, 397

drag and drop, 69-70

font styles, 114

integrating Office applications, cut and paste actions, 735

macros, 814-815, 820

menu commands, 20

moving between open workbooks, 42

navigating tables, 52

navigating worksheets using, 27

Pick From List feature, accessing, 30

saving worksheets, 34

selecting cells, 50

selecting columns and rows, 53

selecting contiguous cells, 55

selecting entire worksheets, 54

undoing changes, 111

Visual Basic Editor, 868-870

keystrokes
  applying operators, 161
  copying formulas, 174

L

Label control (Forms toolbar), 424

labeling rows and columns, 30-31

labels (charts)
  aligning with gridlines, 603
  axis labels, 478-479, 537
  changing, 523
  data labels, 467
    adding to charts, 541
    formatting, 482-483, 540-543
  series labels, 468

Landscape orientation, 142

languages, specifying in spell-checker, 713

LARGE function, 346, 365, 377

large numbers, formatting, 102

largest numbers, calculating, 365

largest value, identifying, 369

layering
  automatic subtotals, 452
  objects (charts), 569-570

layout
  hierarchical lists, 388
  PivotTables, 618

Layout dialog box (PivotTable and PivotChart Wizard), 613-617

LCM function, 305

least common multiple, calculating, 305

least-squares method, calculating best-fit regression line, 366-367

LEFT function, 326

legacy lists
modifying, 388-391
transposing data, 391

legal size paper, 143-144

Legend button (Chart toolbar), 508

legends (charts), 467-468, 544
formatting
eliminating borders, 501
options, 481-482
moving, 544
resizing, 544

Legends tab (Chart Wizard), 481-482

LEN function, 326, 332-333

Less Brightness button (Picture toolbar), 568

Less Contrast button (Picture toolbar), 568

less than operator, 161

less than or equal to operator, 161

letter size paper, 143-144

lifetime charts, creating, 601-602

Line button (Drawing toolbar), 128

line charts, 490

Line Color button (Drawing toolbar), 129

line item milestone management charts, 692-693

Line Style button
Drawing toolbar, 129
Picture toolbar, 568

Linear setting (Trendline dialog box), 526

linear trends, custom fill data series, 72-73

lines
formatting, value axes, 535
grouping, 132-133
ungrouping, 132

Lines and Arrows button (Drawing toolbar), 547

Lines button (Drawing toolbar), 546

LINEST function, 346, 366-367

Link Spreadsheet Wizard, 764-766

linking
Excel data to Access database, 764-766
charts to worksheet cells, 592
external workbooks, 183-185
updating values, 185
Office programs
copying Excel data into PowerPoint, 737-738
hyperlinks for, 746-752
worksheets, 82-83
breaking links, 85-86
locking external links, 85
updating links, 83-85

Links dialog box (Edit menu), 84

liquid measure units, converting between, 222

liquidity ratios, 685

List Box control (Forms toolbar), 425, 435

list management tools, 190, 198-199

List Members list, 861

listings
AddBorders procedure
Do loop, 859-860
modified, 860
AddNameToFooter macro without indents, 862
AddNameToFooter procedure with comments, 864
calculating number of days in month, 853
constants, 844-845
calculating income tax, 811
If-Then structure, 857
loops, 858-859
macro for auto formatting, 833
macro to select and print current region, 810
PERCHANGE function, 855
placing watch on Value property, 869
RemoveDiscontinuedProds procedure, 874
variable UserName, 843

lists
adding
data ranges, 402-403
form controls, Combo Box example, 427-428
avoiding blanks, 387
conditional formatting, 408
formulas, 410-413
interactive approach, 408-410
consolidating data in, 447
creating from single cells, 394-396
custom, 73-75, 388
data entry, 396-397
Data Fields, 388
date-driven, setting up, 393-394
design issues, 386-387, 405
embedding charts in, 595-596

field names, 388, 399
filtering, 397, 416
    Advanced Filter,
        421-424
    AutoFilter, 417-421
    automatic subtotaling,
        450-452
header rows, 388
hierarchical structures, 387
managing data in
    sort options, 413-416
    text to speech features,
        413
modifying
    changing cases, 389
    legacy lists, 388
    Paste Special dialog box
        options, 389-391
    transposing data,
        391-393
printing, 399
records, 388
scrolling, splitting windows,
    399-400
searching data forms for,
    398
sorting, 397
standard layout, 388
subtotals, calculating,
    319-320
troubleshooting, 405, 437
viewing, 399
    custom views, 403-405
    multiple windows, 400-
        401
literal text, 845
literals, formatting code, 100
LN function, 313-314
Load Model option (Solver
    Options dialog box), 657
loans, calculations
    cumulative interest pay-
        ments, 244-245
    future value, 247-248

interest payments, 248-249
payment amounts, 254-255
location offsets, 296-297
locking
    external links, 85
    row size, 33
LOG function, 305
LOG10 function, 305
Logarithmic Scale option,
    518, 521
Logarithmic setting
    (Trendline dialog box), 526
Logarithms, 217
    base 2, complex numbers,
        217
    calculating
        base 10 logarithms, 305
        flexible bases, 305
        natural logarithms,
            313-314
LOGEST function, 346, 368
logic error, 865
logical functions, 278-283
    AND, 278-280
    FALSE, 278
    IF, 278-281
    NOT, 278, 281-282
    OR, 278, 282-283
    troubleshooting, 283
    TRUE, 278
logical tests
    IF function, 280-281
    NOT function, 281-282
    OR function, 282-283
logical values, 160, 266, 273
LOGINV function, 346
LOGNORMDIST function,
    346
looking up last number in a
    column, 683-684

lookup formulas, creating
    with Lookup Wizard,
    293-294
LOOKUP function
    Array form, 287, 294-295
    Vector form, 287, 295
lookup functions, 286-301
    ADDRESS, 286
    AREA, 286
    CHOOSE, 287-288
    COLUMNS, 286
    HLOOKUP, 286, 288-289
    HYPERLINK, 286
    INDEX, 286, 290-292
    INDIRECT, 287
    LOOKUP, 287, 294-295
    MATCH, 287
    OFFSET, 287, 296-299
    ROW, 287
    ROWS, 287
    TRANSPOSE, 287,
        299-300
    VLOOKUP, 287, 300-301
Lookup Wizard, 293-294
    creating lookup formulas,
        293-294
    index formulas, 436
loop structures
    AddBorders procedure
        modified, 860
    description, 858
    Do loop, 859-860
    listing, 858-859
LOWER function, 326,
    333-334, 388-389
lowercase letters, converting
    to uppercase letters, 326-
    327, 333-334, 340

M

Macauley duration, calculating, 246-247

Macro dialog box, 819

Macro Options dialog box, 820

Macro Recorder, 810-816, 835
  description, 838
  inefficiency of, 838

Macro Security button (Security tab), 714

macros. *See also* functions
  adding to toolbar buttons, 718-719
  AutoFit Column, 835
  AutoFormat, 833
  capabilities, 811
  comments, 810
  custom functions, 164
  Custom Header and Footer, 834
  definition, 810
  deleting, 831-832
  descriptions, 815, 820
  digital signatures, 817
  editing, 828-830
  graphics, 826-827
  Macro Recorder, 810-816, 835
  menus, 821-825, 831-832
  naming, 814
  playing, 817-827, 833-834
  Print Current Region, 832-833
  readability, 811
  recording
    absolutely, 813
    cell or object selection, 814
    relatively, 813
    step-by-step, 814-816, 835
    stopping recording, 815

  runtime errors, 833-834
  saving, 816
  security, 816-817
  Sheet-Naming, 830
  shortcut keys, 814-815, 820
  storing, 719, 812-816
  toolbars, 821-825, 831-832
  troubleshooting, 833-834
  viruses, 816-817
  Visual Basic for
    Applications (VBA), 810
  writing
    advantages of, 838
    VBA, 838

Macros dialog box, 815

magnetism units, converting between, 221

Mail Recipient button (Reviewing toolbar), 81

managing data
  auditing data entry
    auditing options, 458-460
    marking invalid data, 457-458
  automatic subtotaling, 450-452
  conditional formatting, 408-413
    formulas, 410-413
    interactive approach, 408-410
  consolidation tables, 447-449
  filtering lists, 416-424
    Advanced Filter, 421-424
    AutoFilter, 417-421
  form controls, 424-435
    calculation tables, 429-432
    charts, 433-435
    control characteristics, 435
    Forms toolbar controls, 428-429

  grouping data, 440-445
    column-based groups, 443
    creating groups, 441
    hierarchical grouping, 441
    layered groupings, 443-444
    multiple summary tables, 444-445
    viewing groups, 442-443
  outlining data, 440
    Auto Outline feature, 446-447
    outlining options/settings, 447
  sort options, 413-416
  text to speech features, 413
  validating data entry, 453-457
    Data Validation dialog boxes options, 454-457
    Formula Auditing toolbar, 453-454

margins, worksheets, 140, 144-145

Margins button (Print Preview toolbar), 139

Margins tab
  Page Setup dialog box, 141
  Print Setup dialog box, 144-146

mass units, converting between, 221

MATCH function, 287, 291-292

math, 304-323. *See also* calculations
  ABS, 304, 307-308
  ACOS, 304, 308-309
  ACOSH, 304
  ASIN, 304, 309-310
  ASINH, 304
  ATAN, 304

ATAN2, 304
ATANH, 304
CEILING, 304
COMBIN, 304, 310-311
COS, 304, 311
COSH, 304
COUNTIF, 304, 311-313
DEGREES, 305, 313
EVEN, 305
EXP, 305
FACT, 305
FACTDOUBLE, 305
FLOOR, 305
GCD, 305
INT, 305
LCM, 305
LN, 313-314
LOG, 305
LOG10, 305
MDETERM, 305
MINVERSE, 305
MMULT, 305
MOD, 305
MROUND, 305
MULTINOMIAL, 305
ODD, 305
PERMUT, 305, 315
PI, 306, 316
POWER, 306
PRODUCT, 306
QUOTIENT, 306
RADIANS, 306
RAND, 306, 316-317
RANDBETWEEN, 306
ROMAN, 306, 317-318
ROUND, 306
ROUNDDOWN, 306
ROUNDUP, 306
SERIESSUM, 306
SIGN, 306
SIN, 306
SINH, 306
SQRT, 306, 318-319
SQRTP1, 306
statistics. *See* statistical
    functions

SUBTOTAL, 306, 319-320
SUM, 307, 320-323
SUMIF, 307, 321-322
SUMPRODUCT, 307
SUMSQUARES, 307
SUMX2MY2, 307
SUMX2PY2, 307
TAN, 307, 322
TANH, 307
TRUNC, 307

matrix-related calculations
    inverse matrices, 305-306
    matrix products of two
        arrays, 305
    maxtrix determinants, 305

**MAX function, 177, 346,
368-369**

**Max Time option (Solver
Options dialog box), 656**

MAXA function, 347

**Maximize button (workbook
taskbar), 11**

**maximum values, extracting
from tables, 195-196**

MDETERM function, 305

**MDURATION function,
236, 249-250**

means, calculating, 349
    arithmetic means, 350
    geometric means, 362-363
    population means, 352

**measurement systems, 216,
220-222, 230**

measurement units
    picas/points, 113-114
    specifying for charts, 478

measures (OLAP), 790

media matrices, 153-154

**MEDIAN function, 347,
369-370**

medians
    calculating, 369-370
    comparison with averages,
        370

menu bar, 20, 724

menus, 20
    adaptive menus, 20
    Chart menu
        3-D View dialog box,
            558-559
        Add Data dialog box,
            511
        Add Trendline dialog
            box, 525-527
        Chart Options, 543
        Chart Type dialog box,
            508
        Source Data dialog box,
            514
    commands, 20
    customizing, 723-724
        creating custom menus,
            725
        deleting custom menus,
            726
        hiding/displaying, 727
        relocating menu bars,
            724
    Data menu
        Advanced Filter dialog
            box, 422
        AutoFilter option, 417
        Consolidate dialog box,
            447-449
        Data Validation dialog
            box, 454
        Group and Outline
            options, 447
        Group and Outline
            submenu, 441
        New Database Query,
            792-793
        Sort dialog box, 413-415
        Subtotals dialog box,
            450-451

design issues, 728
Draw menu
  Group options, 132
  Order option, 131
Edit menu
  Go To Special dialog
    box, 28
  Links dialog box, 84
  Paste dialog box, 511
  Paste Special, 512
  Paste Special dialog box,
    82-83
  Replace dialog box, 75
File menu
  Exit option, 11
  New dialog box, 40
  Page Setup dialog box,
    141-143, 150
  Print dialog box, 137-
    138
  Print Preview, 500
  Save As command, 34
  Save As dialog box,
    38-39
  Save as Web Page
    command, 636
  Save command, 34
Format menu
  AutoFormat feature,
    126-127
  Column/Row Hide
    options, 45
  Conditional Formatting,
    409
  Format Axis dialog box,
    535
  Format Cells dialog box,
    111, 120-126, 710
  Format Chart Title
    dialog box, 544
  Format Column
    Width/Row Height
    dialog boxes, 32
  Format Data Point
    dialog box, 549-551

Format Data Series
  dialog box, 515, 541
Format Floor dialog
  box, 556-557
Format Trendline dialog
  box, 527-529
Format Wall dialog box,
  556
Style dialog box,
  116-118
Help menu, 12
Insert menu
  Chart Wizard, 469
  Insert Hyperlink dialog
    box, 747-749
  Insert Picture dialog
    box, 566
keyboard shortcuts, 20
macros, 821-825, 831-832
menu bars, 20
shortcut menus, 20
Table menu, Show
  Gridlines option, 734
toolbar reference icons, 20
Tools menu
  Analysis ToolPak, 669
  Auditing options,
    459-460
  Goal Seek dialog box,
    647-649
  Options dialog box, 704
  resetting font defaults,
    115
  Solver Parameters dialog
    box, 651-653
  Solver Results dialog
    box, 653-654
  Spelling command, 30
View menu, Page Break
  Preview feature, 140-141
Window menu
  Freeze Panes command,
    43
  Remove Split command,
    45
  Split command, 43

Merge and Center button
  (Formatting toolbar), 18,
  110, 119-120, 153
Merge button (Style dialog
  box), 118
Merge Cells option (Format
  Cells dialog box), 121
Merge Labels option
  (PivotTable and PivotChart
  Wizard), 622
Microsoft Help, 13
Microsoft Access
  forms, 786-787
  Import Spreadsheet
    Wizard, 759-764
  importing Excel data,
    759-764
  Link Spreadsheet Wizard,
    764-766
  linking Excel data, 764-766
  troubleshooting, 786
Microsoft Excel Help button
  (Standard toolbar), 18
Microsoft Query, 774-777
  calculations, 781
  creating joins, 777-779
  limiting information
    returned, 779-781
  starting, 776
  tables, 776-777
  totals, 781
MID function, 327, 334-335
MIN function, 347, 370
  AutoCalculate, 177
MINA function, 347, 371
Minimize button (workbook
  taskbar), 11
minimizing clutter, charts,
  476
minimum values, extracting
  from tables, 196

minus (-) character, outline view, 442

MINUTE function, 203

MINVERSE function, 305

MIRR function, 236

missing parenthesis, finding in formulas, 163

MMULT function, 305

MOD function, 305

MODE function, 347, 371

modified duration, calculating, 249-250

modules, 816
  adding, 852
  deleting, 852
  description, 845
  naming, 852

Modulus (absolute value), 217

MONTH function, 203, 207
  embedding in SUM and IF functions, 212-213

months
  as basis for hierarchical groupings, 441
  in data series, 70

More Brightness button (Picture toolbar), 568

More Contrast button (Picture toolbar), 568

mortgage calculations
  calculating payments, 662-665
  multiple-variable active tables, adding scrollbars, 667-669

mouse device
  adding data to charts, 513
  scrolling, 11

moving
  category labels, 602
  cells
    drag and drop, 68
    Roadrunner Effect, 68
  chart legends, 482, 544
  charts containing objects, 602
  embedded charts, 506-507
  fields, PivotTables, 610
  worksheets, 25

Moving Average setting (Trendline dialog box), 526

Moving Average tool (Analysis ToolPak), 670

MROUND function, 305

multidimensional cubes (OLAP), 791
  data sources, 791-792
  processing, SQL Server, 792

multidimensional tables, creating using drawing tools, 153

MULTINOMIAL function, 305

multiple-combination charts, 594-595

multiplication
  calculating least common multiple, 305
  database functions, 197
  formulas, 162
  function, 306
  operator, 161

multiplier formulas with active tables, 665-666

Multiply option (Paste Special dialog box), 391

My Documents folder, 35

N

N function, 267

NA function, 267

Name box (Formula bar)
  creating named ranges, 58
  viewing cell addresses, 50

Name Define dialog box (Insert menu), 58, 165

names
  cell ranges, 57-58
    naming conventions/ limitations, 59
    removing named ranges, 59
    shortcut, 58
    troubleshooting naming errors, 59-60
    viewing named ranges, 59
  custom menus, 724
  custom toolbars, 720
  if fields, hierarchical lists, 388
  macros, 719, 814
  modules, 852
  PivotTables, 619
  ranges, 164
    advanced filters, 422
    creating, 165
    pasting into formulas, 165-166
    simplifying complex formulas, 436
  variables, 842
  worksheets, 24

natural logarithms
  calculating, 313-314
  complex numbers, 217

navigating
  between data form options, 397
  multiple open workbooks, 41-42
  worksheets
    Go To shortcut, 28
    keyboard shortcuts, 27, 65

negation
  formulas, 162
  operator, 161

negative values in formatting code, 101

NEGBINOMDIST function, 347

nested calculations, 163-164

nested subtotals, 452

nesting hyperlinks, 749

net present value, calculating, 251-252

NETWORKDAYS function, 203, 208-209, 213

New button (Standard toolbar), 16

New Comment button (Formula Auditing toolbar), 454

New Database Query (Data menu)
  Choose Data Source dialog box, 792-793
  Create New Data Source dialog box, 793

New dialog box (File menu), accessing templates, 40

New Toolbar dialog box (Customize dialog box), 720

New Worksheet task pane, 12

Newton option (Solver Options dialog box), 657

Next button (Print Preview toolbar), 139

Next Comment button (Reviewing toolbar), 81

NOMINAL function, 236

non-recorded procedures, creating, 849-851

noncontiguous ranges, 54
  adding to lists, 402-403
  selecting on grouped worksheets, 55-57

None option (Paste Special dialog box), 391

nonprintable characters, removing, 326

nontext values, identifying, 266, 273

normal distribution, calculating, 371-372

Normal style, editing, 116-117

NORMDIST function, 347, 371-372

NORMINV function, 347, 372

NORMSINV function, 347

not equal to operator, 161

NOT function, 278, 281-282

NOW function, 203

NPER function, 236, 250-251

NPV function, 236, 251-252

number and text codes (formatting codes), 97

number arguments, 160

number formats, formatting code for, 99-101

Number of Copies section (Print dialog box), 137

Number tab (Format Cells dialog box), 93-94
  Custom category, 97, 103-105
  custom characters and symbols, 102
  Date category, 95
  Fraction category, 96

numbers
  adding ordinal to automatically, 337-338
  converting
    binary to decimal format, 216, 219
    binary to hexadecimal format, 216
    binary to octal format, 216
    decimal to binary format, 216, 223
    decimal to hexadecimal format, 216
    decimal to octal format, 216
    hexadecimal to binary format, 217, 225
    hexadecimal to decimal format, 217
    hexadecimal to octal format, 217
    octal to binary format, 218, 230
    octal to decimal format, 218
    octal to hexadecimal format, 218
    text strings to, 327
  entering in cells, 32

formatting, 92
    built-in formats, 93-94
    comma style, 92
    conditional formatting
        codes, 103-104
    currency format codes,
        101
    currency style, 92
    custom characters, 102
    custom formats, 93-94,
        97
    dates, 94-99
    decrease decimal option,
        92
    fractions, 96
    increase decimal option,
        92
    large numbers, 102
    numbers and text, 99-
        101
    percent style, 92
    repeating characters,
        104-105
    scientific notation, 93
    specialized formats, 96
    time, 95-99
    viewing built-in codes,
        97
identifying, 266, 273-275
possible combinations of,
    calculating, 310-311
random numbers, 306,
    316-317
rounding, 331-332
truncating, 307
numeric keypad, 64
Numfile text type, 272

O

Object Linking and
    Embedding. See OLE
object-oriented program-
    ming
    collections, 839
    constants, 844-845

functions, 841
methods, 840
objects, 839
overview of, 839
properties, 840
variables, naming, 842
writing code, 841
objects
    charts, troubleshooting
        moving problems, 602
    description, 839
    grouping, shapes and lines,
        132-133
    overlapping, changing order
        of, 131
    ungrouping, 132
OCT2BIN function, 218,
    230
OCT2DEC function, 218
OCT2HEX function, 218
octal numbers
    converting binary numbers
        to, 216
    converting decimal num-
        bers to, 216
    converting hexadecimal
        numbers to, 217
    converting to binary
        format, 218, 230
    converting to decimal
        format, 218
    converting to hexadecimal
        format, 218
ODBC (Open Database
    Connectivity), 767
    data sources, 769-771
odd first periods, calculating
    security values for, 252-254
ODD function, 305
odd numbers, identifying,
    266, 273
ODDFPRICE function, 236

ODDFYFIELD function,
    236
ODDLPRICE function, 236
ODDLYIELD function, 237
ODDPRICE function,
    252-254
Office 2000
    application files, integrating
        data from, 752
    integrating with
        PivotTables with
        Microsoft Query, 608
Office Clipboard, Office
    program integration,
    734-735, 745
offline (local) cubes,
    799-801, 804-805
Offline OLAP Settings
    dialog box, 801
OFFSET function, 287,
    296-299
    COUNTA function, 355-
        356
    IF function, 296-297
    updating charts, 298-299
offsetting categories (charts),
    troubleshooting, 560
OLAP (On-line Analytical
    Processing), 790
    Cube Wizard
        accessing and launching,
            801-802
        creating dimension
            hierarchies, 803
        saving cubes, 804
        selecting cube measures,
            802-803
    dimension hierarchies, 790
    measures, 790

multidimensional cubes, 791-805
   data source connection, 793-794
   data source definition, 792-793
   OLAP PivotCharts, 798-799
   OLAP PivotTables, 794-797
   saving cubes locally, 799-805
   SQL Server, 792
   PivotCharts, creating, 798-799
   PivotTables, 790-791, 795-797
     creating, 794-795, 805
     multidimensional cubes, 791-792
   Server, saving cubes from, 799-801, 804-805

OLE (Object Linking and Embedding), 82

OLE DB, 767-768

On-line Analytical Processing. *See* **OLAP**

Open button (Standard toolbar), 16

Open Database Connectivity (ODBC), 767

Open event, starting code automatically, 871-872

operating environment, 266, 271-272

operators
   arithmetic, 161
   comparison, 161
   comparison operators, 161
     custom AutoFilter, 420-421

defined, 160
keystrokes, 161
operation order, 161-164
reference, 161
text, 161

Option Button control (Forms toolbar), 425, 436

Options dialog box
   adding/removing scrollbars, 710-711
   Chart tab, Plot Visible Cells only option, 592
   Color tab, 707-709
   customizing defaults, 704
     cursor movement, 704-705
     fonts, 706
     function ToolTips, 706
     workbook sheets, 704-705
   date system options, 211
   Error Checking tab, 712
   International tab, 712-713
   resetting font defaults, 115
   Save tab, 712
   Security tab, 713-714
   Spelling tab, 713
   Web Options button, 706
   Zero Values option, 710

Options tab
   Format Data Series dialog box, 549
   Format Trendlines dialog box, 528-529

OR function, 278, 282-283

order of operations, 161-163
   nested calculations, 163-164

Order options (Draw menu), 131

Order setting (Trendline dialog box), 526

ordering data series, 548

ordinals, automating, 337-338

organization-specific information, creating data series from, 73-75

orientation (charts)
   column-based, 473
   row-based, 472
   specifying, 471

origin (charts), 516
   changing, 520-521

Origin text type, 272

outlines
   data, 440
     Auto Outline feature, 446-447
     creating toolbars, 440
     outlining options/settings, 447
     process, 440
   structuring lists, 386
   symbols, 442, 446

Outlining/Grouping toolbar, 440-441
   Group Symbols button, 441
   Hide Detail button, 441
   Select Visible Cells button, 441
   Show Detail button, 441
   Show Outline Symbols button, 441
   Ungroup button, 441

Oval button (Drawing toolbar), 128

overlap settings (charts), 548-549

overlapping objects, changing order, 131

overlays
   adding to charts, 575-578
   pie charts, 580-581

P

P&L, 684-685

Page Break Preview button (Print Preview toolbar), 140

Page Break Preview feature, 140-141

Page Down key, navigating worksheets, 27

Page Layout settings (PivotTable and PivotChart Wizard), 622

Page Number button (Custom Header/Footer dialog boxes), 149

Page Order option (Page Setup dialog box), 150

Page Setup dialog box, 141-142
    Header/Footer tab, 142, 147
    Margins tab, 141
    Page tab, 141-143
    Sheet tab, 142, 150-151

Page tab (Page Setup dialog box), 141-143

Page Up key, navigating worksheets, 27

page view, creating from PivotTable fields, 631-632

palettes, custom workbooks, 706-709

paper size, printing worksheets, 143-144

parameter queries, 781

parentheses ()
    formulas, 162
        finding missing parentheses, 163
        rearranging, 163
    nested calculations, 163-164

Parentheses info type, 267

passwords, adding to worksheets, 35-37

Paste button (Standard toolbar), 17
    adding data, 511

Paste command (chart context menu), adding data, 511

Paste Link option (Paste Special dialog box), 391

Paste Special dialog box, 82
    adding data to charts, 512
    copying Excel data, 735
    linking, 82-83
    modifying lists, 389-391
    pasting PivotTables, 739
    transposing data, 391-393

pasting named ranges into formulas, 165-166

Path and Name button (Custom Header/Footer dialog boxes), 149

patterns, applying to cells, 125-126

Patterns tab
    Format Axis dialog box, 535
    Format Cells dialog box, 125-126
    Format Data Series dialog box, 583
    Format dialog box, 552
    Format Floor dialog box, 556-557
    Format Trendline dialog box, 527
    Format Wall dialog box, 556

PEARSON function, 347

percent change function, 855

Percent Style button (Formatting toolbar), 18, 92

percentages
    calculating operator, 161, 373
    formatting code, 100
    formulas, 162

PERCENTILE function, 347, 373

PERCENTRANK function, 347, 373-374

PERCHANGE function listing, 855

performance
    formulas, 436
    OLAP cubes, 801
        enhancing PivotTables, 802
    optimizing when using fill effects, 560

Period setting (Trendline dialog box), 526

PERMUT function, 305, 315, 347

permutations, calculating, 305, 315

Personal Macro Workbook, 812-813, 816, 830

PERSONAL.XLS! files, Macros, 719

personalizing charts, 498-499

perspective, adding to 3D charts, 559, 574

PI function, 306, 316

picas (font sizes), 113-114

PickFromList feature, 30

Picture tab (Fill Effects dialog box), 554-555

Picture toolbar
accessing, 566
buttons, 567-568

pictures, chart backgrounds, 554-555

Pictures Tab (Web Options button), 706

pie charts, 490-491
exploding, 490
formatting, 579
changing angle of data series, 549
effective design, 580-581
exploding slices, 549-550
overlays, 580-581
spinning slides, 579-580
when not to use, 491

Pivot Table button (PivotTable toolbar), Formulas, Calculated Field options, 628

Pivot Tables, 198-199
obtaining values from, 191, 198-199
troubleshooting, 199

PivotChart Wizard, 611, 798-799

PivotCharts. *See also* **charts**
creating, 611-612, 623-624
customizing, 624-625
hiding/displaying data, 626-628
rearranging fields, 625-626
formatting, 608
OLAP PivotCharts, 798-799

pivoting, 608

PivotTable and PivotChart Wizard
creating PivotCharts, 623-624, 798-799
creating PivotTables, 611-612, 794-795
multiple ranges for, 635-636

formatting options, 613
Layout button, 613-617
PivotTable Options dialog box, 618-623
AutoFormat option, 620-621
Data Options section, 623
For Error Values, Show option, 622-623
Grand Totals for Columns option, 619
Merge Labels option, 622
name options, 619
Page Layout settings, 622
Repeat Item Labels on Each Printed Page option, 622
Set Print Titles option, 622
Subtotal Hidden Page Items option, 620

PivotTable button (PivotTable toolbar), 610

PivotTable Field dialog box, expanding summary options, 618

PivotTable Field List, creating PivotTables, 617

PivotTable Options dialog box (PivotTable and PivotChart Wizard), 618-623
AutoFormat option, 620-621
Data Options section, 623
For Error Values, Show option, 622-623
Grand Totals for Columns option, 619
Merge Labels option, 622
name options, 619

Page Layout settings, 622
Repeat Item Labels on Each Printed Page option, 622
Set Print Titles option, 622
Subtotal Hidden Page Items option, 620

PivotTable toolbar, buttons, 609-610

PivotTables. *See also* **tables**
comparing to PivotCharts, 623-624
creating
multiple ranges, 635-636
new tables from, 613
PivotChart Wizard, 611-612
customizing, 624-629
hiding/displaying columns and rows, 629
hiding/displaying details, 626-628
PivotTable toolbar, 610
data
grouping, 638-639
viewing, 638
dates, 633-634, 638
drilldown, enabling, 629-631, 638
enhancing performance, 436, 802
Excel 2002 improvements, 608
fields, dragging outside table, 631-632
formatting, 613
AutoFormat option, 620-621
handling errors/empty cells, 622-623
label display options, 622
layout options, 622
PowerPoint, 740
formulas/calculations, 628-629

functions, 618
laying out, 618
managing employee hours and costs, 639-643
OLAP, 790-797, 801-805
    analyzing database data, 801-805
    creating, 794-795
pasting into PowerPoint slides, 738-739
placing, 613
quick summaries, 632-633
rearranging data, 610
saving and editing
    adding interactivity, 636-637
    HTML format, 636-638
source data, data handling options, 623
structure, levels of information, 608-609

playing macros, 817-827, 833-834

plot areas (charts), 468-471
    formatting, 551
    identifying data series, 471
    resizing, 519
    selecting source data, 471

Plot Visible Cells only option (Option dialog box), 592

plus (+) character, outline view, 442

PMT function, 237, 254-255, 662-665

Point of Sale. *See* POS

pointing hand cursors, 748

points (font sizes), 113-114

Poisson distribution, calculating, 374-375

POISSON function, 348, 374-375

Polynomial setting (Trendline dialog box), 526

population means, calculating confidence intervals, 352

Portrait orientation, 142

POS (Point of Sale), 679

positive values, formatting code, 101

POWER function, 306

power series, sum of, 306

Power Setting setting (Trendline dialog box), 526

power units, converting between, 221

power, raising numbers to, 226-227

PowerPoint presentations
    copying tables/charts to, 736-739
        cut and paste method, 737
        linking method, 737-738
        PivotTables, 738-739
        selecting cell ranges, 737
    formatting Excel objects in, 740-741
    pasting charts into, 741-742
    pasting data into worksheets, 744
    pasting Excel data into datasheets, 742-744

PPMT function, 237

precedents, tracing, 458-460

Precision option (Solver Options dialog box), 656

predicting values, 360-361

Prefix info type, 267

presentations
    diagrams, 700
    interactive, OFFSET function, 296
    PowerPoint
        copying tables/charts to, 736-739
        formatting Excel objects in, 740-741
        pasting charts into, 741-742
        pasting data into worksheets, 744
        pasting Excel data into datasheets, 742-744

Press and Hold To View Sample button (Chart Wizard), 470

pressure units, converting between, 221

Preview button (Print dialog box), 137-140

previewing
    chart types (Chart Wizard), 510
    font formatting, 112
    print jobs, 138-140
    worksheets, 137-143

Previous button (Print Preview toolbar), 139

Previous Comment button (Reviewing toolbar), 81

PRICE function, 237, 255-256

PRICEDISC function, 237

PRICEMAT function, 237

Print Area option (Page Setup dialog box), 150

print areas, 138
    selecting, 151

Print button (Standard toolbar), 17, 136
  printing charts, 501

Print dialog box (File menu), 136-140
  Number of Copies section, 137
  Preview button, 137-140
  Print Range section, 136-138
  Print What section, 136
  Printer section, 136-137

Print option (Page Setup dialog box), 150

Print Preview (File menu), 500

Print Preview button (Standard toolbar), 139

Print Preview feature, 137-140

Print Preview toolbar, 139-140

print quality, adjusting, 144

print range, choosing, 137-138

Print Range section (Print dialog box), 136-138

Print Setup dialog box (File menu)
  Headers/Footers tab, 147-150
  Margins tab, 144-145

Print Titles option (Page Setup dialog box), 150

Print What section (Print dialog box), 136

Printer section (Print dialog box), 136
  print to file option, 137
  selecting printers, 137

printers, selecting, 137

printing
  charts, 500-501
  comments, 80
  lists, 399
  worksheets, 135-137
    centering, 146
    choosing print range, 137-138
    headers/footers, 147-150
    margin settings, 144-145
    page orientation, 142
    paper size, 143-144
    previewing, 137-140
    print quality adjustments, 144
    printing to file, 137
    scaling printouts, 142-143
    selecting print area, 151
    troubleshooting, 151-152

PROB function, 348

Procedure command (Insert menu), Visual Basic Editor, 851

PRODUCT function, 306

production curves, 591

production models, Solver with Gannt charts example, 658-660

products, complex numbers, 217, 227-228

professional format for charts, 535

profitability ratios, 686-687

Programs menu (Start menu), launching Excel, 10

Project Explorer window, Visual Basic Editor, 846

projects
  compiling, 865
  description, 845
  modules, 852

PROPER function, 327, 335-336

Properties window, Visual Basic Editor, 846

Protect info type, 267

protected worksheets, auditing data, 458

PV function, 237, 256-257

pyramid charts, 497

Q

Quadratic option (Solver Options dialog box), 657

quarters, as basis for hierarchical groupings, 441

QUARTILE function, 348

queries, 777
  calculations, 781
  choosing columns, 771-773
  creating joins, 777-779
  data sources, 769
  editing, 782-783
  filtering data, 773-774
  limiting information returned, 779-781
  Microsoft Query, 774-777
    starting, 776
    tables, 776-777
  ODBC data source definitions, 769-771
  parameters, 781
  saving, 774
  sorting data, 774
  totals, 781

Query Wizard, 769-774
  choosing columns, 771-773
  choosing data sources, 769
  filtering data, 773-774
  saving queries, 774
  sorting data, 774

How can we make this index more useful? Email us at indexes@quepublishing.com

question mark (?) character, custom AutoFilter, 420

Quick Watch dialog box, Visual Basic Editor, 870

quotient, complex numbers, 217

QUOTIENT function, 306

R

radar charts, 495

radians
converting degrees to, 306
converting to degrees, 305, 313

RADIANS function, 306

RAND function, 306, 316-317

RANDBETWEEN function, 306

Random Number Generation dialog box, 671

Random number generation tools (Analysis ToolPak), 670-672

random numbers, generating, 306, 316-317, 671

range borders
editing ranges, 172
moving with fill handles, 172

Range Finder feature, locating parentheses, 163

range names, advanced filtering, 422

range references, 178
anchoring, 179-180
AutoSum formulas, 170

editing
changing formulas directly, 172
dragging range borders, 172
named ranges, 164-166
options, 171

ranges
adding to form controls, 427-428
contiguous, 50
data, charts
modifying, 475
specifying, 471
defined, 52
multiple, creating PivotTables, 635-636
naming, 57-60
conventions/limitations, 59
removing named ranges, 59
shortcuts, 58
troubleshooting, 59-60
viewing named ranges, 59
noncontiguous, 54
selecting, 50
adding content after, 52
grouping worksheets, 55-57, 61
keyboard, 52-53

Rank and Percentile tool (Analysis ToolPak), 670

RANK function, 348, 375-376

ranking values, 373-376

RATE function, 237, 257-258

real coefficients, converting into complex numbers, 216-220

rearranging worksheets, 25

Recalc text type, 272

RECEIVED function, 237, 258-259

Record Macro dialog box, 814-815

recording macros
absolutely, 813
cell or object selection, 814
relatively, 813
step-by-step, 814-816, 835
stopping recording, 815

records
copying, Advanced Filter options, 423
hierarchical lists, 388
searching data forms for, 398
selecting, Advanced Filter options, 423-424

recovering corrupted worksheets, 37

Rectangle button (Drawing toolbar), 128

redirecting broken links, 85

Redo button (Standard toolbar), 17

Reference form (INDEX function), 286, 290-292

reference functions, 286-301
ADDRESS, 286
AREA, 286
CHOOSE, 287-288
COLUMNS, 286
HLOOKUP, 286-289
HYPERLINK, 286
INDEX, 286, 290-292
INDIRECT, 287
LOOKUP, 287, 294-295
MATCH, 287
OFFSET, 287, 296-299

ROW, 287
ROWS, 287
TRANSPOSE, 287, 299-300
VLOOKUP, 287, 300-301

reference operators, 161

references
absolute cell references, 680-683
cell links, 434-435
identifying, 266, 273
rows and columns, 290-292

referencing
cells
absolute referencing, anchoring references, 178-180
links, 428-429
range referencing, 178
relative referencing, 178
data from other workbooks
links, 183-185
updating values, 185
dates, relative referencing, 283
external worksheet data, 181-182

Refresh Data button (PivotTable toolbar), 609-610

refreshing data, 782

regression lines, calculating
intercepts, 364
slope values, 376-377
strait line best-fit, 366-367

Regression tool (Analysis ToolPak), 670

relational databases, 386, 756-758

relative referencing, 178
keyboard shortcuts, 323
timelines, 283

Release text type, 272

Remove All Arrows button (Formula Auditing toolbar), 454

Remove Dependent Arrows button (Formula Auditing toolbar), 454

Remove Precedent button (Formula Auditing toolbar), 454

Remove Split command (Window menu), 45

RemoveDiscontinuedProds procedure listing, 874

removing
custom toolbars, 723
data series, 510
displayed toolbars, 19
nonprintable characters from text, 326
scrollbars from windows, 710-711
window splits, 45

Rename command (shortcut menu), 24

renaming menus, 724

reordering data series, 548

repeating characters, formatting code, 100, 104-105

repeating text, 327

Replace dialog box, editing data, 75

REPLACE function, 327

REPLACEB function, 327

reports (Solver), 653
answer reports, 653-654
hiding report sheets, 655

repositioning chart axes, 521-522

REPT function, 327

Reset Picture button (Picture toolbar), 568

resetting
color palette, 709
toolbars, 723

resizing
charts, plot area, 519
columns, hiding data, 45
embedded charts, 506

resolution (print quality), dots-per-inch, 144

resource pools, 687-689

restoring deleted menus, 728

return types (cells), 269

reverse schedules, 678-680

reversed bar charts, 489

reversing series data (charts), 523-525

Reviewing toolbar, 80

RIGHT function, 327, 336-337

right-clicking
accessing chart objects, 508
accessing worksheets, 22
adding separator bars to toolbars, 722
assigning hyperlinks to objects, 718-719
customizing toolbars, 714-718
opening shortcut menus, 21
rearranging layered objects, 569

Roadrunner Effect, drag and drop, 68

ROMAN function, 306, 317-318

Roman numerals, converting Arabic numerals to, 306, 317-318

rotating images, 573

ROUND function, 306

ROUNDDOWN function, 306

rounding
  functions
    CEILING, 304
    EVEN, 305
    FIXED, 326, 331-332
    FLOOR, 305
    INT, 305
    MROUND, 305
    ODD, 305
    ROUND, 306
    ROUNDDOWN, 306
    ROUNDUP, 306
  relationship to column width, 32

ROUNDUP function, 306

ROW function, 287

Row Hide option (Format menu), 45

Row info type, 268

row-based data series (charts), 472

rows
  adjusting height, 31-32
    AutoFit feature, 32
    dragging boundaries, 32
    Format menu, 32
  blank, avoiding in lists, 387
  formatting, Word documents, 736
  freezing, 42-43
  headings, abbreviating for charts, 475
  hiding/displaying, 45
  hierarchical lists, header rows, 388
  labeling, 30-31
  locking size, 33

PivotTables, hiding/displaying, 629
  selecting, keyboard shortcuts, 53-54
  VBA, removing unwanted rows, 873-874

ROWS function, 287

Run Dialog control (Forms toolbar), 425

runtime errors
  description, 865
  macros, 833-834

S

Sampling tool (Analysis ToolPak), 670

Save As command (File menu), 34

Save As dialog box (File menu), 38
  creating templates from worksheets, 39
  Save Options dialog box, accessing security tools, 36-37

Save as Web Page command (File menu), 636

Save button (Standard toolbar), 16, 35

Save command (File menu), 34

Save Model option (Solver Options dialog box), 657

Save Options dialog box, 35-37

Save tab (Options dialog box), AutoRecover feature, 712

saving
  charts, custom charts, 502
  database queries, 774
  macros, 816
  OLAP multidimensional cubes, saving offline, 799-801, 804-805
  PivotTables
    adding interactivity, 636-637
    HTML format, 636-638
  Solver answer reports, 653-654
  worksheets, 34
    adding passwords and encryption, 35-37
    as templates, 39
    default folders, 35
    file formats, 37-38
    first-time saves, 34-35
    keyboard shortcuts, 34

Scale tab (Format Axis dialog box), 517-518, 523

scaling
  axes in charts
    category (X) axis, 521-523
    value (Y) axis, 516-521
  page breaks, 141
  worksheet printouts, 142-143

scatter charts, 493-494

schedules
  cascading schedules, 677-679
  reverse schedules, 678-680

scientific notation, 93, 100

scope, 851

screen displays
  default blank worksheet, 11
  split screens, 43-45
  workbooks, 11

ScreenTips, 11, 823
  chart elements, 507
  viewing current date/time, 70

Scrollbar control (Forms toolbar), 425, 433-435

scrollbars
  active tables, 667-669
  adding, 710-711
  charts, adding page change indicator, 433-435
  removing, 710-711

scrolling
  buttons, accessing worksheets, 22
  freezing rows or columns, 42-43
  lists, splitting windows, 399-400
  Roadrunner Effect, 68
  workbooks, 11

SEARCH function, 327

SEARCHB function, 327

searching
  help files, 13
  lists, data forms, 398

SECOND function, 203

secondary axes
  adding to charts, 514-515, 575-578
  formatting in charts, 534-535

secondary axes (charts), 531, 549

securities, calculations
  amount due at maturity, 258-259
  discount rate, 245-246
  future value, 247-248
  modified duration, 249-250
  net present value, 251-252
  odd first periods, 252-254
  present value, 256-257
  T-bill prices, 259-260
  T-bill yields, 260-261
  total number of accounting periods, 250-251
  total value, 255-256
  yields, 261-262
  yields at maturity, 262-263

security
  macros, 816-817
  tools
    customized menus, 723-724
    encryption, applying to worksheets, 35-37
    enhanced options, 713-714
    passwords, adding to saved worksheets, 35-37

Security dialog box, 817

Security tab (Options dialog box), 713
  Macro Security button, 714

Select All button, 54

Select All Sheets command (worksheet shortcut menu), 27

Select Changes to Accept or Reject dialog box (Tools menu), 77-78

Select Objects button (Drawing toolbar), 128

Select Visible Cells button (Outlining/Grouping toolbar), 441

Selected Floors option (Format Floors dialog box), 556-557

Selected Trendline command (Format menu), 527-529

Selected Walls option (Format Wall dialog box), 556

selecting
  cells
    cell ranges, 50
    contiguous ranges, 50
    grouped worksheets, 55-57
    keyboard shortcuts, 50-53
    noncontiguous ranges, 54
    vulnerability of selected cells, 52
  charts
    Chart Wizard, 470
    objects, 507
  columns and rows, 53-54
  data for sorting, 415
  data series, 510
  printers, 137
  ranges, grouping worksheets, 61
  records, Advanced Filter options, 423-424
  worksheets, 54

sell in and sell through, 676

Send Backward (Draw menu), 131

Send to Back (Draw menu), 131

Send to Back button (Drawing toolbar), 569-570

How can we make this index more useful? Email us at indexes@quepublishing.com

separation reference operator, 161

separators/separator bars, adding to custom toolbars, 722

Series dialog box (Fill menu), Step Value options, 72

Series In option (Chart Wizard)
    Columns setting, 473
    Rows setting, 472

series labels (charts), 468

series lines, adding to stacked charts, 597-599

series order, charts, 523-525

Series Order tab (Format Data Series dialog box), 548

Series tab (Chart Wizard)
    adding/removing data series, 473
    options, 474-475

SERIESSUM function, 306

Set Print Titles option (PivotTable and PivotChart Wizard), 622

Set Transparent Color button (Picture toolbar), 568

Settings dialog box (Data menu), customizing outlining settings, 447

Settings tab (Data Validation dialog box), 454

Setup button (Print Preview toolbar), 139

shading
    applying to cells, 122-125
    cells, colors and patterns, 125-126
    charts, 566

Shadow button (Drawing toolbar), 129

shapes
    adding to charts, 546-548, 566-568
    converting to text boxes, 547
    grouping, 132-133
    ungrouping, 132

Shapes tab (Format Data Series dialog box), adding 3D shapes, 557

shapes, drawing, 572

Sheet Name button (Custom Header and Footer dialog boxes), 149

Sheet tab (Page Setup dialog box), 142, 150-151

sheet tabs, 22, 46

shortcut keys
    creating, 10
    Go To, 28
    keyboard, navigating worksheets, 27
    macros, 814-815, 820

shortcut menus, 20
    accessing worksheets, 22
    cells, Pick From List feature, 30
    charts, 3-D View dialog box, 574
    deleting hyperlinks, 750-751
    toolbar buttons, Button Editor, 717-718

updating/editing hyperlinks, 750
worksheets
    Rename command, 24
    Select All Sheets command, 27
    Ungroup Sheets command, 27

Show Detail button
    Outlining/Grouping toolbar, 441
    PivotTable toolbar, 610, 626-628

Show Gridlines command (Table menu, Word), 734

Show Iteration Results option (Solver Options dialog box), 657

Show Outline Symbols button (Outlining/Grouping toolbar), 441

Show Watch Window button (Formula Auditing toolbar), 454

Show/Hide Comment buttons (Reviewing toolbar), 81

Shrink to Fit option (Format Cells dialog box, 121

SIGN function, 306

SIN function, 306

sine, complex numbers, 217

single stack thermometer charts, 578-579

single-stack charts, adding series lines, 596-599

SINH function, 306

Sip Blanks option (Paste Special dialog box), 391

size
  fonts, 113-114
  units, converting between, 222

sizing handles
  grouped objects, 132-133
  resizing charts, 506

SKEW function, 348

slices (pie charts), 579-581

slider charts, 153-155

slides (PowerPoint)
  copying data to
    cut and paste method, 737
    linking method, 737-738
    selecting cell ranges, 737
  copying into Word, 745
  formatting Excel objects in, 740-741
  pasting Excel charts into, 741-742
  pasting PivotTables into, 738-739

SLN function, 237

SLOPE function, 348, 376-377

SMALL function, 348, 377

smallest value, identifying, 370-371

Social Security numbers, formatting options, 96

Solver Options dialog box, 656-659

Solver Parameters dialog box (Tools menu), 651-653

Solver Results dialog box (Tools menu), 653-654

Solver tool, 646-657
  accessing/enabling, 650
  analysis options, 656-657
  budget cap example, 650-653

creating/saving answer reports, 653-654
  enabling, 650
  Gantt charts, 657-659
  limitations, 656
  multiple projects, 660-662
  resetting, 654-655

Sort Ascending button (Standard toolbar), 17

Sort Descending button (Standard toolbar), 17

Sort dialog box (Data menu), 413-415

sorting
  automatic subtotaling, 450
  data, 413-416
    selecting data for sorting, 415
    sort sequences, 415-416
  data series in pie charts, 580-581
  database data, 774
  imported Word tables, 745-746
  lists, 397
  rank calculations, 376
  symbols, sort order, 416

source data
  changing/editing, 514
  PivotTables/PivotCharts, handling options, 623
  specifying, 475

Source Data dialog box (Chart menu), changing data source, 514

source tables (charts), setting up, 469

source workbooks, 183-185
  linking to target workbooks, 82-83
    breaking links, 85-86
    locking external links, 85
    redirecting broken links, 85
    updating links, 83-85
  updating values, 185

space inserter, formatting code, 100

spacebar, overwriting cell content, 64

spaces, removing from text, 327, 339-340

special effects
  charts
    adding, 595
    secondary axes, overlays, 575-578
    three-dimensional effects, drawing tools, 153

speech capabilities, managing data, 413

spell checking, cell contents, 30

Spelling button (Standard toolbar), 17, 30

Spelling command (Tools menu), 30

Spelling tab (Options dialog box), 713

Spinner control (Forms toolbar), 425, 435

spinners
  adding to tables, 665-666
  description, 432

spinning pie chart slices, 579-580

split bars, 400

split boxes, 45

Split command (Window menu), 43

splitting
  screen displays, 43-44
    removing splits, 45
    split bars, 44
  windows, 399-400

spreadsheets. *See also* worksheets
  cells. *See* cells
  linking Access databases to Excel spreadsheets, 764-766
  refreshing data, 782

SQL Server, 775
  connecting to, 793-794
  OLAP, 792

SQRT function, 306, 318-319

SQRTP1 function, 306

square roots
  calculating, 306, 318-319
  complex numbers, 217

stacked charts
  column charts, 488
  single-stack charts, adding series lines, 596-599

stacking
  charts, 590-591
  drawn objects, 131

standard deviation, calculating, data sets with multiple data types, 378-379

Standard toolbar
  AutoSum button, 17, 166
  Chart Wizard button, 17, 509
  Copy button, 17
  Cut button, 17
  display options, 15-16
  Drawing button, 17
  Email button, 17
  enabling Watch Window, 180
  Format Painter button, 17
  Hyperlink button, 17
  Microsft Excel Help button, 18

New button, 16
Open button, 16
Paste button, 17
Print button, 17, 136, 501
Print Preview button, 139
Redo button, 17
Save button, 16, 35
Sort Ascending button, 17
Sort Descending button, 17
Spelling button, 17, 30
Undo button, 17
Visual Basic Editor, 845-846
Zoom button, 18

STANDARDIZE function, 348

Stars and Banners button (Drawing toolbar), 547

Start menu, launching Excel, 10

starting
  Microsoft Query, 776
  Excel
    opening screen, 11
    shortcut icons, 10
    Start menu, 10
    Windows Explorer, 10

statements
  description, 839
  typing in lowercase, 849

statistical functions, 344-381
  AVEDEV, 344
  AVERAGE, 344, 349-350
  AVERAGEA, 344
  BETADIST, 344
  BETAINV, 344
  BINOMDIST, 344, 350-351
  CHIDIST, 344, 351-352
  CHIINV, 344
  CHITEST, 344

CONFIDENCE, 344, 352
CORREL, 344, 353-354
COUNT, 344, 354-355
COUNTA, 345, 354-356
COUNTBLANK, 345, 356-357
COUNTIF, 345, 356-357
COVAR, 345, 358
CRITBINOM, 345
DEVSQ, 345
EXPONDIST, 345, 358-359
FDIST, 345, 359-360
FINV, 345
FISHER, 345
FISHERINV, 345
FORECAST, 345, 360-361
FREQUENCY, 345, 361-362
FTEST, 345
GAMMADIST, 345
GAMMAINV, 345
GAMMALN, 346
GEOMEAN, 346, 362-363
GROWTH, 346, 363-364
HARMEAN, 346
HYPGEODIST, 346
INTERCEPT, 346, 364-365
LARGE, 346, 365, 377
LINEST, 346, 366-367
LOGEST, 346, 368
LOGINV, 346
LOGNORMDIST, 346
MAX, 346, 368-369
MAXA, 347
MEDIAN, 347, 369-370
MIN, 347, 370
MINA, 347, 371
MODE, 347, 371
NEGBINOMDIST, 347
NORMDIST, 347, 371-372
NORMINV, 347, 372
NORMSINV, 347

PEARSON, 347
PERCENTILE, 347, 373
PERCENTRANK, 347, 373-374
PERMUT, 347
POISSON, 348, 374-375
PROB, 348
QUARTILE, 348
RANK, 348, 375-376
SKEW, 348
SLOPE, 348, 376-377
SMALL, 348, 377
STANDARDIZE, 348
STDEV, 348, 378
STDEVA, 348, 378-379
STDEVP, 348
STDEVPA, 348
STEYX, 348
TDIST, 349
TINV, 349
TREND, 349, 379
TRIMMEAN, 349
troubleshooting, 381
TTEST, 349
VAR, 349, 380
VARA, 349, 380
VARP, 349, 380
VARPA, 349
WEIBULL, 349
ZTEST, 349

status bar
    AutoCalculate feature, 175
    customizing AutoCalculate
        function, 711-712

STDEV function, 348, 378

STDEVA function, 348, 378-379

STDEVP function, 348

STDEVPA function, 348

step values, custom data series, 72

stepping
    debugging, 866-867
    description, 866

STEYX function, 348

stock charts, 497, 538-539

stock diaries, 497

Stop Recording toolbar, 815

stopping macro recordings, 815

storing macros, 719, 812-816

strings (text strings)
    comparing, 326, 329-330
    concatenating, 326-329
    converting to numeric
        values, 327
    counting characters,
        326-327, 332-337
    finding, 326, 330-331
    managing, 326
    replacing, 327
    searching, 327
    substituting text, 327,
        338-339

structured lists
    adding form controls,
        Combo Box example,
        427-428
    avoiding blanks, 387
    conditional formatting,
        408-413
        formulas, 410-413
        interactive approach,
            408-410
    consolidating data, 447
    creating from single cells,
        394-396
    custom layouts, 388
    data entry forms, 396-397
    Data Fields, 388
    data-driven, 394

design issues, 386-387, 405
field names, 388, 399
filtering, 397, 416
    Advanced Filter,
        421-424
    AutoFilter, 417-421
    automatic subtotaling,
        450-452
header rows, 388
hierarchical structures, 387
inserting data ranges,
    402-403
managing data
    sort options, 413-416
    text to speech features,
        413
modifying, transposing
    data, 391-392
printing, 399
records, 388
scrolling, splitting windows,
    399-400
searching, 398
standard layout, 388
troubleshooting, 405, 437
viewing, 399
    custom views, 403-405
    multiple windows,
        400-401

structuring worksheets, 446

Style dialog box (Format menu), 116-117
    Format Cells dialog box,
        117
    Merge button, 118

styles
    custom, creating/applying,
        117
    default (Normal), editing,
        116-117
    fonts, 114
    merging among workbooks,
        118
    permanent, 153

subfolders, 35

subroutines, 810

**SUBSTITUTE function,
327, 338-339**

**SUBTOTAL function, 306,
319-320**
  charts, 588-590
  syntax, 451-452

**Subtotal Hidden Page Items
option (PivotTable and
PivotChart Wizard), 620**

subtotaling
  automatic, 450-452
  hidden fields in
    PivotTables, 620

**subtotals, adding to charts,
588, 590**

**Subtotals dialog box (Data
menu), 450-451**

**Subtract option (Paste
Special dialog box), 391**

subtraction
  formulas, 162
  operator, 161

**SUM function, 214, 307,
320-321**
  accessing using AutoSum
    feature, 166-168
  AutoCalculate, 177
  automating, 323
  consolidated tables, 449
  embedding
    YEAR/MONTH
    functions, 212-213
  IS BLANK function,
    274-275

**SUM IF formula, chart
controls, 434-435**

**SUMIF function, 307,
321-322**
  accessing using AutoSum
    feature, 168-170

**summary statistics, count
calculations, 354-357**
  blank cells, 356-357
  cells in ranges, 356-357

**summary tables, multiple,
creating for single
worksheet, 444-445**

**SUMPRODUCT function,
307**

**sums, complex numbers,
218, 229**

**SUMSQUARES function,
307**

SUMX2MY2 function, 307

SUMX2PY2 function, 307

surface charts, 495-496

SYD function, 237

symbols
  outline symbols, clearing,
    446
  sort order, 416

syntax
  cell links, IF statement, 431
  database functions, 190-199
    DAVERAGE, 190-193
    DCOUNT, 190,
      193-194
    DCOUNTA, 190
    DFUNCTION,
      191-192
    DGET, 190, 194-196
    DMAX, 190
    DMIN, 190, 196
    DPRODUCT, 190, 197
    DSUM, 191, 197-198
    DVAR, 191
    DVARP, 191
    GETPIVOTDATA,
      191, 198-199

date functions, 202-213
  DATE, 202, 204-205
  DATEVALUE, 202
  DAYS360, 202, 205-206
  EDATE, 206-207
  EOMONTH, 202
  MONTH, 203, 207
  NETWORKDAYS,
    203, 208-209
  NOW, 203
  TODAY, 203, 209-210
  WEEKDAY, 203,
    210-211
  WORKDAY, 203
  YEAR, 203, 211-213
  YEARFRAC, 203
engineering functions,
  216-230
  BESSELI, 216-218
  BESSELJ, 216
  BESSELK, 216
  BESSELY, 216
  BIN2DEC, 216, 219
  BIN2HEX, 216
  BIN2OCT, 216
  COMPLEX, 216,
    219-220
  CONVERT, 216,
    220-222, 230
  DEC2BIN, 216, 223
  DEC2OCT, 216
  DELTA, 216, 223-224
  ERF, 216
  ERFC, 216
  GESTEP, 217, 224
  HEX2BIN, 217, 225
  HEX2OCT, 217
  IMABS, 217
  IMAGINARY, 217
  IMARGUMENT, 217
  IMCONJUGATE, 217,
    225-226
  IMCOS, 217
  IMDIV, 217

IMEXP, 217
IMLN, 217
IMLOG10, 217
IMLOG2, 217
IMPOWER, 217, 226-227
IMPRODUCT, 217, 227-228
IMREAL, 217
IMSIN, 217
IMSQRT, 217
IMSUB, 218, 228-229
IMSUM, 218, 229
external worksheet references, 182
financial functions, 234-263
    ACCRINT, 234
    ACCRINTM, 234
    AMORLINC, 234
    COUPDAYBS, 234
    COUPDAYS, 234
    COUPDAYSNC, 234
    COUPNCD, 234
    COUPNUM, 235, 243-244
    COUPPCD, 235
    CUMIPMT, 235, 244-245
    CUMPRINC, 235
    DB, 235
    DDB, 235
    DISC, 235, 245-246
    DOLLARDE, 235
    DOLLARFR, 235
    DURATION, 235, 246-247
    EFFECT, 235
    FV, 235, 247-248
    FVSCHEDULE, 235
    INTRATE, 236
    IPMT, 236, 248-249
    IRR, 236
    MDURATION, 236, 249-250
    MIRR, 236

NOMINAL, 236
NPER, 236, 250-251
NPV, 236, 251-252
ODDFPRICE, 236
ODDFYIELD, 236
ODDLPRICE, 236
ODDLYIELD, 237
ODDPRICE, 252-254
PMT, 237, 254-255, 662
PPMT, 237
PRICE, 237, 255-256
PRICEDISC, 237
PRICEMAT, 237
PV, 237, 256-257
RATE, 237, 257-258
RECEIVE, 237
RECEIVED, 258-259
SLN, 237
SYD, 237
TBILLEQ, 237
TBILLPRICE, 237, 259-260
TBILLYIELD, 237, 260-261
VDB, 238
XIRR, 238
XNPV, 238
YIELD, 238, 261-262
YIELDDISC, 238
YIELDMAT, 238, 262-263
information functions, 266-275
    CELL, 266-269
    COUNTBLANK, 266, 269-270
    ERROR.TYPE, 266, 270-271
    INFO, 266, 271-272
    IS, functions, 272-273
    ISBLANK, 266, 273-274
    ISERR, 266, 273
    ISERROR, 266, 273
    ISEVEN, 266, 273
    ISLOGICAL, 266, 273
    ISNA, 266, 273

ISNONTEXT, 266, 273
ISNUMBER, 266, 273-275
ISODD, 266, 273
ISREF, 266, 273
ISTEXT, 266, 273
N, 267
NA, 267
TYPE, 267
linked cells, 83
linking to other workbooks, 184
logical functions, 278-282
    AND, 278-280
    FALSE, 278
    IF, 278-281
    NOT, 278-282
    OR, 278
    TRUE, 278
lookup and reference functions, 286-301
    ADDRESS, 286
    AREA, 286
    CHOOSE, 287-288
    COLUMNS, 286
    HLOOKUP, 286, 288-289
    HYPERLINK, 286
    INDEX, 286, 290-292
    INDIRECT, 287
    LOOKUP, 287, 294-295
    MATCH, 287
    OFFSET, 287, 296-299
    ROW, 287
    ROWS, 287
    TRANSPOSE, 287, 299-300
    VLOOKUP, 287, 300-301
math/trigonometry functions, 304-323
    ABS, 304, 307-308
    ACOS, 304, 308-309
    ACOSH, 304
    ASIN, 304, 309-310
    ASINH, 304

ATAN, 304
ATAN2, 304
ATANH, 304
CEILING, 304
COMBIN, 304, 310-311
COS, 304, 311
COSH, 304
COUNTIF, 304, 311-313
DEGREES, 305, 313
EVEN, 305
EXP, 305
FACT, 305
FACTDOUBLE, 305
FLOOR, 305
GCD, 305
INT, 305
LCM, 305
LN, 313-314
LOG, 305
LOG10, 305
MDETERM, 305
MINVERSE, 305
MMULT, 305
MOD, 305
MROUND, 305
MULTINOMIAL, 305
ODD, 305
PERMUT, 305, 315
PI, 306, 316
POWER, 306
PRODUCT, 306
QUOTIENT, 306
RADIANS, 306
RAND, 306, 316-317
RANDBETWEEN, 306
ROMAN, 306, 317-318
ROUND, 306
ROUNDDOWN, 306
ROUNDUP, 306
SERIESSUM, 306
SIGN, 306
SIN, 306
SINH, 306

SQRT, 306, 318-319
SQRTP1, 306
SUBTOTAL, 306, 319-320
SUM, 307, 320-323
SUMIF, 307, 321-322
SUMPRODUCT, 307
SUMSQUARES, 307
SUMX2MY2, 307
SUMX2PY2, 307
TAN, 307, 322
TANH, 307
TRUNC, 307
statistical functions, 344-380
AVEDEV, 344
AVERAGE, 344, 349-350
AVERAGEA, 344
BETADIST, 344
BETAINV, 344
BINOMDIST, 344, 350-351
CHIDIST, 344, 351-352
CHIINV, 344
CHITEST, 344
CONFIDENCE, 344, 352
CORREL, 344, 353-354
COUNT, 344, 354-355
COUNTA, 345, 354-356
COUNTBLANK, 345, 356-357
COUNTIF, 345, 356-357
COVAR, 345, 358
CRITBINOM, 345
DEVSQ, 345
EXPONDIST, 345, 358-359
FDIST, 345, 359-360
FINV, 345
FISHER, 345
FISHERINV, 345

FORECAST, 345, 360-361
FREQUENCY, 345, 361-362
FTEST, 345
GAMMADIST, 345
GAMMAINV, 345
GAMMALN, 346
GEOMEAN, 346, 362-363
GROWTH, 346, 363-364
HARMEAN, 346
HYPGEODIST, 346
INTERCEPT, 346, 364-365
LARGE, 346, 365, 377
LINEST, 346, 366-367
LOGEST, 346, 368
LOGINV, 346
LOGNORMDIST, 346
MAX, 346, 368-369
MAXA, 347
MEDIAN, 347, 369-370
MIN, 347, 370
MINA, 347, 371
MODE, 347, 371
NEGBINOMDIST, 347
NORMDIST, 347, 371-372
NORMINV, 347, 372
NORMSINV, 347
PEARSON, 347
PERCENTILE, 347, 373
PERCENTRANK, 373-374
PERMUT, 347
POISSON, 348, 374-375
PROB, 348
QUARTILE, 348
RANK, 348, 375-376
SKEW, 348
SLOPE, 348, 376-377

SMALL, 348, 377
STANDARDIZE, 348
STDEV, 348, 378
STDEVA, 348, 378-379
STDEVP, 348
STDEVPA, 348
STEYX, 348
TDIST, 349
TINV, 349
TREND, 349, 379
TRIMMEAN, 349
TTEST, 349
VAR, 349, 380
VARA, 349, 380
VARP, 349, 380
VARPA, 349
WEIBULL, 349
ZTEST, 349
text functions, 326-340
CHAR, 326
CLEAN, 326
CODE, 326
CONCATENATE, 326, 328-329
DOLLAR, 326
EXACT, 326, 329-330
FIND, 326, 330-331
FIXED, 326, 331-332
LEFT, 326
LEN, 326, 332-333
LOWER, 326, 333-334
MID, 327, 334-335
PROPER, 327, 335-336
REPLACE, 327
REPLACEB, 327
REPT, 327
RIGHT, 327, 336-337
SEARCH, 327
SEARCHB, 327
SUBSTITUTE, 327, 338-339
T, 327
TEXT, 327
TRIM, 327, 339-340
UPPER, 327, 340
VALUE, 327

time functions, 202-203
HOUR, 203
MINUTE, 203
SECOND, 203
TIME, 203
TIMEVALUE, 203

syntax error, 865

system crashes, recovering corrupted data/worksheets, 37

System text type, 272

T

T function, 327

T-bills, calculations
prices, 259-260
yields, 260-261

t-Test, Paired Heterodastic tool (Analysis ToolPak), 670

t-Test, Paired Two Sample tool (Analysis ToolPak), 670

Tab key, 27, 50

Table menu (Word), Show Gridlines option, 734

tables
active
adding spinners, 665-666
multiple-variable tables, 667-669
amortization, 662-665
AutoFile, 174
automatic subtotaling, 450-452
calculation tables, form controls, 429-432
chart source tables, setting up, 469
consolidating data, 447-449

copying into PowerPoint presentations, 736-738
cut and paste method, 737
linking method, 737-738
copying into Word documents, 734-735
data, 646
data tables, adding to charts, 483-484
formatting, PowerPoint, 740-741
hierarchical grouping, 441
incorporating in charts, 583
lookup function
horizontal lookups, 286-289
vertical lookups, 287, 300-301
Microsoft Query, 776-777
multi-dimensional, creating using drawing tools, 153
PivotTables. *See* PivotTables
summary tables, 444-445
transposing, 391-393, 680-683
Word documents
adding to worksheets, sorting and filtering data, 745-746
copying into Excel, 745
formatting, 736

TAN function, 307, 322

Tangent option (Solver Options dialog box), 657

tangents
calculating, 307, 322
hyperbolic, 307

TANH function, 307

target workbooks, linking to source workbooks, 82-85
breaking links, 85-86
locking external links, 85
redirecting broken links, 85
updating links, 83-85

task panes
Clipboard taskpane, 13-15
Insert Clip Art option, 15
New Worksheet task pane, 12

taskbars, worksheets, closing Excel, 11

TBILLEQ function, 237

TBILLPRICE function, 237, 259-260

TBILLYIELD function, 237, 260-261

TDIST function, 349

telephone numbers, formatting options, 96

temperature measurements, converting between, 221

templates
creating form worksheets, 39, 46
starting workbooks, 40

Templates folder, 46

testing
cells, cell ranges, 272-273
form controls, 428
logical testing
IF function for, 280-281
NOT function, 281-282
OR function, 282-283

text
adding
shapes, 547
toolbar buttons, 715-716
body text, hierarchical lists, 388
editing, 30
entering in cells, 29-30

formatting
charts, legends, 544
data labels, 540-544
Word documents, 736
types (INFO function), 271-272
values, identifying, 266, 273
Word documents, adding to worksheets, 745

text arguments, 160

Text Box button (Drawing toolbar), 128

Text Box tool (Drawing toolbar), 545

text boxes, adding to charts, 586

text files
importing, 785-786
importing data from, 783-785

text formats, formatting code, 99-101

TEXT function, 327

text functions, 326-340
CHAR, 326
CLEAN, 326
CODE, 326
CONCATENATE, 326-329
DOLLAR, 326
EXACT, 326, 329-330
FIND, 326, 330-331
FIXED, 326, 331-332
LEFT, 326
LEN, 326, 332-333
LOWER, 326, 333-334
MID, 327, 334-335
PROPER, 327, 335-336
REPLACE, 327
REPLACEB, 327
REPT, 327
RIGHT, 327, 336-337

SEARCH, 327
SEARCHB, 327
SUBSTITUTE, 327, 338-339
T, 327
TEXT, 327
TRIM, 327, 339-340
UPPER, 327, 340
VALUE, 327

Text Import Wizard, importing data from text files, 783-785

text operators, 161

text placeholders, formatting code, 101

text strings
comparing, 326, 329-330
concatenating, 326-329
converting to numeric values, 327
counting characters, 326-327, 332-337
finding, 326, 330-331
managing, 326
replacing, 327
searching, 327
substituting text in, 327, 338-339

Text to Columns option (Data menu), creating lists, 395

text to speech features, managing data, 413

Text to Speech toolbar, 413

text wrapping, 30, 121

thermometer charts, creating, 576-578
single stacked thermometers, 578-579

Theta argument, 217

thousands separator, formatting code, 100

three-dimensional (3D) boxes, placing charts in, 572

three-dimensional (3D) charts, 487
  formatting, 555
    3D views, 558-559
    data series, 557
    floors, 556-557
    walls, 556
  gradient fills, creating in 3D charts, 582-583
  pie charts, 490
  surface charts, 495
  wire-frame charts, 495
  Z-axis, 468

three-dimensional (3D) effects
  adding to charts
    column depth, 573-575
    perspective, 574-575
  drawing tools, 153

three-dimensional (3D) objects, adding to charts, 575

tick marks (charts), 468, 535-536

Tiled option (Window menu), 42

tiling, 42
  windows, 182, 734

time
  analyses, 598
  formatting options, 95-99
    24-hour clock format, 96
    custom codes, 98-99
  units, converting between, 221
  viewing with ScreenTips, 70

Time button (Custom Header/Footer dialog boxes), 149

TIME function, 203

time functions, 202-203
  HOUR, 203
  MINUTE, 203
  SECOND, 203
  TIME, 203
  TIMEVALUE, 203

time-scale displays, formatting charts, 478

Time-Scale option (Chart Wizard, Axes tab), 479

timelines, conditional formatting, 411-413

TIMEVALUE function, 203

TINV function, 349

titles
  center, 153
  charts, 468, 476-478
    adding, 543-544
    formatting, 543-544
  formatting, 119-120
  merge and center, 119-120

Titles tab
  Chart Options dialog box, 543
  Chart Wizard, 476-477
    naming value (Y) axis, 477-478
    uppercase letters, 478

TODAY function, 203, 209-210

Toggle Grid control (Forms toolbar), 425

Tolerance option (Solver Options dialog box), 656

toolbars
  adding/removing, 19
  attaching to worksheets, 722
  Auditing
    Circle Invalid Data button, 457
    Clear Validation Circles button, 458
  Borders toolbar, Eraser button, 122
  Chart toolbar
    changing chart type, 509
    editing embedded charts, 507-508
  customizing, 714-723
    adding hyperlinks, 718
    adding macros, 718-719
    adding separators, 722
    building custom toolbars, 720-721
    changing button images, 716-718
    deleting buttons, 715
    deleting/removing, 723
    displaying text on buttons, 715-716
    moving buttons, 722
  display options, 15-16
  Drawing toolbar, 128-129
    AutoShapes option, 546
    Bevel tool, 134-135
    buttons, 127-129, 546-547
    displaying/hiding, 129
    Text Box tool, 545
    WordArt button, 570
  floating, 129, 570
  Formatting toolbar
    buttons, 18-19, 109-110
    customizing, 110
    Decrease/Increase Indent buttons, 120

display options, 110
Draw Borders button, 122-125
Fill Color button, 126
Merge and Center button, 119-120
number formats, 92
Forms toolbar, activating, 584
Formula Auditing, buttons, 453-454
images, 824
macros, 821-825, 831-832
Outlining/Grouping toolbar, 440
Picture toolbar
  accessing, 566
  buttons, 568
PivotTable toolbar, 609-610
Print Preview toolbar, buttons, 139-140
reference icons, 20
references to, in menus, 20
Reviewing, comment functions, 80
ScreenTips, 823
Standard toolbar
  accessing functions, 166
  AutoSum button, 166
  buttons, 16-18
  Chart Wizard button, 469, 509
  enabling Watch Window, 180
  Paste button, 511
  Print button, 136, 501
  Print Preview button, 139
  Save button, 35
  Spelling button, 30
  Visual Basic Editor, 845-846
Stop Recording toolbar, 815
Text to Speech toolbar, 413

Toolpak (Analysis ToolPak), 206, 669-672
Tools menu
Accept or Reject Changes, 77-78
Add-Ins, 206, 293
Auditing submenu, 459-460
commands
  Macro, Macros, 819
  Macro, Record New Macro, 814
  Macro, Security, 817
  Macro, Stop Recording, 815
Data Analysis, enabling Analysis ToolPak, 669
displaying/hiding comments, 80
enabling drag and drop, 68
enabling Solver, 650
Extend Lists Formats and Formulas option (Tools menu), enabling/disabling, 388
Goal Seek dialog box, 647-649
Options dialog box
  adding/removing scrollbars, 710-711
  Color tab, 707-709
  cursor movement, 704-705
  customizing defaults, 704
  Error Checking tab, 712
  font type and size, 706
  function ToolTips, 706
  International tab, 712-713
  resetting font defaults, 115
  Save tab, 712
  Security tab, 713-714

Spelling tab, 713
Web Options button, 706
workbook sheets, 704
Options submenu, date system options, 211
Solver Parameters dialog box, 651-653
Solver Results dialog box, 653-654
Spelling command, 30
Track Changes feature, enabling, 76

ToolTips, enabling/disabling, 706
Top 10 AutoFilter, 418-419
Total Pages button (Custom Header/Footer dialog boxes), 149
totals
  PivotTables, 619
  queries, 781
Totmem text type, 272
Trace Dependents button (Formula Auditing toolbar), 454
Trace Error button (Formula Auditing toolbar), 454
Trace options (Tools, Auditing menu), 459-460
Trace Precedents button (Formula Auditing toolbar), 453
tracer arrows, 458
tracing precedents, dependents, 459-460

Track Changes feature
accepting and rejecting changes, 77-78
disabling, 77
enabling, 75-76
Highlight Changes dialog box, 76-77
troubleshooting problems with, 86

tracking changes, 75-77
accepting/rejecting changes, 77-78

transferring
Excel data to Access databases, 759-764
Excel databases into non-Access databases, 766-767

transparent images, creating, 570-573

TRANSPOSE function, 287, 299-300

Transpose option (Paste Special dialog box), 391-393

transposing
data, lists/tables, 391-393
tables, 680-683

Treasury bills. *See* T-bills

tree views, OLAP dimension hierarchies, 796

TREND function, 349, 379

Trendline dialog box, 526

trendlines (charts), 468
adding, 502, 525-527
calculating, 379
formatting, 527-529

trigger cells, conditional formatting, 408-410

trigonometry functions. *See* math/trigonometry functions

TRIM function, 327, 339-340

TRIMMEAN function, 349

troubleshooting
auditing features, access problems, 460
Auto Outline feature, 446, 460
AutoCorrect feature, unwanted corrections, 86
chart formatting, 602-603
charts
adding data, 530
changing chart type, 530
customizing tick marks, 531
data labels, 502, 560
fill effects, 560
formatting axis lines, 560
formatting borders, 560
formatting data points, 560
offsetting categories, 560
secondary axis, 531
selecting chart elements, 501
colors, 53
data management
complex formulas, 436
index formulas, 436
legacy list problems, 437
databases, 786
date function errors, 213
deleted menus, retrieving, 728
formula-related errors, 177-178, 186, 436
information function problems, 275
lists, 405
logical functions, 283
lookup and reference functions, VLOOKUP problems, 301
macros, 833-834
Microsoft Access, 786
PivotTables, 199, 638
printing-related problems, 151-152
range naming errors, 59-60
statistical functions, 381
titles, 153
value axis formatting, 530

TRUE function, 278

TrueType fonts, worksheets, 112-113

TRUNC function, 307

truncating numbers, 307

TTEST function, 349

two-dimensional (2D) charts, 487
advantages of, 573
pie charts, 490

Type field (formatting codes), 97

Type format bar (Format Cells Number tab), 104-105

TYPE function, 267

Type info type, 268

U

Underline button (Formatting toolbar), 18, 110

underlining cell contents, 114

Undo button, 17, 513

undoing
edits, 65
formatting changes, 111

Ungroup button
(Outlining/Grouping
toolbar), 441

Ungroup Sheets command
(worksheet shortcut
menu), 27

Ungroup Sheets option
(worksheet context menu),
56

ungrouping
drawn objects, 132
worksheets, 27

Unhide dialog box, 709, 829

Update button, updating
referenced values, 185

Update File button
(Reviewing toolbar), 81

updating
hyperlinks, 749-752
linked data, 738
links, 83-85

UPPER function, 327, 340,
388-389

uppercase letters
chart titles, 478
converting lowercase letters
to, 327, 340
converting to lowercase,
326, 333-334

Use Automatic Scaling
option (Solver Options
dialog box), 657

Use Labels In option
(Consolidate dialog box),
449

Username variable, listing,
843

V

validating data entry,
453-454
Data Validation dialog box
options, 454-457
marking invalid data, 457

Validation command (Data
menu), 454

Validation option (Paste
Special dialog box), 390

value (Y) axis
formatting, 478-479,
534-535
naming, 476-478
scaling, 516-521

value axes, 468
formatting in charts, 535
naming, 476

value chains
market opportunity value
chain, 695-697
overview, 695
strategic risk factor value
chain, 697-698

VALUE function, 327

value matrixes, 698-700

values
calculating largest, 377
calculating smallest, 377
data sets
identifying largest value,
368-369
identifying median value,
369-370
identifying smallest
value, 370-371
displaying, 871

Values and Number Formats
(Paste Special dialog box),
390

Values option (Paste Special
dialog box), 390

VAR function, 349, 380

VARA function, 349, 380

variables
description, 842
naming, 842
UserName listing, 843
watching in debugging,
869-870

variance, calculating, 380
data sets with multiple data
types, 380
database function, 191
whole population, 380

VARP function, 349, 380

VARPA function, 349

VBA (Visual Basic for
Applications), 810
breakpoints, 867-868
code
starting automatically,
871-872
writing, 841
collections, 839
constants, 844-845
control structures, 856
decision-making, 856-
858
loops, 858-860
functions, 841
Help system, accessing, 847
Immediate window, 868
macro language, creating
custom functions, 164
methods, 840
object-oriented program-
ming, 839
objects, 839
procedures, 848
projects, compiling, 865
properties, 840

removing unwanted rows, 873-874
statements, typing in lower-case, 849
stepping, 866-867
variables, naming, 842

VDB function, 238

Vector form (LOOKUP function), 287, 295

versions, documents, identifying, 46

vertical alignment options, 120

vertical axis. *See* Y-axis

vertical field names (hierarchical lists), 388

vertical lists/tables, transposing to horizontal, 391-393

vertical lookups, 287, 300-301

vertical ranges, returning as vertical ranges, 287, 299-300

vertical scrollbars, adding/removing, 710-711

Very Hidden option (Hide dialog box), 709

View Current Sheet Right-to-Left option (International tab), 712-713

View menu
Custom Views option, 403
Page Break Preview feature, 140-141
Toolbars
Customize dialog box, 714
adding text to buttons, 716
changing button images, 716-717

viewing
charts, Zoom feature, 507
clipboard contents, 14
data in PivotTables, 638
font names, 112-113
groups, expanding/collapsing views, 442-443
lists, 399
custom views, 403-405
multiple windows, 400-401
multiple Office programs, 734
named ranges, 59
OLAP dimension hierarchies
displaying/hiding individual items, 798
drilling down, 796-797
tree view, 796
OLAP PivotTables, 796-797
selected calls, 50
sheet tabs, 46
worksheets
freezing rows or columns, 42-43
right-to-left option, 712-713
splitting the screen, 43-45

views
multiple workbooks
switching between, 41-42
tiling options, 42
three-dimensional, adding to charts, 558-559
worksheets, 40

viruses, macros, 816-817

Visual Basic Editor, 828-830
Auto Syntax Check, 865
code, writing
Auto Quick Info, 862
comments, 864
indents, 862
List Members list, 861
modules
adding, 852
deleting, 852
naming, 852
overview, 845
procedures
function, 852-855
non-recorded, 849-851
Standard toolbar buttons, 845-846
windows, 846-847

Visual Basic for Applications. *See* VBA

visual effects, charts, 595

VLOOKUP function, 287, 301
PivotTables, 639-640
troubleshooting, 301

W

walls (3D charts), formatting, 556

Watch Window, evaluating formulas, 180

watches, placing on statement or variables, 869-870

waterfall charts, 520-521

watermarks, 570-573

Web Options button (Options dialog box), 706

Web pages
enabling encoding, 706
enabling formulas, 706
font settings, 706
graphics, setting defaults, 706
saving PivotTables as, 636-638
selecting browser, 706

Web PivotTables, 636-638

Webdings, inclusion matrices, 154

WEEKDAY function, 203, 210-211

WEIBULL function, 349

weight units, converting between, 221

width, columns, adjusting, 31-32

Width info type, 268

wildcard characters
custom AutoFilter, 420
SUMIF function, 322

Window menu
Arrange command, tiling option, 42
Arrange options, 401
displaying multiple worksheets, 513
Arrange Windows dialog box, 182
Freeze Panes command, 43
Freeze Panes option, 399
New Window option, 401
Remove Split command, 45
Split command, 43

windows
customizing, 710
adding/removing scrollbars, 710-711
status bar settings, 711-712

multiple
arranging, 400-401
working from, 182
splitting, 399-400
tiling, 734
Visual Basic Editor, 846-847

Windows Explorer
identifying file versions, 46
launching Excel from, 10

wire frame charts, 495

wizards
Convert Text to Columns Wizard, 785-786
Data Connection Wizard, 768
Import Spreadsheet, 759-764, 786
Link Spreadsheet, 764-766
OLAP Cube Wizard
accessing and launching, 801-802
creating dimension hierarchies, 803
saving cubes, 804
selecting cube measures, 802-803
PivotTable and PivotChart Wizard, 611-613
Query Wizard, 769-774
choosing columns, 771-773
choosing data sources, 769
filtering data, 773-774
saving queries, 774
sorting data, 774
Text Import Wizard, importing data from text files, 783-785

Word documents
copying charts to, 734-735
copying Excel data to, 734
copying PowerPoint slides to, 745
copying tables/charts to, 734-735
formatting Excel data in documents, 736
pasting data into worksheets, 744
sorting/filtering data, 745-746

word wrapping, 30

WordArt, 566
adding to charts, 575
creating watermarks/draft stamps, 570-573

WordArt button (Drawing toolbar), 570

workbooks, 22
closing, 11
copying cell content between, drag and drop, 68
customizing, color palettes, 706-709
defaults
changing
hiding/displaying cell contents, 710
hiding/displaying worksheets, 709
hiding/displaying zero values, 709-710
external
linking to, 183-185
updating values, 185
grouping worksheets in, 27

linking, 82-83
    breaking links, 85-86
    locking external links, 85
    redirecting broken links, 85
    updating links, 83-85
macros, 816-817
merging styles, 118
modules, 816
multiple
    displaying simultane-
        ously, 513
    switching between,
        41-42
    tiling, 42
    viewing, 40
Personal Macro Workbook,
    812-816, 830
screen displays
    main components, 11
    Minimize/Maximize/
        Close buttons, 11
scrolling, 11
sheets, customizing number
    of, 704-705
starting from templates, 40
structuring, 440
ungrouping worksheets, 27
Word documents,
    formatting, 736

WORKDAY function, 203

worksheets
accessing, 22
adding new sheets, 23
adding text from Word
    documents, 745
adding Word tables, sort-
    ing/filtering data, 745-746
applying custom number
    formats, 94
arranging/rearranging, 25
attaching custom toolbars,
    722-723

AutoFit feature, 33-34
cells. *See* cells
columns
    adjusting width, 31-32
    labeling, 30-31
comments
    adding comments, 79-81
    deleting, 80
    editing comments, 80
copying cell content
    between, drag and drop,
    68
copying data from
    Word/PowerPoint to, 744
corrupted, recovering, 37
creating templates from, 46
customizing, adding hyper-
    links, 718
data entry, data forms,
    396-397
default opening screen dis-
    play, 11
embedded charts, 467,
    484-486, 595-596
    moving, 506-507
    resizing, 506
external, referencing data
    from, 181-182
form controls, 424-427
    multiple-variable tables,
        667-669
    spinners, 665-666
formatting, 108
    adding borders and
        shading, 122-125
    advantages, 108
    alignment, 111
    changing default font,
        152
    fonts, 111-114
    Format Cells dialog box,
        111
    Formatting toolbar,
        109-110

individual characters,
    115
media matrices/plans,
    153-154
page setup options,
    141-142
tips, 156
titles, 119-120
grouping, 25-27, 55-57
    selecting and naming
        ranges, 61
headers/footers
    adding fields, 148-150
    adding text, 147-148
hiding/displaying, 709
highlighting specific con-
    tent, conditional format-
    ting, 408
inserting graphics, 569
linking, 82-83
    breaking links, 85-86
    charts, 592
    locking external links, 85
    redirecting broken links,
        85
    updating links, 83-85
margins, 140
moving, 25
multiple
    summarizing data from,
        183
multiple, advantages of
    using, 23
naming, 24
navigating
    Go To shortcut, 28
    keyboard shortcuts, 27,
        65
New Worksheet task pane
    features, 12
number of, changing
    defaults, 23

PivotTables/PivotCharts
  handling multiple
    PivotTables, 613
  placement options, 613
  referencing calculations,
    628-629
printing, 135-137
  adjusting print quality,
    144
  centering on pages,
    146-147
  choosing print range,
    137-138
  header and footer mar-
    gins, 145
  margin settings, 144-145
  page orientation, 142
  paper size, 143-144
  previewing, 137-140
  previewing page breaks,
    140-141
  printing to file, 137
  scaling printouts,
    142-143
  selecting print area, 151
  troubleshooting, 151-
    152
protected, auditing data,
  458
rows
  adjusting height, 31-32
  labeling, 30-31
saving, 34
  adding passwords and
    encryption, 35-37
  default folder, 35
  file formats, 37-38
  first-time saves, 34-35
  templates, 39
selecting, 54
sheet tabs, coloring, 23-24
starting from templates, 40
structuring, 446

summary tables, creating
  multiple tables, 444-445
taskbar icons, closing Excel,
  11
ungrouping, 27
viewing, 40
  freezing rows and
    columns, 42-43
  hiding/displaying rows
    and columns, 45
  splitting the screen,
    43-45
Word documents, format-
  ting, 736
zero values, 710

wrapping text, 121

writing
  code
    Auto Quick Info, 862
    commenting code, 864
    indents, 862
    List Members list, 861
  macros
    advantages, 838
    VBA, 838

X

X-axis, 467-468
  Error Bars tab (Format
    Data Series dialog box),
    539
  formatting, 478-479
  naming, 476-477
  scaling, 521-523
XIRR function, 238
XLStart folder, 813
XNPV function, 238

Y

**Y Error Bars tab (Format
Data Series dialog box),
538-540**
Y-axis, 467-468
  formatting, 478-479,
    534-535
  naming, 476-478
  scaling, 516-521
**Y-axis Error Bars tab
(Format Data Series dialog
box), 538**
YEAR function, 203
  embedding in SUM and IF
    functions, 211-213
YEARFRAC function, 203
**years, customizing date
system for, 211**
**YIELD function, 238,
261-262**
YIELDDISC function, 238
**YIELDMAT function, 238,
262-263**
yields
  securities, calculating,
    261-262
    yield at maturity,
      262-263
  T-bills, calculating, 260-261

Z

Z axes (charts), 468, 534-535
**z-Test, Two-Sample for
Means tool (Analysis
ToolPak), 670**

Zero Values option (Options dialog box), enabling/disabling, 710

zero-length string, 844

ZIP codes, formatting, 96

Zoom button
Print Preview toolbar, 139
Standard toolbar, 18

Zoom feature, viewing charts, 507

ZTEST function, 349

Your Guide to Computer Technology

informIT

www.informit.com

Sams has partnered with **InformIT.com** to bring technical information to your desktop. Drawing on Sams authors and reviewers to provide additional information on topics you're interested in, **InformIT.com** has free, in-depth information you won't find anywhere else.

ARTICLES

Keep your edge with thousands of free articles, in-depth features, interviews, and information technology reference recommendations—all written by experts you know and trust.

POWERED BY

Safari

ONLINE BOOKS

Answers in an instant from **InformIT Online Books'** 600+ fully searchable online books. Sign up now and get your first 14 days **free**.

CATALOG

Review online sample chapters and author biographies to choose exactly the right book from a selection of more than 5,000 titles.

SAMS   www.samspublishing.com

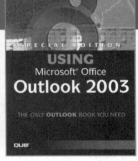